A HISTORY OF AMERICAN FOREIGN POLICY

A HISTORY OF

American Foreign Policy

JOHN HOLLADAY LATANÉ

LATE PROFESSOR OF AMERICAN HISTORY
THE JOHNS HOPKINS UNIVERSITY

and

DAVID W. WAINHOUSE

NEW YORK UNIVERSITY

Second Revision

THE ODYSSEY PRESS NEW YORK

14204

PREFACE TO THE SECOND REVISION

The writing of the first edition of this book was to the late Professor Latané a work of devotion. For many years he had been a keen student of American history and especially of our foreign relations. As the author of *America as a World Power*, *From Isolation to Leadership*, *The United States and Latin America*, and finally of *The History of American Foreign Policy*, he achieved real distinction. Obviously his work on our foreign relations deserved perpetuation.

The first edition of *The History of American Foreign Policy* was published in 1927. A few years later Professor Latané was planning to revise and enlarge the text. Owing, however, to his untimely death, the task of revising fell to another.

In my first revision I brought the account down to 1934. I did not touch, except for a few minor, verbal changes, the first twenty-two chapters. They still remain, in this second revision, as Professor Latané wrote them. Also, much of Chapters XXIII to XXIX remains the work of Professor Latané, though, for this second revision, I have found it advisable to make some changes. Chapters XXX to XXXV were added in the revision made in 1934.

The present edition brings the account down to September, 1939—to the outbreak of the Second World War. For it I have made numerous changes in Chapters XXX to XXXIV and have omitted all of former Chapter XXXV. The last six chapters are entirely new.

The subject matter covered in the chapters dealing with contemporary history is not an exhaustive exposition and no one is more aware of this than the writer. The aim throughout has been to focus the reader's attention on the more important developments in international affairs as they bear directly on our foreign policy. It is yet too early to pass final judgment on the recent events treated, and no attempt is made to solve the complex of problems arising in our foreign policy in a world that has not known such anarchy since the Napoleonic era.

I desire to express my appreciation to Irvin C. Rutter, Special Assistant to the Attorney General, for reading the chapter on Neutrality, and to Professor Clyde Eagleton of New York University for reading the manuscript and offering valuable suggestions. I need hardly add that neither Mr. Rutter nor Professor Eagleton is responsible for the views expressed.

D. W. W.

New York, June 1, 1940

CONTENTS

PART I. REPUBLICAN PRINCIPLES AND IDEALS

PART II. THE DEFIANCE OF THE OLD WORLD

PART III. ROUNDING OUT BORDERS AND LOOKING OVER SEAS

PART IV. SAFEGUARDING THE UNION

PART V. EXPANSION IN CARIBBEAN AND PACIFIC

PART VI. INTERVENTION IN EUROPE

PART VII. THE UNITED STATES IN THE POST-WAR PERIOD

LIST OF MAPS

PART I

REPUBLICAN PRINCIPLES AND IDEALS

AMERICAN FOREIGN POLICY

CHAPTER I

THE FRENCH ALLIANCE

The Colonies seek aid of the enemies of England

OUR Revolutionary ancestors set up a government founded on a new principle, happily phrased by Jefferson in the Declaration of Independence in the statement that "governments derive their just powers from the consent of the governed." This declaration was a challenge to the monarchical governments of the Old World, which were based on the doctrine of the divine right of kings. If the founders of the new government were to secure aid and alliances abroad, it was evident that they must appeal to some motive powerful enough to overcome the natural antipathy of the Old-World monarchies to revolutionary principles. They turned first to France because France was regarded as the natural enemy of England, and because she was still smarting from the loss of her American continental possessions. Spain also was hostile to England, and they turned to Spain, too, but with less success, because Spain was still the greatest of all American powers, and was, therefore, not disposed to encourage rebels in provinces adjacent to her own.

The objective of French diplomacy

When Louis XVI came to the French throne in 1774, he chose as chief minister the aged Count de Maurepas, but the Secretaryship of State for Foreign Affairs was conferred upon the Count de Vergennes, a cold and reserved, but industrious, clear-headed, and patriotic statesman, who largely determined and directed French policy during the period of the American Revolution. From the first, Vergennes' efforts were directed to the restoration of French prestige, which had not recovered from the reverses of the Seven Years' War and which had just suffered a new humiliation in the first partition of Poland. In this act France's recent ally Austria had been *particeps criminis,* so that the two Bourbon thrones of France and Spain, united by the Family Compact of 1761, were for all practical purposes isolated and on the defensive. As a result of the Seven Years' War France had lost Canada and India and had ceded New Orleans and all of Louisiana west of the Mississippi to Spain in compensation for the loss of Florida, while her rival England, as the result of Pitt's brilliant policy, had risen to unforeseen heights of prosperity and now held in her hands the balance of power. The extent of the British Empire, stretching from North America to India, British naval supremacy undisputed since 1763, and the vast wealth that was being accumulated by British commerce were believed to constitute a serious menace, not only to France, but to the rest of Europe. To restore French prestige and the balance of power in Europe became the main objective of French diplomacy.[1]

The revolt of the Colonies foreseen

The idea that the American colonies, rendered more secure by the expulsion of France from Canada, would sooner or later throw off the English yoke was advanced by many thoughtful observers at the close of the French and Indian War. In 1765 Choiseul, the brilliant minister of Louis XV, prepared a memoir for the King which concluded with this significant statement:

> Only the revolution which will occur some day in America, though we shall probably not see it, will put England back to that state of weakness in which Europe will have no more fear of her.[2]

[1] Wharton, *Diplomatic Correspondence of the American Revolution,* I, chap. iv; Corwin, *French Policy and the American Alliance,* particularly chaps. i and ii.

[2] Corwin, p. 40.

Report made by Baron de Kalb

From the beginning the dispute between England and her colonies was closely followed in France. In 1767 Baron de Kalb, who later as a major-general in the American army so gallantly gave his life at the battle of Camden, was sent by Choiseul on a secret mission to America to investigate and report on the rumors of revolt that were coming to Europe. While he did not regard revolution as imminent and thought that foreign intervention would merely hasten reconciliation, he wrote from New York:

> All classes of people here are imbued with such a spirit of independence and freedom from control that if all the provinces can be united under a common representation, an independent state will soon be formed. At all events, it will certainly come forth in time. Whatever may be done in London, this country is growing too powerful to be much longer governed at so great a distance.[3]

Vergennes sends secret agent to America

When Vergennes came into power conditions in America had taken a more serious turn and he was convinced that a rupture was at hand, so he sent over a secret agent of his own. Bonvouloir, the man chosen for this mission, was a soldier of distinction who had visited America before and claimed to know many public men. He was instructed to assure them that France had no designs on Canada, and that her only interest in the movement for independence lay in the establishment of commercial relations.[4]

Vergennes' "Considerations"

Early in March, 1776, Bonvouloir's first report was received, and it convinced Vergennes that the time had come to lend secret aid and encouragement to the Americans. He had, however, to overcome the opposition of Turgot and others who urged the King to stick to his program of economy and internal reform. On March 12 Vergennes submitted to the King a long memoir entitled "Considera-

[3]Wharton, I, 418.

[4]*Ibid.*, p. 333.

tions on the Affairs of the English Colonies in America."[5] He begins the discussion in a judicial tone by stating that it was problematic whether France and Spain should desire the subjection or the independence of the English colonies, for they were threatened in either case by dangers which it was not perhaps in the power of human foresight to anticipate or avert. The most obvious dangers concerned the West Indies and, stated alternatively, were,

> . . . that the English Ministry, beaten on the continent of America, may seek an indemnity at the expense of France and Spain, which would at once efface their shame, and give them the means of reconciliation with the insurgents, to whom it would offer the trade and provisioning of the Isles; [or] that the colonies, having become independent, and preserving no tie with England, may become conquerors from necessity, and that, surcharged with goods, they may seek a forced outlet in the sugar islands, and in Spanish America, which would destroy the ties which attach our colonies to the mother country.

Vergennes thus tried to make it appear that France and Spain were threatened by an attack from England, or the liberated colonies, or from the combined forces of both, and that it was time to adopt a definite defensive policy.

Proposes aid in munitions and money

He proposed to give the insurgents aid in munitions and money, but for the present not to enter into any compact with them. While France and Spain were to avoid compromising themselves, they were not to flatter themselves that they would be free from suspicion. The English, "accustomed to be led by the impulse of their interests, and to judge of others by themselves, will always believe that we are not allowing such a good opportunity of injuring them to escape." He urged the necessity, therefore, of putting the armed forces of the two monarchies in a position which might "either restrain the English, render their attacks uncertain, or insure the means of punishing them."

At the King's request the memoir was submitted to the

[5]Stevens, *Facsimiles of Manuscripts in European Archives Relating to America*, No. 1316; Doniol, *Histoire de la Participation de la France à l'Etablissement des Etats-Unis d'Amérique*, I, 273.

Opposition of Turgot

other ministers, most of whom endorsed fully the views of Vergennes.[6] The only dissenting voice was that of Turgot, who called attention to the state of the finances and the bad condition of the army and the navy. He thought that war should be avoided, if possible, and that to attack England would hasten reconciliation between her and her colonies, thus precipitating the danger most to be feared. He even asserted that it was to the interest of France for England to succeed in subjugating her colonies, because, if they were ruined, England would be weakened thereby, and if they remained strong they would preserve the desire for independence and continue to be an embarrassment to the mother country.[7]

Vergennes' real motives

The arguments which a statesman in Vergennes' position advances do not always reveal his real reasons or motives. There is ample evidence to justify the conclusion that he was convinced that the disruption of the British Empire would be the surest means of restoring French prestige. He strove sincerely, therefore, to establish the complete independence of the United States, and in this purpose he never wavered.[8] But he needed all the arguments he could muster in order to convince others. His insistence on the danger of an attack on the French and Spanish West Indies, especially the danger from an English-American coalition, was probably pure propaganda, intended to influence Louis XVI and his uncle, the King of Spain.[9]

Congress sends Deane to Paris

Meanwhile, as the result of Bonvouloir's mission and of information received by Franklin from friends in Paris that France was inclined to render secret aid to the

---

[6]Stevens, *Facsimiles,* Nos. 1319, 1320.

[7]Wharton, I, 339.

[8]*Ibid.*, pp. 363–364; Phillips, *The West in the Diplomacy of the American Revolution,* 149, 202, 215.

[9]Corwin, chap. vi. For a different view, see Van Tyne, "Influences Which Determined the French Government to Make the Treaty with America, 1778," in *Am. Hist. Rev.*, XXI, 528–541

colonies, Congress decided to send an authorized business agent to Paris, and in February, 1776, Silas Deane, of Connecticut, who had been a member of the first and second Congresses, was elected to fill this important post. He was a graduate of Yale, a man of striking appearance and good manners, and accustomed to a liberal style of living. His instructions, dated March 3, 1776, were drawn up by the Committee of Secret Correspondence, consisting of Benjamin Franklin, Benjamin Harrison, John Dickinson, Robert Morris, and John Jay.[10] He was directed to proceed to Paris in the character of a West Indian merchant, and he was furnished with letters of introduction to various friends of America. He reached Paris in July, and soon established close relations with Caron de Beaumarchais, a secret agent of the French Court.[11] Beaumarchais, famous in literature as the author of two of the most popular comedies of the day, *The Barber of Seville* and *The Marriage of Figaro*, was something more than an adventurer—a man undoubtedly of great talents, and although a pastmaster in the art of intrigue, there was a fascinating combination of boldness, resourcefulness, and chivalry in his nature. Long before the arrival of Deane, he had conceived the idea of becoming the secret agent of the French Court in forwarding supplies to the colonies, and had made journeys to London to confer with Arthur Lee, of Virginia, who had succeeded Franklin as agent for the colony of Massachusetts.

Beaumarchais

Beaumarchais is generally credited with having enlisted Vergennes in the cause and with having finally won the approval of the King. In a memorial to Louis XVI in February, 1776, he said:

> If it be replied that we can not assist the Americans without offending England and without drawing upon us the storm

[10]Wharton, II, 78.

[11]Loménie, *Beaumarchais et Son Temps;* Wharton, I, 364–386.

which I wish to keep off, I reply that this danger will not be incurred if the plan I have so many times proposed be followed—that of secretly assisting the Americans without compromising ourselves. . . . If your majesty has not at hand a more clever man to employ in the matter, I undertake and answer for its execution without any one being compromised, persuaded that my zeal will supply my want of talent better than the talent of another man could replace my zeal.

Secret agent of the French Court

The arguments of Beaumarchais and Vergennes finally prevailed, and two months before the arrival of Deane the King decided to extend secret aid to the colonies and to transact all business with them through the agency of Beaumarchais. On June 10, 1776, a million livres was advanced by the French treasury to Beaumarchais, and on August 11 he received another million, which the French Court persuaded the King of Spain to contribute. Later Spain also advanced military supplies of unknown amount through Beaumarchais.

"Hortalez et Cie"

In pursuance of the plan of secret aid, Beaumarchais established a mercantile house under the fictitious name of "Roderique Hortalez et Cie." When Deane arrived he was semi-officially referred to this firm, from which he soon obtained clothing for 20,000 men, 30,000 muskets, 100 tons of gunpowder, 200 brass cannon, 24 mortars, with shot and shell in proportion. The firm of Hortalez and Co. continued in existence from 1776 to 1783, occupying a large residence on a prominent street formerly owned by the Netherlands government as its embassy. During that period its disbursements are said to have amounted to over 21,000,000 livres, most of which was used in the purchase and shipment of military supplies to America. Beaumarchais' letters are delightfully written and highly entertaining, and there can be no question about his zeal for the American cause or the value of the services which he actually rendered. On September 25, 1776, in a letter to Vergennes, he summarizes in characteristic vein news just received from America by a vessel which reached Nantes twenty-six days from Nantucket: "1st, That Congress is still sitting at Philadelphia, and does not think of withdrawing therefrom. 2nd, That the Americans declared their independence on the 4th July, and have not since changed their mind."

Beaumarchais' zeal for the American cause

After reporting Sir Peter Parker's defeat at Charleston, South Carolina, Lord Dunmore's repulse in Virginia waters, the capture of Ticonderoga and Crown Point, and the sanguinary engagement at New York (battle of Long Island), the details of which were meager, he adds: "It is not true that the Province of Maryland and the County of Sussex on the Delaware have declared for England, as has been reported in the *English Gazette.*" In conclusion, he says that he is making extracts from "a very long memoir by an American deputy [Deane] on the past, present, and future of his country. He is awaiting two other deputies for fresh instructions, and the moment approaches when you will have to say *yes,* or *no.* I would go and hang myself immediately if it were the latter."[12]

As a natural consequence of the dubious and fictitious character of the house of Hortalez and Co., it was difficult, when the time came for a final settlement, to ascertain what supplies received by Congress from Beaumarchais were sent on his own account and what were gifts from the French government, but this subject will be discussed later.[13]

The services of Deane

Although Deane was merely a business agent of Congress, and acted mainly through Beaumarchais, he occupied a semi-official relation to the French government, and frequently addressed communications directly to Vergennes. By force of circumstances, he was sometimes drawn into matters entirely beyond the limits of his commission. He promised commissions to numbers of French officers whom Congress found itself unable to em-

[12]Stevens, *Facsimiles,* No. 898.

[13]Pp.65–71.

ploy, and many of them returned to France disgruntled. He even proposed at one time that Count Broglie should be called to America as commander-in-chief.[14] This was a favorite scheme of Baron de Kalb, but Congress took no notice of the suggestion, and Kalb himself dropped the matter after his arrival in America when he became familiar with the political situation.

His recall and disgrace

After Franklin's arrival in France, the main direction of diplomatic relations passed under his control, and Deane was occupied largely with financial accounts. Deane was recalled by resolution of Congress, passed December 8, 1777,[15] as the result of Arthur Lee's criticisms of his conduct. There is no reason whatever to doubt his honesty or zeal at this time in the service of his country. Although reputed to be a man of wealth when he went to France, he appears to have returned in financial distress. He appealed to Congress for a settlement of his accounts, but they refused to accept his statements, and he returned to Paris in search of papers to substantiate his claims. For a time he lived as a private pensioner of Vergennes. He eventually entered the service of the British Crown, and wrote a series of letters urging the colonies to return to British allegiance.[16]

Plan for foreign treaties

As soon as Congress decided to declare independence, a committee was appointed to prepare a form of treaty to be proposed to foreign powers. Dickinson, Franklin, John Adams, Benjamin Harrison, and Robert Morris constituted this committee,[17] but the main work seems to have been done by John Adams. The draft treaty, consisting of thirty articles.[18] was approved by Congress September

---

[14] Wharton, I, 392.

[15] *Ibid.*, II, 444.

[16] Wharton, I, 559–573. The claim of Deane's heirs was finally reported favorably by the Senate Committee on Revolutionary Claims in 1842, and a settlement based on compromise was made.

[17] Wharton, II, 100.

[18] *Journals of Continental Congress,* V, 576, 768.

17, 1776, and Franklin, Deane, and Thomas Jefferson were commissioned to represent the United States at the French Court. On account of the delicate state of his wife's health, Jefferson declined the post, and Arthur Lee was elected in his place. Deane and Lee were already in France.

Franklin's arrival in France

Benjamin Franklin, at the age of seventy, set sail on the 29th of October on what was to prove to be by far the most important mission of his life. He arrived in Quiberon Bay on board the *Reprisal*, Captain Wickes, about December 4, and proceeded to Nantes. On December 16, 1776, Beaumarchais wrote to Vergennes that while at Havre a few days before, he had learned of Doctor Franklin's arrival:

> Knowing, as I do, this wretched country of gossip and idleness, I tremble lest, on the arrival of that celebrated man at Paris, he should be so surrounded that some indiscretion might be committed. I hastily wrote to Mr. Deane to go and meet his friend, to lock him up until my return, and not to let him speak nor give letters to any one, until I had had the honor of forewarning him, Monsieur le Comte, and of taking your orders regarding this matter. [After reference to some business matters which required his personal attention, he continues:] I then returned, traveling at night, not to keep Mr. Franklin prisoner too long. I made such good speed that I have arrived before him. . . . The excitement caused by Mr. Franklin's arrival is inconceivable. However, that courageous old man allowed his vessel to make two captures on the journey, in spite of the personal risk which he ran. And shall we Frenchmen be afraid?[19]

His fame and popularity

Franklin's arrival in Paris marked a new epoch in the affairs of France as well as of America. It may safely be asserted that even to the present day no American has ever been sent to a foreign post better qualified, by experience, training, and character, for the duties he was to perform than Franklin.[20] A few months later, Adams,

[19]Stevens, *Facsimiles*, No. 911; Doniol, II, 96.

[20]*See* Lay, *Foreign Service of the United States*, 4.

who at times exhibited great jealousy of his colleague, wrote this of Franklin:

> His reputation was more universal than that of Leibnitz or Newton, Frederick or Voltaire, and his character more beloved and esteemed than any or all of them. . . . His name was familiar to government and people, to foreign countries, nobility, clergy, and philosophers, as well as plebeians, to such a degree that there was scarcely a peasant or a citizen, a valet de chambre, coachman or footman, a lady's chambermaid or a scullion in a kitchen, who was not familiar with it, and who did not consider him a friend to human-kind. . . . If a collection could be made of all the gazettes of Europe for the latter half of the 18th century, a greater number of panegyrical paragraphs upon *le grand* Franklin would appear, it is believed, than upon any other man that ever lived.[21]

Financial assistance from the King

On December 23, 1776, Franklin, Deane, and Lee addressed to Vergennes the first formal diplomatic note in our history.[22] Several memoirs asking for aid and urging recognition of independence followed. On January 9, 1777, Vergennes replied to the commissioners, still refusing open aid, but declaring that his Majesty "will signify to them his favorable disposition and good wishes by assigning to them secret assistance which will assure and extend their credit and their purchases."[23] During the course of the year the sum of two million livres was placed by the French treasury with M. Grand, the banker of the United States, subject to Franklin's orders. This was a free gift. Also a loan of one million livres was obtained from the Farmers-General of France, an organization which collected the taxes and enjoyed among other privileges the tobacco monopoly. In the contract for this loan dated March 24, 1777, Franklin and Deane undertook in the name of their government to deliver during the year 1777 five thousand hogsheads of York and James

Loan from the Farmers-General

[21] Wharton, I, 488.

[22] Stevens, *Facsimiles,* No. 607.

[23] *Ibid.,* No. 622; Doniol, II, 116–122.

River tobacco, while the Farmers-General agreed, on their part, to accept bills drawn on them by Franklin and Deane in the course of the ensuing month to the extent of one million livres, and to pay another million as soon as the tobacco arrived.[24] As Congress was able to deliver but a small part of the tobacco promised, only the first million was advanced under this contract, and a considerable sum remained due to the Farmers-General for the first million. This sum was later repaid to the French government, which as a result of the French Revolution succeeded to the rights of the Farmers-General.

Foreign affairs conducted by committees of Congress

The domestic organization of our Revolutionary diplomacy gave rise to many difficulties. Foreign affairs, as well as all other executive business of the government, were conducted by committees appointed by Congress, and under its direct instructions. The Committee of Secret Correspondence already referred to was replaced in April, 1777, by a Committee of Foreign Affairs. The personnel of this committee underwent changes from time to time, which tended to prevent the development of a consistent foreign policy, even had Congress refrained from interference by frequent resolutions and by reference of many foreign questions to special committees. The president of Congress sometimes undertook to conduct its diplomatic correspondence when there was no committee appointed for the purpose. Finally, in 1781, Congress established a Department of Foreign Affairs, and in October of that year Robert R. Livingston assumed the duties of Secretary for Foreign Affairs.[25]

Difficulty of communicating with agents abroad

Great difficulty was experienced in communicating regularly with the representatives abroad. It is estimated that at least one-third of the correspondence failed to reach its destination, the letters being intercepted by the British navy and placed in the British archives. During

[24] Wharton, II, 300.

[25] *Ibid.*, I, 456–457.

one period of eleven months, when Congress had as many as twelve agents on the continent of Europe, not a single letter was received from one of them. Many of the intercepted letters were of course in cipher, but as the keys to most of the ciphers were known to the British Foreign Office, the enemy was as well informed of the plans of Congress as were its agents abroad.[26] The British secret service was also well organized and a number of American-born British subjects who posed as friends of the American cause acted as informants. Some received pay from both sides. The most notorious was Dr. Edward Bancroft, a native of Massachusetts and a friend of Franklin, whose confidence he retained to the end.[27]

John Adams and "militia diplomacy"

When Deane was recalled in November, 1777, John Adams was elected to take his place as one of the commissioners at the Court of France. Adams was a believer in what he called "militia diplomacy." "Militia diplomacy," he once said, "sometimes gains victories over regular troops, even by departing from the rules." He also expressed the opinion in a letter to Congress, hitting at Franklin, that "no man will ever be pleasing at a court in general who is not depraved in his morals or warped from your interests."

Jealousy of Franklin

In matters relating to the conduct of foreign relations, there was the same jealousy or dread of executive authority that there was in matters relating to the control of finance and the army. There was jealousy of Franklin and the unique position of influence which he held at the French Court, just as there was of Washington in the field. It is a well-established rule of diplomacy that an envoy is not to be pressed on a foreign court when it is understood that he will not be received. Under the influence of Richard Henry Lee and Samuel Adams, Con-

---

[26] *Op. cit.*, pp. 461–462.

[27] See the interesting article by Bemis, "British Secret Service and the French-American Alliance," in *Am. Hist. Rev.*, XXIX, 474.

gress sent a number of commissioners to European courts for the purpose of borrowing money, even when it was perfectly clear that those courts would not receive such commissioners. Franklin was utterly opposed to this policy, but he was overruled.[28] Arthur Lee was instructed to go to Madrid, but he was stopped by the Spanish government on the way, although Spain had secretly given a million francs through Vergennes to the American cause. Lee held an alternate commission to Berlin, and this capital he succeeded in reaching, but merely in a private capacity. Frederick the Great refused to receive him, and his visit to Berlin is memorable mainly for the theft of his papers, which was openly acknowledged to have been committed under the direction of the British Minister.

Theft of Arthur Lee's papers at Berlin

This affair was not without its amusing features. Hugh Elliot, the British minister, bribed a German servant to procure duplicate keys to the door and bureau of the room at the inn where Lee and his companion, Sayre, were staying. It had been observed that they were in the habit of going out into the country once or twice a week to dine with a friend, and did not usually return until eleven o'clock at night. During one of these absences the servant entered Lee's room and got possession of his portfolio. The papers were taken to Elliot, who at once set several of his friends to work copying them. While the copying was going on, Elliot to avoid suspicion went to the inn to call on an English nobleman who was staying there, and found to his surprise that Lee and Sayre had that moment returned, several hours earlier than was expected. Elliot boldly engaged them in conversation as long as he could, pretending not to know who they were, and without giving them his name. Finally, Lee went to his room to write some dispatches, and soon raised a cry of robbery, and notified the Berlin police. Later that night the papers were returned by Elliot to one of the servants

[28] Wharton, I, 289–294.

at the inn. The affair created a great sensation, and Elliot at once stated to the German Foreign Minister that the papers had been stolen by an overzealous servant who had heard him remark to some friends that he would give a thousand pounds to see what Lee had in a journal which it was said he kept every day. Elliot offered to resign in case Frederick the Great should be displeased, but that monarch censured him mildly for his vivacity and zeal, and made no formal complaint to the British government. George III, through the Earl of Suffolk, mildly censured Elliot, but the noble Earl added that "in consideration of the loyal zeal" displayed by Elliot "the King has been graciously pleased to take notice of the great expenses in which you involved yourself, and has directed the amount to be made good to you." He enclosed a draft for one thousand pounds.[29]

Unhappy experiences of other agents

The theft of his papers brought Lee and his mission into such publicity that the Prussian government declined to continue the informal negotiations and he accomplished nothing at Berlin. His brother, William Lee, was elected by Congress a commissioner to the Court of Vienna with an alternate commission to Berlin, but he was never permitted to enter either capital, and he spent his time quarrelling with Franklin over the question as to whether he was entitled to his salary as minister or not. Francis Dana was sent to St. Petersburg, John Adams to The Hague, and Ralph Izard to Florence. Adams eventually negotiated a treaty with Holland, but during most of the time these envoys, unable to gain recognition from the powers to which they were sent, took up their residence at Paris, where they relied on Franklin for support, and interfered seriously with his work, demanding that they be kept informed of all his negotiations and giving him advice, which he felt under no obligation to follow.

Early in December, 1777, Franklin, Deane, and Lee

[29]Stevens, *Facsimiles*, Nos. 1451–1482.

Effect of news of Burgoyne's surrender

received dispatches bringing the glorious news of Burgoyne's defeat and surrender. The commissioners wrote home that this news "apparently occasioned as much joy in France as if it had been a victory of their own troops over their own enemies," and they promptly took advantage of the situation to press upon Vergennes the proposals of Congress for a treaty of amity and commerce which they had placed in his hands nearly a year before.[30] A copy of the note to Vergennes was inclosed by Arthur Lee to Count de Aranda, the Spanish ambassador to France, who was favorably disposed to the United States but without much influence on his own government, expressing the hope that a treaty might also be made with Spain and requesting his coöperation.[31] The news from America had moved Louis XVI to consent to negotiations with the American commissioners with this reservation, however:

> His Majesty, united to the King of Spain by ties most intimate and close, does not wish to make any engagement not shared by that Prince, and which is not to be carried out in concert with him. This is why His Majesty, while declaring that he is disposed to entertain the overtures which may be made to him for a negotiation, expressly reserves to himself the power to conclude nothing except conjointly with the King his uncle, relying on what His Catholic Majesty may indicate as the proper time for publicly declaring himself.[32]

The French Court decides to recognize American independence

The decision to recognize the independence of the United States and to negotiate a treaty as soon as the concurrence of Spain could be obtained was communicated to Franklin and his associates, December 12,[33] by Vergennes' secretary Gérard, soon to be appointed first envoy to the United States.

Meanwhile Vergennes had sent a special courier to

[30]Wharton, II, 444.

[31]*Ibid.*, p. 447.

[32]Stevens, *Facsimiles*, No. 1762.

[33]Wharton, II, 452.

Vergennes seeks concurrence of Spanish Court

Spain bearing the news of Burgoyne's surrender and a note to the French ambassador Montmorin, who was instructed to lay it before Florida Blanca, the chief minister of Charles III, and to ask for an early decision. The note begins by referring to the "uneasiness" caused by Burgoyne's surrender and the danger of a reconciliation between England and her colonies. "What wiser course could England take than to try to regain as friends those whom she despairs of having again as subjects?" Borrowing a sentence from one of Beaumarchais' letters he says: "The power which first recognizes the independence of the Americans will be the one to gather all the fruit of this war." He then asks: "Shall we allow the English to re-amalgamate with America without having taken any measures to at least share its affection?" Advancing his favorite argument of the danger of an English-American coalition he says:

> Whatever course we take we shall have difficulty in avoiding war with England. It is not what we may have done in favor of America which hurts her most grievously; it is the re-establishment of the Navy of the two Crowns. Now, if war is to be the necessary result of the present crisis, is it not more expedient to venture on it with the Americans for friends, rather than have them our enemies?

Fully aware of Spain's territorial ambitions he left this question for subsequent discussion in a carefully worded statement with which he brings the note to a close:

> I do not speak here of the stipulations to be made with the Americans. If we treat with them, we have nothing to ask of them for ourselves which can embarrass them—the guarantee of our islands and of our possessions in Western America and mutual freedom of trade while conforming to the regulations established at the places where vessels may touch. Spain may have more matters to arrange, and her commercial stipulations may differ from ours. All that is a matter for discussion when the preliminary question has been decided.[34]

[34]Stevens, *Facsimiles*, No. 1769.

Florida Blanca rejects proposed alliance with France and America

Vergennes' arguments made little impression on Florida Blanca, a resourceful and aggressive minister, who on taking office a few months before had completely reversed the policy of his vacillating predecessor Grimaldi. Florida Blanca was jealous of French influence, indifferent to the Family Compact, and ambitious to develop a distinctive Spanish policy which would free Spain from dependence on France. Furthermore, as a staunch royalist he dreaded the effect on the Spanish colonies of the establishment of a republic near them.[35] He, therefore, rejected Vergennes' proposal for a triple alliance, and such assistance as Spain rendered later was the result of close bargaining. For the present, Florida Blanca announced, the King had decided

> . . . (1) to give abundant aid in money[36] to the Colonists on the express condition of inviolable secrecy; (2) to offer them his protection in case they should have need of it, provided they conduct themselves with fidelity and precaution; (3) and finally to watch attentively the ascendency which the various parties in London may secure, especially in what concerns a cessation of the war against the Americans.[37]

Spanish Court displeased with French policy

While this was the formal reply, Montmorin's dispatch to Vergennes, December 23, 1777, gives a vivid account of his interviews with Florida Blanca and the King, in which they made no effort to conceal their displeasure at the apparent effort of France to force their hand. Florida Blanca declared that they could not commit an act more hostile to the English than that of treating with her colonies and recognizing their independence; that the Spanish fleet was then on its way back from America and that if it

> . . . happened to be taken by the English, it would be one more means in their hands, and one less in ours, which would

[35]Phillips, 48.

[36]Three million livres was promised, but not forthcoming (Wharton, II, 470). In 1780 Jay succeeded after long negotiations in getting a loan of $150,000.

[37]Stevens, *Facsimiles*, No. 1790.

make it absolutely impossible for us to carry on war. Moreover, I cannot persuade myself that the circumstances are as pressing as is thought in France. The American deputies are playing their game. Their aim has always been to compromise us with the English. Whatever precautions may be taken in order that secrecy may be kept, the American deputies have too great an interest to divulge it for it not to leak out; and finally I do not think a reconciliation between the mother country and her colonies is easy. Much time will pass before they can come to an understanding. The present ministry will never dare to take on itself the odium of granting independence, and if the Ministry changes, we shall have time to take our precautions.

His policy was the usual Spanish one of delay. After further argument to the same effect he concluded: "I do not know how all this will end. I quite think we shall be forced into war. If that happens, we shall not be the first to wish for peace," and repeated several times with emphasis and a certain sort of emotion: "Before asking for it we must sell even our last shirt." Montmorin replied in a jocular tone that he hoped it would be the English who would sell their shirts. From this interview Montmorin drew the conclusion that if France should go to war "they will be very angry here, but will, however, follow what may have been decided in France. Be quite sure, Sir, that in whatever manner France is dragged into war, Spain will follow."[38]

The French alliance with America signed

Disregarding the views expressed by the Spanish Court, Vergennes continued negotiations with the American Commissioners, and on February 6, 1778, two treaties were signed on behalf of France by Gérard and on behalf of the United States by Franklin, Deane,[39] and Lee. One was a treaty of amity and commerce, which was to go into effect as soon as ratified; the other was a treaty of alliance, which was to go into effect in case war should take place between

[38]Stevens, *Facsimiles*, No. 1792; Doniol, II, 695.

[39]Although Deane had been recalled he continued to act until April, when he sailed on Count d'Estaing's fleet in company with Gérard, the recently appointed minister to the United States.

France and Great Britain as a result of the treaty of commerce. The object of the alliance was declared to be "to maintain effectually the liberty, sovereignty, and independence absolute and unlimited, of the said United States," and the two parties agreed not to lay down arms until this object was assured. France renounced "forever the possession of the islands of Bermudas, as well as of any part of the continent of North America, which before the treaty of Paris in 1763, or in virtue of that treaty, were acknowledged to belong to the Crown of Great Britain." The United States, on the other hand, was free to conquer the Bermudas or Canada, while France was at liberty to annex any of the British possessions in the Gulf of Mexico. Furthermore, the two parties agreed to guarantee each other's possessions in America including the additions or conquests within the limits specified above. There was a separate and secret act, signed at the same time, reserving the right of the King of Spain to become a party to the foregoing treaties.[40]

The effect of the alliance in America

The French Alliance was of tremendous significance and soon changed the whole aspect of affairs. The dispatches bearing the good news and the texts of the treaties were slow in reaching America, but the treaties were promptly ratified by Congress May 4, 1778.[41] Following the long and disheartening winter of Valley Forge the news of the alliance rekindled enthusiasm and infused a new spirit into the movement for independence. Meanwhile the French Alliance had precipitated a serious crisis in the British Parliament. On February 17, before receiving information of it, Lord North had risen in the House of Commons and, to the amazement of both friends and opponents, had proposed a bill, conceding nearly everything the Americans had demanded, except independence, and providing for the appointnent of commissioners with full powers to

[40](Malloy) *Treaties and Conventions of the United States*, **I, 479–483.**

[41]Wharton, II, 568.

PACIFIC
OCEAN
VANCOUVER ISLAND
UNEXPLORED
Columbia
River
Snake
River
Yellowstone R.
SPANIS
POSSESS
River
Arkansas
Colorado
Rio
Grand
TROPIC OF CANCER
Scale of Miles
0
200
400
600
GENERAL DRAFTING CO. INC., N.Y.
140°
130°
120°
110°
100°
40°
30°
20°

1. NORTH

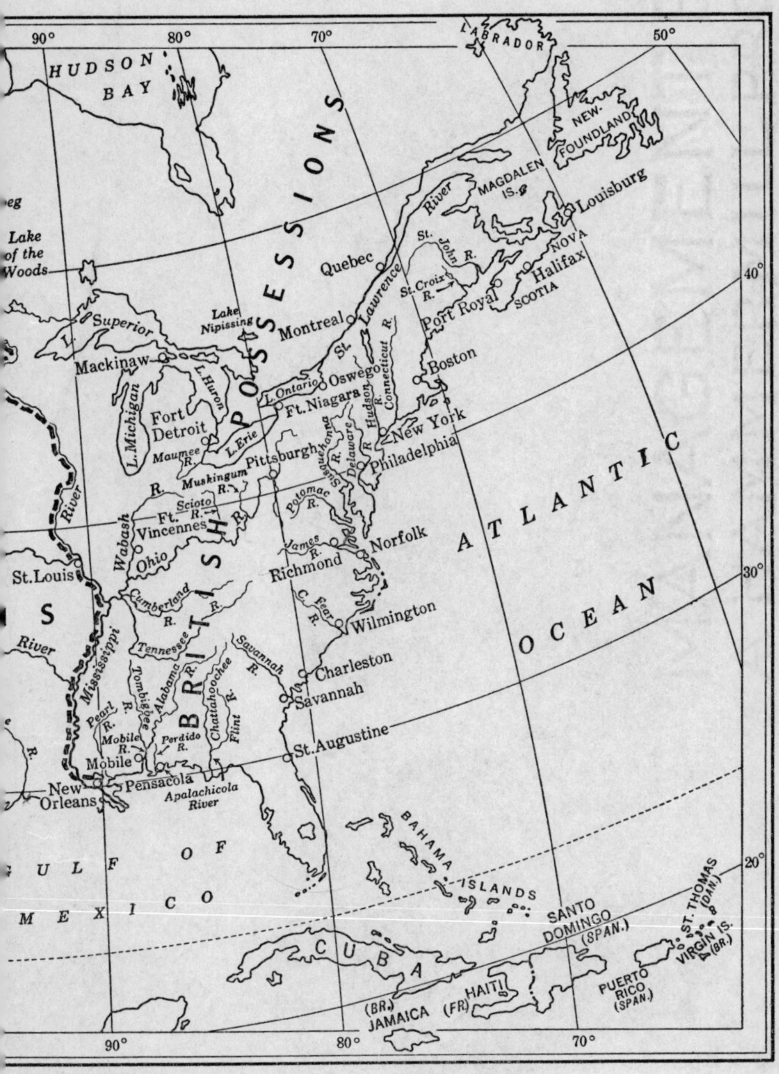
HUDSON BAY
LABRADOR
NEWFOUNDLAND
MAGDALEN IS.
Louisburg
NOVA SCOTIA
Halifax
Port Royal
St. John R.
St. Croix R.
Quebec
Montreal
St. Lawrence River
Lake Nipissing
BRITISH POSSESSIONS
Lake of the Woods
L. Superior
Mackinaw
L. Huron
L. Michigan
Fort Detroit
L. Erie
L. Ontario
Oswego
Ft. Niagara
Connecticut R.
Hudson R.
Boston
New York
Philadelphia
Delaware R.
Susquehanna R.
Pittsburgh
Maumee R.
Muskingum R.
Scioto R.
Ft. Vincennes
Wabash
Ohio
Potomac R.
James R.
Richmond
Norfolk
C. Fear R.
Wilmington
Charleston
Savannah R.
Savannah
St. Augustine
Cumberland R.
Tennessee R.
Tombigbee R.
Alabama R.
Chattahoochee R.
Flint R.
Perdido R.
Pearl R.
Mobile R.
Mobile
Pensacola
Apalachicola River
New Orleans
St. Louis
Mississippi River
ATLANTIC OCEAN
GULF OF MEXICO
BAHAMA ISLANDS
CUBA
JAMAICA (BR.)
HAITI (FR.)
SANTO DOMINGO (SPAN.)
PUERTO RICO (SPAN.)
ST. THOMAS (DAN.)
VIRGIN IS. (BR.)
90°
80°
70°
50°
40°
30°
20°

A IN 1775

treat with the colonies. These measures were debated at length and finally adopted. On March 13 the British government learned of the French treaties and immediately declared war on France. In the face of this great crisis all eyes were turned to Chatham, and Lord North offered to resign and urged the King to call on his great opponent to form a new ministry, but George III flew into a rage and declared that no power in heaven or earth could ever make him stoop to treat with "Lord Chatham and his crew." He would in all probability have been forced to yield, however, had not the tragic death of Chatham, who was stricken as he rose to speak on the floor of the House of Lords, removed the necessity. North continued at the head of the ministry. The peace commissioners reached America just as the British were evacuating Philadelphia. Congress refused to consider their proposals and in October they returned to England.

England declares war on France

The first effort of the French to render military and naval aid was not successful and raised doubts as to the value of the French Alliance. In April, 1778, Count d'Estaing sailed from Toulon with twelve ships of the line and four thousand French soldiers and arrived in the mouth of the Delaware early in July. But Sir Henry Clinton had heard that he was on the way and had evacuated Philadelphia. D'Estaing was too late to intercept Lord Howe's fleet which carried several thousand Tories from Philadelphia to New York. D'Estaing followed Howe to Sandy Hook. He had a great opportunity, with the aid of Washington's army, to destroy the British fleet and shut the British army up in New York, but his pilots reported that his larger ships could not cross the bar. With Washington's approval he decided to abandon the attack on New York and attempt the capture of Newport. Howe with a reinforced fleet followed him and while the two fleets were maneuvering for position a gale dispersed them and after putting in at Boston for repairs d'Estaing

D'Estaing's fleet fails to render effective aid

sailed off for the West Indies to attempt the conquest of the smaller British islands.

French loans secured by Franklin

The most important of the immediate results of the French Alliance was the loan of 18,000,000 livres, secured by Franklin, and advanced in twenty-one instalments from 1778 to 1782. The first advance was made three weeks after the signing of the treaty. The money previously advanced had been in the form of gifts, with the exception of the loan of 1,000,000 livres obtained from the Farmers-General in 1777. In 1781 France made through Franklin a gift of 6,000,000 livres and secured from Holland a loan of 10,000,000 livres for the United States, the interest and principal of which were guaranteed by the French government. This must not be confused with the Dutch loan secured later by John Adams. In 1783, France made another loan of 6,000,000 livres. These loans amounted in all to 35,000,000 livres, or $6,352,500.[42] The total cost of the war to France including naval and military operations, is estimated to have been 1,200,000,000 livres.[43] This vast expenditure, without any compensating gains, undoubtedly hastened the catastrophe toward which the French monarchy was headed.

[42](Malloy) *Treaties and Conventions of the United States*, I, 483–487.
[43]Wharton, II, 526 n.

CHAPTER II

INDEPENDENCE AND BOUNDARIES

Establishment of regular diplomatic intercourse

As a result of the recognition of the independence of the United States, Louis XVI decided to send an envoy to reside near Congress, and on March 28, 1778, M. Conrad Alexander Gérard was appointed first minister plenipotentiary to the United States. He arrived aboard d'Estaing's fleet in July.[1] His reception, being that of the first foreign minister, was the subject of grave discussion in Congress and a formal ceremonial was prescribed.[2] In September, Congress elected Benjamin Franklin minister plenipotentiary to the Court of France and dissolved the mission which had included Lee and Adams. Lee lingered in Europe for two years, a stormy petrel, while Adams returned to the United States. The latter, however, was not allowed to continue long in idleness. On September 27, 1779, he was chosen by Congress to a still more important post, that of minister plenipotentiary for negotiating a treaty of peace and commerce with Great Britain, when that nation should be found ready to recognize the independence of the United States.

Efforts to bring Spain into the war

After the signature of the alliance between France and the United States the next aim of Vergennes was to get Spain into the war on the best terms he could arrange. This was a very difficult task, for Spanish aims and ambitions were very different from those of France and utterly opposed to those of the United States. Louis XVI's announcement to his royal uncle of his decision to form an

[1]Wharton, *Dip. Cor. of Am. Rev.*, I, 422.

[2]*Ibid.*, II, 653.

alliance with the United States[3] had, as Montmorin had predicted, caused indignation and anger at the Spanish Court. But Florida Blanca soon realized that he could use the situation to good advantage and make it the means of driving a hard bargain with Vergennes. Partly to gain time and partly to relieve his sovereign of all appearance of subserviency to French policy he proposed mediation between England and France. The British government encouraged the idea with a view to keeping Spain out of the war as long as possible, but finally rejected the Spanish proposals by laying down impossible conditions.[4]

Secret convention of Aranjuez

The discussion of mediation led, however, to an exchange of views between France and Spain as to the eventual terms of peace, which resulted in the signing on April, 12, 1779, of the secret convention of Aranjuez.[5] By the terms of this agreement the Family Compact was renewed, Spain agreed to enter the war, and it was stipulated that neither party would sign any treaty with the common enemy without the consent of the other. On the subject of American independence France was explicit. Article IV contained the following declarations:

> The very Christian King, in strict execution of the engagements contracted by him with the United States of America, proposes and requests that his Catholic Majesty, on the day he declares war against England, shall recognize the sovereign independence of the United States, and he shall engage not to lay down his arms until this independence is recognized by the King of Great Britain.

The Spanish declaration was, however, non-committal:

> The Catholic King has desired and still desires to gratify the very Christian King, his nephew, and to procure for the United States all the advantages they desire and which it is possible to obtain. But as his Catholic Majesty has as yet not concluded

---

[3]*Op. cit.*, p. 467.

[4]Corwin, *French Policy and the American Alliance,* 180–190.

[5]Wharton, I, 356; Doniol, III, 803.

with them any treaty by which their reciprocal interests have been settled, he reserves the right to do so, and to come to an agreement at that time as to whatever bears on the said independence.

War aims of France and Spain

The treaty then states at length the war aims of France and Spain. The French aims were: (1) the abolition of all treaty stipulations which deprived France of the right to fortify Dunkirk; (2) the expulsion of the English from the island and fisheries of Newfoundland; (3) liberty of commerce with the East Indies; (4) the recovery of Senegal; (5) the possession of the island of Santo Domingo; and (6) either the abolition or the complete execution of the Treaty of Utrecht. The Spanish aims were much more ambitious. They were: (1) the restitution of Gibraltar; (2) the possession of Mobile; (3) the restitution of Pensacola and the eastern coast of Florida; (4) the expulsion of the English from the bay of Honduras; (5) the revocation of the privilege accorded in the treaty of 1763 to the English to cut dye-woods on the coasts of Campeche; and (6) the restitution of the island of Minorca. In a separate article the two powers pledge themselves not to lay down arms or even to make a truce without at least being assured of the restitution of Gibraltar and the removal of the restrictions relative to the fortifications of Dunkirk.

Embarrassing position of Vergennes

Thus Vergennes put himself in the position of being bound to two yokefellows who were pulling in quite different directions. The direct object of the American alliance was the independence of the United States, while the main object of the Spanish alliance was the recovery of Gibraltar. His situation was rendered all the more difficult by the fact that the terms of the American alliance were known, while the terms of the Spanish alliance were kept secret.

The pledge of France not to lay down arms until Gibraltar was recovered was the only obligation assumed that was inconsistent with her prior treaty with the United

States.[6] The Americans had agreed not to make peace without France and France now agreed not to make peace until Gibraltar was won. Vergennes had no right, without the knowledge or consent of the United States, to link the cause of American independence with the recovery of Gibraltar. But affairs in America were in an extremely critical condition and it was of the utmost importance to get Spain into the war.

Vergennes refrained, however, from committing France on the vital questions of the western boundaries of the States and the navigation of the Mississippi River. His efforts later on to harmonize the differences that arose between Spain and the United States on these questions led to charges against him of vacillation, insincerity, and willingness to sacrifice American interests.[7]

Western boundaries and the Mississippi question

As these questions played such an important part in the peace negotiations it is important at this point to review the subject at some length. In the first place it is important to note that most of the earlier discussions in regard to the western lands and the navigation of the Mississippi took place in Philadelphia and not in Paris. Franklin had no special instructions on these points and was too much occupied with other things. When Gérard was sent to Philadelphia as minister plenipotentiary his instructions[8] covered the questions of Canada and the Floridas, but made no reference to western boundaries or the Mississippi.

> The envoys of Congress [said Vergennes] have proposed to the King to enter into an engagement to favor the conquest by the Americans of Canada, Nova Scotia, and the Floridas, and he has reason to think that Congress has taken this project to heart. But the King has considered that the possession of those three countries, or at least of Canada, by England, will be an element of disquiet and anxiety to the Americans, which will make them

[6]Corwin, 205.

[7]Phillips, *The West in the Diplomacy of the American Revolution*, 202.

[8]Wharton, II, 523.

> feel the more the need they have of the alliance and the friendship of the King, and which it is not his interest to remove.

Gérard was instructed therefore to make no engagement relative to such conquest, but if Congress should become too pressing he might acquiesce, provided such conquest should not be made an essential condition of peace.

On the subject of Spanish interests the instructions stated:

> There is one point of great consequence to the King, and which will demand all the dexterity of M. Gérard—the stipulations to be undertaken in favor of Spain. He knows that that power has taken no part in the two treaties, though she has not opposed them, and that up to the present time she has said nothing of the conditions on which she may accede to them in the future. However, we have reason to think that she would desire to acquire the Floridas, a share in the fisheries of the banks of Newfoundland, and Jamaica. . . . The Floridas enter into the plans of conquest of the Americans. It will therefore be necessary to prepare them for the contingency of a surrender of their claims.

Conflict of Spanish and American interests

Gérard appears to have inferred from these instructions that he was given a general mandate to look out for the interests of Spain. His efforts in this direction were soon reinforced, if not inspired, by Juan de Miralles, an Havana merchant, who arrived in Philadelphia with a commission from the captain general of Cuba to act as an observer for his Catholic Majesty.[9] The extensive claims to the Mississippi Valley later advanced by Spain seem to have originated in the brain of Miralles and to have been communicated by him to Gérard who soon became their zealous advocate. These two foreigners soon acquired a remarkable ascendency over certain members of Congress and Gérard's house became a favorite resort for the discussion of all foreign questions, particularly the conflicting interests of the United States and Spain. There was a division of opinion in Congress between the delegates from states

[9]Corwin, 243.

Division of opinion in Congress

with extensive claims to western lands and the delegates from states with restricted boundaries who were jealous of the territorial pretensions of their neighbors. Congress was in great financial straits and some of its members were willing to consider the sacrifice of territory in return for financial aid. John Jay, then president of Congress, and Gouverneur Morris, both of New York, a state whose western land claims were rather shadowy, held repeated conferences with Gérard and Miralles and were frequently entertained at their residences. As to his position at this time Jay some years later made the following statement:

> I was early convinced that provided we could obtain independence and a speedy peace, we could not justify protracting the war, and hazarding the event of it, for the sake of conquering the Floridas, to which we had no title, or retaining the navigation of the Mississippi, which we should not want this age, and of which we might acquire a partial use with the consent of Spain.[10]

In January, 1779, Gérard stated to a committee of Congress that the United States had no more right to the possessions of the English monarch than the King of Spain would have whenever he should become engaged in war with England; that France would never prolong the war a single day to procure for them the possessions they coveted; and that good feeling would never be established with Spain so long as the Americans held these pretensions.[11]

Vergennes position on the Mississippi question

That Gérard's views were not authorized by Vergennes is evident when they are compared with the latter's dispatch of October, 1778, which was received by Gérard in February shortly after the conference above referred to. Vergennes wrote:

> I do not know, I cannot even conjecture the intentions of the Court of Madrid on this subject. But I judge from the situation of the places that the Americans will insist on the free naviga-

[10]Johnston, *Cor. and Public Papers of John Jay*, I, 329.

[11]Corwin, 252.

tion of the Mississippi on account of the settlements which they propose to form on the Ohio, and I assure you that it would appear astonishing to me that anyone should refuse this request. However, there may be local considerations in the negative of which I am ignorant, and which deserve some consideration; you are in a position to obtain information in regard to these either through the Americans themselves or through M. Miralles; and if they appear to be of such a nature as to necessitate Spain's refusal, you will do well to prepare the Americans for it with prudence and tact. But in the contrary case, you ought to prevail upon the Spanish agent, not only to avoid giving his Court prepossessions on this subject, but also to present the case to it in such a manner that it will have no difficulty in giving the consent which the Americans will not fail to ask of it.[12]

Congress defines the boundaries of the United States

Meanwhile, as a result of Gérard's representations and in order to pave the way for an alliance with Spain, Congress decided to abandon the projected conquest of Canada and the Floridas and by a resolution of February 23, 1779, defined the boundaries of the United States as follows:

Northerly by the ancient limits of Canada, as contended for by Great Britain, running from Nova Scotia, southwesterly, west, and northwesterly, to Lake Nepissing, thence a west line to the Mississippi; easterly by the boundary settled between Massachusetts and Nova Scotia; southerly by the boundary between Georgia and East and West Florida; and westerly by the river Mississippi.[13]

The resolution also affirmed the right to navigate the Mississippi to the southern boundary of the United States and demanded a free port or ports below.

Jay's mission to Spain

A few months later, September, 1779, Jay was appointed minister plenipotentiary to negotiate a treaty of alliance and of amity and commerce with Spain. He and Adams had both been nominated for the position of peace com-

[12]Doniol, III, 570.

[13]*Journals of Continental Congress,* XIII, 241. The line from Nova Scotia to Lake Nepissing followed the southern boundary of Quebec as laid down in the proclamation of 1763. (For map, see Howard, *Preliminaries of the Revolution,* p. 4.) By the Quebec Act of 1774 the bounds of that province had been extended to the Ohio River, but the colonies had protested against this as an arbitrary act in derogation of their rights.

missioner to treat with England and for several ballots there was no choice. Finally it was decided to proceed to the election of a minister to Spain and Jay was immediately chosen. Adams was then elected to the other position.[14] Jay's instructions were based on the resolutions of February 23. The most important paragraph was the following:

> That if his Catholic Majesty shall accede to the said treaties [of 1778], and, in concurrence with France and the United States of America, continue the present war with Great Britain for the purpose expressed in the treaties aforesaid, he shall not be precluded from securing to himself the Floridas: On the contrary, if he shall obtain the Floridas from Great Britain, these United States will guaranty the same to his Catholic Majesty: Provided always, that the United States shall enjoy the free navigation of the river Mississippi into and from the sea.[15]

This last clause was to be regarded as an ultimatum. Jay was further instructed to try to obtain some convenient port or ports on the Mississippi below the thirty-first degree for the vessels and merchandise of the inhabitants of the United States. Finally he was told to represent to his Catholic Majesty the great distress of the States in matters of finance and to solicit a loan of five millions of dollars upon the best terms he could, but before making any proposition for a loan he was to endeavor to obtain a subsidy in consideration of the guarantee of the Floridas.[16]

Spain seeks to exclude United States from Mississippi Valley

Jay's mission was a difficult one and it soon revealed the fact that Spain's ambitions were unalterably opposed to the interests and aspirations of the United States. Florida Blanca was reluctant to recognize American independence; he wanted Great Britain to retain Canada as a check on the rising power of the new republic; he insisted on the exclusive right of Spain to navigate the Mississippi; and he denied the claims of the United States to the lands be-

[14] *Secret Journals of Congress*, II, 257.
[15] *Ibid.*, II, 262.
[16] *Ibid.*, II, 263.

tween that river and the Alleghenies. The aim of Spanish diplomacy throughout the war and the peace negotiations was to keep the United States a weak and dependent nation, to confine its territory to the Atlantic seaboard, and to exclude its inhabitants from the Mississippi Valley and the Gulf of Mexico. With Mexico, Cuba, Louisiana, and the Floridas in her possession Spain hoped to build up a powerful empire around the Gulf of Mexico.[17] In fact, Florida Blanca candidly admitted this to Jay, saying, with some degree of warmth, according to the latter's report:

> . . . that unless Spain could exclude all nations from the Gulf of Mexico they might as well admit all; that the king would never relinquish it [i. e., the navigation of the Mississippi]; that the minister regarded it as the principal object to be obtained by the war, and *that obtained,* he should be perfectly easy whether or no Spain procured any other cession; that he considered it far more important than the acquisition of Gibraltar, and that if they did not get it, it was a matter of indifference to him whether the English possessed Mobile or not.[18]

Vergennes instructs Luzerne to support Spanish claims

About the time that Jay was appointed minister to Spain Gérard resigned on account of ill health and the Chevalier de la Luzerne succeeded him as French minister to the United States. Gérard had misled Vergennes as to the real state of opinion on the Mississippi question by representing to him that a large and influential body of intelligent men favored restricting the western boundaries and that the opposition was made up of an anti-French party led by the Adamses and Lees, who were in favor of separate negotiations with England.[19] The idea that there was a strong English party in America opposed to the French Alliance and that public opinion was divided on the question of boundaries probably explains the sudden change in Vergennes' attitude as shown in his instructions to Luzerne. In communicating the substance of these in-

[17] Phillips, 131.
[18] Wharton, IV, 146.
[19] Phillips, 129; Corwin, 265.

structions to Congress Luzerne, who had been in America long enough to realize the trend of public opinion, departed from the argumentative tone of the original and represented himself as merely stating in an impartial way the views of the Spanish Court, France's sole interest being to remove all misunderstanding between her allies. The main points set forth were: (1) that the United States extended no farther west than the limits of settlement laid down in the British proclamation of 1763; (2) that as the territory of the United States did not extend to the Mississippi, they had no right to navigate that river; (3) that it was probable that the King of Spain would conquer the Floridas during the course of the war and that every cause of dispute relative thereto should be removed; and (4) that the lands lying on the east side of the Mississippi, from which settlers were excluded by the proclamation of 1763, were possessions of the crown of Great Britain and therefore subject to Spanish conquest.[20]

Instructions reconsidered and changed

When Vergennes was informed by Luzerne of the real state of feeling in America he realized that open advocacy of Spain's claims would seriously endanger the good relations between France and the United States and he promptly changed his instructions. In a dispatch of June 3, 1780, while repeating his personal belief that Spain had a right to conquer the territory on the east bank of the Mississippi, he held that this was not a matter for France to decide and that Luzerne should do no more than advise individual members of Congress to show greater moderation in the statement of their claims and greater confidence in the magnanimity of the King of Spain. At this time Vergennes held the view that the French guarantee of the territory of the United States was eventual and that its extent could be determined only by the treaty of peace.[21]

At Madrid Florida Blanca informed Jay that the only

[20]*Journals of Continental Congress,* XVI, 114–115; Wharton, III, 488–489.

[21]Corwin, 278–279.

obstacle in the way of a treaty was the pretensions of America to the navigation of the Mississippi and Jay asked Congress for further instructions.[22] The question was referred to a committee and on October 4, 1780, after debate and amendment Congress unanimously adopted the report. Jay was directed to adhere to his former instructions respecting the right of the United States to the free navigation of the Mississippi to the sea, but he was given discretionary powers in regard to regulations governing navigation and free ports below the thirty-first parallel; he was told to adhere strictly to the boundaries of the United States as already fixed by Congress; and finally he was informed that in case Spain should acquire the Floridas, it would be of the greatest importance for the United States "to have the use of the waters running out of Georgia through West Florida into the bay of Mexico," and that as a compensation for this he was authorized to guarantee the possession of the Floridas to Spain.[23]

Jay's negotiations with Florida Blanca

Two weeks later Congress adopted a letter, drafted by James Madison, "To the Ministers Plenipotentiary of the United States at the Courts of Versailles and Madrid, explaining the reasons and principles on which the instructions to Mr. Jay of the 4th instant are founded."[24] In this able document Madison presented probably the strongest case that could be made for claims that were by no means incontestable. The main points of his argument were that by the Treaty of Paris of 1763 all the territory claimed by the United States was expressly and irrevocably ceded to the King of Great Britain; and that the United States in consequence of the revolution in their government were entitled to the benefits of that cession; that the territorial rights of the King of Great Britain within the limits of the United States had accrued to him from the enter-

Madison's argument on claims to western lands

[22] Wharton, III, 724–725.

[23] *Journals of Continental Congress,* XVIII, 900.

[24] *Ibid.,* XVIII, 935–947.

prises, the risks and sacrifices of the present inhabitants and their progenitors; that if the rights to the western lands depended on conquest, the United States had a more extensive claim than Spain could acquire, having by the success of their arms gained possession of all the important settlements on the Illinois and Wabash and established civil government over them, while Spain held no post above Natchez; that the proclamation of 1763 was clearly intended merely to regulate relations with the Indians and did not renounce the cessions made by the Treaty of Paris or affect the boundaries of the colonies as established by their ancient charters; and, finally, that the western territory was by inference included in the guarantee of the French treaty of alliance, which provided for the possible conquest by the United States of Canada and the Bermudas, for

> . . . if it had been understood by the parties that the western territory in question, known to be of so great importance to the United States, and a reduction of it so likely to be undertaken by them, was not included in the general guaranty, can it be supposed that no notice would have been taken of it, when the parties extended their views, not only to Canada, but to the remote and unimportant island of Bermudas?

On right to free navigation of Mississippi

On the subject of the navigation of the Mississippi the argument was not so convincing. The claim was based (1) on devolution from the right stipulated to the King of England by Article VII of the Treaty of Paris, (2) on the natural right of the inhabitants of the upper banks of the river to a free outlet to the sea, and (3) on the usage of nations, quoting a rather doubtful passage from Vattel. Finally he appealed to the generosity of his Catholic Majesty and to the economic interests of Spain and France, pointing out that unless the produce of the western country could find an outlet down the Mississippi to the possessions of Spain and France it would be diverted by way of the Great Lakes and the St. Lawrence into British channels.[25]

[25] *Op. cit.*, pp. 942–946.

Congress offers concessions for Spanish alliance

A few months later, when the Southern States were overrun by the British and general despondency prevailed, Congress at the suggestion of the Virginia delegates, who were acting under instructions of their General Assembly, receded from its former position and by resolution of February 15, 1781, authorized Jay to abandon the claim to the free navigation of the Mississippi below the thirty-first parallel, but at the same time ordered him to exert every possible effort to obtain from Spain the use of the river and of one or more ports. The reason for this action was stated to be to remove every reasonable obstacle to the accession of Spain to the existing alliance between France and the United States.[26]

Jay reluctantly carries out instructions

Jay did not wholly approve of his new instructions. His views on the subject had undergone a change since the days of his conferences with Gérard and Miralles. Spain having entered the war for purposes of her own, he did not believe that concessions of the kind proposed would make her any more zealous in the struggle against England. Furthermore, he had become annoyed and humiliated at the treatment he had received in Spain. Under these circumstances he delayed announcing to Florida Blanca the concession proposed by Congress. Finally, however, being convinced that the Spanish Court had opened his dispatches before they were delivered to him or in some way had learned the nature of his instructions, he submitted an outline of a treaty based on the abandonment of the claim to the navigation of the Mississippi below the thirty-first parallel, announcing to the Spanish minister, however, that

> . . . if the acceptance of it should, together with the proposed alliance, be postponed to a general peace, the United States will cease to consider themselves bound by any propositions or offers, which he may now make in their behalf.[27]

[26]*Op. cit.*, XIX, 152.

[27]Johnston, *Cor. and Public Papers of John Jay*, II, 123–126.

Spain rejects proposal for alliance

Fortunately Jay's efforts proved unsuccessful. As he had expected, the proffered concession did not bring Spain any nearer to an alliance. Jay continued in Spain another year, subjected to official discourtesies and delays. Beyond the loan of $150,000 his mission had been productive of nothing but disappointment and failure. Finally in the spring of 1782, in response to a letter from Franklin, stating that he was needed in the negotiations with England, he left for Paris convinced of the insincerity of the Spanish Court and of its unalterable hostility to the welfare and interests of his country. Thus questions of vital importance to the United States, which from the American and French points of view it was so desirable to settle before entering into negotiations with England, were through the selfish designs of Spain deferred until the end of the war.

Holland drawn into war against England

By the close of 1780 England was at war with the United States, France, Spain, and Holland. There was a preponderance of naval power against her, and on the naval situation the independence of America finally turned. Holland had offended England in several ways. She had permitted John Paul Jones to bring prizes taken from the English into her ports, though finally yielding to the pressure of the British government she had ordered him to leave. In October, 1780, the British captured Henry Laurens, who was on his way to Holland to negotiate a loan and had among his papers the draft of a treaty signed by the chief magistrate of Amsterdam without, however, the authorization of the States-General. The Dutch government was immediately called upon to disavow the document and to punish the signer. It complied with the first demand, but not with the second. On December 20, England declared war.

This incident, however, was not the real reason for the declaration of war. Holland had united with the powers of the North in the Armed Neutrality, which challenged

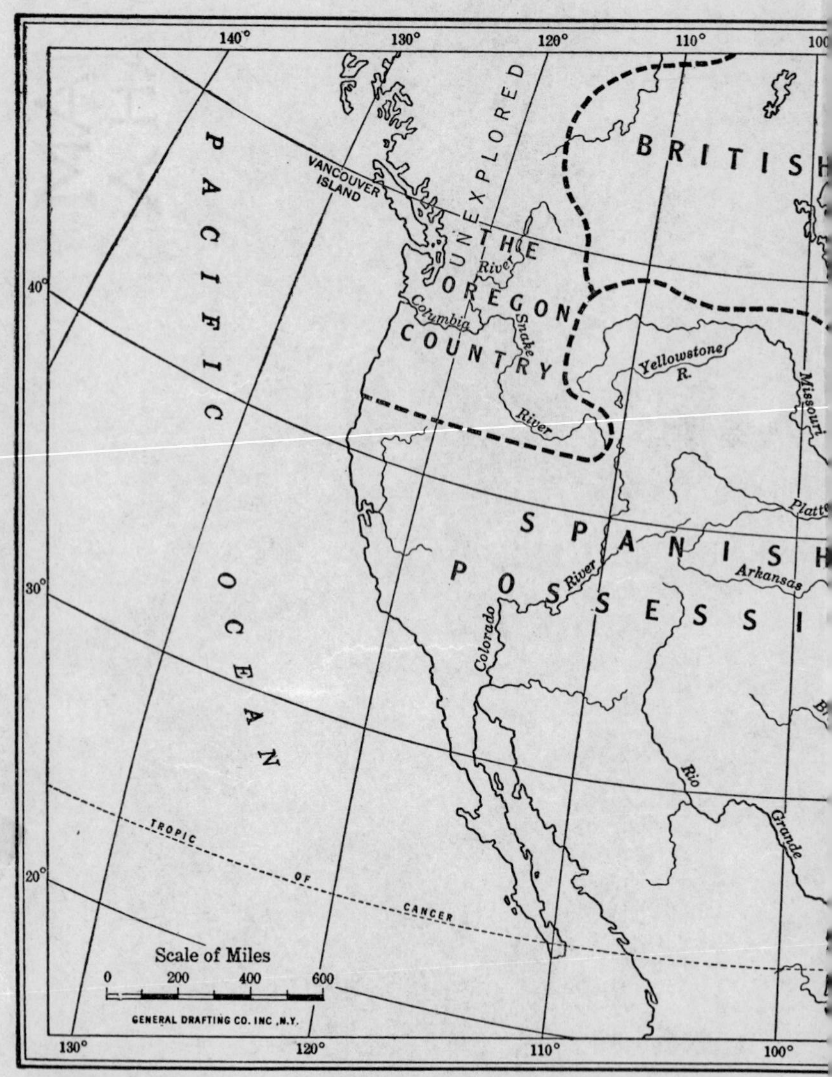

140°
130°
120°
110°
100°
PACIFIC OCEAN
VANCOUVER ISLAND
UNEXPLORED
BRITISH
THE OREGON COUNTRY
River
Columbia
Snake
River
Yellowstone R.
Missouri
Platte
SPANISH POSSESSI
River
Arkansas
Colorado
Rio Grande
40°
30°
20°
TROPIC OF CANCER
Scale of Miles
0 200 400 600
GENERAL DRAFTING CO. INC, N.Y.
130°
120°
110°
100°

2. NORTH A

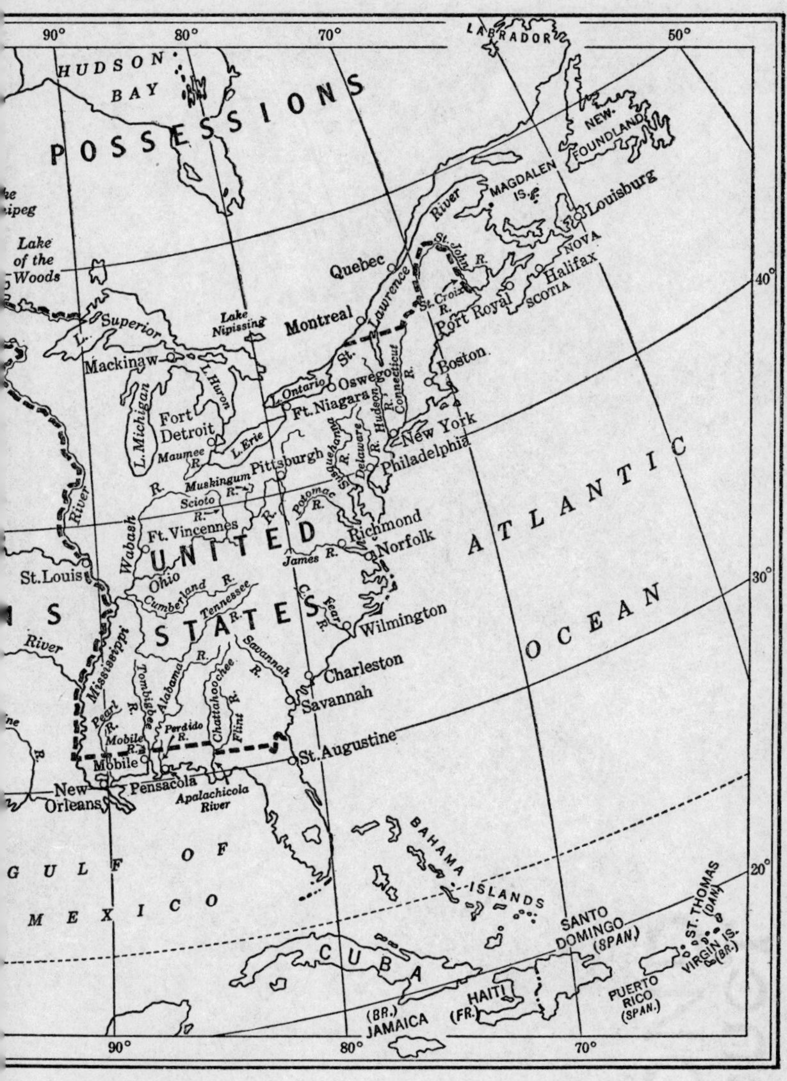
HUDSON
BAY
POSSESSIONS
LABRADOR
NEW FOUNDLAND
MAGDALEN IS.
Louisburg
River
Lake of the Woods
Quebec
St. John R.
NOVA SCOTIA
Halifax
St. Croix R.
Port Royal
Lake Nipissing
Montreal
St. Lawrence
L. Superior
Mackinaw
L. Huron
L. Ontario
Oswego
Connecticut R.
Boston
L. Michigan
Fort Detroit
Ft. Niagara
Hudson R.
Delaware R.
Susquehanna R.
New York
Philadelphia
L. Erie
Maumee R.
Pittsburgh
Muskingum R.
Scioto R.
Potomac R.
Wabash R.
Ft. Vincennes
UNITED STATES
Richmond
James R.
Norfolk
ATLANTIC OCEAN
St. Louis
Ohio
Cumberland R.
Tennessee R.
C. Fear R.
Wilmington
River
Mississippi
Savannah R.
Charleston
Tombigbee R.
Alabama R.
Chattahoochee R.
Flint R.
Savannah
Pearl R.
Mobile R.
Perdido R.
St. Augustine
Mobile
New Orleans
Pensacola
Apalachicola River
GULF OF MEXICO
BAHAMA ISLANDS
ST. THOMAS (DAN.)
VIRGIN IS. (BR.)
SANTO DOMINGO (SPAN.)
CUBA
HAITI (FR.)
PUERTO RICO (SPAN.)
(BR.) JAMAICA
90°
80°
70°
50°
40°
30°
20°

A IN 1783

England's maritime supremacy, and the Dutch island of St. Eustatius in the West Indies had been the principal base for the contraband trade with the United States. England did not care to go to war with Russia and the other associated powers, but she wanted to make an example of Holland, whose commercial rivalry was of more consequence. The moment war was declared the British ministry sent orders to Rodney, who had left New York and was cruising in the West Indies, to destroy St. Eustatius. These orders were ruthlessly carried out.

St. Eustatius devastated by Rodney

The alliance of neutral powers, known as the Armed Neutrality, was based on a declaration of Catherine II of Russia issued in the spring of 1780 and communicated to Denmark, Sweden, Holland, and Portugal, as well as to the belligerent powers of England, France, and Spain. It proclaimed the right of neutrals to trade with countries at war, it adopted the principle that free ships make free goods, it undertook to limit contraband strictly to military supplies, and it declared that no port should be regarded as blockaded unless a sufficient number of vessels were maintained in front of it to make an attempt to enter dangerous.[28] Franklin regarded this move with enthusiasm. Under date of June 3, 1780, he wrote:

The Armed Neutrality

> Russia, Sweden, Denmark, and Holland are raising a strong naval force to establish the free navigation for neutral ships and of all their cargoes, though belonging to enemies, except contraband—that is, military stores. France and Spain have approved of it, and it is likely to become henceforth the law of nations that *free ships make free goods.* England does not like this confederacy. I wish they would extend it still further, and ordain that unarmed trading ships, as well as fishermen and tanners, should be respected as working for the common benefit of mankind, and never be interrupted in their operations even by national enemies; but let those only fight with one another whose trade it is, and who are armed and paid for the purpose.[29]

---

[28] Wharton, III, 608. Also J. B. Scott, *The Armed Neutralities of 1780 and 1800.*

[29] Wharton, III. 761.

Principles approved by Congress

The Congress of the United States approved of the Russian declaration and directed the board of admiralty to prepare and report instructions comformable to its principles for the commanders of the armed vessels of the United States.[30] These resolutions were transmitted by John Adams to the States-General of Holland with the request that they be forwarded to Russia, Sweden, and Denmark, and that the United States be admitted as a party to the confederacy.[31] When Dana was sent to St. Petersburg he was instructed to accede to the Armed Neutrality but in his letter of September 5, 1782, he explained that it was limited to neutrals and to the duration of the war.[32] While the Armed Neutrality was far from being effective, the principles it proclaimed were of fundamental importance and afforded a rallying point for neutrals in future wars.

The end of the war

With no friends left on the continent of Europe and a strong combination of naval powers arrayed against her, England's attempt to reduce her former colonies was assuming a hopeless aspect. The end came October 19, 1781, when Cornwallis surrendered at Yorktown. This result was brought about by the timely appearance in the Chesapeake of the French fleet under Count de Grasse and the rapid movement of Washington with Rochambeau's expeditionary French force from the Hudson to the historic Virginia peninsula, where La Fayette, at the head of an American force, was holding Cornwallis in check. The French Alliance had finally given Washington that superiority on land and sea without which the war would have lingered on indefinitely. There were more Frenchmen, soldiers and sailors, engaged in the operations at Yorktown than there were Americans.

On June 14, 1781, Congress annulled Adams's commis-

---

[30] *Op. cit.*, IV, 80.

[31] *Ibid.*, p. 274.

[32] *Ibid.*, V, 700, and VI, 306. See also Livingston's report on the attitude of the United States, Wharton, VI, 473; and subsequent resolutions of Congress, *ibid.*, pp. 481, 717, 742, and *Secret Journals*, III, 414.

sion as sole plenipotentiary for negotiating peace, and appointed four other commissioners to act in conjunction with him. These were Benjamin Franklin, John Jay, Henry Laurens, and Thomas Jefferson. Adams ascribed this change in part to the French government and in part to Franklin. As he had regarded the day of his appointment as sole plenipotentiary as the proudest moment of his existence, so now he described the year in which he was deprived of it as "the most anxious and mortifying year of my whole life." While waiting in Paris for the time to come for opening negotiations with England Adams had entered upon a correspondence with Vergennes so lacking in tact that the French minister finally informed him that he would receive no further communications on American affairs except through Franklin, who was the sole minister accredited by Congress to the French Court. Shortly afterward Adams received instructions to proceed to Holland for the purpose of negotiating a treaty and securing a loan. For some months he met with little success. The Dutch government was slow to recognize the independence of the United States, notwithstanding the fact that Holland was now at war with England. But the surrender of Cornwallis produced a more favorable condition of affairs and in April, 1782, Adams was given official recognition. Two months later he secured from the bankers of Holland a loan of $2,000,000 and on October 8 he had the satisfaction of signing with the government a commercial treaty, the second in the history of his country. He returned to Paris, much elated over his success, to participate in the final peace negotiations.[33]

Peace commissioners

Meanwhile the first steps in the negotiations with England had been undertaken by Franklin alone. Jefferson had declined the appointment as peace commissioner. Laurens was still a prisoner in the Tower of London, Jay was still in Spain, and Adams had not returned from

Instructions adopted by Congress

[33]Wharton, IV, 224, 401, 526; V, 49, 86, 97, 315, 408, 803

Holland. The instructions to the peace commissioners had been the subject of long debate and serious differences of opinion in Congress. As finally drafted they were brief. The commissioners were told not to accede to any treaty which did not "effectually secure the independence and sovereignty of the thirteen states," and which did not leave the French treaties in full force and validity. On the subject of boundaries they were referred to the instructions of 1779 and 1780 as expressing the desires and expectations of Congress, but they were given a wide discretion. The last paragraph, which in its final form was dictated by the French envoy Luzerne,[34] proved embarrassing to the commissioners and occasioned much controversy. It was:

> You are to make the most candid and confidential communications, upon all subjects, to the ministers of our generous ally the King of France; to undertake nothing in the negotiations for peace or truce, without their knowledge and concurrence; and ultimately to govern yourselves by their advice and opinion.[35]

First overtures of peace

The first approaches to Franklin were made in January, 1782, by David Hartley, a personal friend and a member of Parliament. Hartley broached the question of a separate peace, but this overture was promptly rejected by Franklin.[36] In March and April there took place the exchange of letters between Franklin and Lord Shelburne which led the latter to send a special agent to Paris to confer with Franklin.[37] The man chosen for this mission was Richard Oswald, a retired Scotch merchant, who had extensive interests in America. Franklin proposed to Oswald the cession of Canada by Great Britain to the United States as a desirable basis for a durable peace.[38] This

[34] *Journals of Continental Congress*, XX, 625–626.

[35] *Ibid.*, XX, 651.

[36] Wharton, V, 80, 112.

[37] *Ibid.*, pp. 535–536.

[38] A full account of negotiations to July 1 is given in Franklin's *Journal*, Wharton, V, 535–585.

idea appeared reasonable to Oswald and on his return to London he presented it in an interview with Rockingham, Shelburne, and Fox. Later he reported to Franklin that the Prime Minister and Shelburne did not seem averse to it, but that Fox seemed startled at the proposition.[39]

State of the British ministry

The preliminary negotiations were delayed at this time by a dispute in the British ministry as to whether they should be conducted under the direction of Shelburne, who was Secretary for Colonial Affairs, or of Fox, who was Secretary for Foreign Affairs. About the time that Oswald returned to Paris in May, Fox sent Thomas Grenville over with a commission to open negotiations with France. His instructions, however, related to America as well, and it was evident that Fox wanted to make Grenville the sole negotiator for Great Britain.[40] Not only did Shelburne protest against this arrangement, but it was objected to by Vergennes, who wanted to keep the two sets of negotiations separate. He said to Franklin:

> They want to treat with us for you, but this the king will not agree to. He thinks it not consistent with the dignity of your state. You will treat for yourselves, and every one of the powers at war with England will make its own treaty. All that is necessary for our common security is that the treaties go hand in hand and are signed all on the same day.[41]

The situation was relieved by the death of Rockingham, July 1. Shelburne became Prime Minister, Fox retired, Oswald continued negotiations with Franklin, and Fitzherbert replaced Grenville in the negotiations with France.

Franklin's proposals

On July 9 Franklin submitted to Oswald certain propositions as the basis for a treaty, and with these the real negotiations began. As necessary conditions Franklin demanded: (1) Independence full and complete in every sense, and the withdrawal of all troops; (2) Settlement of

[39]Fitzmaurice, *Life of William, Earl of Shelburne*, II, 140.
[40]*Ibid.*, p. 137.
[41]Wharton, V, 564.

the boundaries; (3) Confinement of the boundaries of Canada to at least what they were before the Quebec Act, if not to still narrower limits; (4) Freedom of fishing on the banks of Newfoundland. The following were stated as advisable stipulations: (1) Reparation for injuries inflicted by the British; (2) Acknowledgment of the error of England in distressing the colonies; (3) Reciprocal freedom of trade; (4) the cession of Canada and Nova Scotia.[42]

Jay objects to form of Oswald's commission

Negotiations continued for some time on the basis of the above proposals. Jay, who reached Paris the latter part of June, was prevented by illness from taking much part in the early negotiations. When he was able to do so he at once raised questions as to the wording of Oswald's commission, which authorized him to treat with the commissioners of the *colonies* or *plantations*.[43] Vergennes and Franklin thought the commission sufficient to warrant proceeding with the negotiations, but Jay insisted that Great Britain must recognize the independence of the United States before entering upon a discussion of the terms of peace.[44] Jay soon became thoroughly distrustful of Vergennes. In a conference with the latter's secretary, Rayneval, the questions of the navigation of the Mississippi and the western lands came up and Rayneval upheld the Spanish point of view. Jay requested Rayneval to put his views in writing. In the memoir which he presented Rayneval proposed that the territory between the Mississippi and the Alleghenies from the northern boundary of the Floridas to the Ohio should be reserved for the Indians, the southwestern portion under the protection of Spain, and the northeastern portion under the protection of the United States. The country north of the Ohio was recognized as belonging to Great Britain, and the right of

---

[42]Fitzmaurice, *Life* of *Shelburne,* II, 166.

[43]Wharton, V, 613.

[44]For Jay's account of the negotiations see his report to Livingston of November 17, 1782, Wharton, VI, 11–49.

the Americans to navigate the Mississippi was denied.[45] Although Rayneval represented these as his personal views Jay was convinced that they afforded conclusive evidence of a determination on the part of Vergennes to subordinate the territorial interests of the United States to the negotiations between Spain and Great Britain. A few days later Jay received from English agents what purported to be a translation of a letter to Vergennes from Marbois, who was then in Philadelphia, in which strong opposition was expressed to the American claim to the Newfoundland fisheries. The authenticity of the letter was later denied and at best it was in the language of Livingston "a mere gossiping letter that bound nobody."[46] About the same time Jay learned that Rayneval had been sent by Vergennes to London on a secret mission. To Jay's way of thinking this mission could have no other object than the consummation of the plot to deprive America of her right to the fisheries, to the navigation of the Mississippi, and to the western lands. He determined, therefore, to make every effort to counteract it and without consulting Franklin he persuaded Benjamin Vaughan, a personal friend of Shelburne and a friend of the American cause, to go at once to London and present the American case to the Prime Minister. As a matter of fact, the object of Rayneval's visit was to sound Shelburne on the general situation and to urge Spain's claims to Gibraltar, though American claims were incidentally discussed.[47]

Jay's suspicions

Separate negotiations

The effect of Vaughan's visit, which was simultaneous with that of Rayneval, was to convince the British cabinet that a serious feud had arisen between the Americans and their allies, which the British government could use to good advantage. They decided, therefore, to make the changes in Oswald's commission to suit the American de-

[45] Wharton, VI, 25.

[46] *Ibid.*, V, 238–241.

[47] Fitzmaurice, *Life of Lord Shelburne*, II, 176–182.

mand and to hurry forward the separate negotiations.[48] It was believed that the elimination of America would greatly facilitate the settlements with France and Spain.

The questions at issue

Adams arrived in Paris October 26. By this time England had conceded the essential points contained in Franklin's proposals to Oswald of July 9. There remained, however, several questions on which agreement was very difficult. These were: (1) the right claimed by the Americans to dry fish on the coasts of Newfoundland and other British possessions, (2) the payment of debts due to British subjects prior to the war, and (3) compensation for the confiscated property of loyalists. As soon as Adams got into the negotiations he insisted on the right to dry fish on British coasts. He declared that he would not sign a treaty on any other terms. By way of concession, however, he said that he would agree to a stipulation permitting British creditors to sue for the recovery of their debts.

The Provisional Treaty of November 30, 1782

The terms were all finally agreed upon and on November 30, 1782, the Provisional Treaty was signed. Laurens, released from the Tower of London, reached Paris in time to affix his name to the treaty. Article I acknowledged the United States, mentioning all thirteen by name to be "free, sovereign, and independent states." Article II defined the boundaries substantially in accordance with the claims of Congress except in one particular: the line from the point where the forty-fifth parallel reaches the St. Lawrence instead of running across to Lake Nipissing was to follow the St. Lawrence and the Great Lakes, thus leaving the large triangle inclosed by Lakes Erie, Ontario, and Huron, to Canada. By Article III, it was agreed that the people of the United States should continue to enjoy unmolested the right to take fish on the Banks of Newfoundland, and that they should have the liberty to take part in the inshore fisheries of all the British dominions in

[48] *Op. cit.*, p. 183.

America, and also "the liberty to dry and cure fish in any of the unsettled bays, harbors and creeks of Nova Scotia, Magdalen Islands, and Labrador, so long as the same shall remain unsettled." John Adams claimed a right to the inshore fisheries and access to the shores for the purpose of drying and curing the catch, while the British regarded it as a privilege. The word *liberty* was finally adopted as a compromise. This fisheries article proved to be a fruitful source of misunderstanding and bad feeling. In fact, as we shall see later, no other controversy in American diplomacy has persisted so long or brought the country so often to the verge of war. Article IV provided that there should be no lawful impediment to the recovery of debts. In Article V it was agreed that Congress should recommend to the legislatures of the states the restitution of the confiscated estates of loyalists. The only other article of importance was number VIII, which declared that, "The navigation of the river Mississippi, from its source to the ocean, shall forever remain free and open to the subjects of Great Britain and the citizens of the United States." Finally there was a secret article relating to West Florida which will be considered in the next chapter.[49]

Violation of instructions of Congress

In signing this treaty without the knowledge or concurrence of Vergennes the commissioners had violated the instructions of Congress. Franklin had at first opposed this course but had finally acquiesced in the decision of Jay and Adams. It took all of his suavity and tact to appease Vergennes. He said to him: "Nothing has been agreed in the preliminaries, contrary to the interests of France; and no peace is to take place between us and England till you have concluded yours." Vergennes' feelings could not have been very deeply wounded, for a few weeks later he made at Franklin's solicitation another loan of 6,000,000 livres to the United States.

[49](Malloy) *Treaties and Conventions of the United States*, I, 580.

France and Spain sign peace with England

Nevertheless the conclusion of the Provisional Treaty made it impossible for France and Spain to continue the war, while the raising of the siege of Gibraltar and Rodney's victory over the French fleet in the West Indies made it imperative for them to make the best terms they could. The preliminaries between England, on the one hand, and France and Spain on the other were signed January 20, 1783. France reverted largely to the *status quo,* while Spain gained Minorca and the Floridas, the latter without definition of boundaries.

How the treaty was received

When the treaty of peace was received by Congress the feeling of the majority was that the commissioners were not justified in departing from their instructions. They were, therefore, thanked for their services, but mildly reproved for their conduct toward France.[50] Jay's course has been the subject of much controversy and opinion is still divided as to whether his suspicions of Vergennes helped the course of negotiations or not.[51] In England, the treaty was regarded as too liberal and caused the overthrow of Shelburne, but the new ministry signed the definitive treaty in the exact terms of the preliminary September 3, 1783.[52] The American commissioners failed, however, in their efforts to form a commercial treaty with Great Britain. The mother country was not yet ready to modify her old commercial system or to grant any privileges to her rebellious offspring.

[50]For an interesting report of the discussion in Congress, See Hunt, *Writings of James Madison*, I, 403–418.

[51]See Corwin, Chap. XV.

[52](Malloy) *Treaties and Conventions of the United States*, I, 586.

CHAPTER III

COMMERCIAL RESTRICTIONS AND WAR DEBTS

Commercial clauses of the French treaty

In establishing their independence the United States looked forward to a happy era of trade expansion and commercial prosperity. Freed from the burdensome restrictions of the English navigation laws they hoped to establish trade relations with all the nations of the civilized world on the basis of "the most perfect equality and reciprocity," to quote the language of the preamble of the commercial treaty with France. But even in this treaty the liberal proposals of Congress were reduced to less liberal terms. The instructions to the American commissioners proposed absolute equality of treatment in each other's ports, that is, that Frenchmen should pay no higher duties or imports in American ports than Americans paid, and *vice versa.*[1] For this proposal was substituted the most-favored-nation clause in the conditional form, Article II:

> The Most Christian King and the United States engage mutually not to grant any particular favor to other nations, in respect to commerce and navigation, which shall not immediately become common to the other party, who shall enjoy the same favor freely, if the concession was freely made, or on allowing the same compensation, if the concession was conditional.

Articles III and IV provided that the citizens or subjects of the contracting parties should not pay in each other's ports higher duties or imports than were paid by the most favored nations. The Americans also proposed absolute freedom of trade with the French West Indies but received

[1] *Journals of Continental Congress*, V, 768.

only limited privileges.[2] American ships of limited tonnage could carry enumerated goods to specified ports, and take back rum and molasses. The enumerated list was liberal and many American ships engaged in the trade.[3]

Treaties with other nations

By the treaty of 1782 with the Netherlands Americans were granted most-favored-nation privileges and admitted to the Dutch West Indies, but the Dutch duties were very high, though not so high in the island possessions as in the home ports. The only other commercial treaties which the agents of Congress succeeded in negotiating during the period of the Confederation were those with Sweden in 1783, Prussia in 1785, and Morocco in 1787. The Swedish and Prussian treaties extended most-favored-nation treatment, but the volume of trade with Prussia was very small and Sweden imposed so many restrictions and prohibitions on commerce that American trade was reduced to almost nothing. American tobacco carried in American ships had to pay much heavier duty than if carried in Swedish ships. Other European countries made the same discrimination, though not in all cases was the duty so high as that charged in Sweden.[4] The Moroccan treaty dealt largely with questions relating to the protection of life and property. Trade with Great Britain and the other countries with whom we had no commercial treaties was subject to arbitrary regulations.

General plan of commercial treaties

On May 7, 1784, Congress elected Jefferson minister plenipotentiary in addition to Franklin and Adams for the purpose of negotiating commercial treaties with European nations. On the same day, Jay, who was on his way back from Europe, was elected Secretary for Foreign Affairs, an

[2]Cf. Articles XII and XIII of the treaty plan (*Journals of Continental Congress*, I, 771) with Article XXX of the treaty.

[3]Bemis, *Jay's Treaty: A Study in Commerce and Diplomacy*, 21 note; Mahan, *War of 1812*, I, 92.

[4]See Jefferson's report of Dec. 16, 1793, on "Commercial Privileges and Restrictions," *Am. State Papers, Foreign Relations*, I, 300. Although made at a later date this report describes conditions substantially as they existed during the period of the Confederation.

office which he held until 1790, when Jefferson assumed the duties of first Secretary of State under the Constitution. The general plan of commercial treaties adopted by Congress in the instructions to the new commission was drafted by Jefferson and contained some notable principles which will be discussed later. The reason why the commissioners met with such scant success will appear in the following pages.[5]

Restrictions encountered by American trade

Europe still believed in the mercantile theory and clung to the system of colonial monopoly. By declaring independence the United States forfeited the lucrative trade which they had carried on as colonies with the British West Indies and after the conclusion of peace Great Britain refused to permit American ships to enter her colonial ports. Her refusal to embody in the definitive treaty of 1783 any commercial clauses was a bitter disappointment to the commissioners and to Congress, and she rejected all proposals for a commercial treaty until 1794 when Jay's unsatisfactory treaty was signed. As Spain and Portugal permitted no direct intercourse between their American possessions and any foreign country, there was not a port in the Western Hemisphere, outside of the few open ports in the French and Dutch West Indies, into which a vessel bearing the American flag could lawfully go. British restrictions which had been substantially the same for ten years were summed up by Jefferson in 1793 as follows:

> Great Britain admits in her islands our vegetables, live provisions, horses, wood, tar, pitch, and turpentine, rice, and bread stuff, by a proclamation of her executive, limited always to the term of a year, but hitherto renewed from year to year. She prohibits our salted fish and other salted provisions. She does not permit our vessels to carry thither our own produce. Her vessels alone may take it from us, and bring us in exchange, rum, molasses, sugar, coffee, cocoa nuts, ginger, and pimento. There are, indeed, some freedoms in the island of Dominica, but, under such circumstances, as to be little used by us. In the

[5]The full reports of their negotiations are in *Dip. Cor., 1783–1789*, II, 195–346.

British continental colonies, and in Newfoundland, all our productions are prohibited, and our vessels forbidden to enter their ports. Their governors, however, in times of distress, have power to permit a temporary importation of certain articles, in their own bottoms, but not in ours.[6]

American commerce dependent on Great Britain

American vessels were permitted to carry to England raw materials, unmanufactured goods, and naval stores produced in the United States. There were certain specified exceptions falling under the head of raw materials, such as oil and other whale products, which were excluded. In spite of all restrictions, in 1790, the first year in which records were kept, over seventy-five per cent of all the foreign commerce of the United States was with Great Britain, and British vessels carried over half of this commerce.[7] Ninety per cent of American imports came from Great Britain, mostly in the form of manufactured goods. England was the only country in which American merchants could get long-term credit. French merchants had not succeeded in replacing England in the American market, and had suffered from the financial chaos that followed the Revolution. Americans preferred English goods and refused to be converted to French tastes, but more important than this was their familiarity with English business methods.

The Confederation unable to gain concessions

Although the states had won their political freedom their economic dependence upon England was almost as great as it had been during the colonial period. This situation continued until the War of 1812 and was an ever-present and dominating factor in the diplomacy of the period. In fact, the commercial status of the states was in some respects worse than it had been before the Revolution, for they had lost many of the rights which they had enjoyed as British subjects, and the principles which they proclaimed in behalf of commercial freedom made little im-

[6] *A. S. P., F. R.*, I, 302.

[7] Bemis, 34.

pression upon the economic system of Great Britain, or of continental Europe. Although the United States was the largest customer England had, the British understood perfectly the dependent position of their former colonies and refused to make any concessions. In vain did the Americans protest and resort to retaliation. Some of the states imposed discriminatory tariff and tonnage duties, while others, in retaliation for the exclusion of their ships from the West Indies, passed laws prohibiting British vessels from taking on American goods in their ports. These efforts all failed because the states, engaged in commercial disputes with one another, would not take uniform and concerted action against England. As Washington said: "One state passes a prohibitory law respecting some article, another state opens wide the avenue for its admission. One assembly makes a system, another assembly unmakes it." The need for a national commercial policy was one of the main arguments advanced in favor of the adoption of the new Constitution.[8]

England continues to hold frontier posts

Commercial relations with Great Britain were furthermore complicated by the disputes that arose out of certain provisions of the peace treaty. As no definite time had been set for the withdrawal of British troops from the territory of the United States, the treaty merely stating that it should take place "with all convenient speed," the British government decided to delay the evacuation of the posts on the American side of the northwest frontier, the principal ones being Oswego, Niagara, Detroit, and Mackinaw. These posts commanded the lucrative fur trade and maintained British ascendancy over the Indians north of the Ohio River. British troops had also taken away thousands of slaves in direct violation of the treaty. As an excuse for holding the posts the British government alleged the failure of the United States to carry out Articles IV and V of the treaty, the one providing that no legal

[8]See Bemis, Chapter II, "Anglo-American Commerce."

obstacle should be opposed to the collection of debts due British merchants and the other that Congress would recommend to the states the restitution within certain limits of the confiscated property of loyalists. It was true that some of the states had failed to carry out fully the first stipulation, but so far as the second was concerned, it was clearly understood from the first that the word *recommend* was used in its ordinary sense and that the United States assumed no obligation to force the states to comply with the recommendation.[9] The British argument was weak and largely an after-thought. The real reason for holding the frontier posts was in the first instance the fur trade, at that time the most profitable industry in North America. Later there was developed the definite project of creating within the boundaries assigned to the United States by the treaty of 1783 a neutral Indian zone which would serve as a buffer between Canada and the United States and exclude the latter from the Great Lakes and the St. Lawrence.[10] Meanwhile British officials were continually tampering with the Indians and inciting them to acts of hostility against the advancing American frontier north of the Ohio. This policy culminated in serious conflicts with the Indians during Washington's first administration.

Mission of John Adams to England

From the close of the Revolution to the organization of the new government under the Constitution British policy on the question of a commercial treaty, as well as on matters relating to the execution of the peace treaty, was one of evasion and delay. The British watched with satisfaction the growing weakness of the Confederation and held it in such slight esteem that they did not even send a minister to the United States until 1791, when Washington's administration had infused new life into the republic and

[9]Jefferson's letter to Hammond of May 29, 1792, sets forth the American side of the dispute ably and fully, *A. S. P., F. R.*, I, 201–237. See also Bemis, 100–102.

[10]Bemis, Chapter VI.

inspired confidence in its future. Meanwhile the Congress of the Confederation had made the mistake of sending a minister to the Court of George III in the person of John Adams. He remained in London from 1785 to 1788, stared at by the populace, but conducting himself with dignity. He made no progress toward the settlement of the disputes that had arisen out of the peace treaty or toward the negotiation of a treaty of commerce but he had ample time to record his impressions of the English as well as to give a detailed account of his official transactions.[11]

Jefferson's mission to France

In striking contrast with Adams's trying experience in London was Jefferson's delightful and interesting sojourn at the Court of France. He succeeded Franklin as minister in 1785 and continued there until October, 1789, witnessing the opening scenes of the great Revolution. In fact, he was consulted by La Fayette and other leaders on the formation of a constitution, but, as he tells us in his autobiography, he was careful not to compromise his official position by interfering in the internal affairs of the country to which he was accredited.[12] His official duties were confined to a few objects: the admission into France of whale oils, salted fish, salted meats, rice, and tobacco on favorable terms, and the free admission of American products into the French islands. Jefferson was as much at home among the French people as Franklin and almost as beloved by them. He parted from his friends with sadness.

> I cannot leave this great and good country without expressing my sense of its preëminence of character among the nations of the earth. A more benevolent people I have never known, nor greater warmth and devotedness in their select friendships. Their kindness and accommodation to strangers is unparalleled, and the hospitality of Paris is beyond anything I had conceived to be practicable in a large city. Their eminence too in science, the communicative dispositions of their scientific men, the

[11] *Dip. Cor. of U. S., 1783–1789*, IV, 151, to V, 369.

[12] Ford, *Writings of Jefferson*, I, 153–155. [Federal Edition, 12 vols.]

politeness of the general manners, the ease and vivacity of their conversation, give a charm to their society to be found nowhere else.[13]

Relations with Spain

Relations with Spain during the period of the Confederation and for some years thereafter were in a very unsatisfactory state, and a subject of constant anxiety and irritation. Although that power had gone to war with England she had refused to become a party to the French-American alliance, and it was only with great reluctance that she finally agreed, after the war was over, to recognize the independence of the United States. Spain had failed to get Gibraltar, her main objective in the war, and she had failed in her efforts to exclude the Americans from the Mississippi Valley. She was all the more determined, therefore, to deny to them the use of the Mississippi as an outlet to the sea. The right to navigate the Mississippi throughout its entire course had been granted to British subjects by the treaty of 1763, to which both France and Spain were parties. In the treaty of 1783 Great Britain confirmed this right to citizens of the United States. Spain held that it was not a right at all, but a privilege extended to Great Britain which she had no power to transfer to a third party.

The West Florida boundary

Another point of dispute was the boundary between the United States and West Florida, which by the treaty of peace with England was fixed at the thirty-first parallel. But in the preliminary treaty of 1782 there was a secret article which was as follows:

It is hereby understood and agreed that in case Great Britain, at the conclusion of the present war, shall recover, or be put in possession of West Florida, the line of north boundary between the said province and the United States shall be a line drawn from the mouth of the river Yassous, where it unites with the Mississippi, due east, to the river Apalachicola.[14]

---

[13] *Op. cit.*, I, 157. The full correspondence relating to Jefferson's French mission is found in *Dip. Cor., 1783–1789*, II, 349, to IV, 149.

[14] (Malloy) *Treaties and Conventions*, I, 584.

This had been the northern boundary of the British province of West Florida as fixed by the royal proclamation of 1767. Great Britain did not recover West Florida and at the close of the war she ceded the province to Spain without defining its boundaries. Spain therefore claimed the whole province as defined by the proclamation of 1767 and by the secret article given above which had come to her knowledge. From 1783 to 1795 this important territory, extending from the Mississippi on the west to the Apalachicola on the east, and from parallel thirty-one degrees on the south to 32° 28′ on the north, was the subject of an apparently irreconcilable dispute.

The Jay-Gardoqui negotiations

When Jay was called from Madrid to Paris in 1782, he left William Carmichael as *chargé d'affaires*, but his duties were largely routine.[15] In 1785 Don Diego de Gardoqui arrived at Philadelphia as Spanish *chargé d'affaires* and soon entered into negotiations with Jay, who was then Secretary for Foreign Affairs. Jay was instructed by Congress to insist on the free navigation of the Mississippi and the boundary of West Florida as fixed by the treaty with England.[16] Gardoqui refused to yield on these points and stated that the king did not regard the treaty of 1783 as binding. Jay asked Congress for new instructions, and proposed in return for liberal commercial privileges, to agree for a term of twenty-five years to "forbear the use" of the right to navigate the Mississippi, leaving the boundary question to future discussion and compromise.[17]

Division of opinion in Congress

This proposal gave rise to a long and vehement debate. The New England and Middle States (Delaware not represented during the discussion), more interested in promoting commercial relations with Spain than in safeguarding the interests of the southwest, voted solidly for releasing Jay from his instructions, while the delegates

[15]For information in regard to Carmichael's mission, see *Dip. Cor., 1783–1789*, VI, 373–417.

[16]*Secret Journals of Congress*, III, 586.

[17]*Dip. Cor., 1783–1789*, VI, 200.

from Maryland, Virginia, North and South Carolina, and Georgia voted with equal unanimity against the change. As the vote by states was seven to five, attention was called to the fact that no treaty could be ratified without the vote of nine states, and it was argued from this that Jay's instructions could not be changed except with the consent of nine states. The point was overruled and the instructions changed.[18] Madison was thoroughly indignant and unbosomed himself in a long letter to Jefferson. He asked him to imagine the effect of a stipulation, which "shuts up the Mississippi twenty-five or thirty years," on the Assembly of Virginia "already jealous of northern politics" and having in it "about thirty members from the western waters."[19] Fortunately Jay was unable to come to terms with Gardoqui even on the basis proposed.[20]

Negotiations at Madrid

When Jefferson became Secretary of State under Washington, William Short was sent to Spain to join Carmichael and they were appointed commissioners plenipotentiary for the negotiation of a treaty. Meanwhile the situation in America was approaching a crisis. The West was in a state of perpetual excitement and irritation,—irritation against Spain for closing the Mississippi and inciting the Indians to attacks on the American frontier, and irritation against their own government for its failure to force once and for all a settlement of the whole Mississippi question. The settlers of Kentucky and Tennessee had lost all patience, and instigated by Gênet, the minister of the French Republic then at war with Spain, had to be restrained by the national government from organizing a military expedition for the purpose of seizing New Orleans.[21] Short, who after Carmichael's resignation had been raised to the rank of minister resident, was proceeding with the discussions at

---

[18]*Secret Journals of Congress,* IV, 81–127.

[19]Hunt, *Writings of Madison,* II, 263.

[20]The Jay-Gardoqui Negotiations are found in *Dip. Cor., 1783–1789,* VI, 65–272.

[21]*A. S. P., F. R.,* I, 454–460.

Madrid,[22] but the situation was so critical that in November, 1794, Washington commissioned Thomas Pinckney, who was then in London, to go to Spain as envoy extraordinary in order to reinforce Short and bring the negotiations to a conclusion. A few months later Godoy, the new Spanish premier, made peace with France, and fearing that England would unite with the United States in an attack on Louisiana, signed with Pinckney the treaty of October 27, 1795. Spain accepted the thirty-first parallel as the boundary of West Florida, and agreed that the navigation of the Mississippi, "from its source to the ocean," should be free to the citizens of the United States. The latter were also given permission for the space of three years to deposit their merchandise at New Orleans, paying only warehouse charges, pending reshipment on ocean-going vessels. This so-called right of deposit, without which the right of navigation was of little benefit, soon became the subject of hot disputes and so continued until the acquisition of Louisiana.[23]

The Spanish treaty of 1795

When Americans tried after the Revolution to revive commercial relations with the Mediterranean countries they found themselves exposed to the depredations of the Barbary corsairs. The north African states of Morocco, Algiers, Tunis, and Tripoli had long been in the habit of levying tribute on the commerce of the Mediterranean, and the powers of Europe had for various reasons acquiesced in the system. Before the Revolution, American commerce had been under British protection and was covered by the payments which Great Britain annually made to these petty powers. The volume of American trade passing through the Straits of Gibraltar had been considerable. About one-sixth of the wheat and flour exported from the colonies, one-fourth of the dried fish and a

The Barbary corsairs

[22] *Op. cit.*, I, 433–444.

[23] On Pinckney's mission see *A. S. P., F. R.*, I, 469, 533–549; also G. L. Rives, "Spain and the United States in 1795," in *Am. Hist. Rev.*, IV, 62–79.

considerable quantity of rice were sold in Mediterranean ports and brought good prices. There were between eighty and a hundred ships engaged in this trade manned by twelve hundred seamen. This trade was of course interrupted during the war.[24] In the instructions to the commissioners to France, Congress had proposed an article placing the Mediterranean commerce of the United States under the protection of the King of France,[25] but all they could obtain was a promise of his good offices.[26]

Negotiations with Tripoli and Morocco

While Adams was in London an ambassador from Tripoli arrived and Jefferson came over from Paris to confer with him. The interview as reported by Adams and Jefferson was not without its humorous features. The ambassador informed them, however, that a treaty of peace with Tripoli would cost them about $150,000 and that Tunis and Morocco would each demand about the same amount, while Algiers would want as much as the three smaller powers combined, approximately half a million. As these sums were considered unreasonable and as Congress had authorized the expenditure of only eighty thousand dollars in negotiations with the Barbary powers, there was not much that the commissioners could do. As Morocco had captured an American vessel the commissioners sent Thomas Barclay as their agent to secure the liberation of the vessel and crew, and if possible, to negotiate a treaty. Through the friendly offices of the Spanish court the vessel was released and Barclay secured what was considered a very liberal treaty from the Emperor of Morocco at the moderate cost of about ten thousand dollars. The treaty was approved and signed by Adams and Jefferson in January, 1787, and duly ratified by Congress.[27]

---

[24]For a view of relations with Barbary powers during the Confederation see Jefferson's report of December 28, 1790, in *A. S. P., F. R.*, I, 104.

[25]*Journals of Continental Congress*, V, 770.

[26]Article VIII of the Commercial Treaty of 1778.

[27]A report of Barclay's negotiations is found in *Dip. Cor., 1783–1789*, V, 168–223.

This treaty did not help matters much, for the other states continued their depredations. Algiers had already seized two American vessels and consigned their crews to slavery. High insurance rates and terror of slavery practically put a stop to all American commerce with the Mediterranean. Jefferson declared that he preferred war to tribute and while in Paris undertook to form an association of nations for concerted operations against the Barbary powers. He drafted a series of articles and submitted them to the ambassadors of the powers concerned, but he could not get the coöperation of the American Congress.[28]

War or tribute

After the adoption of the Constitution the United States finally decided to follow the example of the European powers and purchase peace and protection for its commerce. In 1795, at a cost of about eight hundred thousand dollars the United States secured the release of its citizens from Algiers and a treaty of peace and amity. Treaties with Tripoli and Tunis followed in 1796 and 1797.

The high cost of peace

In directing the negotiation of commercial treaties with the countries of Europe Congress undertook to safeguard American commerce in time of war as well as to promote it in time of peace. In the treaty with France we find stipulations regulating the belligerent right of visit and search, a classification of contraband limiting the right of confiscation strictly to military stores, and the agreement that free ships should make free goods. These provisions are all found in the treaty plan drafted by John Adams and adopted by Congress, September 17, 1776.[29] On May 7, 1784, Congress adopted another plan for commercial treaties, which was embodied in the instructions to Franklin, Adams, and Jefferson.[30] This plan was drafted by Jefferson as chairman of the committee on foreign relations

Neutral rights

[28]Ford, *Writings of Jefferson*, I, 99–103.

[29]*Journals of Continental Congress*, V, 768. Professor Corwin usually so accurate is in error in crediting these stipulations solely to Vergennes (*French Policy and the American Alliance*, 170–171).

[30]Ford, *Writings of Jefferson*, IV, 353; *Secret Journals of Congress*, III, 484.

and on the day that it was adopted he was elected one of the three commissioners to carry it out. The new plan was a remarkable document and a great advance on the Adams plan, but in the intervening years much progress had been made in the definition of neutral rights. In July, 1778, France had announced her adherence to the principle that blockades to be binding must be effectively maintained, and in 1780, the Empress Catherine II of Russia had announced the principles that became the basis of the Armed Neutrality.[31] Jefferson appropriated and applied all of these liberal principles and added others yet more liberal. He undertook to alleviate war by proposing the immunity of unfortified towns and non-combatants generally from attack, the exemption of private property from capture at sea, the abolition of privateering, the prohibition of the seizure of even contraband of war without full payment, the protection of enemy property under the neutral flag, and the proscription of fictitious or paper blockades. Practically every proposal in Jefferson's model treaty has entered into the permanent policy of the United States, though some of it has not yet been realized. One paragraph of the plan, first proposed by Franklin, is worthy of being quoted at length:

Jefferson's treaty plan

Franklin's liberal proposals

> All fishermen, all cultivators of the earth, and all artisans or manufacturers, unarmed and inhabiting unfortified towns, villages, or places, who labor for the common subsistence and benefit of mankind, and peaceably following their respective employments, shall be allowed to continue the same, and shall not be molested by the armed force of the enemy, in whose power, by the events of war, they may happen to fall; but if anything is necessary to be taken from them, for the use of such armed force, the same shall be paid for at a reasonable price; and all merchants and traders exchanging the products of different places, and thereby rendering the necessaries, conveniences, and comforts of human life more easy to obtain and more general, shall be allowed to pass free and unmolested; and neither of the contracting powers shall grant or issue any com-

[31] See p. 37 ante.

mission to any private armed vessels empowering them to take or destroy such trading ships, or interrupt such commerce.[32]

The Prussian treaty of 1785

Franklin had proposed this article for the definitive treaty with England in a letter to Oswald of January 14, 1783,[33] but it had, of course, been rejected. In fact, none of the naval powers were willing to go as far as the American proposals. Prussia as a military power did not object to restrictions on maritime warfare, so Frederick the Great agreed to the incorporation of the entire American plan in the treaty of 1785,—a treaty unique in American diplomacy not only because of the advanced principles it contains but also because no other treaty in our history bears three such distinguished names as Franklin, Adams, and Jefferson. The treaty was, however, of little practical significance and was forgotten by all save a few students of diplomacy until it was brought suddenly to light during the submarine controversy preceding the war with Germany.

Enduring force of early principles

Few persons realize how consistently the United States has striven for these principles throughout its career. Many of them have become a part of international law. The rule that free ships make free goods, that a blockade to be binding must be effective, and the abolition of privateering were finally adopted by the powers of Europe at the close of the Crimean War and embodied in the Declaration of Paris of 1856. The immunity of unfortified towns from bombardment was adopted in one of The Hague conventions of 1907, but unfortunately disregarded in the late war. The exemption of private property from capture at sea has been and is still peculiarly an American policy. The proposal has been urged upon other governments by Presidents Monroe, John Quincy Adams, Pierce, McKinley, and Roosevelt, and it lay at the basis of President Wilson's proposal for the freedom of the seas in the second of his Fourteen Points.

[32]Ford, *Writings of Jefferson*, IV, 354.

[33]Bigelow, *Works of Franklin*, VIII, 246.

Jefferson's views on contraband

In his views on contraband, Jefferson was more than a century ahead of his times, for the experiences of the Great War have brought many thoughtful people to the conclusion he reached in his day:

> The difference between articles of one or another description is a difference in degree only. No line between them can be drawn. Either all intercourse must cease between neutrals and belligerents, or all be permitted. Can the world hesitate to say which shall be the rule?[34]

"Free ships free goods"

While our early treaties adopted the rule, *free ships free goods,* they also included the rule, *enemy ships enemy goods.* These rules were the direct opposite of the rules of international law as stated by Vattel and other writers of the eighteenth century. Vattel states that the property of an enemy found on a neutral vessel may be seized, and that the property of a neutral found on an enemy vessel should be restored.[35] The reasons for the change are stated by Jefferson with his usual lucidity:

> It cannot be denied that according to the general law of nations, the goods of an enemy are lawful prize in the bottom of a friend, and the goods of a friend privileged in the bottom of an enemy; or in other words, *the goods follow the owner.* The inconvenience of this principle in subjecting neutral vessels to vexatious searches at sea has for more than a century rendered it usual for nations to substitute a *conventional* principle *that the goods shall follow the bottom,* instead of the *natural* one before mentioned. France has done it in all her treaties; so I believe had Spain, before the American Revolution. Britain had not done it.[36]

The Armed Neutrality had adopted the principle *free ships free goods*, but that alliance was limited to the period of the war then in progress. In 1783, Congress instructed its ministers abroad that in stipulating for the recognition of this and other neutral rights, they were to avoid com-

[34]Ford, *Writings of Jefferson,* IX, 299.

[35]*Law of Nations,* Ed. of 1758, Book III, Chap. VII, sections 115, 116.

[36]Ford, *Writings of Jefferson,* VIII, 120.

mitting the United States to the support of these rights by force of arms.[37]

Finances of the Confederation

After the Revolution the finances of the Confederation were in such a deplorable condition that Congress was unable to keep up the interest on the foreign loans or to pay any instalments on the principal. Congress had no power to levy import duties and its sole means of raising money at home was to make requisitions on the states. After the war was ended the states paid less attention to the demands of Congress than they had when danger was impending. Had it not been for new loans obtained in Holland it is difficult to see how the government could have been maintained at all. The loan of $2,000,000 secured by Adams in 1782 came in slowly, but another loan of $800,000 was obtained from Dutch bankers in 1784, and two loans of $400,000 each in 1787 and 1788.[38]

The foreign debt

The following estimate of the foreign debt of the United States was reported by a committee of Congress, April 8, 1783:

To the Farmers-General of France. livres	1,000,000	
To Beaumarchais	3,000,000	
To King of France, to the end of 1782	28,000,000	
To same, for 1783	6,000,000	
Livres.	38,000,000	= $7,037,037
Recd. on loan in Holland, 1,678,000 florins		671,200
Borrowed in Spain by Mr. Jay		150,000
Int. on Dutch loan, one year at 4 pr. ct.		26,848
		$7,885,085[39]

Interest on the French loan to the date of the treaty of peace was generously remitted by the King of France in the contract concluded by Vergennes and Franklin, July 16, 1782.[40] In his letter to Congress Franklin stated

[37] Wharton, VI, 482.

[38] Bayley, *National Loans*, in Tenth Census, VII, 309–315.

[39] *Journals of Continental Congress*, XXV, 954.

[40] (Malloy) *Treaties and Conventions*, I, 485.

that this amounted "to the value of near two millions" (livres).[41]

Principal and interest in 1790

By the time the new government under the Constitution was organized the foreign debt had been increased considerably by the accumulation of interest and by the new loans obtained in Holland. On January 1, 1790, it stood as follows:

French loan of eighteen million livres..........	$3,267,000.00
French loan of ten million livres..............	1,815,000.00
French loan of six million livres..............	1,089,000.00
Loan from Farmers-General, balance due......	153,688.89
Loan from Spain in 1781....................	174,017.13
Holland loan of 1782........................	2,000,000.00
Holland loan of 1784........................	800,000.00
Holland loan of 1787........................	400,000.00
Holland loan of 1788........................	400,000.00
Total principal of foreign debts............	10,098,706.02
Balance due France for military supplies......	24,332.86
Arrearages of interest to January 1, 1790......	1,760,277.08
Debt due foreign officers who served in Revolution..................................	186,988.78
Arrearages of interest to January 1, 1790......	11,219.32
	$12,081,524.06

Funding of the debt to France

As a result of Hamilton's reorganization of national finances the government took steps to meet its foreign obligations and the debts were eventually paid. In the case of the French debt the final funding operation took place in 1795, twelve years after the conclusion of peace. The debt was converted into domestic stock, bearing interest at four and one-half and five and one-half per cent. In a report dated December 14, 1795, Oliver Wolcott, who had succeeded Hamilton as Secretary of the Treasury stated that the French debt had been "adjusted to the satisfaction of an authorized agent of the French Republic." The

[41]Bigelow, *Works of Franklin,* VIII, 145.

[42]Bayley, 325.

four and one-half per cent stock was all repaid in 1807 and 1808, and the five and one-half per cent stock was finally paid in 1815.[43]

French subsidies never repaid

The sums advanced as gifts from the King of France were of course not included in the above settlement. Repayment of them was not expected, never demanded, and never offered. These gifts, already referred to, may be summarized as follows:

1776, through Beaumarchais	Livres	1,000,000
1777, through Franklin		2,000,000
1781, through Franklin		6,000,000
1782, interest remitted on loan of 1778, approximately		2,000,000
	Livres	11,000,000[44]

Senator Borah's erroneous statements

Special attention is called to these gifts because no less a person than Senator Borah, chairman of the Foreign Relations Committee of the United States Senate, has declared that they were transformed into loans and repaid. Even when Franklin was quoted as an authority against him, he refused to be convinced and declared on the floor of the Senate with greater eloquence than knowledge:

> If there was any gift of which there has been no settlement, after the most industrious effort I have been unable to find a record of it, and the Treasury Department has been unable to find any record of it, and in my opinion history does not record it.[45]

Senator Borah's speech was remarkable for the number of inaccuracies and misstatements it contained. He confused the gift of six million livres in 1781 with the loan of the same amount in 1783. He also brought into the discussion the Beaumarchais claim and stated that his heirs

[43] *Am. State Papers*, Finance, I, 360, 671.

[44] (Malloy) *Treaties and Conventions*, I, 485, 489.

[45] See Colloquy Between Senators Borah and Bruce, *Congressional Record* January 22, 1925.

had been overpaid by the United States. Only the first gift of one million passed through Beaumarchais' hands, so that even if for the moment we eliminate that, there remain ten million livres advanced as gifts through Franklin which have never been called in question by anyone familiar with the subject.

The Beaumarchais claim

The Beaumarchais claim has entered so largely into the recent discussions of the Revolutionary debt to France that the main facts in regard to it should be stated. It was not included in the settlement of the French debt referred to above, but was handled separately. When Beaumarchais presented his claim for supplies furnished to Congress, Arthur Lee, who had conceived a violent dislike of him, insisted that the military supplies for which he demanded payment were taken from the royal arsenals and forwarded as gifts from the King of France. This view appears to have been shared at first by Franklin and Deane, but when they made inquiry of Vergennes, he replied that the King had furnished nothing; that he had simply permitted Beaumarchais to provide himself from his arsenals, on condition of replacing the articles.

"The lost million"

In 1786, when the accounts of M. Grand, the American banker in Paris, came up for settlement, it was discovered that he had credited the United States with only two million livres received as a gift from the French government prior to the treaty of 1778, whereas in the contract of February, 1783, between Franklin and Vergennes, the amount was put at three million.[46] Franklin, who had returned to the United States, was unable to explain the discrepancy, and wrote to Grand earnestly requesting him "to get this matter explained, that it may stand clear before I die, lest some enemy should afterward accuse me of having received a million not accounted for." The only information Grand could get from Vergennes was that the million in question had been advanced June 10, 1776.

[46](Malloy) *Treaties and Conventions,* I, 489.

As this was before the arrival of Franklin, or even Deane, at Paris, Franklin concluded that the million had been paid to Beaumarchais and that it was a *mystère du cabinet,* which perhaps had better not be further inquired into.[47]

Congress demands an explanation

Thus the "lost million" entered the case, and Congress refused to pay Beaumarchais' claims until the mystery could be cleared up. When Hamilton was Secretary of the Treasury, Beaumarchais' claim was again taken up, and the auditor reported a balance due Beaumarchais of 2,280,231 livres, but again raised the question of the "lost million." At the request of Hamilton, Jefferson directed Gouverneur Morris, United States minister at Paris, to make further inquiries of the French government. Now that the monarchy had been overthrown, the government of the Republic had no objections to revealing the state secrets of the old régime, and Morris was given a copy of the long-sought receipt, which showed that the million in question had been received by Beaumarchais, and that he had agreed to account for it to Vergennes.

Makes only partial payment

After Beaumarchais' death in 1799, the claim was taken up by the French government on behalf of his wife and daughter, and in 1806 Congress passed an act authorizing the payment of $78,886.26, the amount reported by the Treasury officials as due after the deduction of one million livres. Beaumarchais' heirs continued to press for the payment of this million.

The French government repeatedly declared that the million in dispute had been used for secret political purposes in advancing the American cause, and produced papers with the endorsements of Vergennes and the King to the effect that the money had been used for the purposes designated. The opponents of the claim expressed the belief that the money was used for the purchase of supplies intended as free gifts from the King of France. The pay-

[47]Wharton, I, 376–380.

ment of the claim was recommended by Attorney-General C. A. Rodney, by Attorney-General William Pinkney, by Presidents Madison and Monroe, and by various committees of Congress, but no action was taken.

In 1828 the claim was referred to the Committee on Foreign Affairs, of which Edward Everett was chairman. The report, dated April 1, includes all previous reports and most of the important documents bearing on the case.[48] The committee recommended payment of the claim and reported a bill for that purpose. This recommendation shared the fate of the preceding ones.

Final compromise

In 1831, Mr. William C. Rives, United States minister to France, signed a convention adjusting claims of American citizens against France for the illegal seizure of ships and goods during the Napoleonic wars and the claims of French subjects against the United States. The convention embodied a compromise on both sides. American claims were reduced to 25,000,000 francs and French claims to 1,500,000. Out of the latter sum the Beaumarchais heirs, whose claim now amounted with interest to 4,689,241 francs, received in 1835 the sum of 810,000 francs.[49] The dispute was thus officially ended.

Beaumarchais' account erroneously stated by Treasury official

Bayley says that this sum of 810,000 francs, together with the amount paid in 1806, made an over-payment of 1,426,787 livres. Bayley was an official of the Treasury Department, who prepared for the Census Report of 1880 a history of the National Loans of the United States.[50] Now let us see how he arrives at the over-payment. He reaches his conclusion by including not only the million advanced June 10, 1776, but a million advanced by Spain August 11, 1776, and a third million which he says was advanced by France in instalments during the year 1777. He finds the third million in a statement which occurs in

[48] 20th Cong., 1st Sess., House Report No. 220.

[49] Moore, *International Arbitrations*, V, 4460.

[50] *Tenth Census Reports*, Vol. VII, 299–486.

Loménie, *Beaumarchais and His Times*. Nowhere else has it been found. It is certain that it was unknown to the American diplomats, Treasury officials, and committees of Congress that passed on the claim. Bayley's statement of the account is as follows:[51]

The United States	Livres
By shipment of produce	713,996
By payment to M. de Francy	55,000
By bills of exchange of Franklin	2,688,000
By French subsidies paid Beaumarchais	2,000,000
By Spanish subsidies paid Beaumarchais	1,000,000
By grant by Congress April, 1806	434,635
By payment in 1835	810,000
	7,701,631
To Beaumarchais' account for supplies, etc., as stated by himself	6,274,844
	1,426,787

Not over-paid by United States

Whatever may be said of the above method of stating the account, surely there is no ground for the statement of Bayley that Beaumarchais was over-paid *by the United States*. We received supplies, over and above those paid for, to the full value of a million livres, for which we refused to make payment. Our excuse for the refusal was that the French government had paid for them. This the French government persistently denied, and stated that the million in question had been given Beaumarchais to be used for a secret political purpose in the interest of the American cause, and that he had accounted for the same to Vergennes and to the King.

Beaumarchais' heavy losses

Loménie, Beaumarchais' principal biographer, advances the opinion without sufficient evidence, it would seem, that the three millions, which he says Beaumarchais received from France and Spain, were all used in the pur-

[51]*National Loans*, 303.

chase of supplies, but he adds that the losses sustained through the capture of his ships by the Englısh cruisers and through his transactions with individual states of the Union amounted to considerably more than three millions. He thinks, therefore, that Vergennes, who was thoroughly conversant with Beaumarchais' affairs, approved of his asking full payment for the supplies actually delivered, even though some of them may have been originally intended as gifts from the Crown. It is true that Beaumarchais had to assume all the risk of getting the supplies to America, as Congress refused to pay for those captured by the English cruisers. His losses in transactions with Virginia and South Carolina were due to the rapid depreciation of state currency. Jefferson, in a letter to Beaumarchais' agent, expressed his mortification at the losses sustained, through depreciation of the currency, by one "who has merited so well of us."[52]

"The lost million" used for secret service

There is little doubt that Beaumarchais' espousal of the American cause proved his financial ruin. In view of his great services, it is a matter of regret that he and his heirs were not given a full measure of justice. His case has frequently been cited by writers as a notable example of the ingratitude of republics. The exact disposition of the so-called "lost million" can never be established, for, after the account was rendered, the vouchers were destroyed. Modern governments, including that of the United States, handle secret service funds in pretty much the same way.

The "lost million" should be placed in the list of gifts from the French Crown. It was so acknowledged by Franklin in the treaty of 1783, and so regarded by the Treasury officials, who deducted that amount from Beaumarchais' accounts. There was never any question about this. The only question at issue was as to whether it was

[52]Loménie, *Beaumarchais et Son Temps,* II, 200–204; Kite, *Beaumarchais and the War of American Independence,* II, 159, 245; see also Governor Monroe's "Communication to the Legislature Relative to the Claim of the Representatives of Beaumarchais Against the Commonwealth," Richmond, 1802.

used as a secret fund or for the purchase of supplies. In agreeing to the final compromise the United States government committed itself to the view that it had been used as a secret fund and that, therefore, Beaumarchais' heirs were entitled to payment for the supplies delivered

CHAPTER IV

NEUTRALITY AND ISOLATION

Department of State

SHORTLY after the inauguration of Washington, April 30, 1789, Congress took up the work of organizing the new government. It was decided that there should be three executive departments—foreign affairs, treasury, and war. The department of foreign affairs was created July 27, and the duties of the secretary were limited to matters relating to intercourse with foreign nations. Six weeks later, when a bill was introduced to create a home department, which was to have the custody of public records, correspond with the states, and perform a variety of other duties, Congress reconsidered the whole question and decided to combine the duties of the proposed department with those of the department of foreign affairs. At the same time the name was changed to Department of State, a designation sufficiently comprehensive to cover the rather miscellaneous duties assigned to it.[1]

Jefferson first Secretary of State

Jefferson was Washington's choice for Secretary of State and a letter tendering him the office was received early in December, 1789, shortly after he landed in Virginia on a leave of absence from his French mission. He wrote to Washington that he would prefer to return to Paris, but would follow the President's wishes in the matter.[2] A second letter from Washington induced him to accept the position, but he was detained in Virginia by the marriage of his eldest daughter and by business in Richmond, so that he did not reach New York and

[1]Hunt, *The Department of State*, Chapter II.

[2]Ford, *Writings of Jefferson*, I, 158, and VI, 27, 30.

assume the duties of the office until March 21, 1790. Meanwhile Jay, Secretary for Foreign Affairs under the Confederation, had at Washington's request continued in charge of the office, although acceptance of the position of Chief Justice of the United States prevented his being formally commissioned as Secretary of State.

Prospect of war between England and Spain

One of the first important questions that came up for consideration was the course to be pursued by the United States in the probable event of war between Great Britain and Spain over the Nootka Sound incident. A British vessel had been seized by a Spanish officer near Vancouver and Pitt had made an issue of the case, denying emphatically Spain's right to interfere with British trade on that part of the northwest coast of America. If war came Great Britain would probably attempt the conquest of Louisiana from Canada. The United States, whose western lands occupied a strategic position between the two territories, had grievances against both parties. Great Britain still held the frontier posts, while Spain denied to the western settlers the navigation of the Mississippi. Jefferson thought that Spain might be willing to grant independence to Louisiana and the Floridas rather than see them conquered by Great Britain, in which case he would be willing to join Spain and France in guaranteeing their independence and run the risk of war with England. If Spain and France would not enter into such an arrangement he advised strict neutrality.[3]

Washington uncertain what course to pursue

Later came the intimation that Lord Dorchester might ask permission to march troops from Detroit to the Mississippi, and Washington asked for written opinions from Jefferson, Hamilton, and Adams as to what course he should follow. Adams thought that as the United States was not prepared for war, a neutral course should be pursued, and that to give the permission sought would be unfriendly to Spain. Therefore he advised a negative

[3]Ford, *Writings of Jefferson*, VI, 94.

answer. This might deter Great Britain, or if she persisted and marched through without permission, the way would remain open for negotiations.[4] Hamilton advised giving consent, for war was the only alternative and the country was unprepared. He argued the case at great length, discussing the question from the standpoint of international law, and concluded that the right to consent to the passage of troops was less questionable than the right to refuse.[5] Jefferson held that the President had a perfect right to refuse, but that Great Britain would probably ignore the refusal and the United States would then have to go to war immediately or "pocket an acknowledged insult in the face of the world." He advised avoiding a direct answer, for he declared he was "for preserving neutrality as long, and entering the war as late, as possible."[6] Fortunately the Nootka Sound controversy was adjusted and President Washington was relieved of the necessity of making a decision.

War averted

Great Britain, on her part, had considered two alternatives: one was to secure the United States as an ally by promising the free navigation of the Mississippi, and the other was to take advantage of the discontent and unrest in the West and encourage a separatist movement.[7] The crisis had one good result. It probably inclined Pitt to consider more seriously the question of sending a minister to the United States. About the same time Beckwith, an informal agent of the British government, reported, as the result of conferences with Hamilton, that the latter, supported by an influential party, favored more cordial relations with England, while a pro-French, anti-British party was rapidly crystallizing under the leadership of Jefferson. The revival of the movement in Congress, led

Pitt decides to send minister to United States

[4]C. F. Adams, *Works of John Adams*, VIII, 497.
[5]Lodge, *Works of Hamilton*, IV, 20–49.
[6]Ford, *Writings of Jefferson*, VI, 141–143.
[7]Bemis, *Jay's Treaty*, 53.

by Madison, to pass drastic laws discriminating against British commerce has sometimes been cited as the immediate occasion of sending a British minister to the United States, but the decision appears to have been made before news of these measures reached England, and the only effect it had was to hasten his departure.[8]

Arrival of Hammond

The person sent as first British minister to the United States was George Hammond, a young man of twenty-seven, who arrived in October, 1791, and announced through the British consul at Philadelphia that he would present his credentials as soon as he was informed of the appointment of an American minister to the Court of St. James's. A few weeks later the appointment of Thomas Pinckney of South Carolina to this position was announced and Hammond and Jefferson began a discussion of the questions at issue. Jefferson's first step was to request Hammond to communicate his full powers. This forced the British minister to acknowledge that he had no powers to conclude a treaty, but merely to discuss the principles which might serve as a basis for a definitive arrangement.[9] The object of the British ministry seems to have been to delay rather than to facilitate a settlement, and by long-drawn-out negotiations to stave off the hostile legislation contemplated by Congress.

Discussion over non-fulfilment of treaty

The negotiations began with Jefferson's note of December 15, 1791, calling attention to Great Britain's violation of the treaty of 1783: the failure to withdraw from the frontier posts and the carrying off of over three thousand slaves and other property when the British army vacuated New York.[10] Hammond's reply was delayed until March 5, 1792. In the meantime he collected a mass of material to show that the states had failed to remove the obstacles in the way of the recovery of debts due British

[8] *Op. cit.*, pp. 87–88.
[9] *Am. State Papers, Foreign Relations,* I, 189.
[10] *Ibid.*, p. 190.

subjects and that neither they nor Congress had shown any real disposition to carry out the treaty.[11] These infractions of the treaty on the part of the United States afforded, he argued, a perfect justification for his Majesty's delay in evacuating the posts. Jefferson's reply, dated May 29,[12] called attention to the fact that the slaves had been carried off after the treaty had been proclaimed in this country but before any question could have been raised as to the failure of the states to comply with its terms; also that for more than a year after the treaty went into effect British officials in Canada had explained their continued occupation of the posts by saying that orders for evacuation had not arrived. The United States could not, therefore, be charged with prior infraction of the treaty. The rest of the reply was devoted mainly to the subject of pre-war debts and Jefferson after a long argument concluded that no *lawful* impediment had been opposed to the collection of debts and that

> . . . if any instances of *unlawful* impediment have existed in any of the inferior tribunals, they would, like other unlawful proceedings, have been overruled on appeal to the higher courts. If not overruled there, a complaint to the Government would have been regular, and their interference probably effectual.

Hamilton's interference with negotiations

The force of Jefferson's able argument had been almost completely frustrated, before it was delivered, by Hamilton, who was on terms of intimacy with the British minister. Hamilton's whole financial system was based on the continuance of peace with England, from which country ninety per cent of the imports of the United States came. If this trade should be interrupted and the revenue derived from import duties lost, Hamilton believed that financial chaos and political ruin would follow. Therefore he was willing to sacrifice almost anybody or anything to

[11] *Op. cit.*, pp. 193–200.
[12] *Ibid.*, pp. 201–236.

peace with England. This explains his attitude toward Jefferson and his continual interference with the negotiations of his colleague through secret conferences with Hammond. Professor Bemis has recently gone through Hammond's letters in the British Record Office and discovered a great deal of new and valuable material bearing on the negotiations of this period.[13] That Hammond had correctly taken Hamilton's measure is seen from the following quotation from one of his letters:

> Of this gentleman's sincerity I have the surest pledge in the knowledge that any event which might endanger the external tranquillity of the country would be as fatal to the systems he has formed for the benefit of his country as to his present personal reputation and to his future projects of ambition.[14]

Secret conferences with Hammond

In another dispatch to his government he said that he preferred to communicate privately with Hamilton and to have relations with Jefferson only when absolutely necessary. Throughout his negotiations with Jefferson the British minister was in close touch with Hamilton. The latter admitted that there had been serious infractions of the treaty on the part of the United States; he held out the suggestion that if Great Britain would evacuate the posts some arrangement might be made to secure the interests of British fur traders; and he expressed the hope that the West Indies might be opened to American vessels of "light tonnage." Unaware that his arguments were being undermined in advance by Hamilton, Jefferson submitted to him, in advance, his reply to Hammond and asked his advice. Hamilton approved of most of the document but thought that it would be better to extenuate rather than attempt to vindicate the action of the states. Jefferson submitted Hamilton's notes together with his own to Washington who agreed with Jefferson, particu-

[13] Bemis, *Jay's Treaty*, Chap. V, "Jefferson, Hammond, and Hamilton."
[14] *Ibid.*, p. 104.

larly on the question of debts, and let the document stand as originally drafted.[15]

Disloyalty to Jefferson

When Hammond received what he called Jefferson's "extraordinary performance," he ran at once to Hamilton, who tried to soothe him by lamenting "the intemperate violence of his colleague," by stating that the note did not represent the true sentiments of the United States, and finally by declaring that the President had not read it but had relied on Jefferson's assurance that it was in conformity with the opinions of the other members of the cabinet.[16]

Hammond did not undertake to reply to Jefferson's note, but referred the matter to London. No new instructions on this subject appear to have been sent him, for England was soon occupied with the European crisis and Hammond's future relations with Jefferson were on the questions arising out of the war between his country and France.

War between France and England

As the first holder of the office of Secretary of State under the Constitution, Jefferson had an opportunity, which he did not fail to use, of setting precedents and formulating policies that were to be of far-reaching importance. In January, 1793, Louis XVI was executed, and in February, England joined the coalition against France. Thus began a great naval war which was to last almost continuously for twenty-two years, and which finally drew the United States into the maelstrom. Upon Jefferson as Secretary of State devolved the task of developing what has ever since been known as the American system of neutrality. The fact that he did not write the proclamation of neutrality which President Washington issued April 22, 1793, and that he criticised it in a letter to Madison as pusillanimous has been used by his critics to represent him as opposed to the position as-

[15]Ford, *Writings of Jefferson*, VII, 98; Lodge, *Works of Hamilton*, IV, 60.
[16]Bemis, 106.

sumed by the administration and, therefore, deserving of no credit for the system of neutrality that was developed during the months that followed. As a matter of fact, Jefferson never contemplated any other course than neutrality. On March 22, 1793, before he learned of the outbreak of war, he wrote to David Humphreys, minister to Portugal:

Jefferson takes steps to preserve neutrality

> As there appears at present a probability of a very general war in Europe, you will be pleased to be particularly attentive to preserve for our vessels all the rights of neutrality, and to endeavor that our flag be not usurped by others to procure to themselves the benefits of our neutrality.[17]

On April 7, 1793, he wrote to the President that the accounts he had received from Lisbon of the declaration of war between England and France "render it extremely probable that those powers are at actual war, and necessary in my opinion that we take every justifiable measure for preserving our neutrality.[18] On April 20, two days before the proclamation was issued, he wrote to Gouverneur Morris, who had succeeded him as minister to France:

> No country perhaps was ever so thoroughly against war as ours. These dispositions pervade every description of its citizens, whether in or out of Office. They cannot perhaps suppress their affections, nor their wishes. But they will suppress the effects of them so as to preserve a fair neutrality. Indeed we shall be more useful as neutrals than as parties by the protection which our flag will give to supplies of provision.[19]

Arrival of Gênet

Early in April, 1793, "Citizen" Genet arrived at Charleston, South Carolina, as minister of the newly established French Republic, and at once began issuing commissions to privateers to prey on British commerce. On his journey northward he was received with wild

[17]Ford, *Writings of Jefferson*, VII, 266.
[18]*Ibid.*, p. 275.
[19]*Ibid.*, p. 281.

demonstrations of enthusiasm. He entered Philadelphia May 16, escorted by thousands of people.

Washington consults members of cabinet

In the meantime Washington had called a meeting of the cabinet to consider first, whether a proclamation should be issued, and second, whether a minister from the Republic of France should be received. The second question involved the recognition of the new government in France, and we shall consider it in a moment. Jefferson opposed the issuance of a proclamation at that time for reasons which are abundantly stated in his letters. He thought it advisable, in the first place, to wait and see what course England proposed to pursue in regard to neutral trade. It was best, in his judgment, to leave England in doubt as to our attitude, a doubt which, in view of our treaty of alliance with France, she might well have entertained, and thus force her to make concessions not only in the matter of neutral trade but also in the adjustment of many outstanding disputes, such as the retention of the posts in the Northwest. In a letter to Madison, he says:

Jefferson opposes premature declaration

My objections to the impolicy of a premature declaration were answered by such arguments as timidity would readily suggest. I now think it extremely possible that Hammond might have been instructed to ask it, and to offer the *broadest neutral privileges* as the price, which was exactly the price I wanted that we should contend for.[20]

Favors calling Congress

Jefferson also suggested that no action should be taken until Congress could be called. His reasons for this suggestion are set forth at length in a letter to Madison, written a month or more before the cabinet meeting. In it he said:

The idea seems to gain credit that the naval powers combined against France will prohibit supplies even of provisions to that country. Should this be formally notified I should suppose Congress would be called, because it is a justifiable cause of war,

[20] *Op. cit.*, p. 421.

and as the Executive cannot decide the question of war on the affirmative side, neither ought it to do so on the negative side, by preventing the competent body from deliberating on the question. But I should hope that war would not be their choice. I think it will furnish us a happy opportunity of setting another example to the world, by showing that nations may be brought to do justice by appeals to their interests as well as by appeals to arms. I should hope that Congress instead of denunciation of war, would instantly exclude from our ports all the manufactures, produce, vessels and subjects of the nations committing this aggression, during the continuance of the aggression and till full satisfaction made for it. This would work well in many ways, safely in all, and introduce between nations another umpire than arms. It would relieve us too from the risks and the horrors of cutting throats.[21]

Cabinet decides on proclamation

At the cabinet meeting it was unanimously agreed that a proclamation should be issued, "forbidding our citizens to take part in any hostilities on the seas with or against any of the belligerent powers, and warning them against carrying to any such powers any of those articles deemed contraband according to the modern usage of nations, and enjoining them from all acts and proceedings inconsistent with the duties of a friendly nation toward those at war." The proclamation, which was very brief, was drafted, according to Jefferson's own statement, by Edmund Randolph, the Attorney General.[22] It avoided the use of the word "neutrality" out of deference to Jefferson. At Hamilton's request John Jay also drafted a proclamation, which was forwarded to Hamilton a week before the meeting of the cabinet. As this draft is published in the writings of Jay both he and Hamilton have been credited with its authorship.[23] Several historians make the statement that this proclamation was issued by Washington in a condensed form. Anyone who will take the trouble to compare the two documents will see at once that Jay's draft does not bear the slightest resemblance

[21] *Op. cit.*, p. 250.
[22] *Ibid.*, pp. 408, 446.
[23] Johnston, *Cor. and Public Papers of John Jay*, III, 474.

to the proclamation that was issued. Oliver, one of Hamilton's biographers, goes so far as to claim that Hamilton drafted the rules of neutrality. The only possible basis for such a claim is that Hamilton issued a circular of instructions on the subject to customs officers.

Jefferson develops system of American neutrality

The proclamation itself was of minor importance because of its brevity, but the unanimous determination of the cabinet to pursue a neutral course, notwithstanding the French treaties of 1778, was a matter of great consequence, and upon Jefferson devolved the responsibility of carrying out the policy. This he did with great ability. His numerous and detailed instructions to Pinckney at London, and to Morris at Paris, and his letters to Hammond and Gênet, the British and French ministers, are model diplomatic papers, giving evidence of a profound knowledge of international law and a broad grasp of the principles involved.[24] Anyone who reads these letters carefully will see that Jefferson was the real founder of the American system of neutrality. W. E. Hall, a leading English authority on international law, writing a hundred years later, after quoting at length from Jefferson's papers, concludes with this statement:

> The policy of the United States in 1793 constitutes an epoch in the development of the usages of neutrality. There can be no doubt that it was intended and believed to give effect to the obligations then incumbent upon neutrals. But it represented by far the most advanced existing opinions as to what those obligations were; and in some points it even went farther than authoritative international custom has up to the present time advanced. In the main, however, it is identical with the standard of conduct which is now adopted by the community of nations.[25]

Reddaway, another English writer and author of a well-known book on the Monroe Doctrine, says it is a matter

[24]Ford, *Writings of Jefferson*, VII, passim, and *A. S. P., F. R.*, I, passim. Penalties for the violation of neutrality were imposed by the Act of June 5, 1794, which was renewed in 1797 and made permanent by the Act of April 24, 1800.

[25]Hall, *International Law*, Edition of 1904, 591–593.

of just pride to the United States "that at such a moment the pen of Jefferson could formulate against France broad principles of neutrality to which time has added nothing."[26]

Question of recognizing French Republic

On the weighty question of the recognition of the new government set up in France after the execution of Louis XVI, President Washington requested the opinions in writing of the members of his cabinet. He also asked their opinions as to whether Gênet should be received and as to whether the treaties of 1778 should be regarded as still binding. Hamilton and Jefferson replied at great length, taking as usual opposite sides, particularly on the question as to the binding force of the treaties. Hamilton took the view that as the Bourbon monarchy, with which the treaties had been negotiated, had been overthrown, we were under no obligations to fulfill their stipulations and had a perfect right to renounce them.[27] Jefferson took the correct view that the treaties were with the French nation and that they were binding under whatever government the French people chose to set up. This principle, which is now one of the fundamental doctrines of international law, was so ably expounded by Jefferson that his words are well worth quoting:

Jefferson lays down fundamental doctrine

> I consider the people who constitute a society or nation as the source of all authority in that nation, as free to transact their common concerns by any agents they think proper, to change these agents individually, or the organization of them in form or function whenever they please: that all the acts done by those agents under the authority of the nation, are the acts of the nation, are obligatory on them, to enure to their use, and can in no wise be annulled or affected by any change in the form of the government, or of the persons administering it. Consequently the treaties between the United States and France were not treaties between the United States and Louis Capet, but between the two nations of America and France, and the nations remaining in existence, tho' both of them have since changed

[26]P. 15. Reddaway, *The Monroe Doctrine,* 15.

[27]Lodge, *Works of Hamilton,* IV, 74–101.

their forms of government, the treaties are not annulled by these changes.[28]

French treaties binding

Washington gave no definite opinion, but from the subsequent course of events it appears that he agreed with Jefferson that the treaties were binding, but did not apply to an offensive war such as France was waging. The situation was relieved by the fact that France did not ask for a full compliance with the treaty of alliance, thinking doubtless that the food supplies which we could carry under the neutral flag would be more valuable than any military or naval aid we could give. The commercial treaty, permitting French war ships to bring their prizes into American ports, caused greater trouble, however. Gênet assumed that this provision covered the right to convert such prizes into war ships and to commission them in American ports to go out and attack British commerce. Jefferson stoutly denied this interpretation. He wrote to Gênet, June 17, 1793, as follows:

No right to arm prizes in American ports

> None of the engagements in our treaties stipulate this permission. The XVIIth article of that of commerce, permits the armed vessels of either party, to enter the ports of the other, and to depart with their prizes freely; but the entry of an armed vessel into a port, is one act; the equipping a vessel in that port, arming her, manning her, is a *different* one, and not engaged by any article of the Treaty.[29]

Gênet, however, persisted in his course until the government finally demanded his recall.

Doctrine of recognition

The doctrine of the recognition of *de facto* governments so ably expounded by Jefferson was merely a corollary from the statement in the Declaration of Independence that governments derive their just powers from the consent of the governed. If this statement is true, then governments which are based on the consent of the people

[28]Ford, *Writings of Jefferson*, VII, 284–285; cf. Goebel, *Recognition Policy of the United States*, 98.

[29]Ford, *Writings of Jefferson*, VII, 398.

are the governments which other nations should recognize. When Jefferson first heard that the French monarchy had been overthrown and the republic declared, he directed Gouverneur Morris to suspend further payments of our debt to France until a government should be organized "by the will of the nation substantially declared." In a later letter to Morris (December 30, 1792) he said:

> I am apprehensive that your situation must have been difficult during the transition from the late form of government to the re-establishment of other legitimate authority, and that you may have been at a loss to determine with whom business might be done. Nevertheless when principles are well understood their application is less embarrassing. We surely cannot deny to any nation that right whereon our own government is founded that every one may govern itself under whatever forms it pleases, and change these forms at it's own will, and that it may transact it's business with foreign nations through whatever organ it thinks proper, whether king, convention, assembly, committee, president, or whatever else it may chuse. The will of the nation is the only thing essential to be regarded.[30]

Non-intervention

The passage just quoted is also an admirable statement of the philosophical basis of the doctrine of non-intervention, which since the days of Jefferson has been one of the fundamental principles of American foreign policy.

Non-extradition of political refugees

Closely connected with the right of revolution is the question of the extradition of persons guilty of political crimes. In the matter of extradition Jefferson first drew the distinction between ordinary fugitives from justice and political refugees. Oppenheim, a high authority on international law, says that prior to the French Revolution the term "political crime" was unknown in either the theory or the practice of the law of nations. The French Constitution of 1793 granted asylum to foreigners exiled from their country "for the cause of liberty." A year before the adoption of this constitution, Jefferson

[30]*Op. cit.*, VII, 198.

presented his views on the subject in a report to the President March 22, 1792 in which he said:

> Most codes extend their definitions of treason to acts not really against one's country. They do not distinguish between acts against the *government*, and acts against the *Oppressions of the Government*. The latter are virtues: yet have furnished more victims to the Executioner than the former. Because real Treasons are rare: Oppressions frequent. The unsuccessful Struggles against Tyrrany have been the chief Martyrs of Treason laws in all countries. Reformation of government with our neighbors, as much wanting now as Reformation of religion is, or ever was anywhere. We should not wish then to give up to the Executioner the Patriot who fails, and flees to us.[31]

Washington indorsed the report, and the United States has since uniformly followed the principle laid down by Jefferson by refusing to extradite persons guilty merely of political offenses who have sought refuge in our country.

Interference with neutral trade

From the beginning of the war American commerce suffered from the pretensions of belligerents to regulate and control the trade of neutrals. On July 9, 1793, Gênet complained to Jefferson that the British cruisers were seizing French property found on American ships.[32] Jefferson replied that "by the general law of nations, the goods of a friend found in the vessel of an enemy are free, and the goods of an enemy found in the vessel of a friend are lawful prize"; that the contrary rule, free ships make free goods, was a conventional rule established by special treaties to which England had refused in general to give her adherence; and that therefore he would be at a loss to know on what grounds he could protest.[33]

Meanwhile the French National Convention had passed a decree, May 9, 1793, authorizing the commanders of French war vessels and privateers

---

[31] *Op. cit.*, VI, 447–448.
[32] *A. S. P., F. R.*, I, 164.
[33] *Ibid.*, p. 166.

> . . . to seize and carry into the ports of the Republic merchant vessels which are wholly or in part laden with provisions, being neutral property, bound to an enemy's port, or having on board merchandise belonging to an enemy.[34]

France and England order seizure of provisions

As this decree was in direct violation of the commercial treaty of 1778, it was modified within two weeks by a second decree which declared American vessels exempt. A British order in council of June 9, 1793, directed the seizure and detention of "all vessels loaded wholly or in part with corn, flour, or meal, bound to any port in France," in order that such cargo might be purchased on behalf of his Majesty's government, or the masters of such ships might be permitted, on giving due security, to dispose of their cargoes "in the ports of any country in amity with his Majesty." Jefferson instructed Pinckney, September 7, to protest against this order as contrary to international law and a serious interference with the most important of all American industries, for, he declared, it "strikes at the root of our agriculture."[35] The British reply, defending the alleged right to seize provisions, was not received until April, 1794,[36] and was answered by Edmund Randolph[37] who had succeeded Jefferson as Secretary of State, but just at this time Jay was appointed special envoy to England and the discussion of all disputes was transferred to London.

Jefferson's resignation

Jefferson's resignation took effect December 31, 1793. He had accepted office with reluctance and with the intention of retiring at the close of Washington's first administration. His estate was suffering from his prolonged absence and he yearned for the shades of his beloved Monticello. He had been persuaded by Washington to postpone his retirement, but his relations with Hamilton,

[34]For this decree and the texts of the British orders in council that followed, see Moore, *Digest of International Arbitrations*, I, 299–305.

[35]*A. S. P., F. R.*, I, 239. See also his letter to Hammond, *ibid.*, p. 240.

[36]*Ibid.*, p. 449.

[37]*Ibid.*, p. 450.

already strained, grew continually worse. In vain did Washington express his concern at the growing dissensions in his official family and appeal to Jefferson and Hamilton to exercise mutual forbearance.[38] Hamilton not only continued to undermine the Secretary of State by his too free communications to the British minister, of which Jefferson of course was not fully aware, but under the name "Pacificus" and "No Jacobin" he poured forth anonymous attacks in Fenno's *Gazette of the United States* and in the *Daily Advertiser*.[39] At Jefferson's suggestion Madison replied under the name "Helvidius." In July, 1793, Jefferson announced to Washington his intention of resigning, but was persuaded to defer his retirement until the end of the year.[40] Hamilton's resignation followed thirteen months later.

Madison proposes retaliation against England

The last important paper prepared by Jefferson was the elaborate report on "Commercial Privileges and Restrictions."[41] Madison made this the basis for reintroducing on January 3, 1794, a series of drastic resolutions, originally proposed in 1791, placing duties and restrictions, by way of retaliation, on British goods and vessels.[42] Hamilton had not only kept the British minister informed as to the progress and probable contents of Jefferson's report, but he had also collected in advance of its publication a mass of material for controverting its conclusions.[43] This material was now placed in the hands of a Federalist member of Congress from South Carolina, who used it in a speech against Madison's resolutions and was later burned in effigy by his constituents in the streets of Charleston.[44]

While the debate on Madison's resolutions was in prog-

---

[38]Ford, *Writings of Washington*, XII, 171, 172.

[39]Lodge, *Works of Hamilton*, IV, 135–191, 198, 229.

[40]Ford, *Writings of Jefferson*, VIII, 136.

[41]*A. S. P., F. R.*, I, 301–304.

[42]Bemis, 188 n.

[43]*Ibid.*, p. 105 n.

[44]*Ibid.*, p. 190.

ness, news was received of the still more sweeping order in council of November 6, 1793, directing the seizure of "all ships laden with goods the produce of any colony belonging to France, or carrying provisions or other supplies for the use of any such colony."[45] This order went much further than the Rule of 1756, by which Great Britain had declared that trade which was closed to neutrals in time of peace could not be thrown open to them in time of war, for it denied to Americans even the direct trade between their own ports and the French islands. The order created great excitement in the United States and put the Federalists on the defensive. Even Hamilton denounced it as "atrocious" and advised Washington to prepare for war, but to proceed with negotiations, and in the meantime to avoid reprisals.[46] The excitement was somewhat allayed by the news that the order of November 6 had been modified by the subsequent order of January 8, 1794, permitting the direct trade between the French West Indies and the United States in articles non-contraband of war.[47] This enabled American vessels to bring the products of the French West Indies to the United States, and, after payment of duties, export them to Europe, an indirect trade which assumed large proportions and continued until it was stopped in 1806 by Sir William Scott's famous decision in the *Essex* case.

More British orders in council

Before news of the new order of January 8 reached the West Indies about two hundred and fifty American vessels had been seized and one hundred and fifty of these had been condemned.[48] On March 26, 1794, Congress laid an embargo for thirty days on all vessels in American ports bound for any foreign port, and on April 18 extended it for another period of thirty days.

Seizure of American ships in the West Indies

[45]Moore, *Dig. of Int. Arbits.*, I, 304.
[46]Lodge, *Works of Hamilton*, IV, 291.
[47]Moore, I, 305–6; *A. S. P., F. R.*, I, 431.
[48]*A. S. P., F. R.*, I, 429.

Jay's mission to England

In order to avert the impending crisis Washington finally decided to send an envoy extraordinary to England and to endeavor to hold Congress in check until another effort at negotiation should be fully tried. For this important mission he considered John Adams, Jefferson, Jay, and Hamilton. Hamilton realized that the opposition to him was too strong and urged the appointment of Jay.[49] A few days later Washington sent Jay's nomination to the Senate and on May 12 the new envoy sailed for England. Hamilton now dominated the policy of the administration and Jay's instructions, though drafted by Randolph, reflected the views of Hamilton and a small group of Federalist Senators. In an interview with Hammond, Hamilton indicated that he was prepared to accept the principles of the British order of June 8, 1793, and of January 8, 1794. He did not even deny the legality of the order of November 6, 1793, though he condemned the extreme interpretations placed upon it by the vice-admiralty courts of the West Indies, and said that compensation would be demanded for cargoes seized under that order except in cases where the property could be proven to be French. Thus Hamilton departed from the principles embodied in our early treaties and acquiesced in the treatment of provisions as contraband, in the seizure of enemy property on neutral ships, and the Rule of 1756.[50]

His instructions

Jay's official instructions did not, of course, direct him to surrender these principles, but he was given a wide discretion, and Hamilton's views as reported by Hammond to his superiors governed the negotiations.[51] Jay was instructed to press strenuously for compensation for all captures and injuries sustained under the British orders; to adjust all points of difference that had arisen out of the

[49]For a full statement of the Federalist position, see Hamilton's letter to Washington, April 14, 1794, Lodge, *Works of Hamilton,* IV, 282–300.

[50]Bemis, 199–202.

[51]See Articles XVII and XVIII of the Jay treaty.

treaty of 1783; to negotiate, if possible, a commercial treaty which should include reciprocity in navigation and commerce, the principle that free ships make free goods, definition of contraband exempting provisions, definition of blockade, and other liberal stipulations; and to secure the admission of American vessels to the British West Indies. He was told, however, that the President could not undertake at a distance to lay down "irrevocable" instructions.

> You will therefore consider the ideas herein expressed, as amounting to recommendations only which in your discretion you may modify, as seems most beneficial to the United States, except in the two following cases, which are immutable.

First, he was to sign no treaty contrary to our engagements with France, and second, he was not to sign a commercial treaty which did not admit American vessels to the British West Indies.[52]

Jay's treaty

Jay's negotiations with Lord Grenville began the latter part of July, 1794, and continued until November 19.[53] The treaty signed on that date provided for the surrender of the frontier posts and for the appointment of three arbitration commissions to settle (1) the St. Croix River boundary, (2) the claims for confiscated debts, and (3) the reciprocal claims growing out of the illegal seizure of American vessels by British cruisers, and the capture of British vessels by French ships armed in the ports of the United States.

Arbitration provisions

The commissioners on the boundary question later decided that the Schoodiac was the river which the negotiators of the treaty of 1783 intended under the name of St. Croix. The commissioners on the question of debts due British merchants failed to agree upon an award, but by the convention of 1802 the British government agreed to accept $2,664,000 in settlement of these claims. By

[52] *A. S. P., F. R.*, I, 472.

[53] *Ibid.*, pp. 470–525.

far the most important of the arbitrations under the Jay treaty was that relating to neutral rights and duties. The commissioners met in London and the proceedings covered a period of several years. In the settlement of the intricate questions of international law that arose William Pinkney, the acknowledged leader of the American bar, who was one of the arbiters, won new laurels by his able and comprehensive opinions which were described as "finished models of judicial eloquence." American claimants recovered from the British government $11,650,000, the largest award ever made by an arbitration tribunal prior to the Geneva award of 1872. Awards against the United States, on account of the operations of French privateers fitted out within American jurisdiction, amounted to $143,428. John Bassett Moore says:

> Although this amount was relatively small, its payment established the principle that a government is liable in damages for neglect to perform its neutral duties, and thus laid the foundation of the award made in 1872 at Geneva.[54]

Withdrawal of British troops

Jay's treaty laid the foundations of modern international arbitration, but aside from this achievement, which was not appreciated at the time, and the stipulation for the withdrawal of British troops from the frontier posts, his negotiations were marked by failure and surrender of the principles proclaimed in the days of the Revolution. The treaty provided specifically for the seizure of enemy property in neutral ships and for the pre-emption of foodstuffs.[55] In the way of commercial concessions Jay got little, and the West India agreement was more than disappointing. Article XII permitted American vessels of not more than seventy tons burden to trade with the British West Indies, provided they did not carry to Europe either from the West Indies or from the United

Commercial clauses unsatisfactory

[54] *Principles of American Diplomacy*, 313. For a full discussion of the arbitrations under the Jay treaty, see Moore, *Dig. of Int. Arbits.*, I, 299–349.

[55] Articles XVII and XVIII.

States any molasses, sugar, coffee, cocoa, or cotton. This arrangement raised a storm of indignation and Jay was burned in effigy in various parts of the country. The French minister Adet gave a vivid description to his government of one of these performances, which took place in Philadelphia shortly after his arrival. Jay was burned in effigy there by the ship carpenters. He was represented holding a balance in one hand. On the light end was written "Liberty and Independence of America," on the heavier end, "British Gold"; in his other hand he held the treaty, and from his mouth came the words "Pay me what I demand and I will sell you my country."[56] When Hamilton undertook to address a public meeting in New York City in defense of the treaty he was howled down by a mob and driven bleeding from the platform by a volley of stones.[57] The Senate suspended the objectionable article on the West India trade and consented to the ratification of the rest of the treaty by a bare two-thirds vote June 24, 1795. Washington hesitated long before deciding to ratify but finally did so, there being no other practicable course to pursue.[58]

Jay burned in effigy

Could Jay have gotten a better treaty? Professor Bemis, who has made an exhaustive study of the negotiations, concludes that Grenville was an abler and more experienced diplomat than Jay and that the latter was at a disadvantage "because of the intimate relations between the Foreign Office and America's most influential and powerful statesman." He adds:

Hamilton responsible for Jay's treaty

> The terms of his treaty were the result of the powerful influence of Alexander Hamilton, to whom in the last analysis any praise or blame for the instrument must be given. It was the price paid by the Federalists for a peace which they believed

---

[56]*Correspondence of French Ministers,* Edited by F. J. Turner, in *An. Rept. of Am. Hist. Assn.,* 1903, vol. II, 745.

[57]Lodge, *Alexander Hamilton,* 190.

[58]Ford, *Writings of Washington,* XIII, 69.

indispensable to the perpetuation of American nationality. More aptly the treaty might be called Hamilton's treaty.[59]

Edmund Randolph resigns under a cloud

Washington's ratification of the Jay treaty had been hastened by information that reflected seriously on the character and conduct of the Secretary of State. Several dispatches of the French minister Fauchet, giving an account of interviews with Edmund Randolph, had been captured by the British and placed in the hands of members of Washington's cabinet. The dispatches represented Randolph as conspiring with the French minister to defeat the Jay treaty and intimated, though the language was by no means conclusive, that he had suggested the use of French gold.[60] An examination of all the documents bearing on the case would seem to clear Randolph of the latter charge. So far as the other charge is concerned, his opposition to the treaty was well known—in fact, he was the only member of the cabinet who voted against ratification—while his relations with Fauchet were no more intimate than those of Hamilton with the British minister. When Washington confronted Randolph with the compromising documents in the presence of the other members of the cabinet who were already familiar with their contents, Randolph very naturally tendered his resignation.

The secretaryship of state goes begging

The ratification of the Jay treaty proved the final blow to Washington's popularity. The administration had few supporters. Even the secretaryship of state went begging. It was offered in turn to William Paterson, Thomas Johnson, Charles Cotesworth Pinckney, Patrick Henry, and Rufus King, but all declined a position which held no prospect of anything but unpopularity at home and impotency abroad.[61] Finally Timothy Pickering was

[59]Bemis, *Jay's Treaty*, 269–271.

[60]*Cor. of French Ministers* (Turner), 411, 444. For an able defense of Randolph, see M. D. Conway's *Edmund Randolph*, Chaps. XXIII–XXXIV.

[61]Ford, *Writings of Washington*, XIII, 115, 129, 130.

transferred from the War to the State Department and continued to serve as Secretary of State during the greater part of Adams's administration.

The Jay treaty offends France

The Jay treaty caused deep offense to France and greatly embarrassed Monroe, who had assured the French government that no terms inconsistent with the French treaty would be accepted. The French treaty expressly stipulated that the neutral flag should cover enemy goods and that foodstuffs should not be regarded as contraband. To sign a treaty with England embodying the opposite principles, while France was at war with that country, afforded just grounds for complaint. In fact, Jay's general acquiescence in the British system of maritime law amounted practically to a violation of neutrality. Monroe had been sent to France to succeed Gouverneur Morris whose monarchical sympathies had rendered him unpopular about the time that Jay was sent to England. He was selected because of his known friendship for the French Republic and he was kept in ignorance of Jay's instructions. In fact, he was deceived as to the real character of that mission and instructed to allay French suspicions.

> You may say that he [referring to Jay] is positively forbidden to weaken the engagements between this country and France. It is not improbable that you will be obliged to encounter, on this head, suspicions of various kinds. But you may declare the motives of that mission to be, to obtain immediate compensation for our plundered property, and restitution of the posts.

Not a word was said about a commercial treaty. In conclusion he was directed to

> . . . show our confidence in the French republic, without betraying the most remote mark of undue complaisance. You will let it be seen that, in case of war with any nation on earth, we shall consider France as our first and natural ally.[62]

[62] *A. S. P., F. R.*, I, 668.

Monroe's dramatic and enthusiastic reception by the French Convention and the extreme cordiality of the greetings exchanged between him and the presiding officer, followed by the fraternal embrace, caused consternation among the Federalists. When the text of Jay's treaty, withheld from Monroe until after ratification, was finally made known he was in no position to defend it. Regarding Monroe as disloyal to the administration, Washington finally decided on his recall in July, 1796.[63]

Monroe recalled from Paris

France refuses to receive Pinckney

Shortly before Monroe's recall, the French Directory, in retaliation for the Jay treaty, passed a decree, July 2, 1796, announcing that French cruisers would apply to neutral vessels in matters of search and seizure the same rules that their governments permitted the English to enforce. Charles Cotesworth Pinckney was appointed to succeed Monroe, but when he reached Paris the Directory refused to receive him and ordered him to leave France. He retired to Amsterdam to await developments. Many of the Federalists now demanded war, but President Adams and Hamilton realized that the country was unprepared, while the Republicans insisted that there was no ground for war and that strained relations were due to the mismanagement of the Federalists.

The "X Y Z" affair

Adams was determined if possible to reëstablish diplomatic intercourse and in the autumn of 1797 appointed a commission consisting of C. C. Pinckney, John Marshall, and Elbridge Gerry to attempt new negotiations. When the commissioners arrived in Paris, Talleyrand, who was foreign minister, delayed receiving them and when they grew impatient at their treatment they were informed through secret agents, designated in the dispatches when they were later published as X, Y, and Z, that money was what was wanted and that if they would pay sub-

[63]Bond, "The Monroe Mission to France," *J. H. U. Studies,* XXV, Nos. 2 and 3. See also Washington's notes on Monroe's "View of the Conduct of the Executive in the Foreign Affairs of the United States," Ford, XIII, 452.

stantial sums to Talleyrand and his associates they would be recognized and their business attended to. The spirit of Pinckney's emphatic reply, "No, no, no, not a sixpence," was caught by some happy phrase-maker in America who gave currency to it in the form, "Millions for defense, but not a cent for tribute." This phrase appeared for the first time in the form of a toast to Pinckney at a great banquet given in Philadelphia to Marshall who returned home ahead of his colleagues. It became the watchword of the day, and in spite of Pinckney's disclaimers it was inscribed on his tomb in old St. Michael's Church in Charleston.[64]

De facto, but not _de jure_ war with France

As soon as the "X, Y, Z," dispatches were received, the President announced to Congress that he would never send another minister to France without assurances that he would be "received, respected, and honored as the representative of a great, free, powerful, and independent nation." The publication of the dispatches created intense feeling and for the first time in his life John Adams found himself popular. His recommendations were promptly enacted into law by Congress. The Department of the Navy was created, the construction of a large number of ships was ordered, the seizure of French ships was authorized, the treaties of 1778 were abrogated, and the organization of an army of 10,000 men was begun. Washington was appointed to the chief command and accepted on condition that Hamilton be appointed second in command. As the United States could not fight France on land, Hamilton wished to coöperate with England in an attack on the colonies of Spain, France's ally. He proposed to annex Florida and New Orleans to the United States and to help to establish the independence of Spanish America.[65] Adams, however, did not favor

---

[64]The dispatches are in *A. S. P.*, *F. R.*, II, 158–201. The best narrative is in Beveridge, *Life of John Marshall*, II, chaps. VI–IX.

[65]*Life and Cor. of Rufus King*, II, app. 5 and III, app. 3.

this scheme, and hostilities were confined to the sea. In a little over two years United States ships captured about eighty French vessels, most of them merchantmen or privateers, though among them were a few ships of the French navy, such as *L'Insurgente,* which was captured by Captain Truxtun of the *Constellation* after a regular engagement lasting over an hour. Notwithstanding these sea fights neither country declared war. Meanwhile Napoleon had come into power, and in 1800 he authorized a treaty which reëstablished diplomatic relations and adjusted some of the differences.

Diplomatic relations restored

The policy of American isolation

In Washington's day the United States was an experiment in democracy. The vital question was not our duty to the rest of the world, but whether the rest of the world would let us live. The policy of wisdom was to keep aloof from world politics and give as little cause of offense as possible to the great powers of Europe. Washington pointed out that "our detached and distant situation" rendered such a course possible. This policy was justified by events. We were enabled to follow unhindered the bent of our own political genius, to extend our institutions over a vast continent, and to attain a position of great prosperity and power in the economic world. While our Revolutionary fathers had a broader grasp of European politics than any succeeding generation of American statesmen and eagerly sought alliances in the struggle for independence, no sooner was that object attained than they decided to cut loose as speedily as possible from European entanglements. Washington's Farewell Address was foreshadowed by a resolution Congress adopted June 12, 1783, on the subject of the Armed Neutrality:

> Whereas . . . the true interest of the states requires that they should be as little as possible entangled in the politics and controversies of European nations. . . . Resolved, That the ministers plenipotentiary of these United States for negotiat-

ing a peace be, and they are hereby, instructed, in case they should comprise in the definitive treaty any stipulations amounting to a recognition of the rights of neutral nations to avoid accompanying them by any engagements which shall oblige the contracting parties to support those stipulations by arms.[66]

Washington's Farewell Address

Washington's administration closed with the clouds of the European war still hanging heavy on the horizon. Under these circumstances he delivered his famous Farewell Address in which he said:

The great rule of conduct for us in regard to foreign nations is, in extending our commercial relations to have with them as little *political* connection as possible. So far as we have already formed engagements let them be fulfilled with perfect good faith. Here let us stop.

Europe has a set of primary interests which to us have none or a very remote relation. Hence she must be engaged in frequent controversies, the causes of which are essentially foreign to our concerns. Hence, therefore, it must be unwise in us to implicate ourselves by artificial ties in the ordinary vicissitudes of her politics or the ordinary combinations and collisions of her friendships or enmities.

Our detached and distant situation invites and enables us to pursue a different course. If we remain one people under an efficient government, the period is not far off when we may defy material injury from external annoyance; when we may take such an attitude as will cause the neutrality we may at any time resolve upon to be scrupulously respected; when belligerent nations, under the impossibility of making acquisitions upon us, will not lightly hazard the giving us provocation; when we may choose peace or war, as our interest, guided by justice, shall counsel.

Why forego the advantages of so peculiar a situation? Why quit our own to stand upon foreign ground? Why, by interweaving our destiny with that of any part of Europe entangle our peace and prosperity in the toils of European ambitions, rivalship, interest, humor, or caprice?

It is our true policy to steer clear of permanent alliances with any portion of the foreign world, so far, I mean, as we are now at liberty to do it; for let me not be understood as capable of patronizing infidelity to existing engagements. I hold the maxim no less applicable to public than to private affairs that

[66] Wharton, VI, 482.

honesty is always the best policy. I repeat, therefore, let those engagements be observed in their genuine sense. But in my opinion it is unnecessary and would be unwise to extend them.

Taking care always to keep ourselves by suitable establishments on a respectable defensive posture, we may safely trust to temporary alliances for extraordinary emergencies.[67]

Reasons assigned by Washington for isolation

It will be observed that Washington warned his countrymen against *permanent* alliances. He expressly said that we might "safely trust to *temporary* alliances for extraordinary emergencies." Further than this many of those who are continually quoting Washington's warning against alliances not only fail to note the limitations under which the advice was given, but they also overlook the reasons assigned. In a succeeding paragraph of the Farewell Address he said:

With me a predominant motive has been to endeavor to gain time to our country to settle and mature its yet recent institutions, and to progress without interruption, to that degree of strength and consistency which is necessary to give it, humanly speaking, the command of its own fortunes.

The expression "entangling alliances" does not occur in the Farewell Address, but was given currency by Jefferson. In his first inaugural address he summed up the principles by which he proposed to regulate his foreign policy in the following terms: "Peace, commerce, and honest friendship with all nations, entangling alliances with none."

[67]The Farewell Address was prepared with the assistance of Hamilton, to whom much of the phraseology is due. Ford, *Writings of Washington*, XIII, 277, 325.

CHAPTER V

LOUISIANA AND FLORIDA

Spain retrocedes Louisiana to France

One of Napoleon's dreams was the reëstablishment of a colonial empire in America. With this end in view he had little difficulty in persuading the Spanish Queen Maria Louisa of Parma and her weak and indolent husband Charles IV to cede the Province of Louisiana back to France. The chief consideration for this vast transfer of territory, made by the secret Treaty of San Ildefonso, October 1, 1800, was the promise to give Tuscany, under the name of the kingdom of Etruria, to the Queen's nephew and son-in-law, the Prince of Parma. The terms of the treaty were to be kept secret until Napoleon was ready to take over the province, but within six months, President Jefferson heard rumors of the cession, which, it was supposed, included the Floridas.[1] Neither at Paris nor Madrid could our ministers get any confirmation of the rumors.[2]

Jefferson opposes French occupation of New Orleans

As soon as Jefferson was satisfied that Louisiana had been ceded to France, he instructed Livingston, his representative at Paris, to open negotiations for the purchase of New Orleans and the Floridas, stating that the acquisition of New Orleans by a powerful nation like France would inevitably lead to friction and conflict.

> The day that France takes possession of New Orleans fixes the sentence which is to restrain her forever within her low water mark. It seals the union of two nations who in conjunction can maintain exclusive possession of the ocean. From that moment we must marry ourselves to the British fleet and

[1] King's dispatch from London, March 29, 1801, *A. S. P., F. R.*, II, 509.

[2] *Ibid.*, pp. 512–516.

nation. We must turn all our attentions to a maritime force, for which our resources place us on very high grounds: and having formed and cemented together a power which may render reinforcement of her settlements here impossible to France, make the first cannon, which shall be fired in Europe the signal for tearing up any settlement she may have made, and for holding the two continents of America in sequestration for the common purposes of the United British and American nations. This is not a state of things we seek or desire. It is one which this measure, if adopted by France, forces on us, as necessarily as any other cause, by the laws of nature, brings on its necessary effect.[3]

Napoleon attempts recovery of Santo Domingo

During the interval of peace with England, following the peace of Amiens, Napoleon undertook the resubjugation of the French colony of Santo Domingo, which under the leadership of Toussaint L'Ouverture, a full-blooded Negro, had proclaimed its independence in 1795 and had since successfully defied the authority of France. The "Gilded African," as Napoleon called Toussaint, or the "Black Napoleon," as he was dubbed by others, was now imitating step by step the military despotism which the First Consul was establishing in France. In January, 1802, Napoleon's brother-in-law, General Leclerc, landed with an army of ten thousand men, later increased to twenty-five thousand, and undertook the reconquest of the island. Half a million Negroes opposed the French and yellow fever also attacked them. General Leclerc and thousands of his soldiers died and the enterprise had to be abandoned.[4]

Right of deposit at New Orleans suspended

About the same time that the news of General Leclerc's death reached Washington, and before anyone had time to realize what effect the failure of the Santo Domingo expedition would have on Napoleon's plans, information was received that Morales, the Spanish intendant at New Orleans, had issued in October, 1802, a decree withdrawing the right of deposit. Kentucky and Tennessee were

[3]Ford, *Writings of Jefferson*, IX, 365 (April 18, 1802).

[4]Henry Adams, *History of the United States*, I, Chaps. XV and XVI.

again greatly stirred and eager for war. The act of Morales, in their minds prompted by Napoleon, was a foretaste of what might be expected under French rule. The Federalists did all they could to encourage this feeling, thinking that Jefferson would either have to fight France or face a dissolution of the Union. Meanwhile the Spanish minister Yrujo, who was on intimate terms with Jefferson, came to his assistance and assured him that the act was not authorized by the King of Spain, but was due to mistaken zeal on the part of the intendant, and would be inquired into immediately.[5] It was, in fact, later withdrawn.

Monroe sent on special mission to France

Jefferson preserved a calm exterior, and in his annual message to Congress in December, 1802, merely stated that the cession of Louisiana to France, if carried into effect, would make "a change in the aspect of our foreign relations which will doubtless have just weight in any deliberations of the Legislature connected with that subject." A few days later, in response to a resolution of the House, he transmitted a report from the Secretary of State, giving information called for, and Congress promptly appropriated two million dollars "to defray any expenses in relation to the intercourse between the United States and foreign nations." This sum was intended to cover the expenses of a special mission and first payments on any cession of territory that might be obtained. On January 11, 1803, James Monroe was nominated minister extraordinary to act with Livingston in the negotiation of a "treaty or convention with the First Consul of France for the purpose of enlarging and more effectually securing our rights and interests in the river Mississippi and in the territories eastward thereof." But as there was some doubt as to whether the Floridas were included in the cession, and as all the provinces concerned were still in the hands of Spain and the course of events might prevent

[5] *Op. cit.*, I, 421–427.

the cession being carried into effect, Monroe was also given a commission as minister extraordinary to the Spanish Court, to be used, if necessary, jointly with Charles Pinckney in carrying out the same object.[6]

Jefferson contemplates war with France

When Monroe's appointment was announced the British minister asked the President whether he intended to let Monroe go to London and confer with the British ministers about the free navigation of the Mississippi—a right to which Great Britain was also entitled by treaty. Jefferson replied that he hoped for a pacific settlement of the controversy, but he thought it very probable Mr. Monroe might have to cross the Channel; that the United States would never yield its claim to the free navigation of the Mississippi, and that if they should be obliged at last to draw the sword, "they would throw away the scabbard."[7]

Takes steps to form alliance with England

A month after Monroe's departure with his original instructions, Secretary Madison forwarded new instructions, under date of April 18, authorizing him, in the event of failure of the negotiations at Paris, to form an alliance with England. He was advised to begin these negotiations through the British minister at Paris rather than to go to London. The latter course might be taken as the signal for a rupture, and if there was to be war it was desirable to delay matters until suitable terms could be agreed upon with England and until Congress could be convened. The emergency was so great, the note declared, that

> . . . notwithstanding the just repugnance of this country to a coalition of any sort with the belligerent politics of Europe, the advantages to be derived from the coöperation of Great Britain in a war of the United States, at this period, against France and her allies, are too obvious and too important to be renounced.[8]

---

[6]Richardson, *Messages and Papers of the Presidents*, I, 351.

[7]Henry Adams, I, 346.

[8]*A. S. P., F. R.*, II, 555.

By the time these instructions reached Paris, the Louisiana-Purchase Treaty had been signed.

Livingston opens Louisiana negotiations

Meanwhile the negotiations which Livingston was carrying on at Paris had taken a surprising turn. Unable to get any satisfactory replies from Talleyrand, he appealed directly to Napoleon in a note dated February 27, 1803. This note dealt with two subjects: American claims, which he placed at twenty million francs, and the situation created by the suspension of the right of deposit at New Orleans and the cession of Louisiana to France. He asked for some explicit declaration explaining the terms on which France had received Louisiana and recognizing the rights of the United States. In case the cession should include the Floridas he pointed out that the grant to the United States of a free passage through Mobile and Pensacola would greatly strengthen the bonds of friendship between the two nations.[9]

Talleyrand evasive

Talleyrand replied on behalf of the First Consul that it was not believed that the debt could "be raised, by any valuation whatever, to the sum of twenty millions," but every claim established would be promptly and fully paid. Assuming an even loftier tone he continued:

> As to the second question in your memoir, which relates to Louisiana, the First Consul would have preferred its having been the subject of a separate note. Affairs so different in their nature ought to be kept as much as possible apart, and should certainly not be united. It is entirely opposed to the maxims of government, adopted by the republic, to mingle important and delicate political relations with calculations of account and mere pecuniary interests.

He concluded with the statement that the First Consul had decided to send immediately to the United States a minister plenipotentiary, to deal with the questions relating to Louisiana.[10]

---

[9] *Op. cit.*, II, 538.
[10] *Ibid.*, p. 546.

Livingston presses for a reply

If Napoleon had any intention of transferring the negotiations to Washington he soon changed his mind. Events were moving too rapidly in Europe to make negotiations at such a distance safe. Meanwhile Livingston was pressing Talleyrand for some definite reply to his communications on the Louisiana question, but without much prospect of success. Displeased at the appointment of Monroe, which he regarded as a reflection on his handling of the case, he grew bolder, and on April 11 talked very plainly to Talleyrand, telling him that the United States would probably avail itself of Spain's breach of the treaty, in suspending the right of deposit, to take possession of New Orleans and the Floridas; that England would never permit the Floridas to go to France, but would seize them as soon as the transfer took place; and that without the Floridas, Louisiana would be indefensible and would likewise soon fall into the hands of the British. He concluded his argument by referring to the probability of a renewal of the war in Europe. To his amazement Talleyrand suddenly turned to him and asked whether the United States wished the whole of Louisiana. Livingston replied that their wishes extended only to New Orleans and the Floridas, but that it would be good policy on France's part to give them the country above the Arkansas so as to place a barrier between Louisiana and Canada. The French minister then inquired what he would give for the whole. Livingston replied that he had not thought about the subject, but supposed twenty millions might be considered, provided the claims of American citizens were paid. Talleyrand said this sum was too low, but requested him to reflect upon the matter and let him know the next day. As Monroe was expected in two days, Livingston said he would delay any further offer until he arrived.[11]

Talleyrand offers to sell all of Louisiana

The failure of the Santo Domingo expedition and the

[11] *Op. cit.*, II, 552.

Napoleon's reasons for the sale

prospect of the immediate renewal of the war with England now made Napoleon as anxious to get rid of Louisiana as he had been a few months before to acquire it. He concluded that the best thing to do with the province was to give it to the United States, so as to make that country a serious rival of England. On the very morning of Livingston's conversation with Talleyrand, Napoleon had sent for Marbois, Minister of the Treasury, and had ordered him to enter into negotiations at once for the sale not of New Orleans and the Floridas, but of all Louisiana. He fixed the minimum price at fifty million francs. Napoleon's choice of Marbois was due in part to his unwillingness to trust Talleyrand in so large a financial transaction and in part to Marbois' friendship for Livingston and his knowledge of American affairs acquired during several years' residence as consul in Philadelphia.[12]

Further negotiations with Talleyrand

The next day, April 12, Livingston again called on Talleyrand, hoping no doubt to get the negotiation well under way before Monroe should have any part in it. The French minister remarked that the proposition he had made the day before was purely personal, but he again invited Livingston to make an offer. Upon Livingston's declining to do so without consulting Monroe, Talleyrand shrugged his shoulders and changed the conversation. Not willing to be diverted, Livingston continued to press the subject until Talleyrand finally told him that France did not own Louisiana but merely had its acquisition in contemplation. Livingston smiled at this assertion and told him he had seen the treaty, but he added that, if Talleyrand meant to declare officially that Louisiana still belonged to Spain, he would negotiate no further on the subject, and, if Monroe concurred, they would advise their government to take possession. At the boldness of this proposal Talleyrand seemed alarmed.

[12]Sloane, "World Aspects of the Louisiana Purchase," in *Am. Hist. Rev.*, IX, 507; Henry Adams, II, 25–39.

The terms agreed upon

That night Monroe arrived, and the next day, while he was being entertained by Livingston at dinner, Marbois was seen walking in the garden. He declined to come in then but returned later while they were taking their coffee and had a few words with Livingston. As the house was full of guests he suggested that it would be better for Livingston to come to his house any time before eleven that night. As soon as Monroe left, Livingston hastened to Marbois and the negotiation progressed rapidly. Marbois suggested one hundred and twenty million francs, but Livingston said such a sum was out of the question. Marbois then said that if they would name sixty million and agree to assume the American claims, he would communicate the offer to the First Consul and try to get him to accept it.[13]

Jealousy between Livingston and Monroe

From this point on the negotiations are shrouded in mystery. An unfortunate rivalry developed between Livingston and Monroe, each claiming the chief credit for the transaction. Livingston wrote a long letter to Madison, November 15, 1803, to prove that the terms were practically agreed upon before Monroe arrived, while Monroe maintained in a letter dated March 3, 1804, that Napoleon's decision to cede the territory was actually produced by his arrival.[14] From Monroe's brief memoranda it appears that the adjustment of American claims caused some delay. In fact, this question was not settled until the 8th or 9th of May. The three documents covering the entire transaction were all antedated April

The treaties signed

30. The first was the treaty of cession, the second was the convention by which the United States agreed to pay France sixty million francs, and the third was the claims convention by which the United States agreed to pay the claims of its citizens against France, as ascertained by

[13] *A. S. P., F. R.*, II, 552–553.

[14] *Ibid.*, p. 573; Hamilton, *Writings of Monroe*, IV, 148.

the French government, the total payments not to exceed twenty million francs.[15] This last arrangement was a serious mistake. The United States should have distributed the twenty millions directly. Under the convention the awards were made by the French government and as the claims filed were greatly in excess of the sum allotted there was room in the designation of preferred claimants for the kind of jobbery and corruption for which Talleyrand was noted. The scandals growing out of the distribution brought into discredit the diplomatic careers of Livingston and his successor, General Armstrong.[16] Had Livingston given more time to the claims convention he might have been spared the aspersions later cast upon his reputation, but he believed that he was right in securing his main object at any cost, and the soundness of this opinion was confirmed by the course of events.

The claims convention

The purchase of a vast empire of over nine hundred thousand square miles—an area equal in extent to that of the original thirteen states—without the knowledge or authorization of the President, was the most serious responsibility ever assumed by any two American diplomats, but Livingston and Monroe rose nobly to the occasion. They must, however, have had serious misgivings as to how their treaty would be received at home. They had been authorized to obtain New Orleans and as much territory as they could secure *east* of the Mississippi; what they had actually done was to purchase New Orleans and a vast territory of unknown extent *west* of the Mississippi.

The magnitude of the purchase

When Jefferson received the dispatches informing him of the unexpected turn the negotiations had taken, he was quick to grasp the immense importance of the op-

Jefferson approves but doubts constitutional power

[15] *A. S. P., F. R.*, II, 507–509; *Treaties and Conventions*, I, 508–521; Henry Adams, II, 40–42.

[16] Henry Adams, II, 47–49.

portunity which had come to the United States, but he was embarrassed by the fact that there was no clause in the Constitution authorizing the acquisition of territory. As a strict constructionist he determined to secure the passage of an amendment expressly authorizing the purchase and had actually drafted one when he received dispatches from Livingston and Monroe advising him to close the transaction as soon as possible lest Napoleon should change his mind. He immediately dropped the amendment question and advised his political associates that the less said about it the better.[17] Thus Jefferson sacrificed his constitutional scruples on the altar of political expediency. A special session of Congress was called for October 17. The treaties were submitted to

Treaties ratified and money appropriated

both Houses. They were ratified by the Senate, October 20, by a vote of twenty-four to seven, and five days later the House appropriated the fifteen million dollars by a vote of ninety to twenty-five. The main opposition came from the New England Federalists, who foresaw that this doubling of the territorial area of the Union would diminish the importance and influence of their section. A few years later, when the bill for the admission of the State of Louisiana was under discussion, Josiah Quincy of Massachusetts threatened secession in case the bill should pass.

Boundaries not clearly defined

Not the least remarkable feature of the Louisiana Purchase Treaty was the fact that it did not define the boundaries of the ceded territory. It was described, in the language of the Treaty of San Ildefonso, as "the Colony or Province of Louisiana with the same extent that it now has in the hands of Spain, and that it had when France possessed it; and such as it should be after the treaties subsequently entered into between Spain and other states." This language was indefinite and contradictory. French Louisiana had extended as far east as the Perdido,

[17] Ford, *Writings of Jefferson*, X, 3–12.

including Mobile, which had been the capital of the province before the founding of New Orleans, while Spanish Louisiana had included nothing east of the Mississippi except New Orleans and the island on which it stands. Livingston and Monroe had no sooner signed the treaty than they began to inquire as to the extent of the territory they had purchased. From the French government they could get no satisfactory answer. Marbois told Livingston that he was sure Mobile was included. When approached by Livingston, Monroe being ill at the time, Talleyrand was evasive as usual:

> I asked the minister what were the east bounds of the territory ceded to us. He said he did not know; we must take it as they had received it. I asked him how Spain meant to give them possession. He said, according to the words of the treaty. But what did you mean to take? I do not know. Then you mean that we shall construe it in our own way? I can give you no direction; you have made a noble bargain for yourselves, and I suppose you will make the most of it.[18]

Criticisms of the transaction

New England historians have been harsh in their criticisms of Napoleon, Jefferson, and everybody else involved in the Louisiana Purchase. Henry Adams declared:

> The sale of Louisiana to the United States was trebly invalid: if it were French property, Bonaparte could not constitutionally alienate it without the consent of the Chambers; if it were Spanish property, he could not alienate it at all; if Spain had a right of reclamation, his sale was worthless.[19]

Professor Channing, in an interesting discussion of the question, comes to this conclusion:

> In taking Louisiana we were the accomplices of the greatest highwayman of modern history, and the goods which we received were those which he compelled his unwilling victim to disgorge.[20]

---

[18]*A. S. P., F. R.*, II, 561.

[19]*History of the United States*, II, 56.

[20]*The Jeffersonian System*, 79.

Spanish protest met by Madison

As a matter of fact, Spain made a formal protest to the American government against the validity of the cession several weeks before the treaty was ratified. The grounds of the protest were, first, that Napoleon had made a solemn engagement not to alienate Louisiana, and, second, that he had failed to carry out the stipulations relating to the Kingdom of Etruria which formed the main consideration for the transfer.[21] This protest was easily met by Madison who called the attention of the Marquis de Yrujo to a letter which Mr. Pinckney had received from the Spanish minister of state a few months before, in which the minister said:

> By the retrocession made to France of Louisiana, this power regains the said province with the limits it had, and saving the rights acquired by other Powers. The United States can address themselves to the French government to negotiate the acquisition of territories which may suit their interests.[22]

He was relying, no doubt, on Napoleon's keeping his promise not to alienate. Madison's reply was more convincing to the Spanish government of that day than it was to the two historians of our day quoted above, for a few months later Pinckney was informed that

> . . . his majesty has thought fit to renounce his opposition to the alienation of Louisiana made by France, notwithstanding the solid reasons on which it is founded; thereby giving a new proof of his benevolence and friendship towards the United States.[23]

When the Spanish government refused to negotiate with us further in regard to Louisiana and referred us in the most positive and explicit manner to France as the owner of the province, it is sheer nonsense to talk about our having received stolen goods.

---

[21] *A. S. P., F. R.*, II, 569.
[22] *Ibid.*, p. 570.
[23] *Ibid.*, p. 583.

The question of the Floridas

As to whether the Floridas were included in the cession to France, Livingston had been unable to get any definite information until shortly before the signing of the American treaty. His opinion varied with the character of the information or rumors he received from time to time.[24] He finally learned that the Floridas as such were not included, but this left open the question as to whether the eastern boundary of Louisiana extended to the Perdido. His conversations with Marbois and Talleyrand after the signing of the treaty led him to the conclusion that Napoleon had intended to insist on the Perdido as the eastern boundary and that this was the natural interpretation to be placed on the clause "with the same extent . . . that it had when France possessed it." In the hands of France, Louisiana had never had any other eastern boundary but the Perdido. He therefore urged his government to assert its claim to that part of West Florida.[25] Henry Adams criticizes Livingston unsparingly for taking a stand which, he claims, was directly contrary to the known facts of the case. The negotiators, he says, had been sent to buy the east bank of the Mississippi, but they had bought the west bank instead. They were disappointed to find that the Floridas were not included and looked about for some way to retrieve the situation.

The United States claims Perdido as boundary

> Hardly was the treaty signed, when Livingston found what he sought. He discovered that France had actually bought West Florida without knowing it, and had sold it to the United States without being paid for it. This theory, which seemed at first sight preposterous, became a fixed idea in Livingston's mind.[26]

The theory as stated may be preposterous, but that was not the theory on which Livingston proceeded, and the claim he advanced cannot fairly be called preposterous by anyone who makes an unprejudiced examination of the

Treaty of San Ildefonso purposely vague

[24] *Op. cit.*, II, 514, 516, 519, 524, 525.

[25] *Ibid.*, p. 561.

[26] *History of the United States*, II, 68.

documents. The language of the Treaty of San Ildefonso was vague and indefinite, and designedly so. It would have been a simple matter for the negotiators to define the eastern limits of the cession by naming the Iberville or the Perdido, whichever they intended, but they did not do so. The question was deliberately left open, to be decided by the course of events, and in view of the persistently hostile attitude of Spain the United States was fully justified in asserting the claim and waiting for the course of events in Europe to make it good. Livingston's "preposterous theory" was adopted by Monroe, by Madison, and by Jefferson, and was later confirmed by acts of Congress and by decisions of the Supreme Court.[27]

The delivery of Louisiana to the United States

On November 30, 1803, Napoleon's agent, Laussat, received from the Spanish governor formal possession of the Province of Louisiana, and three weeks later, on December 20, handed it over to William C. C. Claiborne who had been appointed by Jefferson to receive it on behalf of the United States. The attitude of the administration on the question of the boundaries of Louisiana was fully stated by Secretary Madison in his dispatches to Livingston of January 31 and March 31, 1804. In the first he wrote:

> It does not appear that, in the delivery of the province by the Spanish authorities to M. Laussat, anything passed denoting its limits, either to the east, the west, or the north; nor was any step taken by M. Laussat, either whilst the province was in his hands, or at the time of his transferring it to ours, calculated to dispossess Spain of any part of the territory east of the Mississippi. On the contrary, in a private conference, he stated positively that no part of the Floridas was included in the eastern boundary; France having strenuously insisted to have it extended to Mobile, which was peremptorily refused by Spain. We learn from Mr. Pinckney that the Spanish government holds the same language to him. To the declaration of M. Laussat, however, we can oppose that of the French minister, made to you, that Louisiana extended to the river Perdido; and to the

[27] Moore, *Digest of International Law*, I, 445.

Spanish government, as well as to that of France, we can oppose the treaty of St. Ildefonso, and of September [April] 30, 1803, interpreted by facts and fair inferences. . . . With respect to the western extent of Louisiana, M. Laussat held a language more satisfactory. He considered the Rio Bravo, or Del Norte,[28] as far as the 30th degree of north latitude, as its true boundary on that side. The northern boundary, we have reason to believe, was settled between France and Great Britain by commissioners appointed under the treaty of Utrecht, who separated the British and French territories west of the Lake of the Woods by the 49th degree of latitude.[29]

Claim to West Florida not pressed

In the second dispatch Madison explained that on the occasion of the transfer the United States government had made no demands in regard to West Florida, not caring to face prematurely the dilemma of submitting to a rejection of its claims or of resorting to force. Mere silence, he said, "would be no bar to a plea at any time that a delivery of a part, particularly of the seat of government, was a virtual delivery of the whole."[30]

Mobile organized as customs district

In February, 1804, Congress passed the so-called Mobile act, authorizing the President "to erect the shores, waters, and inlets of the bay and river of Mobile" into a customs district. This he did by a proclamation issued May 20, in which he designated Fort Stoddert to be the port of entry for the said district.[31] As Fort Stoddert was on the Mobile River just above the thirty-first parallel, its designation as the seat of the customs service did not involve occupation of the disputed territory. The Marquis de Yrujo called on Madison, however, in a great rage, with a copy of the act in his hand, and denounced it as an insulting usurpation of his sovereign's unquestionable rights. A note which he addressed to the Secretary

[28]The Rio Grande.

[29]*A. S. P., F. R.*, II, 574. This had reference, of course, to the southern limits of the Hudson Bay territory, but the commissioners referred to failed to come to an agreement, so that Madison was mistaken. See Bemis, "Jay's Treaty and the Northwest Boundary Gap," in *Am. Hist. Rev.*, XXVII, 479.

[30]*A. S. P., F. R.*, II, 575.

[31]Richardson, *Messages and Papers*, I, 369.

of State was so violent in its denunciations that it was brought to the attention of the Spanish government, and was one of several reasons for requesting his recall. The Marquis had married the daughter of Governor McKean of Pennsylvania, a good Republican, and had been on terms of intimacy with Jefferson and Madison. A long controversy over the question of his recall followed and he remained in this country a year or more after the government had refused to have any further official relations with him.[32]

Monroe's mission to Spain

Meanwhile Monroe had been sent on a special mission to Spain to secure recognition of the Perdido and the Rio Grande as the boundaries of Louisiana, to negotiate for the purchase of the remainder of West Florida and the whole of East Florida, and to arrange for the settlement of claims arising out of the illegal seizure of American vessels. He and Pinckney carried on negotiations with the Spanish government from January to May, 1805, without being able to arrive at a satisfactory agreement on any of the points at issue. Monroe then took formal leave and departed for England.[33]

Diplomatic relations with Spain suspended

In 1808, as a result of Napoleon's occupation of Spain, diplomatic relations between Spain and the United States were suspended and not renewed until after the restoration of Ferdinand VII. During the long period of war in the Spanish peninsula the United States did not recognize either Joseph Bonaparte or the Central Junta which was acting in the name of Ferdinand, who was a prisoner in France. The Junta sent Don Luis de Onís as minister to the United States, but he was given no official recognition until the end of the war. During the same period Mr. Ewing, who had been American chargé d'affaires at Madrid, had only "informal" relations with the Central Junta.[34]

---

[32]Moore, *Dig. of Int. Law*, IV, 508.

[33]*A. S. P., F. R.*, II, 613–669; Cox, *The West Florida Controversy* Chap. IV.

[34]Moore, *Dig. of Int. Law*, I, 131–133.

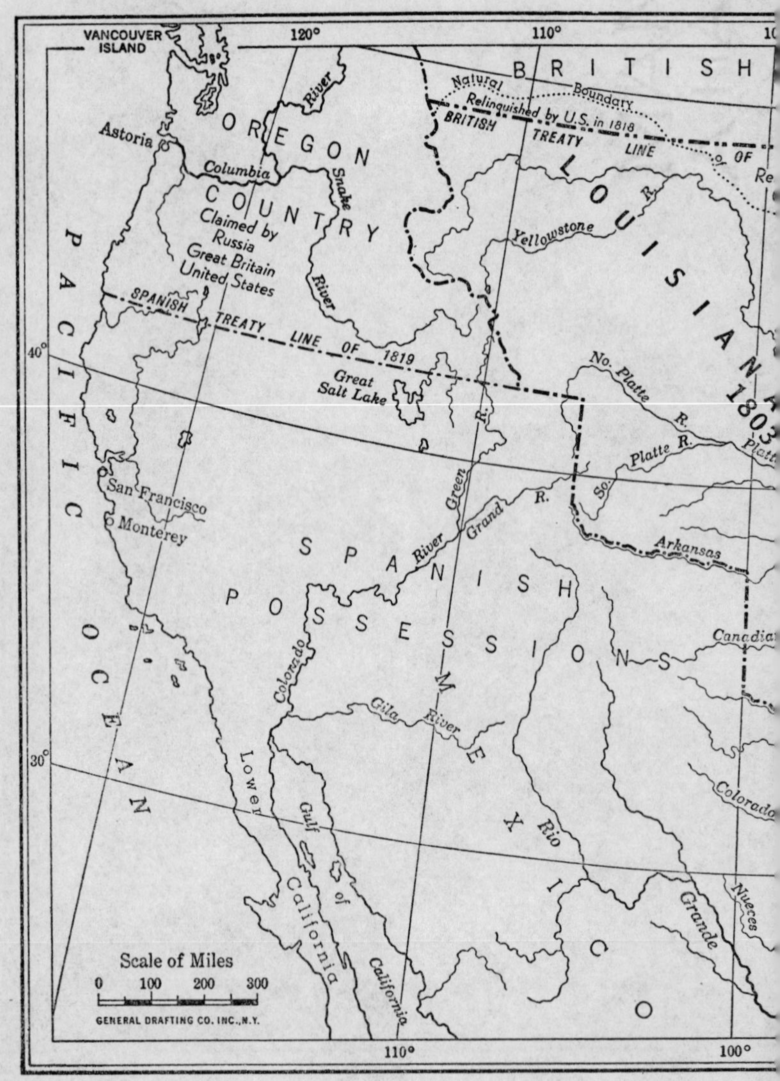

VANCOUVER ISLAND
120°
110°
100°
BRITISH
Natural Boundary
Relinquished by U.S. in 1818
BRITISH TREATY LINE OF
Astoria
OREGON COUNTRY
Claimed by Russia Great Britain United States
Columbia
River
Snake River
LOUISIANA 1803
Yellowstone
R.
PACIFIC OCEAN
SPANISH TREATY LINE OF 1819
40°
30°
Great Salt Lake
No. Platte R.
Platte R.
So.
Green R.
Grand River
San Francisco
Monterey
SPANISH POSSESSIONS
Arkansas
Canadian
Colorado
Gila River
MEXICO
Lower California
Gulf of California
Rio Grande
Nueces
Scale of Miles
0 100 200 300
GENERAL DRAFTING CO. INC., N.Y.

3. FLORIDA

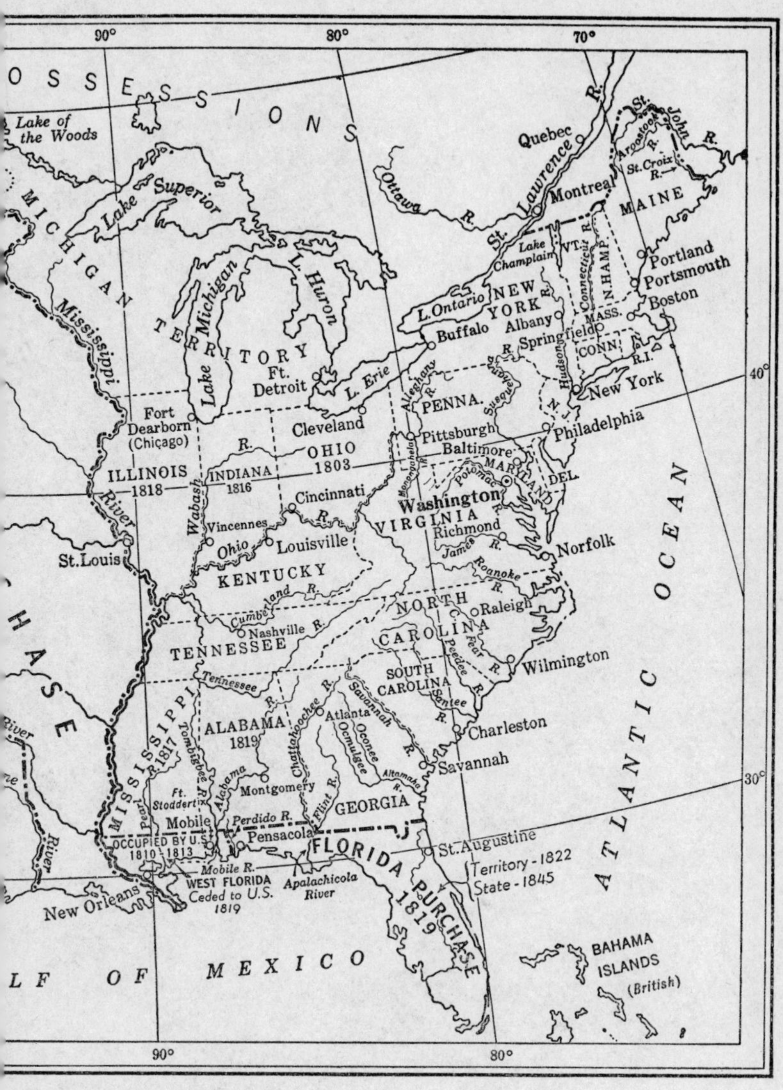

ANA PURCHASES

West Florida occupied by the United States

During this period of relaxation of Spanish power in America, the Floridas became a turbulent frontier, the scene of Indian disturbances, filibustering expeditions, and land speculations.[35] In 1810, the unruly inhabitants of the portion of West Florida lying between the Mississippi and Pearl rivers rose in revolt, captured Baton Rouge, proclaimed their independence, and applied for admission into the American Union. President Madison took military possession of the district and in 1812 it was incorporated in the new State of Louisiana. The same year the strip between the Pearl River and the Mobile district was made a part of the territory of Mississippi. In 1813, during the war with England, the Mobile district was temporarily occupied by American troops, and the following year General Jackson took permanent possession. It was later made a part of Alabama. Spanish Florida, to which the United States had no claim, was invaded by General Jackson in 1814, to prevent the British from seizing Pensacola, and again in 1818, in pursuit of the Seminole Indians.[36]

Diplomatic relations resumed

Thus, when diplomatic relations with Spain were restored after the Napoleonic wars, the United States had incorporated West Florida as far as the Perdido, and had raised a number of perplexing questions by the temporary occupation of the Pensacola region. There remained the unsettled claims covered by the convention of 1802, which Spain had refused to ratify, and later claims arising out of the suspension of the right of deposit and out of the captures made by French privateers within Spanish jurisdiction. Furthermore, a new element had entered into the situation in the revolt of the Spanish provinces in South America and the development of commercial relations between them and the United States. Finally there was the question of Texas. France held that the western

[35]Cox, *The West Florida Controversy* describes this situation in great detail.
[36]Moore, *Int. Arbits.*, V, 4519–4524.

limits of Louisiana extended to the Rio Grande and American statesmen of the day were practically unanimous in claiming Texas as a part of the Louisiana Purchase. This claim was denied by Spain, and has become a subject of endless debate by opposing groups of latter-day Texas and Louisiana historians.

The Florida treaty

Little progress was made toward the settlement of all these differences with Spain until January, 1818, when John Quincy Adams, Secretary of State, made a proposition to De Onís based on terms proposed by Monroe at Madrid in 1805. The negotiations continued for a year, and on February 22, 1819, the so-called Florida treaty was signed.[37] In this treaty the United States secured the Floridas, relinquished Texas, and assumed the claims of its citizens against Spain to the extent of five million dollars. As we already held a large part of West Florida, the language of the treaty was skilfully drawn so as not to impeach our existing title. Article II provided: "His Catholic Majesty cedes to the United States, in full property and sovereignty, all the territories *which belong to him*, situated to the eastward of the Mississippi, known by the name of East and West Florida." Article III established the boundary between the United States and the Spanish possessions to the southwest. It ran in an irregular line from the Gulf of Mexico along the western bank of the Sabine River to the thirty-second degree of latitude, thence north to the Red River, thence along the course of that river to the one-hundredth degree of longitude west of London, or twenty-third from Washington, thence north to the Arkansas River, and along the course of that river to its source, thence due north to latitude forty-two, and by that parallel to the sea. Spain thus renounced in our favor whatever claim she had to the Oregon country.[38]

The ratifications of this treaty were not exchanged until

[37] *A. S. P., F. R.*, IV, 422–626; H. B. Fuller, *The Purchase of Florida.*

[38] (Malloy) *Treaties and Conventions*, II, 1651.

February 22, 1821. The King of Spain withheld his approval on various pretexts for two years.[39] His real reason for keeping matters in suspense was to delay as long as possible the recognition by the United States of the independence of the South American republics.

Ratification delayed

The Texas question

The surrender of Texas was later the subject of bitter controversy. At the time John Quincy Adams was opposed to giving it up. Crawford of Georgia, also a member of the cabinet, held that Florida was so essential to the southeastern states that the chance to obtain it ought not to be lost by pressing the claim to a territory which was of no present value. Clay, representing the sentiment of the West, held that Texas was not only more valuable than Florida, but that it already rightfully belonged to the United States and should not on any account be surrendered. President Monroe was facing a bitter fight over slavery in Missouri and feared that the possession of Texas would prolong that issue and make it more acute. It was claimed later by Adams that General Jackson was consulted and advised surrendering Texas. This he angrily denied. He did, apparently, express his approval of the treaty on the ground that it would put a stop to the Indian warfare on the Florida frontier and avoid a war with Spain. He was so much concerned about the Florida situation that he paid little attention at the time to the southwestern boundary.[40] He little dreamed that this question would rise to plague him in after years. The relinquishment of Texas was an unfortunate mistake that later cost us the war with Mexico and made the Civil War inevitable.

[39] *A. S. P., F. R.*, IV, 650–703.

[40] Moore, *Dig. of Int. Law*, I, 446.

PART II

THE DEFIANCE OF THE OLD WORLD

CHAPTER VI

THE STRUGGLE FOR NEUTRAL RIGHTS

"PEACE, commerce, and honest friendship with all nations, entangling alliances with none." Such was the comprehensive but concise declaration of foreign policy made by Jefferson in his first inaugural address. But the man who declared that peace was his passion had soon to abandon his plan of laying up the navy in the Potomac and wage war against Tripoli. As a result of the chastisement inflicted by Commodore Preble there was no further trouble with the Barbary powers until the War of 1812.

Keynote of Jefferson's policy

Meanwhile England and France, weary of war, signed the Peace of Amiens in March, 1802, but it proved to be merely a truce. In May, 1803, the war was renewed with greater bitterness than ever and with less regard for the rights and interests of neutrals. For some months, however, it did not work any particular hardship on American commerce. In fact, as late as November 8, 1804, Jefferson said in his annual message to Congress:

Renewal of war in Europe

> With the nations of Europe in general our friendship and intercourse are undisturbed, and from the governments of the belligerent powers especially we continue to receive those friendly manifestations which are justly due to an honest neutrality.

So far the British government had not interfered with the direct trade between the French colonies and the United States which she had permitted ever since the order in council of January 8, 1794. American vessels brought the products of the French West Indies to American ports, unloaded, paid the duties and storage charges, and then carried these "Americanized" products to French or other European ports. This trade assumed large proportions and American commerce prospered, especially since the duties paid were in large part refunded on re-exportation. But British planters, shippers, and merchants protested. They claimed that this carriage of the products of hostile colonies to the belligerent and neutral countries of Europe reduced by competition the profits on British colonial articles.[1] When Pitt returned to power in 1804 this question was taken under consideration and orders were finally issued to seize American ships engaged in this practice. In the test case of the *Essex*, May, 1805, Sir William Scott decided that the trade in which the vessel was engaged was in violation of the Rule of 1756, which had been relaxed to cover *bona fide* importations. In the case before him, however, it was shown that the drawback on re-exportation amounted to almost as much as the duty. The continuity of the voyage, therefore, had not been really broken, and the vessel was condemned.

Case of the *Essex*

Monroe's mission to England

A few weeks after the decision in the *Essex* case Monroe returned from his Spanish mission to England and entered upon a long correspondence with the British government, in which he protested against seizures under the Rule of 1756. After the death of Pitt in January, 1806, Fox, who had always been friendly to America, became Secretary for Foreign Affairs, and on February 25, Monroe addressed to him a formal protest against the new policy, which, he said, had been highly injurious to the United States. "About one hundred and twenty of their vessels have been seized, several of which were condemned, all taken from their course, detained, and otherwise subjected to heavy losses and damages."[2] Fox was disposed to be

[1]Mahan, *Sea Power in Its Relations to the War of 1812*, I, 99–101.
[2]*A. S. P., F. R.*, III, 113.

conciliatory and proposed to drop the discussion of the principle, but to suspend the rights claimed by England and leave the Americans in enjoyment of the trade. Monroe insisted on an indemnity for the injuries which had been "severe and unprovoked."[3] The payment of an indemnity by England would, of course, have been a surrender of the principle and Fox could not run counter to public opinion and the opposition in the cabinet. Nevertheless, as will be seen later, a solution of this question would not have been impossible had not other questions of even greater fundamental importance been involved in the general controversy.

The British practice of impressment

The disputes over impressment and blockade played a greater part than the Rule of 1756 in bringing on the War of 1812. The practice of taking British seamen from merchant vessels and forcing them to serve in the navy was one of the main methods of recruiting the British navy in time of war. Discipline in the service was very severe, flogging still existed, and it was found impossible through voluntary enlistments to keep the service up to the required strength. Furthermore, desertions were frequent and many British seamen entered the American merchant marine. Great Britain never claimed the bald right to impress American seamen, but she did claim the right to take her own subjects from American vessels on the high seas, and as it was not always easy to distinguish between an Englishman and an American, and as the British officers were not overscrupulous when they were short of seamen, hundreds of native-born Americans were impressed into the British navy. Great Britain also held the doctrine of indefeasible allegiance and did not recognize the right of her subjects to become naturalized in foreign countries. The real point of the controversy, however, was the right claimed to enforce

[3] *Op. cit.*, III, 117.

her municipal law on American vessels on the high seas. This we strenuously denied.[4]

Early stages of the controversy

As early as 1790, in anticipation of war with Spain, Great Britain impressed a number of American seamen in British ports. As these cases occurred within British jurisdiction the only question raised was that of nationality. Gouverneur Morris, who was then in London on a semi-official mission, took the matter up with the foreign secretary, remarking with characteristic humor, "I believe, my Lord, this is the only instance in which we are not treated as aliens." It was suggested that American sailors should be provided with certificates of citizenship, but Pitt, while approving this plan, remarked that it would be liable to abuse. Several expedients of this kind were tried, especially the act of May 28, 1796, but all proved unsatisfactory. In 1792, Jefferson announced the doctrine on which his country took its stand, when he said: "The simplest rule will be that the vessel being American, shall be evidence that the seamen on board her are such." During the first period of war, 1793–1801, the practice of impressment was the subject of repeated protests by Thomas Pinckney, Jay, and King, who successively represented their country in England, but these protests accomplished nothing in the way of a final solution of the question. The number of impressments during this period was nothing like as great as it was after the renewal of the war. Prior to September, 1801, the number of applications for release which passed through the hands of the American representatives in England was 2,059.[5] Of these 102 were held to be British subjects, 805 were being held for further proof, and 1,142 had been discharged as not being British subjects. These figures afforded a conclusive argument against the propriety of

---

[4]*Op. cit.*, III, 84, 85, 268.

[5]*Ibid.*, p. 85. So given by Madison, but the total does not tally with the figures that follow. Possibly 2,049 was intended.

permitting a belligerent commander to render an impromptu decision on the quarter-deck of an American vessel and put it into immediate execution.[6]

The British blockade of France

The question of blockade was raised in a new form by the British order of May 16, 1806, declaring the coast of France in a state of blockade from the river Elbe to Brest. This blockade was to be absolute only between the Seine and Ostend. Outside these limits neutral vessels might trade provided they had not been laden in any port belonging to or in the possession of his Majesty's enemies, or which going out were not destined to such ports.[7] This order was so worded as to prevent the direct trade between France and her colonies. No protest was made at the time against this blockade, though its legality was later attacked by the United States, which denied that a coast line could thus be shut off from commerce and insisted that an adequate force must be placed before designated ports. Great Britain admitted that a blockade in order to be binding must be effectively maintained, but a dispute arose as to whether the ports along the coast were actually blockaded or only the entrance to the English Channel, a question of fact on which the two governments could never agree. The position of the American government was later stated with great conciseness in the following sentence: "In order to determine what characterizes a blockade, that denomination is given only to a port, where there is, by the disposition of the power which blockades it with ships stationary, an evident danger in entering." While this blockade was overshadowed at the time by the questions of impressment and colonial trade, it assumed great importance six months later when Napoleon retaliated by his famous Berlin decree.

Meanwhile in April, 1806, as the result of remonstrances

[6]Updyke, *The Diplomacy of the War of 1812,* Chap. I. "Impressment"; Mahan, *War of 1812*, I, 114–128.

[7]*A. S. P., F. R.*, III, 267.

Negotiations of Monroe and Pinkney with England

against the decisions of the Admiralty Courts in cases involving the colonial trade, Congress passed an act excluding from American ports, after November 15, certain articles of British manufacture, unless Great Britain would come to some satisfactory agreement before that date. At the same time the President appointed William Pinkney, of Maryland, as commissioner plenipotentiary and extraordinary to act with Monroe, who was given a similar commission, in settling all matters of difference between the United States and England. The two questions particularly emphasized in their instructions were impressment and colonial trade.[8] The opening of negotiations was delayed by the illness of Fox, who died the following September. In the meantime his nephew Lord Holland and Lord Auckland were appointed special commissioners to treat with Monroe and Pinkney. At the first meeting, August 22, the American commissioners, acting in accordance with their instructions, presented the question of impressment. In reporting to their government the attitude of the British commissioners they wrote:

British view of impressment

> On the impressment subject, it was soon apparent that they felt the strongest repugnance to a formal renunciation or abandonment of their claim to take from our vessels on the high seas such seamen as should appear to be their own subjects; and they pressed upon us with much zeal, as a substitute for such an abandonment, a provision that the persons composing the crews of our ships should be furnished with authentic documents of citizenship, the nature and form of which should be settled by treaty; that these documents should completely protect those to whom they related; but that, subject to such protections, the ships of war of Great Britain should continue to visit and impress on the main ocean as heretofore.[9]

It is evident from the report that the British commissioners presented their case with great ability. They began by observing

[8] *Op. cit.*, III, 119.

[9] *Ibid.*, p. 133.

. . . that they supposed the object of our plan to be to prevent the impressment at sea of American seamen, and not to withdraw British seamen from the naval service of their country in times of great national peril, for the purpose of employing them ourselves; . . . that if they should consent to make our commercial navy a floating asylum for all the British seamen who, tempted by higher wages, should quit their service for ours, the effect of such a concession upon their maritime strength, on which Great Britain depended, not only for her prosperity but her safety, might be fatal; . . . that the plan we proposed [for the delivery of deserters] was inadequate in its range and object, inasmuch as it was merely prospective, confined wholly to deserters, and in no respect providing for the case of the vast body of British seamen now employed in our trade to every part of the world.[10]

Refuse to renounce principle

The Americans were willing to lend the aid of local authorities in apprehending and returning deserters from British vessels, provided the British would renounce the claim to impressment.[11] The British commissioners insisted on substituting for "deserters" the phrase "seafaring people quitting their service" and in this form finally agreed to the proposal, but it was rejected by the cabinet.[12] At the same time they were instructed by the cabinet to state to the Americans,

Willing to modify practice

That his Majesty's government, animated by a desire to remove every cause of dissatisfaction, has directed his Majesty's commissioners to give to Mr. Monroe and to Mr. Pinkney the most positive assurances that instructions have been given, and shall be repeated and enforced, for the observance of the greatest caution in the impressing of British seamen; and that the strictest care shall be taken to preserve the citizens of the United States from any molestation or injury; and that immediate and prompt redress shall be afforded upon any representation of injury sustained by them.[13]

The American commissioners accepted this statement as a pledge that the British government intended to suspend

[10]*Op. cit.*, III, 134.
[11]*Ibid.*, p. 137.
[12]*Ibid.*, p. 138.
[13]*Ibid.*, p. 140.

Americans proceed with rest of treaty

the practice of impressment without abandoning the principle, and they consented to proceed with the rest of the treaty. This was a departure from their instructions, for they had been told not to sign any treaty which did not include a renouncement of the alleged right of impressment. On this subject the British cabinet had taken ground unequivocally opposed to the position of the United States. The assurance given above had been accompanied by an opinion from a law officer of the crown stating,

> that the king had a right, by his prerogative to require the service of all his seafaring subjects against the enemy, and to seize them by force wherever found, not being within the territorial limits of another power; that as the high seas were extraterritorial the merchant vessels of other powers navigating on them were not admitted to possess such a jurisdiction as to protect British subjects from the exercise of the king's prerogative over them.[14]

Unsatisfactory treaty signed

In September, the British had requested a suspension of the non-importation act pending the conclusion of the negotiations. On Jefferson's recommendation Congress readily consented to this in December. On the last day of the year the treaty was signed. It defined blockade and contraband in the same terms as the Jay treaty, omitting, however, the clause recognizing the right of preëmption of foodstuffs. It contained no agreement in regard to trade with the British West Indies. It permitted for the period of the war the carriage of the products of the enemy's colonies from the United States to Europe, provided the said products had first been landed and had paid the regular duties in the United States, and provided, further, that on re-exportation, after the drawback, they should remain subject to a duty of not less than two per cent *ad valorem*, and were the *bona fide* property of citizens of the United States.[15] Jefferson was not satisfied

[14] *Op. cit.*, III, 138.
[15] *Ibid.*, pp. 147–151.

with the treaty. Having taken a strong stand on the question of impressment, he was not willing to accept a mere informal understanding coupled with an emphatic reassertion of the right by Great Britain. He therefore withheld the treaty from the Senate, and Madison instructed the commissioners to reopen negotiations along the lines of their original instructions. In the meantime, as long as Great Britain would act in accordance with the informal understanding on the subjects of neutral trade and impressment, the President would recommend to Congress the continued suspension of the non-importation act.[16]

Not submitted to Senate

Before Monroe and Pinkney had an opportunity to take up the negotiations again, Napoleon's Berlin decree of November 21, 1806, and the British order in council of January 7, 1807, had raised new issues that threatened the extinction of neutral trade, while the United States was brought to the verge of war with England by the *Chesapeake-Leopard* outrage. The Berlin decree declared the British Isles in a state of blockade and forbade all commerce and correspondence with them. This measure was declared to be in retaliation for England's illegal blockade order of the previous May, which extended, it was alleged, to "places before which she has not a single vessel of war," to "entire coasts, and a whole empire," which her united forces would be incapable of blockading.[17] Napoleon's decree established a purely fictitious or paper blockade, since his naval forces had been crushed at the battle of Trafalgar and an actual blockade of England was impossible.

Napoleon's Berlin decree

The British order in council of January 7 prohibited the coasting trade with all European ports under the control of France, those which excluded British ships being considered under French control.[18] On November 11,

British orders in council

[16] *Op. cit.*, III, 153, 156.
[17] *Ibid.*, p. 289.
[18] *Ibid.*, p. 267.

1807, another order in council declared an absolute blockade of all European ports from which British ships were excluded.[19] In December, 1807, Napoleon issued his Milan decree by which every ship which submitted to British search or which touched at a British port was ordered to be seized.[20] These decrees and orders were of course directed mainly at the commerce of the United States. An American ship found it difficult to reach a European port without submitting to British search. If, on the other hand, it stopped at a British port and took on British goods, the only condition on which England would allow it to proceed, it rendered itself liable to seizure in accordance with Napoleon's decree on arriving at a continental port.

Blockade and impressment

Instead of stationing her ships before the ports of Europe and maintaining an actual blockade, England found it easier to station them outside of the principal American ports and search the American vessels as they started on their voyages. If they were bound for a forbidden port they were seized and sent to Halifax for adjudication. The searching officers were directed to inforce more rigidly than ever the right of impressment, and it was announced by royal proclamation that

> No letters of naturalization, or certificates of citizenship, do or can in any manner divest our natural born subjects of the allegiance or in any degree alter the duty which they owe to us, their lawful Sovereign.[21]

Number of Americans seized

The number of impressments is impossible to determine with any degree of accuracy. At the beginning of the War of 1812 there were on file in the State Department 6,257 cases of impressed seamen who claimed to be Americans. Lord Castlereagh stated on the floor of the House of Commons that in January, 1811, there were 3,300 men

[19] *Op. cit.*, III, 269.
[20] *Ibid.*, p. 290.
[21] *Ibid.*, p. 268.

claiming to be American citizens serving in the British navy. When the War of 1812 began the British Admiralty report shows that 2,548 impressed American seamen were imprisoned for refusing to serve against their country. Roosevelt estimates the total number as high as 20,000.[22]

The *Chesapeake-Leopard* affair

The depths of our national humiliation were sounded in June, 1807. On the 22nd of that month the United States frigate *Chesapeake* left Norfolk for a cruise to the Mediterranean with four deserters from the British navy aboard. Three of these were native Americans, and the fact that they had deserted from the British navy was known to the officers. The fourth had enlisted under an assumed name. As the ship was proceeding toward the capes, the British war vessel *Leopard* approached and fired a gun as a signal that she wished to communicate with the other ship. Her captain said that he had dispatches and sent British officers aboard. The dispatches were orders from his commanding officer to search the American ship for deserters. The American commander, Commodore James Barron, refused to allow his crew to be mustered and searched by British officers. He had failed to call his men to quarters on the approach of the *Leopard*, and he now tried to gain time, but before the guns could be manned the British fired three broadsides into the *Chesapeake*. Barron hauled down his flag, whereupon the British boarded his ship, mustered the crew, seized the four deserters, but refused to receive the surrender of the *Chesapeake*. Barron was tried by court martial and suspended for five years without pay for neglect of duty in not having his men at quarters when his ship was boarded.

On July 2, President Jefferson issued a proclamation requiring all British war ships to leave American ports and forbidding the furnishing of supplies to them. Four weeks later he summoned Congress in special session,

[22] *Naval War of 1812*, p. 42, note.

but set the date far enough off to give passions time to cool down.

Monroe attempts settlement

A futile correspondence took place between Monroe and Canning, who was now Secretary for Foreign Affairs, on the *Chesapeake-Leopard* affair. Canning informed Monroe of the incident before the latter had time to hear of it through other sources, and Monroe, without waiting for instructions from his government, demanded a disavowal of the act and punishment of the officer responsible for it. He added: "I might state other examples of great indignity and outrage, many of which are of recent date, to which the United States have been exposed off their coast, and even within several of their harbors, from the British squadron; but it is improper to mingle them with the present more serious cause of complaint."[23] This was an unfortunate statement, for it gave Canning the opportunity, which he did not fail to use to the utmost, to insist on a separation of the *Chesapeake-Leopard* case from the general question of impressment. In a sharp note Canning said that his Majesty disclaimed "the pretension of a right to search ships of war, in the national service of any state, for deserters"; he declared that as soon as the facts were fully known reparation would be made for any injury to the sovereignty of the United States; and he expressed thorough accord with Monroe's statement as to the impropriety of injecting into the discussion other causes of complaint, adding in conclusion: "I have only to lament that the same sentiment did not induce you to abstain from alluding to these subjects on an occasion which you were yourself of opinion was not favorable for pursuing the discussion of them."[24] A few days later Canning expressed surprise that the President should have issued his proclamation "without requiring or waiting for any explanation" from the British government. Monroe

Failure of negotiations with Canning

[23] *A. S. P., F. R.*, III, 187.

[24] *Ibid.*, p. 188.

declared that this was "a mere measure of police, which had become indispensable for the preservation of order within the limits of the United States."

Monroe's demands embraced the following points:

Monroe quits London

> That the men taken from the frigate should be restored to it; that the officers who had committed the aggression should be exemplarily punished; that the practice of impressment from merchant vessels should be suppressed; and that the reparation consisting of those several acts should be announced to our government through the medium of a special mission, a solemnity which the extraordinary nature of the aggression particularly required.[25]

In reply Canning insisted that the *Chesapeake-Leopard* incident should be treated apart from the general question of impressment, and he objected to Monroe's attempt to make this particular case, "in which they were in the wrong, instrumental to an accommodation in a case where his government held a different doctrine."[26] On this point the negotiations between Canning and Monroe came to an end, and on October 7 Monroe took formal leave of the King and soon sailed for the United States. Pinkney, who remained in London, was appointed his successor.

Canning sends special commissioner to Washington

Canning now decided to send George H. Rose on a special mission to the United States to settle the dispute over the *Chesapeake* affair. When he reached Washington he demanded, as a preliminary to the negotiation, that the President's proclamation excluding British war ships from American waters should be revoked. The American government very properly took the position that reparation for an acknowledged aggression should precede the withdrawal of the proclamation, and demanded to know what reparation the minister was authorized to offer. Rose refused to comply with this demand and the negotiations ended. He soon returned home.[27]

[25] *Op. cit.*, III, 191.

[26] *Ibid.*, p. 192.

[27] *Ibid.*, pp. 213–220.

Jefferson's embargo policy

In the meantime, as soon as Jefferson learned of the order in council of November 11, 1807, he sent a message to Congress suggesting that an embargo be laid on American commerce, prohibiting absolutely the departure of American ships for foreign ports. He believed that it was better to keep American vessels at home than to send them out with the certainty of capture. The Senate passed the bill within five hours after it was received and three days later it passed the House with amendments, which were concurred in by the Senate the following day, December 22. American vessels were permitted to continue in the coasting trade, but as some of them took advantage of this liberty to make voyages to Europe, a supplementary act was passed January 8, 1808, requiring such vessels to give bond that they would not violate the act. The embargo raised a storm of opposition in New England. Ship owners, unwilling to see their vessels rot in port, assumed the hazard of sending them to sea, for the profits of a successful voyage were very great. By the Bayonne decree of April 17, 1808, Napoleon ordered the seizure of all American vessels found in ports under his control, on the ground that under the embargo act they could not lawfully leave their own country. This was, of course, none of his business, but the decree was carried out and within a year vessels and cargoes of the value of $10,000,000 were seized and condemned.[28] Before the close of Jefferson's administration it was evident that the embargo had failed to produce the desired effect upon either belligerent. Relations with both England and France were strained to the breaking point, and there was as much reason for declaring war against one as against the other. Owing to England's maritime supremacy and the insolent conduct of her officers in impressing seamen within sight of our shores, the popular indignation against her was greater than that against France.

Fails to produce effect on England or France

[28] *Mahan*, I, 189.

Madison elected President

While the embargo policy was still on trial the presidential election of 1808 took place. Madison, Jefferson's choice for the succession, was easily elected, but the Republican majority in Congress was greatly reduced, for the embargo had made New England almost solidly Federalist again. John Quincy Adams supported Jefferson's policy and finding himself in opposition to his party resigned his seat in the United States Senate. He now allied himself with the Republicans and was sent by Madison as minister to Russia.

Repeal of Embargo Act

After the presidential election Jefferson and Madison could no longer control even their own party leaders in Congress, and before the expiration of Jefferson's term, a bill was passed repealing the embargo, the repeal to become effective, out of deference to him, March 15, 1809, ten days after his retirement from office. In its place the non-intercourse act was passed prohibiting commercial intercourse with Great Britain and France, but leaving American ships free to sail to other ports, and authorizing the President to reëstablish intercourse with whichever of the two nations should first suspend its orders or decrees.

Erskine sent to Washington

Within six weeks after Madison's inauguration negotiations were reopened in Washington by the British minister David M. Erskine. He was authorized to offer reparation for the attack on the *Chesapeake* and to promise the withdrawal of the orders in council of January and November, 1807, on three conditions: (1) that the American government would simultaneously withdraw the proclamation excluding British war ships and all non-intercourse and non-importation acts, so far as they affected Great Britain, leaving them in force against France; (2) that the United States would agree for the period of the war to recognize the Rule of 1756; and (3) that Great Britain "for the purpose of securing the operation of the embargo, and of the *bona fide* intention of America to prevent her citizens from trading with France and the powers adopting and acting under the French decrees," should be at liberty to capture all American vessels trading with these powers.[29] In other words, the British government demanded that the British navy should be permitted to assist in enforcing an act of Congress. Erskine was authorized merely to announce these conditions to the United States and to promise that if they were acceded to, Great Britain would send a minister with power to conclude a formal treaty. He did not show the above instructions to Madison, but stated their contents in such a way as to make them appear much less objectionable than they really were. An agreement was soon reached and, on the assurance of Erskine that the orders in council would be withdrawn, on June 10, 1809, President Madison issued a proclamation renewing intercourse with Great Britain. Canning, however, repudiated Erskine's arrangements, but declared that American vessels which had already left port would be allowed to sail to their destinations unmolested. Erskine was recalled and Francis James Jackson appointed to succeed him.[30] The selection of Jackson was most unfortunate. He was ultra British and not at all inclined to be conciliatory.

His agreement repudiated by Canning

Arrival and dismissal of Jackson

When Jackson arrived Madison assumed personal direction of the negotiations and the letters which appeared over the signature of Robert Smith, who was Secretary of State, were in reality written by the President. No sooner had Madison formed an estimate of the character and attitude of Jackson than he determined that the best thing to do was to bring him to the point at once and send him home. He therefore wrote him a letter over Smith's signature, stating that further discussions must be in writing. This aroused the ire of the Englishman. In his next communication Jackson undertook to justify Canning's disavowal of Erskine's agreement on the ground

[29] *A. S. P., F. R.*, III, 300.

[30] *Ibid.*, pp. 295–307.

that the American government knew that Erskine was exceeding his authority. Madison replied that this was the first information he had received that there were any restrictions on Erskine's authority, and requested Jackson to show his full powers before proceeding any further with the negotiation. He further informed the minister that his "improper allusions" and insinuations were inadmissible. Jackson replied hotly that he would find means to vindicate the honor and dignity of His Majesty's government; whereupon Madison informed him that no further communications would be received from him.[31] Jackson confidently expected his government to demand his reinstatement, but they did not take that view of the situation, and he was soon recalled.

Modification of non-intercourse act

Meanwhile in June, 1809, Napoleon had issued a decree stating that in view of the fact that the United States had obtained a withdrawal of the British orders in council, he would withdraw the Milan decree. When he learned shortly afterward that Canning had disavowed Erskine's agreement, he secretly ordered the confiscation of every American ship that should be found in the ports of Spain, France, or Italy. The non-intercourse act was to expire by limitation in 1810, and the question now arose as to what policy should be substituted for it. Nathaniel Macon, who had for a long time been Speaker of the House of Representatives and who was now Chairman of the Committee on Foreign Affairs, reported to the House on December 19, 1809, a bill which had been drawn by Gallatin and approved by the cabinet. This bill opened intercourse with all the world but excluded British and French merchant vessels, as well as naval ships, from American ports. It passed the House but was defeated in the Senate by a combination of the Smith faction with the Federalists. A few days later a measure known as the Macon Bill, Number 2, was introduced. This bill

[31] *Op. cit.*, III, 308–319.

repealed the non-intercourse act and authorized the President, in case either Great Britain or France should withdraw their orders or decrees, to prohibit commerce with the other. This measure was finally enacted into law May 1, 1810.[32]

Tortuous policy of Napoleon

The tortuous policy pursued by Napoleon at this period is very difficult to follow, but he seems to have set to work deliberately to make President Madison believe that he had repealed the objectionable decrees and that it was Madison's duty to force Great Britain to withdraw the orders in council or to go to war with that power. His foreign minister, therefore, informed General Armstrong, the American minister at Paris, that the Berlin and Milan decrees would not be enforced after November 1, 1810, with the understanding that unless the British government should withdraw the orders in council, the United States would revive the non-intercourse act against Great Britain in accordance with the provisions of the Macon bill. This communication was dated August 5, 1810.[33] This move had the desired effect on President Madison. On November 2, 1810, he issued a proclamation announcing that commercial intercourse with Great Britain would cease on February 2, 1811. It was soon evident that Napoleon was not acting in good faith and that American vessels were still subject to unlawful restrictions and seizures. In London Pinkney undertook the task of persuading the British government to withdraw its orders. In his note of December 10, 1810, he presented very ably a strong and severe indictment of the British policy, but in view of the insincerity of Napoleon's act the government refused to recede from its position, and in January Pinkney announced that as Great Britain had failed to appoint a successor to Jackson, he had decided to withdraw, leaving a *chargé d'affaires* to look after the office.

His bad faith

[32] Channing, *History of the United States,* IV, 409–415.

[33] *A. S. P., F. R.,* III, 386.

England offers tardy reparation for *Chesapeake* outrage

After Pinkney had announced his withdrawal but before he left London he was informed that the government had decided to send a minister to the United States and had appointed Augustus J. Foster. The new minister's instructions discussed at length the orders in council representing them as retaliatory measures made necessary by Napoleon's efforts to destroy British commerce with the continent of Europe. He was to urge a repeal of the non-intercourse act on the ground that its enforcement would make the United States virtually an ally of France. He was to offer reparation for the attack on the *Chesapeake:* the restoration of the men taken from her, and pecuniary provision for those who had suffered injury. This tardy reparation was accepted by the United States although dissatisfaction was expressed that the officer who was responsible had merely been removed from one command to another. Even this reparation was delayed by the new dispute arising out of the encounter between the *President* and the *Little Belt,* which was hailed by the American public as a just retribution for the attack on the *Chesapeake.* Foster remained in Washington until war was declared, but as he was not authorized to make any concessions on the vital questions at issue, his mission was not of great significance.[34]

The British tamper with Indians

Another grievance against Great Britain was the Indian situation in the Northwest. The tribes that were hostile to the United States procured arms and ammunition from Canada, and it was generally believed that the British authorities incited them to acts of hostility. In November, 1811, General Harrison defeated a large body of Indians on the Tippecanoe Creek in western Indiana and reëstablished American control over this region.

The Twelfth Congress, which met in extra session November 4, 1811, was dominated by the younger group of Republicans, who elected Henry Clay of Kentucky as

[34]*Op. cit.,* III, 435–500.

Congress bent on war

Speaker. New England was strongly opposed to war and the Middle States were divided, but the South and West dominated Congress and it was soon evident that they were bent on war. In April, 1812, an act was passed, in secret session, establishing an embargo for ninety days. The object of this measure was to retain at home ships and seamen in anticipation of war, and to prevent the carriage of supplies to the British army in Spain. Both objects were defeated by certain Federalist members of Congress, who gave notice of the proposed measure, thus enabling ships to load and put to sea before the President had power to take steps to detain them. It is estimated that flour, grain, and provisions of all kinds to the value of fifteen million dollars, were rushed out of the country in the five days that intervened. This unpatriotic conduct was not confined to any one section of the country. A large amount of flour and grain from the agricultural states of the South was shipped to the Spanish peninsula.

Illicit trade

After war was declared, illicit trade was deliberately encouraged by Great Britain through a system of licenses granted to American ships to carry grain and other provisions to the British naval base at Halifax and to the British army in Spain. Lloyds insured such vessels against capture or detention. Trading with the enemy has existed to some extent in all wars, but it was especially characteristic of the War of 1812. The extent to which New England, where opposition to the war was strong, assisted the enemy is apparent from the dispatches of the British commander in Canada. In August, 1814, General Prevost wrote to his government: "Two-thirds of the army in Canada are at this moment eating beef provided by American contractors. Large droves are daily crossing the lines into lower Canada." Thus desire for gain and lack of patriotism, with the connivance and encouragement of the British government, largely thwarted the efforts of President Madison to keep American produce from the markets of the enemy.[35]

Declaration of war

The declaration of war against Great Britain was passed by Congress June 18, 1812. On the first the President had laid before that body a full statement of grievances against England. They included the impressment of American seamen, the hovering of British cruisers within our territorial waters, and the insolent conduct of officers in searching American vessels, the illegal blockades and restrictions upon American commerce established by the orders in council, the attempt to dismember the Union [referring to the Henry mission to New England in 1809], and finally the intrigues with the Indians of the Northwest. The President made no recommendation. He left the decision as to peace or war with Congress. Five days after the declaration of war the British government, acting under pressure of the manufacturing and commercial interests, withdrew the orders in council, but this was before the days of ocean cables, and the news came too late. The impressment controversy was, moreover, the main cause of the popular feeling against England, and on this question the British government showed no disposition to recede from its position. This issue alone was sufficient to justify war.

[35]Mahan, I, 263–266, 409–411, II, 170–176; Galpin, "The American Grain Trade to the Spanish Peninsula, 1810–1814," in *Am. Hist. Rev.*, XXVIII, 24–44.

CHAPTER VII

AN UNSATISFACTORY BUT DURABLE PEACE

An inconclusive war

The United States fought the War of 1812 without allies, though most of the time England was engaged in a gigantic struggle with Napoleon. No effort was made, however, to form an alliance or even to coöperate with him. While the Americans gained a number of single-ship actions and notable victories on Lake Erie and Lake Champlain, they failed utterly in two campaigns to occupy Canada, and when England, after the first overthrow of Napoleon, was able to put forth her full strength the city of Washington was captured, the capitol and other public buildings burned, and American commerce swept from the seas. Jackson's remarkable victory over Wellington's seasoned troops at New Orleans, while gratifying to the national pride, took place two weeks after the Treaty of Ghent had been signed and had, consequently, no effect on the outcome of the war. An inconclusive contest was followed by an unsatisfactory peace, a peace which was destined to last, however, a hundred years and even to the present day. It was also the beginning of a long era of peaceable relations with the powers of Europe generally, uninterrupted, save by the Spanish War, until the Great War that began just as England and the United States were preparing to celebrate the centennial of the Treaty of Ghent.

A peculiar feature of the War of 1812 was that diplomatic negotiations were carried on while the war was in progress. President Madison had signed the declaration of war with

Diplomatic negotiations during war

great reluctance and he hoped that Great Britain would remove the main grievances rather than go to war. Eight days after the declaration Secretary Monroe wrote to Jonathan Russell, who had been *chargé d'affaires* in London since the withdrawal of Pinkney, expressing the desire of the President to terminate the war on conditions honorable to both parties, and laying down the conditions that would be satisfactory:

> If the orders in council are repealed, and no illegal blockades are substituted for them, and orders are given to discontinue the impressment of seamen from our vessels and to restore those already impressed, there is no reason why hostilities should not immediately cease. . . . As an inducement to the British government to discontinue the practice of impressments from our vessels, you may give assurance that a law will be passed (to be reciprocal) to prohibit the employment of British seamen in the public or commercial service of the United States.[1]

If these terms were acceded to, Russell was authorized to sign an armistice.

Great Britain insists on impressment

The American proposal was transmitted to Lord Castlereagh on August 24, 1812. Five days later he replied that Admiral Warren had already sailed for America with a proposition based on the repeal of the orders in council of June 23, and that as this fact was not known when the American note was dispatched he must decline to enter into a discussion of it. He added:

> I cannot, however, refrain on one single point from expressing my surprise, namely, that as a condition preliminary even to a suspension of hostilities, the government of the United States should have thought fit to demand that the British government should desist from its ancient and accustomed practice of impressing British seamen from the merchant ships of a foreign state, simply on the assurance that a law shall hereafter be passed, to prohibit the employment of British seamen in the public or commercial service of that state.[2]

---

[1] *Am. State Papers, Foreign Relations,* III, 585.

[2] *Ibid.,* p. 589.

Peace overtures rejected by Madison

Admiral Warren's communication was forwarded from Halifax September 30, and Monroe replied October 27, stating that, in view of the withdrawal of the orders in council, the President would agree to an armistice on condition that the British claim to impressment be suspended during the period of the armistice. As Admiral Warren had no authority to bind his government on this question the negotiations came to an end.[3] The Federalists criticized the administration for not acceding to the British proposal, but as impressment had been the chief cause of the war the attitude of the President was correct.

Russian offer of mediation

The Russian government, which had recently become the ally of England and was therefore interested in putting an end to a conflict which lessened England's ability to contend against Napoleon, now came forward with an offer of mediation. On September 20, 1812, the chancellor sent for John Quincy Adams, the American minister at St. Petersburg, and inquired whether his government would accept the mediation of the Czar. Adams replied that he had not up to that time received any official notification that war had been declared, but knowing the reluctance with which his government had gone to war, he was sure they would favorably consider such an offer and he knew of no obstacle in the way of accepting it.[4] Communication was slow in those days and the Russian offer did not reach Washington until March 8, 1813, when it was transmitted through the Russian minister to Secretary Monroe. President Madison decided to accept the offer of mediation and appointed without delay John Quincy Adams, Albert Gallatin, and James A. Bayard as envoys extraordinary and ministers plenipotentiary to negotiate a treaty of peace with representatives of Great Britain at St. Petersburg.

Accepted by United States

The appointments were made during the recess of the

[3] *Op. cit.*, III, 595, 596.

[4] *Ibid.*, p. 625.

Senate, and when that body was convened in special session two months later the right of the President to make the appointments was challenged on the ground that he had the constitutional right only to fill vacancies that happened during the recess of the Senate and that in this case he had created offices that did not exist, and hence no vacancies had occurred.[5] The appointments of Adams and Bayard were finally confirmed, but objection was raised to Gallatin on the ground that the position of Secretary of the Treasury and that of envoy extraordinary were "so incompatible that they ought not to be and remain united in the same person," and he failed of confirmation by one vote.[6] As he had already sailed for Russia, the refusal of the Senate to confirm him created an embarrassing situation. Profiting by Madison's experience his successors in the presidency have refrained from submitting the names of peace commissioners to the Senate for confirmation, but have proceeded under the general powers of the executive to negotiate treaties.[7]

Senate hesitates to confirm peace commissioners

President Madison had, however, acted with undue haste, for the British government rejected the Russian offer on the ground that "the differences with the United States were of a nature *involving principles of the internal government of the British nation*, and which it was thought were not susceptible of being committed to the discussion of any mediation."[8] Fortunately Lord Castlereagh, who was Foreign Secretary, while not disposed to surrender any of the rights claimed by Great Britain, was sincerely desirous of restoring friendly relations with the United States. As his latest biographer says:

Great Britain declines Russian mediation

[5]Corwin, *The President's Control of Foreign Relations*, 49–56.

[6]Updyke, *The Diplomacy of the War of 1812*, 147.

[7]The treaties of peace at the close of the Mexican War, the Spanish War, and the World War were negotiated by commissioners whose names were not submitted to the Senate.

[8]*A. S. P., F. R.*, III, 627.

Certainly no other British statesman did more to lay the foundation of the hundred-years peace which few in either country at that time expected and certainly many did not desire.[9]

Embarrassing position of American commissioners

When Bayard and Gallatin joined Adams in St. Petersburg they found themselves in an embarrassing position, but Castlereagh, while rejecting Russian mediation, let it be known in September, 1813, that he was ready to name plenipotentiaries to treat directly with the Americans. The British still regarded disputes with America as domestic questions with which the powers of Europe had no concern. Castlereagh was determined not to let the question of maritime rights which had caused the American war be brought into discussion with European powers. The mediation of Russia was regarded as particularly objectionable, since Russia in the Armed Neutrality had stood for the same general rights for which the Americans contended. The report that Napoleon intended to urge the admission of American delegates to the Prague conferences also disturbed the British.[10] Meanwhile Gallatin, who was of Swiss origin and had a broad view of the European situation, had exchanged several letters with Alexander Baring, a member of the well-known London banking house, which materially aided in opening the way for direct negotiations.[11]

Castlereagh proposes direct negotiations

Finally, in order to prevent the American question from embarrassing in any way his continental diplomacy Castlereagh sent a letter, dated November 4, 1813, directly to Secretary Monroe under a flag of truce. He expressed the willingness of his government to enter into direct negotiations "for the conciliatory adjustment" of differences "upon principles of perfect reciprocity, not inconsistent with the established maxims of public law,

[9]C. K. Webster, *The Foreign Policy of Castlereagh*, 437.

[10]*Cambridge History of British Foreign Policy*, I, 531.

[11]*A Great Peace Maker: The Diary of James Gallatin*, Appendix I.

and with the maritime rights of the British empire."[12] Although the last clause indicated pretty clearly that the British had no intention of abandoning their claims, President Madison promptly accepted the offer January 5, 1814.[13] As London and Gothenburg had both been mentioned as places for the conference the American government chose the latter.

American commission reorganized

In view of the refusal of the Senate to confirm the appointment of Gallatin, the President reconstituted the commission by adding Henry Clay and Jonathan Russell to Adams and Bayard. Learning later that Gallatin was still in Europe, he reappointed him, his position as Secretary of the Treasury having under the law been vacated by six months' absence and the constitutional objection having been thus removed. Gallatin and Bayard had left St. Petersburg in January and proceeded to London. By the time they arrived Napoleon had been overthrown and the British government was occupied with preparations for the general European negotiations at Vienna. With the European war over, preparations were being made to send Wellington's veterans to America, and the prospects for peace were not favorable. The British were in no hurry to begin negotiations, preferring to delay matters until a decided military success in America would give them the advantage. As there was no longer war on the continent, the British government suggested that some more convenient and accessible place than Gothenburg be chosen for the conference. Gallatin and Bayard at once wrote to Clay and Russell at Gothenburg to get their consent and Ghent was agreed upon before Adams arrived from Russia. By July 6 all five of the American commissioners had reached Ghent, but the British commissioners, who had not been appointed until May 27, kept them waiting a full month.

Ghent selected as place of meeting

[12] *A. S. P., F. R.*, III, 621.
[13] *Ibid.*, p. 622.

The American commissioners

The personnel of the American commission was far superior to that of the British. Adams, Gallatin, and Clay were men of marked ability. Adams had been trained in diplomacy from his youth. At the age of eleven he accompanied his father on his mission to Europe; at fourteen he went to St. Petersburg as private secretary to Dana; later he served as minister to Holland and Prussia, and after a term in the Senate, he had been sent to Russia. His recognized ability and honesty of purpose were handicapped by certain unfortunate traits of character. He was obstinate and contentious, lacking in tact, and disliked by his fellow commissioners. Gallatin was a man of keen intellect, possessed of a sense of humor which Adams lacked, was more conciliatory, and had a better understanding of the European point of view. In fact, without his genial faculty for reconciling opposing views the negotiations would have failed. While Clay was without diplomatic experience, his political shrewdness and persuasive powers added strength to the commission and were usually exerted in support of Gallatin. Bayard and Russell were men of ability though not the equals of their colleagues. The one had served with distinction in the Senate, and the other had gained a valuable knowledge of the questions at issue as *chargé d'affaires* first at Paris and then at London.

The British commissioners

The British plenipotentiaries were Lord Gambier, a sailor of moderate ability, Henry Goulburn, Under-secretary of State for War and Colonies, and William Adams, a Doctor of Laws, and an authority on maritime law, but without much experience in public affairs. In fact, the leading statesmen and diplomats of England were needed in connection with the negotiations at Vienna, in comparison with which those at Ghent were considered of secondary importance. The British commissioners were given very little discretion. They had to consult their government before reaching a decision on any important point and became in fact little more than messengers through whom the decisions of the cabinet were conveyed to the Americans.[14]

American instructions

As the American commissioners could not communicate so readily with their government, a greater responsibility rested upon them. Their instructions were, however, for the same reason, full and detailed. The original instructions of April 15, 1813, were devoted largely to the question of impressment. If Great Britain would agree to put a stop to the practice of impressing seamen from American vessels, the war would cease and the United States would give effective guarantees against the employment of British seamen in the service of the United States. An agreement on this subject was a *sine qua non* of peace. Other subjects on which they were to seek agreement were contraband, blockade, and the Rule of 1756. They were also to provide for the mutual restoration of territory occupied during the war.[15] When the commission was reorganized at the time of the acceptance of the British proposal for direct negotiations, these instructions were renewed with changes of minor importance.[16]

British proposals disconcert American commissioners

The negotiations at Ghent began August 8, 1814. Henry Goulburn opened the conference by mentioning the subjects which seemed likely to be brought into discussion and on which the British commissioners had instructions. These were: (1) impressment, (2) the establishment of definite boundaries for the Indians, (3) a revision of the boundary line between the United States and the adjacent British colonies, and (4) the fisheries, with respect to which he announced that the British government would not renew the privileges granted by the treaty of 1783 without an equivalent.[17] The Americans were greatly disconcerted at the scope of these

[14]*Cambridge History of British Foreign Policy,* I, 534.
[15]*A. S. P., F. R.,* III, 695–700.
[16]*Ibid.,* p. 701.
[17]*Ibid.,* p. 707.

proposals and after some discussion as to their meaning they requested to be permitted to defer their answer to the next day. At the second meeting the Americans said that they had no instructions upon the Indian question or the fisheries, but that there were two subjects not yet mentioned on which they had instructions and which they wished to present for discussion: neutral rights, including blockade, and indemnity for captures both before and subsequent to the war. They objected to discussing the question of Indian boundaries or the fisheries, since these questions had not entered into the disputes that led to the war. They expressed a willingness, however, to hear what the British had to say. On the Indian question the British intention was to assign a definite territory to the Indians south of the Great Lakes to serve as a barrier between the possessions of Great Britain and the United States.

Boundaries and Great Lakes

On the question of boundaries the British commissioners presented their proposals a few days later. They were: (1) that the United States should keep no armed forces on the Great Lakes, (2) that the boundary from Lake Superior to the Mississippi should be revised and the right to navigate that river be confirmed to Great Britain, and (3) that part of Maine be ceded to Great Britain so as to provide direct overland communication between New Brunswick and Quebec.[18] The reason given for the proposal to exclude American naval and military forces from the Great Lakes was that the United States had displayed an aggressive spirit in annexing Louisiana and Florida and in attempts to conquer Canada, and that Great Britain as the weaker power in America would be in constant danger if the United States were permitted to hold the Great Lakes. As the Indians of the Northwest had been the allies of Great Britain it was considered a point of honor to include them in the pacification. This was

[18] *Op. cit.*, III, 709.

announced as a *sine qua non.* The British commissioners had represented their territorial demands as "equally necessary." This was going further than the cabinet intended and when Lord Castlereagh passed through Ghent on his way to Vienna he expressed his disapproval of the peremptory tone of their note on this subject.[19]

Rupture imminent

On the cession of territory and the Indian barrier the Americans were inflexible. They were greatly discouraged, however, and saw no prospect of a favorable termination of the negotiations. If a rupture had to come they were determined that it should take place on these issues, for they were convinced that the President could rally the country to his support in defense of independence and the territorial limits established by the treaty of 1783. Castlereagh saw that the British commissioners had gotten themselves in an awkward position and, if a rupture was to take place, he wanted the responsibility to fall on the Americans. He suspected, however, that their note had been framed in order "to rouse their people upon the question of independence," and as there was every prospect of military success, he was not ready to give way.

Americans stand firm

In the note of September 4 the British commissioners still insisted on the Indian barrier and on acquisition of territory.[20] The Americans, not wishing to break off negotiations at this stage, stated in reply that they were willing to stipulate that the Indians would be restored to the position they occupied prior to the war, and that they were willing to discuss the adjustment of any boundary lines that could be shown to be undefined. The note concluded with this emphatic statement:

> The undersigned, in their former note, stated with frankness, and will now repeat, that the two propositions—first, of assigning in the proposed treaty of peace a definite boundary to the Indians living within the limits of the United States, beyond which boundary they [the United States] should stipulate not

[19]*Cambridge History of British Foreign Policy,* I, 537.

[20]*A. S. P., F. R.,* III, 713.

to acquire, by purchase or otherwise, any territory; secondly, of securing the exclusive military possession of the lakes to Great Britain—are both inadmissible; and that they cannot subscribe to, and would deem it useless to refer to their government, any arrangement, even provisional, containing either of those propositions.[21]

The British more conciliatory

This note put it up squarely to the British to decide whether to continue the war for the sole purpose of creating an Indian barrier. The cabinet was unwilling to break off negotiations on this issue. Accordingly in the reply of September 19 the British disclaimed ever having made the exclusive military possession of the Great Lakes a *sine qua non* and restated their demand in regard to the Indian barrier in a form that amounted to no more than a return to the *status quo*.[22] A few days later the news of the capture and burning of Washington arrived, and this no doubt influenced the Americans in agreeing to the stipulation regarding the Indians which was finally incorporated in the treaty as Article IX. It provided that the United States should put an end, immediately after ratification of the treaty, to hostilities with all the tribes of Indians with whom they might be at war, and restore them to all the possessions, rights, and privileges which they had enjoyed in 1811. This apparent recognition of a British right of protection over Indians living within the jurisdiction of the United States was rendered less objectionable by being stated in reciprocal form. Great Britain agreed, on her part, to do the same for the Indian tribes in Canada.

Agreement regarding Indians

British victories raise demands

During the early part of October, 1814, British expectations of military success in America were high. Washington had been captured and expeditions had been launched against Maine, New York, and New Orleans. Macdonough, by his brilliant victory on Lake Champlain, had already turned back the invading army from Canada.

[21]*Op. cit.*, p. 717.

[22]*Ibid.*, p. 718.

but the news had not reached Europe. On the 21st the British commissioners proposed that all territorial questions be settled on the basis of *uti possidetis*, that is that each party should keep what it held at the conclusion of peace.[23] The Americans promptly rejected this proposal as beyond their powers. They were then invited to present a counter-project. While the Americans were preparing their answer the attitude of the British cabinet underwent a complete change. The reasons for this were threefold: (1) things were not going well at Vienna and there was danger of a rupture in Europe; (2) news was received of the defeat of the British on the Lakes; and (3) the Duke of Wellington gave them some sound advice on the American situation. He had been requested by the government to take the command in America. On November 9, he wrote to Lord Liverpool from Paris:

Wellington's advice to the cabinet

> I have already told you and Lord Bathurst that I feel no objection to going to America, though I don't promise myself much success there. . . . That which appears to me to be wanting in America is not a General, or General officers and troops, but a naval superiority on the Lakes. . . . In regard to your present negotiation, I confess that I think you have no right from the state of the war to demand any concession of territory from America. . . . Why stipulate for the *uti possidetis?* You can get no territory; indeed the state of your military operations, however creditable, does not entitle you to demand any; and you only afford the Americans a popular and creditable ground which, I believe, their government are looking for, not to break off the negotiations, but to avoid to make peace. If you had territory, as I hope you soon will have New Orleans, I should prefer to insist upon the cession of that province as a separate article than upon the *uti possidetis* as a principle of negotiation.[24]

This letter cleared the atmosphere and prepared the way for peace. Meanwhile President Madison had sent to Congress the report of the earlier negotiations setting

[23]*Op. cit.*, p. 724.

[24]Lodge, *One Hundred Years of Peace*, 27.

Madison makes public British demands

forth the exorbitant demands of the British. The publication of this report aroused the fighting spirit of the nation and even the Federalists rallied to the support of the administration in rejecting the idea of a cession of territory. The British cabinet was naturally displeased at what they considered an unheard-of breach of diplomatic procedure in making public negotiations still in progress, but they soon realized that President Madison had scored an advantage. Their demand for territory was severely criticized in Parliament.

Gallatin drafts American proposals

The American project for a treaty, prepared in the main by Gallatin, was presented November 10. In place of *uti possidetis* it proposed the *status quo;* it proposed articles on impressment and blockade; indemnity for acts contrary to international law, including the destruction of unfortified places; it proposed commissions to determine boundaries; and on the fisheries question it held to the rights stipulated by the treaty of 1783.[25]

Treaty of Ghent signed

The British commissioners were disposed to reject most of these proposals, but the cabinet instructed them to waive the *uti possidetis* and the control of the Lakes, and to try to arrive at an agreement. As the American commissioners had been authorized by Monroe's letter of June 25 to sign a peace, if necessary, without an article on impressment, there remained no serious obstacles. On December 24, 1814, the negotiations were concluded by the signing of the Treaty of Peace and Amity. There were no commercial stipulations.[26]

Points in dispute left unsettled

The treaty mentioned scarcely any of the subjects that had caused the war and that had been so hotly contested at Ghent. The harmless article relating to the Indians was all that was left of the British demands, while the Americans had abandoned their claim for damages and failed to secure recognition of their fishing privileges which the

[25] *A. S. P., F. R.*, III, 735.

[26] (Malloy) *Treaties and Conventions of the United States*, I, 612.

British declared had been forfeited. The British claimed that they had surrendered none of their maritime rights, while the Americans held that, since the establishment of peace in Europe, it was no longer necessary to fight against impressment and other objectionable practices which were resorted to only in time of war.[27] Most of the treaty related to the organization of boundary commissions. In Article X the contracting parties agreed to use their best endeavors to promote the abolition of the slave trade. The treaty was favorably received in America. A copy reached New York February 11, 1815, and the news spread quickly through the country concurrently with the accounts of Jackson's great victory over the British at New Orleans on January 8. The people were quite satisfied to let the war close with the battle of New Orleans. The treaty was not so well received in England, but ratifications had scarcely been exchanged when Napoleon's return from Elba absorbed public attention. Such were the unsatisfactory beginnings of a peace that was to last beyond the expectations or hopes of the most optimistic advocates of Anglo-American friendship.

Ratification

Subsequent history of neutral rights

The questions left unsettled by the Treaty of Ghent fall into two classes: (1) those relating to international law, such as impressment, blockade, and neutral rights, and (2) those arising out of the relations between the United States and the British possessions in America, such as boundaries, the fisheries, and the West India trade. As there was not another naval war for forty years, no occasion arose during the period for the revival of the dispute over neutral rights, and when the Crimean war came conditions had changed. At the conclusion of that war the powers of Europe embodied in the Declaration of Paris the rules that blockades to be binding must be effective, that free ships make free goods, and that neutral goods are not liable to capture under the enemy flag, contraband, of course, excepted.

[27] *Cambridge History of British Foreign Policy*, I, 541.

Impressment

The impressment controversy was frequently revived in connection with the British proposals to permit the right of search in time of peace for the purpose of suppressing the slave trade. The United States persistently refused to enter into such an agreement unless Great Britain would abandon the claim to impressment. The British protest over the removal of Mason and Slidell from a British vessel in 1861 and the successful demand for their surrender have been regarded by some writers as a virtual repudiation by Great Britain of the right of impressment.

Disarmament on the Great Lakes

Of the second class of questions one of the most dangerous and the first to be settled was that of armaments on the Great Lakes. The British commissioners at Ghent, after the failure to exclude Americans from the Lakes, had proposed the limitation of armaments, but Adams had objected on the ground that his government had given no instructions on this subject. As the Lakes had been one of the main theaters of the war and had always been of such great strategic importance, it seemed likely that both parties would feel compelled to maintain large naval forces on them. Neither country was inclined to enter upon such heavy expenditures, however, and when Adams, now minister to Great Britain, was authorized by his government to make a proposal similar to the one he had refused to entertain at Ghent, Castlereagh expressed his willingness to enter into such an agreement. The negotiations were then taken up at Washington and resulted in the Rush-Bagot agreement of 1817. By an exchange of notes between the British minister and the Secretary of State it was agreed that naval forces on the Great Lakes should be limited to a few lighter vessels of specified tonnage—a force no more than sufficient for police and customs service.[28] The notes were of such importance that the President

Rush-Bagot agreement of 1817

---

[28](Malloy) *Treaties and Conventions of the United States,* I, 628; Callahan, *The Neutrality of the American Lakes and Anglo-American Relations* (J. H. U. *Studies in Historical and Political Science,* Series XVI, Nos. 1–4).

submitted them to the Senate and the agreement was duly ratified and proclaimed. It may be questioned whether any more enlightened or far-sighted step in the direction of peace was ever taken by two countries similarly situated. It has not merely saved both countries the enormous cost of maintaining navies on these inland waters, but it has prevented hostile demonstrations in times of crisis.

Boundary commissions fail to agree

Of the several boundary commissions created under the Treaty of Ghent the one under Article V, on the boundary from the source of the St. Croix River to the St. Lawrence, was unable to come to an agreement, and the dispute was referred to the King of the Netherlands. His award was not accepted by the United States on the ground that he had exceeded his powers, and the boundary between Maine and New Brunswick remained a dangerous source of trouble until the Webster-Ashburton treaty. The commissioners on the boundary from Lake Huron to the Lake of the Woods likewise failed to agree and this boundary also remained undetermined until the Webster-Ashburton treaty.

Convention of 1818

The commercial convention of 1815, signed on the part of the United States by Adams, Clay, and Gallatin six months after the Treaty of Ghent, merely renewed commercial relations without impairing in any way the British colonial system. Great Britain refused to renew the fishing privileges and refused to admit American vessels to the West Indies. In view of the approaching expiration of this convention the negotiation of a new agreement was undertaken in 1818 and resulted in the signing on October 20 of the very important Convention Respecting Fisheries, Boundary and the Restoration of Slaves.[29] Article I limited the "liberty" of Americans to engage in the inshore fisheries to certain specified parts of the coasts of Newfoundland, Magdalen Islands, and Labrador, but granted it *forever*. It also granted them *forever* the right to dry and

Fisheries

[29] *A. S. P., F. R.*, IV, 348–407.

cure fish in the unsettled bays, harbors, and creeks of Newfoundland and Labrador. This latter provision was indefinite, or became so with the settlement of these coasts, and was the subject of many a long controversy in after years. By this convention the inshore privileges of Americans were more restricted than they were under the treaty of 1783, but they were made perpetual. All subsequent agreements, therefore, rested on this basal treaty.

Northwestern boundary

The convention of 1818 also determined the northwestern boundary from the Lake of the Woods to the Rocky Mountains by running it along the forty-ninth parallel. The dispute over this boundary had its origin in the lack of geographical knowledge of the region on the part of the negotiators of the treaty of 1783, who directed that from the northwesternmost point of the Lake of the Woods the line should follow "a due west course to the River Mississippi." Such a line would, of course, run far north of the course of the Mississippi. After the purchase of Louisiana Secretary Madison attempted a settlement of the question by the adoption of the forty-ninth parallel. Both he and President Jefferson were under the erroneous impression that this line had been adopted by the British and French commissioners appointed under the tenth article of the Treaty of Utrecht, who undertook to establish a boundary line between the Hudson's Bay Company and Louisiana.

Earlier efforts to establish forty-ninth parallel as boundary

It has been pointed out that several books and maps published about the middle of the eighteenth century erroneously stated that the forty-ninth parallel had been agreed upon by the commissioners.[30] The authors of the books and maps referred to probably based their statements on indirect information of the fact that the British commissioners of 1719 had been instructed to agree upon a line from the Lake of the Woods to the forty-ninth parallel and

---

[30] Reeves, *American Diplomacy Under Tyler and Polk,* 195–196.

westward along that parallel. But this line was to be only for the regulation of trade. On this point the instructions were specific:

> But you are to take especial Care in wording such Articles as shall be agreed on with the Commissary or Commissarys of His Most Christian Majesty upon this head, that the said Boundarys be understood to regard the Trade of the Hudson's-Bay Company only, That His Majesty does not thereby recede from His Right to any Lands in America, not comprized within the said Boundarys; And that no pretension be thereby given to the French to claim any Tracts of Lands in America, Southward or South west of the said Boundarys.

No agreement was reached and the instructions to the British commissioners were apparently not published until 1925.[31]

British refuse to extend line beyond Rockies

When Gallatin and Rush took up the question, they proposed that the line should follow the forty-ninth parallel to the Pacific. The British government proposed on its part that it should follow this line "as far as the territories extend." In view of the uncertainty as to the northern limits of Louisiana, this would have left Great Britain free to advance a claim to territory south of the forty-ninth parallel at any point west of the Lake of the Woods. Both sides finally agreed by way of compromise that the line should be run as far west as the Rockies, leaving the Oregon question open.

Joint occupation of Oregon

West of the Rockies the convention of 1818 provided that any country claimed by either party on the northwest coast of America with its harbors, bays, rivers, and creeks, was to be free and open for the term of ten years to the vessels, citizens, and subjects of the two powers, without prejudice to the claims of either. This was the beginning

[31] *British Diplomatic Instructions*, 1689–1789, vol. II—France. Edited for the Royal Historical Society by L. G. Wickham Legg (Camden Society, vol. XXV), 196–205.

of the so-called joint occupation of Oregon which was continued until 1846. The Oregon country was soon clearly defined. By the Florida treaty of 1819 Spain renounced in favor of the United States all claim to territory on the western coast of America north of the forty-second parallel. The only other claimant was Russia, and England and the United States united in opposing her pretensions. The result was that Russia signed a treaty with the United States in 1824 and another with England in 1825, renouncing all claim to territory south of the parallel fifty-four degrees forty minutes. The Oregon country was thus left to the United States and England to be divided amicably or to be contended for by force.

Trade with the British West Indies

In the negotiation of the commercial convention of 1815 Great Britain showed no disposition to relax in the slightest her colonial system and consequently no concessions were made in the matter of the West India trade. It will be recalled that under that system only an enumerated list of American products could be carried to the British West Indies and only in British bottoms. American vessels were excluded. The United States made repeated efforts to have its ships admitted to this trade, but the only concession ever made—that in Article XII of the Jay treaty—had been accompanied by restrictions which caused it to be indignantly rejected. During the period of the Confederation Congress had no power to retaliate and the measures adopted by individual states were ineffective. Soon after the organization of the new government under the Constitution the European wars began and British governors in the West Indies were authorized to throw the trade open to American vessels by proclamation whenever conditions in the islands rendered it necessary. Thus from 1793 to 1812, while the trade was theoretically closed to them, American vessels were as a matter of fact almost continually admitted by proclamation. The temporary suspension during the brief peace following the

Treaty of Amiens caused great hardship and dissatisfaction.[32]

After the War of 1812 the exclusion of American vessels from the West Indies was rigidly enforced and the controversy entered upon a new stage. The commercial convention of 1815, by establishing trade reciprocity between the British Isles and the United States, worked an unforeseen hardship on the American carrying trade. British vessels could carry their cargoes to the United States, load up with provisions, lumber, and other supplies for the West Indies, and there take on sugar and molasses for the homeward voyage. This triangular trade enabled them to make lower freight rates than American vessels could offer in the direct trade from England to the United States. The British vessels could reduce rates on the outward voyage to any point that was necessary to capture the trade, because on the voyage from the United States to the West Indies and from the West Indies home they had no competition and could make a large profit.

Rigid exclusion of American vessels

A demand for countervailing legislation, to employ the term then used, was soon made by the shipping interests and there was much discussion in Congress and in the press as to what form it should take. During the summer of 1816, John Quincy Adams tried to persuade Castlereagh to relax the system, but without success. He therefore advised his government to resort to countervailing legislation. Congress then passed the Navigation Act of March 1, 1817, restricting the importation of West India products to American vessels and to vessels owned by merchants of those colonies. Out of regard for the agricultural interests it did not forbid the export of American goods to those islands in British vessels.[33] Castlereagh decided to make certain minor concessions, but they were so restricted that

Countervailing legislation

[32] F. L. Binns, *The American Struggle for the British West India Carryng Trade*, Chap. I.

[33] *Ibid.*, p. 46.

President Monroe rejected them and in his annual message of December, 1817, laid the matter again before Congress. The Navigation Act of 1818, passed a few weeks later, provided that after September 30 of that year the ports of the United States should be closed to British vessels sailing to or from colonial ports from which American vessels were excluded.

Act of 1818

In the negotiation of the commercial convention of 1818 the American representatives proposed to adjust the dispute on the general basis of reciprocity, but no agreement could be reached and that convention was signed without any clause relating to the West Indies. In May, 1820, Congress took drastic action and passed a law which established non-intercourse in British vessels with all the British colonies in America, including Canada, Nova Scotia, Newfoundland, the Bermudas, and the Bahamas, as well as the West Indies.[34] American vessels now carried their products to the Swedish, Danish, and Dutch islands, from which they were carried in British ships to the British West Indies. The double freights made the goods expensive, however, and the islanders again raised a cry for relief. Meanwhile the effect on Maryland, Virginia, the Carolinas, and Georgia, the states from which most of the exports to the West Indies came, was highly injurious and led to a movement for repeal or modification of the restrictions. Shortly before adjournment in March, 1822, Congress passed a bill authorizing the President to open the ports of the United States to British vessels plying between the United States and West Indian ports so soon as he should be satisfied that those ports had been opened to the vessels of the United States.

Act of 1820

In July, 1822, Parliament passed an act admitting enumerated articles to the West Indies in the vessels of the country where they were produced, but excluding fish and other salted products in the interest of the British North

[34] *Op. cit.*, p. 70.

American provinces. At the same time the King was authorized to deny these privileges to any country which failed to grant reciprocal privileges to British shipping. President Monroe accordingly issued a proclamation, August 24, 1822, opening American ports to British vessels, but he did not remove the discriminating duties to which British ships and cargoes were subject. The British minister at once called attention to this and reminded Adams, the Secretary of State, that the King had the power to withdraw the privileges from countries which did not grant full reciprocity. Adams replied that the President had no authority to remove the duties complained of, and at the same time he called attention to certain features of the British act, particularly the exclusion of fish and salted provisions, which gave the British marked advantages. When Congress met the whole situation was considered, including the correspondence between Adams and Canning, and the act of March 1, 1823, was passed. This act, drafted by Adams, was exceedingly complicated and its meaning not altogether clear. While providing for the removal of the discriminating duties on British vessels it raised an entirely new issue in demanding that American vessels be admitted to British colonial ports on the same terms as vessels importing goods "from elsewhere." Adams interpreted this to include vessels and goods from Canada, Nova Scotia, and other parts of the British Empire. As a member of Parliament remarked, this was as unreasonable as for the British to demand that sugar and rum from the West Indies be admitted to New York on the same terms as sugar and rum from Louisiana. The insistence of Adams on his interpretation of the act prevented Canning and Rush from reaching an agreement in the negotiations of 1824.[35]

Parliament proposes reciprocity

Act of Congress raises a new issue

In 1825, Parliament threw open colonial ports to ships of

[35]The documents covering negotiations from 1822 to 1827 are in *A. S. P., F. R.*, V, 225; and VI, 213–266, 963–984.

Adams fails to meet British terms

foreign countries generally on condition of reciprocity, but with a reduction of duties on goods imported through the United Kingdom. There were now two courses open to the American government, either to renew negotiations or to adopt legislation meeting the conditions of the British act. Adams, who had become President, delayed doing anything for a year. He then sent Gallatin to England with instructions to negotiate an agreement, waiving the demand that American commerce with the West Indies be placed on the same footing with that of the British North American provinces. Before Gallatin reached England, however, the order in council of July 27, 1826, had closed all British colonial ports, except the East Indies and the North American provinces, to American vessels. In March, 1827, President Adams issued a proclamation under authority of the act of 1823, closing American ports to British vessels coming from any of the British colonies or provinces in America. Thus all direct intercourse was forbidden, but American products continued to find their way to the British West Indies through neighboring islands and Nova Scotia, and occasionally directly by proclamations of the local governors.[36] Adams was severely criticized for failure to meet the conditions of the British act of 1825 and for trying when it was too late to obtain concessions which had been offered before that act was passed. The question became one of the chief political issues of the closing years of his administration and undoubtedly contributed to his defeat in 1828.[37]

Gallatin's unsuccessful mission to England

Jackson undertakes settlement of controversy

When Jackson became president he sent Louis McLane as minister to England with instructions to open negotiations on substantially the same terms that Gallatin had proposed. In case the British government displayed a reluctance to reopen negotiations on the ground that the United States had refused to accept the terms proposed in

[36]Binns, 154.

[37]*Ibid.*, pp. 163–184.

the parliamentary act of 1825, he was told to inform them that the views of the previous administration had been submitted to the people of the United States and that the proposals he was to present were the result of "the judgment expressed by the only earthly tribunal to which the late administration was amenable for its acts." These instructions were probably suggested by Jackson himself, but they were signed by Van Buren and were made the principal ground for the refusal of the Senate later to confirm his appointment as minister to England. When McLane took the question up with Lord Aberdeen the latter appeared reluctant to announce a change in British policy without some previous action by the United States. Negotiations were delayed by the opposition of the British North American provinces, which had greatly profited by the exclusion of American vessels from the colonial trade. Finally an understanding was reached and on the recommendation of the President Congress passed an act authorizing him, whenever he should receive satisfactory evidence that the British government would open its ports in the West Indies to American vessels, to admit on the same terms to the United States British vessels coming from those ports. On October 5, 1830, the President issued his proclamation, declaring the acts of 1818, 1820, and 1823 repealed and admitting British vessels from colonial ports. On November 5, a British order in council revoked the order of 1826 and opened British colonial ports to American vessels.

British colonial ports opened to American vessels

Jackson's course was severely criticized by his opponents at the time and it has been criticized by certain historians of later times. The arrangement represented a compromise on both sides, and it did not prove as advantageous to American shipping as had been hoped, for Parliament almost immediately passed an act imposing discriminatory duties on goods imported into the West Indies in favor of the products of the North American dominions. But as

Criticism of Jackson's course

the United States was placed on the same footing as other nations, there were no just grounds of complaint. No duties were placed on American products imported into the British provinces of North America. This regulation encouraged the indirect trade through these provinces to the West Indies. It helped American agriculture and producers generally, but it was injurious to the shipping interests, and this has been the main ground for the criticism of Jackson. In general, the course of the President was approved by the people, and the settlement of a controversy that had lasted for nearly fifty years was regarded as a great diplomatic triumph.[38]

[38]The negotiations under Jackson are given in *British and Foreign State Papers,* XVIII, 1181–1212. See also Binns, 163–188.

CHAPTER VIII

THE DECLARATION OF PRESIDENT MONROE

Napoleon's invasion of Spain

IT WAS inevitable that the American Revolution should sow the seeds of discontent in Spain's American colonies. The effect was not immediate, as is shown by the failure of Miranda's heroic efforts to revolutionize Venezuela and thus make his native land the starting point in the emancipation of the continent. Napoleon's invasion of Spain in 1808 set in motion a train of events which finally resulted in South American independence. When Napoleon overthrew the Spanish monarchy and placed his brother Joseph on the throne, the Spanish people rose en masse, and with the assistance of the British under Wellington carried on a long struggle for independence. During this period they set up a central junta or provisional government, which acted in the name of their sovereign Ferdinand VII, a prisoner in France.

South American wars of liberation

The South American provinces followed the example of the mother country, and they too set up juntas which acted in the name of Ferdinand VII, but actually these juntas were revolutionary bodies, for they largely abolished the rigid colonial system that Spain had imposed upon them and opened up commerce with England and the United States. When Ferdinand was restored to his throne after the first overthrow of Napoleon, he might, by a wisdom hardly to be expected of a Bourbon, have retained the allegiance of his American subjects, but he did not realize the changes that had taken place and insisted on restoring the old system. The colonies then revolted, separately and spasmodically, and thus began the wars of liberation, led by Bolívar in the north and San Martín in the south. By 1822 all of the provinces had established their *de facto* independence, and the Spanish armies had been driven out or captured, except in a few garrisoned towns which held out a little longer.

Sympathy of United States

The struggle of the South American peoples for independence was viewed from the first with feelings of profound satisfaction and sympathy in the United States. From the commencement of the revolution South American vessels were admitted into the ports of the United States under whatever flag they bore. It does not appear that any formal declaration according belligerent rights to the said provinces was ever made, though a resolution to that effect was introduced into the House by committee as early as December 10, 1811.[1] Such formal action was apparently not deemed necessary and, as there was no Spanish minister resident in the United States at that time to protest, our ports were probably thrown open, as a matter of course.[2] The fact that they were accorded full belligerent rights from the first was afterward stated by President Monroe in his annual messages of 1817 and 1818 and in his special message of March 8, 1822.[3]

Commissioners sent to South America

At an early date of the revolution commissioners arrived in Washington seeking recognition of independence, and agents were forthwith dispatched to South America to obtain information in regard to the state of the revolutionary governments and to watch the movements of England and other European powers. Joel R. Poinsett was sent to Buenos Aires in 1811, and the following year Alexander Scott was sent to Venezuela.[4] In 1817, Cæsar A. Rodney, Theodorick Bland, and John Graham were dispatched as

[1]*A. S. P., F. R.*, III, 538.

[2]Moore, *Dig. of Int. Law*, I, 177.

[3]Richardson, *Messages and Papers of the Presidents*, II, 13, 58, 116.

[4]Lyman, *Diplomacy of the United States*, II, 432.

special commissioners to South America. They proceeded to Buenos Aires, where they arrived in February, 1818, and remained until the last of April. Rodney and Graham then returned to the United States while Bland proceeded across the continent to Chile. Their reports were transmitted to Congress November 17, 1818.[5] In 1820, Messrs. J. B. Prevost and John M. Forbes were sent as commercial agents to Chile and Buenos Aires. Reports from them on the state of the revolutions were transmitted to Congress, March 8 and April 26, 1822.[6]

Clay urges recognition

In the meantime a strong sentiment in favor of the recognition of South American independence had arisen in the United States. The struggling colonies found a ready champion in Henry Clay, who, for a period of ten years, labored almost incessantly in their behalf, pleading for their recognition first with his own countrymen and then, as Secretary of State under the Adams administration, with the governments of Europe. His name became a household word in South America and his speeches were translated and read before the patriot armies.

Tries to force the hand of the administration

In spite of the fact that our own political interests were so closely identified with the struggling republics, the President realized the necessity of following a neutral course, and in view of the aid the colonies were receiving from citizens of the United States, called upon Congress for the enactment of a more stringent neutrality law. Clay delivered a vigorous speech in opposition to this measure in January, 1817. His greatest effort in behalf of South America, however, was his speech of March 25, 1818, on the general appropriation bill. He moved an amendment appropriating $18,000 for the outfit and year's salary of a minister to the United Provinces of the Plate.

[5] *A. S. P., F. R.*, IV, 217–270.

[6] *Ibid.*, pp. 818–851. The Carnegie Endowment for International Peace has issued three volumes, edited by Dr. William R. Manning, under the title *Diplomatic Correspondence of the United States Concerning the Independence of the Latin-American Nations* (1925).

Without waiting to hear the report of the three commissioners who had been sent to inquire into the state of the revolutionary governments, he urged that a minister be regularly accredited to Buenos Aires at once. Painting with even more than his usual fire and enthusiasm the beauties and resources of the Southern continent, he said:

> Within this vast region, we behold the most sublime and interesting objects of creation; the loftiest mountains, the most majestic rivers in the world; the richest mines of the precious metals; and the choicest productions of the earth. We behold there a spectacle still more interesting and sublime—the glorious spectacle of eighteen millions of people struggling to burst their chains and be free.[7]

He went on to say that in the establishment of the independence of the South American states the United States had the deepest interest. He had no hesitation in asserting his firm belief that there was no question in the foreign policy of this country, which had ever arisen, or which he could conceive as ever occurring, in the decision of which we had so much at stake. This interest concerned our politics, our commerce, our navigation. There could be no doubt that Spanish America, once independent, whatever might be the form of the governments established in its several parts, those governments would be animated by an American feeling and guided by an American policy. They would obey the laws of the system of the New World, of which they would compose a part, in contradistinction to that of Europe.[8] The House turned a deaf ear to his brilliant rhetoric. The motion was defeated by a vote of 115 to 45, but Clay did not abandon the cause of South America.

His motion defeated

President Monroe seemed strongly inclined toward recognition, but in this he was opposed by Adams and Calhoun, who were unwilling to act in the matter without

[7]Benton's Abridgment, VI, 139.

[8]*Ibid.*, p. 142.

some understanding with England, and if possible with France. Our relations with Spain in regard to the Indian troubles in Florida were in a very strained condition and any action taken at that time in recognition of South America would have involved us in war with Spain and almost inevitably with other European powers. The President, therefore, as a matter of expediency postponed the action which his sympathy prompted, and in his annual message of November 16, 1818, expressed his satisfaction at the course the government had hitherto pursued and his intention of adhering to it for the time being.[9] Under the President's direction, however, efforts were made to secure the coöperation of Great Britain and France in promoting the independence of South America.[10]

Monroe's reasons for delay

In 1819 an amicable adjustment of our differences with Spain seemed to have been reached by the negotiation of a treaty providing for the cession of the Floridas to the United States and the settlement of long-standing claims of American citizens against Spain. An unforeseen difficulty arose, however, which proved embarrassing to the administration. The Spanish monarch very shrewdly delayed ratifying the treaty for two years and thus practically tied the hands of the administration during that time as far as the South American question was concerned.

The Florida treaty

In spite of the awkward position in which the administration found itself, Clay, who was opposed to the treaty on account of its unwarranted surrender of our claims to Texas, continued to plead the cause of South America. Early in the year 1821, a declaration of interest in the South American struggle, introduced by him, was carried by an overwhelming majority, but the administration held back another year until the *de facto* independence of the colonies no longer admitted of reasonable doubt. Mean-

Recognition of the Spanish-American republics

[9]Richardson, *Messages and Papers of the Presidents*, II, 44.

[10]"Adams's *Diary*," September, 1817, to December, 1818; *Letters and Despatches of Castlereagh*, XI, 404, 458.

while the Florida treaty had been ratified. On March 8, 1822, President Monroe, in a special message to Congress, expressed the opinion that the time had come for recognition and asked for the appropriations necessary for carrying it into effect. The President's recommendation was received with approval, and in due course the sum of $100,000 was appropriated for "such missions to the independent nations on the American continent as the President of the United States may deem proper." In accordance with this act Mr. R. C. Anderson of Kentucky was appointed minister to Colombia, Mr. C. A. Rodney of New Jersey to the Argentine Republic, and Mr. H. Allen of Vermont to Chile, in 1824, and Mr. Joel R. Poinsett of South Carolina to Mexico in 1826.

British policy

While the United States government was concerning itself with the political interests of the Spanish provinces, Great Britain was quietly reaping all the commercial advantages to be derived from the situation and was apparently well satisfied to let things follow the drift they had taken. By the destruction of the combined fleets of France and Spain at Trafalgar, in 1805, Nelson had won for Great Britain undisputed control of the Atlantic and laid open the route to South America. Ever since the *assiento* of 1713 had placed the slave trade in her hands, Great Britain had realized the possibilities of South American commerce, and the intercourse, which had been kept up with that continent by smugglers after the termination of the slave monopoly, now that the danger was removed, became more regular and profitable. During the changes of ministry that followed the death of Pitt, the policy of England in regard to South America was weak and vacillating. With Napoleon's invasion of Spain and the national uprising it occasioned, British policy became once more intelligible. It was wisely deemed of more importance to spare the colonies and to win Spain over to the European alliance against Napoleon, than to take her colonies at the cost of driving her permanently into the arms of France. Meanwhile British commerce with the South American states was steadily growing and that too with the connivance of Spain.

Spain interferes with British commerce

At the close of the Napoleonic wars, Spain, fearing that England, through her desire to keep this trade, would secretly furnish aid to the colonies in their struggle for independence, proposed to the British government to bind itself to a strict neutrality. This England agreed to, and when the treaty was signed, there was, according to Canning, "a distinct understanding with Spain that our commercial intercourse with the colonies was not to be deemed a breach of its stipulations."[11] Notwithstanding this tacit compact, British commerce suffered greatly at the hands of Spanish privateers and even Spanish war vessels. Numbers of British merchantmen were captured by Spanish ships, carried into the few ports left to Spain on the Main, and condemned as prizes for trading with the insurgent colonies. Thus at the time of the acknowledgment of South American independence by the United States, a long list of grievances had accumulated in the hands of the British ambassador at Madrid, and in spite of urgent and repeated remonstrances, remained unredressed.

Canning proposes local reprisals

Canning was deterred from making final demands upon the government of Madrid by the consideration that he did not wish to hamper the constitutional government of Spain, which had come into being by the revolution of March, 1820, and against which the other powers of Europe were preparing to act. The condition of affairs on the Spanish Main was, however, critical and demanded instant redress. He decided, therefore, to take matters into his own hands without harassing the government of Spain, and to dispatch a squadron to the West Indies to make reprisals. In a memorandum to the cabinet on this subject, November 15, 1822, in which he outlined his pol-

[11] Stapleton, *Political Life of Canning*, II, 10.

icy, he commended the course of the United States in recognizing the *de facto* independence of the colonies, claiming a right to trade with them and avenging the attempted interruption of that right by making reprisals, as a more straightforward and intelligible course than that of Great Britain, forbearing for the sake of Spain to recognize the colonies, trading with them in faith of the connivance of Spain and suffering depredations without taking redress. It was not necessary, he thought, to declare war against Spain, for "she has perhaps as little direct and available power over the colonies which she nominally retains as she has over those which have thrown off her yoke. Let us apply, therefore, a local remedy to a local grievance, and make the ships and harbors of Cuba, Porto Rico, and Porto Cabello answerable for the injuries which have been inflicted by those ships, and the perpetrators of which have found shelter in those harbors." In conclusion, he declared that the tacit compact, which subsisted for years, by which Spain was to forbear from interrupting British trade with the South American colonies having been renounced by Spain, and the old colonial system having been revived in as full vigor as if she had still a practical hold over her colonies and a navy to enforce her pretensions, "no man will say that under such circumstances our recognition of those states can be indefinitely postponed."[12]

Foresees ultimate recognition

Spain's difficulties

While Great Britain was thus considering the expediency of following the example of the United States in the recognition of Spain's revolted colonies, the powers of central Europe had taken upon them the task of solving the difficulties of that unfortunate country both at home and in America. The restored rule of the Bourbons in Spain had been far from satisfactory to the great mass of the people. In March, 1820, the army which Ferdinand had assembled at Cadiz to be sent against the rebellious colonies, suddenly turned against the government, re-

[12]Stapleton, *Official Correspondence of Canning,* I, 48ff.

fused to embark, and demanded the restoration of the constitution of 1812. The action of the army was everywhere approved and sustained by the mass of the people, and the King was forced to proclaim the constitution and to swear to uphold it. The March revolution in Spain was followed in July by a constitutional movement in Naples, and in August of the same year by a similar movement in Portugal; while the next year saw the outbreak of the Greek struggle for independence. Thus in all three of the peninsulas of southern Europe the people were struggling for the right of self-government. The movement in Greece was, it is true, of an altogether different character from the others, but it was a revolt against constituted authority and therefore incurred the ill-will of the so-called legitimists. The powers of Europe at once took alarm at the rapid spread of revolutionary ideas and proceeded to adopt measures for the suppression of the movements to which these ideas gave rise. The principle of joint intervention on the part of allied governments in the internal affairs of European states had been developed in the years immediately following the overthrow of Napoleon and was the outcome of the wholly anomalous condition in which he had left the politics of Europe. In the hands of Prince Metternich, the genius of reaction against French revolutionary ideas, this principle had become the most powerful weapon of absolutism and now threatened the subversion of popular institutions throughout Europe.

Revolutionary movements in southern Europe

The rapid development of this doctrine of intervention in the seven years immediately following the second fall of Napoleon not only seriously menaced the liberties of Europe, but also threatened to control the destiny of the New World. At the Congress of Vienna Austria, France, Great Britain, Prussia, and Russia had formed a close union and had signed the treaty upon which the peace of Europe rested for the next half century. The agreement made at Vienna was reaffirmed with some minor changes,

The doctrine of intervention

after the second overthrow of Napoleon, at Paris, November 20, 1815. France was now practically excluded from the alliance. This treaty undertook especially to guard against any further disturbance of the peace of Europe by Napoleon or France. One of the most significant features of the treaty, or what was to prove so, was the agreement definitely laid down in the sixth article, providing for meetings of the powers at fixed periods.

Meeting of the allied powers at Aix-la-Chapelle

The first conference held in accordance with this understanding was that at Aix-la-Chapelle in October, 1818. France was readmitted as a member of the Alliance and her territory evacuated by the allied armies. The quintuple alliance thus formed declared that it had no other object than the maintenance of peace; that the repose of the world was its motive and its end. The language of the declaration had been in a large measure neutralized to suit the views of the British government. Lord Liverpool had said to Castlereagh before the meeting of the conference: "The Russian must be made to feel that we have a parliament and a public, to which we are responsible, and that we cannot permit ourselves to be drawn into views of policy which are wholly incompatible with the spirit of our government." The members of the British cabinet, except Canning, did not object seriously to the system of congresses at fixed intervals, but to the declarations publicly set forth by them. Canning, on the other hand, objected to the declarations and to the conferences themselves, "meetings for the government of the world," as he somewhat contemptuously termed them.

It had been generally supposed that the question of the Spanish colonies would come up for discussion at Aix-la-Chapelle. Castlereagh assured the United States, through Bagot, the British minister at Washington, that while England would act with the allied powers at Aix-la-Chapelle in mediation between Spain and her colonies, her mediation would be limited entirely to the employment of her influence and good offices and that she would not take any measures that might assume a character of force.[13]

Meetings at Troppau and Laybach

The revolutions that took place in Spain, Naples, and Portugal in 1820 presented an occasion for another meeting of the allies. In November the representatives of Austria, Russia, and Prussia met in conference at Troppau, and issued a circular setting forth what they had already done for Europe in overthrowing the military tyranny of Napoleon and expressing the determination "to put a curb on a force no less tyrannical and no less detestable, that of revolt and crime." The conference then adjourned to Laybach, where they could, with greater dispatch, order the movements they had decided to take against the revolutionists of Naples. Austria, being more intimately concerned with the political condition of the Italian peninsula than either of the other two powers, was intrusted with the task of suppressing the Neapolitan revolution. The Austrian army entered Naples March 23, 1821, overthrew the constitutional government that had been inaugurated, and restored Ferdinand II to absolute power. The revolution which had broken out in Piedmont was also suppressed by a detachment of the Austrian army.

England dissents

England held aloof from all participation in the proceedings at Troppau and Laybach—though Sir Charles Stuart was present to watch the proceedings. In a circular dispatch of January 21, 1821, the British government expressed its dissent from the principles set forth in the Troppau circular.

Congress of Verona

The next meeting of the allied powers was arranged for October, 1822, at Verona. Here the affairs of Greece, Italy, and, in particular, Spain came up for consideration. At this congress all five powers of the alliance were represented. France was uneasy about the condition of Spain, and England had to send a delegate out of self-

[13]Bagot to Castlereagh, October, 31, 1818. Mem. of a conversation with Adams. *Letters and Despatches of Castlereagh*, Vol. XII, p. 66.

defense, as her interests were largely involved. Castlereagh was preparing to depart for the congress, when his mind gave way under the stress of work and more remotely of dissipation, and he committed suicide. Canning then became Secretary for Foreign Affairs, and Wellington was sent to Verona.

Wellington withdraws

The congress which now assembled at Verona was devoted largely to a discussion of Spanish affairs. Wellington had been instructed to use all his influence against the adoption of measures of intervention in Spain. When he found that the other powers were bent upon this step and that his protest would be unheeded, he withdrew from the congress. The four remaining powers continued their deliberations and finally authorized France to send an army over the Pyrenees for the purpose of restoring Ferdinand to absolute power.[14]

French invasion of Spain

The congress broke up about the middle of December, and the following April, the Duc d'Angoulême led a French army across the Pyrenees. By October the constitutional party had been overthrown and absolutism reigned supreme once more in western Europe. In England alone was there still any semblance of constitutional government.

England breaks with her former allies

The Congress of Verona was the last of the joint meetings of the powers for the discussion of the internal affairs of states. It marked the final withdrawal of England from the European alliance. Henceforth she took up a position distinctly hostile to the principles advocated by her former allies and her policy in relation to Spanish America practically coincided with that of the United States.

[14]For the Congresses of Aix-la-Chapelle, Troppau, Laybach, and Verona, see *Letters and Despatches of Castlereagh,* Vol. XII; *Life of Lord Liverpool,* Vol. III; Stapleton, *Political Life of Canning* and *Official Correspondence of Canning;* Chateaubriand's *Congrès de Verone,* and W. A. Phillips, *The Confederation of Europe, 1813–1823.* The text of an alleged secret treaty signed by the powers at Verona is published in Niles' *Register,* August 2, 1823, Vol. 24, p. 347, and in Elliot's *American Diplomatic Code,* II, 179.

British attitude on Spanish situation

The great majority of the English people sympathized deeply with the constitutional movement in Spain and were ready to take up arms in support of the Spanish people. The protest of England having been disregarded by the powers at Verona, it became necessary for the cabinet, in view of the preparations going on in France for the invasion of the Peninsula, to say what they contemplated doing. In February, 1823, Lord Liverpool circulated among his colleagues a minute prepared by Canning, which gave at length the reasons, military and other, why it would be unwise for England to undertake the defense of Spain. In the first place, the war against Spain was unpopular in France, and if Great Britain should take part in the war, the French government would avail itself of the fact to convert it into an English war and thus render it popular. Second, England would have to undertake the defense of Spain against invasion by land, and her naval superiority would not materially aid the Spaniards or baffle the French. Third, the continental powers were committed to the support of France. Fourth, there was a possibility that the invasion of Spain would be unsuccessful. Fifth, on the other hand, it might meet with success, in which event France might assist Spain to recover her American colonies. Here, he says, England's naval superiority would tell, "and I should have no difficulty in deciding that we ought to prevent, by every means in our power, perhaps Spain from sending a single Spanish regiment to South America, after the supposed termination of the war in Spain, but certainly France from affording to Spain any aid or assistance for that purpose." Sixth, in case of the invasion of Portugal by France and Spain, he thought England would be in honor bound to defend her, in case she asked for aid. The military defense of Portugal would not be so difficult as a land war in Spain.[15]

In accordance with this determination Canning dis-

[15] *Life of Lord Liverpool,* III, 231; *Official Correspondence of Canning,* I, 85.

Opposition to French acquisition of Spanish colonies

patched a letter to Sir Charles Stuart, British ambassador at Paris, March 31, 1823, in which he spoke of recognition of the colonies as a matter to be determined by time and circumstances, and, disclaiming all designs on the part of the British government on the late Spanish provinces, intimated that England, although abstaining from interference in Spain, would not allow France to acquire any of the colonies by conquest or cession. To this note the French government made no reply and England took this silence as a tacit agreement not to interfere with the colonies. The British government continued, however, to watch closely the movements of France.[16]

Canning suggests joint action

As the invasion of Spain drew near to a successful termination, the British government had reason to suspect that the allied powers would next direct their attention to the Spanish colonies with a view to forcing them back to their allegiance or of otherwise disposing of them, that is, by cession to some other European power. It was already in contemplation to call another European congress for the discussion and settlement of this question. As this was a subject of vital interest to the United States, Canning invited the American minister, Mr. Rush, to a conference, August 16, 1823, in which he suggested the expediency of an understanding on this question between England and the United States. He communicated to Rush the substance of his dispatch of March 31 to Sir Charles Stuart. Rush said he understood the import of this note to be that England would not remain passive to any attempt on the part of France to acquire territory in Spanish America. Canning then asked what the United States would say to going hand in hand with England in such a policy. Rush replied that his instructions did not authorize him to give an answer, but that he would communicate the suggestion informally to his government. At the same time he requested to be enlightened as to England's policy in the

[16]Stapleton, *Political Life of Canning*, II, 18.

matter of recognizing the independence of the colonies. Canning replied that England had taken no steps in the matter of recognition whatever, but was considering the question of sending commissioners to the colonies to inquire into the condition of affairs. For the present these commissioners would be sent to Mexico alone.[17]

Mr. Stapleton in his *Life of Canning* simply says that as Rush was not authorized to enter into any formal agreement, Canning thought the delay of communicating with Washington would render such proceeding of no effect and so the matter was dropped.[18] This, however, we learn from Rush's dispatches, is not the whole truth. Several communications passed between them after the conversation above given, which throw a totally different light upon the affair.

His proposals to Rush

In an unofficial and confidential letter to Rush, dated August 20, 1823, Canning asked again if the moment had not arrived when the two governments might come to an understanding in regard to the Spanish-American colonies. He stated the views of England as follows: (1) That the recovery of the colonies by Spain was hopeless; (2) That the question of their recognition as independent states was one of time and circumstances; (3) That England was not disposed, however, to throw any obstacle in the way of an arrangement between the colonies and the mother country by amicable negotiation; (4) That she aimed at the possession of no portion of the colonies for herself; and (5) That she could not see the transfer of any portion of them to any other power with indifference. He added "that if the United States acceded to such views, a declaration to that effect on their part, concurrently with England, would be the most effectual and least offensive mode of making known their joint disapprobation of contrary projects; that it would at the same time put an end to all jealousies

---

[17]Rush, *Residence at the Court of London*, 406.

[18]*Political Life of Canning*, II, 24.

of Spain as to her remaining colonies, and to the agitation prevailing in the colonies themselves by showing that England and the United States were determined not to profit by encouraging it."[19]

Rush without power to act

Prior to the formal recognition of South America, the United States had repeatedly expressed the wish to proceed in the matter hand in hand with Great Britain,[20] but that act placed the United States on an altogether different footing from England. Canning seemed to forget in the wording of his proposal that the United States had already, in the most formal manner, acknowledged the independence of the Spanish colonies. In reply Rush reminded him of this fact and of the desire of the United States to see the colonies recognized by England. In other respects, he believed that the views unfolded by Canning in his note were shared by the United States, but he added that he had no authority to avow these principles publicly in the manner suggested.

Monroe's view of Canning's proposals

As soon as Rush's first dispatch was received President Monroe realized fully the magnitude of the issue presented by the proposal of an Anglo-American alliance. Before submitting the matter to his cabinet he transmitted copies of the dispatch to ex-Presidents Jefferson and Madison and the following interesting correspondence took place. In his letter to Jefferson of October 17, the President said:

> I transmit to you two despatches which were receiv'd from Mr. Rush, while I was lately in Washington, which involve interests of the highest importance. They contain two letters from Mr. Canning, suggesting designs of the holy alliance, against the Independence of S°. America, & proposing a co-operation, between G. Britain & the U States, in support of it, against the members of that alliance. The project aims, in the first instance, at a mere expression of opinion, somewhat in the

[19] Rush, *Residence at the Court of London*, 412.

[20] *Letters and Despatches of Castlereagh*, XI, 458, Bagot's reports of interviews with Adams.

abstract, but which, it is expected by Mr. Canning, will have a great political effect, by defeating the combination. By Mr. Rush's answers, which are also enclosed, you will see the light in which he views the subject, & the extent to which he may have gone. Many important considerations are involved in this proposition. 1st Shall we entangle ourselves, at all, in European politicks, & wars, on the side of any power, against others, presuming that a concert, by agreement of the kind proposed, may lead to that result? 2d If a case can exist in which a sound maxim may, & ought to be departed from, is not the present instance, precisely that case? 3d Has not the epoch arriv'd when G. Britain must take her stand, either on the side of the monarchs of Europe, or of the U States, & in consequence, either in favor of Despotism or of liberty & may it not be presum'd that, aware of that necessity, her government has seiz'd on the present occurrence, as that, which it deems, the most suitable, to announce & mark the commenc'ment of that career.

My own impression is that we ought to meet the proposal of the British govt. & to make it known, that we would view an interference on the part of the European powers, and especially an attack on the Colonies, by them, as an attack on ourselves, presuming that, if they succeeded with them, they would extend it to us. I am sensible however of the extent & difficulty of the question, & shall be happy to have yours, & Mr. Madison's opinions on it.[21]

Jefferson's far-sighted opinion

Jefferson's reply dated Monticello, October 24, displays not only a profound insight into the international situation, but a wide vision of the possibilities involved. He said:

The question presented by the letters you have sent me, is the most momentous which has ever been offered to my contemplation since that of Independence. That made us a nation, this sets our compass and points the course which we are to steer through the ocean of time opening on us. And never could we embark on it under circumstances more auspicious. Our first and fundamental maxim should be, never to entangle ourselves in the broils of Europe. Our second, never to suffer Europe to intermeddle with cis-Atlantic affairs. America, North and South, has a set of interests distinct from those of Europe, and peculiarly her own. She should therefore have a system of her own, separate and apart from that of Europe. While the last

[21]Hamilton, *Writings of James Monroe,* VI, 323–325; Webster, *Castlereagh,* 439.

is laboring to become the domicile of despotism, our endeavor should surely be, to make our hemisphere that of freedom. One nation, most of all, could disturb us in this pursuit; she now offers to lead, aid, and accompany us in it. By acceding to her proposition, we detach her from the bands, bring her mighty weight into the scale of free government, and emancipate a continent at one stroke, which might otherwise linger long in doubt and difficulty. Great Britain is the nation which can do us the most harm of any one, or all on earth; and with her on our side we need not fear the whole world. With her then, we should most sedulously cherish a cordial friendship; and nothing would tend more to knit our affections than to be fighting once more, side by side, in the same cause. Not that I would purchase even her amity at the price of taking part in her wars. But the war in which the present proposition might engage us, should that be its consequence, is not her war, but ours. Its object is to introduce and establish the American system, of keeping out of our land all foreign powers, of never permitting those of Europe to intermeddle with the affairs of our nations. It is to maintain our own principle, not to depart from it. And if, to facilitate this, we can effect a division in the body of the European powers, and draw over to our side its most powerful member, surely we should do it. But I am clearly of Mr. Canning's opinion, that it will prevent instead of provoking war. With Great Britain withdrawn from their scale and shifted into that of our two continents, all Europe combined would not undertake such a war. For how would they propose to get at either enemy without superior fleets? Nor is the occasion to be slighted which this proposition offers, of declaring our protest against the atrocious violations of the rights of nations, by the interference of any one in the internal affairs of another, so flagitiously begun by Bonaparte, and now continued by the equally lawless Alliance, calling itself Holy.[22]

Madison's suggestion

Madison not only agreed with Jefferson as to the wisdom of accepting the British proposal of some form of joint action, but he went even further and suggested that the declaration should not be limited to the American republics, but that it should express disapproval of the late invasion of Spain and of any interference with the Greeks, who were then struggling for independence from Turkey.[23] Monroe, it appears, was strongly inclined to act on Madison's

[22] Ford, *Writings of Thomas Jefferson,* XII, 318.

[23] Hamilton, *Writings of James Madison,* IX, 161–162.

suggestion, but his cabinet took a different view of the situation. From the diary of John Quincy Adams, Monroe's Secretary of State, it appears that almost the whole of November was taken up by cabinet discussions on Canning's proposals and on Russia's aggressions in the northwest. Adams stoutly opposed any alliance or joint declaration with Great Britain. The composition of the President's message remained in doubt until the 21st, when the more conservative views of Adams were, according to his own statement of the case, adopted. He advocated an independent course of action on the part of the United States, without direct reference to Canning's proposals, though substantially in accord with them. Adams defined his position as follows: "The ground that I wish to take is that of earnest remonstrance against the interference of the European powers by force with South America, but to disclaim all interference on our part with Europe; to make an American cause and adhere inflexibly to that."[24]

Opposition of Adams

His reasons

Adams's dissent from Monroe's position was, it is claimed, due partly to the influence of Clay, who advocated a Pan-American system, partly to the fact that the proposed coöperation with Great Britain would bind the United States not to acquire some of the coveted parts of the Spanish possessions, and partly to the fear that the United States as the ally of Great Britain would be compelled to play a secondary part. He probably carried his point by showing that the same ends could be accomplished by an independent declaration, since it was evident that the sea power of Great Britain would be used to prevent the reconquest of South America by the European powers. Monroe, as we have seen, thought that the exigencies of the situation justified a departure from the sound maxim of political isolation, and in this opinion he was supported by his two predecessors in the presidency.

[24]W. C. Ford, "*Genesis of the Monroe Doctrine,*" in Mass. Hist. Soc. *Proceedings*, second series, XV, 392.

In the light of subsequent events

The opinions of Monroe, Jefferson, and Madison in favor of an alliance with Great Britain and a broad declaration against the intervention of the great powers in the affairs of weaker states in any part of the world, have been severely criticized by some historians and ridiculed by others, but time and circumstances often bring about a complete change in our point of view. After our entrance into the great world conflict several writers raised the question as to whether the three elder statesmen were not right and Adams and Clay wrong.[25] If the United States and England had come out in favor of a general declaration against intervention in the concerns of small states and established it as a world-wide principle, the course of human history during the next century might have been very different, but Adams's diary does not tell the whole story. On his own statement of the case he might be justly censured by posterity for persuading the President to take a narrow American view of a question which was world-wide in its bearing. An important element in the situation, however, was Canning's change of attitude between the time of his conference with Rush in August and the formulation of the President's message. Two days after the delivery of his now famous message Monroe wrote to Jefferson in explanation of the form the declaration had taken: "Mr. Canning's zeal has much abated of late." It appears from Rush's correspondence that the only thing which stood in the way of joint action by the two powers was Canning's unwillingness to extend immediate recognition to the South American republics. On August 27, Rush stated to Canning that it would greatly facilitate joint action if England would acknowledge at once the full independence of the South American colonies. In communicating the account of this interview to his government Rush concluded:

Canning's failure to press his proposals

[25]See especially G. L. Beer, *The English-Speaking Peoples*, 79.

> Should I be asked by Mr. Canning, whether, in case the recognition be made by Great Britain without more delay, I am on my part prepared to make a declaration, in the name of my government, that it will not remain inactive under an attack upon the independence of those states by the Holy Alliance, the present determination of my judgment is that I will make such a declaration explicitly, and avow it before the world.[26]

About three weeks later Canning, who was growing restless at the delay in hearing from Washington, again urged Rush to act without waiting for specific instructions from his government. He tried to show that the proposed joint declaration would not conflict with the American policy of avoiding entangling alliances, for the question at issue was American as much as European, if not more. Rush then indicated his willingness to act provided England would "immediately and unequivocally acknowledge the independence of the new states." Canning did not care to extend full recognition to the South American states until he could do so without giving unnecessary offense to Spain and the allies, and he asked if Mr. Rush could not give his assent to the proposal on a promise of future recognition. Mr. Rush refused to accede to anything but immediate acknowledgment of independence and so the matter ended.[27]

Interview with Prince Polignac

As Canning could not come to a formal understanding with the United States, he determined to make a frank avowal of the views of the British cabinet to France and to this end he had an interview with Prince Polignac, the French ambassador at London, October 9, 1823, in which he declared that Great Britain had no desire to hasten recognition, but that any foreign interference, by force, or by menace, would be a motive for immediate recognition; that England "could not go into a joint deliberation upon the subject of Spanish America upon an equal footing with other powers, whose opinions were less formed upon that

[26] Rush, *Residence at the Court of London*, 419.

[27] *Ibid.*, pp. 429, 443.

question." This declaration drew from Polignac the admission that he considered the reduction of the colonies by Spain as hopeless and that France "abjured in any case, any design of acting against the colonies by force of arms."[28] This admission was a distinct victory for Canning, in that it prepared the way for ultimate recognition by England, and an account of the interview was communicated without delay to the allied courts. The interview was not communicated to Rush until the latter part of November, and therefore had no influence upon the formation of Monroe's message of December 2.[29]

Proposed conference on Spanish colonies

Before the close of the year the British government appointed consuls to the South American states, and about the time of their departure, an invitation was sent to the courts of St. Petersburg, Paris, and Vienna to a conference to be held at Paris to "aid Spain in adjusting the affairs of the revolted colonies." A copy of this invitation was also handed to the British ambassador at Madrid, but in such a form as to leave him in doubt as to whether his government was invited to the conference or not.[30] While the discussion as to the proposed conference was going on and before Canning had announced what action his government would take in the matter, President Monroe's message arrived in Europe.

Encroachments of Russia on northwest coast

Spanish America was not the only part of the western continent threatened at this time by European aggression. On the 4th of September, 1821, the Emperor of Russia had issued a ukase, in which he claimed the northwestern coast of North America down to the fifty-first degree. This claim was incompatible with the pretensions of both England and the United States, and was stoutly opposed by them. This was a part of the territory known as the Oregon country, which continued in dispute between

[28] *Political Life of Canning*, II, 26.
[29] Rush, *Residence at the Court of London*, 448.
[30] *Political Life of Canning*, II. 33.

England and the United States until 1846. In July, 1823, Adams declared to Baron Tuyll, the Russian minister to the United States, "that we should contest the right of Russia to any territorial establishment on this continent, and that we should assume distinctly the principle that the American continents are no longer subjects for any new European colonial establishments." This language was incorporated substantially in the President's message.

Monroe's message

The Monroe Doctrine is comprised in two widely separated paragraphs that occur in the message of December 2, 1823. The first, relating to Russia's encroachments on the northwest coast, and occurring near the beginning of the message, was an assertion to the effect that the American continents had assumed an independent condition and were no longer open to European colonization. This may be regarded as a statement of fact. No part of the continent at that time remained unclaimed. The second paragraph relating to Spanish America and occurring near the close of the message, was a declaration against the extension to the American continents of the system of intervention adopted by the Holy Alliance for the suppression of popular government in Europe.

The language used by President Monroe is as follows:

Declaration against further colonization

1. At the proposal of the Russian Imperial Government, made through the minister of the emperor residing here, a full power and instructions have been transmitted to the minister of the United States at St. Petersburg to arrange by amicable negotiation the respective rights and interests of the two nations on the northwest coast of this continent. A similar proposal had been made by His Imperial Majesty to the government of Great Britain, which has likewise been acceded to. The government of the United States has been desirous by this friendly proceeding of manifesting the great value which they have invariably attached to the friendship of the emperor and their solicitude to cultivate the best understanding with his government. In the discussions to which this interest has given rise and in the arrangements by which they may terminate, the

occasion has been judged proper for asserting, as a principle in which the rights and interests of the United States are involved, that the American continents, by the free and independent condition which they have assumed and maintain, are henceforth not to be considered as subjects for future colonization by any European powers.[31]

Against political interference

2. In the wars of the European powers in matters relating to themselves we have never taken any part, nor does it comport with our policy so to do. It is only when our rights are invaded or seriously menaced that we resent injuries or make preparation for our defense. With the movements in this hemisphere we are of necessity more immediately connected, and by causes which must be obvious to all enlightened and impartial observers. The political system of the allied powers is essentially different in this respect from that of America. This difference proceeds from that which exists in their respective governments; and to the defense of our own, which has been achieved by the loss of so much blood and treasure, and matured by the wisdom of their most enlightened citizens, and under which we have enjoyed unexampled felicity, this whole nation is devoted. We owe it, therefore, to candor and to the amicable relations existing between the United States and those powers to declare that we should consider any attempt on their part to extend their system to any portion of this hemisphere as dangerous to our peace and safety. With the existing colonies or dependencies of any European power we have not interfered and shall not interfere. But with the governments who have declared their independence and maintained it, and whose independence we have, on great consideration and on just principles, acknowledged, we could not view any interposition for the purpose of oppressing them, or controlling in any other manner their destiny, by any European power in any other light than as the manifestation of an unfriendly disposition toward the United States. In the war between those new governments and Spain we declared our neutrality at the time of their recognition, and to this we have adhered, and shall continue to adhere, provided no change shall occur which, in the judgment of the competent authorities of this government, shall make a corresponding change on the part of the United States indispensable to their security.[32]

Reception of message in England

The President's message reached England while the discussion in regard to the proposed congress at Paris was still going on. It was received with enthusiasm by

[31]Richardson, *Messages and Papers of the Presidents,* II, 209.
[32]*Ibid.*, p. 218.

the liberal members of Parliament. Lord Brougham said:

> The question with regard to South America is now, I believe, disposed of, or nearly so; for an event has recently happened than which none has ever dispersed greater joy, exultation, and gratitude over all the free men of Europe; that event, which is decisive on the subject, is the language held with respect to Spanish America in the message of the President of the United States.

Sir James Mackintosh said:

> This coincidence of the two great English commonwealths (for so I delight to call them; and I heartily pray that they may be forever united in the cause of justice and liberty) cannot be contemplated without the utmost pleasure by every enlightened citizen of the earth.[33]

Canning's chagrin

They evidently had reference to the second clause alone, the one relating to Spanish America. The other clause, the one against European colonization in America, seems not to have attracted much attention. Canning, however, saw the bearing of it and objected to the principle it set forth, which was directed against England as much as against the allies. He was evidently a little taken aback at the turn his proposal had taken. The President's message really settled the question before Canning had announced what action his government would take. Some little chagrin is apparent in the tone of his letter to Sir William à Court, British minister at Madrid, December 21, 1823:

> While I was yet hesitating [he says], what shape to give to the declaration and protest which ultimately was conveyed in my conference with P. de Polignac, and while I was more doubtful as to the effect of that protest and declaration, I sounded Mr. Rush (the American minister here) as to his powers and disposition to join in any step which we might take to prevent a hostile enterprise on the part of the European powers against Spanish America. He had no powers; but he would have taken

[33]Wharton, *Dig. of Int. Law*, I, 276.

upon himself to join with us if we would have begun by recognizing the Spanish-American states. This we could not do, and so we went on without. But I have no doubt that his report to his government of this *sounding*, which he probably represented as an overture, had a great share in producing the explicit declaration of the President.[34]

He refuses to attend proposed conference

The conference with Prince Polignac here referred to was that of October 9 quoted above. It was not until after the receipt of President Monroe's message in Europe that Canning framed his answer to the Spanish communication informing him of the proposed meeting in Paris for the discussion of the South American question In that reply he stated to the Spanish government very fully his views upon the question at issue. He said that while England did not wish to precede Spain in the matter of recognition, yet she reserved to herself the privilege of recognizing the colonies when she deemed it best for her interests and right to them. He said that these views had been communicated fully from time to time to the powers invited to the congress and he concluded with the statement: "It does not appear to the British cabinet at all necessary to declare that opinion anew, even if it were perfectly clear (from the tenor of M. Ofalia's instruction) that Great Britain was in fact included in the invitation to the conference at Paris."[35]

Allies abandon plans

While Canning and Monroe acted independently of each other, the expression that each gave to the views of his government was rendered more emphatic and of more effect by the knowledge of the other's attitude in the matter. Another point to be noted is that Monroe's message was made public, while Canning's answer was for some time known only to the diplomatic corps.

The determination of both England and the United States to oppose the intervention of the allies in South America had the desired effect. Conferences in answer

[34] *Op. cit.*, I, 272.

[35] *Political Life of Canning*, II, 42.

to the invitation of Spain were held in Paris, but they were participated in only by the ordinary representatives of the powers invited, resident in that capital, and their only result was to advise Spain not to listen to the counsels of England.

Canning announces independent course of action

All further discussion that took place between England and Spain in reference to recognition of the colonies by Great Britain was confined to the status of the revolutionary governments, and upon this point their views were so divergent that Canning finally announced to the Spanish government that "His Majesty would, at his own time, take such steps as he might think proper in respect to the several states of Spanish America without further reference to the Court of Madrid; but at the same time without any feeling of alienation towards that court, or of hostility towards the real interests of Spain."[36]

Great Britain decides on recognition

The French troops continuing to occupy Spain after the time stipulated by treaty, Canning sought an explanation from France, but without satisfactory results. He therefore determined at a cabinet meeting held December 14, 1824, to recognize Mexico and Colombia forthwith. On January 1, 1825, after the ministers had left England with instructions and full powers, the fact of recognition was communicated officially to the diplomatic corps and two days later it was made public. That this recognition was a retaliatory measure to compensate England for the French occupation of Spain was understood at the time and was distinctly avowed by Canning two years later.[37] In a speech delivered December 12, 1826, in defense of his position in not having arrested the French invasion of Spain, he said:

Canning's boast

> I looked another way—I sought for compensation in another hemisphere. Contemplating Spain, such as our ancestors had

[36]*Op. cit.*, II, 54.

[37]*Official Corresp. of Canning*, II, 242. Letter to Granville. On the general question of recognition, see *Life of Lord Liverpool*, III, 297–304.

known her, I resolved that, if France had Spain, it should not be Spain *with the Indies*. I called the New World into existence to redress the balance of the Old.

In spite of the great indebtedness of South America to Canning, this boast falls somewhat flat when we remember that the Spanish colonies had won their independence by their own valor and had been recognized as independent governments by the United States two years before Great Britain acted in the matter.

Clay's efforts in behalf of further recognition

The United States government did not relax its efforts in behalf of the South American states with the recognition of England, but continued to exert itself in order to secure the acknowledgment of their independence by the other powers of Europe, particularly Spain.[38] Secretary Clay tried to get the other members of the alliance to use their good offices with Spain for the purpose of inducing her to recognize her late colonies, but the Emperor of Russia, the head of the alliance, continued to preach to Spain "not only no recognition of their independence, but active war for their subjugation." To the request of the United States he replied that, out of respect for "the indisputable titles of sovereignty," he could not prejudge or anticipate the determination of the King of Spain.[39] It was some ten years before Spain could be persuaded to renounce her ancient claims.

---

[38] *A. S. P., F. R.*, V, 794–796, VI, 1006–1014.

[39] *Ibid.*, pp. 850 ff.

CHAPTER IX

RELATIONS WITH FRANCE AND THE BRITISH EMPIRE

Jackson's election to the presidency

Jackson's election to the presidency marked the triumph of Western or frontier democracy over the more conservative East. It was a period of growth and internal expansion, and the rapid settlement of the Southwest gave rise to frontier problems which assumed serious proportions under his successors. The abolition of slavery in the British West Indies and the efforts of the British government to suppress the African slave trade through international coöperation were coincident with the consolidation of the slave power in America and its dominance in national politics. The slavery conflict absorbed more and more of the attention of American statesmen and tended to increase isolation in general questions of international concern. Jackson, whose anti-British sentiments had been so manifest throughout most of his career, had less difficulty with England than might have been expected. Fortunately the Canadian troubles did not begin until the administration of his successor, and the only very serious outstanding dispute with England—the West India question—was adjusted early in his administration. His moderation in handling this question was doubtless due to his disapproval of everything Adams had done.

The only international dispute in which Jackson displayed his characteristic energy and arbitrary method of procedure was not with England, but with France. The settlement of the long-standing controversy over the

The French Spoliation Claims

French Spoliation Claims, following the adjustment of the West India question with England, established his reputation for the energetic and successful handling of diplomatic questions. The claims against France arose from the illegal seizure and condemnation of American vessels under the Napoleonic decrees. When Gallatin was sent to France and instructed in 1816 to present these claims, the restored Bourbon government was not disposed to do anything. In fact, they declined even to consider any claims except those for vessels and cargoes destroyed at sea without having been condemned by the Council of Prizes, and delayed action on these. When the question was taken up again by Gallatin's successor, James Brown, he was met with counter claims on the part of France for the seizure of certain French vessels, for the alleged violation of Articles VII and VIII of the Louisiana treaty, which granted France most-favored-nation treatment, and for supplies furnished by Beaumarchais during the American Revolution. In regard to the Louisiana treaty the point at issue was whether France could claim the benefit of concessions made to other nations by way of reciprocity. The United States has always taken the position that a nation cannot claim under the most-favored-nation clause benefits granted to others through reciprocity treaties, unless that nation is willing to grant a full equivalent.

The Claims Convention of 1831

When Jackson became President, William C. Rives was sent as minister to France and he was instructed to press for a settlement of the Spoliation Claims. The claims which he presented were divided into five classes and amounted in all to $12,047,286, without interest.[1] The negotiations were interrupted by the Revolution of July, 1830, which brought Louis Philippe to the throne. The new government was more favorably disposed to a settlement, and a claims convention was signed July 4,

[1] Moore, *Int. Arbits.*, V, 4458.

1831.[2] The agreement represented a compromise on both sides. Rives agreed to accept twenty-five million francs, while France was to deduct one million five hundred thousand francs in satisfaction of all claims, including that of Beaumarchais' heirs which alone amounted with interest to more than four and a half million francs. In return for a reduction of duties for a period of ten years on French wines imported into the United States, France agreed to abandon her interpretation of the disputed articles of the Louisiana treaty. The convention met with great satisfaction in the United States and was promptly ratified.

The French Chamber fails to make appropriation

The French Chamber of Deputies failed, however, to make provision for carrying out the convention. When the first payment fell due February 2, 1833, Jackson directed the Secretary of the Treasury to draw a draft through the Bank of the United States on the French Minister of Finance for the amount. The French government let the draft go to protest, and the Minister of Foreign Affairs complained to Rives of the procedure of the United States, reminding him that under the French constitutional system, as well as under that of the United States, the financial clauses of a treaty could not be carried into effect without the coöperation of the legislature. At the next meeting of the Chamber a bill carrying the necessary appropriation was presented by the government, but defeated by a narrow majority.

Jackson recommends reprisals

Jackson was not the kind of man to submit quietly to what he considered a plain violation of an agreement. When Edward Livingston was presented as Rives' successor at the Court of France, King Louis Philippe expressed his good feeling toward the United States and assured him that the convention would be faithfully executed. In reporting this to the President, Livingston suggested that the display of "a strong national feeling on

[2](Malloy) *Treaties and Conventions*, I, 523.

the subject" in the next message to Congress might have a good effect on the Chamber of Deputies and would help to establish "the national reputation for energy." Jackson's exhibition of energy in his annual message of December 1, 1834, probably went far beyond Livingston's expectations. He reviewed the whole case at length, declared that further negotiations were out of the question, and asked authority to make reprisals in case France delayed meeting her obligations any longer.[3] The message created a great stir in Congress. The President's opponents, under the leadership of Clay, tried to make political capital out of it, but the only action they could get was a mild resolution, that "it is inexpedient at present to adopt any legislative measures in regard to the state of affairs between the United States and France."

Rupture of diplomatic relations

When Jackson's message reached France it created great surprise and indignation. The French minister was recalled from Washington, Livingston was offered his passports, and the Chamber of Deputies was informed that diplomatic intercourse with the United States had been suspended. On March 25, 1835, the Chamber of Deputies passed an act for carrying out the convention with the proviso that no payments should be made until satisfactory explanations of the President's message should be received. The President refused to make such explanations, but declared in his annual message of December 7, 1835, that, "The conception that it was my intention to menace or insult the government of France is as unfounded as the attempt to extort from the fears of that nation what her sense of justice may deny would be vain and ridiculous."[4] This was as far as he would go in the direction of an apology or explanation.

At this point the British government offered to act as

[3]Richardson, *Messages and Papers*, III, 97.

[4]Jackson's messages were accompanied by the correspondence, most of which appears in Richardson, *Messages and Papers*, III, 147–222.

mediator. Jackson accepted the offer with the understanding that no apologies would be expected, and the dispute was soon adjusted. On February 15, 1836, the British *chargé d'affaires* at Washington informed the Secretary of State that

British mediation

> The French government has stated to that of his Majesty that the frank and honorable manner in which the President has in his recent message expressed himself with regard to the points of difference between the governments of France and of the United States has removed those difficulties, upon the score of national honor, which have hitherto stood in the way of the prompt execution by France of the treaty of the 4th July, 1831.[5]

The incident was thus closed and diplomatic relations were resumed.[6]

Canadian insurrection of 1837

In 1837, unsuccessful revolutions took place in both Upper and Lower Canada. The dissatisfaction was due mainly to the fact that the council or upper house of the legislature was in both provinces appointed by the royal governor. In Lower Canada racial and religious elements entered into the situation; the English, whose control was maintained through the governor and council, constituted only about one-third of the population, while the French Catholics made up the rest and had a majority in the assembly. In Upper Canada the contest was between the original settlers who owned large estates and the more recent immigrants. The leader of the insurrection was a Scotchman, William Lyon Mackenzie, who after the collapse of the movement escaped with many of his followers across the border into the United States, where they were received by the people with open expressions of sympathy. In a short time the whole border was aflame with excitement, and in Buffalo, Rochester, Troy, St.

[5]*Op. cit.*, III, 221.

[6]This controversy is covered quite fully in Moore, *Int. Arbits.*, V, 4447–4485, and in *British and Foreign State Papers*, XXII, 595–686, 964–993; XXIII, 1295–1341; and XXIV, 1086–1155.

Albans, Burlington, and Middlebury meetings were held, resolutions of sympathy adopted, money, provisions, and ammunition collected, volunteer companies organized, and other preparations made for aiding the revolt against Great Britain. In Buffalo the flag of the insurgents was raised over the Eagle Tavern where Mackenzie established his headquarters. The United States government at once took steps to check these hostile preparations. Secretary of State Forsyth wrote to the governors of New York, Vermont, and Michigan, requesting them to arrest all parties preparing for an invasion of Canada, and the district attorneys were instructed to prosecute all those who committed acts in violation of the neutrality laws of the United States.

The attack on the *Caroline*

Meanwhile Mackenzie and his followers, realizing that they could not invade Canada from the United States, crossed over to Navy Island in the Niagara River and proclaimed a provisional government. Here a number of Americans joined them and the fortification of the island was undertaken. The governor of Upper Canada sent Colonel McNab to Chippewa, opposite the island, to prevent a landing on the mainland. On December 29, 1837, McNab was informed that the steamship *Caroline*, which had been hired by the insurgents to bring them ammunition and supplies, was lying at Navy Island. He at once ordered Captain Drew of the Royal Navy to collect a force of volunteers and destroy the *Caroline*. That night Drew and his men drifted down the river in open boats, but when they arrived at the island they found that the *Caroline* was over on the American shore tied to the wharf at Schlosser. Without considering whether his orders justified an attack within American jurisdiction, Drew crossed over, boarded the ship, and put the crew to flight with bullets and cutlasses. He then towed the ship out into the current, set her afire, and let her go over the falls. In the mêlée several of the crew were wounded and an American named Amos Durfee was killed.[7]

Protest and answer

As soon as information of this incident was received at Washington General Winfield Scott was sent to the border with letters to the governors of New York and Vermont asking them to call into service the militia for the purpose of defending the frontier, and the attention of the British minister, Henry S. Fox, was called to this "extraordinary outrage" committed on the persons and property of citizens of the United States within the jurisdiction of the State of New York.[8] Fox waited to receive a report from the governor of Upper Canada before replying to the American note. He then inclosed the report to Forsyth. The governor acknowledged that the force that destroyed the *Caroline* was under the command of Colonel McNab; but declared that the piratical character of the *Caroline* was fully established; that the ordinary laws of the United States were not at the time enforced along the frontier; and that the destruction of the vessel was an act of necessary self-defense. In May, 1838, Andrew Stevenson, the American minister at London, presented a demand for reparation to Lord Palmerston, who merely acknowledged the receipt of the note and promised that it would receive consideration.[9]

The case of Alexander McLeod

The demand of the United States had not been met when in 1840 a Canadian named Alexander McLeod made the boast under the influence of liquor in a New York tavern that he had killed Amos Durfee. He was taken at his word, examined before a magistrate, and committed to jail in Lockport. He was later indicted by a grand jury to stand trial in the court of Niagara County. McLeod's arrest created great excitement on both sides of the border. The British minister at Washington called

[7] *British and Foreign State Papers*, XXVI. 1373.

[8] *Ibid.*, p. 1376.

[9] 25 Cong., 2 Sess., House Exec. Docs. 64, 74, 305; 26 Cong., 2 Sess.. House Exec. Doc. 33, House Report, 162.

upon the government of the United States "to take prompt and effectual steps for the liberation of Mr. McLeod." He said that it was well known that "the destruction of the steamboat *Caroline* was a public act of persons in Her Majesty's service obeying the orders of their superior authorities"; that it could not for this reason be made the ground for legal proceedings; and that it was "quite notorious that Mr. McLeod was not one of the party engaged in the destruction of the steamboat *Caroline*."

Forsyth advances excuse of state jurisdiction

Forsyth replied that the offense with which McLeod was charged had been committed within the State of New York; that the jurisdiction of each state in the United States was, within its proper sphere, perfectly independent of the Federal government; and that the latter could not interfere. The question of McLeod's absence from the scene of the offense could, he said, be settled by legal evidence. If the destruction of the *Caroline* was a public act, done under authority, the government of the United States had never been so informed, and it would be proper that the court before which McLeod was to be tried should pass on its validity. In reply Fox said that the *Caroline* was a hostile vessel engaged in piratical warfare against Her Majesty's people; that the place where it was destroyed "was nominally within the territory of a friendly power; but the friendly power had been deprived, through overbearing piratical violence, of the use of its proper authority over that portion of territory."

Great Britain demands of Federal government immediate release of McLeod

The correspondence was referred by the House of Representatives to the Committee on Foreign Affairs. This committee made a report which the Whigs declared was sensational and a deliberate attempt to inflame the people against Great Britain. The Democrats, however, stood by the report. The date set for the trial of McLeod was the fourth Monday in March, 1841. Van Buren's term ended and Harrison's began on the 4th of March, and Webster became Secretary of State. The British minister,

Fox, was instructed to make known to the government of the United States that Her Majesty's government entirely approved his course and the language adopted by him in his official correspondence, and that he was again to demand the immediate release of Mr. Alexander McLeod. This demand was made because the attack on the *Caroline* was an act of a public character; because it was a justifiable use of force for the defense of British territory against unprovoked attack by "British rebels and American pirates"; because it was contrary to the practice of civilized nations to hold individuals responsible for acts done by the order of the constituted authorities of a state; and because Her Majesty's government could not admit the doctrine that the Federal government had no power to interfere and that the decision must rest with the State of New York. The relations of foreign powers were with the Federal government. To admit that the Federal government had no control over a state would lead to the dissolution of the Union so far as foreign powers were concerned and to the accrediting of foreign diplomatic agents, not to the Federal government, but to each separate state.[10]

Webster's handling of the case

Webster received the note quietly, sent the Attorney-General to Lockport to see that McLeod had skilful and eminent counsel and to say that if the defense were overruled, it was the wish of the President that the case be removed by writ of error to the Supreme Court of the United States. On account of some defect in the procedure, the trial was postponed, greatly to the annoyance of Webster, who was receiving in every mail from Europe news of an alarming kind. Cass wrote from Paris that Great Britain was in earnest, that her minister was instructed to leave Washington if McLeod were hanged, and that the British Mediterranean fleet had been ordered to assemble at Gibraltar and sail thence to Halifax.

[10]*British and Foreign State Papers,* XXIX, 1126.

While waiting for the case to come to trial, Webster answered the note of the British minister. He reminded him that in the United States as in England persons held under judicial process could be released only by judicial process. In neither country could the executive interfere directly or forcibly to release a prisoner. He said that the avowal that the destruction of the *Caroline* was a public act gave the case a new aspect; that the government of the United States did not doubt that after this avowal individuals concerned in the act ought not by the principles of public law and the general usage of civilized states, to be held personally responsible in the ordinary tribunals of law. The President, however, did not regard the destruction of the *Caroline* as a justifiable use of force. The government of the United States could not admit that it had not both the will and power to preserve its own neutrality and force the observance of its own laws on its own citizens. It was jealous of its rights, especially of the absolute immunity of its territory against aggression from abroad.[11]

The trial and acquittal of McLeod

McLeod's case was taken before the Supreme Court of New York. The court decided that it had jurisdiction, that McLeod could not be discharged, that the expedition was murder and arson in time of peace, and it remanded the prisoner for trial according to the ordinary forms of law. This decision raised excitement along the border to fever heat. Notwithstanding threats of violence on both sides, when the trial of McLeod took place at Utica good order prevailed. The jury brought in a verdict of not guilty, and McLeod was released and allowed to depart in peace.[12]

In order to avoid similar complications in the future Webster drafted a statute, which was enacted and approved August 29, 1842, providing for *habeas corpus* pro-

[11]*Op. cit.*, XXIX, 1129.

[12]A full account of the trial is given in Niles' *Register*, LXI, 104–108, 119–128, 187–191.

ceedings before a Federal judge in all cases of prisoners claiming to have committed the acts for which they are held under the commission or order of a foreign state; if not released, the prisoners to be remanded to the local court for trial, with the right of appeal to the circuit court of the United States and to the Supreme Court.[13]

Act for removal of such cases to Federal courts

The *Caroline* incident was finally closed by an exchange of notes between Mr. Webster and Lord Ashburton a few days before the signature of the treaty of August 9, 1842. Webster called attention to the fact that although five years had elapsed since the incident occurred, no atonement or apology had been made for the offense to the dignity and sovereignty of the United States. He did not raise the question as to the lawfulness or unlawfulness of the employment in which the ship was engaged, but confined himself solely to the violation of American territory. Lord Ashburton replied with a long discussion of the case, in which he took exception to the "rather highly colored description" of the occurrence given by Webster, but expressed regret that "some explanation and apology" had not been made at the time of the occurrence. He concluded with the statement that,

Great Britain expresses regret for *Caroline* affair

> Her Majesty's government earnestly desire that a reciprocal respect for the independent jurisdiction and authority of neighboring states may be considered among the first duties of all governments, and I have to repeat the assurance of regret they feel that the event of which I am treating should have disturbed the harmony they so anxiously wish to maintain with the American people and government.[14]

Webster said later that it took him two days to persuade Lord Ashburton to use the word "apology." Webster accepted Ashburton's statement in a letter written for the American public which was as skilfully worded as that of Lord Ashburton. In fact, he made it appear that

[13] *5 U. S. Statutes at Large,* 539.

[14] *British and Foreign State Papers,* XXX, 195.

the British explanation and apology went much further than they really did. In conclusion he declared that the subject would not be made a topic of further discussion between the two governments.[15]

The northeastern boundary dispute

The disputes growing out of the Canadian rebellion were coincident with disturbances of a serious character along the Maine-New Brunswick frontier, where the boundary line established by the treaty of 1783 had never been determined. That treaty defined the northeast boundary of the United States as follows: "From the northwest angle of Nova Scotia viz., that angle which is formed by a line drawn due north from the source of the St. Croix River to the Highlands; from the said Highlands which divide those rivers that empty themselves into the river St. Lawrence, from those which fall into the Atlantic Ocean, to the northwesternmost head of the Connecticut River." This language was hopelessly vague and indefinite. It was not known what river was intended under the name St. Croix and it was impossible for any two surveyors to agree upon what series of hills constituted the aforesaid "Highlands" or upon the location of the northwest angle of Nova Scotia. The commissioners appointed under Article V of the Jay treaty decided that the Schoodiac was the river intended as the starting point of the boundary, but there remained the question as to the location of the northwest angle of Nova Scotia and the line from that point to the head of the Connecticut River. The location of this boundary, together with other parts of the boundary to the Lake of the Woods, was referred to commissions organized under provisions of the Treaty of Ghent. The commissioners on the northeast boundary were unable to agree and in 1827 a special convention was signed submitting the dispute to arbitration. The King

[15]On the general subject see Tiffany, *Relations of the United States to the Canadian Rebellion of 1837–1838*; Reeves, *American Diplomacy Under Tyler and Polk*, Chap. i.

of the Netherlands, who was selected as arbiter, decided upon an arbitrary division of the territory, which, on the ground that he had exceeded his powers, the United States Senate refused to accept. Great Britain appears to have been willing at first to accept this award, but later withdrew her consent.[16]

The "Aroostook War"

In 1837, it was reported that the British colonial authorities were planning to construct a railroad through the disputed territory in order to afford direct overland communication between Halifax and Quebec. This aroused opposition in the United States. Petty disputes had in the meantime been continually arising between the authorities of Maine and New Brunswick, and these were brought to a head suddenly in the summer of 1838 when an unusually large number of British lumbermen began operations on the Aroostook River. The authorities of Maine ordered them to withdraw from American territory, but they refused to do so, and assembled in considerable numbers for the purpose of maintaining their position by force. The governor of Maine sent a body of militia to enforce the authority of the state, and the New Brunswick authorities procured a detachment of British regulars to back up their position. The situation became very serious, and bloodshed was narrowly averted. General Scott was sent to the scene of the trouble in order to restrain the Maine authorities, and the question was quickly taken up by the British Foreign Office and the American State Department. The so-called "Restook War" came at a very unfortunate moment, for the relations between the two countries were already strained to the utmost by the Canadian insurrection and the attack on the *Caroline*.[17]

The situation was so grave, however, that the diplomats found it necessary to take up seriously the settlement of

[16]Moore, *Int. Arbits.*, I, Chaps. i–iv.

[17]Sprague, *The Northeastern Boundary and the Aroostook War, passim.*

Surveyors unable to agree upon line

the boundary question. Palmerston, the British Foreign Secretary, and Forsyth, the American Secretary of State, began a new series of surveys for the purpose of determining the angle and the Highlands. For three years, 1839–1842, the matter was under discussion, and the surveyors attempted in vain to locate a line which would correspond with the line of the treaty.[18] In 1841, the Whig party came into control of the government in Washington, and about the same time Peel succeeded Melbourne as Prime Minister of England. Daniel Webster became Secretary of State, and Lord Aberdeen succeeded Palmerston as Foreign Secretary. When Webster came into office the most pressing question was the McLeod case. The suppression of the slave trade and the question of the right of search also added greatly to his difficulties. Aberdeen's tone was much more conciliatory than Palmerston's and as soon as the McLeod affair was settled, Webster devoted himself earnestly to the boundary question. He proposed through the British minister at Washington to drop the mass of data accumulated by surveyors and historians and to try to reach an agreement by direct negotiation. In other words, he considered it hopeless to reach an agreement on the proper interpretation of the treaty of 1783, and proposed that the two governments should agree on a conventional line.

Mission of Lord Ashburton

Peel decided to accept Webster's overtures and at the same time determined to send a special envoy to the United States with full power to settle the questions in dispute. For this important mission he and Aberdeen, after careful consideration, chose Alexander Baring, Lord Ashburton, head of the famous London banking house. Ashburton was not a professional diplomat, but he was a man of great ability and experience, had married an American wife, and was favorably known in the United States through having financed the Louisiana Purchase.

[18] Moore, *Int. Arbits.*, I, 141–144.

His instructions

It was thought that he would be *persona grata*. In his instructions of February 8, 1842, the objects of his mission were stated in the order of importance as follows: the northeastern boundary, the Oregon boundary, the northwestern boundary, the *Caroline* incident, and the right of search for the suppression of the African slave trade. He was apparently given a free hand and this was accepted as proof of England's desire that the questions at issue should be settled in a friendly and satisfactory way. In fact, Webster stated after his first interview with Ashburton that the latter had come without instructions and with full powers. Supplementary instructions were, however, sent him on March 31, telling him that it was deemed essential that the proposed line of communication between Halifax and Quebec should be preserved, and that he must insist on the line of the Upper St. John, thus claiming far more than was assigned to Great Britain by the award of the King of the Netherlands.[19] Against these new instructions he at once protested. Fortunately he had time to correspond with his government, for Webster was having trouble with the commissioners of Maine and had to ask for a delay. There were constitutional difficulties in the way of disposing by treaty of territory claimed by a state without the consent of that state. Massachusetts, of which Maine had formerly been a part, was also an interested party. Webster finally gained the consent of Maine and Massachusetts to the compromise he and Lord Ashburton had informally agreed upon, by promising them each $150,000 and an equal division of the part of "the disputed territory fund" which Great Britain was to hand over to the United States.[20] The agreement to make these payments was incorporated in the fifth article of the treaty—an unusual stipulation, to which Lord

Opposition of Maine and Massachusetts overcome

[19]*Cambridge History of British Foreign Policy,* II, 249; E. D. Adams, "Lord Ashburton and the Treaty of Washington," in *Am. Hist. Rev.,* XVII, 768.

[20]Moore, *Int. Arbits.,* I, 147–151.

Ashburton at first objected as a matter with which Great Britain had no concern, but when Webster explained that it would insure the votes of those states in the Senate for ratification he withdrew his objection.

Webster-Ashburton Treaty: north-eastern boundary

The boundary line as drawn in Article I of the treaty began at the monument set up by the commissioners under Article V of the Jay treaty; it then ran due north following the line marked by the surveyors in 1817 and 1818 under Article V of the Treaty of Ghent to the St. John; up the channel of that river to the mouth of the St. Francis; up the St. Francis to Lake Pohenagamook; from this point it followed an arbitrary line in a southwesterly direction to the intersection of parallel forty-six degrees twenty-five minutes with the southwest branch of the St. John; up that branch to the Highlands; thence along the Highlands to the northwest source of the Connecticut River known as Hall's Stream; and down the middle of that stream to the boundary marked by Valentine and Collins prior to the year 1774 as the forty-fifth degree of north latitude; and thence along that line to the St. Lawrence.

Webster's statement of gains

By the adoption of the last line Rousse's Point on Lake Champlain and lands supposed to be within the limits of New Hampshire, Vermont, and New York, which were really north of the correctly ascertained forty-fifth parallel, were confirmed to the United States. In his letter of July 15, 1842, to the Maine commissioners Webster said that by the treaty there would be assigned to the United States 7,015 square miles, and to Great Britain 5,012 square miles of the 12,027 in dispute; that this was 893 square miles less than the United States would have received under the award of the King of the Netherlands, but that this land was in the mountains and not very valuable; and that while the portion of the disputed area assigned to the United States was in quality seven-twelfths, in value it was at least four-fifths of the whole.[21]

[21] *The Works of Daniel Webster*, VI, 276.

Lake of the Woods boundary

The determination of the boundary from the St. Lawrence to the Lake of the Woods did not present so many difficulties and was more easily disposed of. The treaty confirmed the forty-ninth parallel, already agreed upon in 1818, as the boundary from the Lake of the Woods to the Rocky Mountains. The Oregon question, which was so soon to produce another crisis, does not appear to have entered seriously into the negotiations and was omitted from the treaty.[22]

The "red-line map"

One incident connected with the boundary negotiations which was discussed in the Senate debates and later, when they were published, in the press, placed Webster in an embarrassing position. This was his use of the famous "red-line map," which was supposed to be a copy of the one used by the commissioners who negotiated the treaty of 1783. The commissioners used Mitchell's Map,[23] but no copy was annexed to the treaty. After the signing of the preliminary treaty Vergennes sent a map to Franklin and requested him to mark on it the boundaries of the United States. Franklin returned the map with the statement that he had marked the boundaries "with a strong red line."[24] In 1842, shortly before the opening of the Webster-Ashburton negotiations, Jared Sparks discovered in the French archives Franklin's letter to Vergennes and at once began a search for the map referred to.

Jared Sparks discovers the wrong map

He found a small map of North America, made by D'Anville in 1746, on which had been drawn a heavy red line intended apparently to mark the boundaries of the United States. This line assigned Great Britain even more than she claimed. There was nothing whatever to identify the map, but Sparks at once sent it to Webster, and Webster immediately instructed Everett to "forbear to press the search after maps in England or elsewhere," which he had

[22]Adams, *Am. Hist. Rev.*, XVII, 770, 781.

[23]Wharton, *Dip. Cor. of Am. Rev.*, VI, 133.

[24]*Ibid.*, p. 120.

been told earlier to undertake. Webster did not make known the discovery to Lord Ashburton, but he used the map to good purpose in persuading Maine and Massachusetts to agree to the boundary compromise and in securing the ratification of the treaty by the Senate. When these facts became known he was severely criticized both in America and in England for witholding the map from Lord Ashburton, but he replied that he did not think it his duty to submit to the British representative a piece of doubtful evidence which might prejudice the claim of the United States or precipitate another controversy.

The British Museum map

It was not known at the time that in 1839 the Director of the British Museum had called Palmerston's attention to a map with a red line marked "boundary as described by Mr. Oswald," and that the map had been immediately removed from the British Museum to the Foreign Office. This was the copy of Mitchell's Map actually used by Oswald in the negotiations of 1782 and the line marked on it followed very closely the boundary claimed by the United States. After the ratification of the Webster-Ashburton treaty this map was shown by Aberdeen to Everett who described it in a dispatch March 31, 1843, in which he says:

> The line giving our boundary as we have always claimed it, that is, carrying the northwestern angle of Nova Scotia far to the north of the St. John's is drawn very carefully in a bold red line, full a tenth of an inch broad; and in four different places along the line distinctly written "the boundary described by Mr. Oswald."[25]

This map was later restored to the British Museum where it is now preserved.[26]

[25]Benton, *Thirty Years' View,* II, 671. On March 21, Palmerston had made an elaborate attack on the treaty in the House of Commons, in which he criticized the Government for witholding this map (*Hansard* LXVII, 1162). This speech probably attracted Everett's attention.

[26]Moore, *Int. Arbits.,* I, 154–157.

Unjust criticism of Webster

Thus it appears that during the negotiations each party had exclusive control of evidence which strongly sustained the position of the other. It is doubtful, however, whether Lord Ashburton knew of the British Museum map, and in view of the unsatisfactory character of the cartographic and historical evidence Webster would appear to be fully justified in deciding upon a conventional line which, after all, in view of the existing settlements and private rights, probably satisfied the equities of the case better than any line which might have been in the minds of the negotiators of 1782. He had agreed to this course before the map turned up. After his return to England Lord Ashburton wrote:

> The public are very busy with the question whether Webster was bound in honor to damage his own case by telling all. I have put this to the consciences of old diplomatists without getting a satisfactory answer. My own opinion is that in this respect no reproach can fairly be made.[27]

British efforts to suppress the slave trade

The question of search in connection with the suppression of the slave trade, though appearing last in Ashburton's instructions, assumed great prominence in the negotiations and came near disrupting them. After the emancipation act of 1833, abolishing slavery in the British colonies, Lord Palmerston undertook to secure international coöperation for the suppression of the slave trade, and by 1839 Great Britain had signed treaties granting her the right of search with Hayti, Uruguay, Venezuela, Bolivia, Argentina, Mexico, Texas, Denmark, and the Hanse Towns. In 1841 a quintuple treaty was signed by Great Britain, France, Austria, Prussia, and Russia, which provided that

> . . . the high contracting parties agree by common consent that those ships of war which shall be provided with special warrants and orders . . . may search every merchant

[27] E. D. Adams, *Am. His. Rev.*, XVII, 780.

vessel belonging to any of the high contracting parties which shall on reasonable ground be suspected of being engaged in the traffic in slaves.[28]

Cass opposes British plan

General Cass, the American minister at Paris, protested against the ratification of the quintuple treaty by France. He acted without instructions but based his protest on a passage in the President's message to the effect that the United States could "not consent to interpolations into the maritime code at the mere will and pleasure of other governments." In addressing the French government Cass used much stronger language. He said that if France should accept Aberdeen's interpretation that the treaty imposed a duty on France to violate the American flag, then the United States "would prepare themselves with apprehension, indeed, but without dismay, with regret, but with firmness, for one of those desperate struggles which have sometimes occurred in the history of the world." The French government delayed ratifying the treaty for several years and Cass was given credit for defeating the British plan, but other considerations entered into the decision of the French government. President Tyler approved of Cass's note and Webster wrote him to that effect. Cass published anonymously a pamphlet on the right of search which attracted great attention in Europe and America and was reprinted in this country in Niles' *Register* under the author's name. When Webster failed to secure a renunciation of the British practice of search and impressment in the treaty of 1842 Cass announced his intention of resigning his mission and entered upon a very bitter correspondence with Webster which attracted wide attention. Although criticized severely by John Quincy Adams and others for having identified himself with the slave-holding interests, Cass's position that the right of search could be exercised only by

[28]*Cambridge History of British Foreign Policy,* II, 244.

a belligerent was sound from the standpoint both of American policy and international law.[29]

Efforts to prevent abuse of American flag

The engagements England entered into were largely nugatory as long as the United States held aloof, for all that a slaver of any nationality had to do to claim exemption from search was to hoist the American flag. On March 11, 1840, Lieutenant Paine of the United States Navy, who had been assigned to duty on the African coast to prevent this abuse of the American flag, signed with Commander Tucker of the Royal Navy an agreement authorizing the officers of either squadron to detain all vessels under the American flag engaged in the slave trade, those vessels found to be American property to be handed over to the American officers and all others to the British.[30] The activity of the British officers in carrying out this agreement soon gave rise to vehement protests to the United States government against the search of American vessels in time of peace. Stevenson, the American minister in London, was instructed to protest against the search of American vessels by British cruisers. A very hot correspondence ensued between him and Lord Palmerston. In a note dated April 16, 1841, Stevenson declared:

The United States renews protest against search

> The subject has been too repeatedly urged upon the consideration of your Lordship and her Majesty's government, to render a recapitulation of the arguments either necessary or proper. The determination of the United States has been distinctly announced that they could admit no cognizance to be taken by foreign ships, of those belonging to their citizens, on the ocean, and under their flag, either for the purpose of ascertaining whether their papers were genuine or forged, or whether the vessels were slavers or not. That the admission of any such pretension would, in effect, be surrendering the right of search. . . . It becomes my duty therefore again distinctly to express to your Lordship the fixed determination of my govern-

[29] Rives, *Am. Dipl. Under Tyler and Polk*, 33–38; McLaughlin, *Lewis Cass*, Chap. VI.

[30] *British and Foreign State Papers*, XXIX, 624

ment, that their flag is to be the safeguard and protection to the persons and property of its citizens, and all under it, and that these continued aggressions upon the vessels and commerce of the United States cannot longer be permitted.

In reply to the British argument that since the United States had by act of Congress declared the slave trade to be piracy, Great Britain had a right to search vessels suspected of being engaged in the trade, Stevenson said:

The British government reaffirms its position

In making the slave trade piracy, the government of the United States have not thereby made it an offense against the law of nations, inasmuch as one nation cannot increase or limit offenses against public law.[31]

In one of his notes Palmerston referred to the agreement made between Tucker and Paine, but Stevenson replied that he had no knowledge of it except that received from his Lordship and no reason to suppose that such authority had been confided by the American government to any of its naval officers. Palmerston then sent him a copy of the agreement.[32] In Palmerston's last note to Stevenson, August 27, 1841, he reiterated the British position, declaring that

. . . the examination of the papers of merchantmen suspected of being engaged in slave trade, even though they may hoist an United States' flag, is a proceeding which it is absolutely necessary that British cruisers employed in the suppression of the slave trade should continue to practice, and to which her Majesty's government are fully persuaded that the United States government cannot, upon consideration, object.[33]

Change of government

Matters had thus come to an *impasse*, but the tension was fortunately relieved by the changes of government which took place just at this time. Palmerston was succeeded by Aberdeen, who was much more conciliatory in the tone of his dispatches. The correspondence on the

[31] *Op. cit.*, XXX, 1142.

[32] *Ibid.*, p. 1151.

[33] *Ibid.*, p. 1153. The full correspondence is in vol. XXIX, 621–656, 1188–1193, and XXX, 1128–1181.

right of search continued but Stevenson was soon succeeded by Edward Everett, and by the time he arrived the situation had been greatly aggravated by the case of the *Creole*. The *Creole* was an American vessel bound from Hampton Roads to New Orleans with a few passengers and one hundred and thirty-five slaves on board. During the voyage the slaves rose in revolt, wounded several of the crew, killed one of the passengers, and took the vessel into the port of Nassau in the British Bahamas. The local authorities arrested those slaves who were implicated in the murder and set the rest free.[34] This act caused intense indignation in the United States, especially in the South. The Northern abolitionists, however, applauded the act. Webster found himself in the uncomfortable position of having to instruct Everett to make a formal protest to the British government and to secure some guarantee against similar occurrences in the future. Aberdeen's reply was formal, and commended the action of the colonial officials. This note, received in the midst of the Webster-Ashburton negotiations, came dangerously near causing a rupture. Ashburton wrote to Aberdeen, May 12, that "for the present it must not be published here, as it does not suit our present purpose to irritate the Southern people."[35]

Case of the *Creole*

Ashburton hoped to secure a separate treaty covering the right of search and the African slave trade. He realized fully the sensitiveness of the American people and of American statesmen on the subject of the British practice of search and he wrote to Aberdeen that the American attitude on the efforts to suppress the slave trade was due to a fear of the renewal of impressment. Webster proposed that a clause be inserted in the treaty, or a declaration be made by Great Britain, to the following effect:

Webster-Ashburton negotiations on slave trade and impressment

[34]Moore, *Int. Law*, II, 358–361; *British and Foreign State Papers*, XXX, 181–193.

[35]E. D. Adams, in *Am. Hist. Rev.*, XVII, 774.

. . . that in the event of our being engaged in a war in which the United States shall be neutral, impressment from her merchant vessels navigating the high seas will not be practiced, provided that provision be made by law or other competent regulation, that during such war no subject of the crown be entered into the merchant service of America, that shall not have been resident at least five years in the United States.

Ashburton put up a strong argument to Aberdeen in favor of such a declaration.

Impressment, as a system, is an anomaly hardly bearable by our own people. To a foreigner it is undeniable tyranny, which can only be imposed upon him by force, and submitted to by him so long as that force continues. . . . The population of America has more than doubled since the last war, and that war has given her a navy which she had not before, a navy very efficient in proportion to its extent. Under these circumstances can impressment ever be repeated? I apprehend nobody in England thinks it can.[36]

Aberdeen rejected the proposal, stating that it would be "tantamount to an absolute and entire renunciation of the indefeasible right inherent in the British Crown to command the allegience and services of its subjects wherever found." The American government was determined not to permit the right of search unless Great Britain would renounce the alleged right of impressment.

Settlement of the *Creole* case

Webster and Ashburton had also hoped to cover the *Creole* case by including in the proposed article on extradition "mutiny and revolt on board ship," but Aberdeen struck those words out.[37] The prospect for a treaty seemed almost hopeless, but Ashburton and Webster continued their labors. Negotiations in regard to the *Creole* were brought to a close a few days before the treaty was signed by an exchange of notes. Webster set forth the American case in a way that was, Lord Ashburton stated, "mainly calculated to cover his popularity in the South."

---

[36] *Op. cit.*, p. 775.

[37] *Ibid.*, p. 777.

His own reply, Ashburton added, was intended to "evade any engagement," while upholding British principles with regard to slavery. He, however, gave his pledge that instructions would be sent to the governors of her Majesty's colonies that there should be "no officious interference with American vessels driven by accident or by unlawful violence into those ports."[38] The case of the *Creole* was submitted to the mixed claims commission of 1853. The commissioners disagreed, but the umpire awarded the United States the sum of $110,330. This decision gave rise to an animated debate in Parliament, but Great Britain paid for the liberated slaves.[39]

Conclusion of Webster-Ashburton treaty

Finally on August 9, 1842, Webster and Ashburton signed two treaties, one dealing with the boundary, the provisions of which have already been described, and the other dealing with the suppression of the slave trade and extradition. After the two treaties were dispatched to England for ratification Webster decided that in order to secure ratification by the Senate it would be better to combine them in one. This was done.[40] Article VIII provided for joint cruising squadrons on the coast of Africa "to enforce, separately and respectively, the laws, rights, and obligations of each of the two countries for the suppression of the slave trade," under such orders as would "enable them most effectively to act in concert and coöperation." Article IX pledged the two contracting parties to use their influence with other powers in bringing about the closing of slave markets wherever they existed. The treaty was ratified by the Senate by a vote of thirty-nine to nine within ten days after it was received. It was freely criticized in both countries. In England it was referred to as "Ashburton's capitulation," while many Americans were dissatisfied with the boundary compromise

[38] *British and Foreign State Papers*, XXX, 181–193.

[39] Moore, *Int. Arbits.*, I, 417.

[40] Adams, 779.

and the failure to secure a renunciation of the British practice of search.[41] It should be said in behalf of the negotiators, however, that they had tided over a dangerous crisis and that this result had been brought about by discarding the usual formalities of diplomacy and discussing the points at issue in a very free and informal manner. There were no protocols of their conferences and the notes exchanged were discussed and agreed upon before being made official. President Tyler followed the negotiations closely and had no small share in bringing them to a happy conclusion.

Crisis tided over

Comment of Lord Bryce

Lord Bryce has left an interesting comment on the Anglo-American diplomacy of this period:

> Neither American nor British interests were always in the keeping of men so tactful and prudent as Webster and Ashburton. There were moments when the stiff and frigid attitude of the British Foreign Secretary exasperated the American negotiators, or when a demagogic Secretary of State at Washington tried by a bullying tone to win credit as the patriotic champion of national claims. But whenever there were bad manners in London there was good temper at Washington, and when there was a storm on the Potomac there was calm on the Thames. It was the good fortune of the two countries that if at any moment rashness or vehemence was found on one side, it never happened to be met by the like quality on the other.[42]

[41]Webster undertook an elaborate vindication of the treaty in a speech in the Senate April 6 and 7, 1846.

[42]Dunning, *The British Empire and the United States,* Introduction (by Lord Bryce), XXXVII.

PART III

ROUNDING OUT BORDERS AND LOOKING OVER SEAS

CHAPTER X

OREGON AND TEXAS

THE Democratic platform of 1844 declared:

The "Roaring Forties"

> That our title to the whole of the territory of Oregon is clear and unquestionable; that no portion of the same ought to be ceded to England or any other power; and that the re-occupation of Oregon and the re-annexation of Texas at the earliest practicable period are great American measures, which this convention recommends to the cordial support of the Democracy of the Union.[1]

This declaration illustrates the spirited diplomacy of what Professor Dunning calls the "Roaring Forties."[2] It was fortunate for both countries that the unyielding and aggressive nationalism of Palmerston had been replaced by the more conciliatory policy of Peel and Aberdeen.

Conflicting claims to Oregon

The Oregon question, brushed aside during the Webster-Ashburton negotiations by more pressing issues, brought the two countries within the brief space of four years nearer to war than they had been since 1812. Both countries had indisputable claims to territory on the north-west coast, but the claims overlapped to such an extent that it was difficult to draw a line of demarcation. The control of the Columbia River and the territory that drained into it was the main point of contention throughout the controversy. The American claims to this region, as stated officially by John Quincy Adams in 1823, were based

> . . . upon its discovery from the sea and nomination by a citizen of the United States; upon its exploration to the sea by

[1]Stanwood, *History of the Presidency*, 215.

[2]*The British Empire and the United States*, chap. iii.

Captains Lewis and Clarke; upon the settlement of Astoria, made under the protection of the United States, and thus restored to them in 1818; and upon the subsequent acquisition of all the rights of Spain, the only European power who, prior to the discovery of the river, had any pretensions to territorial rights on the Northwest coast of America.[3]

Origin of these claims

Various Spanish explorers are credited with having sailed as far north as Oregon as early as the sixteenth century, and it is possible that Drake may have followed the coast that far north, but the evidence in regard to these voyages is doubtful. An English expedition under Captain Cook sailed up the coast in 1778, and ten years later an American, Captain Gray, followed the same route. Gray returned in 1792 and explored the Columbia River for some miles inland, naming it after his ship. In 1793 Alexander Mackenzie crossed over the mountains from Canada and explored the upper waters of the Frazer River. In 1805, Lewis and Clarke crossed from the head waters of the Missouri to the Columbia and followed its course to the sea. England laid great stress on the Nootka Sound agreement of 1790, by which Spain conceded to the British the right to trade north of the Spanish settlements in California.[4] In 1811, John Jacob Astor launched his fur-trading project, and the little settlement known as Astoria was made at the mouth of the Columbia. As soon as his agents heard that the War of 1812 had begun they sold out to their rivals, the Northwest Company of Canada, and a British squadron a little later took formal possession in the name of their sovereign. At the close of the war the United States insisted on the restoration of Astoria in accordance with the general terms of the Treaty of Ghent. Though at first surprised at the demand, the British government restored the place in 1818.[5]

Astoria

[3]Schafer, "British Attitude toward the Oregon Question," in *Am. Hist. Rev.*, XVI, 288.

[4]Garrison, *Westward Extension*, chap. xi.

[5]Schafer, 281–285.

The British insist on line of Columbia River

In the negotiations that led to the joint-occupation agreement of 1818 the British hoped to establish a line south of the forty-ninth parallel both east and west of the Rockies. They tried first to secure recognition of their claim to territory as far south as the Columbia in the hope that this would influence the determination of the line east of the mountains to a point on the Mississippi due south of the Lake of the Woods. The claim to access to the Mississippi was, of course, based on the clause in the treaty of 1783 giving Great Britain the right to navigate that river. In his instructions to Bagot, Castlereagh said:

> It being obvious that altho' the rights of the respective parties in the interior and on the coast may have taken their origin in circumstances wholly unconnected, that where a line is to be drawn through a territory so wild and uncultivated as that westward of the Mississippi, towards the Pacific, it is for the convenience of both governments first to enquire what their respective rights are upon the sea-coast to which such frontier line is to be drawn, before they proceed to trace the intermediate boundary.[6]

The Americans hold to the forty-ninth parallel

The Americans, on the other hand, realizing that their claim to the valley of the Columbia had been greatly strengthened by the restoration of Astoria, were disposed to let that question rest for the present, and to press for the adoption of the forty-ninth parallel east of the mountains, hoping that in the course of time this would help them to establish the same line west of the mountains. For this reason the United States rejected the British proposal of an arbitration of the whole dispute and pressed for direct negotiations on the boundary from the Lake of the Woods to the Rockies. They succeeded in getting the forty-ninth parallel and proposed to extend it west of the mountains to the sea, but the British insisted on the line of the Columbia River. The Oregon dispute was temporarily postponed by the joint-occupation agreement, which

[6] *Op. cit.*, p. 284.

Spain and Russia eliminated

was to last for ten years. The following year Spain relinquished in favor of the United States all rights north of the forty-second parallel. This defined clearly the southern boundary of the Oregon country, and a few years later its northern limits were fixed at fifty-four degrees and forty minutes by the American and British treaties of 1824 and 1825 with Russia. Great Britain and the United States were now the sole claimants.

Canning endeavors to recover lost ground

In 1826, in view of the approaching expiration of the agreement of 1818, the negotiations were renewed, but Canning insisted on the midstream of the Columbia River from its mouth to the forty-ninth parallel; from that point to the Rockies he was willing to adopt the forty-ninth parallel as the boundary. In a letter to Lord Liverpool, July 7, 1826, he referred to the restoration of Astoria as "absolutely unjustifiable."

> Compare the bill of sale by which the settlement, or blockhouse, of Astoria was made over for a valuable consideration, by a company half British and half American, to a wholly British Company, with the first article of the Treaty of Ghent stipulating the restoration of places "taken" in war; and read Lord Bathurst's despatch directing the surrender to the Yankees of the settlement so bought and sold.[7]

Unfortunately for the British argument, it was after this private commercial transaction that a British naval officer came along and "took" the place, thus bringing it within the scope of the terms of the Treaty of Ghent. Canning urged Liverpool to retrieve the blunder by maintaining their ground. "If we retreat from that, the cession of Astoria will have been but the first symptom of weakness, the first of a series of compliances with encroachments which, if not resisted, will grow upon success." Looking to the future, he declared,

> That the trade between the Eastern and Western Hemispheres direct across the Pacific, is the trade of the world most sus-

[7] *Op. cit.*, p. 291.

ceptible of rapid augmentation and improvement. . . . I should not like to leave my name affixed to an instrument by which England would have foregone the advantages of an immense direct intercourse between China and what may be, if we resolve not to yield them up, her boundless establishments on the N. W. Coast of America.[8]

His vision of the future of the Pacific

Canning died the following year, just two days after Gallatin had signed with Grant and Addington the Convention of August 6, 1827, which extended the joint occupation arrangement indefinitely, subject to termination by either party on twelve months' notice. Canning's Oregon policy was maintained by his successors for nearly twenty years. In the negotiations of 1842, Lord Ashburton was authorized to accept the forty-ninth parallel as the boundary from the Rocky Mountains to the Columbia, but from that point it must follow the middle of the river to the sea. Ashburton stated to Webster, as his personal opinion that, if the United States could secure from Mexico the harbor of San Francisco, Great Britain would not object, provided she got the line of the Columbia. Webster did not consider this proposition favorably, though it was known that he favored the acquisition of California. So the Oregon question was dropped. The following year Webster took up the California question, and in a letter to Everett suggested a tripartite treaty between the United States, Great Britain, and Mexico, by which Mexico was to cede Upper California to the United States for a liberal sum, and out of this sum the claims of American citizens and British subjects against Mexico were to be paid. He coupled with it certain concessions in the matter of the Oregon boundary.[9]

His policy followed by his successors

Ashburton's reason, as stated to his government, for not pressing the Oregon question was the fear that such a

[8] *Op. cit.*, pp. 291–292.

[9] *Ibid.*, pp. 293–294.

Proposals for reopening Oregon negotiations

course would endanger the negotiations in regard to the northeastern boundary, which he considered of much greater importance. When the latter question was out of the way, Lord Aberdeen instructed Fox, the British minister at Washington, October 18, 1842, to propose to Webster that Everett be given instructions to enter into negotiations on the Oregon question in London.[10] Webster agreed to this proposal, and a few weeks later President Tyler announced in his annual message that he intended to urge upon the British government the importance of an early settlement of the question. Aberdeen remonstrated against this statement as misleading, since the President had before him when he wrote his message the British proposal and Webster's assent to it.[11] Webster's retirement delayed matters and no instructions were sent to Everett. In the President's annual message of 1843 the statement of the previous year in regard to the Oregon question was repeated, to the further annoyance of Fox and Aberdeen. Fox was now succeeded by Pakenham and, in view of the apparent reluctance of the American government to open negotiations in London, the new minister was authorized to consent to the negotiations taking place in Washington.[12] Upshur's sudden death and Calhoun's attention to the Texas treaty caused another delay. The negotiations were finally taken up in August and September, 1844. Pakenham offered the United States a free port or ports on Vancouver or the mainland south of the forty-ninth parallel, but insisted on the line of the Columbia. Calhoun refused to surrender the claim to the valley of the Columbia, and the negotiations came to an end.[13]

During these negotiations the presidential campaign was

[10] *British and Foreign State Papers,* XXXIV, 49–50

[11] *Ibid.*, p. 52.

[12] *Ibid.*, p. 56.

[13] *Ibid.*, pp. 60–86.

"Fifty-Four Forty or Fight"

in full swing, and the Democratic slogan was "Fifty-Four Forty or Fight." Since England persisted in rejecting the forty-ninth parallel, which was a fair division and which the United States had repeatedly proposed, there was nothing to do but seize the whole territory and let England fight if she wanted to. Such was the Democratic argument, but it was believed that England would agree to the forty-ninth parallel rather than go to war. No one had ever seriously maintained that the United States had a valid claim to the whole territory.

President Polk's position

In January, 1845, Pakenham proposed arbitration, but Calhoun replied that the President still hoped that the question might be settled by direct negotiations. Nothing further was done during Tyler's administration. In view of the platform on which Polk had been elected, the paragraph of his inaugural address devoted to Oregon was briefer and milder than might have been expected. The most significant passage was the statement that it would be his

> . . . duty to assert and maintain by all constitutional means the right of the United States to that portion of our territory which lies beyond the Rocky Mountains. Our title to the country of Oregon is "clear and unquestionable," and already are our people preparing to perfect that title by occupying it with their wives and children.

The British position

When the subject of the President's address came up in the House of Commons, Peel reviewed the efforts to arrive at a settlement in a conciliatory tone, and expressed regret at the means adopted by the new President to make known his views. He concluded with a statement of policy which had evidently been carefully considered and agreed upon, for Aberdeen made the same statement in the House of Lords. Peel said:

> I feel it my imperative duty on the part of the British government to state in language the most temperate, but at the same

time the most decided, that we consider we have rights respecting this territory of Oregon which are clear and unquestionable. We trust still to arrive at an amicable adjustment . . . but, having exhausted every effort to effect that settlement, if our rights shall be invaded, we are resolved and we are prepared—to maintain them.[14]

Polk again proposes forty-ninth parallel

These were solemn words, solemnly spoken, and the situation was one that would have led to war had not both parties desired to avoid a conflict. Polk and Buchanan, his Secretary of State, now had the embarrassing problem of withdrawing from the "Fifty-Four Forty or Fight" position. The Mexican situation made a settlement with England a matter of vital importance. Buchanan reopened the Oregon question in a note to Pakenham dated July 12, 1845. In a long argument he asserted "exclusive rights over the whole territory in dispute as against Great Britain," but he added that the President "found himself embarrassed, if not committed, by the acts of his predecessors," who "had uniformly proceeded upon the principle of compromise in all their negotiations." The President, therefore, had instructed him to propose "that the Oregon territory shall be divided between the two countries by the 49th parallel of north latitude from the Rocky Mountains to the Pacific Ocean; offering, at the same time, to make free to Great Britain any port or ports on Vancouver's Island, south of this parallel, which the British government may desire."[15]

British minister indignantly rejects proposal

Pakenham was so indignant at the proposal to run the line through the island of Vancouver that he made the mistake of rejecting the proposal without referring it to London, and requested Buchanan to submit another proposal "more consistent with fairness and equity, and with the reasonable expectations of the British government."[16] Polk then directed Buchanan to withdraw the

[14] *Cambridge History of British Foreign Policy*, II, 258.

[15] *British and Foreign State Papers*, XXXIV, 100–101.

[16] *Ibid.*, p. 110.

American proposal. Buchanan did so in a long note, in which he again reviewed the controversy. He also took exception to the language of the British minister and to the summary manner in which the proposal had been rejected. In conclusion, however, he said:

> In taking this step, the President still cherishes the hope that this long-pending controversy may yet be finally adjusted in such a manner as not to disturb the peace or interrupt the harmony now so happily subsisting between the two countries.[17]

Polk looks John Bull in the eye

In his annual message of December 2, 1845, Polk reviewed the controversy, again emphasizing the repeated offers of the United States to compromise on the forty-ninth parallel, and declared:

> The civilized world will see in these proceedings a spirit of liberal concession on the part of the United States, and this government will be relieved from all responsibility which may follow the failure to settle the controversy.

He requested authority to give England the required year's notice of the termination of the joint-occupation agreement, and asked Congress to take the necessary steps for the protection of American citizens in the territory and "the maintenance of our just title." In his private Diary he made this note:

> The only way to treat John Bull is to look him in the eye. . . . If Congress falters or hesitates in their course, John Bull will immediately become arrogant and more grasping in his demands.

Rejects offer of arbitration

Meanwhile Pakenham had requested Buchanan to renew the proposition which had been rejected. This Buchanan refused to do, and Pakenham then proposed arbitration again.[18] Several notes on the subject were exchanged, but

[17] *Op. cit.*, XXXIV, 130.

[18] *Cambridge History of British Foreign Policy*, II, 259.

the proposal was declined. In communicating the President's decision Buchanan said:

> He believes that as there are no two nations on earth more closely bound together by the ties of commerce, so there are none who ought to be more able or willing to do each other justice, without the interposition of any arbitrator.[19]

England agrees to forty-ninth parallel

The resolution of Congress authorizing the President to serve notice of the denunciation of the convention of 1827 was communicated to the British government in a courteous way so as to leave the door open to further negotiation, but Polk let it be known that any proposition would have to come from England. He also let it be known that, notwithstanding his withdrawal of the offer of the forty-ninth parallel, he would submit to the Senate a proposition of that kind coming from Great Britain. Peel and Aberdeen finally sent over to Pakenham a draft treaty dividing the territory by the forty-ninth parallel from the Rockies to the Straits of Fuca and along the straits to the ocean, thus retaining the whole of Vancouver's Island for Great Britain. The treaty also granted to the Hudson's Bay Company the right to navigate the Columbia River from the forty-ninth parallel to the sea. The President threw the responsibility upon the Senate by submitting the treaty before it was signed. On June 12 the Senate, by a vote of 37 to 12, advised the acceptance of the British proposal, and on June 15 the treaty was signed in the exact form submitted by Peel and Aberdeen. Polk was relieved at having the dispute ended, for war with Mexico had already been declared, and there was now no danger of British interference either in Mexico or California.

The Texas question, linked with that of Oregon in the Democratic platform of 1844, had far wider ramifications. It assumed, in fact, the dignity of a world problem, for it

[19]*British and Foreign State Papers,* XXXIV, 137–145.

The Texas question

involved not merely the United States, Texas, and Mexico, but Great Britain and France as well. The efforts of these two great European powers to prevent the annexation of Texas to the United States constitute one of the most interesting and important chapters in the international politics of that day. It is, moreover, a new chapter, for the documentary material relating to the subject in the archives of Texas, Mexico, and Great Britain has only recently been made available.[20] The exploration of these archives has brought about a remarkable reversal of the earlier verdict of history on this period of American diplomacy. All the older accounts were colored by the violent prejudices of contemporary anti-slavery agitators and writers who professed to see in the movement for annexation nothing but a slaveholders' conspiracy to acquire more territory, and who closed their eyes to all evidences of the diplomatic intrigues of England and France—intrigues which, if successful, would have excluded the United States not only from Texas, but from California and Oregon as well. American historians, with rare exceptions, for half a century perpetuated without investigation the anti-slavery tradition, and denounced Tyler and Polk in intemperate and ofttimes violent language for having gained for their country the great Southwest and access to the Pacific. The explanation is simple enough. The acquisition of territory resulting from the Mexican War reopened the slavery question in Congress and started a new phase of the great sectional debate which hastened, if it did not make inevitable, the Civil War. The victorious North looked back upon the Mexican War as a crime perpetrated on an innocent neighbor by the slaveholding South. General Grant expressed the prevailing opinion in his personal memoirs, when he said:

The traditional view

[20]*Diplomatic Correspondence of the Republic of Texas*, edited by G. P. Garrison (An. Rpts., Am. Hist. Assn., 1907, 1908); E. D. Adams, *British Interests and Activities in Texas, 1838-1845* (1910); Justin H. Smith, *The Annexation of Texas* (1911), and *The War with Mexico*, 2 vols (1919).

Grant and Foster

The Southern Rebellion was largely the outgrowth of the Mexican War. Nations like individuals are punished for their transgressions. We got our punishment in the most sanguinary and expensive war of modern times.

John W. Foster quotes this with approval and emphasizes the slaveholders' conspiracy idea.[21] In striking contrast with the views of Grant and Foster is the statement of the case by John Bassett Moore:

Dissenting views of John Bassett Moore and

No acquisition of territory by the United States has been the subject of so much honest but partisan misconception as that of the annexation of Texas. By a school of writers whose views have had great currency, the annexation has been denounced as the result of a plot of the slave-power to extend its dominions. But, calmly surveying the course of American expansion, we are forced to conclude that no illusion could be more complete. It would be more nearly correct to say that, but for the controversy concerning slavery, there would have been no appreciable opposition in the United States to the acquisition of Texas. Such local antagonism as might have existed to the disturbance of the balance of power in the Union would have been overwhelmed by the general demand for an extension of boundaries so natural and, except for the slavery question, in every respect so expedient.[22]

James G. Blaine

It is interesting to note in this connection that James G. Blaine recorded a judgment on the annexation of Texas and the Mexican War wholly at variance with that prevailing in his day. Although a violent partisan in the days of Reconstruction, he usually took a liberal view of questions of foreign policy. In his memoirs he wrote:

It was wiser policy to annex Texas, and accept the issue of immediate war with Mexico, than to leave Texas in nominal independence to involve us probably in ultimate war with England. The entire history of subsequent events has vindicated the

[21] *A Century of American Diplomacy*, 321.

[22] *Principles of American Diplomacy*, 350. The same statement occurs in the edition of 1905, so that Moore came to this conclusion from a study of the material in the State Department before that in the foreign archives had been fully explored.

wisdom, the courage, and the statesmanship with which the Democratic party dealt with this question in 1844.[23]

Tyler and Polk not the only intriguers

While it may be assumed that the American people have become reconciled in the course of two generations to the possession of Texas and California, nevertheless the view still prevails very generally that these territories were acquired by methods of intrigue and conspiracy, which have left a blot on the national escutcheon. There should be some satisfaction, however, in knowing that Tyler and Polk were not the only intriguers and conspirators; that Lord Aberdeen made every effort to form an alliance against the United States for the purpose of making Texas a cotton-growing dependency of Great Britain; that Louis Philippe encouraged the scheme with a view to extending to America his favorite principle of the balance of power; that Texas, discouraged by the refusal of the Van Buren administration to receive her into the Union, was on the point of being seduced by the European offers of protection; that the Mexican leaders played fast and loose with the situation in order to gain political advantage at home; and that through this maze of diplomatic intrigue Tyler and Polk led the country to a successful issue. But success however great does not justify dishonorable methods. Were the methods employed dishonorable, or did the contemporary opinions of the anti-slavery party merely become crystallized into a national tradition when that party acquired the ascendancy in the Union? This question can be answered only by a review of the case with the new material recently brought to light before us.

Whatever claim the United States had to Texas as a part of the Louisiana Purchase was, as we have seen, surrendered to Spain in the so-called Florida treaty of 1819.[24] By the time this treaty was ratified in 1821, Mexico had

[23] *Twenty Years in Congress,* I, 40.

[24] *Ante*, p. 118.

Spanish treaty of 1819 unexecuted when Mexico becomes independent

revolted against Spain and set up a *de facto* government, which was recognized by the United States in 1822.[25] Article IV of the Florida treaty had provided for the appointment of a commission to survey and mark the southwestern boundary, but as a result of the Mexican revolution this article remained unexecuted. Was the Spanish treaty binding upon the United States and Mexico and should they proceed to mark the boundary in accordance with the provisions of Article IV? This was the first question that arose after the recognition by the United States of Mexican independence.

Both Mexico and United States delay marking boundary

The first Mexican minister sent to Washington was instructed to say that the Mexican government recognized the treaty of 1819 as valid and was disposed to carry out the provisions for surveying and marking the boundary.[26] But the United States was in no hurry to take this view of the case. American settlers were already going into Texas, and there was a widespread feeling that a great mistake had been made in surrendering the country to Spain. John Quincy Adams, the Secretary of State who had negotiated the treaty, was now a candidate for the presidency, and his enemies were charging him with the responsibility for the loss of Texas. That is probably the reason why the Mexican envoy could get no acknowledgment from the American government that it regarded the treaty of 1819 as binding under the change of sovereignty. At any rate, no step was taken by the United States toward settling the boundary question until after the presidential election.

Clay proposes different boundary

When Adams became President in March, 1825, he appointed Henry Clay Secretary of State and Joel R. Poinsett minister to Mexico. Poinsett was instructed by Clay to regard the treaty of 1819 as "obligatory upon

[25]Manning, *Early Diplomatic Relations Between the United States and Mexico*, 12, 277.

[26]*Ibid.*, p. 277.

both the United States and Mexico," but as the boundary outlined in that treaty was unsatisfactory and liable to lead to disputes he was directed to find out whether the Mexican government would be willing to establish a new line—that of the Brazos, or the Colorado, or the Snow Mountains, or the Rio Grande.[27] If he found the Mexican government unwilling to negotiate a new line, he was to arrange to carry out the treaty of 1819. During the negotiations it developed that while the Mexican government expressed its willingness to abide by the treaty of 1819, it was in reality delaying a settlement with the hope of ultimately gaining the extreme limits claimed by Spain before the negotiation of that treaty. Meanwhile American settlers were pouring into Texas and receiving liberal grants of land from the Mexican government. Under these circumstances, President Adams decided to make an offer for the purchase of Texas. On March 15, 1827, Clay wrote to Poinsett that the extensive grants of land made to citizens of the United States "without any sort of equivalent, judging according to our opinions of the value of the land," authorized the belief that but little value was placed upon the province of Texas by the Mexican government. Poinsett was, therefore, authorized to offer one million dollars for the line of the Rio Grande, or half that sum for the line of the Colorado.[28] Poinsett made no formal attempt to carry out these instructions. He believed that the sum proposed was too small, and on sounding certain members of the government he found that there was little chance of gaining the consent of either house of the Mexican congress to a sale of any part of Texas. He abandoned the idea of purchase, therefore, and on January 12, 1828, signed a treaty recognizing, and providing for the marking of, the boundary of the treaty of 1819. This treaty was promptly

Adams offers to purchase Texas, whole or part

[27] *Op. cit.*, pp. 286–288.

[28] *Ibid.*, pp. 306–308.

ratified by the United States Senate, but the Mexican government delayed action until the period set for the exchange of ratifications had expired, and as a result of this delay the treaty did not go into effect until 1832.[29]

Jackson renews offer of purchase

About six months after Jackson became President, Van Buren instructed Poinsett to renew the overtures for the purchase of Texas. Four possible lines for the new boundary were suggested. For the first line, running through the center of the Grand Prairie between the Nueces and the Rio Grande, he was authorized to offer four million dollars, or if he "should find it indispensably necessary, to go as high as five millions." For the other proposed lines he was to offer proportionate amounts.[30] Poinsett regarded it as useless to attempt another negotiation, and no effort was made to carry out the instructions until the arrival of his successor, Colonel Anthony Butler.

The Texan Revolution

Rumors that Butler was authorized to renew negotiations for the purchase of Texas reached Mexico before he did and aroused great indignation. In April, 1830, the Mexican Congress, in response to this feeling, passed a law suspending land grants to colonists and prohibiting further immigration into Texas from the United States. It was found impossible to enforce this law, and its only effect was to produce friction and hasten revolution. In 1835, the Texans drove out the Mexican troops. The following year an army under General Santa Anna, the President of Mexico, undertook the reconquest of the province, but was defeated by the Texans under General Sam Houston at the battle of San Jacinto, April 21, 1836. A month earlier the Republic of Texas had adopted a constitution recognizing the institution of slavery. This constitution did not introduce slavery, as is frequently stated. Various measures looking to the gradual extinction of slavery had been taken, and General Guerrero had issued a decree in

Status of slavery

[29] *Op. cit.*, pp. 312–322.

[30] *Ibid.*, pp. 336–346.

1829 abolishing slavery in Mexico, but this had later been modified so as not to include Texas. The constitution of Texas annulled all legislation relating to the extinction of slavery. Many of the colonists were from the slave-holding states, and there were a large number of slaves in the province, but a study of the early stages of the colonization of Texas discovers no evidence of the "conspiracy" to extend slave territory. That was not the motive that led settlers into the country. Some of the leaders, like Austin, came from free states, while others came from the mountains of Virginia, Tennessee, and Kentucky, where slavery as an institution had gained little foothold. Adventurous spirits were drawn to Texas because it was a good frontier. The advance to the Southwest was typical of the general westward movement.[31]

American sympathy for Texas

The Texas struggle for independence was regarded with interest and sympathy in the United States, and the government found it difficult to enforce its neutrality acts. Sam Houston, Davy Crockett, and other men of prominence, as well as hundreds unknown to fame, went down to join the revolutionary army. When the constitution of Texas was submitted to the people in September, 1836, they were also called upon to vote on the question of annexation to the United States, and the result showed that they were overwhelmingly in favor of it. But the moment was not favorable. The slavery question was rapidly becoming a fundamental issue in American politics, and John Quincy Adams, who had earlier favored the annexation of Texas, was now leading a bitter fight for the right of the abolitionists to have their petitions presented and read before Congress. The movement for annexation delayed the recognition of Texan independence. Jackson displayed unwonted caution, and notwithstanding the fact that both House and Senate had passed resolutions favorable to recognition, in his message of

Jackson delays recognition

[31]Garrison, *Westward Extension*, 23–34.

December 21, 1836, he urged delay "at least until the lapse of time or the course of events shall have proved beyond cavil or dispute the ability of the people of that country to maintain their separate sovereignty and to uphold the government constituted by them."[32] On the last day of his administration Jackson approved the general appropriation act, which made provision for "the outfit and salary of a diplomatic agent to be sent to the Republic of Texas, whenever the President of the United States may receive satisfactory evidence that Texas is an independent power, and shall deem it expedient to appoint such minister." On March 7, 1837, the independence of Texas was recognized when President Van Buren appointed a *chargé d'affaires* to that republic.[33] There is no evidence connecting Jackson with any secret intrigues in regard to the revolution or annexation. There is little doubt that he hoped to see Texas come into the Union, but he realized the danger of hasty action and he was determined to uphold the dignity and honor of the United States.[34]

Van Buren rejects offer of annexation

In August, 1837, the Republic of Texas, acting through its minister at Washington, made a formal proposal to the Van Buren administration to negotiate a treaty of annexation. The offer was promptly declined in no uncertain terms. Secretary Forsyth replied to the Texas minister that so long as Texas and Mexico remained at war a consideration of the proposal would involve the question of war between the United States and Mexico, and that in view of the treaty of amity and commerce with Mexico, even to reserve the overture for future consideration "would imply a disposition on our part to espouse the quarrel of Texas."[35]

---

[32]Richardson, *Messages and Papers of the Presidents,* III, 265.

[33]Moore, *Dig. of Int. Law,* I, 101.

[34]Barker, "President Jackson and the Texas Revolution," in *Am. Hist. Rev.,* XII, 788.

[35]The full correspondence will be found in 25 Cong., 1 Sess., House Exec. Doc. No. 40.

John Quincy Adams reviews Texas question

On January 4, 1838, resolutions were introduced in the Senate and House by Preston and Waddy Thompson, both of South Carolina, the one authorizing, and the other directing, the President to take the necessary steps for the annexation of Texas by treaty. The Senate resolution was tabled June 14 by a vote of 24 to 14, and the House resolution was talked to death by John Quincy Adams, who spoke in opposition to it every day for three weeks. He complained later that Congress adjourned before he could finish his speech, and reviewed the entire subject in 1842 in an address to his constituents which runs through several numbers of Niles' *Register*.[36] He boasted of the fact that as Secretary of State he had tried to secure the recognition of the claim of the United States to the whole of Texas, and in the negotiation of the treaty of 1819 had stood out for the line of the Rio Grande until overruled by the other members of the cabinet and directed by President Monroe to abandon it. Later, in 1825, as President he had tried to purchase Texas with the consent of the owner. But at that time slavery did not exist in Texas.[37] Without slavery and with the consent of Mexico he would still favor annexation.

Threats of nullification

As soon as it became known in 1843 that President Tyler was contemplating annexation, Adams presented the following resolution to the Committee on Foreign Relations:

> That any attempt of the government of the United States, by an act of Congress or by treaty, to annex to this Union the republic of Texas, or the people thereof, would be a violation of the Constitution of the United States, null and void, and to which the free States of this Union and their people ought not to submit.

The committee refused to report the resolution to the House, but Adams, Giddings, and other anti-slavery lead-

[36]Vol. LXIII, 136–140, contains the first instalment.

[37]This statement, as we have already pointed out, was not correct.

ers issued an address to the people of the free states, in which they declared:

Threats of secession in case Texas should be annexed

> We hesitate not to say that annexation, effected by any act or proceeding of the federal government, or any of its departments, would be identical with dissolution. It would be a violation of our national compact, its objects, designs, and the great elementary principles which entered into its formation, of a character so deep and fundamental, and would be an attempt to eternize an institution and a power of nature so unjust in themselves and abhorrent to the feelings of the people of the free states, as, in our opinion, not only inevitably to result in a dissolution of the union, but fully to justify it; and we not only assert that the people of the free states "ought not to submit to it," but we say with confidence, THEY WOULD NOT SUBMIT TO IT.[38]

Tyler favors annexation

Tyler's decision to take up the Texas question was reached in the summer of 1843. Although from the first strongly in favor of annexation, he delayed taking action in the matter because he did not believe he could get a treaty ratified by the Senate. Since his break with the Whigs there was strong personal as well as political opposition to him in that body. He had, therefore, rejected President Houston's renewed overtures in 1841 and again in 1842. But during the summer of 1843 a truce had been brought about between Texas and Mexico through the efforts of the British and French ministers in Mexico, and the growing influence of Great Britain and France in Texas began to cause serious apprehensions in Washington. Furthermore, following the armistice President Houston instructed Isaac Van Zandt, his representative in Washington, to state "that the subject of annexation was not open to discussion." Various interpretations have been given of Houston's apparently shifting policy during the years 1841–1844, but the truth seems to be that he did not care for Texas to appear any longer as a suppliant, and he believed that the United States could be forced to take

Houston's policy

[38]Niles' *Register*, LXIV, 174–175. (Capitals in the original.)

the initiative. In order to spur on annexation sentiment in the United States, he made good use of Great Britain's prominence in arranging the armistice, and took no pains to conceal his negotiations with the European powers.[39]

Alleged British schemes for abolition in Texas

What caused most alarm in Washington, however, were the reports that Great Britain was negotiating with Texas for the abolition of slavery. These reports came mainly from Ashbel Smith, the Texas representative in London. On January 25, 1843, he wrote a "confidential" letter to Van Zandt, the Texas *chargé* in Washington, which was probably communicated to some member of Tyler's cabinet, in which he said:

> It is the purpose of some persons in England to procure the abolition of slavery in Texas. They propose to accomplish this end by friendly negotiation and by the concession of what will be deemed equivalents. I believe the equivalents contemplated are a guarantee by Great Britain of the independence of Texas—discriminating duties in favor of Texan products and perhaps the negotiation of a loan, or some means by which the finances of Texas can be readjusted. They estimate the number of slaves in Texas at 12,000 and would consider the payment for them in full, as a small sum for the advantages they anticipate from the establishment of a free state on the southern borders of the slave holding States of the American Union.[40]

Report of Aberdeen's views

A little later an extract from one of Smith's letters to Anson Jones, Secretary of State of Texas, was placed in Calhoun's hands. It reported Lord Aberdeen as stating in an interview with Smith that it was the well-known policy and wish of the British government to abolish slavery everywhere, and that its abolition in Texas was deemed very desirable not only from the standpoint of British interests, but also with reference to its future influence on slavery in the United States.[41]

Fearing that there was danger in delay, President Tyler

[39]Garrison, chap. viii; Reeves, chap. v.

[40]*Dip. Cor. of the Republic of Texas,* Part III, 1105.

[41]"Correspondence of Calhoun," *An. Report of Am. Historical Association,* 1899, Vol. II, 866.

Houston receives American overtures cautiously

directed Secretary Upshur to propose negotiations for a treaty of annexation. This he did in a letter to Van Zandt of October 16, 1843. The latter replied that he would have to write home for instructions. President Houston showed no eagerness to seize the opportunity. In fact, he questioned the likelihood of ratification, and stated that the acceptance of the proposal would alienate England, and that, if the treaty should then be rejected by the Senate, Texas would be left "in an extremely awkward situation." Upshur replied that measures had been taken to ascertain the views of Senators and "it is found that a clear constitutional majority of two-thirds are in favor of the measure."[42] Houston then demanded that before entering into negotiations United States forces be placed near the Texas border and in the Gulf so as to be in a position to render aid in case of attack from Mexico. This demand was finally complied with.[43]

The Texas question in the House of Lords

Meanwhile a discussion had taken place in the House of Lords in August, 1843, between Lord Brougham and Lord Aberdeen on the subject of abolition in Texas, and its ultimate effect on slavery in the United States. Upshur at once protested through Everett against certain statements which seemed to imply an intention on the part of the British government to foster abolition in Texas as a preliminary to a general attack on slavery in the United States, and directed him to demand an explicit statement or explanation of British policy.[44] Lord Aberdeen's reply to Everett was not very satisfactory,[45] and the rumors as to British designs continued to arouse bad feeling in Washington. In order to quiet matters, Lord Aberdeen felt it incumbent upon him to make a definite statement to the American government, which he did in a dispatch

[42] 28 Cong., 1 Sess., Sen. Ex. Doc. No. 341, p. 47

[43] *Ibid.*, pp. 74–81.

[44] *Ibid.*, p. 27.

[45] *Ibid.*, p. 38.

to Pakenham, December 26, 1843. He declared that it must be well known to the United States and to the whole world

Aberdeen defines his policy

> . . . that Great Britain desires, and is constantly exerting herself to procure, the general abolition of slavery throughout the world. But the means which she has adopted, and will continue to adopt, for this humane and virtuous purpose, are open and undisguised. She will do nothing secretly or underhand. She desires that her motives may be generally understood and her acts seen by all.
>
> With regard to Texas, we avow that we wish to see slavery abolished there, as elsewhere; and we should rejoice if the recognition of that country by the Mexican government should be accompanied by an engagement on the part of Texas to abolish slavery eventually, and under proper conditions, throughout the Republic. . . .
>
> Great Britain, moreover, does not desire to establish in Texas . . . any dominant influence . . . . and she has no thought or intention of seeking to act directly or indirectly, in a political sense, on the United States through Texas.[46]

Calhoun replies to Aberdeen

This dispatch was not transmitted to the American government by Pakenham until February 26, 1844. Two days later Secretary Upshur met his tragic death in the explosion on board the *Princeton*, and his successor, Calhoun, did not enter upon his duties until April. 1. On the 18th he addressed a reply to Pakenham, in which he expressed the deep concern of the President at the avowal of Lord Aberdeen of Great Britain's desire to see slavery abolished in Texas, and of her efforts to make the abolition of slavery one of the conditions of the recognition by Mexico of Texan independence. He stated that the President had felt it to be "the imperious duty" of the Federal government "to adopt in self-defense the most effectual measures to defeat" the British policy, and the President

> . . . directs me to inform you that a treaty has been concluded between the United States and Texas, for the annex-

[46] *Op. cit.*, p. 48; *British and Foreign State Papers*, XXXIII, 232.

ation of the latter to the former, as a part of its territory, which will be submitted without delay to the Senate for its approval. This step has been taken as the most effectual, if not the only means of guarding against the threatened danger.

Calhoun concluded his note with an array of census statistics showing a great increase in deafness, blindness, insanity, and idiocy among negroes in the states which had abolished slavery, from which he drew the conclusion that so far as the United States was concerned the British policy of emancipation would be neither wise nor humane.[47]

Pakenham protests against Calhoun's conclusions

The day after receiving this note Pakenham made a rejoinder protesting in the name of his government against assigning to it any share of responsibility for the annexation of Texas. He declared that a false inference had been drawn from Lord Aberdeen's dispatch. In a second letter Calhoun stated that he had carefully read the dispatch again and could find nothing in it to weaken the President's inference that Great Britain was endeavoring through diplomacy to bring about abolition in Texas.[48] Calhoun has been severely criticized for identifying the cause of annexation with the defense of slavery, but it is not probable that this Pakenham correspondence affected the vote either way.

Tyler submits annexation treaty to Senate

The treaty of annexation was signed April 12, 1844, and laid before the Senate with a message from the President and accompanying documents April 22.[49] It was doomed from the first, partly because of political and personal opposition to President Tyler, and partly because of its presentation at an unpropitious moment—the eve of the presidential campaign. The Whig party held its convention in Baltimore the first of May, and amid great enthusiasm nominated Henry Clay for President. Shortly before the meeting of the convention Clay had announced

[47] 28 Cong., 1 Sess., Sen. Doc. No. 341, p. 50; *British and Foreign State Papers*, XXXIII, 236.

[48] *British and Foreign State Papers,* XXXIII, 240–245.

[49] 28 Cong., 1 Sess., Sen. Doc. No. 341, pp. 1–119.

his opposition to annexation on the ground that it would involve the country in war with Mexico. By a strange coincidence Van Buren, the leading candidate for the Democratic nomination, made a similar announcement the same day. His opposition to annexation was well known and had been anticipated by Clay, who was afraid of the Texas issue and hoped thus to eliminate it from the campaign. The nomination of Polk by the Democrats four weeks later and the emphatic demand in the platform for the "reannexation of Texas at the earliest practicable period" came as a complete surprise and proved Clay's undoing.

The treaty rejected

A week after the adjournment of the Democratic convention the Senate rejected the treaty by a vote of thirty-five to sixteen. Of the twenty-nine Whigs in the Senate all save one, Henderson of Mississippi, voted against the treaty, thus endorsing the position of their candidate. Of the twenty-three Democrats only fifteen voted for the treaty; seven voted with the Whigs, and one absented himself when the vote was taken. The split in the Democratic ranks was due partly to opposition to Tyler and partly to dissatisfaction resulting from the defeat of Van Buren. Aside from this it was a party vote. It was at any rate not sectional, for five votes from the free states were cast for the treaty and fifteen from the slave states against it.[50] Strange to say, opposition to the annexation of Texas played a minor part in the defeat of the treaty. Van Zandt and Henderson, who negotiated the treaty on behalf of Texas, wrote to their government two days after its rejection as follows:

Annexation merely deferred

> You will see from the speeches made during the discussion that the majority of those who voted against ratifying the treaty, are in favor of annexing Texas at some future period. . . The question of the annexation of Texas to this government has become strictly a party question between the demo-

[50] Garrison, 120; Smith, *Annexation of Texas*, 272.

crats and whigs in the pending contest for the next Presidency, and should the former party succeed in electing their nominee we can not doubt that Texas can be annexed under his administration, if she desire it.[51]

British interest in Texas

Meanwhile Great Britain and France had not been inactive spectators of the course of events in America. There were many reasons why Great Britain should oppose the annexation of Texas by the United States. In the first place, she did not care to see the area, wealth, and population of the United States so greatly increased; in the second place, she did not care to see the Mexican republic, where she had large interests, subjected to the danger of absorption by her more powerful northern neighbor; and in the third place, she did not care to see the hold of the United States on the Gulf of Mexico strengthened. Her opposition to the extension of slavery has already been discussed. These were general considerations.[52] A more impelling motive was undoubtedly this: that England wished to encourage the development of Texas as a cotton-growing country from which she could draw a large enough supply to make her independent of the United States. If Texas should thus devote herself to the production of cotton as her chief export crop, she would, of course, adopt a free-trade policy, and thus create a considerable market for British goods. Great Britain would thus be enabled to make an important flank movement against America's tariff; for if British goods were allowed free entrance into Texas, it would be very difficult to prevent their being smuggled across the border into the United States.[53]

For the above reasons, therefore, Great Britain consistently opposed the annexation of Texas to the United States, and entered into negotiations with France, Mexico,

[51] *Diplomatic Correspondence of the Republic of Texas,* Part II, 284.

[52] Smith, *Annexation of Texas,* 382.

[53] *Dip. Cor. of Republic of Texas,* Part III, 1104–1105.

Steps taken by Britain to prevent American annexation

and the Republic of Texas for the express purpose of preventing the consummation of American policy. As soon as it became evident that Tyler contemplated taking definite measures looking toward annexation, Lord Aberdeen instructed the British ambassador at Paris to confer with Guizot, and to say that since the government of Louis Philippe had recognized the new republic, and "the interests of the two countries in that part of America were, in all respects, the same," he presumed that France, like England, "would not look with indifference upon any measure, by which Texas should cease to exist as a separate and independent state." He proposed, therefore, "that the representatives of the two governments at Washington and in Texas should be instructed to hold the same language; deprecating all interference on the part of the United States in the affairs of Texas," and "at the same time, warning the Texian government not to furnish the United States with any just cause of complaint."[54] Guizot appears to have concurred entirely with the views of the British government, and on February 10, 1844, Pageot, the French minister at Washington, was instructed to inform the government of the United States that even should the people of Texas wish to be annexed, France "could not view such an event with indifference."

French policy in accord with British

Guizot made the interesting statement in the Chamber of Deputies that the new republic had been recognized in order to obtain raw materials on better terms than the United States would give, to secure lower duties than the American rates, and to acquire valuable markets. He also dwelt upon the idea of a balance of power in America, and urged the value of Texas as a barrier against the United States. Besides these reasons, it was the general policy of Louis Philippe to cultivate friendly relations with England. He felt, according to Edward Everett, that "without the goodwill of the present British govern-

[54]Smith, *Annexation of Texas*, 383.

ment his own would sink." Although, therefore, the French government cared much less about Texas than did the British government, it determined to protest formally against the annexation of Texas to the United States. Pageot's instructions to this effect reached him at Washington about the time that Calhoun signed the annexation treaty. He conferred fully with Pakenham, the British minister, about the matter, and they concluded that a mere protest, "unsupported by an intimation of more decisive measures of resistance," would be insufficient to check the intentions of the American government. Furthermore, they both thought that any step taken by them at this time would arouse a popular outcry which would weaken the anti-annexation strength in the Senate, and thus do more harm than good. They agreed, therefore, that no protest should be made.[55]

The Murphy memorandum

In May, 1844, Lord Aberdeen had an important conversation with Murphy, the Mexican representative at London. A memorandum of what was said, drawn up by Murphy in French, was modified by Aberdeen in English. The important part of this, with Aberdeen's modifications in italics, was as follows:

> Lord Aberdeen expressed a wish to see Mexico acknowledge the independence of Texas. "If Mexico," he said, "will concede this point, England (and I have reason to believe that France will join with her in this determination) will oppose the annexation of Texas and moreover *he would endeavor that* France and England will unite in guaranteeing not only the independence of Texas, but also the boundary of Mexico. On the other hand should Mexico persist in declining to recognize Texas, the intentions of England to prevent the annexation of that country to the United States might not be put in execution." Upon my remarking that it was not at all probable that the American Government would be willing to drop the annexation affair, even should the American Senate reject the Treaty for the present, Lord Aberdeen replied that *provided that England and France were perfectly agreed,* "it would matter little to England

[55] *Op. cit.*, pp. 387–388.

whether the American Government should be willing to drop this question or not, and that, should it be necessary, she would go to the last extremity in support of her opposition to the annexation; but that for this purpose it was essential that Mexico be disposed to acknowledge the independence of Texas, because otherwise an agreement in policy between her and England would be impossible."[56]

Aberdeen proposes joint guarantee of Texan independence

It was soon evident that the treaty would not be ratified by the Senate. Lord Aberdeen then came forward with a proposition that as soon as the treaty should be rejected, England and France should unite with Texas and Mexico in a diplomatic act, or perpetual treaty, guaranteeing the independence of Texas and the boundary that should be determined between Texas and Mexico. The United States would be invited to unite in this act, but it was not expected that the government of that country would agree to it. So far as Mexico was concerned, Lord Aberdeen said she would be forced into acquiescence in case she should be unwilling to join. Both Louis Philippe and Guizot stated that France would join in the act, and President Houston of Texas directed his representative in London to give the necessary pledges for Texas.[57]

Failure of the plan due to France's withdrawal

The diplomatic act, however, was never signed. At the suggestion of Pakenham and Pageot, England and France decided to await the result of the presidential election in the United States. The plan was, therefore, indefinitely postponed. There is no evidence, however, that England intended to abandon the plan. Most of the evidence on the subject leads to the conclusion that France's withdrawal was directly responsible for the breakdown of the plan for joint action. This latter view seems to be confirmed by the course of affairs in France. When the attitude of the French government became

---

[56] *Op. cit.*, p. 389. The full French text is given in Adams, *British Interests and Activities in Texas*, 168–169.

[57] *Dip. Cor. of Republic of Texas*, Part III, 1154; Smith, *Annexation of Texas*, 391.

known a great outcry was raised in France, bad faith toward the United States was charged, and Guizot, "the man of England," was accused not only of sacrificing the interests of his own country, but of promoting those of her ancient enemy, England. It was argued that Texas would eventually be either American or English; that what France had to fear was a preponderance on the ocean and not on the American continent. Thiers argued that it was better for a small state like Texas to belong to the American Union than to remain independent, for in the latter case it would fall under the domination of England. If Texas could be incorporated with the United States it would develop as Louisiana had done, and France would have her share of trade. The leading newspapers of France openly denounced the whole scheme of joint action with England. The attitude of the French press and the opposition in the Chamber of Deputies undoubtedly had their effect on Guizot and on Louis Philippe.[58]

Opposition of the French Chamber and of the press

French government disclaims hostility to United States

In July, 1844, William R. King, the American minister, dined with Louis Philippe, and in the course of conversation the latter inquired why the annexation treaty had been rejected. This gave Mr. King an opening. He replied that the treaty had been temporarily defeated on account of "political considerations of a domestic nature," but that annexation "would certainly be consummated at no distant period." Louis Philippe, while expressing his desire to see the young republic remain independent, assured Mr. King that France "would not proceed to the extent of acts hostile or unfriendly to the United States in reference to the Texas question." Shortly afterward Mr. King had an interview with Guizot, in which he told him that he had received from reliable

[58]Smith, *Annexation of Texas*, 395–399; G. L. Rives, "Mexican Diplomacy on the Eve of War with the United States," in *Am. Hist. Rev.*, XVIII, 278–280. For a different view, see Adams, *British Interests and Activities in Texas*, chap. viii.

sources reports that England and France were contemplating a joint protest against the annexation of Texas. Guizot replied "with considerable animation if not some impatience" that no steps of this kind had been taken, that France's interests in the question were purely commercial and differed from those of England, and that the rejection of the treaty had now banished the subject. Mr. King replied that he was gratified by Guizot's assurances; that Texas must be annexed in order to guard against the danger of England's controlling it; that this view prevailed not only in the Democratic party, but was held by the great majority of American people, and that consequently the project of annexation was by no means dead.[59]

Calhoun's use of the French disclaimer

In acknowledging Mr. King's dispatch, Calhoun made the most of the French disclaimer. He made it appear that the assurances given by Louis Philippe and Guizot were much stronger than they really were, and he entered into a long discussion of British policy for the purpose of showing that it was wholly selfish and opposed to the true interests of France. The President, he wrote, "highly appreciates the declaration of the King, that, in no event, would any steps be taken by his government in the slightest degree hostile, or which would give to the United States just cause of complaint." The annexation of Texas he declared to be "merely a question of time and mode." If accomplished peacefully it would inure to the benefit of all parties concerned, including Mexico; if delayed, or temporarily defeated through the interference of other powers, it would probably involve sooner or later a fierce and bloody conflict.

His defense of slavery

While England's motives in opposing annexation were in part commercial, like those of France, one of her leading motives was undoubtedly the hope, expressed by Lord Aberdeen, that Negro slavery might be abolished in Texas, and ultimately, by consequence, in the United States and throughout the whole of

[59]Smith, *Annexation of Texas,* 399–400.

this continent. France could have no interest in the consummation of such a scheme. Emancipation in the West Indies, he declared, had turned out to be a costly experiment. He then proceeded to quote statistics from *Blackwood's Magazine* to show that there had been a serious decline in the tropical productions of Great Britain and a corresponding increase in "those countries which have had the good sense to shun her example." Her object, therefore, in attacking slavery was to regain her superiority by destroying "the capacity of those who had outstripped her in consequence of her error." What possible motive could France and the other continental powers have in furthering British policy? Was it not better for them to be supplied with tropical products from the United States, Brazil, and Cuba at low prices, than to be dependent on one great monopolizing power?[60] We shall see presently the uses to which this letter was put.

Aberdeen notifies Mexico of change in British policy

Meanwhile, the Murphy memorandum had produced in Mexico an effect which was just the opposite of that intended. Santa Anna used it to prove that England would back him to the limit, and announced his intention of reconquering Texas.[61] At the same time the government of Texas delayed final action on the British proposals, probably to await the outcome of the presidential election in the United States. In these circumstances the lukewarm attitude of France compelled Lord Aberdeen to modify his policy. On October 23, he instructed Bankhead to inform the Mexican government that since it would not consent to recognize the independence of Texas, the proposed concert between England and France, "as set forth in the memorandum," had been abandoned. He declared, however, that the annexation of Texas to the United States would be "an evil of the greatest magni-

[60] 28 Cong., 2 Sess., Sen. Doc. No. 1, p. 39.

[61] Adams, *British Interests and Activities in Texas,* 184.

tude" to Mexico, and that it could be avoided only by the immediate recognition of the new republic. It was evident that Aberdeen had not completely abandoned his policy and was very reluctant to do so.[62]

The Texas question in the election of 1844

In the presidential campaign of 1844, Polk's open advocacy of annexation threatened to draw off Clay's Southern following, so as the contest progressed Clay wrote letters to his Southern friends in which he undertook to hedge on the Texas question. While this shifting of position enabled him to carry North Carolina and Tennessee, it caused him to lose New York, where the abolitionist candidate polled over fifteen thousand votes, drawing enough votes from Clay to leave Polk a majority of a little over five thousand. The contest was so close that had Clay carried New York he would have been elected.

Effect of Polk's election on England and France

On November 25, the result of the American election was announced in the London newspapers. The result was sufficiently decisive to convince England and France that they could not continue their opposition without risking a war with the United States. In an interview with the British ambassador, Guizot remarked, as Calhoun had suggested, that the annexation of Texas concerned Great Britain more than it did France, to which the British ambassador replied: "As both Governments have recognized Texas, you would no doubt join with England in negotiations to secure recognition from Mexico." Guizot answered: "Undoubtedly we will use our best efforts for that purpose, and will even refuse to recognize the annexation of Texas to the United States; but, as a question of peace or war, I am not prepared to say that its junction with the American states is of sufficient importance to us to justify us in having recourse to arms in order to prevent it."[63]

Aberdeen continued "to urge Mexico by every available

[62] Smith, *Annexation of Texas*, 402.

[63] *Ibid.*, p. 404.

Tyler proposes annexation by joint resolution

argument, and in every practicable manner, to recognize without delay the independence of Texas," and he hoped to the last that Texas might decide against annexation and that Mexico might listen to reason.[64] But the people of Texas were overwhelmingly in favor of annexation, and the election of Polk was a clear indication of the wishes of the people of the United States. Tyler did not wait for the inauguration of his successor, but determined to act at once. In his annual message of December, 1844, he proposed that Texas be annexed by joint resolution, as this method would require only a majority and not two-thirds of the Senate. Among the papers accompanying his message was Calhoun's dispatch to King, already referred to.[65] The publication of this dispatch created a sensation in Europe and tended to widen the rift between England and France. It also convinced Aberdeen that further interference on his part would be likely to inflame public opinion in the United States and lead to serious results. The annexation resolution passed the House in January, 1845, but Benton held it up in the Senate until March 1, when it was finally adopted. It was promptly approved by Tyler. When news of the passage of the resolution reached Texas, President Jones and Secretary Smith were still conferring with the French and British *chargés* over the terms of a proposed treaty with Mexico.

The people of Texas vote for union with United States

The people of Texas still had a chance to choose between independence and union with the United States. The Texas Congress unanimously rejected the proposed treaty with Mexico, and when a convention of the republic met, July 4, it adopted an ordinance agreeing to annexation with only one dissenting vote.[66]

Justin H. Smith, who has devoted more time and attention to this intricate subject and examined more docu-

[64]Adams, *British Interests and Activities in Texas*, 193–218.

[65]*Ante*, p. 255.

[66]Reeves, *Am. Diplomacy Under Tyler and Polk*, chap. vii.

ments bearing upon it than any other investigator, draws the following conclusion:

General conclusion

In short, then, it appears that Great Britain was so anxious to prevent the annexation of Texas that she stood ready, if supported by France, to coerce Mexico and fight the United States; that the French government were at first no less willing than England to agree upon decisive measures; that the determination of the American people to resent vigorously such dictation—a course sure to arouse the many Frenchmen who were against the British, against the King or against Guizot—caused that power to fall back; that in consequence England wavered and then withdrew; and that all this grand effort at international concert resulted only in a sort of conspiracy to divert the people of Texas from the destiny actually preferred by the majority. And it is interesting to note, first, that probably the decisive element in the affair was the readiness of a large number of Americans to plunge into a war for which the nation was wholly unprepared; and, secondly, that after these diplomatic events had been taking place for months, it was loudly asserted by opponents of Tyler's administration, not only that England had no schemes afoot with reference to Texas, but that every idea of a European concert against annexation was transparent moonshine.[67]

[67] *Annexation of Texas,* 413. cf. *Cambridge History of British Foreign Policy,* II, 254–256.

CHAPTER XI

THE DIPLOMACY OF THE MEXICAN WAR

Mexico severs diplomatic relations

A FEW days after the passage of the joint resolution for the annexation of Texas, the Mexican minister made a formal protest in the name of his government and asked for his passports. The United States minister to Mexico was denied all official intercourse and, after a delay of several months, withdrew from the country. Diplomatic relations were thus severed by act of the Mexican government.[1] In view of the previous declaration of the Mexican minister of foreign affairs that "the passage of an act for the incorporation of Texas with the territory of the United States must be considered by Mexico as equivalent to a declaration of war,"[2] the abrupt severance of diplomatic relations was a serious step and not justified by the circumstances. The independence of Texas had been recognized not only by the United States, but by England, France, and other powers, and for several years Mexico had made no effort to reconquer her former province.

Polk proposes to send a special envoy

Its annexation by the United States was not a *casus belli*, and the severance of diplomatic relations under all the circumstances made war extremely likely if not inevitable. As the independence of Texas had never been recognized by Mexico, there had, of course, been no agreement as to the boundary between the two countries. Mexico still claimed the whole of Texas. Texas claimed

[1]*Messages and Papers of the Presidents*, IV, 388.

[2]Reeves, 157.

the Rio Grande as her southwest boundary, and as the result of the annexation this was the boundary which President Polk felt it his duty to maintain. Before stationing troops on this frontier, however, he decided to make an effort to reëstablish diplomatic relations, and in September, 1845, Secretary Buchanan instructed Mr. Black, the American consul, "to ascertain from the Mexican government whether they would receive an envoy from the United States, intrusted with full power to adjust all the questions in dispute between the two governments."[3] To this overture the foreign minister replied under date of October 15, 1845:

Mexico agrees provisionally

> Although the Mexican nation is deeply injured by the United States, through the acts committed by them in the department of Texas, which belongs to this nation, my government is disposed to receive the commissioner of the United States who may come to this capital with full powers from his government to settle the present dispute in a peaceable, reasonable, and honorable manner. . . . What my government requires above all things is, that the mission of the commissioner of the United States and his reception by us, should appear to be always absolutely frank, and free from every sign of menace or coercion. And thus, Mr. Consul, while making known to your government the disposition on the part of that of Mexico to receive the commissioner, you should impress upon it, as indispensable, the previous recall of the whole naval force now lying in sight of our port of Vera Cruz. Its presence would degrade Mexico, while she is receiving the commissioner, and would justly subject the United States to the imputation of contradicting, by acts, the vehement desire of conciliation, peace, and friendship, which is professed and asserted by words.[4]

Appointment of John Slidell

The fleet was promptly withdrawn from Mexican waters, and John Slidell was sent to Mexico with a commission as envoy extraordinary and minister plenipotentiary. His instructions, drafted by Buchanan, were dated November 10, 1845.[5] The subjects committed to his care

[3] 29 Cong., 1 Sess., Sen. Doc. No. 337, p. 8.

[4] *Ibid.*, p. 12.

[5] 30 Cong., 1 Sess., Sen Doc. No. 52, p. 71

were, in the order stated, the claims of American citizens against Mexico, the settlement of the boundary in the upper stretches of the Rio Grande, and the purchase of California. It has been usual for American historians to represent the claims of American citizens against Mexico as having been trumped up for the occasion, but such was not the case. They arose out of outrages committed on the persons and property of Americans and had been continuously pressed upon the attention of the Mexican government. In 1837, President Jackson had laid these claims before Congress and declared that the outrages on which they were based were of such a character as to justify immediate war, but as he was reluctant to resort to the last extremity, he proposed that one more demand be made upon Mexico before resorting to reprisals.[6] The Senate, by a unanimous vote, concurred in by the House, directed him to make the demand. After much delay, Mexico finally signed a convention, April 11, 1839, for the submission of the claims to a mixed commission. The sum of $2,026,139.68 had been awarded American claimants when the term of the commission as set by the treaty expired, leaving claims amounting to $3,336,837.05 unadjudicated. After the payment of a few instalments of interest the Mexican government defaulted in its payments. In 1843, an effort was made to organize another commission to continue the work of the first, but the Mexican government insisted that the commission should sit in Mexico, while the Senate of the United States considered it unreasonable that the claimants, all of whom were citizens of the United States, should be compelled to go to Mexico with their documents and testimony.[7]

American claims against Mexico

After reviewing fully the question of the claims, the

[6]*Messages and Papers of the Presidents,* III, 278.

[7]Moore, *Dig.* of *Int. Arbits.,* II, 1245; 30 Cong., 1 Sess., Sen. Doc. No. 52, p. 74.

Slidell's instructions

instructions to Slidell continued: "The fact is but too well known to the world that the Mexican government are not now in a condition to satisfy these claims by the payment of money." The United States would be willing, however, to assume the claims of its citizens if Mexico would agree to a satisfactory adjustment of the Rio Grande boundary. From the mouth of the river to the Paso there was no doubt, it was contended, as to the validity of the Texas claim. The congress of Texas had, however, claimed the Rio Grande as its boundary from the mouth to the source. This included a large part of New Mexico, but as the Texans had not established control over the upper valley of the river, the United States did not regard this claim as valid. In view of the remoteness of the Santa Fé valley and the difficulty of avoiding frontier disputes in case it should be divided by the line of the Rio Grande, it was thought that Mexico might be willing to part with the whole of New Mexico for a fair consideration. Mr. Slidell was, therefore, authorized to offer for the province the sum of five million dollars in addition to the assumption by the United States of all claims of American citizens against Mexico. If, however, Mexico should be unwilling to part with any territory west of the Rio Grande, Slidell was authorized to agree to assume the claims, provided Mexico would agree to the line claimed by the congress of Texas.[8]

New Mexico

California

On the subject of California the instructions declared: "The government of California is now but nominally dependent upon Mexico, and it is more than doubtful whether her authority will ever be reinstated." Mr. Slidell was instructed to use his best efforts to obtain a cession of that province, and he was authorized to offer for a boundary running due west from the southern extremity of New Mexico to the Pacific the sum of twenty-five millions in addition to the assumption of claims. If

[8] 30 Cong., 1 Sess., Sen. Doc. No. 52, p. 78.

he could not get the whole of California, he was authorized to offer twenty millions for a line commencing at any point on the western boundary of New Mexico and running due west to the Pacific, provided it gave the United States the bay and harbor of San Francisco.[9]

Alleged British designs on California

The instructions in regard to California were premised on the statement that, "From information possessed by this department, it is to be seriously apprehended that both Great Britain and France have designs upon California." It was true that both Great Britain and France were pressing Mexico for the payment of the claims of their subjects, that Mexico had recognized these claims and agreed to pay them, but had defaulted, and that there were constant rumors of proposals to satisfy these claims by land cessions in California. Few persons at all familiar with the situation believed that California would long continue a dependency of Mexico, and the general belief was that it would fall either to England or to the United States. In fact, the Mexican government had little authority over the province and, as a British consul wrote to his government, it was "at the mercy of whoever may choose to take possession of it." British residents of California and British naval officers on the Pacific station had long urged their government to acquire the province, but Great Britain was at this time

Aberdeen's instructions

singularly indifferent to colonial expansion, and Aberdeen, under date of December 31, 1844, instructed his agents in California to remain entirely passive in the event of an insurrection against Mexico, adding:

> It is, however, of importance to Great Britain, while declining to interfere herself, that California, if it should throw off the Mexican yoke, should not assume any other which might prove inimical to British interests.[10]

---

[9]*Op. cit.*, p. 79.

[10]Adams, *British Interests and Activities in Texas*, 248.

On the same day he wrote to the same effect to the British minister in Mexico, concluding his dispatch with a more specific instruction:

But on the other hand you will keep your attention vigilantly alive to every credible report which may reach you of occurrences in California, especially with respect to the proceedings of the United States citizens settled in that Province, whose numbers are daily increasing, and who are likely to play a prominent part in any proceeding which may take place there, having for its object to free the Province from the yoke of Mexico.[11]

Mexico offers California to England

The soundness of Polk's apprehensions as to the possibility of California being offered to some European power is confirmed by the fact that in May, 1846, just on the eve of war with the United States, the president of Mexico offered to transfer California to Great Britain in return for a loan. The offer reached England just after a change of ministry, but Palmerston, who had returned to the foreign office, did not reverse Aberdeen's policy. The acceptance of the offer at that time would in fact have been equivalent to a declaration of war against the United States. Palmerston's reply was that

Her Majesty's Government would not at present feel disposed to enter into any Treaty for the acquisition of California; and the more so, because it seems, according to recent accounts, that the Mexican Government may by this time have lost its authority and command over that Province, and would therefore be unable to carry into effect its share of any arrangement which might be come to regarding it.[12]

California rapidly coming under American control

The view has been too often taken by American historians that Polk forced war upon Mexico in order that he might have an excuse for taking California. An impartial examination of the documents and other evidence in the case does not warrant such a conclusion. In fact,

[11] *Op. cit.*, p. 249.

[12] *Ibid.*, p. 263.

it was quite evident to most observers, European as well as American, that if peace continued California would in a few years be controlled by emigrants from the United States who would bring the province into the Union after the manner of Texas.[13] Had the British proposal of 1844 for guaranteeing the independence of Texas not been thwarted by the stupid obstinacy of Mexico, the fate of the entire Pacific slope might have been different, for if the United States had become engaged in war with Great Britain, France, and Mexico combined, it is probable that Great Britain, with her strong foothold in Oregon, would have extended her sway over the entire Pacific Coast.

Mexico refuses to receive Slidell

Slidell was cautioned against pressing the purchase of California unless he should "discover a prospect of success." He arrived at Vera Cruz sooner than he was expected and at a very inopportune time for the government of President Herrera, which was tottering to its fall. Furthermore, the general purport of his instructions had in some unexplained way become known, and Herrera was being denounced as a traitor for having agreed to receive him. Consul Black was informed that Slidell's appearance at the capital might cause the overthrow of the government, and he was urged to pursuade him not to leave Vera Cruz or even embark at this time. But the envoy was already on his way to the City of Mexico, where he arrived on December 6, 1845.[14] Herrera referred the question to the Council, and that body decided that Slidell should not be received. The reasons assigned were that Mexico had agreed to receive a commissioner to negotiate on the subject of Texas alone, and the United States had sent an envoy extraordinary and minister plenipotentiary, thus implying the full resumption of diplomatic relations prior to the settlement of the Texas question which had caused the rupture. Objection was

[13] Smith, *The War with Mexico*, I, 325–327.

[14] 29 Cong., 1 Sess., Sen. Doc. No. 337, pp. 17–18

also raised to Slidell's credentials on the ground that his appointment had not been confirmed by the Senate.[15]

Change of government in Mexico

Before the end of the month Herrera's government was overthrown, and General Paredes assumed the position of temporary president. The new ruler assumed, as was expected, an aggressive attitude of hostility to the United States, and publicly swore to defend every foot of the territory of Mexico, including, of course, the whole of Texas.[16] When the change of government was reported at Washington, Buchanan instructed Slidell not to leave Mexico without demanding recognition from the new government. Paredes declined, however, to reverse the decision of his predecessor. The reasons assigned were substantially the same, but the note was more peremptory in tone.[17]

General Taylor ordered to advance to the Rio Grande

Meanwhile, on receipt of Slidell's first dispatches telling of the popular clamor against his reception, President Polk ordered General Zachary Taylor to advance from Corpus Christi to the Rio Grande and to take up a position opposite Matamoros for the purpose of preventing the Mexicans from occupying the left bank. He was instructed to act on the defensive and to forbear to exercise the right which the United States had in common with Mexico to the free navigation of the river, as the exercise of this right would probably precipitate a conflict. He was not to treat Mexico as an enemy unless that country assumed that character either by a declaration of war or an open act of hostility.[18] While this order was dated January 13, 1846, it was March 8 before Taylor was ready to leave Corpus Christi and March 28 before he reached the Rio Grande. A month later a Mexican force crossed the river and fell on a detachment

[15] *Op. cit.*, p. 19. He was appointed during the recess of the Senate.

[16] Smith, *The War with Mexico*, I, 98–101.

[17] 29 Cong., 1 Sess., Sen. Doc. No. 337, pp. 54–61.

[18] The order, dated January 13, 1846, is published in 29 Cong., 1 Sess., Sen. Doc. No. 337, p. 82.

of American troops under Thornton, killing and wounding some and capturing the rest. There is little doubt that Mexico deliberately chose war.

Mexicans, confident of victory, choose war

On March 21, a week before Taylor reached the Rio Grande, Slidell's request to be received had been deliberately and finally rejected by the government of Paredes. Furthermore, the Mexicans were confident that they would win, and in this opinion they were backed by foreign observers and correspondents. Even so well informed an officer as Captain Elliot, former British minister to Texas, wrote: "If the war should be protracted and carried beyond the Rio Grande, I believe that it would require very little skill and scarcely any exposure of the defending force to draw the invading columns well forward beyond all means of support from their own bases and depots into situations of almost inextricable difficulty."[19] Not only the Mexican press, but leading British and French journals freely predicted the failure of American arms. The London *Times*, referring sarcastically to the United States, said: "The invasion and conquest of a vast region by a state which is without an army and without credit is a novelty in the history of nations."[20] The United States army at this time numbered 7,200 men, while that of Mexico numbered approximately 32,000.[21] Accustomed as the Mexicans were to frequent revolutions and almost continuous fighting, they had an overweening confidence in themselves and a corresponding contempt for the Americans whose offers to settle disputes through financial negotiations appeared to them to indicate weakness.

Relative military strength

The supposed inferiority of Taylor's army encouraged the Mexicans to hasten the attack. They also counted much on the general unpreparedness of the United

---

[19] Smith, *The War with Mexico*, I, 107.

[20] *Ibid.*, p. 109.

[21] *Ibid.*, pp. 139, 157.

Mexican reliance on anti-slavery party and foreign intervention

States, on anti-slavery opposition to the war, and on European intervention. The well-known opposition of England and France to American annexation of Texas and to American expansion in general convinced them that one or two Mexican victories would be followed by the intervention of these powers. Their hopes of British intervention were based strongly on the Oregon dispute. Great Britain had rejected Polk's offer to compromise on the forty-ninth parallel, and Polk's message to Congress had committed him to a position which made a peaceable solution of the controversy appear impossible. In fact, the Mexican representative in London reported that Lord Aberdeen would like to see Mexico fight the United States and win.[22] The unexpected settlement of the Oregon dispute shortly after the beginning of the war removed the hope of immediate British intervention, but the Mexicans still hoped to win, and even Taylor's early victories did not completely dispel their illusions as to the military inferiority of the United States.

Return of Santa Anna

The military disasters led, however, to the overthrow of Paredes and the return of Santa Anna from exile. Polk had been led to believe that the return of Santa Anna to power would pave the way for peace, and he had sent a secret agent to Havana to confer with him. The terms proposed were a liberal cash payment for New Mexico and California, and permanent friendly relations with Mexico. If Santa Anna on regaining power would agree to negotiate, the President would at once stop military operations and send a minister. Santa Anna responded in cordial though rather vague terms to these proposals, and President Polk issued orders to the commander of the blockading squadron off Vera Cruz to let him through.[23] Whatever his inten-

[22]*Op. cit.*, I, 114–115.
[23]*Ibid.*, I, 201–203.

tions may have been, when Santa Anna reached Mexico he found the people more bent on war than ever, and the political foundations of his own power so unstable that he soon concluded that the only safe place for him was at the head of the army. On September 17, when he was appointed commander-in-chief of "The Liberating Army," he declared: "Every day that passes without fighting at the north is a century of disgrace for Mexico."[24] Polk was deceived and disappointed, and had to prepare for a longer war than he had anticipated.

American forces occupy California

In the meantime, the expedition under General Kearny had taken Santa Fé and was on its way to California. When he reached that province he found that the American fleet under Commodore Stockton had already taken possession of San Francisco and Monterey, and that some other Mexican garrisons had been driven from the country. This result had been brought about with the assistance of a small force of Americans raised by Captain John C. Frémont, who had crossed the continent with a party of fifty or sixty soldiers on an exploring expedition with a view to locating an overland route from the Mississippi to the Pacific. Kearny soon completed the conquest begun by Fremont and Stockton. Thus the vast region of California and New Mexico was won by a few hundred men with little effort or loss of life.

Scott's expedition against the City of Mexico

As neither Taylor's victories nor the conquest of New Mexico and California had brought the Mexican government to the point of entertaining peace proposals, Polk decided to send an expedition against the City of Mexico by way of Vera Cruz. Taylor was a Whig and his victories had brought him such great popularity that his name was already being mentioned for the presidency. Polk decided, therefore, to entrust the new expedition to another general. He was embarrassed by the fact that there was no Democrat in the army of sufficiently

[24]*Op. cit.*, I, 218–224.

high rank to be placed in command, so he finally chose another Whig, General Winfield Scott. The expedition of 12,000 men commanded by Scott disembarked near Vera Cruz March 9, 1847, and three weeks later forced the town to surrender. Although not fully prepared for an immediate advance, Scott determined to hurry his troops away from the coast in order to escape the yellow fever season which was fast approaching. About the middle of April he defeated Santa Anna in a three days' fight at Cerro Gordo, and a month later his advance captured and occupied Puebla. Santa Anna retired to the City of Mexico. Scott was greatly embarrassed at this time by having to delay military operations in order to reorganize his army. The terms of about one-third of his troops had expired, and he had to send these men home and await the arrival of new volunteers.

Mission of Nicholas P. Trist

There began now one of the most singular series of negotiations in the history of American diplomacy. Taylor's glorious victory at Buena Vista in February and Scott's capture of Vera Cruz in March encouraged Polk to believe that the Mexican government would welcome peace. After the rejection of his previous overtures, and in the absence of definite information as to the disposition of the Mexican authorities, he did not care to subject the United States to the possibility of another rebuff by the appointment of a public commissioner, but he decided to send to the headquarters of the army "a confidential agent, fully acquainted with the views of the government, and clothed with full powers to conclude a treaty of peace with the Mexican government, should it be so inclined." For this mission he selected Nicholas P. Trist, chief clerk of the State Department, a man of agreeable manners and appearance who had long been associated with public men and affairs. He had read law under Jefferson, whose granddaughter he married. He had served for a number of years as consul at Havana and spoke the Spanish language fluently.[25] His instructions, drafted by Buchanan April 15, 1847, and accompanied by a projét of a treaty, authorized him to offer a sum not exceeding thirty millions of dollars for New Mexico and Upper and Lower California, with the understanding that the United States would assume all the claims of its citizens against Mexico, and with the proviso that Mexico would grant to the United States and its citizens the right of transit across the isthmus of Tehuantepec. The acquisition of Lower California and the right-of-way across the isthmus of Tehuantepec were not made indispensable conditions of peace, but the instructions stated:

His instructions

> The extension of our boundaries over New Mexico and Upper California, for a sum not exceeding twenty millions of dollars, is to be considered a *sine qua non* of any treaty. You may modify, change, or omit the other terms of the projét if needful, but not so as to interfere with this ultimatum.[26]

Misunderstanding as to Trist's powers

As soon as the proposed treaty should be accepted and ratified by the Mexican government, Trist was instructed to communicate this fact to the commanders of the land and naval forces of the United States; and he was informed that orders had been issued to them by the Secretaries of War and the Navy to suspend hostilities upon the receipt of such notice. Marcy's dispatch to General Scott was so worded as to give the latter an entirely erroneous impression of the powers intrusted to Trist, and aroused the wrath of the old general. It read as follows:

> Mr. Trist is clothed with such diplomatic powers as will authorize him to enter into arrangements with the government of Mexico for the suspension of hostilities. Should he make known to you, in writing, that the contingency has occurred in consequence of which the President is willing that further

[25] On Trist's mission, see McCormac, *James K. Polk*, 487–554

[26] 30 Cong., 1 Sess., Sen. Doc. No. 52, pp. 81–89.

active military operations should cease, you will regard such notice as a direction from the President to suspend them until further orders from the department, unless continued or recommenced by the enemy.[27]

Conflict of authority

This order, considered by itself and apart from Trist's instructions, which were not communicated to Scott, practically subordinated the commanding general to "the chief clerk of the Department of State," as Scott stated in a letter to Trist, and he further declared that in view of the perilous situation of the army in the heart of the enemy's country he would not recognize Trist's authority in a military question, such as an armistice, unless the latter were clothed with military rank superior to his as well as with diplomatic functions. "I shall demand, under the peculiar circumstances," he added, "that, in your negotiations, if the enemy should entertain your overtures, you refer that question [i.e., of an armistice] to me, and all the securities belonging to it."[28]

Scott appeals to the Secretary of War

Scott forwarded his correspondence with Trist to the Secretary of War, and Marcy replied at length censuring him for his hasty misconstruction of the order, and calling attention to the paragraph which directed him to forward the dispatch, which Trist bore, to the commander of the Mexican forces and to inform him that an officer of the Department of State, "next in rank to its chief," was at his headquarters. Thus it was not intended that Trist should make overtures to the enemy except through Scott, and the orders in regard to an armistice were not to go into effect until a treaty had actually been signed and ratified by the Mexican government.[29]

The misunderstanding was due to Trist, who on his

[27] *Op. cit.*, p. 119.

[28] *Ibid.*, p. 120.

[29] *Ibid.*, p. 121.

A reconciliation effected

arrival at Vera Cruz May 6, 1847, forwarded to Scott Marcy's orders, together with Buchanan's dispatch sealed, and a tactless letter asking Scott to forward the dispatch to the Mexican government. This Scott refused to do and returned the dispatch to Trist. For the next two months the quarrel between Trist and Scott continued, and, as they were not on speaking terms, they bombarded each other with ill-tempered letters, and laid their cases before their superiors at Washington. The President was much displeased and talked of recalling both, but the Cabinet persuaded him that it would be bad policy to do so. Late in June, Trist and Scott arrived at an understanding and their relations became cordial. Scott wrote to Marcy that he found Trist "able, discreet, courteous, and amiable," while Trist wrote to Buchanan that he had "entirely misconceived" Scott's character. Each made the request that the correspondence relating to the quarrel be suppressed.[30] How the reconciliation was effected is not known, as Trist's letter of July 7 was never received and Scott sent no communication to the Secretary of War for several weeks.[31]

Trist's abortive negotiations with Santa Anna

While this altercation was in progress, Trist asked Bankhead, the British minister, to transmit to the Mexican government the dispatch which Scott refused to forward.[32] This Bankhead consented to do, and in a few days received a reply that the question of peace negotiations would have to be referred to the Mexican Congress. Santa Anna tried to get that body to assume the responsibility of authorizing negotiations, but Congress shirked the duty and adjourned without taking definite action.[33] Santa Anna then sent secret agents who in-

[30] *Op. cit.*, pp. 135, 302.

[31] Reeves, *American Diplomacy Under Tyler and Polk*, 314–317; Smith, *The War with Mexico*, II, 128–130.

[32] 30 Cong., 1 Sess., Sen. Doc. No. 52, pp. 181–185.

[33] *Ibid.*, p. 302.

timated to Trist that if he would let him have $10,000 immediately and promise to pay a million as soon as a treaty should be ratified by Mexico, he would appoint commissioners to meet Trist at once. Trist laid this proposal before Scott, with whom he had recently become reconciled, and Scott advanced the $10,000 out of his fund for secret expenses. But Santa Anna's generals opposed negotiations and he hesitated. Meanwhile Scott continued his advance on the City of Mexico, still expecting that Santa Anna would offer to negotiate. On August 20, he defeated the Mexicans in the battles of Contreras and Churubusco, and called on the city to surrender. In order to avoid an assault on the city, Santa Anna asked for a truce, and the terms of a short armistice were signed August 24. In the negotiations that followed, Trist found to his surprise that the Mexicans refused steadfastly to give up the territory between the Rio Grande and the Nueces, and rather than break off negotiations he proposed an extension of the armistice for forty-five days in order that he might refer this question to Washington. This was in direct violation of his instructions, which made the Rio Grande boundary a *sine qua non*. As soon as Santa Anna realized that he could not accept the American demands without sacrificing his influence with both army and people, he began strengthening the defenses of the city and violating in other ways the armistice. To Scott's demand for an explanation he replied in a warlike tone intended to arouse the Mexicans, and hostilities were resumed. The general view of the armistice taken at the time, even by the authorities at Washington, was that Trist and Scott were the mere dupes of Santa Anna, who wanted to gain time in order to collect his scattered forces and strengthen his defenses. Santa Anna undoubtedly wanted peace, but he loved political power and dreaded exile or death, so he gave way before the

Armistice signed but not kept by Mexicans

taunts of his political enemies and decided to stake all on another fight.[34]

Overthrow of Santa Anna and reopening of negotiations

Hostilities were resumed September 8, and on the 13th the Americans stormed and carried the great natural fortress of Chapultepec in the bloodiest battle of the war. The next day the City of Mexico was occupied and Santa Anna's army dispersed. He soon resigned the presidency, and Peña y Peña, the former foreign minister, reluctantly consented at the request of the Moderado party to assume the executive authority. Peña's constitutional status was questionable, and the political situation was one of great confusion. He finally decided to negotiate, and notified Trist that he would appoint commissioners, but the meeting of the Mexican Congress on November 2 caused further delay. Before Trist met the commissioners he received on November 16 Buchanan's letter dated October 4, informing him that in view of the failure of his earlier negotiations and of the bad faith of the Mexican government in the matter of the armistice, the President had come to the conclusion that his continued presence with the army could be productive of no good, but might do much harm by encouraging the delusive hopes of the Mexicans. He was, therefore, ordered to return to the United States by the first safe opportunity. In conclusion Buchanan said:

Trist ordered home

> Should you have concluded a treaty before this dispatch shall reach you, which is not anticipated, you will bring this treaty with you to the United States, for the consideration of the president; but should you, upon its arrival, be actually engaged in negotiations with Mexican commissioners, these must be immediately suspended; but you will inform them that the terms which they may have proposed, or shall propose, will be promptly submitted to the president on your return. You are not to delay your departure, however, awaiting the communication of

---

[34]Smith, II, 137–139.

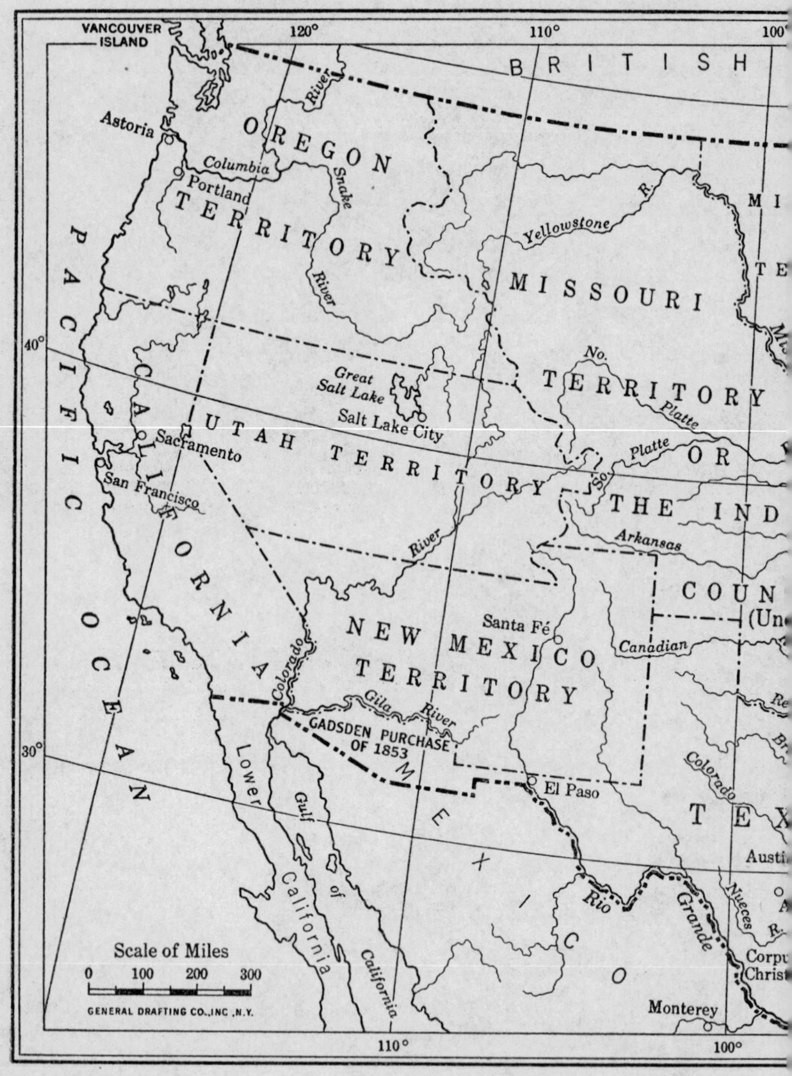
VANCOUVER ISLAND
120°
110°
100°
BRITISH
Astoria
OREGON
Columbia
Portland
TERRITORY
River
Snake
River
Yellowstone
R.
MISSOURI
TERRITORY
No.
Platte
So.
Platte
OR
THE IND
Arkansas
COUN
(Un
PACIFIC OCEAN
40°
30°
CALIFORNIA
Great Salt Lake
Salt Lake City
UTAH TERRITORY
Sacramento
San Francisco
River
NEW MEXICO TERRITORY
Santa Fé
Canadian
Colorado
Gila River
GADSDEN PURCHASE OF 1853
El Paso
MEXICO
Lower California
Gulf of California
Rio Grande
Colorado
Nueces
R.
TEX
Austi
Corpu
Christ
Monterey
Scale of Miles
0 100 200 300
GENERAL DRAFTING CO., INC., N.Y.

4. EX

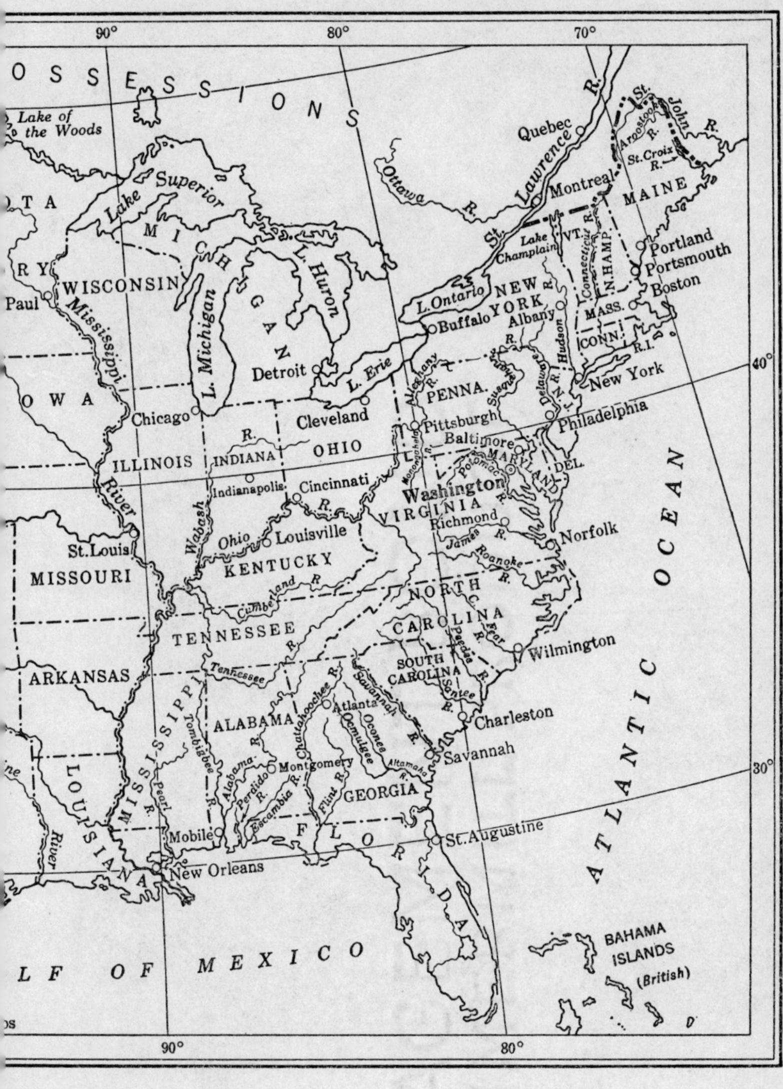

90°
80°
70°
Lake of the Woods
Lake Superior
MICHIGAN
L. Michigan
L. Huron
WISCONSIN
Mississippi River
IOWA
Chicago
Detroit
L. Erie
Cleveland
ILLINOIS
INDIANA
Indianapolis
OHIO
Cincinnati
Ohio R.
Wabash
Louisville
KENTUCKY
St. Louis
MISSOURI
Cumberland R.
TENNESSEE
Tennessee R.
ARKANSAS
MISSISSIPPI
Tombigbee R.
ALABAMA
Alabama R.
Montgomery
Mobile
Pearl R.
LOUISIANA
New Orleans
Quebec
St. Lawrence R.
Montreal
Ottawa R.
L. Ontario
Buffalo
NEW YORK
Albany
Hudson R.
Lake Champlain
VT.
N. HAMP.
Connecticut R.
MAINE
St. John R.
Aroostook R.
St. Croix R.
Portland
Portsmouth
Boston
MASS.
CONN.
R.I.
New York
PENNA.
Allegheny R.
Susquehanna R.
Delaware R.
N.J.
Pittsburgh
Philadelphia
Baltimore
MARYLAND
DEL.
Potomac R.
Washington
VIRGINIA
Richmond
James R.
Norfolk
Roanoke R.
NORTH CAROLINA
C. Fear R.
Wilmington
SOUTH CAROLINA
Pedee R.
Santee R.
Charleston
Savannah R.
Atlanta
Chattahoochee R.
Oconee
Ocmulgee
Altamaha R.
Savannah
GEORGIA
Flint R.
Perdido R.
Escambia R.
FLORIDA
St. Augustine
OF MEXICO
ATLANTIC OCEAN
BAHAMA ISLANDS (British)
40°
30°

to 1850

any terms from these commissioners, for the purpose of bringing them to the United States.[35]

His departure delayed

When Trist received this letter he had no other thought than to obey the order of recall, but his departure was delayed by two considerations: Scott could not well spare a detachment to escort him to the coast, and his testimony was wanted in the court-martial proceedings against General Pillow. He wrote to Buchanan to this effect, and at the same time expressed the opinion that to require the Mexican authorities to send commissioners to Washington would have a disastrous effect upon the peace party and was altogether impracticable. He, therefore, urged Buchanan to send a commission to Mexico at once.[36]

Decides to disregard order of recall

In the meantime he thought it unwise to make public announcement of his recall because of the effect it would have on the peace party, but he requested Edward Thornton, who was temporarily in charge of the British legation, to inform the Mexican authorities and to tell them that any proposals they might make would be forwarded to Washington immediately by the commanding general. When Thornton returned he informed Trist that commissioners had been appointed to meet him, that Peña had shown great disappointment and concern at the idea of having to sue for peace at Washington, and that he believed the party then in power to be sincerely desirous of peace. After conference with General Scott, Trist finally decided to disobey the order of recall and enter into negotiations with the Mexican commissioners. In a long letter to Buchanan, dated December 6, 1847, he based the reasons for his decision on the conviction:

First, that peace is still the desire of my government; secondly, that if the present opportunity be not seized at once, all chance

[35] 30 Cong., I Sess., Sen. Doc. No. 52, p. 93.

[36] *Ibid.*, pp. 228–230.

Reasons assigned

of making a treaty at all will be lost for an indefinite period—probably forever; thirdly, that this (the boundary proposed by me) is the utmost point to which the Mexican government can, by any possibility, venture. I also state, that the determination of my government to withdraw the offer to negotiate, of which I was made the organ, has been taken with reference to a supposed state of things in this country entirely the reverse of that which actually exists.[37]

A grave crisis

This decision required courage of a high order. Even a successful negotiation, as the event proved, could hardly be expected to avert the wrath of Polk and Buchanan whose orders he was deliberately disobeying, and in carrying on negotiations with the enemy after the withdrawal of his powers he was violating a criminal statute of the United States and would undoubtedly be prosecuted if he failed to secure a satisfactory treaty. The crisis was graver than he thought, for about this time the Mexicans got the impression from the American papers that the Whigs favored easier terms than Trist proposed, and, furthermore, hope of British influence in favor of Mexico was again revived. The Mexican authorities, therefore, delayed the negotiations, but the arrival of Doyle, the new British minister, dispelled the hope of British aid, for he promptly informed them that nothing more than good offices could be expected of his government. In fact, Doyle and Thornton did everything that was possible to pave the way for peace.[38]

The Treaty of Guadalupe Hidalgo

After further delay, the peace negotiations finally began, and the treaty was signed at the small suburb of Guadalupe Hidalgo, February 2, 1848. Its main provisions were in accordance with the instructions and project which Trist had received when he started for Mexico nearly a year earlier. The United States got New Mexico and California, the boundary line running from

[37]*Op. cit.*, pp. 231–266.

[38]Smith, *The War with Mexico*, II, 237–238.

the mouth of the Rio Grande up the middle of that river to the southern boundary of New Mexico, thence westerly along that boundary to its western termination, thence northward to the first branch of the Gila River, thence down the middle of said branch and said river to the Rio Colorado, thence along the division line between Upper and Lower California to the Pacific. In consideration of this extension of boundaries the United States agreed to pay Mexico fifteen million dollars and to assume the claims of its citizens.[39]

Ratification advised by Polk

The treaty was carried to Washington with unusual speed and delivered to the President February 19. Meanwhile there had developed a strong feeling that Mexico was being treated too leniently and that more territory should be demanded. Bancroft expressed the opinion that the United States should "rescue a large part of Mexico from anarchy" by annexing it, and Cass talked of rescuing the whole. After conferring with his cabinet, Polk decided that Trist's irregular conduct had no real bearing on the question, and on February 22 he transmitted the treaty to the Senate with the recommendation that it be ratified with certain modifications. It was received at first with derision and scorn, and the President was called upon "to communicate to the Senate, in confidence, the entire correspondence between Mr. Trist and the Mexican commissioners." In complying with this resolution the President again expressed the opinion that the treaty should be ratified, notwithstanding "the exceptionable conduct of Mr. Trist." The treaty was opposed by the annexationists of the South and West as taking too little from Mexico and by the anti-annexationists of New England as taking too much. To the way of thinking of the latter group the country was too large already. The Committee on Foreign Relations wanted to throw the treaty out as the

[39](Malloy) *Treaties and Conventions of the United States,* I, 1107.

work of a discredited agent and send an imposing commission to negotiate another treaty, but Polk told them bluntly that this would be "worse than an idle ceremony." The American people wanted peace, and when it was made clear that a rejection of the treaty would throw Mexico into a state of hopeless chaos and make peace impossible, the Senate, on March 10, advised ratification, with amendments, by a vote of 38 to 14. Article X, relating to Mexican land grants in the ceded territory, was stricken out as not authorized by Trist's instructions, and a secret article, extending the time for the exchange of ratifications under certain contingencies, was also eliminated.[40]

The Senate consents

Europe surprised at mild terms of the treaty

The war had been conducted with humanity and peace had been negotiated with moderation. Europe was surprised at the mild terms imposed on Mexico and at the withdrawal of a victorious army from a country of vast natural resources which lay at the mercy of the conqueror. Rarely has a nation shown such self-restraint. The unparalleled success of the American arms did not sweep Polk off his feet. He was not influenced by the foolish clamor against hauling down the flag which half a century later influenced McKinley in his decision to keep the Philippines Polk could not, however, forgive Trist, or even do him simple justice. Although the treaty was accepted, the man who negotiated it was not even permitted to exchange ratifications, but was ordered home in disgrace, dismissed from the public service, and denied even his salary from the time of his first recall. He was too proud and sensitive to press his claim, and he soon sank into obscurity. Justice was denied him for more than twenty years. Finally, when he was a feeble old man, Congress made an appropriation for the payment of his claim, and President

Trist suffers injustice

[40] 30 Cong., I Sess., Sen. Doc. No. 52, pp. 1–66; Smith, *The War with Mexico*, II, 243–248.

Grant appointed him postmaster at Alexandria, Virginia.[41]

Subsequent controversies arising out of the treaty

Three articles of the treaty of Guadalupe Hidalgo gave rise to diplomatic controversies. They were Article V, which described the boundary and provided for its survey; Article VI, which made certain pledges in regard to the construction of a canal or railway along the Gila River; and Article XI, under which the United States assumed the obligation of preventing Indian incursions into Mexican territory and restoring Mexican citizens captured by the Indians. When, after many delays, the boundary commissioners met at El Paso in December, 1850, a long discussion was precipitated by the discovery that Disturnell's map of Mexico, referred to in the treaty, was inaccurate. It placed El Paso on parallel thirty-two degrees fifteen minutes, whereas by astronomical observation it was shown to be on parallel thirty-one degrees forty-five minutes. The question was as to whether the southern boundary of New Mexico should be located according to degrees of latitude or eight miles north of El Paso, as marked on the map. The Mexican commissioner, Condé, refused to accept the line as marked on the map, and Bartlett, the American commissioner, finally agreed upon a compromise. Lieutenant Gray, the American surveyor, had been delayed by illness and when he arrived he refused to accept the Bartlett-Condé compromise. As his authority was equal to that of the commissioner, the question was referred to Washington. President Fillmore, following the recommendation of Secretary of the Interior Stuart, upheld the Bartlett-Condé compromise, but the Democrats in Congress, led by the Senators from Texas and California, opposed it and demanded an in-

The Mesilla Valley

---

[41] 41 Cong., 2 Sess., Sen. Rep. No. 261, July 14, 1870; U. S. Stat. at Large, XVII, 643, Act of April 20, 1871, appropriating $14,559.90 on account of salary, outfit, and contingent expenses.

vestigation of Bartlett's conduct. The area in dispute, the Mesilla Valley, embraced five or six thousand square miles of territory. Its agricultural value was insignificant and its loss would not have excited political controversy had it not been vitally connected with the question of a transcontinental railroad.[42]

The project of a transcontinental railroad

The discovery of gold in California shortly after its acquisition by the United States and the rush of settlers to the Pacific Coast aroused popular interest in the question of a transcontinental railroad. The pioneer advocate of this project was Asa Whitney, of New York, who as early as 1845 had advocated the building of a railroad westward from the Great Lakes by means of land grants from the public domain. The rival project of a railroad by a southern route had been advocated in the Memphis Convention of 1845 by James Gadsden, president of the South Carolina Railroad Company.[43]

The mission of James Gadsden

The Democratic administration of President Pierce was largely dominated by Jefferson Davis, the Secretary of War, who was greatly interested in the southern route. The Bartlett-Condé line was promptly rejected, and Gadsden was sent as minister to Mexico for the purpose of securing a better boundary. His selection was due to Jefferson Davis, who informed him of his appointment before he was officially notified by Secretary of State Marcy.[44]

Its object

The object of Gadsden's mission, as stated in Marcy's instructions of July 15, 1854, was to secure territory south of the Gila River which would give the United States a practicable route for a railroad, to secure a release from the obligations of Article XI, which Mexico had interpreted to mean that the United States must

---

42 P. N. Garber, *The Gadsden Treaty*, 11–17.

43 *Ibid.*, pp. 17–18.

44 *Ibid.*, pp. 74–81

pay for all damage done by Indian incursions, and to arrange a settlement of all claims between the two governments.[45]

Santa Anna in need of money

Santa Anna had recently returned from exile and been elected President again by an overwhelming majority. He was greatly in need of money, and Gadsden wrote to Marcy soon after his arrival that the important question was the amount of money to be paid and not the amount of territory to be ceded.[46] Gadsden was authorized to offer $50,000,000 for Lower California and the northern parts of the states of Coahuila, Chihuahua, and Sonora, and proportionate amounts for smaller cessions.[47] The filibustering expedition of William Walker into Lower California just before the opening of the negotiations created a state of feeling among the Mexicans very unfavorable to Gadsden's mission. He succeeded, however, in accomplishing his main object—the acquisition of ample territory for a railroad. For the territory south of the Gila River, which is still known as the "Gadsden Purchase," the treaty provided that the United States should pay Mexico $15,000,000. The treaty was signed December 30, 1853. It reached Washington at an unfavorable moment. The country was wrought up over the Kansas-Nebraska Bill. The treaty encountered the opposition of the anti-slavery Senators and of those who favored a northern railroad route. It was amended in several particulars. The amount of the payment was cut down to ten millions, and in this form the treaty was sent back to Mexico. Santa Anna was in urgent need of money and the treaty was finally ratified.[48]

The "Gadsden Purchase"

[45] *Op. cit.*, pp. 83–85.
[46] *Ibid.*, p. 89.
[47] *Ibid.*, pp. 91–92.
[48] *Ibid.*, pp. 109–143; (Malloy) *Treaties and Conventions*, I, 1121.

CHAPTER XII

CUBA AND MANIFEST DESTINY

The origin of the Cuban question

THE Cuban question, like that of South American independence, had its origin in the Napoleonic invasion of Spain and the resulting paralysis of Spanish power in America. The declaration of President Monroe, enforced by the well-known attitude of England, dealt the death-blow to Spanish hopes of recovering the Southern continent. Hence the islands of Cuba and Porto Rico, which had remained loyal to the King, were clung to with all the greater tenacity as the sole remains of the imperial possessions over which the successors of Ferdinand and Isabella had ruled for three centuries. The "Ever-faithful Island of Cuba" was rewarded for her loyalty by the concession of certain liberties of trade and invited to send representatives to the Spanish Cortes—a privilege which was subsequently withdrawn. Spain was now too weak to protect her two West Indian dependencies—the remains of her former glory, but her very weakness secured their possession to her. The naval and commercial importance of Cuba, "the pearl of the Antilles," made it a prize too valuable to be acquired by any one of the great maritime powers without exciting the jealousy and opposition of the others. Henceforth, to borrow the figure of a contemporary journalist, Cuba was to be the trans-Atlantic Turkey, trembling to its fall, but sustained by the jealousies of those who were eager to share the spoils.

The strategic importance of Cuba, commanding to a large extent the commerce of the West Indies and of the Central American states, and, what was of vital interest to us, the traffic of the Mississippi valley, attracted at an early period the attention of American as well as of European statesmen. In a letter to President Madison in 1809, Jefferson, in speaking of Napoleon's policy in regard to the Spanish-American colonies, said:

The strategic importance of the island

> That he would give up the Floridas to withhold intercourse with the residue of those colonies cannot be doubted. But that is no price; because they are ours in the first moment of the first war; and until a war they are of no particular necessity to us. But, although with difficulty, he will consent to our receiving Cuba into our Union, to prevent our aid to Mexico and the other provinces. That would be a price, and I would immediately erect a column on the southern-most limit of Cuba, and inscribe on it a *ne plus ultra* as to us in that direction.[1]

President Madison expressed his views on the Cuban question in a letter to William Pinkney, October 30, 1810:

First statement of American policy

> The position of Cuba gives the United States so deep an interest in the destiny, even, of that island, that although they might be an inactive, they could not be a satisfied spectator at its falling under any European government, which might make a fulcrum of that position against the commerce and security of the United States.[2]

This was the first statement in the evolution of a Cuban policy consistently adhered to by the United States until the successes of the Mexican war superinduced larger ideas of the mission and destiny of the Union.

Reports of British designs

As early as 1817 fears as to the fate of Cuba were raised in the minds of the American public by newspaper reports to the effect that England had proposed a relinquishment of her claim against Spain for the maintenance of the British army during the Peninsular

[1]H. A. Washington, *Writings of Thomas Jefferson*, V, 443.

[2]Madison's Works, II, p. 488.

campaign, amounting to £15,000,000, in return for the cession of the island.[3] Reports of this nature were circulated for several months on both sides of the Atlantic, but the question did not assume any very great importance until 1819, when the treaty for the cession of the Floridas to the United States was being negotiated with Spain. It was then insisted by the British press that the acquisition of the Floridas would give the United States such a preponderating influence in West Indian affairs as to render necessary the occupation of Cuba by Great Britain as the natural and only offset.[4] The Florida treaty was ratified after some delay, which, however, does not appear to have been caused by the British government, as was supposed at the time. The British papers, nevertheless, continued to condemn in strong terms the treaty as well as the inaction of their government in not making it a pretext for the seizure of Cuba.

British reaction to Florida treaty

Suspicious movements of British squadron

As the preparations of France for the invasion of Spain in 1823 progressed the fate of Cuba became a question of absorbing interest in America. There was little hope that the island would continue a dependency of Spain. It was rumored that Great Britain had engaged to supply the constitutional government of Spain with money in her struggle with France and would occupy Cuba as a pledge for its repayment. Both Spanish and French journals spoke of British occupation of Cuba as a matter no longer to be doubted, and the presence in the West Indies of a large British squadron, sent nominally for the purpose of suppressing piracy, seemed to lend color to the reports.[5] The British press was clamoring for the acquisition of Cuba. The *Packet*

---

[3]Niles' *Register*, under date November 8, 1817.

[4]For a full discussion of the question see the pamphlet by J. Freeman Rattenbury, entitled, "The Cession of the Floridas to the United States of America and the Necessity of Acquiring the Island of Cuba by Great Britain." London, 1819.

[5]Niles' *Register*, March and April, 1823.

declared: "The question then comes to this, shall England occupy Cuba, or by permitting its acquisition by the United States (which they have long desired) sacrifice her whole West India trade? There can be no hesitation as to the answer."

British government disclaims all designs on Cuba

The British government, however, officially disclaimed all designs upon Cuba, but this disclaimer did not fully reassure the American government, and our representatives abroad were instructed to exercise a close scrutiny upon all negotiations between Spain and England. In the spring of 1823, Mr. Forsyth was succeeded by Mr. Nelson at the Court of Madrid. In his instructions to the new minister, which went much beyond the usual length and were occupied almost exclusively with a discussion of the Cuban question, John Quincy Adams used the following remarkable words:

Views of John Quincy Adams

"In looking forward to the probable course of events for the short period of half a century, it seems scarcely possible to resist the conviction that the annexation of Cuba to our Federal Republic will be indispensable to the continuance and integrity of the Union itself." We were not then prepared for annexation, he continued, "but there are laws of political as well as physical gravitation; and if an apple, severed by the tempest from its native tree, cannot choose but fall to the ground, Cuba, forcibly disjoined from its own unnatural connection with Spain, and incapable of self-support, can gravitate only toward the North American Union, which, by the same law of nature, cannot cast her off from its bosom."[6]

President Monroe consulted Jefferson on the subject of Spanish-American affairs and the entanglements with European powers likely to arise therefrom. Jefferson replied, June 11, 1823:

[6]32 Cong., 1 Sess., H. Ex. Doc. No. 121; *Brit. and For. State Papers*, XLIV, 114–236.

Jefferson's opinion

Cuba alone seems at present to hold up a speck of war to us. Its possession by Great Britain would indeed be a great calamity to us. Could we induce her to join us in guaranteeing its independence against all the world, except Spain, it would be nearly as valuable as if it were our own. But should she take it, I would not immediately go to war for it; because the first war on other accounts will give it to us, or the island will give itself to us when able to do so.[7]

Danger of French interference in Cuba

During the summer of 1825 a large French squadron visited the West Indies and hovered for several weeks about the coasts of Cuba. This action on the part of the French government, without explanation, excited the alarm of both England and the United States and drew forth strong protests from Mr. Canning and from Mr. Clay. Canning wrote to Granville, the British minister at Paris, that he could not consent to the occupation of Havana by France, even as a measure of protection against possible attacks from Mexico and Colombia.[8] Again some two months later he wrote:

As to Cuba you cannot too soon nor too amicably, of course, represent to Villéle the impossibility of our allowing France (or France us, I presume) to meddle in the internal affairs of that colony. We sincerely wish it to remain with the mother-country. Next to that I wish it independent, either singly or in connection with Mexico. But what cannot or must not be, is that any great maritime power should get possession of it. The Americans (Yankees, I mean) think of this matter just as I do.[9]

Secretary Clay' pronouncement

The expressions of the United States, as to the designs of France, were as emphatic as those of England. Mr. Clay declared "that we could not consent to the occupation of those islands by any other European power than Spain under any contingency whatever."[10]

In this connection Canning wished to bring about

---

[7]H. A. Washington, *Writings of Jefferson*, VII, 288

[8]*Official Corresp. of Canning*, I, 265.

[9]*Ibid.*, p. 275.

[10]*A. S. P., F. R.*, V, 855. Also Wharton's *Digest*, Sec. 60.

the signature, by England, France, and the United States, of "ministerial notes, one between France and the United States, and one between France and Great Britain, or one tripartite note signed by all, disclaiming each for themselves, any intention to occupy Cuba, and protesting against such occupation by either of the others."[11] The government of the United States held this proposal under advisement, but on France declining, it was dropped.[12] In 1826, when an attack upon Portugal was feared, Canning advised, in case of such an attack, the immediate seizure of Cuba by Great Britain as more effective than half a dozen Peninsular campaigns.[13]

Canning proposes tripartite agreement

The Cuban question was involved in the long debate on the proposal of the executive of the United States to send delegates to the congress of Spanish-American republics assembled at Panama in 1826. This debate occupied the attention of Congress during the winter and spring of 1826, and was engaged in with great earnestness. One of the chief objections to the proposed mission was the fact that the question of Cuba and Porto Rico would come up and that the United States government had already committed itself to the foreign powers on that subject. The report of the Senate Committee on Foreign Relations declared that,

The Cuban question in Congress

> The very situation of Cuba and Porto Rico furnishes the strongest inducement to the United States not to take a place at the contemplated congress, since, by so doing, they must be considered as changing the attitude in which they hitherto have stood as impartial spectators of the passing scenes, and identifying themselves with the new republics.[14]

The Southern members were united in their opposition to the Panama mission, and in fact to any closer

[11]Stapleton, *Political Life of Canning,* III, 154.

[12]Mr. Clay to Mr. King, October 25, Wharton's *Digest,* Sec. 60.

[13]Canning to Earl of Liverpool, October 6, 1826.

[14]*A. S. P., F. R.,* V, 863.

Attitude of Southern members

alliance with the new republics, for the reason that the latter had adopted the principle of emancipation and any further extension of their influence would jeopardize the institution of slavery in the United States. For the same reason they were opposed to the transfer of Cuba to any other European power. If a change from its connection with Spain were necessary they favored annexation by the United States, and meantime they were strongly opposed to the government entering into any engagement with foreign powers or in any way committing itself on the Cuban question.[15]

The declaration of Mr. Clay against the interference of England and France in the affairs of Cuba was consistently adhered to under the administrations of Jackson and Van Buren.

Secretary Forsyth guarantees Cuba to Spain

In 1838–39, the British government dispatched special commissioners to Cuba and Porto Rico to report on the condition of the slave trade. The presence of these agents in Cuba gave rise to reports that Great Britain contemplated revolutionizing the island, or at least occupying it for the purpose of suppressing the slave trade. The United States gave Spain to understand that we would not consent to British control in whatever way it might be brought about. Mr. Forsyth wrote to Mr. Vail, our representative at Madrid, July 15, 1840:

> You are authorized to assure the Spanish government, that in case of any attempt, from whatever quarter, to wrest from her this portion of her territory, she may securely depend upon the military and naval resources of the United States to aid her in preserving or recovering it.[16]

Again, Mr. Webster in January, 1843, wrote to Mr. Campbell, United States consul at Havana:

---

[15] Benton's *Abridgment*, VIII, 427, 428, and IX, 90–218.

[16] 32 Cong., 1 Sess., H. Ex. Doc. No. 121; Wharton *Dig. of Int. Law*, sec. 60.

> The Spanish government has long been in possession of the policy and wishes of this government in regard to Cuba, which have never changed, and has repeatedly been told that the United States never would permit the occupation of that island by British agents or forces upon any pretext whatever; and that in the event of any attempt to wrest it from her, she might securely rely upon the whole naval and military resources of this country to aid her in preserving or recovering it.[17]

Webster repeats the guarantee

A copy of this letter was also sent to Washington Irving, our representative at Madrid, to make such use of as circumstances might require.[18]

Mexican war marks change in policy

During the first period of our Cuban diplomacy the efforts of this government were directed toward preventing the acquisition of the island, or the establishment of a protectorate over it, by Great Britain or France. With the Mexican war, however, and the growing conviction of "manifest destiny," our foreign policy assumed a much bolder and more aggressive character, and during the next fifteen years all manner of schemes for the southward extension of our territory were suggested and many of them actually undertaken. Cuba became an object of desire, not only in the eyes of the slave-holding population of the South as an acquisition to slave territory, but of a large part of the nation, because of its strategic importance in relation to the interoceanic transit routes of Central America, which seemed the only feasible line of communication with our rapidly developing interests in California. Consequently various attempts were made to annex the island to the United States, both by purchase from Spain and forcibly by filibustering expeditions.

In June, 1848, under the administration of President Polk, Mr. Buchanan, Secretary of State, wrote to our minister at Madrid, directing him to open negotiations

[17]Wharton's *Digest*, Sec. 60.

[18]Mr. Upshur, who succeeded Mr. Webster as Secretary of State, wrote to Mr. Irving to the same effect, October 10, 1843.

President Polk offers to purchase Cuba

with the Spanish government for the purchase of Cuba. After referring to the dangers of British occupation and to the advantages of annexation, he said: "Desirable, however, as this island may be to the United States, we would not acquire it except by the free will of Spain. Any acquisition not sanctioned by justice and honor would be too dearly purchased." He stated that the President would stipulate for the payment of $100,000,000, as a maximum price.[19] This offer was rejected by the Spanish government. The Minister of State after several months' delay finally replied "that it was more than any minister dare to entertain any such proposition; that he believed such to be the feeling of the country, that sooner than see the island transferred to any power, they would prefer seeing it sunk in the ocean."

Under the Whig administration of Taylor and Fillmore no effort was made for the purchase of Cuba. On August 2, 1849, Mr. Clayton wrote to Mr. Barringer that the government did not desire to renew the negotiation for the purchase of Cuba made by the late administration, since the proposition had been considered by the Spanish government as a national indignity; that should Spain desire to part with Cuba, the proposal must come from her.

Lopez prepares filibustering expedition

About this time active preparations were going on for the invasion of Cuba by an armed expedition under the Cuban patriot Narciso Lopez. On August 11, 1849, President Taylor issued a proclamation warning all citizens of the United States against taking part in such expedition and saying, "No such persons must expect the interference of this government in any form on their behalf, no matter to what extremities they may be reduced in consequence of their conduct."[20] A few days

[19]Mr. Buchanan to Mr. Saunders, June 17, 1848, 32 Cong., 1 Sess., H. Ex. Doc. No. 121; *Brit. and For. State Papers*, XXVI.

[20]Richardson, *Messages and Papers of the Presidents*, V, 7.

later the entire force of Lopez was arrested by the United States marshal just as it was on the point of leaving New York.

Southern leaders interested in the enterprise

Nothing daunted, Lopez traveled through the southern and southwestern states secretly enlisting men and making arrangements for their transportation to Cuba. Many men of prominence at the South were in open and avowed sympathy with the enterprise. In the spring of 1850, Lopez called upon Gen. John A. Quitman, Governor of Mississippi, who had served with great distinction in the Mexican war, and offered him, in the name of his compatriots, the leadership of the revolution and the supreme command of the army. Quitman's sympathies were thoroughly enlisted in the movement, but he declined the honor on account of the serious aspect of political affairs, particularly what he considered the encroachments of the Federal government upon the rights of the states. He made liberal contributions of money, however, and gave Lopez sound advice about his undertaking, insisting that he must have an advance column of at least 2,000 men to maintain a footing on the island until reinforcements could go to their aid.[21]

Unfortunately for Lopez he did not follow the advice of Quitman. A company of volunteers altogether inadequate for the successful accomplishment of the enter-

[21] J. F. H. Claiborne, *Life and Corresp. of John A. Quitman*, II, 55–56, and Appendix, p. 385.

In June the Grand Jury of the United States Circuit Court at New Orleans found a bill against John A. Quitman, John Henderson, Governor of Louisiana, and others, for setting on foot the invasion of Cuba. Quitman's view of state sovereignty did not admit the right of the United States courts to proceed against the chief executive of a sovereign state. He sought the advice of friends throughout the South as to what course he should pursue. None of them admitted the right of the United States courts to indict him and several of them advised him that it was his duty to assert the principle of state sovereignty even to the point of calling out the state militia to protect him against arrest. Others advised him to submit under protest so as to avoid an open breach. This course was finally adopted, and when the United States marshal appeared on the 3rd of February, 1851, to take him into custody, he yielded, causing at the same time an address to be issued to the people of Mississippi, in which he resigned the office of governor. After proceedings which lasted two months, Henderson was acquitted and the charges against Quitman and the others dismissed.

Lopez attempts to land in Cuba

prise was collected at New Orleans. There Lopez chartered a steamer, the *Creole*, and two barks, the *Georgiana* and the *Susan Loud.* Three-fourths of the volunteers had served in the Mexican war. The first detachment comprising 250 men left New Orleans in the bark *Georgiana*, April 25, 1850, under the command of Col. Theodore O'Hara. They proceeded to the island of Contoy off the coast of Yucatan in the territory of Mexico. There they were joined three weeks later by Lopez and 450 followers in the *Creole.* The entire command, with the exception of the crews of the two barks and a few others to guard the stores, embarked in the *Creole* and effected a landing at Cardenas, but the natives did not come to the aid of Lopez and after holding the town for twelve hours he reluctantly reëmbarked and headed for Key West. The *Creole* was pursued by the *Pizarro*, a Spanish war vessel, which steamed into the harbor just as she cast anchor. For a few moments the Spaniards seemed to be on the point of preparing to open fire on the *Creole*, but when they saw the United States custom-house officers take possession of her they changed their minds and left the harbor.

Release of captured Americans demanded

The two barks, which had been left with a small guard at the island of Contoy, were captured by Spanish war ships, taken to Havana, condemned as prizes and the men put on trial for participation in the Lopez expedition. As these men had committed no act of hostility against Spain, and had, moreover, been seized on neutral territory, the United States government at once issued its protest and demanded their release. The Spanish government replied that these men had been described as pirates by the President of the United States in his proclamation warning citizens against joining the expedition and were, therefore, beyond the pale of the protection of the United States. After heated negotiations which lasted several months and seriously threatened the peace of the two countries, the prisoners were released, but it was declared to be an act of grace on the part of the Queen and not a concession to the demands of the United States.[22]

The final expedition dispersed and Americans executed

Lopez was prosecuted by the United States government for violation of the neutrality laws, but escaped conviction and at once set about organizing another expedition. On August 3, 1851, the third and last expedition of Lopez, consisting of over 400 men, left New Orleans. After touching at Key West the steamer proceeded to the coast of Cuba and landed the expedition at Bahia Honda. The main body under Lopez proceeded into the country where they had been led to expect a general uprising of the Cubans. Col. W. S. Crittenden, who had served with bravery in the Mexican war, was left in command of a smaller body to bring up the baggage. This detachment was attacked on the 13th and forced to retreat to the place where they had landed, where about fifty of them obtained boats and tried to escape. They were, however, intercepted off the coast, taken to Havana, sentenced before a military court, and executed on the 16th.

Lopez taken and put to death

The main body under Lopez was overcome and dispersed by Spanish troops on the 24th. Lopez was taken prisoner, tried, and executed. Many of his followers were killed or died of hunger and fatigue and the rest made prisoners. Upon receipt of this news Commodore Parker was at once ordered to proceed in a frigate to Havana to inquire into the charges against the prisoners executed, and the circumstances of their capture, trial, and sentence. To these inquiries the captain-general replied that he considered those executed as pirates, that they had been so denounced by the President of the United States in his proclamation, that he was not at liberty to furnish a copy of the court records, but

[22] 31 Cong., 2 Sess., Sen. Ex. Doc. No. 41.

would send them to Madrid and to the Spanish minister at Washington.[23]

Anti-Spanish demonstration in New Orleans

When the news of the executions at Havana reached New Orleans the excitement was intense. The office of the Spanish consul was broken into, portraits of the Queen and Captain-General of Cuba defaced, the Spanish flag torn in pieces, and the consul burned in effigy in LaFayette Square. The consul had to flee from the city for safety and the property of certain Spaniards residing in New Orleans was destroyed. A long correspondence ensued between the two governments. The United States agreed to pay an indemnity for injuries to the public property of Spain, but not for the destruction of property belonging to Spanish residents, who were entitled only to the same protection afforded our own citizens.[24]

Action of British and French governments

A few weeks after the last Lopez expedition the British and French representatives at Washington notified our government that orders had been issued to their squadrons in the West Indies to repel by force any attempts at the invasion of Cuba from any quarter. Our government replied that such action on the part of England and France could "not but be regarded by the United States with grave disapproval, as involving on the part of European sovereigns combined action of protectorship over American waters."[25]

Proposal of a tripartite agreement

In order to allay the uneasiness caused by the attempts of filibusters, supposed to be encouraged or at least connived at by the government of the United States, the Spanish government requested Great Britain and France, in January, 1852, to secure the signature

---

[23] 32Cong., 1 Sess., H. Ex. Doc. No. 1.; also 2d Annual Message of Fillmore, December 2, 1851, Richardson, *Messages and Papers of the Presidents,* V, 113.

[24] 32 Cong., 1 Sess., H. Ex. Doc. No. 1.

[25] Mr. Crittenden to Comte de Sartiges, October 22, 1851. See also Pres. Fillmore to Mr. Webster and Mr. Webster's reply. 2 Curtis's *Life of Webster,* 551.

by the American government in conjunction with them of an abnegatory declaration with respect to Cuba.[26] Accordingly in April, 1852, the British and French ministers at Washington brought the subject to the attention of this government in notes of the same date, suggesting a tripartite convention for the guarantee of Cuba to Spain.[27]

To this proposal Mr. Webster replied in part as follows:

Secretary Webster's reply

> It has been stated and often repeated to the government of Spain by this government, under various administrations, not only that the United States have no design upon Cuba themselves, but that, if Spain should refrain from a voluntary cession of the island to any other European power, she might rely on the countenance and friendship of the United States to assist her in the defense and preservation of that island. At the same time it has always been declared to Spain that the government of the United States could not be expected to acquiesce in the cession of Cuba to an European power.

He reminded them, furthermore, that "the policy of the United States has uniformly been to avoid, as far as possible, alliances or agreements with other states, and to keep itself free from national obligations, except such as affect directly the interests of the United States themselves."[28]

Everett's final rejection of the proposal

The matter was again urged upon the United States by the British and French governments in notes to Mr. Webster, dated July 9, 1852, in which the indefeasibility of the Spanish title to the island and its bearings upon the neutrality of the proposed Central American canals were dwelt upon. The death of Mr. Webster postponed for some time the answer of the United States, but

[26] *Brit. and For. St. Pap.*, XLIV. Lord Howden to Earl Granville. January 9, 1852.

[27] Comte de Sartiges to Mr. Webster, April 23, 1852, 32 Cong., 2 Sess., Sen. Ex. Doc. No. 13.

[28] Mr. Webster to Comte de Sartiges, Apru 29, 1852. To Mr. Crampton, same date, to same effect.

the proposal was finally rejected in a notable dispatch prepared by Webster's successor, Edward Everett.

Foreign policy of President Pierce

With the growth of the slavery conflict, which had now become paramount to all other questions, the annexation of Cuba had become a party issue, and the return of the Democratic party to power, in 1853, was hailed by the Southern extremists as a signal for the acquisition of the long-coveted prize. This expectation was further heightened by the declaration of President Pierce, in his inaugural address, that the policy of his administration would "not be controlled by any timid forebodings of evil from expansion," and that the acquisition of certain possessions not within our jurisdiction was "eminently important for our protection, if not in the future essential for the preservation of the rights of commerce and the peace of the world."

Soulé appointed minister to Spain

William L. Marcy, of New York, was appointed Secretary of State and for the mission to Spain the President selected Pierre Soulé of Louisiana, a Frenchman by birth and education, who had been exiled for political reasons. His appointment under the circumstances created unfavorable comment both in this country and in Europe, and his sojourn of several days at Paris on the way to his post at Madrid caused the French government some annoyance. Louis Napoleon advised the Court of Madrid not to receive him, as his views on the Cuban question were well known to be of a radical character.

Marcy's instructions

In his instructions to Mr. Soulé, July 23, 1853, Mr. Marcy emphasized the importance of our relations with Spain in view of the rumors of contemplated changes in the internal affairs of Cuba and of the recent interposition of England and France. He directed him to try to negotiate a commercial treaty with Spain favorable to our trade with Cuba, and pointed out the urgent necessity of allowing a "qualified diplomatic intercourse between the captain-general of that island and our consul at Havana, in order to prevent difficulties and preserve a good understanding between the two countries."[29] The difficulty of settling disputes arising in Cuba had been the subject of frequent remonstrances on the part of the United States. The captain-general was clothed with almost "unlimited powers for aggression, but with none for reparation." He exercised no diplomatic functions and was in no way subject to the authority of the Spanish minister at Washington.

Soulé granted authority to propose purchase of Cuba

Upon the arrival of Mr. Soulé in Spain, he found that Mr. Calderon, the head of the cabinet, was strongly opposed to any commercial treaty or agreement which would promote intercourse between the United States and the dependencies of Spain, and equally averse to allowing the captain-general any diplomatic powers.[30] Mr. Soulé was by nature hot-headed and impetuous and could suffer anything sooner than enforced inactivity. Whatever may have been the intentions of the executive in sending him, he had come to Madrid for the purpose of consummating the long-cherished scheme of acquiring Cuba. Accordingly, on February 23, 1854, he wrote to Mr. Marcy that the affairs of the Spanish government were about to reach a crisis, that a change of ministry was imminent, and that contingencies involving the fate of Cuba were likely to arise which might be of great interest to the United States. He, therefore, asked for definite instructions. Relying upon these representations and upon Mr. Soulé's judgment, Mr. Marcy transmitted in due time the necessary powers, authorizing him to negotiate with Spain for the purchase of Cuba, or for its independence, if such an arrangement would be more agreeable to Spanish pride, in which event the United

[29] 32 Cong., 2 Sess., H. Ex. Doc. No. 93, p. 3.

[30] Mr. Soulé to Mr. Marcy, November 10, and December 23, 1853, and January 20, 1854.

States would be willing to contribute substantial aid to the result.

The *Black Warrior* affair

In the meantime, however, the *Black Warrior* affair had strained the relations of the two countries almost to the point of rupture. This case. involving the seizure of an American steamer by Spanish officials at Havana for an unintentional violation or neglect of custom-house regulations, was of an unusually exasperating character.

Soulé demands redress

As soon as the department at Washington was fully informed of this outrage, Mr. Marcy forwarded all the documents in the case to Mr. Soulé and directed him to demand of the Spanish government a prompt disavowal of the act and the payment of an indemnity to the owners of the vessel and of the cargo, the extent of the injury being estimated at $300,000. On April 8, Mr. Soulé presented a formal demand on the part of his government. No answer to this note having been received, on the 11th he repeated his demands much more emphatically, calling for an indemnity of $300,000, insisting that all persons, whatever their rank or importance, who were concerned in the perpetration of the wrong, be dismissed from Her Majesty's service, and finally declaring that non-compliance with these demands within forty-eight hours would be considered by the government of the United States as equivalent to a declaration that her Majesty's government was determined to uphold the conduct of its officers.

Spirited correspondence with Calderon

Mr. Calderon replied, on the 12th, that whenever Her Majesty's government should have before it the authentic and complete data, which it then lacked, a reply would be given to the demand of the United States conformable to justice and right; that the peremptory tone of Mr. Soulé's note suggested to the government of Her Majesty "a suspicion that it was not so much the manifestation of a lively interest in the defense of pretended injuries, as an incomprehensible pretext for exciting estrangement, if not a quarrel between two friendly powers." To this note Mr. Soulé replied that the suggestion made as to the motives of the United States in seeking redress was "but little creditable to the candor of Her Catholic Majesty's government, and comes in very bad grace from one who, like your excellency, cannot but be aware that the records of this legation, as well as those of Her Catholic Majesty's department of state, are loaded with reclamations bearing on grievances most flagrant, which have never been earnestly attended to and were met at their inception with precisely the same dilatory excuses through which the present one is sought to be evaded."

Unsatisfactory outcome

Meanwhile the aspects of the case were altogether changed by a private agreement between the Havana officials and the owners of the *Black Warrior*, by which the ship and her cargo were released. Mr. Soulé continued, however, according to instructions from Washington, to demand compensation for the damages sustained by the owners and passengers not compensated for by the return of the ship and cargo, and also reparation for the insult to the United States flag. The Spanish government, however, refused to recognize any ground for reparation after the restitution of the ship and cargo, and persisted in contradicting, without the support of any evidence whatever, the facts as presented by the United States, although they were all certified to in proper legal form.

The President considers extraordinary mission to Spain

On June 24, Mr. Marcy wrote that the President was far from satisfied with the manner in which our demands were treated by the Spanish government, but that before resorting to extreme measures he was determined to make a final appeal to Spain for the adjustment of past difficulties and for the guarantee of more friendly relations in the future. Although satisfied with the spirited manner in which Mr. Soulé had performed the duties of his mission, the President was considering the expediency of reinforcing the demands of the United States by the appointment of an extraordinary commission of two distinguished citizens to act in conjunction with him. He instructed him, therefore, not to press the affair of the *Black Warrior*, but to wait until the question of the special commission could be laid before Congress.

Change of ministry in Spain

During the summer there was a change of ministry in the Spanish government, which, as was not infrequently the case, was attended with more or less serious disorders. In August, Mr. Marcy wrote that in view of the unsettled condition of affairs in Spain and for other reasons not stated, the purpose of sending a special mission had, for the present at least, been abandoned. Without pressing matters Mr. Soulé was, nevertheless, to avail himself of any opportunity which might be presented, of settling the affairs in dispute and of negotiating for the purchase of Cuba.

Under the same date he proposed to Mr. Soulé the plan of consulting with Mr. Mason and Mr. Buchanan, our ministers at Paris and London, for the purpose of overcoming any obstacles that England and France might interpose. This suggestion led to the celebrated meeting at Ostend and the so-called manifesto.

The conference at Ostend

In accordance with the instructions of the President, Messrs. Soulé, Mason, and Buchanan proceeded to make arrangements for the proposed conference, which was held at Ostend, in Belgium, October 9, 10, 11, 1854. They then adjourned to Aix-la-Chapelle for a week, where the reports of their proceedings were prepared.

The "Manifesto"

The greater part of the report is taken up with an enumeration of the advantages that would accrue to the United States from the acquisition of Cuba, and an elaborate exposition of the ways in which the interests of Spain would be promoted by the sale. The only specific recommendation of the report was that a proposal should be made through the proper diplomatic channel to the Supreme Constituent Cortes about to assemble, to purchase Cuba from Spain, the maximum price to be $120,000,000. The report then proceeds to discuss the question, what ought to be the course of the American government should Spain refuse to sell Cuba? The ministers declared:

> After we shall have offered Spain a price for Cuba far beyond its present value, and this shall have been refused, it will then be time to consider the question, does Cuba, in the possession of Spain, seriously endanger our internal peace and the existence of our cherished Union?
>
> Should this question be answered in the affirmative, then, by every law, human and divine, we shall be justified in wresting it from Spain if we possess the power; and this upon the very same principle that would justify an individual in tearing down the burning house of his neighbor if there were no other means of preventing the flames from destroying his own home.

Drafted for political effect

The report also recommended that all proceedings in reference to the negotiations with Spain "ought to be open, frank, and public." This recommendation, together with the general character of the report, indicates that its authors were rather bent on making political capital of the affair at home than on seriously furthering negotiations at Madrid. As a matter of fact, the Ostend Manifesto made Buchanan an acceptable presidential candidate to the southern wing of the Democratic party and played no small part in securing for him the nomination in 1856.[31]

Repudiated by Marcy

The objectionable features of the report were politely but firmly repudiated by the administration in Marcy's reply to Soulé and Soulé promptly resigned his mission. This fact was generally overlooked at the time, while the unfortunate publicity given to the proceedings at

---

[31]The correspondence relating to the *Black Warrior* case and to the Ostend conference is contained in 33 Cong., 2 Sess., H. Ex. Doc. No. 93.

Ostend brought endless censure upon President Pierce and Secretary Marcy.

Friendly relations with Spain restored

In spite of the "jingo" policy attributed to the Pierce administration, the complications arising out of the seizure of the *Black Warrior* were not made a *casus belli*, as might easily have been done. After Mr. Soulé's return to the United States the negotiations were continued by his successor. The conduct of the officials concerned in the seizure was disavowed, and the indemnity claimed by the American citizens concerned was paid. The administration closed on terms of comparative friendship with Spain, although there were numbers of claims still unadjusted. The Cuban question figured conspicuously in the campaign of 1856. The platform of the Democratic party was strongly in favor of acquisition, while the new Republican platform stigmatized the Ostend Manifesto as the highwayman's plea.

President Buchanan urges upon Congress the purchase of Cuba

Until the Buchanan administration all negotiations for the purchase of Cuba had been undertaken on the authority of the executive alone. An effort was now made to get the two houses of Congress to concur in an appropriation for this purpose. It was thought that united action on the part of the legislative and executive branches of the government would produce some impression on Spain. Accordingly, in his second, third, and fourth annual messages, President Buchanan brought the matter to the attention of Congress, but his appeal met with little encouragement In January, 1859, Senator Slidell, the chairman of the Senate Committee on Foreign Relations, reported a bill carrying $30,000,000 to be placed at the disposal of the President as a preliminary sum for the purchase of Cuba.[32]

Slidell's report

This report created violent opposition, and in February the bill was withdrawn by Mr. Slidell at the urgent request of his friends.

[32]Sen. Report No. 351, 35 Cong., 2 Sess.

The Civil War intervenes

The annexationist and filibustering schemes of the decade immediately preceding the War of Secession were prompted by two motives. The one was the extension of slave territory, or at least the thwarting of the schemes of emancipation for Cuba which Great Britain was urging upon the Spanish government. The other was to secure, by the occupation of this strong strategic position, undisputed control over the proposed interoceanic canal routes of Central America and communication by this means with the new states on the Pacific Coast. These motives for annexation were removed, the one by the abolition of slavery in the United States, and the other by the construction of the great transcontinental railroads which established direct overland communication with the Pacific states.

CHAPTER XIII

NEGOTIATIONS FOR AN ISTHMIAN CANAL

The dream of centuries

THE cutting of the isthmus between North and South America was the dream of navigators and engineers from the time when the first discoverers ascertained that nature had neglected to provide a passage. Yet the new continent which so unexpectedly blocked the way of Columbus in his search for the Indies opposed for centuries an insurmountable barrier to the commerce of the East and the West. The piercing of the isthmus always seemed a perfectly feasible undertaking, but the difficulties in the way proved greater than at first sight appeared. There were (1) the physical or engineering problems to be solved, and (2) the diplomatic complications regarding the control of the canal in peace and its use in war. The weakness of the Spanish American states, whose territories embraced the available routes, and their recognized inability either to construct or protect a canal made what might otherwise have been merely a question of domestic economy one of grave international import. In this respect, as in others, the problem presented the same features as the Suez Canal. To meet these difficulties three plans were successively developed during the nineteenth century: (1) a canal constructed by a private corporation under international control, (2) a canal constructed by a private corporation under the exclusive control of the United States, and (3) a canal constructed, owned, operated, and controlled by the United States as a government enterprise. The Clayton-

Engineering and diplomatic problems

Bulwer treaty provided for the construction of a canal in accordance with the first plan; several unsuccessful attempts were made to raise the necessary capital under the second plan; while the third plan was the one under which the gigantic task was actually accomplished.

The Nicaragua route

The comparative merits of the Nicaragua and Panama routes long divided the opinion of experts. American engineers generally favored that through Nicaragua. The length of the Nicaragua route, from Greytown on the Atlantic to Brito on the Pacific by way of the San Juan River and through Lake Nicaragua, is about 170 miles. The elevation of the lake above the sea is about 110 feet. Its western shore is only twelve miles from the Pacific, with an intervening divide 154 feet above the sea. From the southeast corner of the lake flows the San Juan River, 120 miles to the Atlantic, with an average fall of about ten inches to the mile. The serious objections to this route are: (1) the lack of harbors at the terminals, Brito being a mere indentation on the coast, rendering the construction of immense breakwaters necessary, while at Greytown the San Juan broadens out into a delta that would require extensive dredging; and (2) the enormous rainfall at Greytown, exceeding that known anywhere else on the western continent—nearly twenty-five feet.

The Panama route

The Panama route from Colon on the Atlantic to Panama on the Pacific is about fifty miles in length, with a natural elevation nearly double that of Nicaragua. There are natural harbors at each end which with improvements are able to accommodate the heaviest shipping. The Panama Railroad, built along the line of the proposed canal, in 1850-55, gave this route an additional advantage. There were, however, certain disadvantages: (1) the unhealthfulness of the vicinity, rendering labor scarce and inefficient; (2) the heavy rainfall, ten to twelve feet at Colon; and (3) the treacherous character of the geologic structure, due to its volcanic origin, through which the cut had to be made. The impossibility of making even approximate estimates of the cost of the work in such a deadly climate and through such an uncertain geologic formation was one of the greatest difficulties to be overcome. The De Lesseps plan provided for an open cut throughout at the sea-level, at an estimated cost of $170,000,000. The work was begun in 1884 and prosecuted until 1888, when the gigantic scheme collapsed, after the company had expended about $300,000,000 and accomplished less than one-third of the work.

The legal status of an interoceanic canal

Great as the engineering problems of the various canal schemes have been shown to be, the importance to the world's commerce of the object in view would, in all probability, have led to their solution and to the construction of a canal long before the United States undertook the Panama enterprise, had it not been for difficulties of an altogether different character, complications arising out of the question as to the status of the canal in international law. The diplomatic difficulties in the case of an interoceanic canal are very great. It cannot be regarded as a natural strait, like the Dardanelles, the Danish Belts, or the Straits of Magellan, which were for a long time held under exclusive jurisdiction, but are now free to all nations. Nor, on the other hand, could an isthmian canal be compared to the Kiel Canal, which is within the territory of Germany, and which, although open to commerce, was specially designed to meet the needs of the German navy. Such canals as this are built by the capital of the country through which they pass, and are protected and controlled by its government. The status of the Kiel Canal was changed by the Treaty of Versailles. Article 380 threw the canal "open to the vessels of commerce and of war of all nations at peace with Germany on terms of entire equality."

No one of the republics to the south of us, through whose territory it was proposed to build a canal, could raise the capital for its construction or insure its protection when completed. No company chartered by one of these governments could have raised the necessary capital without some further guarantee. Hence it was that all companies organized for this purpose had to secure their charters from some more powerful nation, such as the United States or France, and their concessions from one of the Central American states. This rendered necessary a treaty between the state granting the concession or right to construct a canal through its territory and the state chartering the company. The claims of other states to equality of treatment in the use of such a canal constituted another element that had to be considered.

Diplomatic complications

First announcement of American policy

With the establishment of the independence of the Spanish-American republics the question of the construction of a ship canal across the isthmus became a matter of general interest, and it was one of the proposed subjects of discussion at the Congress of American Republics summoned by Bolivar to meet at Panama in 1826. In the instructions to the United States commissioners to that congress, Mr. Clay authorized them to enter into the consideration of that subject, suggesting that the best routes would likely be found in the territory of Mexico or of the Central Republic. As to the diplomatic status of the canal, he said:

> If the work should ever be executed so as to admit of the passage of sea vessels from ocean to ocean, the benefits of it ought not to be exclusively appropriated to any one nation, but should be extended to all parts of the globe upon the payment of a just compensation or reasonable tolls.[1]

Resolutions of the Senate

In 1835, and again in 1839, the United States Senate passed resolutions authorizing the President to enter into negotiations with other nations, particularly Central America and New Granada, for the purpose of protecting

[1]*Report of International American Conference,* Vol. IV (Hist. App.), 143.

by treaty either individuals or companies who might undertake to open communication between the two oceans, and of insuring "the free and equal navigation of the canal by all nations." Presidents Jackson and Van Buren both commissioned agents with a view to carrying out these resolutions, but without success.

Interest of Louis Napoleon in the Nicaragua route

While a prisoner at Ham in 1845, Prince Louis Napoleon Bonaparte secured from the government of Nicaragua a concession granting him power to organize a company for the construction of a waterway to be known as "Le Canale Napoléon de Nicaragua." After his escape from Ham, he published in London a pamphlet entitled "The Canal of Nicaragua, or a Project for the Junction of the Atlantic and Pacific Oceans by means of a Canal."[2]

Canal treaties

Although the United States government was a party to endless negotiations in regard to an inter-oceanic canal, there were only three treaties of any practical importance prior to the close of the nineteenth century, by which it acquired rights and assumed obligations on that account.[3] These were (1) the treaty with New Granada (Colombia) of 1846; (2) the Clayton-Bulwer treaty with England of 1850; and (3) the treaty with Nicaragua of 1867. Only the first two of these will be considered in the present chapter.

The United States acquires right-of-way across Panama

The treaty with New Granada was signed at Bogotá, December 12, 1846, and ratified by both governments in 1848. It did not differ materially from the general draft of treaties, except in the thirty-fifth article, which was of a special character and related to the Isthmus of Panama. By this article "the government of New Granada guarantees to the government of the United States that the right-of-way or transit across the Isthmus of Panama, upon any modes of communication that now exist or

[2]Snow: *Treaties and Topics in American Diplomacy*, 328.

[3]Our treaties with Mexico and Honduras, although covering the case of canal constructions, were of no practical importance, as the routes through these countries were not feasible.

that may be hereafter constructed, shall be open and free to the government and citizens of the United States," for the transportation of all articles of lawful commerce upon the same terms enjoyed by the citizens of New Granada.

Guarantees neutrality and sovereignty of the isthmus to Colombia

> And in order to secure to themselves the tranquil and constant enjoyment of these advantages, and for the favors they have acquired by the 4th, 5th, and 6th articles of this treaty, the United States guarantee positively and efficaciously to New Granada, by the present stipulation, the perfect neutrality of the before-mentioned isthmus, with the view that the free transit from the one to the other sea may not be interrupted or embarrassed in any future time while this treaty exists; and, in consequence, the United States also guarantee, in the same manner, the rights of sovereignty and property which New Granada has and possesses over the said territory.[4]

Panama railroad built by Americans

This treaty was to remain in force for twenty years, and then, if neither party gave notice of intended termination, it was to continue in force, terminable by either party at twelve months' notice. This treaty was in full force when the Panama revolution of 1903 took place. Under the protection of this treaty the Panama Railroad Company, composed mainly of citizens of the United States, secured a charter from New Granada, and between 1850 and 1855, constructed a railroad across the isthmus along the line of the proposed Panama canal. In consequence of the riot at Panama in 1856, efforts were made by the United States to modify this treaty so as to give the United States greater control and power to protect the means of transit, but without success.[5] Other attempts to modify it in 1868 and 1870 likewise failed.[6]

Four years after the signature of the above treaty with Colombia, and two years after its ratification by the

[4]Correspondence in relation to the Proposed Interoceanic Canal, the Clayton-Bulwer Treaty, and the Monroe Doctrine. Government Printing Office, 1885, p. 5. Referred to hereafter as "Collected Correspondence."

[5]*Ibid.*, pp. 23–27.

[6]*Ibid.*, pp. 27 and 40.

The Clayton-Bulwer convention

Senate, the United States and Great Britain executed what is popularly known as the Clayton-Bulwer treaty. It is of great importance to understand clearly the circumstances under which this treaty was negotiated.[7]

British occupation of the Nicaraguan coast

For very obvious reasons, the Isthmus of Panama was for many years the objective point of all canal schemes, but as the engineering difficulties of this route began to be fully appreciated, attention was directed more and more to that through Nicaragua. The occupation by Great Britain, under the assumption of a protectorate, of the territory about the mouth of the San Juan River, which belonged to Nicaragua and Costa Rica, and in which the Atlantic terminus of the canal would fall, was a source of no little uneasiness and perplexity to the United States. In June, 1849, Mr. Hise, *chargé d'affaires* of the United States in Central America, negotiated without the authorization or knowledge of his government a treaty with Nicaragua which gave the United States exclusive rights in the construction of a canal through the territory of that state.[8] This treaty was not submitted to the Senate, but was made use of in the negotiations that were opened shortly thereafter with Great Britain for the purpose of ousting her from her position of control over the mouth of the San Juan. A few months later, September 28, 1849, Mr. Squier signed with Honduras a treaty which ceded Tiger Island, in the Bay of Fonseca, to the United States, thus giving us a naval station on the Pacific side of the isthmus. This treaty, like that negotiated by Mr. Hise, was unauthorized and never submitted to the Senate.[9] Both treaties were used, however, in bringing England to the signature of the Clayton-Bulwer treaty. This activity in treaty making was occasioned by the acquisition of

The United States in need of a route to California

[7](Malloy) *Treaties and Conventions*, I, 659.
[8]Collected Correspondence, 94.
[9]*Ibid.*, p. 14.

California and the rush to the gold fields by way of the isthmus.

Discussion of the Nicaragua route

During the period that elapsed between Mr. Bancroft's withdrawal from London and Mr. Lawrence's arrival as the representative of the United States, Mr. Clayton instructed Mr. Rives, who was on his way to Paris, to stop in London and hold a conference with Lord Palmerston on the Central American question. At this date the United States was striving simply for equal rights in any waterway that might be opened through the isthmus and not for any exclusive rights. Mr. Rives declared to Lord Palmerston "that citizens of the United States had entered into a contract with the state of Nicaragua to open, on certain conditions, a communication between the Atlantic and Pacific oceans by the river San Juan and the Nicaragua lake; that the government of the United States, after the most careful investigation of the subject, had come undoubtedly to the conclusion that upon both legal and historical grounds the state of Nicaragua was the true territorial sovereign of the river San Juan as well as of the Nicaragua lake, and that it was, therefore, bound to give its countenance and support, by all proper and reasonable means, to rights lawfully derived by their citizens under a grant from that sovereign." He further said:

Objections to British control of Mosquito coast

That the United States would not, if they could, obtain any exclusive right or privilege in a great highway, which naturally belonged to all mankind, for they well knew that the possession of any such privilege would expose them to inevitable jealousies and probable controversies which would make it infinitely more costly than advantageous; that while they aimed at no exclusive privilege for themselves, they could never consent to see so important a communication fall under the exclusive control of any other great commercial power; that we were far from imputing to Her Britannic Majesty's government any views of that kind, but Mosquito possession at the mouth of the San Juan could be considered in no other light than British possession, and his lordship would readily comprehend that such a state of things, so long as it was continued, must necessarily give rise to dissatisfaction and distrust on the part of other commercial powers.[10]

Terms of the Clayton-Bulwer treaty

The negotiations thus opened by Mr. Rives were continued by Mr. Lawrence upon his arrival in England, but were shortly thereafter transferred to Washington, where Mr. Clayton succeeded in arranging with Sir Henry Lytton Bulwer the terms of a convention which was signed April 19, 1850. The intention of the two governments, as declared in the preamble, was to set forth "their views and intentions with reference to any means of communication by ship canal which may be constructed between the Atlantic and Pacific oceans by the way of the river San Juan de Nicaragua, and either or both of the lakes of Nicaragua or Managua, to any port or place on the Pacific Ocean."

Self-denying provisions

By the first article Great Britain and the United States bound themselves never to obtain or maintain any exclusive control over the said ship canal; never to erect or maintain any fortifications commanding the same or in the vicinity thereof, or to colonize or exercise dominion over Nicaragua, Costa Rica, the Mosquito coast, or any part of Central America; and never to make use of any alliance, connection, or influence with any of these states to obtain any unequal advantages in regard to commerce or navigation through the said canal.

Neutralization of the canal under international guarantee

The second article provided for the neutralization of the canal in the event of war between the contracting parties. The third guaranteed protection for the persons and property of the parties legally undertaking the construction of the canal. The fourth related to gaining the consent of the states whose territory the canal should traverse. The fifth article provided for the neutralization and protection of the canal so long as it was managed

[10]*Op. cit.*, pp. 11 and 12.

without discrimination against either of the contracting parties, and stipulated that neither of them would withdraw its protection without giving the other six months' notice. In the sixth article the contracting parties promised to invite every state with which they were on terms of friendly intercourse to accede to this convention. In the seventh article the contracting parties agreed to lend their support and encouragement to the first company offering to construct the canal in accordance with the spirit and intention of this convention. The eighth article was of special importance. It declared that "the governments of the United States and Great Britain having not only desired, in entering into this convention, to accomplish a particular object, but also to establish a general principle, they hereby agree to extend their protection, by treaty stipulations, to any other practicable communication, whether by canal or railway, across the isthmus which connects North and South America, and especially to the interoceanic communications, should the same prove practicable, whether by canal or railway, which are now proposed to be established by the way of Tehuantepec or Panama."[11]

A general principle

Such are the main stipulations of the celebrated Clayton-Bulwer treaty, which remained in force until 1901, and which during that period probably called forth more discussion than any treaty which the United States had ever signed.

Criticism of the treaty

In after years a large number of people on this side of the Atlantic, forgetting the object and aim of the treaty and the circumstances under which it was negotiated, thought that the United States conceded too much and violated the principle of the Monroe Doctrine in giving England a position and interest in America which she did not before possess. This opinion was held by some prominent statesmen at the time the treaty was negotiated, notably

[11] *Op. cit.*, p. 99.

by Buchanan, who poured forth severe criticism and ridicule upon it. While it was before the Senate for ratification he wrote to a friend:

Buchanan's statement

> If Sir Henry Bulwer can succeed in having the two first provisions of this treaty ratified by the Senate, he will deserve a British peerage. The consideration for our concessions is the relinquishment of the claim to the protectorate of the Mosquito shore—so absurd and unfounded that it has been ridiculed even by the London *Times.* Truly Sir Henry has brought this claim to a good market when he found a purchaser in Mr. Clayton. The treaty altogether reverses the Monroe Doctrine, and establishes it against ourselves rather than European governments.[12]

Let us see what the interests of the two signatory powers were at that time in Central America. The United States had recently acquired California by the treaty of Guadalupe Hidalgo, and the rapid development of the Pacific states made the canal a question of greater importance to the United States than ever before. The great transcontinental railroads, which some fifteen years later established direct overland communication with the Pacific states, were then hardly thought of.

British interests in Central America

England's interest in the canal, on the other hand, was rather a prospective one, but farsighted as usual she had provided for future contingencies by occupying several years before, under the guise of a protectorate over the Mosquito Indians, Greytown at the mouth of the San Juan River, the Atlantic terminus of the canal. In addition to the Mosquito coast, England at this time held the Bay Islands and Belize, or British Honduras. The United States, it is true, had never recognized the claims of Great Britain to dominion over the Mosquito coast. These claims, which dated back to the eighteenth century when British wood-cutters in search of mahogany, and smugglers entered the territory occupied by the Mosquito

[12]Mr. Buchanan to Hon. John A. McClernand, April 2, 1850, *American Hist. Rev.*, Oct., 1899.

Indians and established cordial relations with them, had been abandoned by the treaty of 1786 with Spain, but were revived in 1841, when a ship of war was sent to San Juan del Norte to announce the protection of England over the lands of the Mosquito king and to raise the Mosquito flag.[13] In 1848, the English and Indians drove the Nicaraguans out of the town and changed the name to Greytown.

The United States uniformly denied the rights of the Mosquito king to sovereignty over the district, and consequently the pretensions of the inhabitants of Greytown to political organization or power derived in any way from the Mosquitos. In his instructions to Mr. Hise soon after the occupation of Greytown, Secretary Buchanan said:

Criticism of British policy

> The object of Great Britain in this seizure is evident from the policy which she has uniformly pursued throughout her history, of seizing upon every available commercial point in the world whenever circumstances have placed it in her power. Her purpose probably is to obtain control of the route for a railroad or canal between the Atlantic and Pacific oceans by way of Lake Nicaragua. . . . The government of the United States has not yet determined what course it will pursue in regard to the encroachment of the British government. . . . The independence as well as the interests of the nations on this continent require that they should maintain an American system of policy entirely distinct from that which prevails in Europe. To suffer any interference on the part of the European governments with the domestic concerns of the American republics, and to permit them to establish new colonies upon this continent, would be to jeopard their independence and ruin their interests. These truths ought everywhere throughout this continent to be impressed upon the public mind; but what can the United States do to resist such European interference whilst the Spanish-American republics continue to weaken themselves by civil divisions and civil war, and deprive themselves of doing anything for their own protection.

Whatever the rights of the case, Great Britain was in actual possession of the Atlantic terminus of the proposed

[13] Wharton's *Digest*, Sec. 295.

The United States unable to use force against England

canal, and the United States was not prepared forcibly to oust her, even if such a course had been deemed advisable. The United States had no rights in the case at this time by treaty with Nicaragua or otherwise, none of the statesmen of that day having been broad enough in their views or bold enough to consider the territory of Nicaragua as "a part of the coast-line of the United States." All that could be opposed to England's *de facto* possession was the Monroe Doctrine, and England held that her claim antedated the declaration of that principle of American diplomacy. Mr. Clayton cannot, therefore, be justly charged with a violation of the Monroe Doctrine, for the effect of the treaty was to leave England weaker territorially on this continent than she was before.

The Nicaragua-Costa Rica boundary

The Clayton-Bulwer treaty left open several minor questions that required adjustment before the canal enterprise could be pushed forward with success. Chief among these were the dispute between Nicaragua and Costa Rica in regard to their boundary line and the controversy between Great Britain and Nicaragua in regard to the territory claimed by the Mosquito Indians. In April, 1852, Mr. Webster and Sir John Crampton agreed upon a basis for the settlement of Central American affairs, and drew up and signed a proposal to be submitted to Nicaragua and Costa Rica.[14] This proposed basis for a treaty was rejected by Nicaragua, which left the questions involved in the same unsettled position.

Divergent interpretations of the Clayton-Bulwer treaty

A much more serious obstacle to the accomplishment of the objects of the Clayton-Bulwer treaty than the failure of the above proposal arose from the wide divergence of opinion between the British and American governments in regard to its interpretation. The discussion involved two principal points: (1) Whether the abnegatory clauses of the first article were merely prospective in character and directed against future acquisitions in Central America,

[14]Collected Correspondence, 102.

or whether they required Great Britain to abandon her protectorate over the Mosquito coast at once; and (2) whether the Bay Islands came within the purview of the treaty. It was expressly stipulated that Belize or British Honduras was not included in Central America and therefore not affected by the treaty one way or the other. A declaration to this effect was filed at the state department by the British minister, Sir Henry Bulwer. In reply, Mr. Clayton, after conference with the chairman of the Senate Committee on Foreign Relations, acknowledged that British Honduras did not come within the scope of the treaty, but at the same time carefully refrained from affirming or denying the British title to that settlement or its alleged dependencies.[15] This left open the question as to whether the Bay Islands were dependencies of Belize or of the Republic of Honduras.

Status of the Bay Islands

Shortly after the failure of the Crampton-Webster proposals, Great Britain took advantage of the uncertainty that existed in regard to the status of the Bay Islands and by a formal proclamation, issued July 17, 1852, converted her settlements on those islands into "the Colony of the Bay Islands." When the United States government expressed its surprise at this proceeding, the British government replied that the Bay Islands were dependencies of Her Majesty's settlement at Belize and therefore, by explicit agreement, not within the scope of the Clayton-Bulwer treaty.[16]

Dallas-Clarendon treaty

In 1856 an effort was made to terminate the difficulties arising out of the different constructions put upon the Clayton-Bulwer treaty by the negotiation of a supplementary convention. On October 17 of that year a treaty was signed in London by the American minister and Lord Clarendon, known as the Dallas-Clarendon treaty. It provided (1) for the withdrawal of the British protectorate

[15] *Op. cit.*, p. 234, also Wharton's *Digest*, II, 190.
[16] Collected Correspondence, 248.

over the Mosquito Indians; (2) it regulated the boundaries of the Belize settlements on the basis of a compromise; and (3) it provided for a cession of the Bay Islands to Honduras, upon condition of the ratification of a treaty already negotiated between Great Britain and Honduras, which virtually erected an independent state of the islands, exempt in many particulars from the sovereignty of Honduras, and under the protectorate of Great Britain.

Senate amendments unacceptable to Great Britain

The first two clauses were acceptable to the United States Senate, but it was deemed proper to amend the third by striking out all that part of it which contemplated the concurrence of the United States in the British treaty with Honduras, and simply to provide for a recognition by the two governments of the sovereignty of Honduras over the islands in question.[17] Great Britain rejected this amendment and the Dallas-Clarendon treaty fell through. Great Britain and the United States were thus thrown back upon the Clayton-Bulwer treaty with its conflicting interpretations.

New British proposal

In October, 1857, the President was notified informally that the British government had decided to dispatch Sir William Ouseley, a diplomatist of well-recognized authority and experience, to Central America to make a definite settlement of all matters in dispute between the United States and England; that the efforts of the new plenipotentiary would be directed to those objects which had been dealt with in the Dallas-Clarendon treaty of 1856, viz., the cession of the Bay Islands to Honduras, the substitution of the sovereignty of Nicaragua for the protectorate of England over the Mosquitos and the regulation of the frontiers of Belize; that it was the intention of Her Majesty's government to carry the Clayton-Bulwer treaty into execution according to the general tenor of the interpretation put upon it by the United States, but to do so by separate negotiation with the

[17] *Op. cit.*, p. 286.

Central American republics, in lieu of a direct engagement with the Federal government.[18]

Great Britain suggests arbitration as alternative

President Buchanan replied that he would be satisfied with this course and that upon receiving an official assurance to that effect, he would change the character of the message he had already prepared for Congress. On the 30th of November, 1857, the British government submitted to the United States the alternative of referring the Clayton-Bulwer treaty to the arbitration of any European power which the United States might prefer to select or of adjusting matters by negotiations with the Central American republics, as already outlined in Sir William Ouseley's prospective mission.[19]

Walker's invasion of Nicaragua

At this stage of the negotiations matters were further complicated (1) by the negotiation of the Cass-Yrissari treaty of November 16, 1857, between the United States and Nicaragua for protection of the transit route and (2) by the invasion of Nicaraguan territory by a band of filibusters under General Walker, bent on the subversion of the lawful government of the country. The treaty was not ratified, however, and the Walker expedition was arrested by the interposition of the United States navy.

Abrogation of Clayton-Bulwer treaty proposed by Buchanan

The United States government not having given any definite answer to the British proposal to submit the treaty to arbitration, the British government delayed dispatching Sir William Ouseley on his mission. In the negotiations which took place during this delay the question of the abrogation of the Clayton-Bulwer treaty was discussed between the two governments. In his message of December 8, 1857, President Buchanan had suggested abrogation of the treaty by mutual consent as the wisest course that could be pursued in view of the increasing complications to which the varying constructions of it were giving rise. The British government took up this sug-

[18] *Op. cit.*, pp. 262–263.

[19] *Ibid.*, p. 276.

gestion and expressed its willingness to concur in such a course, but also expressed the opinion that the initiative should be taken by the government which was dissatisfied with its provisions.

The British reply

The British minister was, however, directed by his government to make it perfectly clear to the government of the United States, that to abrogate the treaty was to return to the *status quo ante* its conclusion in 1850; that Great Britain had no kind of jealousy respecting American colonization in Central America, and did not ask or wish for any exclusive privileges whatever in that quarter.[20] Finally, Sir William Ouseley was dispatched on his mission, and during the years 1859 and 1860 succeeded in negotiating treaties with Guatemala, Honduras, and Nicaragua, the provisions of which were in substantial accord with the rejected Dallas-Clarendon treaty.[21]

Final settlement satisfactory to United States

The treaty which he signed with Nicaragua on January 28, 1860, though restoring to that republic nominal sovereignty over the Mosquito territory, reserved to the Indians the right of retaining their own customs, assigned boundaries to that reservation in all probability greatly beyond its true limits, and confirmed grants of land previously made in that territory. Notwithstanding these facts, in his annual message of December 3, 1860, President Buchanan declared that the United States government was satisfied with the final settlement. His words were:

> The discordant constructions of the Clayton-Bulwer treaty between the two governments, which at different periods of the discussion bore a threatening aspect, have resulted in a final settlement entirely satisfactory to this government.[22]

The Civil War caused an indefinite postponement of all canal projects. The history of the Panama Canal will be discussed in a later chapter.

[20] *Op. cit.*, p. 280.

[21] *Ibid.*, pp. 294–302.

[22] Richardson, *Messages and Papers*, V, 639.

CHAPTER XIV

RELATIONS WITH CHINA AND JAPAN

A special policy for eastern Asia

IN EASTERN Asia and the Pacific the United States has from the first come into direct contact with the great world powers and been forced, although at times reluctantly, to play the game of world politics. Here was a field in which neither isolation nor the Monroe Doctrine could be successfully applied. A new policy had to be developed.

It is a fact not generally recognized by Americans that in the three great political and commercial areas with which we have close relations we have three separate and distinct policies: the policy of isolation, which is still supposed to dominate our relations with Europe; the Monroe Doctrine, which has kept Latin America free from European exploitation and maintained the open door, but which has latterly taken on an imperialistic aspect; and the policy of coöperation in eastern Asia and the Pacific, which was first developed by Seward during the period of the Civil War, then suffered to lapse, was revived again by John Hay, and finally made the basis of the Washington treaties of 1922.

Aim of American policy in the East

The consistent aim of American policy in the East has been to secure most-favored-nation treatment for American citizens and American commerce, or the open door as opposed to foreign spheres of influence. This policy had its beginning when Commodore Kearny, of the American navy, at the close of the Opium War in 1842, secured from the Chinese commissioner a pledge of most-favored-nation treatment. In our efforts to maintain favorable trade relations with China we have not infrequently taken advantage of the coercive measures of other powers without assuming moral responsibility for their acts, at times we have coöperated with these same powers, and at other times we have pursued a policy of isolation. We have never attained anything in Asia by isolation. As a recent writer says:

"An isolated policy in Asia tends inevitably to a surrender of most-favored-nation treatment or a defiance of all comers. It is essentially belligerent."[1]

Beginnings of American trade with China

American trade with China began almost with the establishment of independence. The first vessel bearing the United States flag to make the voyage to the Far East was the *Empress of China*, which left New York February 22, 1784, for Canton with a cargo of ginseng. Her return home in May, 1785, aroused great interest and, although she reported very modest profits, other vessels were soon fitted out for the voyage to China in Boston, Providence, New York, Philadelphia, Baltimore, and Norfolk. Under the special favors extended to the China trade by Congress in the acts of 1789 and 1791 it grew rapidly. At the same time American whalers were meeting with great success in the Pacific. The China trade and the whaling industry both suffered from the Embargo of 1807 and the War of 1812, but both revived after 1815.[2]

Early success

Between the War of 1812 and Britain's Opium War with China American trade with the Orient flourished as at no other period. Until the British break with China in 1839 none of the powers had resorted to coercive measures, and as long as all foreign merchants had to compete in gaining the good will of the Chinese authorities, the Americans seemed to have the advantage. All suffered injustice at times, but during this early period

[1]Tyler Dennett, *Americans in Eastern Asia*, 678.

[2]*Ibid.*, chap. i; Callahan, *American Relations in the Pacific and Far East*, 10.

Americans suffered far less than they did when their competitors resorted to measures of coercion.

Establishment of consular relations

Major Samuel Shaw of Boston, a distinguished Revolutionary officer, who had gone out as supercargo on the *Empress of China,* made a full report on conditions at Canton and the prospects for American trade to John Jay, Secretary of Foreign Affairs, and on Jay's recommendation he was elected by Congress to the position of consul at Canton. When Washington became President he renewed Shaw's appointment, and the latter served until his death in 1794. Shaw and his successors for more than fifty years were resident merchants who served without compensation save the fees of the office, which prior to 1836 rarely amounted to $500 a year.[3] The Chinese regarded all traders with contempt, and theoretically refused to have official relations with the consul, though they expected him to exercise despotic control over his own countrymen at Canton.[4]

The diplomatic mission of Edmund Roberts

The first American diplomatic mission to the Far East was not to China, but to Annam, Siam, and Muscat. The murder of the crew of the *Friendship* of Salem, Massachusetts, in 1831, by natives of Sumatra, was the immediate occasion for the dispatch of a special agent by the government of the United States. President Jackson selected Edmund Roberts of New Hampshire, a large shipowner who had spent much time abroad and had visited the Oriental countries. He left in the U.S.S. *Peacock* in 1832 provided with autographed letters from the President of the United States to the sovereigns of Muscat, Siam, and Annam, and with powers to negotiate treaties. He touched at Manila and also at Canton. When the *Peacock* appeared off the latter port the Chinese authorities, on learning that it was a war vessel, issued an edict ordering it to depart and return home at once. Mr.

[3]Dennett, 61.

[4]*Ibid.*, pp. 62, 75.

Roberts paid no attention to this edict and remained for six weeks after it was issued. He then went to Annam or Cochin-China. Here various technical obstacles were thrown in the way of direct intercourse with the higher officials, and in order to impress them with his importance Mr. Roberts resorted to the device of adding to his name by way of titles the names of the counties in his native state of New Hampshire, and was proceeding with the names of towns, mountains, and rivers, when the agents, telling him that it would not do to append more titles than the provincial governor possessed, consented to bear his letter to that functionary. He met with a more favorable reception in Siam, and negotiated a treaty bearing the date March 20, 1833. He was also successful in negotiating a treaty with the Sultan of Muscat. Mr. Roberts then returned to the United States, and the treaties which he had negotiated were ratified by the Senate. He was almost immediately sent out on a second mission in a man-of-war to exchange ratifications. He was received with great ceremony at Siam, and the squadron then proceeded to Canton, where an Oriental plague broke out in the vessels and Mr. Roberts died at Macao June 12, 1836. He was the pioneer in American diplomacy in the Orient.[5]

His resourcefulness

Japan not visited by Roberts

It seems at first sight strange that China was not included in Roberts' mission, but none of the powers had treaties with China at that time, and there was apparently no demand from the merchants for a treaty. While Roberts was in Batavia he received instructions to proceed to Japan for the purpose of negotiating a treaty, but he considered that too great a task for an expedition which was too small to impress the Japanese and without funds or presents for the Shogun.[6]

Early intercourse with China was attended with many

[5]Foster, *American Diplomacy in the Orient,* 45–55.

[6]Dennett, 131, 133.

hardships. The Emperor and official classes refused to recognize the equality of other nations and insisted on treating Europeans as the subjects of vassal nations and their envoys as tribute bearers. No barbarian or "foreign devil" was permitted to have an interview with the Emperor without performing the kowtow.

Efforts of Great Britain to establish diplomatic intercourse with China

Until 1842 European trade with China was confined to the single port of Canton, and was carried on under the disadvantage of all sorts of troublesome regulations and interference on the part of the Chinese local officials. Notwithstanding these disadvantages, the commerce between Europe and China had by the latter part of the eighteenth century assumed large proportions. It was mainly in the hands of the Portuguese, the British, and the Dutch. The British trade was a monopoly in the hands of the East India Company, and consisted largely of trade in opium, tea, and silk. Various acts of hostility against British merchants led in 1793 to the dispatch of Lord Macartney to China with the object of establishing diplomatic communication with the Chinese court. After many preliminary negotiations, Lord Macartney finally insisted on visiting Peking, and the Chinese reluctantly consented. The flag which waved from the mast of the junk that bore him and his attendants up the Peiho bore the legend "tribute-bearers from the country of England." He was told that he could not be admitted into the Emperor's presence without performing the kowtow. This he refused to do. He offered, however, that if a mandarin of equal rank with himself would perform the kowtow before the picture of George III which he was carrying to Peking as a present to the Emperor, he would bow down in the same manner before the "Son of Heaven." This offer was declined, but the Emperor finally consented to receive Lord Macartney on condition that he would perform the same obeisance as he would before his own sovereign. This he did, but he accomplished little or

Lord Macartney has trouble over the kowtow

nothing, and was kept under such strict espionage that his sojourn in Peking amounted almost to imprisonment.[7]

Futile missions of Amherst and Napier

The continued disordered state of affairs in China and the hostility to merchants led Great Britain in 1816 to send a second ambassador in the person of Lord Amherst. As he declined to perform the kowtow before the Emperor, he was not admitted to the imperial presence, and his mission was likewise a failure.[8] The Chinese were totally ignorant of the wealth, civilization, and military power of Europe, and treated all foreigners with utter contempt. The hardships which were inflicted on the merchants at Canton were the subject of reiterated complaint. When the monopoly of the East India Company came to an end about 1833, Great Britain sent Lord Napier to Canton as minister to superintend the foreign trade. He was not properly backed up by his government, and after being subjected to untold annoyances and insults, died at Macao a few months after his arrival.[9]

The dispute over opium

Meanwhile the opium trade between British India and China had assumed large proportions, and the Chinese officials made repeated efforts to put a stop to it. The complaints of the Chinese mandarins finally moved Captain Elliot (afterward Admiral Sir Charles Elliot), superintendent of trade at Canton, to agree to surrender to the Chinese authorities all opium in the hands of Englishmen. This was in 1839. Over 20,000 chests of opium, valued at \$300-\$500 a chest, were handed over to the Chinese officials and destroyed, but the merchants refused to sign a bond that they would refrain from dealing in opium in the future, a stipulation on which Lin, the Chinese imperial commissioner, insisted. In consequence of their refusal the merchants were finally driven from Canton. The

---

[7] Morse, *International Relations of the Chinese Empire,* I, 53–54.

[8] *Ibid.,* pp. 55–57.

[9] *Ibid.,* pp. 118–138.

British fleet, which arrived soon after their expulsion, backed up the merchants, and the controversy soon developed into the famous Opium War, which began in 1840. To the Chinese opium was the sole cause of the war; to the foreigners concerned, especially the English, opium was an incident. They did not believe in the sincerity of the Chinese officials, but thought that the interference with the trade was merely another demand for "squeeze." In spite of earlier decrees they had found little difficulty in getting opium admitted through bribery. But the Chinese government was now in earnest, though the foreigners did not realize it. While many Americans and some English abstained on conscientious grounds from trading in opium, they were in full sympathy with the demand for the readjustment of China's relations with the foreign merchants, and all united in a long chapter of grievances which grew out of the legitimate trade and had no connection with opium.[10]

Other grievances

The Opium War and the treaty of Nanking

Soon after the rupture the British fleet captured Chusan and in 1841 the Bogue forts fell. Canton was now at the mercy of the fleet. At this point Ki Shen, who had succeeded Lin as imperial commissioner, agreed to cede Hongkong and to pay an indemnity of $6,000,000. When this news reached Peking, Ki Shen was dismissed and military operations were resumed. Canton was soon taken by the British, and later Amoy, Ningpo, Tinghai, Shanghai, and several smaller coast towns. The British then advanced against Nanking, the southern capital of China, which would undoubtedly have fallen into their hands had not the imperial government proposed peace. By the treaty of 1842, signed at Nanking, it was provided that the four ports of Amoy, Foochoo, Ningpo, and Shanghai should be open to British trade on the same conditions as Canton; that Hongkong should be ceded to

---

[10]Morse, I, 250 note.

the British crown; that the Chinese government should pay to Great Britain a war indemnity of $21,000,000.[11]

Opinion in the United States

The government of the United States was naturally an interested observer in the events leading to the Opium War and in the outcome of that struggle. In an address before the Massachusetts Historical Society in November, 1841, John Quincy Adams took the ground that Great Britain was entirely justified in going to war, but the state of public opinion in America is shown by the fact that this address excited a great deal of adverse criticism and that the *North American Review* refused to publish it. Whatever the state of public opinion in America, the government of the United States was eager to profit by the coercive measures which Great Britain employed. During the war the United States kept a naval squadron in Chinese waters. Commodore Kearny, who was in command of this squadron, showed great firmness and skill in compelling the authorities at Canton to pay damages amounting to several hundred thousand dollars for injuries suffered by Americans during the war on account of mob violence. As soon as he heard that the British treaty provided for a new tariff and new trade regulations, he communicated with the governor of Canton, and asked that citizens of the United States in their trade should "be placed upon the same footing as the merchants of the nation most favored." He was given every assurance that American commerce would receive favorable treatment. A member of the British commission later wrote:

Commodore Kearny secures promise of most-favored-nation treatment

> The Chinese government promised, on the representation of the American Commodore, Kearny, previous to the treaty of Nanking, that whatever concessions were made to the English should also be granted to the United States. The throwing open the ports of China to Europe and America was not, therefore, the result of our policy, but had its origin in the anxious

[11] *Op. cit.*, I, 301–304.

forethought of Americans, lest we might stipulate for some exclusive privileges.[12]

The United States decides to send a minister to China

During the war the question of sending an American diplomatic representative to China was agitated by the merchants of Boston. When Dr. Peter Parker, who had been in China for some years as a medical missionary, was in Washington in April, 1841, he urged Secretary Webster to send a minister and suggested the name of John Quincy Adams. On December 30, 1842, President Tyler, having received news of the terms of the British treaty, sent a special message to Congress, written by Daniel Webster, in which he recommended that an appropriation be made for dispatching a commissioner to China for the purpose of negotiating a treaty of commerce. In the same message he discussed the situation in the Hawaiian Islands and requested an appropriation for a consul. The Pacific was beginning to loom large on the diplomatic horizon. When it came to the naming of a minister, Webster suggested Edward Everett, then minister to Great Britain, probably with a view to succeeding him at the Court of St. James's. Webster was at this time anxious to withdraw from Tyler's cabinet. On Mr. Everett's declining the offer, Caleb Cushing, a member of Congress from Massachusetts, was selected.[13] Cushing was a shrewd lawyer and a man of great ability and probably better fitted to cope with Chinese diplomacy than Everett. Fletcher Webster, son of the Secretary of State, was appointed secretary of the delegation, and Dr. Peter Parker and Rev. E. C. Bridgman, two missionaries, were made interpreters.

Caleb Cushing finally chosen

Futile efforts to reach Peking

The expedition, consisting of a frigate, a sloop of war, and a steam frigate, reached Macao February 24, 1844, where Mr. Cushing established himself in the house of a former Portuguese governor, and created "a profound sen-

[12]Foster, 74–76; Dennett, 108–111.

[13]Fuess, *Life of Caleb Cushing*, 2 vols., published in 1923.

sation in the colony by the novelty and magnitude of his mission as well as by his attractive personal qualities." A little later, however, he reported regretfully that a French embassy, "arranged on a scale of much greater expense than that of the United States," had also arrived. Three days after his arrival Cushing sent a note to the provincial governor expressing his intention of proceeding to Peking to deliver the President's letter to the Emperor. This note started a correspondence which lasted for three months. The Chinese government had no desire to negotiate a treaty, and was displeased at the arrival of the American mission. The imperial governor informed Mr. Cushing that he would have to wait until the august Emperor's will could be ascertained, and that a man-of-war could not be permitted under any circumstances to go to Tientsin. Mr. Cushing was equal to the occasion. He replied that the American consul had notified the Chinese government several months in advance that he was coming for the purpose of negotiating a treaty, and that if it had been the desire of the Emperor to negotiate at the frontier, he would have sent a commissioner to Canton for that purpose. He added that if the governor did not think it advisable for him to go to Tientsin in a war ship, he would proceed to Peking overland. In reply the governor said that the way overland was long and the crossing of the rivers dangerous, and he urged the envoy to "tranquillize himself" at Macao until the Emperor's pleasure could be learned. After two and a half months Mr. Cushing was informed of the Emperor's decision. It was stated that his going to Tientsin and to the capital would be utterly irregular, as Americans had never gone through the form of bearing tribute to the Emperor, but that a commissioner with the imperial seal, Kiying, had been appointed and was traveling with all speed to Canton to meet him. On June 9, Cushing received a letter from Kiying advising him of his arrival and adding that "in a few days we shall take each other

Imperial commissioner sent to negotiate with Cushing

by the hand, and converse and rejoice together with indescribable delight." As Mr. Foster says, Cushing accepted this as a somewhat exaggerated figure of speech, but his relations with Kiying were quite satisfactory. The latter was anxious to conclude the treaty before the arrival of the French mission, which was expected in a few days, and an agreement was reached without serious difficulty. On July 3, 1844, the treaty was signed at a temple in the suburbs of Macao occupied by the Chinese embassy. Strange to say, Mr. Cushing had not set foot on Chinese territory, nor had he had any personal intercourse with a single high Chinese official except the members of the embassy. The treaty was negotiated and executed on what was practically Portuguese territory.[14]

The treaty of 1844

The Cushing treaty was in many respects superior to the English, and it was immediately used by the French as a model for theirs, negotiated a few weeks later. Not only did it contain more advantageous provisions in regard to the conduct of trade, but in Article XXI it guaranteed to Americans in clear and explicit terms the rights of extraterritoriality.

Guarantee of extra-territoriality

> Subjects of China who may be guilty of any criminal act towards citizens of the United States shall be arrested and punished by the Chinese authorities according to the laws of China; and citizens of the United States who may commit any crime in China shall be subject to be tried and punished only by the consul, or other public functionary of the United States, thereto authorized, according to the laws of the United States.

It was further provided in Article XXV that,

> All questions in regard to rights, whether of property or person, arising between citizens of the United States in China, shall be subject to the jurisdiction of, and regulated by the authorities of their own government. And all controversies occurring in China between citizens of the United States and the subjects of any other government shall be regulated by the treaties existing between the United States and such governments, respectively, without interference on the part of China.

[14]Foster, 78–86; Dennett, 146–156; 28 Cong., 2 Sess., Sen. Docs. 58 and 67.

Fixes status of foreigners in China

It appears that the principle of extraterritoriality had in substance been granted to the English, although it was not included in the Treaty of Nanking or that of the Bogue, but was referred to in the Regulations of Trade. It was apparently conceded to the United States in lieu of a cession of territory, such as the English got at Hongkong.[15] Cushing's clear statement of the doctrine fixed the status of foreigners in China as it has remained even to our own day, for under the most-favored-nation clause other nations soon claimed for their subjects the privileged status enjoyed by Americans.

Contrast with earlier conditions

While Mr. Cushing was still at Macao, a mob attacked the foreign settlement, and in defense an American killed a Chinaman. The Chinese authorities demanded the surrender of the American, which Mr. Cushing naturally refused. A jury of Americans impaneled by the consul decided that the act had been committed in self-defense. This was the first criminal case that arose in China after the negotiation of the treaties. It will be recalled that in 1821 a member of the crew of an American ship had been executed by the Chinese authorities. The sailor in question, Terranova, was an Italian by birth but was serving on an American merchant vessel. He dropped or threw an earthen jar overboard which struck on the head of a woman in a boat, causing her to fall overboard and be drowned. His surrender was demanded by the Cantonese authorities and was refused, but when the Chinese authorities stopped all American trade it was agreed that a trial should be conducted aboard the ship by Chinese officials. They refused to allow any testimony for the defense to be taken or to hear any argument, and adjudged him guilty. The sailor was put in irons by the ship's officers but not surrendered. As trade with the Americans was still suspended, the ship's officers finally agreed to a second trial to take place in the city. At this trial by

[15]Dennett, 162–165.

Chinese officials Terranova was condemned and executed within twenty-four hours by strangulation. His body was then returned to the ship and American trade reopened. In 1780, a French seaman had been put to death by Chinese authorities, and in 1784, an English sailor was surrendered to the Chinese and executed by strangulation.[16]

Extra-territoriality a serious restriction on Chinese soverignty

These and other cases afforded grounds for the demand for exemption from the local jurisdiction. At the time it was doubtless a just demand and a necessary one, for the Chinese government did not recognize the law of nations or any of the obligations of international intercourse. Now that China has become a member of the community of nations the principle of extraterritoriality imposes a serious restriction upon her sovereignty which it is not likely that she will much longer tolerate.

The American treaty forbids opium trade

The American treaty differed from the English in declaring the opium trade illegal and providing that citizens of the United States engaging in it should "be dealt with by the Chinese government without being entitled to any countenance or protection from that of the United States." The influence of the American missionaries was shown in Article XVII, which in addition to agreeing to provide places of residence and business in the five treaty ports, also made provision for hospitals, churches, and cemeteries. In fact, under this treaty, American missions grew more rapidly than American commerce.[17]

Difficulty of enforcing treaties

The British, American, and French treaties were signed by China with great reluctance, and more or less trouble was experienced in carrying them out at all five of the treaty ports. The population of Canton was particularly unruly and the opposition to the treaties so great that foreigners were unable to secure the rights and privileges which had been granted them. The conditions of life at Shanghai were much better than at Canton, and it soon

[16]Morse, I, 104; Dennett, 86.

[17]Dennett, 168–169.

became the most important of the five ports. Foreigners were assigned ample space within the city walls and given full freedom to go a limited distance into the surrounding country. In the efforts to advance their interests in China the British and French were more and more inclined to resort to force, while the United States relied on the promises and good faith of China without fully realizing that the imperial government could exercise little effective control over local conditions at the treaty ports. The Taiping Rebellion, which began about 1850, developed into the greatest civil war in history, and for more than a decade paralyzed the activities of the central government. This situation had in it the possibility of grave peril for China. The empire appeared to be in a state of dissolution, and there was danger that foreign powers might appropriate portions of it. The first American to perceive this danger and to outline the true American policy was Humphrey Marshall, a relative of the great Chief Justice and the American commissioner in China, who wrote to Secretary Marcy in 1853:

The Taiping Rebellion

Sound American policy

> It is my opinion that the highest interests of the United States are involved in sustaining China—maintaining order here, and gradually engrafting on this worn-out stock the healthy principles which give life and health to governments, rather than to see China become the theatre of widespread anarchy, and ultimately the prey of European ambition.[18]

American representatives in China

The American treaty had provided for a revision of its terms at the expiration of twelve years, and England and France were even more insistent than the United States in their demands for the redress of existing grievances and the extension of commercial privileges. During this period the United States was represented in China by five commissioners: A. H. Everett, 1845-1847; John W. Davis. 1848-1850; Humphrey Marshall, 1852-1854; Robert M. McLane, 1854; Peter Parker, 1855-1857. The salary was

[18] *Op. cit.*, p. 215.

small and it was difficult to get men to accept the position or to hold it long.[19] As a result of these frequent changes American policy lacked continuity. Marshall was succeeded by Robert M. McLane, who went to China without definite instructions and resigned on account of ill health in less than a year. He recommended joint action with England and France in a blockade of the principal rivers and ports as the only effective means of securing redress and a revision of the treaties, but Secretary Marcy replied that the President had "serious objections to uniting with Great Britain and France in what you call the aggressive policy—that is the bringing together a united naval force of the three powers in order to obtain the revision of the treaties with China, securing larger commercial privileges by intimidation, or possibly by force."[20] The murder of a French missionary named Chapdelaine in 1853 was made use of by the French in furthering their demands. The French representative promptly called upon Commissioner Yeh at Canton for redress. In reply the commissioner declared that under the treaty mission work was restricted to the five treaty ports, and furthermore that the province of Kwangsi, where the murder occurred, was in a state of disturbance as a result of the Taiping Rebellion. As a matter of fact, the murder of Père Chapdelaine was an official act of the Emperor's representative. Three years later the *Arrow* episode, involving the boarding of a Hongkong-registered vessel, bearing the British flag, by Chinese officials and the removal of the Chinese crew, gave England an excuse for using pressure upon the Chinese government.[21]

Refusal of United States to coöperate with England and France

The Crimean War doubtless delayed the action of England and France. Just at this time Commodore Perry's expedition to Japan, which will be described later,

Perry proposes naval base in the East

[19] *Op. cit.*, pp. 189–192.

[20] *Ibid.*, p. 240.

[21] Morse, I, 422–480.

had an important influence on American policy in China. Not only did Perry force an entrance into Japan, but he made every effort to commit his government to the policy of maintaining a naval base in the East. "I assume," he wrote, "the responsibility of urging the expediency of establishing a foothold in this quarter of the globe, as a measure of positive necessity to the sustainment of our maritime rights in the East." He suggested the occupation of the Bonin Islands, Lew Chew, and Formosa as the first step. He made the Lew Chew Islands the rendezvous for his squadron during his stay in the East and secured a coaling station at Napa.[22] President Pierce did not take kindly to this suggestion and declined to consent, without the authority of Congress, to the occupation and retention of an island in that distant quarter, Had Japan refused to yield to intimidation it is probable that the United States would have found it necessary to adopt Perry's policy, but the signing of the treaty removed the necessity for the time being, and the squadron returned home. Dr. Peter Parker, while commissioner to China from 1855 to 1857, was eager to seize Formosa, a measure which he considered justifiable in view of China's failure to live up to her treaty obligations, but he was unable to convince his government of the justice or expediency of such a step.[23]

Doctor Parker suggests seizure of Formosa

Great Britain and France decide on coercive measures

After the Crimean War, Great Britain and France decided to bring matters to a conclusion in China, and early in 1857 they appointed plenipotentiaries to succeed their resident commissioners. Great Britain appointed the Earl of Elgin and France appointed Baron Gros. Lord Elgin's instructions were to demand, (1) reparations for injuries to British subjects; (2) a complete execution of treaty stipulations; (3) compensation for losses occasioned by the late disturbances; (4) the residence of the

[22]Dennett, 270–274.
[23]*Ibid.*, p. 284.

British plenipotentiary at Peking and his right to communicate directly in writing with the high officials there; (5) the revision of treaties, with provision for increased facilities of trade, such as the opening of additional ports. Baron Gros's instructions were to the same effect, except that special stress was laid on obtaining reparation for the murder of Père Chapdelaine.[24]

The United States declines invitation to coöperate

At the same time the British government proposed through Lord Napier at Washington that the United States should "authorize their naval and political authorities in China to act heartily in concert with the agents of the two allied powers." It was proposed to destroy the Barrier forts below Canton and to blockade the Yangtze as far as the Grand Canal and the mouth of the Peiho. The Buchanan administration, which had just come into power, declined to become a party to this alliance or to resort to measures of coercion. Secretary Cass replied that a military expedition against China could not be undertaken without the consent of Congress which alone had the right to declare war, and further that the relations of the United States with China did not justify war. The United States would agree, however, to appoint a minister plenipotentiary, but he would not be authorized to negotiate jointly with England and France or to sign jointly with them a treaty with China.[25]

For the new post of envoy extraordinary and minister plenipotentiary the President selected his friend William B. Reed of Pennsylvania. The instructions of the new minister, prepared by Cass, began with this remarkable paragraph:

Cass's remarkable instructions to Reed

Communicate freely with the British and French ministers and make known to the Chinese that the President believes that the objects of the Allied Powers are "just and expedient." Confine yourself to firm representations to the Chinese, bearing

[24]Morse, I, 485–488.

[25]Dennett, 298–302.

in mind that the government of the United States is not at war with China, and leaving to the government to determine what shall be the next step in case your representations are fruitless.[26]

He was also told to demand satisfaction for the claims of Americans and modifications of the Cushing treaty which would enlarge the opportunities for trade and safeguard the lives and property of American citizens in the open ports. Finally he was authorized to act as mediator between the belligerents, if the opportunity should present itself. Thus while the American government refused to resort to force and expressed its good will and pacific intentions to China, it lent its approval to the measures adopted by England and France and stood ready to claim under the most-favored-nation principle the full benefit of whatever concessions and privileges these powers might extort from China by force. If it considered the claims of the allied powers "just and expedient," it should have coöperated with them; if, on the contrary, it did not consider war justifiable, it should not have committed itself in advance to the course of action proposed by them.

The United States ready to profit by coercive measures of the allies

Delay caused by the Indian Mutiny

Lord Elgin arrived at Hongkong early in July, 1857, accompanied by a large squadron. He had intended to proceed as speedily as possible to the north and bring pressure to bear on the Peking authorities, but the delay of Baron Gros in reaching China and the Indian Mutiny compelled him to postpone this movement. In fact, he had to send two regiments and three hundred marines back to Calcutta. During the summer, the powers were marking time diplomatically. In October, Baron Gros arrived and the decision was made "to use force at Canton to bring the local government to terms" before proceeding north. In December, Elgin and Gros sent simultaneous notes to Commissioner Yeh. Mr. Reed also sent a note demanding a revision of the treaty of 1844. The Russian

[26] *Op. cit.*, p. 306.

representative was seeking a new treaty which would admit Russia to the open ports on the same terms as the other powers. So far Russia's trade had been limited to the overland route. Commissioner Yeh's reply to these notes was unsatisfactory and evasive. He refused to concede a single point, and stated that a revision of the treaties was unnecessary.[27]

The occupation of Canton

On December 28, the allied navies began the bombardment of Canton, and a week later the city was taken and occupied. Yeh was captured and sent as a prisoner to Calcutta where he died the following year. The British and French now faced an embarrassing situation. They had exerted all the force at their command and yet no concessions had been made to them. They did not have troops enough to administer a great city like Canton, so they turned it over to Yeh's successor on his agreeing to administer it with the assistance of a foreign committee. Most of the troops were then withdrawn.[28]

The demands of the powers

On February 11, 1858, Lord Elgin and Baron Gros addressed notes to the "senior secretary of state at Peking," demanding among other things the residence of envoys at Peking, the opening of more ports, the suppression of piracy, and the protection of Christians. They declared their intention of proceeding to Shanghai, and agreed to negotiate there if Chinese plenipotentiaries should meet them before the end of March. The American and Russian ministers agreed to lay their demands before the Chinese government at the same time. All four ministers then proceeded to Shanghai. On March 25, they received joint dispatches from the Nanking Viceroy forwarding replies from Peking. Lord Elgin and Baron Gros were informed that Commissioner Yeh, having mismanaged affairs, was disgraced, and that another had been appointed in his place; that Chinese ministers of

[27]Morse, I, 489–499.
[28]*Ibid.*, pp. 500–505.

state were prohibited by law from having any relations with foreigners; and finally that the ambassadors were to return to Canton and there open negotiations with the new commissioner.

The Chinese reply

The reply to the American envoy was to the same effect, except that it expressed strong approval of the friendly attitude taken by the American authorities. The Russian envoy was informed that as the treaties with Russia had never granted the right to trade at the five ports, he had no reason to interfere in the Canton question, and he was ordered to proceed to the Amur, on the Russian frontier, where Chinese commissioners would meet him to settle questions relating to the frontier. The attack on Canton, the spread of the Taiping Rebellion, the impotency of the Chinese government produced absolutely no effect upon its attitude toward foreigners. Foreign relations were still to be conducted at the point farthest removed from Peking, and between the envoys and the imperial government there was to be no direct intercourse.[29]

The foreign envoys proceed to the Peiho

In view of the unsatisfactory character of the replies just quoted, the four envoys decided to proceed to the Peiho. Baron Gros suggested that notes similar in tone to those already presented be forwarded to the Chinese government, that they demand that Chinese plenipotentiaries be appointed to meet them either at Tientsin or Peking, and that they declare emphatically that they would carry on no further negotiations at Canton. The Chinese government was to be given six days within which to make a favorable answer, and if one was not received in that time the foreign powers would proceed to take possession of the Taku forts. The American and Russian envoys were instructed not to resort to force, but they agreed to act jointly with Great Britain and France until hostile measures were actually resorted to. The notes were forwarded on April 24, 1858, but the Chinese government in reply merely authorized the Viceroy of Pechili

[29] *Op. cit.*, I, 507–510.

to negotiate with them. Lord Elgin and Baron Gros were not satisfied that he was provided with full powers and refused to confer with him. Mr. Reed, however, took a different view of the situation and began negotiations with the Viceroy. A coldness had arisen between him and Lord Elgin as a result in part of the latter's assumption of leadership in all matters relating to the combined missions. As the relations between Reed and his Russian colleague were cordial, the four envoys tended to separate into pairs. Reed's negotiations, which were not meeting with much success, were interrupted May 20 by the attack of the British and French navies on the Taku forts. After a bombardment of two hours the forts were taken and the allies proceeded up the river. Lord Elgin and Baron Gros were followed by Mr. Reed and the Russian minister in a Russian steamer which bore both the Russian and American flags. At Tientsin the British and French plenipotentiaries established themselves in a large temple, while the American and Russian ministers secured comfortable quarters in a private residence. The advance up the Peiho at last produced an effect on the government at Peking. Commissioners with full powers were immediately sent to Tientsin and negotiations began early in June. The Russian and American treaties were signed first, on the 13th and 18th, and the British and French on the 26th and 27th. The approval of the treaties by the Chinese government was received July 4 and the foreign ministers withdrew to Shanghai, where negotiations on the tariff and trade regulations were to be completed.[30]

The attack on the Taku forts

Separate treaties signed at Tientsin

In all the negotiations with China Lord Elgin had played the leading rôle, and his treaty established the primacy of Great Britain among the powers having relations with China. Mr. Reed secured in the American treaty a comprehensive most-favored-nation clause which gained

[30] *Op. cit.*, I, 512–530; Dennett, 311–314.

for the United States all that had been won from China by the armed forces of the two allied powers. In one respect Mr. Reed departed from his instructions. The prohibition of the opium trade which appeared in the Cushing treaty was omitted from the treaty of Tientsin. The trade was not legalized in the texts of any of the treaties, but in the revised tariff a rule appeared fixing the duty on opium and limiting its sale by the importer to the port of entry. Only natives could carry it into the interior. In view of the fact that Americans had persistently violated the opium provision of the Cushing treaty, Mr. Reed concluded, not entirely without British persuasion apparently, that it would be better to legalize the traffic under heavy duties and restrictions as to its sale by foreigners.[31]

Prohibition of opium omitted from the American treaty

China delays exchange of ratifications

The American treaty received the approval of the Senate, and was ratified by the President December 21, 1858. Mr. Reed having resigned, John E. Ward of Georgia was appointed minister to China, and upon him devolved the duty of exchanging ratifications. This proved to be a difficult task. When he reached Shanghai he announced to the Chinese commissioners his intention of going to Peking for the purpose of exchanging ratifications. To this the Chinese raised objections and there was nothing in the treaty to justify his demand, but he relied on the fact that the British and French treaties specifically named Peking as the place for the exchange of ratifications. In the meantime, the British were having difficulties with the Chinese officials over the situation at Canton. The Cantonese were not pleased with the treaties and continued to commit acts of hostility. As a result the British still held the city and the Chinese government demanded that they restore it to the Chinese authorities before exchanging ratifications.[32]

Lord Elgin and Baron Gros had left China after the

---

[31] Dennett, 314–326.

[32] *Ibid.*, pp. 334–336; Morse, I, 571–572.

signature of the treaties, but when their successors went to Shanghai to arrange for the journey to Peking, where ratifications were to be exchanged, they met with unexpected obstacles. The various accounts of the events leading up to the renewal of hostilities between the Anglo-French forces and China are contradictory and difficult to reconcile. In June, 1859, the British, French, and American ministers proceeded to the mouth of the Peiho. Here they were told by the local officials that orders had been received not to permit any foreigners to ascend the river. The British then decided to force an entrance to Tientsin and from that point to open negotiations with Peking. On June 24 an ultimatum was sent ashore in which Admiral Hope of the British navy demanded that the obstructions which had been placed in the river be removed and that his ships be allowed to pass. Failing to receive a reply, on the following day he attempted to force a passage. During the combat that followed the forts, which had been greatly strengthened, had the better of the contest, and serious loss was inflicted on the British. Six of the English gunboats were put out of action, four of them being sunk. Twenty-five sailors and 64 marines were killed, and 93 sailors and 252 marines wounded. Admiral Hope himself received a severe wound. When Commodore Tatnall of the American frigate *Powhatan* learned of Admiral Hope's wound, he at once got in his gig and proceeded up the river to express his sympathy. The batteries opened fire upon him, killing his coxswain, and when he went aboard Admiral Hope's gunboat the crew of his gig, finding only three of the British able to fight, took a turn at the guns which were firing on the forts. Tatnall also sent a steamer to assist in towing some of the English launches into the battle line, exclaiming by way of explanation for his unneutral conduct, "Blood is thicker than water."[33]

England and France renew hostilities

"Blood thicker than water"

[33]Morse, I, 576–579; Foster, 246–248; Dennett, 338–340.

The American envoy receives a rebuff

Mr. Ward, the American envoy, was a little later invited to land at Peitang, a few miles north of Taku, with the promise that he would then be conveyed to Peking. He was conveyed overland to the capital city late in July, and an audience with the Emperor was arranged, Mr. Ward receiving every assurance that the kowtow would not be required, but when the time came he found that this ceremony could not be dispensed with; so he refused to have the audience, and on the following day he received an imperial mandate ordering him to quit Peking and to exchange ratifications at Peitang. Returning to that point, he exchanged ratifications on the 16th of August. Neither the American treaty nor the instructions of the State Department named Peking as the place for the exchange of ratifications, so that Mr. Ward was acting within his discretion in exchanging them at Peitang.[34] Shortly after the exchange of ratifications Mr. Ward returned to the United States, having tendered his resignation several months before.[35]

British explanation of China's action

British writers have claimed that the real explanation of China's action at this time was the stipulation in the British treaty in regard to the residence of foreign envoys at Peking, and that the rupture at Taku had been brought about by the determination of the Chinese government to reopen the discussion on this and one or two other points before the exchange of ratifications with Great Britain. The other treaty powers could claim for their envoys residence at Peking only under the most-favored-nation clause, so that if the Chinese government could secure the elimination from the British treaty of the clause stipulating the residence of her minister at Peking, that right could be denied to all the foreign envoys. The fact that the Taiping Rebellion was at its lowest ebb in 1859 and

---

[34]Morse, I, 580; Foster, 248–253; Dennett, 340–343.

[35]The correspondence of Ward, together with that of Reed, is found in 36 Cong., 1 Sess., Sen. Ex. Doc. No. 30.

that the imperialists had recaptured a great many cities had no doubt some influence on the conduct of the Chinese government.[36]

After the repulse of the British at Taku, Admiral Hope informed the British minister that he did not have a sufficient force at his disposal to enable him to continue operations, and the expedition, with the British and French ministers, withdrew to Shanghai. When the reports of these proceedings were received by the British and French governments, they decided to send Lord Elgin and Baron Gros back to China with formidable squadrons and a sufficient number of troops to force their way to Peking. On August 1, 1860, the allied forces landed at Peitang, in order to take the Taku forts in the rear. This task was accomplished in about three weeks, and they immediately proceeded up the river to Tientsin. Here envoys met them and proposed to open negotiations, but the allies pushed on to Peking. When they forced an entrance into the city they found that the royal family had fled. As they did not care to take military possession of the city, they decided to destroy the beautiful summer palace. There was some talk of destroying the winter palace too, but they concluded that that would prevent the return of the Emperor. They then opened negotiations with Prince Kung and other plenipotentiaries, and finally signed the two conventions of Peking. The Emperor had to express deep regret for the breach of friendly relations caused by the Chinese military authorities at Taku in June, 1859. The British insisted on the permanent residence of their envoy at Peking, and the Chinese government was forced to pay indemnities to both governments. The signing of these conventions marked the end of the twenty years' struggle for the establishment of foreign intercourse with China. Prior to the Opium War China had dictated to foreigners the conditions

Lord Elgin and Baron Gros return to China

The capture of Peking

China at the mercy of the powers

[36]Morse, I, 580–587.

of trade. After 1860 the foreign powers dictated to China.[37]

Commodore Perry's expedition to Japan

Commodore Perry's famous expedition to Japan in 1852-1854 was a radical departure from the general policy of attending strictly to our own business. There were, it is true, certain definite grievances to redress, but the main reason for the expedition was that Japan refused to recognize her obligations as a member of the family of nations and, except for the Dutch trading station on the little island of Deshima in the harbor of Nagasaki, closed her ports to all intercourse with the outside world. This policy of exclusion or isolation had been adopted in the seventeenth century when the Spanish and Portuguese religious orders were expelled and the native Christians suppressed. The Dutch had been permitted to continue at Nagasaki because they were willing to trade without attempting to carry on religious propaganda, so for over two centuries they had enjoyed a practical monopoly of Japanese trade. The United States had no direct trade with Japan, but some American cotton reached Japan through Chinese merchants. American sailors who had from time to time been shipwrecked on the coasts of Japan had failed to receive the treatment usually accorded by civilized nations, and this afforded a pretext for the dispatch of an expedition; but the real reasons for this remarkable move have so far not been satisfactorily explained by any of the numerous writers who have described the expedition in such detail. Proponents of the economic interpretation of history might make out a good case here for the influence of King Cotton, but while the expedition was carried out under the Democratic administration of Pierce, it was dispatched by the Whig administration of Fillmore. Commodore Perry's own personality was undoubtedly an important factor, as is shown by the fact that, owing to the illness of Webster,

Objects and motives

[37] *Op. cit.*, I, 589–616.

Perry was permitted to draft his own instructions which, whether revised or not we do not know, were signed by the Acting Secretary of State. One paragraph of these instructions shows that Perry was far-sighted enough to see the true basis of future American policy in the Pacific, but governments as a rule act under the spur of present interests rather than the lure of remote possibilities. The paragraph referred to is as follows:

Perry's statement

> Recent events—the navigation of the ocean by steam, the acquisition and rapid settlement by this country of a vast territory on the Pacific, the discovery of gold in that region, the rapid communication established across the isthmus which separates the two oceans—have practically brought the countries of the East in closer proximity to our own; although the consequences of these events have scarcely begun to be felt, the intercourse between them has already greatly increased and no limits can be assigned to its future extension.[38]

Previous efforts to reach Japan

The decision to send a naval force to Japan for the purpose of establishing commercial intercourse was not made suddenly. Edmund Roberts had received a commission to go there in 1832. After Cushing's successful negotiations with China in 1844, Commodore Biddle was sent to Japan with two ships. He spent ten days in Yedo Bay in July, 1846, but was unable to establish relations with the government. He was informed that no trade could be allowed except through the Dutch at Nagasaki, and that every nation had a right to manage its own affairs in its own way. He was warned to leave as soon as possible and to consult his own safety by not appearing again upon the coast.[39] In 1851, Commodore Aulick, in command of the U. S. squadron in the East, was commissioned by Webster to negotiate a treaty with Japan, but he was prevented by illness from carrying out his instructions.

[38]Dennett, 262–263.

[39]Callahan, 75.

Perry's squadron at Yedo

Finally, in 1852, Commodore Matthew Calbraith Perry, a younger brother of the hero of the fight on Lake Erie, was given a strong squadron and commissioned to negotiate a treaty with Japan. The expedition sailed from Norfolk in November, 1852. On his arrival at Canton Perry took on board Dr. S. Wells Williams as chief interpreter, and in July, 1853, sailed into the bay of Yedo. As Perry's flagship, the *Susquehanna*, a new steam frigate, the first that had ever been seen in Japanese waters, steamed quietly up the bay in the face of a strong head wind, without sails, and with smoke curling from its funnels, the Japanese were struck with consternation. As soon as the ships anchored, a boat came out carrying the vice-governor of Uraga, who requested to see the commander of the squadron. He was told that the commander could not confer with any except one of the highest officials of the empire. The vice-governor was, therefore, received by one of Perry's aids. The Americans were informed that their ships must proceed to Nagasaki, the only place where business could be transacted with foreigners. They replied that the squadron had come on a friendly mission with a messenger from the President of the United States to the Emperor, and that it would remain where it was until his business was transacted. The following day the governor of Uraga came on board. Perry refused to see him in person, but designated two of his commanders to confer with him. He repeated the demands that had been made by the vice-governor the day before, but he was finally told that if the Japanese government did not appoint a suitable person to receive the documents addressed to the Emperor, Commodore Perry would himself go on shore with a sufficient force to deliver them in person. After a delay of several days the governor finally returned and stated that a high official would be appointed to receive the President's letter, but that a reply to the letter would be transmitted to Nagasaki

Told to go to Nagasaki

and delivered through the Dutch. To this answer was made that Commodore Perry would not go to Nagasaki and would not receive any communication through the Dutch. A few days later Perry was received on shore by an official of very high rank, who was attended by about five thousand soldiers. Perry was accompanied by his officers and a body of sailors and marines. The squadron had taken position in front of the place set for the meeting, and within easy cannon range. The dispatches were presented to the Japanese officials with great ceremony, and Perry informed them that in view of the importance of the business to be considered he would not wait for a reply but would return to the same place the following spring to receive the answer of the Emperor. The governor asked whether he would return with all his vessels. Perry replied: "All of them and probably more, as these are only a portion of the squadron."[40]

Perry finally received on shore

Perry then went to Chinese waters to supply and refit his squadron. The Taiping Rebellion was in progress, and the American minister was very anxious that Perry's squadron should remain in Chinese waters, but Perry was so much impressed with the importance of his mission to Japan and with the fear that the commanders of the Russian or French squadron, then in Chinese waters, might proceed to Japan and reap the fruit of his efforts, that he shortened his stay in China and left during the winter for Japan. In February, 1854, the fleet, now double its size on the first visit, entered the Bay of Yedo. As the vessels steamed impressively up the bay, Japanese officials tried in vain to persuade Perry to stop, and after he came to anchor he was informed that commissioners had been appointed to negotiate with him at a point in the outer bay. He replied that he would not return to the lower bay, and that if the commissioners were not willing to treat with him at his present anchorage, he would

The Japanese forced to negotiate a treaty

[40]Foster, 150–158.

proceed to Yedo and carry out the negotiations there. The commissioners finally appeared and after an interchange of receptions and festivities the terms of a treaty were agreed upon and signed on March 31, 1854. Treaties with other countries soon followed. The British treaty was signed October 14, 1854, the Russian treaty January 26, 1855, and later in the year a treaty with Holland.[41]

Significance of Perry's visit

Perry's visit marks an era in the history of Japan. Later the Japanese people were so much impressed with its significance that they formed an association to erect a monument to his memory. The money was contributed by the Japanese people, the Emperor himself subscribing to the fund, and the dedication took place July 14, 1901, the forty-eighth anniversary of Perry's first visit. The United States sent a squadron, commanded by Rear-Admiral Rodgers, a grandson of Perry, to participate in the exercises. There was also present Rear-Admiral Beardslee, who was a midshipman in Perry's fleet. The monument was erected on the spot where Perry held his first conference with the Japanese plenipotentiaries.[42]

Treaty concessions meager

Perry's treaty was a brief document and, notwithstanding the circumstances of its negotiation, it was much easier on Japan than Cushing's treaty had been on China. It conceded few commercial privileges. Japan agreed to open two ports to American vessels and trade, and to protect and restore shipwrecked sailors. The treaty contained a most-favored-nation clause, but no extraterritorial provision. The omission of the latter seems to have been due to Dr. S. Wells Williams, whose experience in China had led him to the conclusion that the principle of extraterritoriality was wrong. It was, however, inserted three years later in the first treaty negotiated by Townsend Harris. Perry had merely opened a crack in

---

[41]*Op. cit.*, pp. 159–166. The official documents relating to the expedition are found in 33 Cong., 2 Sess., Sen. Ex. Doc. No. 34.

[42]Foster, 169.

the door. The real basis of foreign trade and intercourse with Japan was laid by Townsend Harris in the treaties of 1857 and 1858, which became the models which the other powers followed.[43]

Shogun and Emperor

In the early negotiations with Japan Commodore Perry was not aware of the peculiar character of the Japanese government and of the fact that he was dealing with the Shogun and not with the Emperor. The negotiators of the European treaties labored under the same ignorance, and it was not until Townsend Harris was in the midst of his negotiations that he began to realize the true situation. For centuries the chief executive power of Japan had been in the hands of the Tycoon or Shogun, who resided at Yedo (the modern Tokio), while the Emperor lived in seclusion at Kioto. Furthermore, for two hundred and fifty years the Shogunate had been hereditary in the powerful Tokugawa family. When the Shogun was forced to agree to the treaties with the United States and other foreign powers, the feudal barons raised a great outcry against him and appealed to the Emperor. When the Shogun tried to carry out the treaties, many of the barons resisted, and one of the most powerful, the Prince of Nagato, undertook to close the straits of Shimonoseki and expel the foreigners from his dominions. The representatives of the powers decided upon a joint naval expedition with the object of punishing the Prince and opening the straits. The British proposed this expedition and took the leading part in it, furnishing nine vessels, but the other powers coöperated, France furnishing three vessels, Holland four, and the United States one. The expedition was undertaken with the tacit approval of the Shogun whose authority the Prince of Nagato had defied, and on its return to Yokohama the Shogun made various concessions to the foreign powers and agreed to an

The Shimonoseki expedition

[43] Dennett, 355–364; Treat, *Diplomatic Relations Between the United States and Japan, 1853–1865,* chap. iii.

indemnity of $3,000,000 to pay the expenses of the expedition.[44]

Political transformation of Japan

With the pressure of the foreign powers the position of the Shogun became more and more difficult. Resistance was useless, yet every concession he made to the foreigners was denounced by the nobles. Japan was fast drifting into civil war or anarchy. Finally, in 1867, the ruling Shogun, by a remarkable act of self-abnegation, resigned his position and restored the government of the country to the Emperor. The young Emperor, who had shortly before come to the throne, adopted the year-name Meiji, which means Enlightened Government, and his reign was to prove one of the most remarkable in history. In the course of a generation Japan was transformed from a feudal state into a modern industrial nation. Although the Shogun had been overthrown for making concessions to foreigners, one of the first acts of the young Emperor was to invite the foreign representatives to Kioto and receive them in person. When he and his advisers were faced with the responsibility they had to do precisely what the Shogun had done. The nobles patriotically supported the Emperor, for they understood that only a centralized government could successfully cope with the foreigner.[45]

The coöperation of the United States in the Shimonoseki expedition was a radical departure from American practice and tradition. The indemnity convention signed at the close of the expedition and the tariff convention negotiated by the same powers with Japan two years later are among the very few treaties prior to the World War negotiated and signed by the United States jointly with other powers. Yet both conventions were approved and ratified by the Senate.

Seward's policy of coöperation

Seward's policy of coöperation may have been dictated by the exigencies of the Civil War, but whatever his motives or intentions, as soon as he left the State

[44]Dennett, 400–401; Foster, 192–195.

[45]Longford, *Transformation of Japan*.

Department the government reverted to the policy of isolation, and not until the Boxer uprising a generation later did the United States again coöperate with other powers in the Far East.

Anson Burlingame at Peking

In China the United States was ably represented during the Civil War by Anson Burlingame, who developed with great success a policy of peaceful coöperation. The Taiping Rebellion was still in progress and China in danger of dissolution. Extensive concessions in the treaty ports could easily be obtained. Burlingame established friendly relations with the British, French, and Russian ministers and impressed upon them the importance of preserving and guaranteeing "the territorial integrity of the Chinese Empire," [46] a phrase borrowed a generation later by John Hay and used by him to such good effect. Burlingame's later career reads like a romance. When he announced in 1867 his intention of resigning and returning to the United States to reënter political life, the Chinese government asked him if he would be willing to head a mission to the western powers. He accepted the proposal and was soon accredited as the first Chinese ambassador to America and Europe. He arrived in the United States with a large train of attendants, and from the moment the commission landed in San Francisco until its departure from New York for Europe it received a continuous series of ovations. It then proceeded to London, Paris, Berlin, and St. Petersburg, attracting great attention and meeting with marked success. A few days after reaching the Russian capital Mr. Burlingame was stricken with pneumonia and died, thus ending his brilliant career.

His mission to the western powers

The immigration provisions of the Burlingame treaty

While in Washington in July, 1868, Burlingame, acting on behalf of China, negotiated with Seward a treaty, Article V of which contained the following clause:

The United States of America and the Emperor of China cordially recognize the inherent and inalienable right of man

[46] Dennett, 373.

to change his home and allegiance, and also the mutual advantage of the free migration and emigration of their citizens and subjects respectively from the one country to the other for purposes of curiosity, of trade, or as permanent residents.

At this time several thousand Chinese were engaged in the construction of the transcontinental railroad, and the rapid development of California was made possible by Chinese labor. But public opinion was soon to undergo a radical change on the question of Chinese immigration, and appeals were soon made to Congress for the abrogation or modification of the Burlingame treaty. In 1876, a joint committee of the two Houses of Congress, under the chairmanship of Senator Oliver P. Morton, visited California and made a thorough investigation of the question. The majority report, favoring restriction, and the minority report, opposing it, set forth fully all the arguments used for the next twenty-four years.[47]

The Chinese exclusion acts

In 1878, Congress passed a bill which so greatly restricted Chinese immigration that President Hayes vetoed it, on the ground that it was in direct violation of the Burlingame treaty. Two years later a commission, with President Angell of the University of Michigan at its head, was sent to China to secure the consent of the Chinese government to modification of the Burlingame treaty. The new treaty of 1880 provided for restrictions on the immigration of Chinese laborers, but expressly provided that Chinese subjects "proceeding to the United States as teachers, students, merchants, or from curiosity" should be allowed to come and go of their own free will, and should be accorded all the rights, privileges, and immunities accorded to the citizens and subjects of the most-favored-nation. This treaty paved the way for the exclusion act of 1882. Some of the subsequent exclusion acts, notably those of 1888 and 1892, passed on the eve of presidential elections, were in plain violation of treaty stipulations,

[47] 44 Cong., 2 Sess., Sen. Rep. 689; also 45 Cong., 2 Sess., Misc. Doc. No. 20.

and all were harshly administered. Even those Chinese who came within the four privileged classes were frequently treated with inexcusable severity. Unfortunately the subject of Chinese immigration has too frequently been handled as a political rather than as a social or economic question.

PART IV

SAFEGUARDING THE UNION

CHAPTER XV

THE DIPLOMACY OF THE CIVIL WAR

The blockade

HISTORIANS of the Civil War have described military operations in great detail, but they have paid less attention to the blockade and to the attitude of foreign governments. During the first two years of the war, that is, from Bull Run to Gettysburg, the Southerners had decidedly the advantage in the field, and very few foreign observers believed that the North would ever succeed in conquering the South. The outcome was, in fact, the result of the naval superiority of the North and the acquiescence of England and France, although with reluctance, in the greatest commercial blockade that had ever been undertaken—a blockade which seriously disturbed their trade and industry.

Faith of the South in King Cotton

In seceding from the Union the Southern States based their hope of success on two beliefs: one that the Northerners would prove indifferent fighters, and the other that the dependence of Europe on the cotton supply of the South would compel early recognition of independence and, if the war continued long, intervention. It is difficult for us to realize at this day the infatuation with which the latter idea was cherished. Senator Hammond, of South Carolina, voiced a widespread belief when he said in the United States Senate, March 4, 1858:

> If there were no other reason why we should never have war, would any sane nation make war on cotton? Without firing a gun, without drawing a sword, should they make war on us we could bring the whole world to our feet. . . . What

would happen if no cotton was furnished for three years? I will not stop to depict what every one can imagine, but this is certain: England would topple headlong and carry the whole civilized world with her, save the South. No, you dare not make war on cotton. No power on earth dares to make war upon it. Cotton *is* King. Until lately the Bank of England was king, but she tried to put her screws as usual, the fall before the last, upon the cotton crop, and was utterly vanquished. The last power has been conquered. Who can doubt, that has looked at recent events, that cotton is supreme?[1]

Reliance on British recognition

William H. Russell, of the London *Times*, who was in Charleston during the exciting days of April, 1861, was very much impressed with the fact that the Southerners were staking everything on their faith in cotton. "These tall, thin, fine-faced Carolinians," he writes, "are great materialists. Slavery perhaps has aggravated the tendency to look at all the world through parapets of cotton-bales and rice-bags, and though more stately and less vulgar, the worshippers here are not less prostrate before the 'almighty dollar' than the Northerners." Describing a dinner given in his honor by the British consul, he says:

It was scarcely very agreeable to my host or myself to find that no considerations were believed to be of consequence in reference to England except her material interests, and that these worthy gentlemen regarded her as a sort of appanage of their cotton kingdom. "Why, sir, we have only to shut off your supply of cotton for a few weeks, and we can create a revolution in Great Britain. There are four millions of your people depending on us for their bread, not to speak of the many millions of dollars. No, sir, we know that England must recognize us."

Recording a conversation with Edmund Rhett, he says: "Mr. Rhett is also persuaded that the Lord Chancellor sits on a cotton bale."[2]

It was not until the return of Yancey from his unsuccessful mission to Europe that the leaders of the Confederacy

[1]This and other quotations to the same effect have been collected by C. F. Adams in *Studies Military and Diplomatic*, chap. vii.

[2]Russell, *My Diary North and South*, 118, 148.

Cotton not supreme

realized their mistake. In a speech in New Orleans in March, 1862, he said: "It is an error to say that Cotton is King. It is not. It is a great and influential power in commerce, but not its dictator."[3] Six months later, in a speech at Crawfordville, Georgia, Alexander Stephens said:

> The great error of those who supposed that King Cotton would compel the English ministry to recognize our government and break the blockade, and who will look for the same result from the total abandonment of its culture, consists in mistaking the nature of the kingdom of the potentate. His power is commercial and financial, not political.[4]

These quotations will explain how it was that the South entered on the war without taking into consideration the possibilities of the blockade, which was in reality destined to be the determining factor in the contest.

Lincoln's blockade proclamation

On April 15, 1861, President Lincoln issued a proclamation calling upon the States for troops for the purpose of "repossessing" the forts in the South seized by the Confederates. Two days later Jefferson Davis, President of the Confederate States, by public proclamation invited applications for letters of marque and reprisal, thereby indicating the intention of waging war on the high seas against the commerce of the United States.[5] On April 19, President Lincoln, acting, he said, "in pursuance of the laws of the United States and of the law of nations," issued a proclamation announcing that he had "set on foot a blockade" of the Confederate ports from South Carolina to Texas, and eight days later he included the coasts of North Carolina and Virginia. He also declared that if any person, acting under the pretended authority of the Confederate States, should molest a vessel of the United States, such person would be "held amenable to the laws

[3]C. F. Adams, *Studies Military and Diplomatic,* 260.

[4]*Ibid.,* p. 261 n.

[5]Richardson, *Messages and Papers of the Confederacy,* I, 60.

of the United States for the prevention and punishment of piracy." In order to avoid the appearance of a paper blockade, since an effective blockade of the entire coast of the Confederacy was impossible at this time, the proclamation directed that a vessel approaching or attempting to leave a blockaded port "be duly warned by the commander of one of the blockading vessels, who will indorse on her register the fact and date of such warning, and if the same vessel shall again attempt to enter or leave the blockaded port she will be captured and sent to the nearest convenient port for such proceedings against her and her cargo as prize as may be deemed advisable."[6]

Vessels to be warned before seized

Lord Lyons' advice to Seward

Lord Lyons, the British minister at Washington, had tried to convince Seward that any interference with British trade would be disastrous to the Northern cause in England, and he had gone so far as to hint at British intervention in case of serious interference. Neither he nor Lord Russell believed that an effective blockade would be possible, and they regarded the attempt to establish one as less objectionable than the closing of Southern ports as ports of entry by act of Congress, which had been seriously considered. In reaching the conclusion that it would be impossible for the North to blockade effectively over 3,000 miles of coast, Lyons and Russell overlooked the fact that cotton could be shipped in large quantities from only seven Southern ports: Norfolk, Wilmington, Charleston, Savannah, Mobile, New Orleans, and Galveston. An effective blockade of these ports was not an impossible task.[7] When, in July, 1861, both Houses of Congress passed the "Southern Ports Bill," authorizing the President to close the ports by proclamation irrespective of the blockade,[8] both England and France protested. The French minister Mercier stated to Seward that his

The "Southern Ports Bill"

[6]Richardson, *Messages and Papers of the Presidents,* VI, 14, 15.

[7]E. D. Adams, *Great Britain and the American Civil War,* I, 244, 253.

[8]*U. S. Statutes at Large,* XII, p. 255 (Sect. 4 of the act).

government would regard such a measure as a paper blockade, and on August 12, Lord Lyons presented formal instructions declaring that "Her Majesty's Government would consider a decree closing the ports of the South actually in possession of the insurgent or Confederate states as null and void, and that they would not submit to measures taken on the high seas in pursuance of such decree."[9] In the face of these protests Seward was able to dissuade the President from declaring the Southern ports closed to foreign ships. The non-intercourse proclamation of August 16 interdicted all commerce between the States in insurrection and other parts of the Union, but did not put into effect section 4 of the bill, against which England and France had protested.[10] England and France thus committed themselves to recognition of a commercial blockade, however extensive, provided it should be effectively maintained and not a mere paper blockade.

Great Britain issues declaration of neutrality

In the meantime, as a result of Davis's proclamation of April 17, calling for privateers, and of Lincoln's proclamation of April 19, giving notice of an intended blockade, Great Britain faced a maritime war, and at once began to take steps for the protection of her commerce. The two proclamations were sufficient evidence of belligerent status to warrant action. Accordingly, on May 13, the Queen of England issued a declaration of neutrality,[11] which was followed by similar declarations from France, Spain, and the Netherlands in June, from Brazil in August, and from the other maritime powers in due course.[12] This action did not commit the powers to a recognition of the independence of the Confederacy nor to the reception of diplomatic agents. It merely extended

[9]Adams, *Great Britain and the American Civil War*, I, 250.
[10]Richardson, *Messages and Papers of the Presidents*, VI, 37.
[11]*British and Foreign State Papers*, LI, 165.
[12]Moore, *Dig. of Int. Law*, I, 185.

to the Confederates the rights of belligerents, that is, it entitled their flag to recognition on the high seas and their ships of war and commerce to the same privileges in neutral ports as were accorded the ships of the North.

Delay in making diplomatic appointments

Lincoln had delayed sending new ministers abroad for reasons not altogether clear, possibly from lack of a definite foreign policy, or possibly through the influence of Seward who hoped to avoid war and was reluctant to inaugurate new missions abroad until the situation became clearer at home. For more than two months the new administration was represented at London by Dallas of Pennsylvania, and at Paris by Faulkner of Virginia, both holdovers from the Buchanan administration, and the latter a Southern sympathizer.[13] The Confederate government had acted with much greater promptness and had dispatched a mission to Europe in March.

Charles Francis Adams sent to England

Charles Francis Adams, who was finally chosen by Lincoln and Seward as minister to England, was of distinguished lineage. His father and grandfather had both been ministers to England as well as Presidents of the United States. He inherited much of their ability and also a full measure of their stern, uncompromising Puritanism. The Adams family was not kindly disposed to England. Neither John Adams nor his son had found the atmosphere of London congenial. In fact, their experiences had been anything but pleasant, and Charles Francis was to have a still more unpleasant sojourn in England. His mission was more important than that of either of his forebears,

[13]When Faulkner finally returned home he was cordially received by Seward at the State Department, his accounts were audited, and he was paid the balance due. He then parted with Seward, intending to join his young son (afterward a U. S. Senator) and daughter, whom he had left at Barnum's Hotel, Baltimore, and then to make his way to his home at Boydville, Berkeley County (now West Virginia). Before he could leave Washington, however, he was arrested by order of Secretary Stanton and detained as a prisoner of State. Six months later he was exchanged for Congressman Alfred Ely, of New York, who had been captured while witnessing the battle of Bull Run. An ex-minister was considered a fair exchange for a Congressman. (Ex-Senator Charles J. Faulkner is my authority for this incident.) Cf. Bancroft's *Life of Seward,* II, 268.

and was in the end to prove more successful. The fate of the United States turned largely on the policy of England, and a single false step on the part of the American minister might have been fatal. Adams bore on his shoulders a load almost as great as that borne by Lincoln and under more trying circumstances, for he was surrounded by people who either sympathized openly with the Confederacy, or were at least sceptical as to the possibility of the Union being restored.

Regards the declaration of neutrality as unfriendly

Adams reached London late on the evening of May 13, 1861, the very day on which the British Cabinet decided to recognize the Confederates as belligerents. The next day, when he picked up his morning paper, he was confronted by the text of the declaration of neutrality. This did not seem to him a very propitious beginning of his mission. Dallas had been instructed by Seward to "use all proper and necessary measures" to prevent recognition of the Confederates, and after an interview with Lord Russell, he had reported that no action in the way of recognition even of belligerency would be taken before the arrival of Adams. So he understood Russell, but the latter denied later that any pledge had been given. When Adams arrived the step had been taken, and he felt that it was an unfriendly and discourteous act. This feeling was intensified by the knowledge that a few days before Russell had received the Confederate commissioners, though "unofficially."[14] His son and biographer came to the conclusion late in life that the issuance of the declaration before the arrival of Adams was most fortunate, for his instructions were based on the Lincoln-Seward theory that the war was a local insurrection with which foreign nations had no concern, whereas the British government was confronted by the proclamations of Davis and Lincoln which made recognition of *de facto* war inevitable. Had the declaration been issued after

Protest would have been futile

[14]C. F. Adams, *Charles Francis Adams* (American Statesmen).

the protest which Adams would undoubtedly have made, an immediate rupture would in all probability have resulted.[15] Furthermore, had Great Britain delayed taking any action until after the battle of Bull Run, she would probably have recognized the Confederacy at once as an independent state and not merely as a *de facto* belligerent government.

Resentment against England unreasonable

The British recognition of belligerency was deeply resented in the United States and was made the subject of reiterated complaint. It was considered an unfriendly act and the first step toward ultimate recognition of independence. The American government contended that war did not exist in the international sense; that the United States had not relinquished its sovereignty over the Southern States; that the Confederates were insurgents or rebels; and that there was no reason why any foreign power should take official cognizance of them. This contention was not only directly at variance with the well-known practice of the United States in according recognition to *de facto* governments, but it was also untenable in international law, for President Lincoln's proclamation of a blockade "in pursuance of the law of nations" was an official acknowledgment to the nations of the world, though not so intended, that a state of public war existed. His proclamation directed the search and seizure of ships of other nations attempting to enter blockaded ports. Such rights over commerce are accorded only to belligerents and are never admissible in time of peace. The United States has upon every other occasion in its history denied the validity of the so-called pacific blockade, as in the attempt of England and Germany in 1902 to coerce Venezuela when it insisted that a blockade which affected the ships of third parties was an act of war.[16] Further-

[15]Statement made by Charles Francis Adams, Junior, in his public lectures at the Johns Hopkins University on the James Schouler Foundation in 1914. Cf. E. D. Adams, *Great Britain and the American Civil War*, I, 111–112.

[16]Post, p. 490.

State of war recognized by the Supreme Court

more, the Supreme Court of the United States, at its December term in 1862, declared that the President's proclamation of a blockade April 19, 1861, was "itself official and conclusive evidence to the Court that a state of war existed" and confirmed as valid prizes all vessels found guilty of violating that proclamation. The fact that British subjects had millions of dollars of property in the South and that their vessels and goods were threatened with seizure in case they attempted to leave or enter a Confederate port, made it necessary for the British government to take cognizance of the war and to warn its subjects officially that, if they wished to avoid the confiscation of their property, they must observe the rules of neutrality. If Great Britain erred in thinking that a state of war existed from the date of Lincoln's proclamation, she erred in company with the Supreme Court of the United States.[17]

Status of the Declaration of Paris

When the war began the powers of Europe were much concerned as to what attitude the two belligerents would assume in regard to privateering and blockades and what treatment they would accord to the neutral flag and to neutral goods. The principal European powers had reached an understanding among themselves on these points at a conference at Paris in 1856 following the Crimean War. The declaration then adopted provided:—"1. Privateering is and remains abolished; 2. The neutral flag covers enemy's goods, with the exception of contraband of war; 3. Neutral goods, with the exception of contraband of war, are not liable to capture under the enemy's flag; 4. Blockades, in order to be binding, must be effective." The United States was invited to give its adherence to this declaration, but declined on grounds stated at length by Mr. Marcy, who was then Secretary of State. He said that while the United States was well

[17]Moore, *Dig. of Int. Law*, I, 190; Woolsey, *International Law*, Ed. of 1878, p. 304.

known to be in thorough accord with the last three propositions, it could not consent to the first, unless coupled with a declaration exempting the private property of belligerents, other than contraband of war, from capture; that without this amendment the United States, whose policy was against maintaining a large naval establishment in time of peace, would have to continue, in attacking the commerce of its enemies, to depend largely on privateers. Marcy's amendment was not accepted by the signers of the Declaration of Paris.[18]

Seward's position

As soon as Seward learned of Davis's intention to issue commissions to privateers, he took steps to arrange for the immediate adherence of the United States to the Declaration of Paris. In a circular note to the representatives of the United States abroad he directed them to sign formal acts of adherence with the Marcy amendment, if there was any chance of securing it, but if not, then unconditionally.[19] This was a very clever move on the part of Mr. Seward. According to his view all citizens of the United States, loyal or disloyal, were alike bound by the law of nations and the treaties entered into by the United States, and, therefore, if the powers would admit the United States as a signatory of the Declaration of Paris, privateering on the part of the Confederacy would be a violation of international agreement and could not be recognized by the powers of Europe. But England and France had already committed themselves on this point and were not to be caught in any such trap. Lord Lyons had been instructed by his government, as soon as war began, to secure, if possible, the assent of the Confederacy to the rules of 1856 regarding the neutral flag, neutral goods, and blockades. The matter was brought to the attention of President Davis through the British consul at Charleston, and as a result the Confederate Congress

The attitude of the Confederacy

[18]Moore, *Dig. Int. Law,* VII, 561–568.
[19]*Ibid.,* pp. 570–573.

passed a resolution maintaining the right of privateering, but acceding to the Declaration of Paris on the other points. England thus practically agreed not to interfere with privateering by the Confederates. When Seward heard of the negotiations he asked for the removal of the consul, and on Lord Russell's refusal to withdraw him, President Lincoln revoked his exequatur on the ground that he had invited the insurgents to become a party to an international agreement similar to a treaty.[20]

Refusal of England and France to adopt Seward's view

When Seward's note was brought to the attention of the French minister, he agreed to sign a convention covering the Declaration of Paris, provided that it did not implicate his government, directly or indirectly, in the internal conflict then existing in the United States. The British government likewise agreed to sign such an agreement, provided it was to be prospective and was not to "invalidate anything already done." When asked by Mr. Adams to explain his meaning, he said: "It would follow logically and consistently, from the attitude taken by Her Majesty's Government, that the so-called Confederate States, being acknowledged as a belligerent, might, by the law of nations, arm privateers, and that their privateers must be regarded as the armed vessels of a belligerent." In other words, the Declaration of Paris was not a part of international law at that time, but simply a treaty agreement, and could bind only those powers which had formally accepted it. When the position of England and France was clearly understood, Seward let the matter drop.[21]

Privateering plays an insignificant part

Seward might have spared himself all trouble and anxiety on the subject of privateering, however, for privateering played no appreciable part in the war. This was due to two things: first, the blockade, which after

[20]For the case of Mr. Robert Bunch, British Consul at Charleston, see Moore, *Dig. Int. Law*, V, 20–21.

[21]Moore, *Dig. Int. Law*, VII, 574–583; C. F. Adams, "Seward and the Declaration of Paris," in *Proceedings of Mass. Hist. Society*, XLVI.

a few months was sufficiently effective to prevent Confederate privateers from bringing their prizes into Confederate ports; and second, the refusal of England and France to permit either belligerent to bring prizes into their ports. The principal object of privateering is gain, and unless prizes can be taken into port and condemned and sold, there is no incentive to privateering. Mere commerce-destroying is not a lucrative occupation. As soon, therefore, as the blockade became strong enough to make it exceedingly dangerous for a privateer to attempt to bring a prize into a Confederate port the practice ceased. While a number of small sailing vessels were commissioned, they soon disappeared. The most important were the *Jeff Davis*, which after making a few captures off the New England coast was wrecked on the coast of Florida; the *Beauregard*, captured; the *Judah*, burned by the Federals at Pensacola; the *Savannah*, captured; and the *Petrel*, sunk by a shell from the United States frigate *St. Lawrence*. By the end of 1861 the privateers had all disappeared. Thereafter the work of commerce-destroying was carried on by vessels owned by the Confederate government and commanded by officers of the Confederate Navy, with results that exceeded anything before experienced in naval warfare. The Confederate cruisers, such as the *Alabama*, *Florida*, and *Shenandoah*, were referred to at the time by Northern writers as privateers, corsairs, or pirates, and these terms, perpetuated by historians, have created great confusion as to the principles of international law involved.[22]

The Confederate cruisers not privateers

Confederate mission seeks recognition

Before the outbreak of hostilities the Confederate government had taken steps to gain admission into the family of nations. On March 16, 1861, Mr. Toombs, Secretary of State, directed W. L. Yancey, P. A. Rost. and A. Dudley Mann to go to London as soon as pos-

[22]J. R. Soley, *The Blockade and the Cruisers*, 168–172; C. F. Adams, "Seward and the Declaration of Paris," 9–20.

sible, and thence to the other European capitals, to press the claims of their country to full recognition as an independent power.[23] On May 3, through the courtesy of Mr. Gregory, a member of Parliament, the commissioners were granted a private interview by Lord Russell at his home. They reported that "neither England nor France will recognize the independence of the Confederate States at present, but that England in reality is not averse to a disintegration of the United States, and both of these powers will act favorably toward us upon the first decided success we may obtain"[24] Mr. Rost then proceeded to Paris, where, in an interview with M. Thouvenel, the French Minister of Foreign Affairs, he received greater encouragement. He was informed that England and France had agreed to pursue the same course, and he received the impression that recognition was a mere matter of time.[25] The commissioners reported, however, that the slavery question would probably embarrass the governments of Europe in dealing with the question of recognition of independence. Yancey finally grew impatient at the delay and resigned, while Mann was commissioned to Belgium and Rost to Spain.

Slavery an embarrassment

The capture of Mason and Slidell

Meanwhile, on August 28, 1861, President Davis had appointed James M. Mason, of Virginia, as special commissioner to England, and John Slidell, of Louisiana, as commissioner to France. Mason and Slidell ran the blockade at Charleston October 12, and proceeded to Havana, whence they sailed November 7 on the English Mail Steamer *Trent* for Southampton. On the following day, when passing through the Bahama channel, the *Trent* was overhauled by the United States man-of-war *San Jacinto*, commanded by Captain Wilkes, and the Confederate commissioners, together with their secre-

[23]Richardson, *Messages and Papers of the Confederacy*, II, 3–11.

[24]*Ibid.*, p. 34.

[25]*Ibid.*, p. 42.

taries, were forcibly removed despite the protests of the captain of the ship. They were taken to Fort Warren, in Boston harbor, and there placed in confinement.[26] The act of Captain Wilkes met with almost universal approval at the North. He was officially commended by the Secretary of the Navy, feted at Boston and New York, and voted a gold medal by the House of Representatives. Neither Seward nor Lincoln appears to have realized at the time the serious nature of the situation, though Seward made the following entry in his diary under date of November 30:

> In the capture of Messrs Mason and Slidell on board a British vessel, Captain Wilkes having acted without any instructions from the government, the subject is therefore free from the embarrassment which might have resulted if the act had been specially directed by us.[27]

Reception of the news in England and America

Lincoln's oft-quoted remark on hearing of the capture, that he feared the prisoners would prove white elephants on his hands, evidently had reference to the demand he foresaw would be made for their execution as traitors rather than to any idea of having to surrender them to Great Britain. The storm of indignation that swept over Great Britain when news of the capture was received was paralleled only by the wave of enthusiasm that went over the United States. Fortunately there was no Atlantic cable at the time, for an immediate demand for the surrender of the captives would have resulted in war.

Regarded as a blunder by Adams

As it was, the time required for the exchange of dispatches left Mr. Adams in London and Lord Lyons, the British minister in Washington, in very trying positions. Mr. Adams from his point of view in England regarded the act of Wilkes as a very serious blunder.

[26]Mason's detailed account of his experiences from his capture to his arrival in London is printed in *The Public Life and Diplomatic Correspondence of James M. Mason*, by his daughter, 209–246.

[27]Seward, *The Diplomatic History of the War for the Union* (Vol. V of the Works of William H. Seward, Edited by George E. Baker), 46.

In a private letter to Motley in Vienna, dated December 4, he wrote:

It ought to be remembered that the uniform tendency of our own policy has been to set up very high the doctrine of neutral rights, and to limit in every possible manner the odious doctrine of search. To have the two countries virtually changing their ground under this momentary temptation would not, as it seems to me, tend to benefit the position of the United States. Whereas, a contrary policy might be made the means of securing a great concession of principle from Great Britain. Whether the government at home will remain cool enough to see its opportunity, I have no means of judging.[28]

Gloomy forebodings

When he learned of the general exultation in his country over the act of Captain Wilkes, he wrote with "an indescribably sad feeling" to his son that he feared the act would prove to be the final calamity in the contest. He complained that his countrymen had little comprehension of the state of public opinion in England:

Putting ourselves in the place of Great Britain, where would be the end of the indignation that would be vented against the power committing it? Yet it seems everywhere to have been very coolly taken for granted that because she did outrageous things on the ocean to other powers, she would remain quiet when such things were done to her. A little observation of her past history ought to have shown that she never sees the right until half a century after she has acted wrong. She now admits her error in our revolution, and in the last war. Now she is right in principle and only wrong in point of consistency. Our mistake is that we are donning ourselves in her cast-off suit, when our own is better worth wearing, and all for what? Why to show our spite against two miserable wretches.[29]

Influence of environment on Adams's sons

The opinions of Adams's sons afford an interesting example of the influence of environment. Henry, who was with his father in London, wrote to his brother Charles Francis in America:

If the administration ordered the capture of those men, I am satisfied that our present authorities are very unsuitable

[28]C. F. Adams, "The Trent Affair," 38.

[29]*A Cycle of Adams Letters*, 1861–1865, I, 81.

persons to conduct a war like this or to remain in the direction of our affairs. It is our ruin. Do not deceive yourself about the position of England. . . . This nation means to make war. Do not doubt it. What Seward means is more than I can guess. But if he means war also, or to run as close as he can without touching, then I say that Mr. Seward is the greatest criminal we've had yet.[30]

About the same time Charles Francis, Junior, wrote from America: "The English precedents so clearly justify us that I cannot fear difficulty from that cause."[31]

Lord Lyons awaits instructions

Lord Lyons, who was patiently awaiting instructions in Washington, was the type of diplomat who had no opinions, so far as the general public or even his more intimate associates could gather, except those of his government. His career was so utterly devoid of anything in the nature of an indiscretion that his biography is almost lacking in essential elements of human interest.[32] He boasted in after years that during his five years in Washington he had "never taken a drink, or made a speech," a remarkable record for a bachelor! In the trying weeks following the capture of Mason and Slidell, Lord Lyons maintained absolute silence, and no one could abstract from him the slightest expression of opinion as to what action his government would be likely to take.

Great Britain demands surrender of Mason and Slidell

Finally, on December 18, he received Lord Russell's dispatch instructing him to demand the surrender of Mason and Slidell on the ground that they had been "forcibly taken from on board a British vessel, the ship of a neutral power, while that vessel was pursuing a lawful and innocent voyage—an act of violence which was an affront to the British flag and a violation of international law." Lord Lyons broke the force of the blow by communicating the contents of this dispatch to Seward orally and with the utmost tact. The firmness with which he officially

[30] *Op. cit,* I, 75.

[31] *Ibid.,* p. 78.

[32] Lord Newton, *Life of Lord Lyons,* 2 vols., 1913

communicated the dispatch two days later left no doubt in Seward's mind as to the real intentions of England.[33]

Russell's dispatch modified at request of the Queen

The dispatch as originally drafted by Russell, after conference with the Cabinet, was rather harsh and somewhat too peremptory in character, but it was submitted to the Queen who sought the advice of the Prince Consort. The latter was in the last stages of an illness from which he died within a fortnight. He suggested changes in the wording of the dispatch so as to render it less offensive to American pride, and the Queen, who was eager to spare him all anxiety, persuaded the cabinet to make the changes proposed.[34] The American government was given seven days in which to reply; if at the end of that time the British demand was not complied with, Lord Lyons was instructed to leave Washington and repair immediately to London. At the same time England made extensive naval preparations and sent eight thousand troops to Canada.

Seward yields to the British ultimatum

On December 28, Seward replied to the British demand. He agreed to surrender Mason and Slidell, but on grounds wholly different from those set forth in the British dispatch. His note was clever, if we recognize the fact that it was intended primarily for the American people, but it was not a great state paper because it did not meet the British contention that the *Trent* was engaged in an innocent voyage from one neutral port to another, and had a right to carry the persons in question. Whether the latter were classed as diplomatic agents or as quasi-diplomatic agents, they certainly were not embodied in the military forces of the Confederacy. Seward argued at length that Mason and Slidell, their secretaries and their dispatches, were contraband of war and therefore liable to seizure, but that the removal of these men from the *Trent* without bringing the ship itself before a prize

[33]Lord Newton, *Life of Lord Lyons*, I, 65–75.
[34]*Ibid.*, p. 61.

court for trial was irregular and therefore not justified. He asserted the right to prevent a contraband person "from proceeding in his unlawful voyage and reaching the destined scene of his injurious service," but, he added, the captured person might be innocent and was therefore entitled to a fair trial. But as to the mode of procedure, he said, "the books of law are dumb." Nevertheless, he maintained, the vessel should have been taken into port and judicial proceedings instituted to try the controversy, but even then there was this difficulty: "Only courts of admiralty have jurisdiction in maritime cases, and these courts have formulas to try only claims to contraband chattels, but none to try claims concerning contraband persons."

His confused and sophisticated reasoning

Seward's argument to prove that the Confederate agents were contraband of war was, of course, beside the mark. The case would fall to-day under the head of "unneutral service," but that topic had not been clearly developed by the international law writers of that day, and even under the modern doctrine of unneutral service neither the *Trent* nor the agents she bore would be liable to seizure. The Declaration of London, Article 47, provides:

> . . . any individual embodied in the armed force of the enemy, and who is found on board a neutral merchant vessel may be made a prisoner of war, even though there be no ground for the capture of the vessel.

On solid ground at last

The greater part of Seward's argument was illogical and confused. At the end, in strange contradiction to what had gone before, he finally got his feet on solid ground. In surrendering the captives, he declared he was really defending "an old, honored, and cherished American cause":

> If I decide this case in favor of my own government, I must disavow its most cherished principles, and reverse and forever

abandon its essential policy. The country cannot afford the sacrifice. If I maintain these principles, and adhere to that policy, I must surrender the case itself. It will be seen, therefore, that this government could not deny the justice of the claim presented to us in this respect upon its merits. We are asked to do to the British nation just what we have always insisted all nations ought to do to us.[35]

How the decision was received

During the interval between the reception of the British note and the reply, Lincoln and Seward had time to warn the friends of the administration of what was coming, and some of the leading newspapers began to prepare the public by raising questions as to the validity and wisdom of Wilkes's procedure. The North acquiesced in the decision of the government, though with great reluctance and disappointment and increased hatred of England. The Confederates, who had followed the controversy with intense interest, hoping that it would lead to a rupture between the United States and England and hasten recognition, were likewise greatly disappointed at the outcome.

Reception of Mason and Slidell in England

Mason and Slidell were taken from Fort Warren January 1, 1862, and transferred to a British man-of-war, which after a stormy voyage landed them at the Bermudas. They reached England on the 29th, and were cordially received by the friends of the Confederacy, among whom were Messrs. Lindsay, Gregory, and other members of Parliament.[36] The great majority of the upper classes, including many of the nobility, were strongly in sympathy with the South. As the stock of cotton diminished and the distress of the factory operatives in Lancashire increased, the British ministry was urged by the friends of the South to offer mediation, and in case of its rejection by the North to follow it up by

[35]Seward, *Dip. Hist. of the War for the Union*, 295–309.

[36]*Confederate State Department Correspondence, Official Records of Union and Confederate Navies*, Series II, Vol. III, 331. Cited hereafter as *Confed. State Dept. Cor.*

recognition of independence and the breaking of the blockade.

Interview with Lord Russell

At Mr. Mason's request he was granted an unofficial interview by Lord Russell at the latter's house February 10, 1862. Having been cautioned by members of Parliament that the government was a little sensitive at the emphasis placed on cotton as a factor in the determination of its foreign policy, he omitted that topic and confined himself largely to a discussion of recognition and the blockade. In reporting to his government the result of his interview with Lord Russell, he said: "On the whole, it was manifest enough that his personal sympathies were not with us, and his policy inaction."[37] The interview was followed by a number of communications from Mr. Mason on the subject of the blockade, inclosing lists of vessels entering and clearing from Cuban ports engaged in commerce with the Confederate States. He argued from these facts that the blockade was not effective, and therefore in violation of the fourth article of the Declaration of Paris, which at the request of England and France both belligerents had agreed at the commencement of the war to observe. Lord Russell merely acknowledged the receipt of the communication.

Attitude of Louis Napoleon

On April 11, Mr. Lindsay, M. P. for Liverpool, and one of the largest ship-owners in England, had an interview with the French Emperor in the interests of the Confederacy, in which he discussed the blockade. The Emperor agreed with him that it was not effective and said that he would long since have taken the necessary steps to put an end to it, but that he could not obtain the concurrence of the British ministry, and that he was unwilling to act alone. He declared that he was prepared to send a formidable fleet to the mouth of the Mississippi if England would send an equal force; that they would demand free ingress and egress for their

[37] *Op. cit.*, p. 343.

merchant vessels with their cargoes of goods and supplies of cotton, which were essential to the world.[38] He authorized Mr. Lindsay to make his views known to the British ministry. Lord Russell refused to receive this communication through Mr. Lindsay, on the ground that he could not communicate with a foreign power except through the regular diplomatic channels. In an interview with Mr. Slidell on the 18th of April the Emperor complained that Lord Russell had sent his previous proposition in regard to joint action on the blockade to Lord Lyons, and that the latter had communicated it to Mr. Seward; that for this reason he was unwilling to communicate officially with the British ministry again until he knew that England was in accord with him.[39]

Interview with Slidell

In July, 1862, Slidell had another interview with the French Emperor, which encouraged him to send a formal note to the foreign secretary asking for recognition, and he requested Mason to make simultaneously a like demand on the British government. In accordance with this suggestion, Mason addressed a formal note to Russell July 24, and at the same time requested a personal interview. The interview was declined, and in answer to the demand for recognition Russell said that in view of the capture of New Orleans and the advance of the Federals up the Mississippi, Her Majesty's Government were still determined to wait. When this correspondence was received by Benjamin, he instructed Mason to continue in London, but to refrain from further communication with Lord Russell until he himself should invite correspondence, or until some important change in British policy should occur.[40]

England declines to be hurried into recognition

---

[38]*Op. cit.*, p. 393; Richardson, *Messages and Papers of the Confederacy*, II, 236–239.

[39]*Confed. State Dept. Cor.*, 397.

[40]*Ibid.*, pp. 481, 500–504; also in Richardson, *Messages and Papers of the Confederacy*, II, 289–310.

CHAPTER XVI

THE MENACE OF EUROPEAN INTERVENTION

Pope's defeat at Bull Run

POPE'S defeat at Bull Run, August 30, 1862, and Lee's advance into Maryland soon drew the attention of the British ministry again to the subject of recognition and led to a very interesting correspondence between Palmerston and Russell, the latter having accompanied the Queen to Gotha. On September 14, 1862, the Prime Minister wrote that the Federals "got a very complete smashing," and if Washington or Baltimore should fall into their hands, he asked whether England and France should not "address the contending parties and recommend an arrangement upon the basis of separation." Russell replied on the 17th:

Correspondence between Russell and Palmerston

> I agree with you that the time is come for offering mediation to the United States government, with a view to the recognition of the independence of the Confederates. I agree further, that, in case of failure, we ought ourselves to recognize the Southern States as an independent State. For the purpose of taking so important a step, I think we must have a meeting of the Cabinet.

He thought that the step should be taken in conjunction with France, and, if possible, with Russia and other powers. To this note Palmerston replied:

> Your plan of proceedings about the mediation between the Federals and Confederates seems to be excellent. Of course, the offer would be made to both the contending parties at the same time; for, though the offer would be as sure to be accepted by the Southerners as was the proposal of the Prince of Wales by the Danish Princess,[1] yet, in the one case as in the other,

[1]This was written shortly after the Prince of Wales's marriage had been arranged.

there are certain forms which it is decent and proper to go through.

A question would occur whether, if the two parties were to accept the mediation, the fact of our mediating would not of itself be tantamount to an acknowledgment of the Confederates as an independent state.[2]

While Palmerston and Russell were considering the date for the Cabinet meeting, Russell, who had returned to England, received from Lord Granville, who had taken his place in attendance upon the Queen at Gotha, a long letter in which he said:

Granville opposes change of policy

It is premature to depart from the policy which has hitherto been adopted by you and Lord Palmerston; and which, notwithstanding the strong antipathy to the North, the strong sympathy with the South, and the passionate wish to have cotton, has met with such general approval from Parliament, the press, and the public.

Russell forwarded this letter to Palmerston, who replied October 2:

The condition of things which would be favorable to an offer of mediation would be great success of the South against the North. That state of things seemed ten days ago to be approaching. Its advance has been lately checked, but we do not yet know the real course of recent events, and still less can we foresee what is about to follow; ten days or a fortnight more may throw a clearer light upon future prospects.[3]

Russell's memorandum

The Cabinet meeting was called for October 23, and in the meantime Lord Russell circulated among the members a confidential memorandum raising the question

. . . whether it is not a duty for Europe to ask both parties, in the most friendly and conciliatory terms, to agree to a suspension of arms for the purpose of weighing calmly the advantages of peace against the contingent gain of further bloodshed, and the protraction of so calamitous a war.[4]

[2]Walpole, *Life of Lord John Russell.* II, 360–361.

[3]*Ibid.*, p. 362.

[4]*Ibid.*, p. 363.

Gladstone's Newcastle speech

While things were in this status, Gladstone, who was Chancellor of the Exchequer, made his famous speech of October 7 at Newcastle, in which he said:

> There is no doubt that Jefferson Davis and other leaders of the South have made an army; they are making, it appears, a navy; and they have made, what is more than either—they have made a nation. . . . We may anticipate with certainty the success of the Southern States so far as their separation from the North is concerned.[5]

Coming from a prominent member of the Cabinet, the natural construction put upon this speech was that the British ministry had decided to recognize the Confederacy. Whatever his intention, the speech aroused the friends of the North and set the tide of public opinion strongly against the proposed change of policy. Sir George Cornewall Lewis, another member of the Cabinet, circulated among his colleagues in answer to Russell's memorandum a counter-memorandum, objecting to the proposed offer of mediation, which he referred to as "the most singular action for the restitution of conjugal rights he had ever heard of." Furthermore, the news of General Lee's check at Antietam and his subsequent retirement across the Potomac made the time unfavorable for an offer of mediation. When the members of the Cabinet convened on the 23d, the Prime Minister was absent and no formal meeting was held.[6] In the informal discussion that took place, Russell and Gladstone stood alone and the subject was indefinitely postponed.[7] Al-

Action postponed

[5]Morley, *Life of Gladstone*, II, 81.

[6]Maxwell, *Life and Letters of the Earl of Clarendon*, II, 265.

[7]C. F. Adams discussed this cabinet meeting in an interesting way in one of his Oxford lectures, 1913, published in *Trans-Atlantic Historical Solidarity*, chap. III. He represented the postponement of the cabinet meeting as due to the personal pique of Lord Palmerston, who, he thought, resented Gladstone's presumption in making an unauthorized announcement of policy, and decided to rebuke him. Further investigations which Mr. Adams made while he was in England, convinced him, however, that he was wrong. With characteristic frankness he acknowledged his mistake and set forth his final conclusions in an address before the Mass. Hist. Society entitled "A Crisis in Downing Street," 1914.

though Palmerston did not care to press the matter in the face of opposition, he was apparently of the same opinion as Gladstone as to the outcome of the war, for on October 20 he wrote to Lord Clarendon:

Palmerston's position

> As to the American War, it has manifestly ceased to have any attainable object as far as the Northerns are concerned, except to get rid of some more thousand troublesome Irish and Germans. It must be owned, however, that the Anglo-Saxon race on both sides have shown courage and endurance highly honorable to their stock.[8]

Lincoln decides to turn the war into a crusade against slavery

President Lincoln took advantage of General Lee's retreat from Maryland to issue the proclamation of emancipation and turn the war into a crusade against slavery. The abolitionists had long been urging this step, and he had been seriously considering it for some months. From the outset slavery had been an embarrassing subject to the diplomats of both North and South. President Lincoln and Congress both solemnly declared that the war was being waged solely for the Union and that there was no intention to interfere with slavery in any state in which it existed. The Confederates were equally emphatic in declaring that they were fighting for States Rights and independence. The theory underlying Seward's treatment of the question was that, as the sovereignty of the United States had not been overthrown, slavery was a domestic question with which foreign powers had nothing to do.[9] He, therefore, instructed his representatives abroad to avoid all discussion of slavery. In his first instructions to Adams, April 10, 1861, he said:

Earlier instructions on question of slavery

> You will not consent to draw into debate before the British government any opposing moral principles which may be supposed to lie at the foundation of the controversy between those States and the Federal Union.[10]

[8]Maxwell, *Life of the Earl of Clarendon*, II, 267.

[9]Bancroft, *Life of Seward*, II, 317, ff.

[10]Seward, *Diplomatic History of the War for the Union*, 208.

In his instructions to Dayton, minister to France, April 22, 1861, he said:

> The new president, as well as the citizens through whose suffrages he has come into the administration, has always repudiated all designs whatever and wherever imputed to him and them of disturbing the system of slavery as it is existing under the Constitution and laws. The case, however, would not be fully presented if I were to omit to say that any such effort on his part would be unconstitutional, and all his actions in that direction would be prevented by the judicial authority, even though they were assented to by Congress and the people.[11]

Reasons for the delay

To have declared the abolition of slavery to be the object of the war would have driven the loyal slave-holding border states into the Confederacy, and the administration considered it of greater importance to secure these states than to win the anti-slavery support in England and France by yielding to the abolitionist demands. In January, 1862, Seward wrote to Adams:

> Every demonstration against slavery puts our assured position in Maryland, Kentucky, Missouri, and Virginia at hazard, and tends to combine the revolting States in mass.[12]

In a dispatch to Adams, May 28, 1862, Seward finally raised the embargo on the discussion of slavery. "I am aware," he began, "that in regard to this point I am opening a subject which was early interdicted in this correspondence." The reasons he assigned for the change of instructions were that the Confederates "persist in invoking foreign arms to end a domestic strife, while they have forced slavery into such prominence that it cannot be overlooked." The burden of his dispatch was that slaves were escaping from bondage and taking refuge with the Federal armies at the rate of a hundred a day. "If the war should continue indefinitely, every slave will

[11] *Op. cit.*, p. 227.

[12] Bancroft, *Life of Seward,* II, 328.

become, not only a freeman, but an absentee." The government was already considering measures for providing them with domiciles at home and abroad. If the Southerners should attempt to prevent the escape of their slaves a servile war would result and disorganize the whole industrial system of the insurrectionary region. It was to the interest of Europe, therefore, to cease encouraging the insurgents and prolonging the war by holding out hopes of intervention, for—

Seward warns Europe of danger of emancipation

> Let it next be considered that the European systems of industry are largely based upon the African slave labor of the insurrectionary states employed in the production of cotton, tobacco, and rice, and on the free labor of the other States employed in producing cereals, out of which combined productions arises the demand for European productions, materials, and fabrics. The disorganization of industry, which is already revealing itself in the insurrectionary states, cannot but impair their ability to prosecute the war, and at the same time result indirectly in greater distress in Europe.[13]

This peculiar argument might well have been used by Mason and Slidell to persuade England and France to intervene and save slavery. Adams was instructed to use it as occasion might arise.

Europe fails to see moral issue

In view of the emphatic declarations of the United States government that abolition was not the aim of the war, and of the Confederates that their sole aim was independence, it is not strange that Englishmen and Frenchmen failed to see any moral issues involved. British opinion was well summarized by Palmerston when he remarked to an American: "We do not like slavery, but we want cotton, and we dislike very much your Morrill tariff." Slidell reported that anti-slavery sentiment in the abstract was quite as general in France as in England, and that while he often heard expressions of regret that slavery existed in the Confederacy, he did not believe the

[13]*Dip. Cor. of U. S.*, 1862, p. 104.

question would affect the action of the Emperor one way or the other.[14]

Seward opposed emancipation proclamation

On July 13, 1862, Lincoln informed Seward that he had decided to issue a proclamation of emancipation. On July 22, the question was discussed at the Cabinet meeting. Seward opposed the measure, declaring that it would be regarded as a sign of weakness to issue it just after the greatest disaster of the war; it would be "the government stretching forth her hands to Ethiopia, instead of Ethiopia stretching forth her hands to the government"; the proclamation should be "borne on the bayonets of an advancing army, not dragged in the dust behind a retreating one." In a letter to his wife he said:

> Proclamations are paper, without the support of armies. It is mournful to see that a great nation shrinks from a war it has accepted, and insists on adopting proclamations, when it is asked for force. The Chinese do it without success.

He also expressed the fear that a proclamation of emancipation might bring on a slave insurrection and cause a cessation in the production of cotton, and thus give England and France an excuse for intervening.[15] Lincoln decided to await the first victory.

The preliminary proclamation

Antietam afforded him the opportunity for which he was waiting, and on September 22, 1862, he issued the preliminary Proclamation of Emancipation, in which he declared that the object of the war was still the restoration of the Union; that he would again urge upon Congress at its next session the adoption of a plan of compensated emancipation for the states not then in rebellion against the United States; that he would also continue his efforts "to colonize persons of African descent with their consent upon this continent or elsewhere, with the previously obtained consent of the governments existing there"; and

[14]Bancroft, *Life of Seward*, II, 330. For a full discussion of the French attitude toward slavery see West, *Contemporary French Opinion on the American Civil War*.

[15]Bancroft, *Life of Seward*, II, 333–335.

. . . that on the 1st day of January, A. D. 1863, all persons held as slaves within any state or designated part of a state the people whereof shall then be in rebellion against the United States shall be then, thenceforward, and forever free.[16]

This proclamation made very little impression in England and France and called forth a good deal of ridicule from the friends of the South. The *Spectator* (London) said:

Received with ridicule in England

> The government liberates the enemy's slaves as it would the enemy's cattle, simply to weaken them in the coming conflict. . . . The principle is not that a human being cannot justly own another, but that he cannot own him unless he is loyal to the United States.[17]

The *Saturday Review* said:

> The President has virtually acknowledged his military failure, and his desperate efforts to procure military support will probably precipitate the ruin of his cause.[18]

The *Times* regarded the proclamation as Lincoln's "last card"—a deliberate attempt to incite a servile insurrection. In an editorial of October 21, it asked:

Lincoln's "last card"

> Is the reign of the last President to go out amid horrible massacres of white women and children, to be followed by the extermination of the black race in the South? Is Lincoln yet a name not known to us as it will be known to posterity, and is it ultimately to be classed among that catalogue of monsters, the wholesale assassins and butchers of their kind?[19]

In France the liberal press received the proclamation with favor, though they regarded it as a halfway measure. The Imperialists condemned it, though not in as harsh terms as the British papers. The *Constitutionnel* declared that Lincoln did not condemn slavery in principle:

Reaction of the French press

[16] *Messages and Papers of the Presidents*, VI, 96.

[17] Bancroft, *Life of Seward*, II, 339.

[18] *Ibid.*, p. 340.

[19] For this and other quotations from the British press see E. D. Adams, *Great Britain and the American Civil War*, II, 101, ff.

> Far from condemning slavery, he promises to maintain it; he offers a premium to encourage it in favor of States which from now until the first of January next, reënter the Union, so that if the proclamation could attain the end it proposes, and if, supposing the impossible, all the Confederate States laid down their arms within the next three months, slavery would be in fact and by right maintained in all the territories. . . . Who then will dare to say again that the North fights for the suppression of Slavery?[20]

The final proclamation produces effect abroad

The final proclamation of January 1, 1863, convinced the world that the North was committed to the cause of abolition. The workers in the cotton mills, who had suffered untold hardships from the blockade and who in the earlier stages of the war had felt very little sympathy for the North, were now stirred to the depths and thronged the meetings that were everywhere held for the purpose of indorsing the new policy of Lincoln. These demonstrations strengthened the hands of the members of Parliament and the Cabinet who opposed the recognition of the South. The Protestant churches of England and France were also stirred by the final proclamation. In February, 1863, seven hundred and fifty Protestant pastors of France issued an address to pastors of all evangelical denominations in England asking them to stir up "a great and peaceful demonstration of sympathy for the black race." An Antislavery Conference of Ministers of Religion, held at Manchester in June, adopted a reply which was signed by nearly four thousand clergymen.[21]

Lincoln's efforts to colonize freedom in tropical countries

Lincoln's views on slavery did not differ fundamentally from those of the average non-slaveholding white of the border states. He did not believe that the black and white races could live together in political equality. Like many of the statesmen of the border states, who a generation before had supported the American Colonization Society, he believed it would be necessary to colonize the

[20]West, *Contemporary French Opinion on the American Civil War*, 86.
[21]Bancroft, *Life of Seward*, II, 341–342.

liberated slaves in some tropical country, and immediately after the adoption of the Emancipation Proclamation, he submitted a proposal to the Cabinet. Seward was not favorable to the scheme, but it fell to him to pave the way for it. In a circular dispatch of September 30, 1862, he directed the American ministers to England, France, Holland, and Denmark to propose treaties providing places of refuge in their West India possessions for the liberated slaves who might voluntarily emigrate.[22] The powers addressed refused their consent. Lincoln's attempts to establish Negro settlements at Chiriqui on the Isthmus of Panama, and on Île à Vache, an island off the coast of Haiti, turned out tragically and failed to point a solution to the problem that weighed so heavily on his mind and heart.[23]

Louis Napoleon discusses mediation

In the meantime Slidell had been urging Louis Napoleon to act, and on October 28, 1862, was granted a long interview with him at St. Cloud. The Emperor declared that his "sympathies were entirely with the South," but "that if he acted alone England, instead of following his example, would endeavor to embroil him with the United States, and that French commerce would be destroyed." He inquired of Slidell: "What do you think of the joint mediation of France, England, and Russia? Would it, if proposed, be accepted by the two parties?" Slidell replied that he had no faith in England, and believed that Russia would incline strongly to the Northern side, that France might be outvoted, and that he would prefer the joint mediation of France and England without Russia. The Emperor said:

> My own preference is for a proposition of an armistice of six months, with the Southern ports open to the commerce of the world. This would put a stop to the effusion of blood, and

[22]*Dip. Cor. of U. S.*, 1862, p. 202.

[23]Bancroft, *Life of Seward*, II, 347; Nicolay and Hay, *Abraham Lincoln*, VI, 354–367.

hostilities would probably never be resumed. We can urge it on high grounds of humanity and the interest of the whole civilized world. If it be refused by the North, it will afford good reason for recognition and perhaps for more active intervention.[24]

The British Cabinet rejects his proposal

A few days later the Emperor made the proposition he had outlined to Slidell to the British government through his ambassador at London. Russell presented it to the Cabinet November 11, and we have a detailed account of the meeting in a letter from Sir George Cornewall Lewis to Lord Clarendon. Russell stated, according to Lewis, that he had received a telegram from St. Petersburg informing him that Russia had already answered the French proposal, that she declined to be a party to a joint representation, but would support it by her minister at Washington, provided it would not cause irritation. Russell then urged the acceptance of the French proposal, declaring that the success of the Democrats in the recent elections afforded a most favorable opportunity for intervention. "The proposal was now before the Cabinet, who proceeded to pick it to pieces. Everybody present threw a stone at it of greater or less size, except Gladstone, who supported it, and the Chancellor and Cardwell, who expressed no opinion." Palmerston, who had at first said a few words in support of the plan, capitulated when he saw that the feeling of the Cabinet was against it.[25] Slidell was quick to learn of the rejection of the French proposal, for on November 28, he wrote in disgust to Mason: "Who would have believed that Earl Russell would have been the only member of the Cabinet besides Gladstone in favor of accepting the Emperor's proposition?"[26]

Seeing that there was no immediate prospect of action

[24]*Confed. State Dept. Cor.*, 574; Richardson, *Messages and Papers of the Confederacy*, II, 345.

[25]Maxwell, *Life of the Earl of Clarendon*, II, 268.

[26]Adams, "A Crisis in Downing Street," 421.

from England, Slidell, on January 8, 1863, addressed a memorandum to the Emperor urging him to recognize the independence of the Confederate States in the hope that other powers would follow his lead.[27] In view of the crushing defeat of the Union army at Fredericksburg, Napoleon thought that the time was favorable for mediation, and the day following the presentation of Slidell's memorandum a dispatch was sent to Mercier, his representative at Washington, making a formal offer of mediation in courteous terms. The offer was politely, but very positively, declined by Seward, and Napoleon was afraid to go any further without the coöperation of England.[28]

The French Emperor's offer of mediation declined

General Lee's rapid advance into Maryland and Pennsylvania in June, 1863, revived hope once more among the friends of the South in England. On June 30, Roebuck introduced in the House of Commons a resolution calling upon the government to enter into negotiation with foreign powers for coöperation in the recognition of the Confederacy. The debate on the resolution continued until July 13, when the mover, convinced that an overwhelming majority of the House were against it, withdrew it from further consideration.[29] Notwithstanding the general state of expectancy that news would shortly be received that Lee had taken Baltimore or Washington, the Cabinet did not intend to have its hand forced, or to change without the fullest consideration the policy it had decided upon in October and November preceding. The Antietam campaign, and not the Gettysburg campaign, was the turning point in the history of the Confederacy. A few days after the withdrawal of Roebuck's motion came the news of the fall of Vicksburg and the defeat of Lee at Gettysburg. Even this news was re-

Roebuck's resolution in the House of Commons

[27]*Confed. State Dept. Cor.*, 640; Richardson, *Messages and Papers of the Confederacy*, II, 391.

[28]Seward, *Diplomatic History of the War for the Union*, 376.

[29]Rhodes, *History of the U. S.*, IV, 374–375; E. D. Adams, *Great Britain and the American Civil War*, II, 170–177.

News of Gettysburg

garded not so much in the light of a Confederate defeat as evidence of an indefinite prolongation of the war and the impossibility of either side winning a decisive victory. A few weeks later Mason, acting under instructions from his government, terminated his mission in London and withdrew to Paris to wait for something to turn up.

Napoleon's Mexican policy

Napoleon's Mexican venture undoubtedly furnishes the secret of his friendly feeling for the Confederacy. The success of his scheme to erect a throne for Maximilian of Austria in Mexico and to establish French influence once more on the western continent, was deliberately calculated on the overthrow of the American Union. The Confederate government quickly caught at the suggestion of an alliance between Maximilian and the South with the power of France to back it, but Napoleon was afraid of the American navy and did not care to go to the full length of recognizing the Confederacy as an independent power without the coöperation of England. His designs on Mexico, however, made England very cautious about entering into any agreement with him.[30]

Attempt to build a Confederate navy in France

Early in 1863 Napoleon authorized the building of a Confederate navy in France, provided the destination of the ships could be kept secret. A number of ships were actually in process of construction, but when a few months later a shipyard clerk betrayed the secret to John Bigelow, American consul at Paris, the Emperor became frightened and withdrew his sanction of the scheme. Only one of the vessels, the *Stonewall,* was ever delivered to the Confederates.[31]

England had allowed the *Florida* and *Alabama* to leave her ports in 1862 in spite of almost overwhelming evidence that they were intended for the Confederate government.

---

[30]Post, 401–406.

[31]*Confed. Navy Dept. Cor.*, Official Records of the Union and Confederate Navies, Series II, Vol. II, 464, 590, 691, 431–438; John Bigelow, *France and the Confederate Navy;* Bulloch, *Secret Service of the Confederate States in Europe*, II, chaps. i and ii.

They destroyed ships and cargoes to the value of many millions and almost drove Federal commerce from the seas.[32] In the summer of 1863, Adams called Lord Russell's attention to two ironclads on the docks at Birkenhead, which were being built under a disguise for the Confederacy. He submitted affidavits obtained by the American consul at Liverpool, but Russell replied that the evidence was not sufficient to justify proceedings against the vessels. Finally, on September 5, when one of the ironclads was on the point of departure, Adams made a final protest which amounted to an ultimatum. In it he said: "It would be superfluous in me to point out to your lordship that this is war."[33] Three days later he received the brief but satisfactory reply: "Lord Russell presents his compliments to Mr. Adams, and has the honor to inform him that instructions have been issued which will prevent the departure of the two ironclad vessels from Liverpool."[34] These were formidable vessels, and Captain Bulloch, who contracted for their construction, was convinced that they could break the blockade at Charleston and Wilmington.[35] Their detention was a serious blow to the Confederacy. There remained little hope of securing any more ships abroad.

Adams stops ship-building program in England

Until the last year of the war blockade running was carried on on a large scale. Boats were specially constructed for this purpose, and a favorite port of rendezvous for the blockade runners was the British port of Nassau in the Bahamas. Goods could be shipped from England to Nassau and there be transferred to blockade runners, which at night would slip through the Federal squadrons into Charleston, Wilmington, or to some port in Florida. A great many blockade runners also went out from

Blockade running

[32] Post, 426–429.
[33] *Dip. Cor. of U. S.*, 1863, 418.
[34] *Ibid.*, p. 419.
[35] Bulloch, *Secret Service of the Confederate States in Europe*, I, chap. vii.

Havana. At first the United States government hesitated to seize a neutral ship bound for a neutral port and there seemed no legal way to break up the Nassau trade, but finally the Federal navy seized several ships, including the *Springbok*, an English ship bound from London for Nassau with a cargo composed in part of contraband goods destined for the Confederacy. She was taken to New York, and the case was tried in the United States District Court, which condemned both ship and cargo. This and several similar prize cases were appealed to the Supreme Court of the United States, and a decision was rendered at the December term in 1866.[36] The *Springbok* was released as having a neutral destination, but the cargo was condemned on the ground that its ultimate destination was the Confederacy. This decision was based on an application or extension of the doctrine of continuous voyage which had originally been laid down by the English Admiralty Court. The Supreme Court held that the destination of the goods rather than that of the ship determined their liability to capture. There seems to have been no clear conception on the part of the court that in separating the goods from the ship they were laying down a new doctrine. The owners of the cargo of the *Springbok* appealed to Lord Russell, but he declined to interfere, holding that not only the cargo but the ship itself was liable. This extension of the doctrine of continuous voyage was adopted by Great Britain during the Boer War, and in the World War it became an issue of vital importance.[37]

The prize cases before the Supreme Court

The doctrine of continuous voyage

In the fall of 1864 Secretary Benjamin informed President Davis that future negotiations with the European powers must be on the basis of emancipation and government seizure of cotton, with which to purchase ships

---

[36] 5 Wallace, 1–62.

[37] Moore, *Dig. of Int. Law*, VII, 719–739; Briggs, *The Doctrine of Continuous Voyage*, 63–79.

to break the blockade. Davis hesitated to act without the authorization of Congress, but Benjamin justified his proposition as a war measure. He believed that by the adoption of a policy of emancipation and a promise to ship cotton the recognition of France and perhaps of England might yet be obtained. He proposed to negotiate treaties with England and France, pledging the government to these policies. With reluctance Davis finally agreed to the plan, hoping after a diplomatic triumph to secure the ratification of the proposed treaties.[38]

Benjamin proposes emancipation as basis of foreign negotiations

The mission of Duncan F. Kenner

For obvious reasons it was not deemed expedient to act through Mason and Slidell alone. They had been sent to Europe to act along totally different lines, and could hardly be expected after so long an absence from the country to appreciate the necessity which changed conditions rendered inexorable. Then, too, their pro-slavery views were so pronounced that they might not be willing to advocate the new policy with any genuine enthusiasm. These considerations, together with the fact that communication through the blockade was now too difficult to permit of free correspondence between the Confederate government and its agents abroad, led Benjamin to propose that one man of recognized ability and prominence be sent to Europe with full authority to act independently or even to dismiss other diplomatic agents. For this important mission President Davis selected Duncan F. Kenner, of Louisiana, one of the largest slaveholders in the South, who had been educated in Europe and spoke French fluently, and who was at this time chairman of the ways and means committee of the Confederate House of Representatives.[39]

It was of the utmost importance that the nature of Kenner's mission should be kept secret, and therefore the Confederate Congress was not consulted and the new

---

[38]Callahan, *Diplomatic History of the Southern Confederacy,* chap. xi.

[39]*Confed. State Dept. Cor.,* 1253–1256.

Benjamin's instructions to Kenner

move was made solely on the authority of the President. Kenner was clothed with full powers to make treaties with the governments of Europe binding the Confederate States to the adoption of a system of gradual emancipation and also to negotiate for the sale of cotton. In the dispatches which he bore to Mason and Slidell the true character of his mission was disguised under general terms. Mr. Benjamin said: "If there be objections not made known to us, which have for four years prevented the recognition of our independence notwithstanding the demonstration of our right to assert, and our ability to maintain it, justice equally demands that an opportunity be afforded us for meeting and overcoming those objections, if in our power to do so." He then instructed Mason and Slidell to consider any communication which Kenner might make verbally "on the subject embraced in this dispatch as emanating from this Department under the instructions of the President."

Conference with Mason and Slidell

Mr. Kenner was delayed in finding a safe way of getting out through the blockade. After trying Wilmington, N. C., he boldly went to New York in disguise, where he had been well known in racing circles prior to the war, and through the aid of a friend in that city secured passage on a ship for England. He arrived in London the latter part of February, 1865, and, learning that Mason was in Paris, proceeded at once to that city. Having arranged a conference with Mason and Slidell, he found with them W. W. Corcoran, but being informed that he was in their confidence, he stated at length the character of his mission. Both Mason and Slidell were greatly astonished at his instructions, and Mason was disinclined at first to coöperate, but finally did so when informed as to the full extent of Kenner's powers.[40] Mason shortly afterward started for London, while Slidell sought an interview with the Emperor. The latter still insisted that he

[40]Callahan, 265.

was willing and anxious to act with England, but would not move without her. When the emancipation question was laid before him he said that "he had never taken that into consideration, that it had not and could not have any influence on his action; but that it had probably been differently considered by England."[41]

Napoleon uninfluenced by slavery question

In an interview with Lord Palmerston at his house, March 14, 1865, Mr. Mason endeavored to sound him as to what the attitude of England would be toward Mr. Benjamin's proposition. "I returned again and again," he says, "during the conversation to this point, and in language so direct that it was impossible to be misunderstood, but I made no distinct proposal, in terms of what was held in reserve under the private note borne by Mr. Kenner. Lord Palmerston listened with interest and attention while I unfolded fully the purpose of the dispatch and of my interview. In reply he at once assured me that the objections entertained by his government were those which had been avowed and that there was nothing 'underlying' them."[42]

Palmerston unmoved by the proposal

The move came too late. Sherman's march through Georgia and into the Carolinas had destroyed all confidence in the success of the Confederacy. Kenner's mission was grasping at a straw. It was followed shortly by the news of Lee's surrender and Lincoln's assassination. The South had overestimated the potency of cotton and staked too much on European intervention.

[41] *Confed. State Dept. Cor.,* 1270.
[42] *Ibid.,* pp. 1272–1276.

CHAPTER XVII

THE POST-BELLUM DIPLOMACY OF SEWARD

Seward continues to direct foreign policy under Johnson

At the moment that Lincoln was assassinated, a savage attack by an unknown assailant was made on Seward, who was confined to his bed by a broken jaw, the result of being thrown from his carriage by runaway horses. Although painfully cut about the face and throat by the knife of the would-be assassin, he finally recovered, was retained as Secretary of State by Johnson, and served throughout the whole of his administration. Thus, fortunately for the country, Lincoln's death did not involve any changes in foreign policy. The Civil War left standing two very serious disputes, the one with England over the so-called "*Alabama* Claims," which will be considered in a separate chapter, and the other with France over the presence of her troops in Mexico. The latter dispute was handled by Seward with consummate ability. The other major achievement of the post-war period of his Secretaryship of State was the purchase of Alaska. Efforts, in the end unsuccessful, to acquire Santo Domingo and the Danish West Indies also absorbed much of his attention.

Foreign intervention in Mexico

The attempt of Louis Napoleon during the Civil War to establish an empire in Mexico with Maximilian of Austria on the throne was a direct challenge of the Monroe Doctrine and a serious menace to republican institutions in the new world. The immediate occasion for foreign intervention was the refusal or inability of Mexico to meet her financial obligations. She had signed a convention with Great Britain in 1842, and subsequently with

Spain and France, recognizing her indebtedness and agreeing to set aside a percentage of the customs duties at Vera Cruz and Tampico for the payment of interest and principal, but as a result of repeated revolutions and changes in government she had defaulted in her payments. Some of the claims were based on outrages committed on the persons and property of subjects of the three European powers resident in Mexico, but the claims of the bondholders bulked largest. Matters were brought to a climax in July, 1861, when President Juarez, who had only recently been recognized by Great Britain and the United States, published a decree suspending for two years all payments on the foreign debts.[1] The European powers demanded the repeal of this decree within twenty-four hours, and when the demand was not complied with they immediately severed diplomatic relations and began making preparations for bringing pressure to bear on Mexico by means of a joint military expedition.

The debt situation

The government of the United States, which had just entered upon the Civil War and had its hands tied so far as Mexico was concerned, regarded the contemplated intervention with apprehension and suspicion. In September, Seward authorized the negotiation of a treaty with Mexico providing for the assumption by the United States of the interest on the foreign debt of Mexico for the term of five years, the money so advanced to be secured by a mortgage on the public lands and mineral rights in Lower California, Chihuahua, Sonora, and Sinaloa.[2] This plan met with objections from England and France as well as from the Senate of the United States, and it was dropped. In the meantime the European powers were proceeding with their plans. On October 31, 1861, a convention was signed at London by Spain, France, and Great Britain, as a preliminary to joint intervention.

Seward proposes assumption of interest payments

[1]*Brit. and Foreign State Papers*, LII; 37 Cong., 2 Sess., H. Ex. Doc. No. 100.
[2]37 Cong., 2 Sess., H. Ex. Doc. No. 100, p. 22.

The most important article of the convention in view of its subsequent violation by the Emperor Napoleon, was the second, which declared that:

The Convention of London

> The high contracting parties bind themselves not to seek for themselves, in the employment of coercive measures foreseen by the present convention, any acquisition of territory, or any peculiar advantage, and not to exercise in the subsequent affairs of Mexico any influence of a character to impair the right of the Mexican nation to choose and freely to constitute the form of its own government.

The fourth article, recognizing that the United States also had claims against Mexico, provided:

> . . . that immediately after the signing of the present convention, a copy of it shall be communicated to the government of the United States, that that government shall be invited to accede to it. . . . But, as the high contracting parties would expose themselves, in making any delay in carrying into effect articles one and two of the present convention, to fail in the end which they wish to attain, they have agreed not to defer, with a view of obtaining the accession of the government of the United States, the commencement of the above-mentioned operations beyond the period at which their combined forces may be united in the vicinity of Vera Cruz.[3]

Seward's reply to the invitation to coöperate with the three allied European powers in the demonstration against Mexico was dated December 4, 1861. He said:

Seward refuses to coöperate with the powers against Mexico

> First. As the undersigned has heretofore had the honor to inform each of the plenipotentiaries now addressed, the President does not feel himself at liberty to question, and he does not question, that the sovereigns represented have undoubted right to decide for themselves the fact whether they have sustained grievances, and to resort to war against Mexico for the redress thereof, and have a right also to levy the war severally or jointly.

In the second place, Mr. Seward expressed the satisfaction of his government that the allied powers had

[3] 37 Cong., 2 Sess., H. Ex. Doc. No. 100. pp. 186–187.

clearly repudiated in the convention all idea of carrying on the war for their own ambitious ends and all intention of exercising in the subsequent affairs of Mexico any influence of a character to impair the right of the Mexican people to choose and freely to constitute the form of their own government.

It is true, as the high contracting parties assume, that the United States have, on their part, claims to urge against Mexico. Upon due consideration, however, the President is of opinion that it would be inexpedient to seek satisfaction of their claim at this time through an act of accession to the convention. Among the reasons for this decision which the undersigned is authorized to assign, are, first, that the United States, so far as it is practicable, prefer to adhere to a traditional policy recommended to them by the father of their country and confirmed by a happy experience, which forbids them from making alliances with foreign nations; second, Mexico being a neighbor of the United States on this continent, and possessing a system of government similar to our own in many of its important features, the United States habitually cherish a decided good-will toward that republic, and a lively interest in its security, prosperity, and welfare. Animated by these sentiments, the United States do not feel inclined to resort to forcible remedies for their claims at the present moment, when the government of Mexico is deeply disturbed by factions within, and exposed to war with foreign nations. And of course, the same sentiments render them still more disinclined to allied war against Mexico, than to war to be waged against her by themselves alone.[4]

Vera Cruz occupied by foreign troops

In pursuance of the London convention, Vera Cruz was occupied in the early part of 1862 by a Spanish force of 6,000 men; a French force of 2,500, which was largely reinforced soon afterward; and a force of 700 British marines. But things did not go well with the allies. The British and Spanish soon began to suspect the French of ulterior designs, and on April 9, 1862, it was officially announced by the representatives of the Three Powers "that not having been able to agree about the interpretation which ought to be given in the present circumstances to the

[4] *Op. cit.*, pp. 187–190; *Brit. and For. State Papers*, LII, 394.

convention of the 31st of October, 1861, they have resolved to adopt for the future an entirely separate and independent line of action."[5]

Withdrawal of British and Spanish contingents

The British and Spanish governments, convinced of the duplicity of France, approved the action of their representatives and ordered the immediate withdrawal of their forces and agents from Mexican soil.

The government of Louis Napoleon thus left to its own devices by the withdrawal of Great Britain and Spain, and by the helpless condition, for the time being, to which the War of Secession had reduced the government of the United States, greatly reinforced its Mexican expedition and placed General Forey in command.

The misfortunes which had overtaken Mexico and the dangers that threatened the permanence of her republican institutions, had now thoroughly alarmed her sister republics of Central and South America, and a correspondence began between them relative to organizing an international American conference to oppose European aggression.

During the remarkable series of events that took place in Mexico in the spring of 1862, Mr. Seward consistently held to the opinion well expressed in a dispatch to Mr. Dayton, June 21, 1862:

Statement of American policy

> France has a right to make war against Mexico, and to determine for herself the cause. We have a right and interest to insist that France shall not improve the war she makes to raise up in Mexico an anti-republican and anti-American government, or to maintain such a government there. France has disclaimed such designs, and we, besides reposing faith in the assurances given in a frank, honorable manner, would, in any case, be bound to wait for, and not anticipate a violation of them.[6]

The French advance

For some months the French troops gradually extended their military operations and occupied a greater extent

---

[5] 37 Cong., 3 Sess., H. Ex. Doc. No. 54, p. 48.

[6] *Ibid.*, p. 530.

of territory without, however, any material change in the situation. The Juarez government still held the capital. In the spring of 1863, however, military operations were pushed forward with greater activity, and in June, General Forey organized a junta of government composed of thirty-five Mexican citizens designated by decree of the French Emperor's minister. The members of this supreme junta were to associate with them two hundred and fifteen citizens of Mexico to form an assembly of two hundred and fifty notables. This assembly was to occupy itself with the form of the permanent government of Mexico. The junta appointed an executive body of three, of whom General Almonte was the head.

On the 10th of July, 1863, the capital of Mexico was occupied by the French army, and on the following day the Assembly of Notables declared:

The crown of Mexico offered to Maximilian of Austria

> 1. The Mexican nation adopts as its form of government a limited hereditary monarchy, with a Catholic prince.
> 2. The sovereign shall take the title of Emperor of Mexico.
> 3. The imperial crown of Mexico is offered to his imperial and royal highness the Prince Ferdinand Maximilian, Archduke of Austria, for himself and his descendants.
> 4. If, under circumstances which cannot be foreseen, the Archduke of Austria, Ferdinand Maximilian, should not take possession of the throne which is offered to him, the Mexican nation relies on the good will of his majesty, Napoleon III, Emperor of the French, to indicate for it another Catholic prince.[7]

The crown of Mexico was formally offered to Maximilian by a deputation of Mexicans, October 3, 1863; but Maximilian replied that he could not accept the proffered throne until the whole nation should "confirm by a free manifestation of its will the wishes of the capital." This was a wise decision, had it been given in good faith and had it been wisely adhered to, but the sequel shows that the archduke was either not sincere in his protestations or

[7] 38 Cong., 2 Sess., Sen. Ex. Doc. No. 11, pp. 254–268.

else was woefully deceived by representations subsequently made to him. Six months later he accepted the crown without the question having been submitted to the wishes of any but a very small portion of the Mexican people.

The French government repudiates designs on independence of Mexico

In spite of the declaration of the Mexican Assembly, which showed so unmistakably the hand of Napoleon, the French government continued to repudiate the designs imputed to it against the independence of Mexico, and Mr. Seward continued to express, officially, at least, the satisfaction of the American government at the explanations vouchsafed by France.

The probable acceptance of the crown by Maximilian was, however, the subject of frequent communications between the governments of France and the United States.

In the course of a somewhat familiar conversation with M. Drouyn de Lhuys, the French Minister of State, in August, 1863, Mr. Dayton expressed the fear that in quitting Mexico France might leave a *puppet* behind her. De Lhuys replied: "No; the strings would be too long to work."

The French scheme linked with the fortunes of the Confederacy

The chances of Maximilian's success in Mexico had been from the first deliberately calculated on the probable success of the Southern Confederacy; and, therefore, the cause of the Juarez government and the cause of the Union were considered the same. The active sympathy of the Unionists with the Mexican republic made it difficult for the administration to maintain neutrality. This difficulty was further enhanced by the doubt entertained in the United States as to the intentions of France. In this connection Seward wrote to Dayton, September 21, 1863, as follows:

> The President thinks it desirable that you should seek an opportunity to mention these facts to M. Drouyn de Lhuys, and to suggest to him that the interests of the United States, and, as it seems to us, the interests of France herself, require

that a solution of the present complications in Mexico be made, as early as may be convenient, upon the basis of the unity and independence of Mexico.[8]

United States urged to recognize Maximilian

In reply, the French minister declared that the question of the establishment of Maximilian on the Mexican throne was to be decided by a majority vote of the entire nation; that the dangers of the government of the Archduke would come principally from the United States, and the sooner the United States showed itself satisfied, and manifested a willingness to enter into peaceful relations with that government, the sooner would France be ready to leave Mexico and the new government to take care of itself, which France would, in any event, do as soon as she with propriety could; but that she would not lead or tempt the Archduke into difficulty, and then desert him before his government was settled. He said that the early acknowledgment of that government by the United States would tend to shorten, or perhaps to end, all the troublesome complications of France in that country; that they would thereupon quit Mexico.

Seward's reply

To this communication, Mr. Seward replied that the French government had not been left uninformed of the opinion of the United States that the permanent establishment of a foreign and monarchical government in Mexico would be found neither easy nor desirable; that the United States could not anticipate the action of the Mexican people; and that the United States still regarded Mexico as the scene of a war which had not yet ended in the subversion of the government long existing there, with which the United States remained in the relation of peace and friendship.[9]

Feeling in Congress

About the time that the crown was offered to Maximilian, Senator McDougall, of California, introduced a

[8] *Op. cit.*, p. 464.

[9] *Ibid.*, pp. 471–473.

resolution declaring "that the movements of the government of France, and the threatened movement of an emperor, improvised by the Emperor of France, demand by this republic, if insisted upon, war." This resolution was not carried, but some days later, on the 4th of April, 1864, the House of Representatives passed by a unanimous vote a resolution declaring its opposition to the recognition of a monarchy in Mexico. Mr. Seward, fearing a rupture with France on this account, took pains to inform the government of that country, through Mr. Dayton, that this action of the House was in no way binding on the executive, even if concurred in by the Senate.

The formal acceptance of the crown of Mexico by Maximilian took place April 10, 1864, at Miramar, the palace he had built near Trieste, in the presence of the Mexican deputation. The next day the Emperor and Empress of Mexico, as they styled themselves, set out for their new dominions by way of Rome, where they received the blessing of the Pope.

France resents resolution of the House

The resolution of the House referred to above came very near producing the rupture that Mr. Seward was striving to avert, or at least to postpone, during the continuance of the war of secession. When Mr. Dayton visited M. Drouyn de Lhuys just after the resolution reached Europe, the remark which greeted him when he entered the room was: "Do you bring us peace, or bring us war?" Mr. Dayton replied that he did not think France had a right to think that the United States was about to make war against her on account of anything contained in that resolution; that it embodied nothing more than the principles which the United States had constantly held out to France from the beginning.[10]

Confederate agents circulate reports

The Confederate agents were taking advantage of the resolution to stir up trouble between the United States and France. In fact, they had long caused reports to be

[10] *Dip. Cor.*, 1864, part III, 76.

spread in Europe, and had succeeded in gaining credence for them, to the effect that the United States government was only awaiting the termination of domestic troubles to drive the French from Mexico. The French naturally concluded that if they were to have trouble with the United States, it was safest for them to choose their own time. Napoleon was all the while coquetting with the Confederate government, and holding above Mr. Seward's head a veiled threat of recognition of Confederate independence. The Confederate government quickly caught at the suggestion of an alliance between Maximilian and the South with the power of France to back it. A Confederate agent was actually accredited to the government of Maximilian, but did not reach his destination. Although Napoleon's calculations were based on the overthrow of the Union, and although he had assumed at the outset, with England and Spain, an attitude decidedly unfriendly to the Federal government, nevertheless he was not willing to go the full length of recognizing the Confederacy as an independent power while the issue of the conflict was still in doubt.

Napoleon's friendly attitude to the Confederacy

In speaking of Slidell's movements in Europe and the encouragement given him in France, Mr. Bigelow wrote to Mr. Seward, February 14, 1865:

> I am strongly impressed with the conviction that, but for the Mexican entanglement, the insurgents would receive very little further countenance from the imperial government, and that a reconciliation of the national policies of the two countries on that question would speedily dispose of all other sources of dissatisfaction.

Ex-Confederate officers received in Mexico

Shortly after the surrender of General Lee, several Confederate officers of high position and influence went to Mexico and identified themselves with the government of Maximilian. Dr. Wm. M. Gwin, a former United States Senator from California, organized a plan for colonizing the states of northern Mexico with ex-Confederates. This scheme was the subject of several representations to the French government on the part of Mr. Seward. He reminded them that the sympathies of the American people were already considerably excited in favor of the republic of Mexico; that they were disposed to regard with impatience the continued intervention of France in that country; and that any favor shown to the proceedings of Doctor Gwin by the titular Emperor of Mexico or by the imperial government of France would tend greatly to increase the popular impatience. He further requested an assurance that the pretenses of Doctor Gwin and his associates were destitute of any sanction from the Emperor of France.

Immigration from Southern States encouraged

Among the most prominent Confederates connected with this scheme were Matthew F. Maury, the distinguished geographer and naval officer, who became a naturalized Mexican citizen and was appointed Imperial Commissioner of Immigration and an honorary councillor of state; and General John B. Magruder, who was charged with the supervision of the survey of lands for colonization. It was hoped that the prominence of these men and the high rank they had held under the Confederate government would, in the general uncertainty that prevailed as to the treatment of the South by the victorious Union party, induce many persons to emigrate to Mexico. Maximilian issued a special decree, September 5, 1865, regarding colonization with a view to inducing Southern planters to emigrate to Mexico with their slaves—the latter to be reduced to a state of *peonage*, regular slavery being prohibited by the laws of the empire. This scheme was altogether impracticable.

Seward refuses to receive envoy from Maximilian

In July, 1865, Maximilian finally made an effort to secure recognition of his government by the United States. On the 17th of July, the Marquis de Montholon, the French minister at Washington, called at the department of state and informed Mr. Seward that a special agent had arrived at Washington, bearing a letter signed by Maximilian and addressed to the President of the United States, a copy of which the marquis presented to the Secretary of State. On the 18th, Mr. Seward returned the copy of the letter to the Marquis de Montholon, and said that, as the United States was on friendly relations with the republican government of Mexico, the President declined to receive the letter or to hold any intercourse with the agent who brought it. The French government expressed to its representative at Washington its annoyance and embarrassment at this step, and said that Maximilian should have taken measures to learn the disposition of the United States before sending the agent.[11]

On the 3rd of October, 1865, Maximilian issued a decree at the City of Mexico, the first article of which declared:

> All persons belonging to armed bands or corps, not legally authorized, whether they proclaim or not any political principles, and whatever be the number of those who compose the said bands, their organization, character and denomination shall be tried militarily by the courts-martial; and if found guilty even of the only fact of belonging to the band, they shall be condemned to capital punishment, within the twenty-four hours following the sentence.

The United States protests against Maximilian's policy

The United States, through Mr. Bigelow, protested to France against this decree, as repugnant to the sentiments of modern civilization and the instincts of humanity. M. Drouyn de Lhuys replied with a touch of sarcasm:

> Why do you not go to President Juarez? We are not the government of Mexico and you do us too much honor to treat us as such. We had to go to Mexico with an army to secure certain important interests, but we are not responsible for Maximilian or his government. He is accountable to you, as to any other government, if he violated its rights, and you have the same remedies there that we had.[12]

[11] *Dip. Cor.*, 1865, Part III.

[12] 39 Cong. 1 Sess., Sen. Ex. Doc. No. 5. p. 3.

Seward assumes a firmer tone

The American government was now relieved from the burden of civil war, and for several months the correspondence of Mr. Seward had been assuming a more decided tone. On September 6, 1865, he reminded the French government that the attention of the country was now no longer occupied by the civil war, and that henceforth both the Congress and the people of the United States might be expected to give a very large share of their attention to questions of foreign policy, chief among which was likely to be that of their relations with France in regard to Mexico. About this time Major General Schofield was sent to Paris on a mission, the precise object of which was long a matter of mystery. It appears from John Bigelow's memoirs that Grant, Schofield, and a number of other army officers were bringing great pressure to bear upon the government to intervene by force and drive Maximilian from Mexico. Seward, with his usual political sagacity, concluded that the best method of holding Grant and his followers in check was to send Schofield to Paris on an informal mission. According to the latter, Seward said to him: "I want you to get your legs under Napoleon's mahogany and tell him he must get out of Mexico." Seward knew perfectly well that Schofield would not be as belligerent in the presence of the Emperor as he was in Washington, and above all he had confidence in Bigelow's tact and ability to handle Schofield when he arrived in Paris. The plan worked beautifully. Neither Bigelow nor Schofield reported just what took place at the interview with the Emperor, but we may be sure that Schofield did not say in Paris what he had intended to say when he left Washington. After Bigelow returned from Paris in 1867, he had a conversation with Seward in which the latter said:

His clever handling of the war party

> I sent General Schofield to Paris to parry a letter brought to us from Grant insisting that the French be driven head over heels and at once out of Mexico. It answered my purpose. It

gave Schofield something to do, and converted him to the policy of the Department by convincing him that the French were going as fast as they could. That pacified Grant and made everything easy.[13]

Finally, on December 16, 1865, Seward addressed what was practically an ultimatum to France. He pointed out the likelihood that Congress, then in session, would direct by law the action of the executive on this important subject, and stated that:

Exerts pressure on France

It has been the President's purpose that France should be respectfully informed upon two points, namely: First, that the United States earnestly desire to continue and to cultivate sincere friendship with France. Second, that this policy would be brought into imminent jeopardy, unless France could deem it consistent with her interest and honor to desist from the prosecution of armed intervention in Mexico, to overthrow the domestic republican government existing there, and to establish upon its ruins the foreign monarchy which has been attempted to be inaugurated in the capital of that country.

In conclusion he added:

It remains now only to make known to M. Drouyn de Lhuys my profound regret that he has thought it his duty to leave the subject, in his conversation with you, in a condition that does not authorize an expectation on our part that a satisfactory adjustment of the case can be effected on any basis that thus far has been discussed.

As late as November 29, 1865, the French government, through the Marquis de Montholon, still insisted on recognition of Maximilian by the United States as the only basis for an arrangement for the recall of the French troops.[14]

The French response

The formal reply to Mr. Seward's note of December 16 was received through the Marquis de Montholon, January 29, 1866. M. Drouyn de Lhuys still insisted that the French expedition had in it nothing hostile to

[13]Bigelow, *Retrospections of an Active Life*, IV, 42; Bancroft, *Life of Seward*, II, 435.

[14]39 Cong., 1 Sess., Sen. Ex. Doc. No. 6, p. 98.

the institutions of the new world, and assuredly still less to those of the United States. He called attention to the fact that the United States had acknowledged the right of France to make war on Mexico, and continued: "On the other part, we admit, as they do, the principle of non-intervention; this double postulate includes, as it seems to me, the elements of an agreement." He also contended that the right to make war implied the right to secure the results of war; that they had to demand guarantees, and these guarantees they could not look for from a government whose bad faith they had proven on so many occasions; that they found themselves engaged in the establishment of a regular government, which showed itself disposed to keep its engagements; that the Mexican people had spoken, and that the Emperor Maximilian had been called to the throne by the will of the people of the country.[15]

Seward's ultimatum

Mr. Seward's counter-reply was dated February 12, 1866. He declared that the proceedings in Mexico were regarded in the United States as having been taken without the authority, and prosecuted against the will and opinions of the Mexican people; that the United States had not seen any satisfactory evidence that the people of Mexico had spoken and called into being or accepted the so-called empire, and that the withdrawal of the French troops was deemed necessary to allow such a proceeding to be taken. He concluded with a virtual ultimatum:

> We shall be gratified when the Emperor shall give to us . . . definite information of the time when French military operations may be expected to cease in Mexico.[16]

Napoleon yields

Napoleon finally decided that, in view of the European situation, he could not risk a war with the United States,

[15] 39 Cong., 1 Sess., H. Ex. Doc. No. 93.

[16] *Ibid.*, also *Dip. Cor.*, 1865, part III.

and in the issue of April 5, 1866, the *Moniteur* announced that the Emperor had decided that the French troops should evacuate Mexico in three detachments: the first to leave in November, 1866; the second in March, 1867; and the third in November, 1867. In the course of a conversation with Mr. Bigelow the day following, M. Drouyn de Lhuys acknowledged that this statement was official. The decision of the Emperor was officially made known to the United States in a note of April 21, 1866. Seward had very fortunately left a loophole in his dispatch of February 12, in the statement that the United States would continue to pursue its policy of neutrality after the French evacuation. De Lhuys said:

> We receive this assurance with entire confidence and we find therein a sufficient guarantee not any longer to delay the adoption of measures intended to prepare for the return of our army.[17]

Effect of the European situation

American historians have usually attributed Napoleon's backdown to Seward's diplomacy supported by the military power of the United States, which was, of course, greater then than at any other time in our history. All this undoubtedly had its effect on Napoleon's mind, but it appears that conditions in Europe just at that particular moment had an even greater influence in causing him to abandon his Mexican scheme. Within a few days of the receipt of Seward's ultimatum Napoleon was informed of Bismarck's determination to force a war with Austria over the Schleswig-Holstein controversy. Napoleon realized that the territorial aggrandizement of Prussia, without any corresponding gains by France, would be a serious blow to his prestige and in fact endanger his throne. He at once entered upon a long and hazardous diplomatic game in which Bismarck outplayed him and eventually forced him into war. In order to have a free hand to meet

[17] 39 Cong., 1 Sess., H. Ex. Doc. No. 93, p. 42.

the European situation he decided to yield to the American demands.

About the time that the French government announced its intention of withdrawing its forces from Mexico, it was found that troops were being enlisted in Austria for the Mexican "foreign legion." The United States government at once took measures to prevent the French troops from being replaced by Austrians by declaring to the Austrian government through Mr. Motley, "that in the event of hostilities being carried on hereafter in Mexico by Austrian subjects, under the command or with the sanction of the government of Vienna, the United States will feel themselves at liberty to regard those hostilities as constituting a state of war by Austria against the republic of Mexico; and in regard to such war, waged at this time and under existing circumstances, the United States could not engage to remain as silent and neutral spectators."[18]

The United States protests against the substitution of Austrian troops

Motley fails to carry out instructions

Mr. Motley seems to have been somewhat surprised and puzzled at the sudden and emphatic change of tone in the instructions of his government, and failed to carry them out in the spirit intended by Mr. Seward. This brought forth a sharp reprimand. Mr. Seward expressed his strong disapproval of the position taken by Mr. Motley in his communication of the instructions of the department to the Austrian government, and directed him to carry out his instructions according to the strict letter, adding:

> I refrain from discussing the question you have raised, "Whether the recent instructions of this department harmonize entirely with the policy which it pursued at an earlier period of the European intervention in Mexico."

Mr. Motley was instructed to withdraw from Vienna in case troops were sent from Austria to Mexico. The embarkation of troops for this purpose was stopped. Austria was in a great state of excitement over the ap-

[18]Wharton's *Digest,* I, 328.

proaching war with Prussia, and, besides needing all her available troops at home, did not care to antagonize the United States.

Delay in departure of French troops

When the time came for the withdrawal of the first contingent of French troops, no action to that end was taken by the French government, and the United States had once more to seek an explanation. The Emperor assured the American government, however, that he had decided from military considerations to withdraw all his troops in the spring in a body, as the recent successes of the insurgents would render any large reduction of his forces perilous to those who remained. He further stated that he had counselled Maximilian to abdicate.[19]

Maximilian refuses to leave Mexico

To the surprise of everyone, however, Maximilian seemed to think that honor demanded that he should remain in Mexico and share the fate of his supporters. His government soon collapsed and he fell into the hands of the Juarez government. Foreseeing the inevitable capture of Maximilian, Seward had instructed Campbell, the recently appointed minister to Mexico, to proceed with all speed to the headquarters of Juarez and to urge clemency in the case of Maximilian and his followers. Campbell got as far as New Orleans, but delayed his departure on various pretexts until Seward finally demanded his resignation.

He had, however, sent a special message through to Juarez. Later the governments of France, Austria, and Great Britain appealed to Seward to use his good offices to prevent the execution of Maximilian. Seward then requested Mr. Romero, the Mexican minister at Washington, to urge Juarez, as a matter of policy, to spare the life of Maximilian.

His capture and execution

On June 14, before this appeal reached Juarez, Maximilian was tried by court-martial and sentenced to death. The execution was set for the 16th, but at the request of Maximilian's counsel it was suspended by order of President Juarez until the 19th in order to

[19] 40 Cong., 1 Sess., H. Ex. Doc. No. 30.

allow the prince to arrange his private affairs. At 7 o'clock on the morning of June 19, 1867, he was shot.[20]

Seward's views on territorial expansion

Seward was the greatest advocate and prophet of territorial expansion who ever held the office of Secretary of State. As early as 1846 he declared:

> Our population is destined to roll its resistless waves to the icy barriers of the North, and to encounter oriental civilization on the shores of the Pacific.

In a speech at St. Paul in 1860 he said:

> I can look southwest and see amid all the convulsions that are breaking the Spanish-American republics, and in their rapid decay and dissolution, the preparatory stage for their reorganization in free, equal, and self-governing members of the United States of America.

He further predicted that the City of Mexico, the ancient Aztec capital, would be "the ultimate central seat of power of the North American people."[21] His actual efforts at annexation were, however, limited to Alaska, the Hawaiian Islands, and certain of the West Indies.

Treaty for purchase of Danish West Indies

The experience of the navy during the Civil War demonstrated the importance of securing coaling stations and naval bases in the West Indies. The Danish Islands of St. Thomas, St. John, and Santa Cruz had been a favorite resort for vessels of the United States, most of the other West Indian islands being favorably disposed to the Confederates. In December, 1865, Seward, who had not wholly recuperated from his injuries, went on a cruise for his health, in the course of which he visited St. Thomas and also Santo Domingo. On his return he immediately opened negotiations with the Danish minister, who received authorization to sell the Danish group for $15,000,000. Seward thought this too much, but the following year, 1867, a treaty was concluded with Denmark providing for

[20] 40 Cong., 1 Sess., Sen. Ex. Doc. No. 20.

[21] Bancroft, *Life of Seward*, II, 470–471.

the cession of the islands of St. Thomas and St. John for $7,500,000 on condition that the inhabitants should by popular vote give their consent. In undertaking these negotiations the United States was influenced on the one hand by the desire to acquire a naval base, and on the other by the fear that these islands might fall into the hands of one of the greater European powers. The plebiscite in St. John and St. Thomas was overwhelmingly in favor of the cession, and the treaty was promptly ratified by the Danish Rigsdag, but the Senate of the United States took no action until March, 1870, when Senator Sumner presented an adverse report from the Committee on Foreign Relations and the treaty was rejected.[22]

Defeated by the Senate

In 1867, Admiral Porter and Mr. F. W. Seward, the Assistant Secretary of State, were sent to Santo Domingo for the purpose of securing the lease of Samana Bay as a naval station. Their mission was not successful, but the following year the President of the Dominican Republic sent an agent to Washington proposing annexation and requesting the United States to occupy Samana Bay at once. In his annual message of December 8, 1868, President Johnson advocated the annexation of Santo Domingo and a joint resolution to that effect was introduced in the House, but it was tabled without debate by an overwhelming vote.[23] The annexation of Santo Domingo became a favorite policy of the Grant administration, and in view of Sumner's opposition had an important bearing on the controversy that arose over the settlement of the *Alabama* Claims.[24]

Proposal to annex Santo Domingo

Seward's only successful effort at annexation was the purchase of Alaska. The treaty for the cession of this vast territory, which Russia had held by right of discovery

Alaska and the fur trade

[22]*Op. cit.*, II, 479–486.
[23]*Ibid.*, pp. 486–489.
[24]Post, 446–449.

and occupation for more than a century, was signed before the public even suspected that the matter was under consideration. There was no popular demand for the acquisition of this "frozen zone," about which Americans knew little and cared less. The only interest ever displayed in the region was that of a few fishermen on the Pacific coast who requested the government to arrange with Russia for them to have access to the ports and harbors of Russian America, and a small group of Californians who wished to obtain a franchise for engaging in the fur trade. Seward instructed Cassius M. Clay, minister at St. Petersburg, to confer with the Russian government on the subject of this concession. Russian America had been for over half a century under the control of a Russian company, which had subleased the fur trade to the Hudson's Bay Company. This lease was to expire in 1867, and the Russian government was in doubt as to whether to renew the lease, to organize an expensive colonial government, or to sell the territory. It had never yielded a revenue.

Russian offer to sell eagerly seized by Seward

When Clay brought the subject of the proposed concession to the attention of the Russian government in February, 1867, Stoeckl, who had been Russian minister to the United States for some years, happened to be in St. Petersburg on a visit. He returned to Washington in March with authority to negotiate a sale. He proposed ten million dollars as a fair price; Seward offered five. They compromised on seven million. It then appeared that the Russian-American Company had certain interests which would have to be taken into consideration. Seward finally offered $7,200,000 provided Russia would assume these liabilities and give the United States a free title. The Russian minister cabled the offer to his government, and on March 29 received a favorable reply. He went at once to Seward's house to inform him and suggested that they arrange the terms next day. Seward's enthusiasm was so great that he said: "Why wait till to-morrow, Mr. Stoeckl? Let us make the treaty to-night." They immediately summoned their assistants and Sumner, chairman of the Senate Committee on Foreign Relations, to meet them at the State Department, settled down to work at midnight, and at four o'clock in the morning had the treaty ready for signature.[25]

A few hours later the treaty was submitted by the President to the Senate where it encountered little opposition, only two senators voting against it. It was ratified and proclaimed June 20, 1867. On July 6, President Johnson sent a message to Congress requesting an appropriation of $7,200,000 in gold for the purpose of carrying out the treaty. Probably owing to the violent conflict between the President and Congress no immediate action was taken, but the President went ahead and took possession of Alaska. The formal transfer was made by the Russian officials to General Rousseau on October 11, 1867. When Congress met in November strong opposition to the purchase developed in the House. For the next six months the time and attention of Congress were absorbed in the impeachment proceedings. Finally, on May 18, 1868, two days after the vote on the main count in the impeachment of the President, General Banks reported from the Committee on Foreign Affairs a bill making the necessary appropriation. Two months later, after considerable discussion, the bill passed the House by a vote of 113 to 43. It passed the Senate with little or no opposition and became a law July 27, 1868.

The treaty ratified

A remarkable fact, which aroused suspicion at the time, was that this appropriation was put through by the chief enemies of the administration and the leaders of the impeachment movement. General Banks was chairman of the Foreign Affairs Committee of the House, and Thaddeus Stevens was chairman of the Committee on Appro-

Charges of bribery

[25] Bancroft, *Life of Seward*, II, 474–477.

priations, while John W. Forney, whose papers, the Washington *Chronicle* and the Philadelphia *Press,* attacked the President with such vehemence that he had to resign the position of secretary of the Senate, was at the same time strongly supporting the Alaskan purchase. By the time Congress met in December, 1868, charges of bribery in connection with the purchase were being freely circulated. It had been discovered that the draft sent abroad had been for less than $7,200,000. The House ordered an investigation, but the report of the committee was unsatisfactory and inconclusive.[26] The discrepancy was nothing like as great as charged. The sum of $7,035,000 was sent abroad and $165,000 was deposited in bank by the Russian minister. Of this sum, the committee found that $26,000 had been paid to Robert J. Walker, $3,000 to a brother of John W. Forney, and $1,000 to a California newspaper man. Walker was a brilliant man, but an unscrupulous character. He had been Secretary of the Treasury under Polk, Governor of Kansas under Buchanan, and confidential financial agent of President Lincoln in Europe during the Civil War. Walker's testimony before the committee was to the effect that he had received $26,000, of which $5,000 went to F. P. Stanton, as his fee for pressing the bill. The impression left was that Walker was well paid for very little work, and explained the rumors that he was the disbursing agent through whom the money was paid to congressmen and newspapermen. Both Walker and Stanton stoutly denied this. Walker testified that he expressed to Stoeckl his warm appreciation of Forney's support, and that Stoeckl authorized him to give Forney $3,000. This sum Forney indignantly refused. But the $3,000 was later paid to D. C. Forney, a junior partner in the *Chronicle.*

Facts brought out in the investigation

Seward's testimony

Seward was questioned by the committee, and answered in very guarded terms, but with the greatest apparent

[26] 40 Cong., 3 Sess., House Reports, No. 35.

frankness. "I do not know *from Mr. Walker* that he was ever paid a cent." When asked, "Have you any knowledge of any money or presents, directly or indirectly, being made from the fund at the disposal of the Secretary of State, or any other fund, to subsidize or propitiate the press, or any person connected therewith, anywhere?"—Seward glibly replied, "On the contrary, I have knowledge that no fund *at the State Department* went to subsidize any press anywhere."

Professor Dunning's discovery

Nearly half a century after these transactions the late Professor Dunning discovered among the Johnson papers in the Library of Congress a memorandum in the President's own handwriting which affords at least a clue to some of the mysteries which the House committee was unable to solve. Writing with President Johnson was difficult, not so much because of his illiteracy as because of an injury to his right arm. He wrote very little and the length of this memorandum bears witness to the importance he attached to the statements so laboriously recorded. It is as follows:

Johnson's memorandum

On the 6th Sept. Sundy 1868 Mr. Seward and myself rode out some seven or eight miles on the Road, leading to Malsboro Md—near place called old fields, we drove out into a shady grove of oak trees—While there taking some refreshment, in the current of conversation on various subjects, the Secretary asked the question if it had ever occurred to me how few members there were in congress whose actions were entirely above and beyond pecuniary influence. I replied that I had never attempted to reduce it to an accurate calculation, but regretted to confess that there was a much smaller number exempt than at one period of life I had supposed them to be—He then stated you remember that the appropriation of the seven $ million for the payment of Alaska to the Russia Govnt was hung up or brought to a dead lock in the H of Reps—While the appropriation was thus delayed the Russian minister stated to me that John W. Forney stated to him that he needed $30,000 that he had lost $40,000, by a faithless friend and that he wanted the $30,000 in gold—That there was no chance of the appropriation passing the House of Reps without certain influence was brought to bear in its favor—The 30,000 was paid hence the advocacy of the appropriation in the Chronicle—He also stated that $20,000 was paid to R. J. Walker and F. P. Stanton for their services—N. P. Banks chairman of the committee on foreign relations $8000, and that the incoruptable Thaddeous Stevens received as his 'sop' the moderate sum of $10,000—All these sums were paid by the Russian minister directly and indirectly to the respective parties to secure appropriation of money the Govnt had stiputed to pay the Russian Govnt in solemn treaty which had been ratified by both Govnts.— Banks and Stevens was understood to be the counsel for a claim against the Russian Govnt for Arms which had been furnished by some of our citizens—known as the Perkins Claim—Hence a fee for their influence in favor of the appropriation &c—Banks was chairman of the Committee on foreign retions—[27]

With what pleasure the President recorded these statements so damaging to the character and reputation of his worst enemies may easily be imagined. For that reason the memorandum should be used with care. Furthermore, it was based on hearsay evidence and is not altogether in accord with Seward's testimony before the House committee a few months later. Seward was, however, not a frank witness, and he may very well have denied all knowledge of transactions which he learned of through third parties. No one who reads the testimony given before the committee can fail to be impressed with the general probability of the memorandum. If Forney had received $30,000 direct from Stoeckl, the latter was doubtless embarrassed when Walker suggested that Forney should be paid. So the $3,000 was sent which Forney spurned, but managed to divert to his brother. The joke was on Walker, for he insisted to the end of his days that Forney was one of the few incorruptible men in public life.

Not far from the truth

Another explanation of the purchase of what was generally regarded as a useless "frozen zone," which was current for many years, was that the United States paid

[27]Dunning, "Paying for Alaska," in *Pol. Sci. Quarterly*, Sept., 1912, pp. 385-386.

the $7,200,000 to Russia as an expression of appreciation of Russia's friendly attitude during the Civil War, especially the dispatch of a formidable Russian fleet to American waters during the winter of 1862-1863 when England and France were threatening intervention. This naval demonstration doubtless had a favorable effect on the fortunes of the Union, but that was not the object of the visit. Russia thought a general war not improbable, and she did not want it to find her fleet in her own ports, where it might be blocked either by ice or the British navy. It was a weak fleet, but capable, if properly handled, of doing great damage to British commerce. She, therefore, sent it to winter in American ports, from which it could readily attack the weaker possessions and commerce of England.[28]

The Russian fleet legend

---

[28]Golder, "The Russian Fleet and the Civil War," in *Am. Hist. Rev.*, XXI, 801.

CHAPTER XVIII

THE "ALABAMA" CLAIMS AND THE TREATY OF WASHINGTON

Definition of the *Alabama* Claims

Of the numerous vessels purchased or built abroad for the Confederate States navy the *Alabama* was the most famous both on account of her career as a commerce destroyer and on account of the circumstances attending her construction and departure from British waters. As a consequence all claims against Great Britain on account of injuries inflicted on the commerce of the United States by Confederate cruisers purchased or built within British jurisdiction were called generically "the *Alabama* Claims."

The *Florida*

The *Oreto*, or *Florida*, was the first regular war vessel built for the service of the Confederate States abroad. She was built by a Liverpool firm under contract for Captain James D. Bulloch, the principal Confederate naval agent in Europe. According to his statement she was twice inspected by the Custom House authorities on orders from the Foreign Office. While the general appearance of the ship indicated the purposes for which she was constructed, she was registered as an English ship, commanded by an Englishman, and had no armament aboard. Bulloch had consulted eminent counsel and had been informed that the British foreign enlistment act of 1819 made it an offense to equip, fit out, or arm a vessel within British jurisdiction to cruise against the commerce of a friendly state, but that the mere building of a ship, without arming and equipping it, was no offense.[1] This

[1]Bulloch, *Secret Service of the Confederate States in Europe*, I, 67; for the full text of the act, see Fenwick, *Neutrality Laws of the United States*, appendix, p. 184. Bulloch was a native of Georgia and an uncle of Theodore Roosevelt. The latter in his *Autobiography*, 15–16, gives a vivid picture of his early recollections of his "Uncle Jimmie."

was the construction which had been placed upon the act by British officials and courts, but it left open the question as to whether the foreign enlistment act was the full measure of England's obligations as a neutral. The government so interpreted it, and took no steps to detain the *Oreto*. She left Liverpool in March, 1862, under temporary command of an English captain and under the British flag. Her armament was shipped about the same time on another British vessel which proceeded to the point of rendezvous, a small desert island on the edge of the Bahamas. Here the *Oreto* received her armament and crew, took the name *Florida*, and hoisted the Confederate flag. During her career as a commerce destroyer, she captured over forty American merchant vessels, most of which were destroyed and the others released under bond.[2]

Construction placed on the foreign enlistment act

Meanwhile Bulloch had contracted for another ship, the *Alabama*. She was built by the Lairds at the Birkenhead Ironworks above Liverpool on the opposite side of the Mersey. Her dockyard number was "290" and by this designation she was known until she was launched, when she was christened the *Enrica*. When delivered to the Confederates her name was changed to the *Alabama*. Bulloch contracted for her in his own name and took small pains to conceal the fact that she was being built for the Confederacy. In fact, he tells us in his narrative that he always attributed his success in getting the *Alabama* built and then sent to sea to the fact that no mystery or disguise was attempted. "I was well advised as to the law, and had the means of knowing with well-nigh absolute certainty what was the state of the negotiations between the United States minister and Her Majesty's Government."[3] In vain did the American consul at Liverpool collect evidence as to the purpose for which

The building of the *Alabama*

[2]C. F. Adams, "The Treaty of Washington" in *Lee at Appomattox and Other Papers*, 44–45.

[3]Bulloch, I, 229.

Adams protests against permitting the ship to depart

Number 290 was being built and in vain did the American minister, Charles Francis Adams, protest. The British government stood on a strict interpretation of the statute. Adams finally retained a Queen's counsel of eminence, R. P. Collier, and submitted to him the affidavits collected by the American consul. He gave a written opinion, in which he said:

> "It appears difficult to make out a stronger case of infringement of the foreign enlistment act, which, if not enforced on this occasion, is little better than a dead letter. It well deserves consideration whether, if the vessel is allowed to escape, the Federal government would not have serious grounds of remonstrance."[4]

Collier's opinion and the affidavits on which it was based were submitted by Adams to Lord Russell who referred them, together with the reports of the commissioners of customs, to the law officers of the Crown. The papers were given to the Queen's Advocate who was on the verge of insanity, and they lay in his private house unexamined for five days. As soon as his condition became known, the papers were sent for and referred to the Attorney-General and the Solicitor-General, who promptly recommended "that without loss of time the vessel be seized by the proper authorities." This report was made July 29. It came too late. That very morning the *Alabama* had put to sea, ostensibly on a trial trip and without clearance papers, but she did not return.[5] As in the case of the *Florida*, the *Alabama* went out under a British captain; her armament was sent out on a second ship, and her officers and crew on a third. This time the place of rendezvous was the Azores. Here, beyond British jurisdiction, the three component parts of a hostile expedition were combined, but Great Britain held that, as the *Alabama* was not armed when it left her shores

While the government hesitates the *Alabama* puts to sea

[4] *Dip. Cor.*, 1862, p. 152.

[5] Moore, *Dig. of Int. Arbits.*, I, 678–682.

she was not guilty of having violated any generally accepted rule of international law, and in this opinion she was probably right.

Her career as a commerce destroyer

Captain Bulloch had expected to command the *Alabama* himself, but shortly before she left England Captain Raphael Semmes arrived with orders to take command. Bulloch had performed too successfully his duties as naval agent in England and France to be spared for sea duty. The *Alabama* was devoted solely to commerce destroying, which her commander reduced to a science. By periodically shifting his activities from one part of the seas to another, he successfully eluded pursuit and continued the work of destruction for two years. During this period the *Alabama* sailed seventy-five thousand miles, thrice the distance around the globe. Her itinerary was roughly as follows: the North Atlantic, the West Indies, the Gulf of Mexico, the coast of Brazil, the Cape of Good Hope, the Indian Ocean, the Straits of Malacca, Ceylon, the Arabian Gulf, Madagascar, Cape Town, St. Helena, Brazil, and the English Channel.[6] She destroyed fifty-seven prizes and released under ransom-bond a large number of others which had neutral cargo aboard or more passengers than could be safely provided for.[7] While the actual value of the prizes destroyed was estimated at only $6,750,000, the *Alabama* caused such alarm among shipowners and so increased the rates of insurance that American commerce was rapidly driven from the seas.

American resentment

The failure of the British government to detain the *Alabama* was resented in the United States as further evidence of an unfriendly attitude. When the torch was applied to American vessels on the high seas, this feeling of resentment rapidly grew into a deep-seated national hatred of England. The complicity of the British government was conclusively attested, in the minds of most

[6]Sinclair, *Two Years on the Alabama*, 3–4.

[7]Semmes, *Service Afloat, passim.*

Americans, by the further fact that the Confederate cruisers, or pirates, as the Northerners preferred to call them, were accorded friendly reception in British colonial ports. As soon as reports were received of the destruction of American merchantmen, Mr. Adams was instructed by Secretary Seward to demand redress of the British government, and although Earl Russell disclaimed all responsibility for damages, Mr. Adams continued to present the claims as they arose.[8]

Russell's defense of British policy

Russell claimed that Great Britain had been sincere in her efforts to live up to her general international duties and to inforce the foreign enlistment act; that her subjects had a right to sell munitions of war to both sides, and that far larger supplies had been sent to the North than to the South; that it was difficult to see why a ship was more an instrument of war than cannon, muskets, swords, bayonets, gunpowder, or projectiles; and, finally, that large numbers of Her Majesty's subjects had fought and fallen in the ranks of the Federal army in violation of the foreign enlistment act, that bounties had been offered them to enlist, and that it was confidently asserted, though Her Majesty's government had no proof, that agents of the Federal government were employed within the United Kingdom to engage subjects of Her Majesty to emigrate to the United States for the purpose of enlisting.[9]

Russell finally became irritated by the persistent and somewhat intemperate nature of Adams's communications, and in a note dated September 14, 1863, in which he again called attention to the fact that "the *Alabama* was not fitted out at Liverpool as a vessel of war," said:

"When the United States government assume to hold the government of Great Britain responsible for the captures made by vessels which may be fitted out as vessels-of-war in a foreign

[8]*Dip. Cor.*, 1863, pp. 16, 29, 38, 58, 371, 421.

[9]*Ibid.*, pp. 39, 104, 424.

port, because such vessels were originally built in a British port, I have to observe that such pretensions are entirely at variance with the principles of international law and with the decisions of American courts of the highest authority; and I have only, in conclusion, to express my hope that you may not be instructed again to put forward claims which her Majesty's government cannot admit to be founded on any grounds of law or justice."[10]

His reply to Adams's demands

Seward insisted on continuing to present the claims to make a record for future use, if for no other purpose.

The demand for a reckoning with England

At the close of the Civil War public opinion in the victorious North was set on a reckoning with England, and not at all disposed to be conciliatory or even reasonable. Fortunately Seward, though determined to press for a settlement, realized fully the complexities of the issues at stake and the necessity for patience and calmness. Furthermore, there were two other subjects of dispute, antedating the Civil War, which had to be adjusted if peace was to be preserved. One was the San Juan water boundary between the island of Vancouver and the mainland, which had been described in indefinite terms in the treaty of 1846, and upon which no agreement had since been reached. The question at issue was whether the boundary should follow the channel to the east or that to the west of San Juan Island.[11]

Dissatisfaction with the Canadian reciprocity treaty of 1854

The other question arose out of the decision of the United States to terminate the Canadian Reciprocity and Fisheries Convention of 1854. The twelve months' notice required by the terms of the convention was given to England March 17, 1865. This convention had been concluded by Secretary Marcy and Lord Elgin who had been sent over on a special mission to adjust the differences that had arisen between the United States and Canada on the subjects of the fisheries, commerce, and navigation. The treaty restored to American fishermen

[10] *Op. cit.*, p. 431.

[11] Moore, *Dig. of Int. Arbits.*, I, 196–235.

for the period of its duration the inshore privileges which had been surrendered in the convention of 1818. In return it granted to Canadian fishermen reciprocal privileges on the Atlantic Coast of the United States north of the thirty-sixth parallel. It also granted to citizens of the United States the free navigation of the St. Lawrence and the free use of the St. John River for their lumber. Finally the reciprocity provision permitted the admission of enumerated products of the United States and the British colonies, mainly raw materials, into each country free of duty.[12]

Peculiar circumstances of its negotiation

Lord Elgin's mission to Washington in 1854 created quite a stir in social as well as in political circles. He was told by Marcy on his arrival that it was quite hopeless to secure the ratification of the terms he proposed. He, therefore, set to work to win over the necessary number of senators and apparently he succeeded. His secretary, Laurence Oliphant, has left a highly amusing, though somewhat exaggerated, account of the methods employed. In his memoir he says:

> It was at the height of the season when we were in Washington, and our arrival imparted a new impetus to the festivities, and gave rise to the taunt, after the treaty was concluded, by those who were opposed to it, that "it had been floated through on champagne." Without altogether admitting this, there can be no doubt that, in the hands of a skillful diplomatist, that beverage is not without its value.

He then quotes the following entry made in his journal at the time:

> Got away from the French minister just in time to dress for dinner at the President's. More senators, and politics, and champagne, and Hard Shells and Soft Shells. I much prefer the marine soft-shell crab, with which I here made acquaintance for the first time, to the political one. Then with a select party

[12](Malloy) *Treaties and Conventions,* I, 668; C. C. Tansill, *The Canadian Reciprocity Treaty of 1854,* Johns Hopkins University Studies in Historical and Political Science, XL, No. 2.

of senators, all of whom were opposed in principle to the treaty, to Governor A's where we imbibed more champagne and swore eternal friendship, carefully avoiding the burning question, and listened to stories good, bad and indifferent, till 2 A. M., when, after twelve hours of incessant entertainment, we went home to bed thoroughly exhausted.[13]

The treaty never regarded with favor

The treaty was ratified by the Senate, but it soon gave rise to charges of unfairness, and the general trade relations between the two countries were soon changed by Canadian tariffs on manufactures and the adoption of a protective tariff by the United States at the beginning of the Civil War. But the main impulse to the denunciation of the treaty seems to have sprung from the general hostility to England. On January 18, 1865, Congress directed that the twelve months' notice of abrogation be given.

Seward threatens to terminate Great Lakes agreement

As a result of abortive Confederate raids from Canada in 1864, Seward had also served notice through Mr. Adams of the intention of the United States to terminate, at the end of six months, the Rush-Bagot agreement of 1817 establishing disarmament on the Great Lakes. But in March, 1865, in view of the changed situation along the Lakes, Seward instructed Adams to withdraw this notice, and since that time the agreement has been regarded by both governments as in full force.[14]

The Fenian movement adds fuel to the flames

The Fenian movement, having for its object the establishment of an independent republic in Ireland, received the enthusiastic support of the Irish population of the United States, who took advantage of the widespread hostility to England to further their cause. In 1865, Fenian conventions were held in several American cities, and a general convention in New York went so far as to elect a president of the so-called Irish republic. In June, 1866, a few thousand Fenians undertook to invade Canada, but they were repulsed by the Canadian volun-

[13]Quoted by Tansill, p. 77.

[14]Moore, *Dig. of Int. Law*, V, 323.

teers. While the government of the United States may have been lax in the matter of precautionary measures, when the actual invasion took place it acted with promptness and energy. Several hundred Fenians were arrested, the arms which had been collected were seized, the frontier garrisons were strengthened, and the President issued a proclamation condemning the enterprise. The British government, through its minister at Washington, expressed the "warmest acknowledgment" of the promptness and sincerity of these measures.[15] At the same time many Irishmen, who had become naturalized in the United States, returned to Ireland to participate in the Fenian movement, and they were treated by the British government as British subjects. The writ of *habeas corpus* was suspended and many of them were thrown into prison. They appealed to the United States and Adams was called upon to take up their cases. The latter had little taste for this duty, and complained to Seward that his chief function was to rescue Irishmen from punishment which in most cases they richly deserved. In 1868, a protocol was signed by which Great Britain agreed to recognize and treat naturalized American citizens of British origin "as in all respects and for all purposes citizens of the United States." As this agreement had to await preliminary legislation by Parliament, it was not finally embodied in a treaty until 1870. But the willingness of the British government to recede from its historic claim of indefeasible and perpetual allegiance produced a better feeling in the United States and helped to relieve the tension of the Irish situation. Seward believed it would pave the way for the settlement of other disputes.[16]

The trouble over Irish-American citizens

A proposal to arbitrate the claims arising out of the Civil War had been made by Adams as early as October,

[15]Bancroft, *Life of Seward*, II, 494; *Dip. Cor.*, 1866, I, 245.

[16](Malloy) *Treaties and Conventions*, I, 691; Moore, *Int. Arbits.*, I, 501.

1863. No reply had been made at the time, but two years later, when the claims were under discussion, Lord Russell, referring to this proposal, said that there were but two questions by which the claim for compensation could be tested:

Russell refuses to arbitrate claims

> The one is, Have the British government acted with due diligence, or, in other words, in good faith and honesty, in the maintenance of the neutrality they proclaimed? The other is, Have the law officers of the Crown properly understood the foreign enlistment act?

He declared that neither of these questions could, with any regard to the dignity of the British nation, be put to a foreign government; that Her Majesty's government were the sole guardians of their own honor, and that the law officers of the Crown must be held to be better interpreters of a British statute than any foreign government could be presumed to be. He added the somewhat ambiguous statement that,

> Her Majesty's government, however, are ready to consent to the appointment of a commission, to which shall be referred all claims arising during the late civil war, which the two governments shall agree to refer to the commission.[17]

His ambiguity equaled by Seward's

Seward accepted this statement as implying that the *Alabama* claims were among those which the British government would not be willing to refer to such a joint commission. This was undoubtedly what Russell meant. On this construction of the offer Seward declined it, but he directed Adams to inquire whether this interpretation of Russell's note was correct. Assuming that it was, he authorized Adams, in language scarcely less ambiguous than Russell's, to say that the proposition for arbitration made in 1863 would not be renewed by the United States.[18]

[17] *Dip. Cor.*, 1865, Part I, 545.

[18] *Ibid.*, p. 565.

Russell's stand unreasonable

Russell's refusal to discuss the question of liability for the *Alabama* claims was regarded as a mistake by many public men in England who sincerely desired to remove all grievances and ill feeling, and who, furthermore, believed that serious questions of international law and policy were involved which could be discussed without any loss of dignity or honor on the part of Her Majesty's government.

The House votes to repeal the neutrality act

Meanwhile public opinion in the United States was assuming a more determined character. In 1866, the House of Representatives unanimously passed a bill to modify the neutrality act of 1818. This act forbade the "furnishing, fitting out, or arming," of any vessel within the limits of the United States, with the intent that such vessel should be used against a friendly nation. The House bill repealed this section and substituted a declaration that nothing in the neutrality act or any other law should be so construed as to prohibit citizens of the United States from selling vessels or steamships, built within the limits of the United States, to the inhabitants of other countries or to governments not at war with the United States. The main reasons assigned by the committee for the proposed change were that the United States was under no obligation to inforce principles of neutrality which were not accepted or acted upon by other states, and that the restrictions imposed by the British foreign enlistment act of 1819 were nominal compared with those of the American statute. This statement was exaggerated. The British act was modeled after the American and the language of the two did not differ materially, but it is true that the American act had been much more strictly construed. In the Senate the bill was twice read and then referred to the Committee on Foreign Relations, where it slept.[19] The measure was avowedly intended as a threat to Great Britain that unless she should recognize the just

Intended as a threat to England

[19]Fenwick, *Neutrality Laws of the United States*, 48–51.

grievances of the United States and render full satisfaction, she might look forward, the first time she became engaged in war, to a flank attack on her commerce from vessels built in the United States for her enemies.

Lord Stanley proposes arbitration

In 1866, there was a change of government in England and Lord Stanley, who succeeded Lord Russell in the Foreign Office, was more favorably disposed toward a settlement of the controversy. He instructed the British minister at Washington to inform Mr. Seward that, while the British government was still unwilling to admit liability for the *Alabama* claims, they would be willing to adopt the principle of arbitration, provided the two governments could agree on an arbiter and on the points to be submitted. The subject of the alleged premature recognition of the Confederate States was not, however, one that the British government would be willing to refer to arbitration, since this was a question as to which every state was the sole judge of its duty. Seward declined to accept arbitration with the limitations proposed and restated the position he had constantly maintained from the beginning,

> . . . that the Queen's proclamation of 1861 which accorded belligerent rights to insurgents against the authority of the United States, was not justified on any grounds, either of necessity or moral right, and therefore was an act of wrongful intervention, a departure from the obligation of existing treaties, and without the sanction of the law of nations.[20]

Seward suggests conference on all questions

Seward did not present the question of the conduct of Great Britain as a subject for general pecuniary reparation, but as one of the grounds on which liability to individual claimants might be maintained. He further called attention to the fact that there were several other questions which might "at any moment become a subject of exciting controversy," and suggested that if Her Majesty's government desired to lay a broad foundation for

[20] Moore, *Int. Arbits.*, I, 498–499.

friendly relations, it might be expedient to attempt a "comprehensive settlement" by means of a conference on all questions at issue.

Reverdy Johnson succeeds Charles Francis Adams

In May, 1868, Charles Francis Adams relinquished the post as minister to England, which he had so long and so ably filled. He was succeeded by Reverdy Johnson, of Maryland, who had served with distinction in the Senate and was recognized as one of the most eminent of American lawyers. In accordance with Seward's instructions, Johnson entered at once into negotiations with Lord Stanley for the adjustment of pending differences, and within three months after his arrival in England signed three conventions: one on the subject of naturalization, one for the submission of the San Juan water boundary to arbitration, and a third providing for the arbitration of all claims of the citizens or subjects of one government against the other. The naturalization convention, as already stated, was after some delay ratified by both governments in 1870. The other two conventions failed. The claims convention was unsatisfactory to Seward, who objected to several features, especially the designation of London as the place for the meeting of the tribunal.[21]

The Johnson-Clarendon convention

On the receipt of detailed instructions from Seward, Johnson immediately renewed the claims negotiations with Lord Clarendon, who had succeeded Lord Stanley, and on January 14, 1869, signed a new convention. This convention provided for the settlement of all claims arising since the convention of 1853, which had in a similar way settled a number of miscellaneous claims of long standing. The President and the Queen were each to appoint two commissioners, and these were to choose an arbiter. In case they could not agree, each side was to name an arbiter and one of these was to be chosen by lot. While the terms of the convention mentioned they did not specially emphasize the *Alabama* claims. Seward had more-

[21] *Op. cit.*, I, 502–503.

over dropped the national claims based on the premature recognition of belligerency, but it was provided that the official correspondence which had taken place between the two governments in connection with any claim should be laid before the commission. In this way the old arguments on the subject of the recognition of belligerency could be reviewed, but only as a means of establishing the private claims. The commission was given no authority to consider other than individual claims. Seward was undoubtedly eager to settle this dispute, which had been handled by him since its inception, before leaving office. Grant had already been elected President, and the new administration would come in on March 4.[22]

Favorably received by Seward

Seward was delighted with the Johnson-Clarendon convention, but he soon realized the difficulties in the way of ratification. The administration of Andrew Johnson was unpopular, and Seward shared a large measure of its unpopularity. When Reverdy Johnson was sent to England, the American people knew nothing of the change of attitude on the part of the British government, and they, therefore, misinterpreted the cordiality of the speeches he made on his arrival. Seward wrote to him that his speeches had "fallen upon the ear of the American people in an hour when party spirit is raging very high." He added this bit of wisdom gained by his own experience:

> Political adversaries, finding your negotiations crowned with complete success, contrary to their own predictions, will begin to cavil at the several treaties which you will have made, on the ground that they fall short of what might and ought to have been secured. This is the habitual experience of diplomacy.[23]

Rejected by the Senate

The treaties were to meet a worse fate than Seward anticipated. When the terms of the Johnson-Clarendon convention became known, it was charged that Johnson

[22]Bancroft, *Life of Seward*, II, 497–500; Adams, "The Treaty of Washington," 92–101.

[23]Moore, *Int. Arbits.*, I, 506.

had fallen under the influence of Southern sympathizers. The public was annoyed at the international subordination of the *Alabama* claims and at the failure to include the claim for national damages. The provision for the choice of an arbiter by lot met with objection and ridicule. The treaty went over to the next administration, and when the vote was finally taken in the Senate April 13, 1869, it stood 54 to 1 against ratification.

Sumner's speech

The sensational feature of the debate was Sumner's speech. Although delivered in executive session, it was released for publication by authority of the Senate. The speech had little or no influence on the vote, for it was evident that the Senate was overwhelmingly opposed to the treaty, but it was an important factor in the subsequent negotiations. Sumner revived the national claims which Seward had dropped. He estimated the direct damages, or individual losses, at $15,000,000.

> But this [he said] leaves without recognition the vaster damage to commerce driven from the ocean, and that other damage, immense and infinite, caused by the prolongation of the war, all of which may be called *national* in contradistinction to *individual*.

The amount of damages claimed

The indirect damage to American commerce was put by him at $110,000,000, which he said was "only an item in our bill." He declared that the "rebellion" had been "suppressed at a cost of more than four thousand million dollars," that through British intervention the war was doubled in duration, and that England was "justly responsible for the additional expenditure." He added:

> To my mind our first duty is to make England see what she has done to us. How the case shall be settled, whether by money more or less, by territorial compensation, by apology, or by an amendment of the law of nations, is still an open question; all may be combined.[24]

[24]Pierce, *Memoir and Letters of Charles Sumner*, IV, 385–388; Adams, "The Treaty of Washington," 98–103; Rhodes, *History of the United States*, VI, 337–343; Moore, *Int. Arbits.*, I, 509–512.

Sumner as chairman of the Foreign Relations Committee thus placed the liability of Great Britain, because of the recognition of Confederate belligerency, at a sum well over two billion dollars, and intimated that this huge sum could be liquidated by the cession of Canada, for it was well known that that was what was in his mind. By the almost unanimous vote against the Johnson-Clarendon convention, taken immediately after Sumner's speech, the Senate indorsed his views, and by releasing the speech for publication proclaimed them to the world. On reading the speech and noting the vote of the Senate, Charles Francis Adams said:

The significance of Sumner's speech

> The practical effect of this is to raise the scale of our demands of reparation so very high that there is no chance of negotiation left, unless the English have lost all their spirit and character.[25]

John Bright, who had been the staunchest friend of the Union in England, said that Sumner was "either a fool himself or else thought the English public and their public men to be fools." He concluded that the speech was Sumner's bid for the presidency.[26]

In the meantime President Grant had appointed Hamilton Fish, of New York, as Seward's successor in the Department of State. Fish and Sumner were friends, and Grant was known to have intense feelings on the *Alabama* question. He is reported to have said that he did not care whether England paid our "little bill" or not, thus implying a threat that he was prepared to settle the score in other ways. Sumner reported that Grant was in full accord with his speech. However this may have been, the two men differed so greatly temperamentally that there was little possibility of close personal or political relations between them, and in fact a divergence of views on important policies was soon apparent. Grant

Grant's attitude on the claims

[25]Adams, "The Treaty of Washington," 103

[26]Rhodes, VI, 341.

was self-possessed and taciturn, while Sumner was excitable and rhetorical, and in tense states of feeling was so extreme in his utterances that even his friends at times questioned his sanity. Sumner had been seventeen years in the Senate and eight years chairman of the Committee on Foreign Relations. In view of Fish's comparative unfamiliarity with foreign affairs, Sumner seems to have assumed that he as chairman of the Senate committee would largely direct the foreign policy of the government. In this conviction he was confirmed by the appointment of his friend John Lothrop Motley as minister to England. Motley was his choice, and when Grant and Fish consented to appoint him, Sumner naturally concluded that his views were to prevail in the settlement with England.[27]

Sumner's dominant position

When the time came to prepare Motley's instructions, Fish's well-trained legal mind recoiled from the extreme position of Sumner's speech. He delayed the final draft as long as possible, but finally, on May 15, 1869, it was presented to the President and Cabinet and approved. On the subject of the British proclamation of May 13, 1861, the instructions read:

Fish's instructions to Motley

The President recognizes the right of every power, when a civil conflict has arisen within another state, and has attained a sufficient complexity, magnitude, and completeness, to define its own relations and those of its citizens and subjects toward the parties to the conflict, so far as their rights and interests are necessarily affected by the conflict.

The necessity and propriety of the original concession of belligerency by Great Britain at the time it was made have been contested and are not admitted. They certainly are questionable, but the President regards that concession as a part of the case only so far as it shows the beginning and the animus of that course of conduct which resulted so disastrously to the United States. It is important in that it foreshadows subsequent events.[28]

[27]For an illuminating discussion of the principal actors in this drama, see Adams, "The Treaty of Washington," 105–113.

[28]J. C. B. Davis, *Mr. Fish and the Alabama Claims*, 35.

This was not only an abandonment but a repudiation of the main contention of Sumner's speech. As soon as the latter learned of the substance of the instructions, May 13 apparently, he rushed in a highly excited state to the house of Mr. J. C. Bancroft Davis, the Assistant Secretary of State, and exclaimed: "Is it the purpose of this administration to sacrifice me—me, a senator from Massachusetts?" Two days later he went to Fish, still highly excited, and threatened that he would make Motley resign, to which Fish replied: "Let him resign. I will put a better man in his place." This brought Sumner to a more reasonable frame of mind, and he proposed a substitute for the paragraphs quoted above, but as the substitute embodied the extreme doctrine of the Senate speech, Fish refused to accept it. On May 17, Sumner sent Fish another draft, accompanied by a letter, in which he said:

Repudiation of Sumner's speech

> As chairman of the Senate Committee, I ought not in any way to be a party to a statement which abandons or enfeebles any of the just grounds of my country as already expounded by Seward, Adams, and myself.

He further expressed his regret that Motley was not allowed "to speak according to his own enlightened discretion."[29]

Motley departs from his instructions

Motley went to England thoroughly imbued with the proclamation legend and the views of Sumner, to whom he owed his appointment. In his first interview with Lord Clarendon he departed from the letter of his instructions and laid undue stress on the proclamation "as being the fountain head of the disasters which had been caused to the American people, both individually and collectively, by the hands of Englishmen." He also stated that measures extending belligerent rights to insurgents "must always be taken with a full view of the

[29]*Op. cit.*, pp. 31–34.

grave responsibilities assumed."[30] His first dispatch giving an account of the interview was received in Washington just as President Grant was considering a proclamation recognizing the belligerency of the Cuban insurgents. A few weeks later such a proclamation was signed by Grant while on a visit to New England and sent to Fish to issue, but the latter considered it premature and withheld it for further directions. It was never issued. Motley's later dispatches revealed the fact not disclosed in the first that his interview with Lord Clarendon had been reduced to writing and that Motley's interpretation had therefore been substituted for the original instructions. This made Grant very angry. Motley's arraignment of the Queen's proclamation, if indorsed by the administration, would give Spain good grounds for action in the event of the issuance of the contemplated Cuban proclamation. Grant, therefore, told Fish to recall Motley at once, but Fish, wishing to avoid an open breach with Sumner, persuaded the President to let Motley continue for the present, with the understanding that no further negotiations in regard to the *Alabama* claims would be intrusted to him. Future negotiations on this subject were to be conducted in Washington.[31]

Grant in anger orders Motley's recall

Sir John Rose confers with Secretary Fish

While the subject of Motley's disregard of his instructions was still perplexing the administration, Sir John Rose, a member of the Canadian ministry and also a member of the commission which had been appointed to settle the claims of the Hudson's Bay and Puget Sound companies against the United States, arrived in Washington and was presented to the Secretary of State. Rose was in the confidence of Lord Clarendon, and one of the main objects of his visit was to sound the government on the subject of the *Alabama* claims. He suggested that the Duke of Argyll and Mr. Forster, both staunch friends of

[30] *Op. cit.*, pp. 118–119.

[31] *Ibid.*, pp. 125–127; Adams, 117–122.

the Union during the war, be sent over as special envoys to effect a peaceful settlement. An account of the interview was later recorded by the Assistant Secretary of State. According to this trustworthy authority:

> Mr. Fish said that the time had not arrived; that the British people were too much irritated by the rejection of the treaty, and by Mr. Sumner's speech, and that our people were too much carried away with the idea of paying off the cost of the war with the amount of damages that Mr. Sumner's speech had made out against Great Britain. He said that when the excitement subsided, the appointment as special envoy of some man of high rank, authorized to express some kind word of regret, would pave the way for a settlement; and he outlined to Sir John the exact scheme for settlement which was adopted a year and a half later.[32]

Breach between Grant and Sumner

Another subject was soon injected into the situation which led in a few months to a complete severance of all personal and political relations between the President and the chairman of the Senate Committee on Foreign Relations. This was the proposed annexation of Santo Domingo, a scheme very dear to the President's heart. An annexation treaty, negotiated at the instance of the President, was laid before the Senate January 10, 1870. Before sending the treaty to the Senate, Grant had an interview with Sumner at the latter's house, in the presence of several prominent men, and departed with the conviction that the senator had agreed to support the treaty. This was the impression made on the others present. When the treaty came up for consideration a few months later, Sumner led the fight against it, and it was rejected June 30 by a vote of 28 to 28, two-thirds being necessary for ratification. The next day Motley was asked to resign. He refused and was finally removed.[33] Motley's literary friends and admirers have created a legend that he was sacrificed to Grant's spite

Recall of Motley

[32] Davis, *Mr. Fish and the Alabama Claims*, 45–46.
[33] *Ibid.*, pp. 49–54.

for Sumner. As a matter of fact, Motley had been retained in order to avoid a breach with Sumner, and when the breach came, although on another issue, there was no longer any reason for letting him continue at a post where he had long since been relieved of all but routine duties. Years later Grant declared that he had regretted many times that he had not stuck to his original determination when he first told Fish to recall Motley.

In his annual message of December 5, 1870, Grant expressed his regret that there had been no adjustment of the claims against Great Britain and that the two governments were so far apart in their views. He suggested that a commission be authorized to establish the amounts of the several claims and that they be paid by the United States, so that the government might have the ownership and control of all demands against Great Britain. He also brought up again the question of the annexation of Santo Domingo, and requested Congress to authorize him to appoint a commission to negotiate a new treaty. This proposal afforded Sumner an opportunity to vent his spleen against the administration. In a speech, which he ostentatiously called "Naboth's Vineyard," he accused the President of trying to commit the country to "a dance of blood" and used language that was intemperate and had the effect of angering Grant still more. Three weeks later the papers relating to the recall of Motley were, by order of the President, sent to the Senate. They contained allusions to Sumner which he considered insulting. The same day that the Motley papers were sent to the Senate, January 9, 1871, Sir John Rose returned to Washington and reopened conferences with Fish.[34]

Sumner's "Naboth's Vineyard" speech

The night of his arrival Sir John dined with Mr. Fish, Mr. Bancroft Davis being the only other guest. After

[34] *Op. cit.*, p. 59; Adams, 169–171; Pierce, *Memoir and Letters of Charles Sumner*, IV, 426 ff.

dinner the first conference was held. Sir John Rose said that he was authorized to state that, if it would be acceptable to the United States to refer all subjects of dispute to a joint commission, his government would send out a commission composed of persons of the highest rank. Mr. Fish inquired whether the British government was prepared to admit liability for the *Alabama* claims. Sir John replied in the negative, but stated that the British government would be willing to submit the question of liability to arbitration. After a long discussion Sir John said that the British government could not take the initiative in the matter of the *Alabama* claims, but he made a proposal in the following form, that

Rose and Fish agree on basis of negotiation

> . . . the British government should propose a commission for the settlement of the San Juan boundary, the fisheries, and other Canadian questions, and that the United States should accede, provided the claims for the acts of the vessels should be also considered.

To this Mr. Fish agreed.[35]

Fish consults Sumner

Before proceeding further Mr. Fish considered it expedient to confer with the chairman of the Senate Committee on Foreign Relations to see if there was a reasonable hope of securing the ratification of a treaty negotiated on the proposed basis. In view of the strained relations growing out of the Motley embroglio Mr. Fish took the precaution of getting a mutual friend and member of the Foreign Relations Committee to sound Sumner and see if he would be civilly received. The result was satisfactory, and on January 15, Fish called by appointment at Sumner's house and laid Rose's proposals before him. Sumner said that he was not ready to give an answer but would send one at an early date. Two days later Fish received Sumner's memorandum, drawn up in four paragraphs, the important one being the second:

[35] Davis, *Mr. Fish and the Alabama Claims*, 59–64.

Sumner's ultimatum

The greatest trouble, if not peril, being a constant source of anxiety and disturbance, is from Fenianism, which is excited by the proximity of the British flag in Canada. Therefore the withdrawal of the British flag cannot be abandoned as a condition or preliminary of such a settlement as is now proposed. To make the settlement complete, the withdrawal should be from this hemisphere, including provinces and islands.[36]

The question of Canadian independence

It should be said in justice to Sumner that his ultimatum was not as astounding then as it appears to be to-day. During the interval between Rose's visits to Washington, Fish had upon a number of occasions discussed with Sir Edward Thornton, the British minister, the question of Canadian independence. Many Englishmen considered the colonies a liability, and Sir Edward declared that England was willing to see them independent, but he said it was impossible to connect the question of Canadian independence with the *Alabama* claims. "Independence means annexation. They are one and the same thing." President Grant himself had suggested to Fish as a basis of settlement the following concessions by Great Britain:

(1) the payment of actual losses incurred through the depredations of British Confederate commerce-destroyers; (2) a satisfactory revision of the principles of international law as between the two governments; and (3) the submission to the voters of the Dominion of the question of independence.[37]

Fish decides to ignore Sumner

But Fish had now dropped the Canadian question from the discussion and had decided to proceed with the negotiations on the basis of an expression of regret on the part of Great Britain, a revision of the principles of international law, and the payment of claims. To such a settlement Sumner was now the chief obstacle. On January 24, Secretary Fish, after conferring with several Democratic senators and receiving assurances of their

[36]*Op. cit.*, pp. 134–137.

[37]Adams, 161.

support, had another interview with Rose, during the course of which he showed him confidentially Sumner's memorandum, and stated that if the British government was willing to send out commissioners on the basis indicated, no effort would be spared "to secure a favorable result, even if it involved a conflict with the chairman of the Committee on Foreign Relations."[38]

Removal of Sumner from his chairmanship

The British commissioners arrived in New York February 22, 1871, and on the 27th the joint commission was organized in Washington. On March 4, the new Congress convened, and a few days later, when the Senate committees were reorganized, Sumner was dropped from the chairmanship of the Committee on Foreign Relations. This action had been desired by the President for some time, but it was not actually decided upon until after the ultimatum of January 17. While this document was known only to a few senators who discreetly kept it secret lest it should arouse Irish sentiment against the negotiations, Sumner's opposition to the administration and his violent denunciations of the President were known to all, so that when the administration leaders demanded his removal the Senate readily acquiesced.[39]

The Treaty of Washington

The way was now open for a settlement. The Treaty of Washington was signed May 8, 1871, and ratified by the Senate May 24. The commissioners who acted on behalf of the United States were Secretary Fish, General Schenck, who had been appointed to succeed Motley as minister to England, Justice Nelson of the Supreme Court, Judge Hoar of Massachusetts, and ex-Senator Williams of Oregon. The British commissioners were Earl de Grey and Ripon, Sir Stafford Henry Northcote, Sir Edward Thornton, minister to the United States, Sir John Alexander Macdonald, premier of Canada, and Montague Bernard, Chicele Professor of International Law

[38] Moore, *Dig. of Int. Arbits.*, I, 530.

[39] Davis, 139–145; Adams, 166, 180.

at Oxford. Lord Tenterden and Mr. Bancroft Davis acted as secretaries. The negotiations were conducted with great informality and in excellent spirit. The results were embodied in a treaty of unusual length, running to forty-three articles. It dealt with the fisheries, the navigation of lakes, canals, and rivers, the system of bonded transit for goods, and the San Juan water boundary, but the important part for the present discussion comprised Articles I-XI, which provided for the submission of the *Alabama* claims to arbitration. The tribunal was to consist of five members appointed in the following manner: one by the President of the United States, one by the Queen of England, one by the King of Italy, one by the President of the Swiss Confederation, and one by the Emperor of Brazil.[40]

Submission of Alabama claims to arbitration

The treaty contained two remarkable concessions on the part of Great Britain. The first was an expression of "the regret felt by Her Majesty's government for the escape, under whatever circumstances, of the *Alabama* and other vessels from British ports, and for the depredations committed by those vessels." The second was the adoption of rules which were to govern the arbitrators. They were three in number:

The three rules governing the award

A neutral Government is bound—

First, to use due diligence to prevent the fitting out, arming, or equipping, within its jurisdiction, of any vessel which it has reasonable ground to believe is intended to cruise or to carry on war against a Power with which it is at peace; and also to use like diligence to prevent the departure from its jurisdiction of any vessel intended to cruise or carry on war as above, such vessel having been specially adapted, in whole or in part, within such jurisdiction, to warlike use.

Secondly, not to permit or suffer either belligerent to make use of its ports or waters as the base of naval operations against the other, or for the purpose of the renewal or augmentation of military supplies or arms, or the recruitment of men.

Thirdly, to exercise due diligence in its own ports and waters,

[40](Malloy) *Treaties and Conventions*, I, 700.

and, as to all persons within its jurisdiction, to prevent any violation of the foregoing obligations and duties.[41]

Explanation of England's soncessions

In agreeing to the above rules Great Britain surrendered her case, and an award against her became a foregone conclusion. The reason for this concession is not far to seek. The ten months preceding the signature of the Treaty of Washington had been disquieting ones for Great Britain. They were the months of the Franco-Prussian war. When Sir John Rose was sent back to Washington in January, 1871, Paris was under siege by the German army and England was a powerless spectator of the triumph of Bismarck's policy. The entire political system of Europe was in process of reorganization and no one could foresee the outcome. Had England been drawn into war she would undoubtedly have suffered the effects of the policy she had pursued during the American civil war. "*Alabamas*" would have been procured by her enemies in American ports and the United States would have had its revenge. This was probably what Grant had in mind when he said he did not care whether England paid "our little bill" or not. The British government decided, therefore, to remove the grievances of the United States and to arrive at an understanding as to the rules that should govern in future wars. The three rules above quoted were adopted with this proviso:

The three rules to be binding in the future

> The high contracting parties agree to observe these rules as between themselves in future, and to bring them to the knowledge of other maritime powers, and to invite them to accede to them.

Organization of the Geneva Tribunal

On December 15, 1871, the arbitrators met at Geneva for the purpose of organizing and exchanging the cases and evidence submitted by the two governments. The members of the tribunal were Charles Francis Adams,

[41] *Op. cit.*, I, 703.

named by the United States, Sir Alexander Cockburn, named by England, Count Sclopis of Italy, Jacques Stoempfli of Switzerland, and Viscount d'Itajuba of Brazil. Count Sclopis was chosen president of the court. Bancroft Davis was the agent of the United States in charge of the American case, while Lord Tenterden held a similar position for his government. The United States was represented by able counsel: Caleb Cushing, William M. Evarts, and Morrison R. Waite. The British counsel were Sir Roundell Palmer and Professor Montague Bernard. After organizing and exchanging cases the tribunal adjourned until April in order to give time for the preparation of the counter-cases. By special agreement these were delivered by the agents to the secretary of the tribunal, and the arbitrators did not convene in final session until June 15, 1872.[42]

The claim for indirect damages revived

In the meantime, soon after the exchange of the original cases in December, an unfortunate controversy arose, which came dangerously near disrupting the entire proceeding. The American case, prepared by Bancroft Davis, included the claims for indirect damages, and as soon as this fact became known there was a great outcry in the British press and even in Parliament. The British commissioners who had negotiated the Treaty of Washington declared severally that it was their understanding that the indirect claims had been dropped by the United States. These claims had been brought forward by the United States commissioners on March 8, objected to by the British, and not brought forward again. They took this to be a waiver. Furthermore, Lord Ripon stated in the House of Lords that the language used in the treaty was expressly intended to exclude those claims. Why Bancroft Davis and Fish, for Fish had examined and approved the American case, included the indirect claims has never been satisfactorily explained. Davis

[42]Davis, *Mr. Fish and the Alabama Claims,* 87 ff.

stated years later that the insistence of Sumner on "the unsound canon of international law touching the rights of a neutral" in his speech of April, 1869, and Motley's adoption of it in his interview with Clarendon made it of vital importance to have the question settled once and for all by the tribunal. He added:

Explanation of Bancroft Davis

> The gigantic claims for indemnity for a breach of that unsound canon, coming from the chairman of the Senate Committee on Foreign Relations, would, if not overruled, have been dangerous to the United States as a neutral in the future.[43]

This was a rather lame excuse. Political considerations probably weighed more in the mind of Fish, who thought that the American people would resent the tacit abandonment of what Sumner had taught them to believe were their just demands. At any rate, the American case contained a long and severe indictment of the course pursued by the British government, and set forth at length the resulting national injuries, indirect claims, and consequential damages.[44]

Fish's probable motive

As the time approached for the reconvening of the arbitration tribunal, there was serious doubt as to whether the British would continue the case, but Secretary Fish threw out intimations that his government was willing to have the indirect claims overruled.[45] When the arbitrators reassembled at Geneva in June they were greatly perplexed over the question, the British government having expressly refused to allow the indirect claims to be submitted. Mr. Adams finally suggested a solution of the difficulty. It was informally agreed that the tribunal should exclude the indirect claims from consideration on the ground that under the principles of international law applicable to such cases they did not afford ground for

Adams suggests a solution

[43] *Op. cit.*, p. 106.

[44] Adams, "The Treaty of Washington," 188 ff.; Moore, *Dig. Int. Arbits.*, I, 560 ff.

[45] Moore, I, 642.

pecuniary damages.[46] The tribunal then assembled, excluded the indirect claims, and proceeded to the consideration of the claims for direct damages. The decision, rendered September 14, 1872, awarded the United States the sum of $15,500,000 in gold in satisfaction of all claims referred to the tribunal. This award was signed by Charles Francis Adams and the three neutral arbitrators, but not by the British representative, Sir Alexander Cockburn. The British government, however, promptly paid the award.[47]

The award

[46] *Op. cit.*, I, 643–646.

[47] *Ibid.*, pp. 653–659; (Malloy) *Treaties and Conventions*, I, 717–722. For the full report of the Geneva Arbitration, see *Papers Relating to the Treaty of Washington*, 4 vols., published as Part II of *Foreign Relations*, 1873.

CHAPTER XIX

FISHERIES, FUR SEALS, AND ALASKAN BOUNDARY

The Newfoundland fisheries

THE Newfoundland fisheries have been the subject of more protracted dispute than any other question in American diplomacy. From the negotiations at Paris in 1782 to the decision of the Hague Court in 1910 the fishing rights exercised by citizens of the United States in the waters of British North America afforded a perpetual source of friction and at times brought the United States and England to the verge of war. By the treaty of 1783 American fishermen were given the "liberty" to engage in the inshore fisheries of the British dominions in North America and to resort to the unsettled portions of certain coasts for the purpose of drying their catch.[1] These inshore privileges were not renewed by the Treaty of Ghent, Great Britain claiming that they had been nullified by the war, but the subject was covered by the convention of 1818. By the terms of this agreement the inshore privileges were restricted to certain specified parts of Newfoundland, Magdalen Islands, and Labrador, but they were granted in perpetuity.[2] By the reciprocity convention of 1854 most of the rights enjoyed by Americans under the treaty of 1783 were renewed for the term of the convention. This convention, it will be recalled, was denounced in pursuance of an act of Congress in 1866 and conditions reverted to the basal convention of 1818.[3]

[1] *Ante*, p. 44.
[2] *Ante*, p. 159.
[3] *Ante*, pp. 431–432.

The subject was referred to the joint high commissioners who drafted the Treaty of Washington in 1871 and by Articles XVIII–XXV of that agreement American fishermen were again admitted to the inshore privileges renounced in the convention of 1818, while Canadian fishermen were given similar privileges on the coasts of the United States north of the thirty-ninth parallel, and the United States agreed to admit Canadian fish and fish oil free of duty. As the British claimed that the inshore privileges granted to Americans were more valuable than the concessions made to Canadians, it was agreed that the amount of additional compensation, if any, to be paid by the United States should be referred to a commission of arbitration. The commissioners met at Halifax and in 1877 awarded Great Britain the sum of $5,500,000 for the twelve years during which the fisheries agreement was necessarily to run. The American member of the commission dissented and the government of the United States protested against the award as excessive, but finally paid it.[4]

Inshore privileges renewed for a consideration

The fisheries articles terminated

The Congress of the United States decided, however, to forestall any demands for future payments by terminating the fisheries agreement. The Treaty of Washington provided that Articles XVIII–XXV should remain in force for ten years, subject to termination thereafter on two years' notice from either party. In pursuance of a joint resolution of Congress, March 3, 1883, the President gave the necessary notice to the British Government and in 1885 the agreement came to an end.[5] In order to avoid difficulties that would inevitably arise from the termination of the agreement in the midst of the fishing season, Secretary Bayard, who had come into office with President Cleveland, agreed to a British proposal of a *modus vivendi*, under which the inshore privileges of

[4]Moore, *Int. Arbits.*, I, 725–753.

[5]Moore, *Dig. of Int. Law,* I, 808.

Americans were to continue pending the appointment of a joint commission to consider the whole question anew. In his annual message of December 8, 1885, President Cleveland recommended that provision be made for such a commission, but the Senate voted against the recommendation. Efforts were then made through diplomatic negotiations to arrive at an agreement as to the interpretation of the convention of 1818, but without success.[6] The Canadian authorities then began seizing American vessels for alleged encroachment on waters and coasts not open to them under the agreement of 1818. Between 1886 and 1888 the dispute reached a serious crisis. It was aggravated by the exceedingly bitter fight between the Democrats and the Republicans in the campaign of 1888, in which the Irish vote figured prominently, and by the contemporaneous seizure by United States revenue cutters of British vessels on the charge of violating the laws of the United States for the protection of the fur seals in the waters of Alaska.

Seizure of fishing vessels

In the lengthy correspondence that took place between the two governments from 1886 to 1888 as to the proper construction of the convention of 1818 a number of interesting and difficult questions were raised. What was the meaning of the word "bays" as used in the convention? Did the term include only bodies of water not more than six marine miles wide at the mouth, or all bodies called bays? Was the three-mile line marking the limit of territorial jurisdiction to follow the sinuosities of the coast, or was it to be drawn three miles out from the line running from headland to headland? Were American vessels that put into British ports for purposes specified in the convention forbidden to obtain supplies or to engage in traffic which was permitted to other vessels under general commercial privileges extended since 1818?[7]

Difficulty of interpreting the convention of 1818

[6] *Op. cit.*, I, 809.

[7] *Ibid.*, pp. 810–866.

Bayard-Chamberlain treaty rejected by the Senate

In November, 1887, British commissioners came to Washington to confer with commissioners appointed by the President. As a result of these negotiations the Bayard-Chamberlain Treaty was signed February 15, 1888, and promptly submitted by President Cleveland to the Senate with a message recommending its approval. In view of the approaching presidential election the treaty became the subject of political debate and was the first treaty ever discussed by the Senate in open session. When the vote was finally taken, August 21, it stood 27 for the treaty and 30 against. As the treaty was rejected without any attempt at amendment, President Cleveland concluded that the Senate did not approve of his method of settling the question and two days later sent a special message to Congress in which he reviewed the controversy and asserted that he was by no means disposed to abandon the interests and rights of Americans or to neglect their grievances. He suggested, therefore, as the only feasible method of procedure, a plan of retaliation in the following words:

President Cleveland suggests retaliation

> I recommend immediate legislative action conferring upon the Executive the power to suspend by proclamation the operation of all laws and regulations permitting the transit of goods, wares, and merchandise in bond across or over the territory of the United States to or from Canada.[8]

Congress did not act on the recommendation.

Indiscreet letter of the British minister

On the 24th of October, 1888, the New York *Herald* made public letters that had passed during the early part of September between one Charles F. Murchison, of California, and Lord Sackville, the British Minister at Washington. Murchison, who represented himself as a former British subject, now a naturalized American, sought advice from the British minister as to how he should vote in the coming election. Sackville replied

[8]Richardson, *Messages and Papers of the Presidents*, VIII, 620.

that he considered Cleveland more friendly to England than Harrison, the Republican candidate. The British minister had been made the subject of a hoax. Murchison was a fictitious name. The Republicans published the correspondence with the intention of turning the Irish vote against Cleveland.[9]

When Secretary Bayard brought the subject to the attention of the British minister, the latter declared that his reply had been strictly private and was not intended for publication. Meanwhile he had given out a very indiscreet interview to the representative of the New York *Tribune*. As the presidential election was only a few days off, the subject assumed great political importance. President Cleveland, therefore, acted with unusual promptness. On October 25, Mr. Bayard cabled the facts to Mr. Phelps, especially emphasizing the fact that in the interview Lord Sackville had reflected upon the motives of the President and the Senate in their handling of the questions relating to Canada and the fisheries. Mr. Phelps promptly communicated his instructions to Lord Salisbury, who declined to take any action until the receipt of the precise language of Lord Sackville and his explanation. Mr. Phelps's cablegram giving an account of this interview was received October 28, and on the following day Mr. Bayard made a detailed report of the entire incident to the President. On October 30, Mr. Bayard was instructed by the President to hand to Lord Sackville his passports.

Lord Sackville given his passports

Further discussion of the case

In the correspondence which followed between Mr. Phelps and Lord Salisbury, the latter took the position that a private letter which had become public only by a betrayal of confidence was not sufficient ground on which to demand the recall of a minister. The interview he regarded in a more serious light, but he declined to ac-

[9]For the text of Lord Sackville's letter see *For. Rels.*, 1888, part 2, pp. 1667–1668.

quiesce in the demand of the United States for the recall of Lord Sackville until he should receive a copy of the alleged interview and have had time to hear Lord Sackville's explanation. The last phase of the controversy took the form of an interesting discussion as to the difference between the recall of a minister and his dismissal. Lord Salisbury denied the right of the United States to insist on the recall of Lord Sackville, which he said would imply a censure of his conduct by both governments. He admitted, however, the right of the United States to dismiss him at pleasure, which, of course, would imply no censure of his conduct on the part of his own government.[10]

The fisheries question referred to the Hague Court

The fisheries question was referred with the Alaskan boundary dispute and other matters to the joint high commission which met at Quebec in the summer of 1898, but no agreement was reached. It was finally referred to the Hague Court by a special agreement signed at Washington January 27, 1909.[11] The questions referred to the Court included all the controversial points that had been raised in the correspondence of 1886–1888 as well as some that had arisen later. One of the most important questions was as to the right of the Canadian and Newfoundland governments to impose upon American fishermen, without the consent of the United States, local regulations making the exercise of the privileges to which they were entitled under the convention of 1818 conditional upon the payment of light or harbor dues, or reporting at custom houses.

The decision a compromise

The decision of the tribunal, rendered September 7, 1910, was somewhat of a compromise. It applied to bays the ten-mile rule, that is, that it was not expedient to permit foreign vessels to fish in bays unless there was at least four miles of water beyond the three-mile limit. The court named a number of bays where

[10] *Op. cit.*, pp. 1669–1718.

[11] *Am. Journal of Int. Law*, IV, 948–954.

there might be difficulty in determining the limits and specified the headlands between which the lines should be drawn. It held that Great Britain or the dominion governments had a right to regulate the exercise of the privileges enjoyed by American fishermen, but that such regulations should be subject to review by a mixed commission of experts.[12] Such a commission was organized in pursuance of the award and made a permanent body. Disputes are now settled as they arise and there is no longer an accumulation of grievances. Furthermore, the fisheries, in the early days the chief industry of New England, have in recent years declined in relative importance, so that it is highly improbable that the question will ever again loom large in American diplomacy.[13]

The Bering Sea controversy

The Bering Sea controversy, which reached a crisis about the same time as the Northeastern fisheries dispute, involved a totally different question—the claim of the United States to exercise jurisdiction over fur seals beyond the three-mile limit. This claim arose out of the interpretation placed by officials on the Russian treaty of cession of 1867. That treaty described the western limit of the territories and dominion of Alaska by a line running through the center of Bering Strait to the North Pole and extending from Bering Strait in a southwesterly direction midway between certain designated islands "to the meridian of one hundred and ninety-three degrees west longitude, so as to include in the territory conveyed the whole of the Aleutian Islands east of that meridian." Did Russia intend to convey dominion over that part of Bering Sea lying east of this line, or merely the islands which were too numerous to name?[14]

The fact that Russia had claimed exclusive dominion over Bering Sea gave some color to the interpretation

[12] *Op. cit.*, pp. 954–1000.

[13] *Ibid.*, V, 1–31, contains Lansing's review of the dispute and the decision.

[14] (Malloy) *Treaties and Conventions*, II, 1521.

The Russian claim to exclusive jurisdiction

that she now conveyed a part of this dominion to the United States. By an imperial ukase issued in 1821 Russia had proclaimed exclusive jurisdiction over these waters and prohibited foreign vessels from approaching within one hundred Italian miles of the Aleutian Islands or the American coast as far south as the fifty-first degree of north latitude. Against this claim both the United States and England protested vigorously and successfully. In the treaty of 1824 between the United States and Russia it was agreed that the respective citizens or subjects of the high contracting parties should not be disturbed or restrained in fishing or navigating in any part of the Pacific Ocean, and further that Russia would make no establishments on the coast south of latitude fifty-four forty and the United States would make none north of that degree of latitude. The following year Russia signed a similar treaty with England. These treaties did not state whether or not Bering Sea was included in the term Pacific Ocean.[15]

Ambiguity of the act of Congress

By act of Congress in 1868, the territory of Alaska was erected into a customs district and the customs and navigation laws were extended to the "mainland, islands, and waters of the territory ceded." The act also prohibited the killing of certain fur-bearing animals "within the limits of Alaska Territory, or in the waters thereof." The ambiguity of this language later gave rise to a serious controversy.[16]

The value of the seal herd

At the time of the cession of Alaska to the United States the most valuable products came from the seal herd which frequented the Pribilov Islands. This was the largest known herd in the world and it had been protected by Russian law from the indiscriminate slaughter which had gone so far toward exterminating the seals in other parts of the world. The Alaskan seal was of great

[15]Moore, *Dig. of Int. Law*, I, 890–892.

[16]Moore, *Int. Arbits.*, I, 763.

commercial value, as is seen by the fact that during the first twenty years of American ownership the revenue derived by the government from the Pribilov herd amounted to more than the purchase price of the entire territory of Alaska.[17]

The habits of the seal

The habits of the seal are interesting. The herd returns from its winter cruise the last of May or first of June. The old males arrive at the islands first and take positions along the shore amid great confusion and after desperate struggles with the younger males, whom they drive off to themselves. The females then arrive and seek their places under the protection of the old males. Soon after landing they give birth to their young, each bearing a single "pup." The females range as far as two hundred miles to sea in quest of food, returning regularly to the care of their young. In the late autumn, the whole herd leaves the islands for its long annual swim to the south. As the seal is a polygamous animal, large numbers of males may be killed off each year without endangering the herd, but the proper selection of the ones destined for slaughter can be made only on land. Pelagic sealing involves the indiscriminate slaughter of male and female and of many animals whose fur is of slight value.[18]

Act of 1869

By acts of March 3, 1869, and July 1, 1870, Congress declared the Pribilov Islands a government reserve and forbade the killing of any fur seal upon the islands or in the waters adjacent thereto, except during the months of June, July, September, and October. It also prohibited the use of firearms or any means tending to drive them away. The Secretary of the Treasury was authorized to lease for a period of twenty years the right to engage in the taking of fur seals, provided not more than one hundred thousand were to be taken annually. The

[17] J. Stanley-Brown, "The Bering Sea Controversy from an Economic Standpoint," in the *Yale Review,* II, 196; Foster, *Diplomatic Memoirs,* II, 22.

[18] J. B. Henderson, Jr., *American Diplomatic Questions,* 10–12.

monopoly was accordingly leased to the Alaska Commercial Company for an annual sum of $55,000 and, in addition, sixty-two and a half cents for each skin taken.[19]

During the term of this lease the value of seal-skins rose from $2.50 in 1870 to $30 in 1890, and the business had become so profitable that foreigners of several nationalities, who of course were excluded from the islands, had resorted to pelagic sealing and the herd was in danger of extermination. As early as 1872 the attention of the treasury officials was called to the fact that expeditions from British Columbia, Hawaii, and even distant Australia were engaged in waylaying the seals in their migrations north and south and even intercepting them in the Straits between the Aleutian Islands. Secretary Boutwell replied:

Pelagic sealing

> I do not see that the United States would have the jurisdiction or power to drive off parties going up there for that purpose, unless they made such attempts within a marine league of the shore.[20]

The United States asserts exclusive jurisdiction

In 1881, the collector of the port of San Francisco inquired of the Secretary of the Treasury the extent of American dominion in Bering Sea, especially the meaning of the terms "waters thereof" and "waters adjacent thereto." Mr. French, the acting secretary, replied that all the waters east of the water line described in the treaty of 1867 were "considered as comprised within the waters of Alaska Territory." This was the first time that the United States had ever advanced the doctrine of *mare clausum* and the ruling was made by a subordinate official of the Treasury Department, apparently without any conference with the Department of State. This ruling was confirmed in 1886 by Mr. Manning, Secretary of the Treasury under President Cleveland, and in August the

[19]Moore, *Int. Arbits.*, I, 764–767.

[20]Moore, *Dig. of Int. Law*, I, 894.

revenue cutter *Corwin,* which had been sent to Bering Sea to protect the seals, seized three British Columbian vessels engaged in catching seals between sixty and seventy miles from land. The cases were tried before Judge Dawson of the United States Court at Sitka. The master and mate of each vessel were sentenced to imprisonment for thirty days and fined $500 and $300 respectively, and the vessels were condemned and ordered to be sold for having been "found engaged in killing fur seal within the limits of Alaska Territory and in the waters thereof in violation of section 1956 of the Revised Statutes of the United States."[21] As Judge Dawson had acted on the advice of the attorney-general of the United States, the government stood committed to the policy of maintaining absolute jurisdiction over the part of Bering Sea east of the treaty line of demarcation.[22]

British sealers seized and condemned

As soon as the British government learned of the seizures, a formal protest was made through Sir Lionel Sackville-West, the British minister at Washington. A diplomatic issue was thus squarely presented and President Cleveland ordered all further proceedings against the vessels suspended pending a settlement of the dispute. This order was disregarded by the United States marshal at Sitka, who thought it "not genuine," and during the summer of 1887 other seizures were made.[23] No captures were made during the summer of 1888. In the meantime Secretary Bayard requested the governments of France, Great Britain, Germany, Japan, Russia, and Sweden and Norway, to coöperate with the United States "for the better protection of the fur-seal fisheries in Bering Sea." He made this request, he said,

A diplomatic settlement attempted

> . . . without raising any question as to the exceptional measures which the peculiar character of the property in ques-

[21]*Op. cit.,* I, 895–896.

[22]Henderson, 18.

[23]Moore, *Int. Arbits.,* I, 775.

tion might justify this government in taking, and without reference to any exceptional marine jurisdiction that might properly be claimed for that end.[24]

Canada objects

Favorable responses were received from France, Great Britain, Japan, and Russia, and the general terms of a convention between the United States, Great Britain, and Russia had been verbally agreed on when, in May, 1888, the negotiations were suddenly suspended by Great Britain at the request of the Canadian government. Lord Salisbury informed Mr. Phelps very frankly that the British government would not execute a convention without the concurrence of Canada and that such concurrence could not be reasonably expected."[25]

In the fall of 1888 a committee of the House of Representatives investigated the Bering Sea question and reported a bill expressly declaring that the waters of Alaska included all the waters of Bering Sea east of the line of the treaty of 1867. This bill passed the House, but as amended by the Senate and finally enacted into law March 2, 1889, it assumed the form of a meaningless resolution:

A Delphic utterance

> That section 1956 of the Revised Statutes of the United States is hereby declared to include and apply to all the Dominion of the United States in the waters of Bering Sea.[26]

The Harrison administration came into office two days after this Delphic utterance and soon adopted the policy, "When in doubt, err on the side of your country's cause." During the following summer the seizures in Bering Sea were renewed and excitement ran high in Canada. The British government made another and a more emphatic protest. To this protest Mr. Blaine, Secretary of State under the Harrison administration, replied at length in a

Blaine's specious argument

[24]Moore, *Dig. of Int. Law,* I, 896.

[25]*Ibid.,* p. 897.

[26]Moore, *Int. Arbits.,* I, 766.

dispatch dated January 22, 1890. He advanced two arguments in defense of the position assumed by his government: (1) that the seized vessels were engaged in a pursuit that was in itself *contra bonos mores,* and one that involved "a serious and permanent injury to the rights of the government and people of the United States"; and (2) that the seal fisheries had been controlled exclusively by Russia, without interference and without question, from their original discovery until 1867, and in like manner by the United States from 1867 to 1886, when certain Canadian vessels asserted their right to engage in and "by their ruthless course to destroy" this valuable industry. "Whence did the ships of Canada derive the right to do in 1886 that which they had refrained from doing for more than ninety years?" He asked whether England would permit foreign vessels to engage in the pearl fisheries of Ceylon which extended more than twenty miles from the shore line. "The law of the sea," he concluded, "is not lawlessness," and cannot be permitted to justify acts immoral in themselves. "One step beyond that which her Majesty's government has taken in this connection, and piracy finds its justification."[27]

Lord Salisbury's reply

Lord Salisbury replied May 22, 1890, that in time of peace no nation was privileged to seize and search upon the high seas the private vessels of a friendly nation, save under suspicion of piracy; that even in the case of the slave trade the United States had held that the vessels of one nation could not be searched by another in the absence of a special international agreement; that Her Majesty's government could not admit that the killing of fur seals was *contra bonos mores* until it should be forbidden by international agreement; that fur seals were indisputably animals *ferae naturae* and therefore *res nullius* until caught; and finally he quoted from the corre-

[27]*For. Rel.,* 1890, pp. 366–370.

spondence of Great Britain and the United States on the subject of the Russian ukase of 1821 to prove that the Russian claim to exclusive jurisdiction in Bering Sea had never been acknowledged, and he also undertook to prove by a long list of British vessels which had engaged in sealing that neither Russia nor the United States had enjoyed the seal fisheries uninterruptedly.[28]

The issue defined

In reply Mr. Blaine undertook to prove that Bering Sea was not included in the term "Pacific Ocean" as used in the correspondence on the subject of the Russian ukase of 1821 and that therefore neither the United States nor Great Britain had questioned Russia's exclusive jurisdiction over Bering Sea. Lord Salisbury held that Bering Sea was included in the term "Pacific Ocean" in the correspondence of 1821–1825, that Russia had therefore acquired no rights by prescription, and that the United States in attempting to close Bering Sea was relying on the discredited doctrine of *mare clausum.* Although Blaine expressly disavowed this doctrine, the American case really rested on it, for his main contention was that Russia had acquired exclusive rights over Bering Sea by prescription and that she had ceded these rights to the United States with the Territory of Alaska.[29]

Lord Salisbury proposes arbitration

As the dispute had now narrowed itself down to this one issue, Lord Salisbury proposed that it be submitted to arbitration and the proposal was accepted by the American government. Pending an agreement upon the terms of arbitration a *modus vivendi* was agreed upon June 15,1891, to cover the approaching sealing season. It was agreed that the killing of seals by British subjects should be prohibited until the following May, and Americans should be permitted to kill only 7,500, a number considered necessary for the subsistence and care of the natives.[30]

---

[28] *Op. cit.*, pp. 419–424.

[29] *Ibid.*, pp. 437–448, 456–465.

[30] *For. Rel.*, 1891, pp. 552–570.

It was also agreed that British and American commissions of scientists should be sent to the islands for the purpose of studying the seal.

Organization of the tribunal

The treaty of arbitration was finally signed at Washington February 29, 1892. It provided for seven arbitrators: two to be named by the President of the United States, two by the Queen of England, one by the President of France, one by the King of Italy, and one by the King of Norway and Sweden. The President of the United States appointed Justice Harlan of the Supreme Court and Senator John T. Morgan. The American agent was John W. Foster. Both Great Britain and the United States were represented by able and distinguished counsel: Sir Charles Russell, Sir Richard Webster, and Christopher Robinson of Canada for Great Britain; Edward J. Phelps, James C. Carter, Henry W. Blodgett, and Frederic R. Coudert for the United States. The tribunal met in Paris in April, 1893, and the proceedings occupied several months. Five questions were submitted for discussion:

Questions submitted for arbitration

1. What exclusive jurisdiction in the sea now known as Behring's Sea and what exclusive rights in the seal fisheries therein, did Russia assert and exercise prior and up to the time of the cession of Alaska to the United States?

2. How far were these claims of jurisdiction as to the seal fisheries recognized and conceded by Great Britain?

3. Was the body of water now known as Behring's Sea included in the phrase "Pacific Ocean," as used in the Treaty of 1825 between Great Britain and Russia; and what rights, if any, in the Behring's Sea were held and exclusively exercised by Russia after said Treaty?

4. Did not all the rights of Russia as to jurisdiction, and as to the seal fisheries in Behring's Sea east of the water boundary, in the Treaty between the United States and Russia of the 30th March, 1867, pass unimpaired to the United States under that Treaty?

5. Has the United States any right, and if so, what right of protection or property in the fur-seals frequenting the islands of the United States in Behring Sea when such seals are found outside the ordinary three-mile limit?[31]

[31](Malloy) *Treaties and Conventions,* I, 748–749.

Russian documents falsely translated

The first part of the American case, as printed and circulated among the members of the tribunal and opposing counsel, was based on what turned out to be false translations of Russian documents. The Russian who had been employed to do this work seems to have thought that by making out a strong case he could curry favor with the American government and thus secure permanent employment in the Alaskan archives. Fortunately the fraud was discovered by Mr. Foster before the oral arguments began and the documents were immediately withdrawn.[32] The first part of the American case was thus completely undermined. Questions 1 and 2 were accordingly decided adversely to the United States, Senator Morgan alone refusing to concur. On the third point it was unanimously decided that the term "Pacific Ocean" in the treaty of 1825 included Bering Sea. The fourth question no longer had any significance, though the tribunal decided that all the rights of Russia had passed to the United States. In the oral argument the counsel of the United States had taken a firm stand on the right of protection and property in the seal herd frequenting the Pribilov Islands, and Mr. Carter had made a particularly brilliant argument in the course of which he covered the whole range of the common and civil law searching for analogies. He discussed domesticated animals and animals *ferae naturae,* swarms of bees, flocks of wild geese which pass from Canada to the United States in winter, deer, elk, buffalo, and other migratory animals. Rarely have American lawyers exhibited before an international tribunal such great erudition or forensic talent. Although their case was weak in point of strict law, it was not without a certain degree of moral strength, and they made the most of it. They showed themselves in every way worthy of their brilliant opponents. The

[32]Foster, *Diplomatic Memoirs,* II, 40–41.

court took a strictly legal view of the questions submitted and on the fifth point decided that

> . . . the United States has not any right of protection or property in the fur-seals frequenting the islands of the United States in Bering Sea, when such seals are found outside the ordinary three-mile limit.

The decision adverse to the United States

In this decision Justice Harlan and Senator Morgan did not concur.[33]

The arbitrators draft regulations

By the terms of the arbitration convention the tribunal had been authorized, in the event of a decision adverse to the United States, to prescribe concurrent regulations for the protection of the seals outside jurisdictional limits. After deciding against the United States on all questions of law, the arbitrators drafted a set of regulations which were later put into effect by both governments. There remained the question of damages due Great Britain for the seizure of ships and other interference with the Canadian sealers. This question was later referred to a special board of arbitration and the sum of $473,151.26 was awarded Great Britain.[34]

The seals in danger of extermination

The regulations for the protection of the seals proved inadequate, however, and scientific commissions were again sent to the islands to make a thorough investigation, but the American and British experts disagreed as to the causes of the rapid decline of the herd, and Great Britain refused to agree to further restrictions. As the regulations prescribed by the Paris arbitrators were to be revised every five years the question was referred to the joint high commission which met at Quebec in the summer of 1898, but no agreement was reached. After the expiration of the regulations seals were slaughtered in the sea in great numbers by Canadians, while Americans were prohibited by act of Congress from engaging in pelagic

[33]Moore, *Int. Arbits.*, I, 914–922.

[34]*For. Rel.*, 1898, pp. 371–373.

sealing. There seemed to be no way of saving the herd from extermination except by international agreement, and the Canadians, to whom Great Britain left the determination of the question, refused to agree to restrictions. Under these circumstances President Roosevelt suggested to Congress, in his annual message of 1906, the extermination of the herd by the United States "in the most humane way possible" in order "to put an end to the hideous cruelty now incident to pelagic sealing."

The agreement of 1911

Finally, on July 7, 1911, a convention was signed at Washington by Great Britain, Russia, Japan, and the United States, prohibiting pelagic sealing in the Pacific north of the thirteenth parallel of north latitude, including the seas of Bering, Kamchatka, Okhotsk, and Japan. Great Britain and Japan were each to receive fifteen per cent of the skins taken on the islands and shores of the United States and of Russia, and the United States, Great Britain, and Russia were each to receive ten per cent of the skins taken on the islands and shores of Japan. The convention was to continue in force for fifteen years and thereafter until terminated by twelve months' notice given by one or more parties.[35]

The Alaskan boundary dispute

The Alaskan boundary dispute may be regarded as having aggravated the fisheries and fur-seal controversies in their later stages, or it may be regarded as having been in large measure produced by the bad feeling that had been engendered by those controversies. The immediate cause of the boundary dispute, however, was the discovery of gold in the Klondike in 1897. The shortest and quickest route to the gold-bearing region lay through the southern strip of Alaska by way of Dyea and Skagway on the headwaters of Lynn Canal. At this time the boundary line between this coastal strip and British Columbia had never been surveyed. The question had been brought to the attention of Congress by President Grant and by succeed-

[35] *Treaties and Conventions*, III, 2966.

ing Presidents, but owing mainly to the expenses of a survey in that rugged and deserted country the matter had been indefinitely deferred by both governments. With the rush of gold hunters to the Klondike the question of determining the boundary assumed an unforeseen importance.

The United States acquired Alaska in 1867 with the boundaries that had been agreed on by Russia and Great Britain in the treaty of 1825. The language of this treaty was indefinite in several particulars. The first part of the boundary line was to run from the southernmost point of Prince Edward Island, which point lies in latitude fifty-four degrees and forty minutes, to the mouth of Portland Channel and up the said channel to the fifty-sixth degree of north latitude. This left in doubt the ownership of certain islands at the mouth of Portland Channel, and there was the further difficulty that Portland Channel does not extend as far north as the fifty-sixth degree. But the main difficulty lay in the determination of the range of mountains extending from the last named point to the one hundred and forty-first degree of west longitude, approximately Mount St. Elias. The boundary was to follow the summit of this range unless it should prove to be at a distance of more than ten marine leagues from the ocean, in which case the line was to follow the sinuosities of the coast and never exceed the distance of ten marine leagues therefrom.[36]

Description of the boundary vague and indefinite

There was no dominant range of mountains parallel to the coast corresponding to the language of the treaty, though such a range was prominently marked on the maps of Vancouver and other cartographers prior to 1825.[37] The intention of the negotiators of 1825 was to exclude the British from deep water north of latitude fifty-four forty. The correspondence shows that the British ne-

The intent of the negotiators of 1825

[36]Moore, *Dig. of Int. Law*, I, 466.

[37]Maps and charts accompanying the case and counter case of the United States before the Alaskan Boundary Tribunal, nos. 4 and 5.

gotiator tried to get an outlet and failed. But with the discovery of gold in the Klondike the Canadians pushed their outposts down to Lynn Canal and claimed Dyea and Skagway. Serious difficulties threatened from the conflict of authority over the collection of customs, and the boundary question was referred to the joint high commission which met at Quebec in 1898 for the purpose of arranging an agreement on the subject of commercial reciprocity and the fisheries. The commission not only failed to reach an agreement, but it developed here for the first time that the Canadians had set up an entirely new theory as to the meaning of the treaty of 1825. They contended that the ten marine leagues should be measured from the general line of the ocean coast and not from tide water. This interpretation would throw the boundary line across the heads of inlets and channels in such a way as to give the Canadians access to deep water.[38]

Canada sets up a new interpretation

Modus vivendi of 1899

In October, 1899, Secretary Hay agreed to a *modus vivendi* which gave the Canadians temporary possession of several points which had always been regarded as within American jurisdiction. Although this provisional line was agreed to "without prejudice to the claims of either party" pending the submission of the dispute to arbitration, Secretary Hay was freely criticized for making even a temporary concession, on the ground that it tended to discredit claims which were too well established to admit of reasonable doubt. As a matter of fact, the official maps issued over a long period of years by the British and Canadian governments substantiated the American claims.[39]

Roosevelt agrees to limited arbitration

When Roosevelt became President he was not willing to submit the question to a mixed tribunal of the ordinary

[38]*Op. cit.*, No. 27; Foster, "Alaskan Boundary" in *Nat. Geog. Mag.*, November, 1899, p. 453.

[39]See series of eight maps from British sources, showing the progressive advance of the Canadian frontier between 1884 and 1898, *United States Atlas*, No. 28.

type with an outside umpire to determine all points of difference. He was ready to fight rather than to surrender a foot of what he considered American territory, however remote and valueless it might be. He finally agreed to a form of arbitration in which Canada could not gain and the United States could not lose. By a convention signed January 24, 1903, the dispute was referred to a mixed commission of three American citizens and three British subjects. The American members appointed were Elihu Root, Secretary of War; Senator Henry Cabot Lodge, of Massachusetts; and ex-Senator George Turner, of Washington. The British members were Lord Alverstone (formerly Sir Richard Webster), Lord Chief Justice of England; Sir Louis Jette, Lieutenant-Governor of the Province of Quebec; and Allen B. Aylesworth, of Toronto. As there was little doubt as to the position of the three American and the two Canadian members of the tribunal, the case was really before Lord Alverstone. If he decided in favor of the claims of the United States, there would be an end of the controversy. If he sustained the Canadian view there would be an even division, and the United States could make good its claims only by force.

The delicate position of Lord Alverstone

The commission met in London in September, 1903, and, by a vote of 4 to 2, the Canadian members dissenting, decided all the important points in favor of the United States. It held that it was the intention of the treaty of 1825 to shut England out from access to tide water.[40] This decision was a great disappointment to the Canadians, some of whom felt that Lord Alverstone had sacrificed their interests in order to promote the British policy of friendly relations with the United States. Some critics went so far as to say that Lord Alverstone had accepted a place on the commission with the tacit understanding that he was to decide the case in favor of the United

Criticism of the decision

[40] Alaskan Boundary Tribunal, Proceedings, I, 29–32; *For. Rel.*, 1903, pp. 543–545.

States. This he indignantly denied at the time and later again in his autobiography. In this connection John Bassett Moore says:

> In reality, the Canadian contentions in regard to the Alaskan boundary fundamentally lacked merit, and, like those of the United States in the fur-seal arbitration, derived color chiefly from the fact that a government was willing to take the chance of presenting them.[41]

---

[41]*Principles of American Diplomacy,* 320.

PART V

EXPANSION IN CARIBBEAN AND PACIFIC

CHAPTER XX

THE REASSERTION OF THE MONROE DOCTRINE

President Cleveland's bold assertion of the Monroe Doctrine

As a result of Blaine's unsuccessful attempt to force Great Britain to relinquish her rights under the Clayton-Bulwer treaty, the Monroe Doctrine had fallen somewhat into disrepute when in 1895 it was suddenly revived in a striking and sensational way by President Cleveland's intervention in the Venezuelan boundary controversy. The dispute between Great Britain and Venezuela in regard to the boundary line between the latter and British Guiana was of long standing. In 1814, by treaty with the Netherlands, Great Britain acquired "the establishments of Demerara, Essequibo, and Berbice," now known as British Guiana. From that time on the boundary line between British Guiana and Venezuela was a matter of dispute. Venezuela always claimed the line of the Essequibo River.

In 1840, Sir Robert Schomburgk, acting under the instructions of the British government, established a line some distance to the west of the Essequibo River and marked it by monuments on the face of the country. Venezuela at once protested. The British government explained that the line was only tentative and the monuments set up by Schomburgk were removed.

British encroachment on Venezuela

Various other lines were from time to time claimed by Great Britain, each one extending the frontier of British Guiana farther and farther to the west. The *British Colonial Office List*, a government publication, in the issue for 1885, put the area of British Guiana at about 76,000 square miles. In the issue of the same list for 1886 the same statement occurs in reference to British Guiana with the change of area to "about 109,000 square miles." Here was a gain of 33,000 square miles without any statement whatever in explanation of how this additional territory had been acquired.

Refusal to arbitrate

After the failure of repeated efforts on the part of Venezuela to secure an adjustment with England, she finally came to the conclusion in 1882 that the only course open to her was arbitration of the controversy. She persistently urged arbitration, but Great Britain refused to submit to arbitration any but a comparatively small part of the territory in dispute. In 1887, Venezuela suspended diplomatic relations with Great Britain, protesting "before her British majesty's government, before all civilized nations, and before the world in general, against the acts of spoliation committed to her detriment by the government of Great Britain, which she at no time and on no account will recognize as capable of altering in the least the rights which she has inherited from Spain and respecting which she will ever be willing to submit to the decision of a third power."

Cleveland decides to intervene

After repeated efforts to promote the reëstablishment of diplomatic relations between Venezuela and Great Britain and after repeated offers of its good offices for the purpose of bringing about an adjustment of the controversy, President Cleveland finally determined to intervene in a more positive manner with a view to forcing, if need be, a settlement of the controversy. This resolution on the part of the American executive, with a full statement of its views on the general principles involved in the dispute, was forwarded to Mr. Bayard for transmission to the British government in Mr. Olney's dispatch of July 20, 1895.[1] After reviewing the history of the controversy Mr. Olney stated in the following concise form what he considered the important features of the situation as it then existed:

[1]*For. Rel.*, 1895–96, Part I, p. 552.

Olney's dispatch of July 20, 1895

1. The title to territory of indefinite but confessedly very large extent is in dispute between Great Britain on the one hand and the South American republic of Venezuela on the other.

2. The disparity in the strength of the claimants is such that Venezuela can hope to establish her claim only through peaceful methods—through an agreement with her adversary either upon the subject itself or upon an arbitration.

3. The controversy, with varying claims on the part of Great Britain, has existed for more than half a century, during which period many earnest and persistent efforts of Venezuela to establish a boundary by agreement have proved unsuccessful.

4. The futility of the endeavor to obtain a conventional line being recognized, Venezuela for a quarter of a century has asked and striven for arbitration.

5. Great Britain, however, has always and continuously refused to arbitrate, except upon the condition of a renunciation of a large part of the Venezuelan claim and of a concession to herself of a large share of the territory in controversy.

6. By the frequent interposition of its good offices at the instance of Venezuela, by constantly urging and promoting the restoration of diplomatic relations between the two countries, by pressing for arbitration of the disputed boundary, by offering to act as arbitrator, by expressing its grave concern whenever new alleged instances of British aggression upon Venezuelan territory have been brought to its notice, the government of the United States has made it clear to Great Britain and to the world that the controversy is one in which both its honor and its interests are involved and the continuance of which it cannot regard with indifference.

His interpretation of the Monroe Doctrine

The greater part of the dispatch was taken up with a discussion of the bearing of the Monroe Doctrine upon the case and the most striking feature of it was that the Monroe Doctrine was appealed to by name. Mr. Olney's statement of the Monroe Doctrine is worthy of the most careful consideration as it was the fullest and most definite official construction of its meaning and scope that had been given to the world. He said:

That America is in no part open to colonization, though the proposition was not universally admitted at the time of its first enunciation, has long been universally conceded. We are now concerned, therefore, only with that other practical application of the Monroe Doctrine the disregard of which by an European power is to be deemed an act of unfriendliness towards the United States. The precise scope and limitations of this rule cannot be too clearly apprehended. It does not establish any general protectorate by the United States over other American states. It does not relieve any American state from its obligations as fixed by international law, nor prevent any European power directly interested from enforcing such obligations or from inflicting merited punishment for the breach of them. It does not contemplate any interference in the internal affairs of any American state or in the relations between it and other American states. It does not justify any attempt on our part to change the established form of government of any American state or to prevent the people of such state from altering that form according to their own will and pleasure. The rule in question has but a single purpose and object. It is that no European power or combination of European powers shall forcibly deprive an American state of the right and power of self-government and of shaping for itself its own political fortunes and destinies.

Lord Salisbury's reply

Lord Salisbury's reply to Mr. Olney was given in two dispatches of the same date, November 26, 1895, the one devoted to a discussion of the Monroe Doctrine, the other to a discussion of the rights of the controversy as between Great Britain and Venezuela. In the first dispatch Lord Salisbury argued that Mr. Olney's views went far beyond the scope of the Monroe Doctrine, that no attempt at colonization was being made, and that no political system was being imposed upon any state of South America. He also denied that the Monroe Doctrine was a part of international law, since it had not received the consent of other nations, and he utterly repudiated Mr. Olney's principle that "American questions are for American decision."

In the second dispatch of the same date Lord Salisbury enters fully into the rights of the controversy between Great Britain and Venezuela, controverting the arguments of the earlier part of Mr. Olney's dispatch, which he characterizes as *ex parte*.

In view of the very positive character of Mr. Olney's dispatch and of the assertion that the honor and interests of the United States were concerned, the refusal of Great Britain to arbitrate placed the relations of the two countries in a very critical position. The American executive, however, had intervened for the purpose of settling the controversy, peaceably if possible, forcibly if need be, and President Cleveland did not now shrink from the logic of events. In a message to Congress, December 17, 1895,[2] he laid before that body Mr. Olney's dispatch of July 20, together with Lord Salisbury's reply. He not only reaffirmed the soundness of the Monroe Doctrine and its application to the case in question, but claimed for that principle of American diplomacy a place in the code of international law.

Cleveland submits the question to Congress

In regard to the applicability of the Monroe Doctrine to the Venezuelan boundary dispute Mr. Cleveland declared:

The Monroe Doctrine at stake

> If a European power by an extension of its boundaries takes possession of the territory of one of our neighboring republics against its will and in derogation of its rights, it is difficult to see why to that extent such European power does not thereby attempt to extend its system of government to that portion of this continent which is thus taken. This is the precise action which President Monroe declared to be "dangerous to our peace and safety," and it can make no difference whether the European system is extended by an advance of frontier or otherwise.

In regard to the right of the United States to demand the observance of this principle by other nations, Mr. Cleveland said:

Its relation to international law

> Practically the principle for which we contend has peculiar, if not exclusive, relation to the United States. It may not have been admitted in so many words to the code of international law, but since in international councils every nation is entitled to the rights belonging to it, if the enforcement of the Monroe Doctrine is something we may justly claim, it has its place in the code of international law as certainly and as securely as if it were specifically mentioned; and when the United States

[2]Richardson, *Messages and Papers of the Presidents*, IX, 655.

is a suitor before the high tribunal that administers international law the question to be determined is whether or not we present claims which the justice of that code of law can find to be right and valid. The Monroe Doctrine finds its recognition in those principles of international law which are based upon the theory that every nation shall have its rights protected and its just claims enforced.

Authority to appoint a boundary commission requested

Mr. Cleveland concluded that the dispute had reached such a stage as to make it incumbent upon the United States to take measures to determine with sufficient certainty for its justification what was the true divisional line between the republic of Venezuela and British Guiana. He therefore recommended that Congress make an appropriation for the expenses of a commission, to be appointed by the executive, which should make the necessary investigations and report upon the matter with the least possible delay. "When such report is made and accepted," he continued, "it will, in my opinion, be the duty of the United States to resist by every means in its power, as a willful aggression upon its rights and interests, the appropriation by Great Britain of any lands or the exercise of governmental jurisdiction over any territory which after investigation we have determined of right belongs to Venezuela." "In making these recommendations," he added, "I am fully alive to the responsibility incurred and keenly realize all the consequences that may follow."

The publication of this message and the accompanying dispatches created the greatest excitement both in the United States and in England, and called forth the severest criticism of the President's course.

Criticism of President Cleveland and Secretary Olney

The main grounds of this criticism were the contentions:

(1) That the Monroe Doctrine was not a part of international law and therefore its observance as such could not be urged upon other nations.

(2) That it was not even an established principle of American diplomacy, since the original declaration was

merely a protest against apprehended aggression on the part of a combination of European powers which had long since ceased to threaten this continent.

(3) That even granting that the Monroe Doctrine was a declaration of American policy, it was merely a policy and imposed no obligation on the government to enforce it except where our interests were directly concerned.

(4) That the occupation of a few thousand acres of uninhabited territory by Great Britain, even if it did rightfully belong to Venezuela, was not a matter that affected the interests of the United States one way or the other or that threatened the permanence or stability of American institutions.

(5) That granting the wisdom and correctness of the President's position, the language of his message and of Mr. Olney's dispatch was indiscreet at best and unnecessarily offensive to British pride.

Their positions misrepresented

It may be well to consider these objections in detail. In regard to the first point it may be said that neither President Cleveland nor Mr. Olney asserted or maintained that the Monroe Doctrine was a part of international law by virtue of its assertion by President Monroe and succeeding Presidents. The position they took was that the Monroe Doctrine was an American statement of a well-recognized principle of international law, viz., the right of a state to intervene in a controversy between other states, when it deems its own interests threatened. Mr. Cleveland declared: "The Monroe Doctrine finds its recognition in those principles of international law which are based upon the theory that every nation shall have its rights protected and its just claims enforced." Mr. Olney's analysis of the doctrine was clearer and more specific. He said: "That there are circumstances under which a nation may justly intervene in a controversy to which two or more other nations are the direct and immediate parties is an admitted canon of international law."

After discussing the general principle of intervention, he adds: "We are concerned at this time, however, not so much with the general rule as with a form of it which is peculiarly and distinctively American."[3]

The Monroe Doctrine a sound policy

In answer to the second objection it is only necessary to refer to accepted works on public law and to the official correspondence of the State Department to show that the Monroe Doctrine had for three-quarters of a century been the cardinal principle of American diplomacy.[4]

The third point, namely as to the expediency of enforcing the Monroe Doctrine in all cases of European aggression on this continent, raises an important question. If, however, the Monroe Doctrine is a wise principle and one which it is our interest to maintain, it is right that it should be asserted on every occasion of its violation. The force of precedent is so great that in the present state of international law, it would be dangerous to do otherwise.

In the fourth place, while it was perfectly true that the occupation of the disputed territory by Great Britain could not in itself conceivably endanger the peace and integrity of the United States, yet as the open violation of a principle upon which we had laid so much stress we could not in honor and dignity have overlooked it.

Vague and rhetorical language

As to the tone of Mr. Olney's dispatch and of Mr. Cleveland's message, it must be acknowledged that while the positions assumed were in the main correct, the language was in some cases unfortunate, either from vagueness or generalization. Thus Mr. Olney's statement, that "3,000 miles of intervening ocean make any permanent political union between a European and an American state unnatural and inexpedient,"—whatever he may have meant by it—appeared in view of Great Britain's

[3]Olney to Bayard, July 20, 1895.

[4]Moore, *Digest of Int. Law,* VI, 368–604, especially Mr. Fish's Report on Relations with the Spanish-American Republics of July 14, 1870, pp. 429–431. The latter is also published in Richardson, *Messages and Papers,* VII, 70–78.

connection with Canada, to be a direct threat and calculated to give offense. Likewise Mr. Cleveland's reference to "the high tribunal that administers international law" was too rhetorical a figure for a state paper.

The move vindicated by its success

It has, indeed, been suggested that President Cleveland and Mr. Olney deliberately undertook to play a bluff game in order to browbeat the British government. In any case, it should be remembered that the test of a diplomatic move is its success, and judged from this standpoint Mr. Cleveland's Venezuelan policy was vindicated by the results. The British government at once adopted the most friendly attitude and placed valuable information in its archives at the disposal of the commissioners appointed by President Cleveland to determine the true boundary line. On November 12, 1896, before the final report of this commission was made, a complete accord was reached between Great Britain and the United States by which the terms of a treaty to be ratified by Great Britain and Venezuela were agreed on, the provisions of which embraced a full arbitration of the whole controversy.

Lord Salisbury changes front

Lord Salisbury's sudden change of front has been the subject of much interesting speculation. How far he was influenced by the South African situation has never been revealed, but it undoubtedly had its effect. President Cleveland's message was sent to Congress December 17. Before the end of the month came Doctor Jameson's raid into the Transvaal, and on the 3rd of January the German Kaiser sent his famous telegram to Paul Kruger. The attention of England was thus diverted from America to Germany, and Lord Salisbury doubtless thought it prudent to avoid a rupture with the United States in order to be free to deal with the situation in South Africa.

The Anglo-Venezuelan treaty provided that an arbitral tribunal should be immediately appointed to determine the true boundary line between Venezuela and British Guiana. This tribunal was to consist of two members

The question submitted to arbitration

nominated by the judges of the Supreme Court of the United States and two members nominated by the British Supreme Court of Justice and of a fifth selected by the four persons so nominated, or in the event of their failure to agree within three months of their appointment, selected by the King of Sweden and Norway. The person so selected was to be president of the tribunal, and it was expressly stipulated that the persons nominated by the Supreme Court of the United States and England respectively might be members of said courts. Certain general rules were also laid down for the guidance of the tribunal.[5]

Triumph of American diplomacy

A treaty embodying substantially these proposals was signed by the British and Venezuelan representatives at Washington, February 2, 1897. The decision of the tribunal which met in Paris gave a large part of the disputed area to Great Britain and this occasioned further criticism of President Cleveland's action in bringing the United States and England to the verge of war on what was termed an academic issue. The award was a matter of secondary importance. The principle for which the United States contended was vindicated when Great Britain agreed to arbitrate. It was a great triumph of American diplomacy to force Great Britain just at this time to recognize in fact, if not in words, the Monroe Doctrine, for it was not long before Germany showed a disposition to question that principle of American policy, and the fact that we had upheld it against England made it easier to deal with Germany.

The Venezuelan episode of 1902

The attention of Europe and America was drawn to Venezuela a second time in 1902 when Germany made a carefully planned and determined effort to test out the Monroe Doctrine and see whether we would fight for it. In that year Germany, England, and Italy made a naval demonstration against Venezuela for the purpose of forcing her to recognize the validity of certain claims of their

[5] *For. Rel.*, 1896, p. 254.

subjects which she had persistently refused to settle. How England was led into the trap is still a mystery, but the Kaiser thought that he had her thoroughly committed and that if she once started in with him she could not turn against him. But he had evidently not profited by the experience of Napoleon III in Mexico forty years earlier under very similar circumstances.

Origin of German claims

In the case of Germany, though the facts were somewhat obscured, the real purpose of the intervention was to collect claims which originated in contract between German subjects and the government of Venezuela. One claim was for the recovery of interest seven years in arrears on five-per-cent bonds, for which Venezuelan customs were pledged as security. Another was for seven-per-cent dividends guaranteed by the Venezuelan government on the capital stock of a railroad built by German subjects at a cost of nearly $20,000,000. There were still other claims amounting to about $400,000 for forced loans and military requisitions.[6]

The State Department informed of the German demands

These claims were brought to the attention of the United States government by the German ambassador on December 11, 1901. Their dubious character, regarded from the standpoint of international law, led Germany to make what purported to be a frank avowal of her intentions to the United States, and to secure for her action the acquiescence of that government. Her ambassador declared that the German government had "no purpose or intention to make even the smallest acquisition of territory on the South American continent or the islands adjacent." This precaution was taken in order to prevent a subsequent assertion of the Monroe Doctrine. In conclusion the German ambassador stated that his government had decided to "ask the Venezuelan government to make a declaration immediately, that it recognizes in principle the correctness of these demands, and is willing

[6] *For. Rel.*, 1901, p. 193; 1903, p. 429.

to accept the decision of a mixed commission, with the object of having them determined and assured in all their details." At the same time the British government demanded a settlement of claims for the destruction of property and for the ill-treatment and imprisonment of British subjects in the recent civil wars, as well as a settlement of the foreign debt.

Secretary Hay's reply

On December 16, 1901, Mr. Hay replied to the German note, thanking the German government for its voluntary and frank declaration, and stating that he did not consider it necessary to discuss the claims in question; but he called attention to the following reference to the Monroe Doctrine in President Roosevelt's message of December 3, 1901:

> This doctrine has nothing to do with the commercial relations of any American power, save that it in truth allows each of them to form such as it desires. In other words, it is really a guarantee of the commercial independence of the Americas. We do not ask under this doctrine for any exclusive commercial dealings with any other American state. We do not guarantee any state against punishment if it misconducts itself, provided that punishment does not take the form of the acquisition of territory by any non-American power.

Germany, Great Britain, and Italy decide to blockade Venezuela

A year later, after fruitless negotiations, the German government announced to the United States that it proposed, in conjunction with Great Britain and Italy, to establish a pacific blockade of Venezuelan harbors. The United States replied that it did not recognize a pacific blockade which adversely affected the rights of third parties as a valid proceeding. The powers then proposed to establish a "warlike blockade," but "without any declaration of war." This device was resorted to at the suggestion of the German government, in order to avoid a formal declaration of war, which could not be made without the consent of the Bundesrath. Meanwhile, Venezuela's gunboats had been seized and her ports blockaded, acts which Mr. Balfour admitted on the floor of the House of Commons constituted a state of war; and on December 20 a formal blockade was announced in accordance with the law of nations, which created a status of belligerency.[7]

Diplomatic intervention of the United States

The hostilities thus commenced were brought to a close by the diplomatic intervention of the United States. Acting under instructions from Washington, the American minister Herbert W. Bowen succeeded in persuading Venezuela to recognize in principle the claims of the foreign powers and to refer them to mixed commissions for the purpose of determining the amounts.[8] Great Britain and Italy agreed to this arrangement, but the German Kaiser remained for a time obdurate. What followed Germany's refusal to arbitrate is described in Thayer's *Life and Letters of John Hay* in the following words:

The Roosevelt Holleben interview

> One day, when the crisis was at its height, he [President Roosevelt] summoned to the White House Dr. Holleben, the German Ambassador, and told him that unless Germany consented to arbitrate, the American squadron under Admiral Dewey would be given orders, by noon ten days later, to proceed to the Venezuelan coast and prevent any taking possession of Venezuelan territory. Dr. Holleben began to protest that his Imperial master, having once refused to arbitrate, could not change his mind. The President said that he was not arguing the question, because arguments had already been gone over until no useful purpose would be served by repeating them; he was simply giving information which the Ambassador might think it important to transmit to Berlin. A week passed in silence. Then Dr. Holleben again called on the President, but said nothing of the Venezuelan matter. When he rose to go, the President asked him about it, and when he stated that he had received nothing from his government, the President informed him in substance that, in view of this fact, Admiral Dewey would be instructed to sail a day earlier than the day he, the President, had originally mentioned. Much perturbed, the Ambassador protested; the President informed him that not a stroke of a pen had been put on paper; that if the Emperor would agree to

[7]*For. Rel.*, 1903, pp. 419, 454; Moore, *Digest of Int. Law*, VII, 140.

[8]Moore, *Digest of Int. Law*, VI, 590.

arbitrate, he, the President, would heartily praise him for such action, and would treat it as taken on German initiative; but that within forty-eight hours there must be an offer to arbitrate or Dewey would sail with the orders indicated. Within thirty-six hours Dr. Holleben returned to the White House and announced to President Roosevelt that a dispatch had just come from Berlin, saying that the Kaiser would arbitrate. Neither Admiral Dewey (who with an American fleet was then maneuvering in the West Indies) nor any one else knew of the step that was to be taken; the naval authorities were merely required to be in readiness, but were not told what for.

On the announcement that Germany had consented to arbitrate, the President publicly complimented the Kaiser on being so stanch an advocate of arbitration. The humor of this was probably relished more in the White House than in the Palace at Berlin.[9]

Thayer's account derived from Roosevelt

The Holleben incident, as narrated for the first time by Thayer, was immediately called in question. It will be noted that Thayer does not in any way quote Hay in the matter, and in the three volumes of *Diaries and Letters of John Hay*, privately printed by Mrs. Hay in 1908, there is no reference of any kind to the incident. It is evident that Thayer got his report of the interview directly from Roosevelt himself. It is said on good authority that while Colonel Roosevelt had no documentary evidence to support his statements at the time that he gave them to Thayer, such evidence came to hand in an interesting way shortly after the appearance of the book. Two German-Americans who had been intimate friends of Holleben promptly wrote to Colonel Roosevelt protesting, not against the facts as stated, but against the use that was made of them. Both correspondents stated that they had been told of the interview at the time by Holleben. Admiral Dewey confirmed the statement as to the preparedness of the fleet in a letter dated May 23, 1916, which was published four days later in the New York *Times*. In it he said:

---

[9]Thayer, *Life and Letters of John Hay*, II, 286–288.

I was at Culebra, Porto Rico, at the time in command of a fleet consisting of over fifty ships, including every battleship and every torpedo-boat we had, with orders from Washington to hold the fleet in hand and be ready to move at a moment's notice. Fortunately, however, the whole matter was amicably adjusted and there was no need for action.

Dewey's statement

In a speech delivered to several thousand Republican "Pilgrims" at Oyster Bay, May 27, 1916, Colonel Roosevelt made the following interesting comments on Dewey's letter:

Just to-day I was very glad to see published in the papers the letter of Admiral Dewey describing an incident that took place while I was President. When we were menaced with trouble I acted up to my theory that the proper way of handling international relations was by speaking softly and carrying a big stick. And in that particular case Dewey and the American fleet represented the big stick. I asked, on behalf of the nation, the things to which we were entitled. I was as courteous as possible. I not only acted with justice, but with courtesy toward them. I put every battleship and every torpedo-boat on the sea under the American flag and Dewey, with instructions to hold himself ready in entire preparedness to sail at a moment's notice. That didn't mean that we were to have war. Dewey was the greatest possible provocative of peace.[10]

Roosevelt's comment

After the agreement to arbitrate had been made, the situation was further complicated by the demands of the blockading powers that the sums ascertained by the mixed commissions to be due them should be paid in full before anything was paid upon the claims of the peace powers. Venezuela insisted that all her creditors should be treated alike. The Kaiser, from what motives it is not quite clear, suggested that this question should be referred to President Roosevelt, but as the United States was an interested party, Secretary Hay did not think it would be proper for the President to act, and it was finally agreed that the demands for preferential treatment should be submitted to the Hague Court.

The demand for preferential treatment

[10]Washington *Post*, May 28, 1916.

The award of the mixed commissions

During the summer of 1903 ten mixed commissions sat at Caracas to adjudicate upon the claims of as many nations against Venezuela. These commissions simply determined the amount of the claims in each case. The awards of these commissions are very instructive, as they show the injustice of resorting to measures of coercion for the collection of pecuniary claims which have not been submitted to arbitration. Belgian claimants demanded 14,921,805 bolivars and were awarded 10,898,643; British claimants demanded 14,743,572 and were awarded 9,401,267; German claimants demanded 7,376,685 and were awarded 2,091,908; Italian claimants demanded 39,844,258 and were awarded 2,975,906; Spanish claimants demanded 5,307,626 and were awarded 1,974,818; United States claimants demanded 81,410,952 and were awarded 2,313,711.[11]

The decision of the Hague Court

The decision of the Hague Court, which was rendered February 22, 1904, held that the three allied powers were entitled to preferential treatment; that Venezuela had recognized in principle the justice of their claims while she had not recognized in principle the justice of the claims of the pacific powers; that the neutral powers had profited to some extent by the operations of the allies, and that their rights remained for the future absolutely intact.[12] This decision, emanating from a peace court, and indorsing the principle of armed coercion, was received with no small degree of criticism.

Discussion of the Venezuelan incident in Parliament

During the discussions on the Venezuelan situation that took place in Parliament in December, 1902, the members of the government repeatedly repudiated the charge of the opposition that they were engaged in a debt-collecting expedition, and tried to make it appear that

[11]Venezuelan Arbitrations of 1903, 58 Cong., 2 Sess., Sen. Doc. No. 316, and *For. Rel.*, 1904, p. 871.

[12]*For. Rel.*, 1904, p. 506. For a full report of the case see 58 Cong., 3 Sess., Sen. Doc. No. 119.

they were protecting the lives and liberties of British subjects. Lord Cranborne declared:

I can frankly tell the House that it is not the claims of the bondholders that bulk largest in the estimation of the government. I do not believe the government would ever have taken the strong measures to which they have been driven if it had not been for the attacks by Venezuela upon the lives, the liberty, and the property of British subjects.

During the same discussion, Mr. Norman said:

The use of the British navy for collecting debts

This idea of the British fleet being employed to collect the debts of foreign bondholders is assuredly a mistaken one. It was said by Wellington once that the British army did not exist for the purpose of collecting certain debts. It is still more true of the British fleet that it does not exist for the purpose of collecting debts of bondholders. People who lend money to South American republics know what the security is and what they are likely to get in return, and they ought not to have the British fleet at their backs.

To this Mr. Balfour, the prime minister, replied:

I do not deny—in fact, I freely admit—that bondholders may occupy an international position which may require international action; but I look upon such international action with the gravest doubt and suspicion, and I doubt whether we have in the past ever gone to war for the bondholders, for those of our countrymen who have lent money to a foreign government; and I confess that I should be very sorry to see that made a practice in this country.

Protest of the Argentine Republic

Against President Roosevelt's contention that the coercion of an American state was not contrary to the Monroe Doctrine, provided that it did "not take the form of acquisition of territory by any non-American power," Signor Drago, Minister of Foreign Relations of the Argentine Republic, vigorously protested in a note dated December 29, 1902.[13] This note contained a restatement of the "Calvo Doctrine," which takes its name from a celebrated Argentine publicist. In his well-

[13] *For. Rel.*, 1903, p. 1.

known book on international law, Calvo contends that a state has no right to resort to armed intervention for the purpose of collecting the private claims of its citizens against another state. This doctrine, which has received the indorsement of most of the Latin-American states, was applied to public bonds in the note above referred to and is now usually known as the "Drago Doctrine." Signor Drago held, first, "that the capitalist who lends his money to a foreign state always takes into account the resources of the country and the probability, greater or less, that the obligations contracted will be fulfilled without delay. All governments thus enjoy different credit according to their degree of civilization and culture, and their conduct in business transactions," and these conditions are measured before making loans. Second, a fundamental principle of international law is the entity and equality of all states. Both the acknowledgment of the debt and the payment must be left to the nation concerned "without diminution of its inherent rights as a sovereign entity."

The "Drago Doctrine"

He said further:

> As these are the sentiments of justice, loyalty, and honor which animate the Argentine people and have always inspired its policy, your excellency will understand that it has felt alarm at the knowledge that the failure of Venezuela to meet the payment of its public debt is given as one of the determining causes of the capture of its fleet, the bombardment of one of its ports and the establishment of a rigorous blockade along its shores. If such proceedings were to be definitely adopted they would establish a precedent dangerous to the security and the peace of the nations of this part of America. The collection of loans by military means implies territorial occupation to make them effective, and territorial occupation signifies a suppression or subordination of the governments of the countries on which it is imposed.

The doctrine so ably expounded by Doctor Drago attracted much attention during the next few years and was given a place on the program of the Third Pan-American

Conference held at Rio de Janeiro in July, 1906. Doctor Drago had made his proposal as "a statement of policy" for the states of the American continents to adopt. After full discussion the Rio Conference decided to recommend to the governments represented "that they consider the point of inviting the Second Peace Conference at The Hague to consider the question of the compulsory collection of public debts; and, in general, means tending to diminish between nations conflicts having an exclusively pecuniary origin."[14]

The question submitted to the Rio Conference

As a result of this action the United States modified the regular program prepared by Russia for the Second Hague Conference by reserving the right to introduce the question of an "agreement to observe certain limitations in the use of force in collecting public debts accruing from contracts." General Horace Porter presented to the Hague Conference a resolution providing that the use of force for the collection of contract debts should not be permitted until the justice of the claim and the amount of the debt should have been determined by arbitration. A large number of reservations were introduced, but the following resolutions were finally adopted by the votes of thirty-nine states, with five states abstaining from voting:

Resolutions of the Second Hague Conference

The contracting powers agree not to have recourse to armed force for the recovery of contract debts claimed from the government of one country by the government of another country as being due to its nationals.

This undertaking is, however, not applicable when the debtor state refuses or neglects to reply to an offer of arbitration, or, after accepting the offer, prevents any "compromis" from being agreed on, or, after the arbitration, fails to submit to the award.[15]

---

[14] *Am. Journal of Int. Law*, II, 78.

[15] *Am. Journal of Int. Law*, II, Supplement, p. 82.

CHAPTER XXI

THE WAR WITH SPAIN

New era introduced by Spanish War

THE war with Spain marked the end of the long period of political, financial, and economic reconstruction that followed the Civil War. The attention of the American people, absorbed for more than a generation by internal problems, was directed once more to questions of foreign policy which had lain dormant for half a century. Expansion to the South, at a standstill since the Mexican War, was resumed, and the long-delayed but inevitable advance into the Caribbean, a favorite policy of the 'fifties, was at last begun. The project of an Isthmian canal, laid aside at the beginning of the Civil War, was now taken up with a definiteness of purpose which insured success. In a brief quarter of a century the United States established itself so firmly in the Caribbean that its control of this important strategic area was no longer questioned, a fact which has occasioned no little alarm to its southern neighbors. With the Spanish War the United States also resumed policies in regard to the Pacific, which had been prominent in the 'fifties. Not only were the Hawaiian Islands annexed—an old project —but also the Philippines, which brought America into intimate relations with eastern Asia, then the storm center of world politics. John Hay's "Open Door" was but the restatement of a policy which found earlier expression in the first American treaty with China, signed in 1844, and in Commodore Perry's famous expedition to Japan ten years later. Expansion in the Caribbean and in the Pacific made inevitable the construction of a canal through the Isthmus and the building of a big navy.

The Cuban question

The war with Spain was fought primarily for the liberation of Cuba. After the Civil War the United States abandoned the idea of annexing Cuba and limited its efforts to urging upon Spain the abolition of slavery and securing a more liberal government for the island and better trade relations. But the "Ten Years' War," that broke out in 1868 and was almost coterminous with Grant's eight years in the presidency, made it extremely difficult to pursue this policy or to remain on friendly terms with Spain. The harsh methods adopted by Spain for the suppression of the insurrection and the failure of Spanish officials to accord to American citizens in Cuba the rights to which they were entitled by international law and treaty gave rise to disputes of a serious nature.[1] A few months after the beginning of his administration President Grant tendered his good offices to Spain for the purpose of bringing the struggle to a close on a basis of independence. While Spain did not in form reject the offer, she imposed conditions which were utterly impracticable.[2]

President Grant's policy

Grant then determined to recognize the so-called Cuban Republic as a *de facto* government, and in August, 1869, he actually signed a proclamation recognizing Cuban belligerency, but Secretary Fish regarded this step as premature and withheld the proclamation for a more opportune moment. It was never issued.

The Spanish Republic

When the Spanish Republic was proclaimed in 1873 the United States was the first power to accord recognition. As soon as the republican government was established, the American minister, General Sickles, acting under instructions from his government, presented himself in the uniform of a major-general of the United States army to the president of the assembly and formally recog-

[1]41 Cong., 2 Sess., Sen. Ex. Doc. No. 7.

[2]41 Cong., 2 Sess., House Ex. Doc. No. 160.

ized the republic. Congress also passed a joint resolution congratulating the people of Spain on the step they had taken, and it seemed at last that relations with Spain were on a good footing. General Sickles urged upon the new government the abolition of slavery and the concession of self-government to Cuba. But these cordial relations were rudely interrupted a few months later by the case of the *Virginius*, an American-registered vessel seized on the high seas by the Spanish war vessel *Tornado*, and taken into the port of Santiago, Cuba, where the vessel was summarily condemned as being engaged in a filibustering expedition, and fifty-three of her passengers and crew were executed. The *Virginius* was carrying men and supplies to the insurgents, but in the absence of a recognized state of war Spain had no right to seize her beyond the territorial waters of Cuba, and the execution of citizens of the United States and England captured under such circumstances was without excuse. The case gave rise to a long controversy, which threatened to end in war, but Spain finally proved to the satisfaction of the United States that the *Virginius* had been fraudulently registered as an American vessel and was not entitled to carry the American flag. Spain agreed to pay indemnities to the families of those who had been executed.[3]

The case of the *Virginius*

In 1875, President Grant determined to take steps to bring the Cuban struggle to a close and restore peace to the island. On November 5, Secretary Fish addressed a circular note to the ministers of the United States at London, Paris, Vienna, Rome, Lisbon, and St. Petersburg, for the purpose of sounding the European powers on the subject of American intervention in Cuba. This move was unsuccessful. Even England expressed her disapproval of the proposed action. The substance of Fish's note appeared unofficially in the press of Europe and America in December, 1875, and he was sharply criticized

Secretary Fish sounds the European powers on Cuba

[3]*For. Rel.*, 1874, 1875, 1876, *passim.*

in this country for having consulted the powers of Europe on what had been uniformly treated since the days of John Quincy Adams and Henry Clay as a purely American question. Congress called for the correspondence and Fish replied that "no correspondence had taken place during the past year with any European government, other than Spain, in regard to the island of Cuba," but that the note of November 5 had been orally communicated to several European governments by reading the same.[4] He did not submit the replies of the American ministers reporting what the foreign ministers had said. Such reports of interviews are usually regarded as a part of the "correspondence" with foreign powers. At any rate, when in 1896 the Senate called for the note of November 5, 1875, and all correspondence with foreign governments relating to it, President Cleveland transmitted the dispatches which Fish had suppressed. They form a document of 137 printed pages.[5] The "Ten Years' War" lingered on until 1878, when, both sides exhausted, the terms of an unsatisfactory pacification of the island were proclaimed by Spain.

His misleading response to Congressional resolution

In February, 1895, the final insurrection against Spanish rule in Cuba began, and soon developed the same features as the "Ten Years' War." The policy of Maximo Gomez, the insurrectionary chief, was to fight no pitched battles but to keep up incessant skirmishes, to destroy sugar plantations and every other source of revenue with the end in view of either exhausting Spain or forcing the intervention of the United States. With the opening of the second year of the struggle, General Weyler arrived in Havana as governor and captain-general, and immediately inaugurated his famous "Reconcentration" policy. The inhabitants of the island were directed by proclamation to assemble within a week in the towns occupied

Cuban insurrection of 1895

[4]44 Cong., 1 Sess., House Ex. Doc. No. 100.

[5]54 Cong., 1 Sess., Sen. Ex. Doc. No. 213.

by Spanish troops under penalty, if they refused, of being treated as rebels. The majority of those who obeyed the proclamation were women and children who, as a result of being cooped up in crowded villages under miserable sanitary conditions and without adequate food, died by the thousands.[6] In the province of Havana alone 52,000 perished.

American sympathy aroused

Public opinion in the United States was thoroughly aroused by the execution of policies which not only excited sympathy for the unfortunate inhabitants of Cuba, but which paralyzed the industries of the island and destroyed its commerce. American citizens owned at least fifty millions of property in the island, and American commerce at the beginning of the insurrection amounted to one hundred millions annually. Furthermore, numbers of persons claiming American citizenship were thrown into prison by Weyler's orders. Some of them were native Americans, but the majority were Cubans who had sought naturalization in the United States in order to return to Cuba and claim American protection.

Other Cubans, including many who were still Spanish subjects, established themselves in American ports and furnished the insurgents with arms and supplies. On June 12, 1895, President Cleveland issued a proclamation calling attention to the Cuban insurrection and warning all persons within the jurisdiction of the United States against doing any of the acts prohibited by the American neutrality laws. Notwithstanding all the efforts of the administration, illegal expeditions were continually being fitted out in the United States, and while the great majority of them were stopped by port officials or intercepted by the navy, some of them succeeded in reaching the coasts of Cuba. President Cleveland's proclamation recognized insurgency as a status distinct from belligerency. It merely put into effect the neutrality laws of the United

Cleveland's proclamation on state of insurgency

[6] 58 Cong., 2 Sess., Sen. Doc. No. 25, p. 125.

States. It did not recognize a state of belligerency and therefore did not bring into operation any of the rules of neutrality under international law. President Cleveland consistently refused to recognize the Cubans as belligerents. In February, 1896, Congress passed a joint resolution, by a vote of 64 to 6 in the Senate and 246 to 27 in the House, recognizing a state of war in Cuba, and offering Spain the good offices of the United States for the establishment of Cuban independence. Notwithstanding the overwhelming majority which this resolution had received, the President ignored it, for it is a well-recognized principle that Congress has no right to force the hand of the President in a matter of this kind. It amounted merely to an expression of opinion by Congress.

Refuses to recognize state of belligerency

In April, 1896, Secretary Olney addressed a note to the Spanish minister in which the United States offered to mediate between Spain and the insurgents for the restoration of peace on the basis of autonomy. Spain rejected this offer, claiming that Cuba already enjoyed "one of the most liberal political systems in the world," and suggesting that the United States could contribute greatly to the pacification of the island by prosecuting "the unlawful expeditions of some of its citizens to Cuba with more vigor than in the past."[7] In his last annual message to Congress, President Cleveland reviewed the Cuban situation at length and, in conclusion, declared:

Olney's offer of mediation rejected

> When the inability of Spain to deal successfully with the insurgents has become manifest and it is demonstrated that her sovereignty is extinct in Cuba for all purposes of its rightful existence, and when a hopeless struggle for its reëstablishment has degenerated into a strife which means nothing more than the useless sacrifice of human life and the utter destruction of the very subject-matter of the conflict, a situation will be presented in which our obligations to the sovereignty of Spain will be superseded by higher obligations, which we can hardly hesitate to recognize and discharge.

Cleveland's warning to Spain

[7]*Spanish Dip. Cor. and Docs.* (translation, Washington, 1905), pp. 7, 8.

President McKinley offers good offices

The McKinley administration, which began March 4, 1897, soon directed its attention to the Cuban question. It was unfortunate that with this question rapidly approaching a crisis the State Department was in feeble hands. John Sherman, the veteran senator from Ohio, was appointed Secretary of State by McKinley in order to make a place in the Senate for Mark Hanna, who had so successfully conducted McKinley's campaign. General Woodford was sent to Madrid to succeed Hannis Taylor, and he was instructed to tender again the good offices of the United States, to remind Spain of the resolution passed by the previous Congress, and to warn her that another Congress was soon to assemble.[8] Six days after the receipt of General Woodford's note the Spanish ministry resigned, and on October 14 the liberal ministry of Sagasta assumed office. Its first act was to recall General Weyler, and to appoint General Blanco to succeed him as governor and captain-general of Cuba. The new ministry promised to grant autonomy to Cuba, and President McKinley in his message of December 6, 1897, declared his intention of allowing time for the new policy to be tested.

Spain promises autonomy

It was soon evident that the grant of autonomy had come too late. The Cubans would no longer be satisfied with anything short of independence. On January 13 1898, there was serious rioting in Havana, deliberately planned as a demonstration against the autonomy scheme, and Consul-General Fitzhugh Lee cabled his government that it was evident that autonomy would prove a failure, that he doubted whether Blanco could control the situation, and that it might be necessary to send warships for the protection of Americans in Havana. The suggestion as to warships met with a prompter response than General Lee had expected. The United States battleship *Maine* was immediately dispatched to Havana, where she arrived January 25 and was assigned an anchorage by the port

The *Maine* sent to Havana

[8] *For. Rel.*, 1898, p. 568.

officials.[9] While she was lying quietly at anchor in Havana harbor, attention was suddenly diverted from Cuba to Washington by the Dupuy de Lôme incident. On February 9, 1898, the New York *Journal* published in facsimile a letter from the Spanish minister at Washington to a friend in Cuba which severely criticized President McKinley's policy and referred to him as "a would-be politician who tries to leave a door open behind him while keeping on good terms with the jingoes of his party." The letter was genuine, though surreptitiously acquired, and was of such a character that it could not be overlooked. When called on for an explanation, Señor de Lôme admitted having written the letter but questioned the accuracy of the translation. He claimed that the language which he had used was permissible under the seal of private correspondence. When General Woodford, acting under instructions from Washington, informed the Spanish Minister of Foreign Affairs that the President expected the immediate recall of Señor de Lôme, he was informed that the latter's resignation had already been accepted by cable.[10]

The Dupuy de Lôme incident

Before the excitement over this incident had subsided, the battleship *Maine* was suddenly blown up in Havana harbor on the night of February 15, and two of her officers and two hundred and fifty-eight of her crew were killed. After a careful examination of witnesses and of the wreck, an American naval court of inquiry reported that the destruction of the ship was due to a submarine mine.[11] A Spanish board of inquiry, after examining a number of witnesses who had seen or heard the explosion, made a brief report the following day to the effect that the ship had been destroyed by an explosion in the forward magazine. It is generally admitted that the American report

The blowing up of the *Maine*

[9] *For. Rel.*, 1898, p. 1025.

[10] *Ibid.*, pp. 1007–1020.

[11] 55 Cong., 2 Sess., Sen. Doc. No. 207.

was correct, but the responsibility for the mine has never been disclosed.

As soon as the report of the court of inquiry was made public, the American people, who had displayed great self-control, threw aside all restraint and the country witnessed an outburst of patriotic fervor such as had not been seen since 1861. "Remember the *Maine*" became a watchword, and the demand for war was overwhelming.

McKinley makes final effort at diplomatic settlement

President McKinley decided, however, to make one more effort at a diplomatic settlement. He proposed an armistice between Spain and the insurgents pending negotiations for a permanent adjustment through the friendly offices of the President of the United States. In reply the Spanish government made counter-propositions to the effect that the questions arising out of the destruction of the *Maine* be submitted to arbitration and that the pacification of the island be left to a Cuban parliament. Meanwhile, the governor-general would be authorized to accept a suspension of hostilities, provided the insurgents should ask for it and agree to disarm. This was simply an invitation to the insurgents to submit, in which case Spain would consider what degree of autonomy was needed or practicable.

Submits the question to Congress

The President considered the Spanish reply as a rejection of his proposal and determined to submit the entire question to Congress.[12] This meant war, for public feeling in America was at the highest pitch of excitement, the "yellow" press was clamoring for war, and it was with the greatest difficulty that the President, who really wanted peace, had held Congress in check. The message to Congress was held back a few days in consequence of a telegram from General Lee, who urged that he be given time to get Americans safely out of Havana. During this period of delay the representatives of Germany, Austria-Hungary, France, Great Britain, Italy, and Russia made a formal appeal to the President

[12] *For. Rel.*, 1898, p. 731.

for peace, and the Pope persuaded the Queen of Spain to authorize General Blanco to suspend hostilities. This concession did not meet fully the American ultimatum and seemed too much like another play for time. The Spanish minister was, therefore, simply informed that the President would notify Congress of this latest communication. President McKinley was later severely criticized for not giving greater consideration to this note and for merely alluding to it in his message instead of transmitting it in full. Had he given it greater consideration, war might have been delayed a few months, but it would not have been averted, for Spain was not willing to make concessions that the Cubans at this late date would have regarded as satisfactory.

The powers of Europe appeal to the the President for peace

In his message to Congress of April 11, 1898, President McKinley referred to the *Maine* only incidentally as "a patent and impressive proof of a state of things in Cuba that is intolerable." He suggested forcible intervention as the only solution of the question and declared that it was justified, not only on grounds of humanity, but as a measure for the protection of the lives and property of American citizens in Cuba, and for the purpose of putting a stop to a conflict which was a constant menace to our peace.[13] Two days later the House passed a resolution by vote of 324 to 19, directing the President to intervene at once to stop the war in Cuba with the purpose of "establishing by the free action of the people thereof a stable and independent government of their own in the island." On the same day the Senate Committee on Foreign Relations reported a resolution demanding the immediate withdrawal of Spain from the island of Cuba, but the minority report urging in addition the immediate recognition of the Cuban republic as then organized was at first embodied in the Senate resolution by a vote of 67 to 21. It was feared by members of the Senate that if we liberated

The President's message

Prompt action of the House

[13]Richardson, *Messages and Papers of the Presidents*, X, 147.

Cuba without first recognizing the so-called republic of Cuba, the island would inevitably be annexed by the United States. After two days of hot debate, the Senate reconsidered, and the House resolution prevailed. On April 19, the anniversary of the battle of Lexington and of the first bloodshed of the Civil War in the streets of Baltimore, the fateful resolutions were adopted in the following terms:

The Senate finally concurs

Resolutions demanding the withdrawal of Spain from Cuba

Resolved by the Senate and House of Representatives of the United States in Congress assembled,

First, That the people of the island of Cuba are, and of right ought to be, free and independent.

Second, That it is the duty of the United States to demand, and the Government of the United States does hereby demand, that the Government of Spain at once relinquish its authority and government in the island of Cuba, and withdraw its land and naval forces from Cuban waters.

Third, That the President of the United States be, and he hereby is, directed and empowered to use the entire land and naval forces of the United States, and to call into the actual service of the United States the militia of the several States to such extent as may be necessary to carry these resolutions into effect.

Fourth, That the United States hereby disclaims any disposition or intention to exercise sovereignty, jurisdiction, or control over said island except for the pacification thereof, and asserts its determination, when that is accomplished, to leave the government and control of the island to its people.[14]

As soon as these resolutions were approved by the President, the Spanish minister asked for his passports, thus severing diplomatic relations, and Woodford was directed to leave Madrid. The North Atlantic Squadron, then at Key West under command of Rear-Admiral William T. Sampson, was immediately ordered to blockade the northern coast of Cuba, and Commodore George Dewey was ordered from Hong Kong to Manila Bay for the purpose of capturing or destroying the Spanish fleet. During the war that followed, foreign public opinion,

[14]*U. S. Statutes at Large,* XXX, 738.

outside of England, was decidedly hostile to the United States, but in the face of the victories of Santiago and Manila Bay this sentiment underwent a marked change, and Spain abandoned whatever hopes she had cherished of European intervention. By the end of July, 1898, the American as well as the European press was beginning to ask why the war should not be brought to a close.

Effects of American victories on European opinion

After the surrender of Santiago General Miles embarked for Porto Rico with a force of 16,000 men, and in a two weeks' campaign overran most of that island with the loss of three killed and forty wounded. A large number of troops had also been sent to the Philippines. It was evident, therefore, that while the war had been undertaken for the liberation of Cuba, the United States did not feel under any obligation to confine its military operations to that island. Having met all the demands of honor, Spain asked the French government to authorize the French ambassador at Washington to arrange with the President of the United States the preliminary terms of peace. The negotiations begun on July 26 resulted in the protocol of August 12, in which Spain agreed to the following demands: first, the immediate evacuation of Cuba and the relinquishment of Spanish sovereignty; second, the cession of Porto Rico and one of the Ladrones by way of indemnity; and third, the occupation by the United States of "the city, bay, and harbor of Manila pending the conclusion of a treaty of peace which shall determine the control, disposition, and government of the Philippines."[15]

Spain makes move for peace

By the terms of the protocol Paris was selected as the place of meeting for the peace commissioners, and here negotiations were opened on October 1. The United States delegation was composed of William R. Day, who resigned the office of Secretary of State to head the mission; Cushman K. Davis, chairman of the Senate Com-

Peace negotiations at Paris

[15] *Spanish Dip. Cor. and Docs.*, p. 206; *For. Rel.*, 1898, p. 819.

mittee on Foreign Relations; William P. Frye, president *pro tem* of the Senate; Senator George Gray of Delaware; and Whitelaw Reid, editor of the New York *Tribune;* with John Bassett Moore, Assistant Secretary of State, as secretary. An entire month was taken up with the Cuban question, the Spanish commissioners striving in vain to saddle the Cuban debt either on the United States or on the people of Cuba. The Philippine question occupied most of the next month. When the commissioners were appointed, President McKinley had not fully made up his mind on this important question. His first intention seems to have been to retain the bay and city of Manila as a naval base and a part or possibly the whole of Luzon. Public sentiment in the United States in favor of acquiring the whole group made rapid headway, and after an extended trip through the South and West, during which he sounded opinion on this question, the President instructed the commissioners to demand the entire group. The commissioners were later authorized to offer $20,000,000 for the cession. This offer, which was recognized by the Spanish commissioners as an ultimatum, was finally accepted under protest. On other points the United States secured what had been demanded in the protocol, and the treaty was signed December 10, 1898.[16]

The question of the Philippines

The debate in the Senate

The treaty was submitted to the Senate January 4, 1899, and precipitated a memorable debate which lasted until February 6. The principal opposition came from Senator Hoar of Massachusetts, who declared that the proposal to acquire and govern the Philippine Islands was in violation of the Declaration of Independence, the Constitution, and the whole spirit of American institutions. The treaty could not be ratified without the aid of Democrats, and the result was in doubt when Bryan went to Washington and advised his friends in the Senate to vote for ratification, saying that the status of the Philip-

[16] 55 Cong., 3 Sess., Sen. Doc. No. 62.

pines could be determined in the next presidential campaign. The outbreak of hostilities between the Filipinos and the American troops occupying Manila put an end to the debate, and on February 6 the treaty was ratified.

When the United States demanded the withdrawal of Spain from Cuba, it was with the declaration that "The United States hereby disclaims any disposition or intention to exercise sovereignty, jurisdiction, or control over said island except for the pacification thereof, and asserts its determination, when that is accomplished, to leave the government and control of the island to its people." Never has a pledge made by a nation under such circumstances been more faithfully carried out. The administration of Cuba during the period of American military occupation was a model of its kind. General Leonard Wood, the military governor, and his associates found the cities and towns crowded with refugees and *reconcentrados*, and governmental affairs in a state of the utmost confusion. They established order, relieved distress, organized hospitals and charitable institutions, undertook extensive public works, reorganized the system of public schools, and put Havana, Santiago, and other cities in a sanitary condition. In a hospital near Havana, Major Walter Reed, a surgeon in the United States army, demonstrated the fact that yellow fever is transmitted by the bite of a mosquito. This discovery was at once put to the test in Havana, and the city was rendered free from yellow fever for the first time in one hundred and forty years.[17]

Leonard Wood's model administration of Cuba

In the organization of a government for the island, the first step was to take a census of the inhabitants, determine the proper basis of suffrage, and hold municipal elections for the purpose of organizing local government. This work having been successfully accomplished, a constitutional convention, summoned by General Wood,

Dispute over relations with the United States

[17]*Report of the Military Governor of Cuba,* 8 vols., 1901.

convened in the city of Havana, November 5, 1900. By February 21, 1901, the convention had agreed upon a constitution modeled in general after that of the United States. The new constitution provided for the recognition of the public debts contracted by the insurgent government, but was silent on the subject of future relations with the United States. This subject had been brought to the attention of the convention early in February by General Wood, who had submitted for incorporation in the constitution certain provisions which had been drafted in Washington. The convention objected to these proposals on the ground that they impaired the independence and sovereignty of the island, and that it was their duty to make Cuba "independent of every other nation, the great and noble American nation included."

The United States, however, had no intention of withdrawing from the island until this matter was satisfactorily adjusted. A provision, known as the Platt Amendment, was therefore inserted in the army appropriation bill of March 2, 1901, directing the President to leave the control of the island to its people so soon as a government should be established under a constitution which defined the future relations with the United States substantially as follows:

The Platt Amendment

I. That the government of Cuba shall never enter into any treaty or other compact with any foreign power or powers which will impair or tend to impair the independence of Cuba, nor in any manner authorize or permit any foreign power or powers to obtain by colonization or for military or naval purposes or otherwise, lodgment in or control over any portion of said island.

II. That said government shall not assume or contract any public debt, to pay the interest upon which, and to make reasonable sinking fund provision for the ultimate discharge of which, the ordinary revenues of the island, after defraying the current expenses of government shall be inadequate.

III. That the government of Cuba consents that the United States may exercise the right to intervene for the preservation of Cuban independence, the maintenance of a government adequate for the protection of life, property, and individual liberty, and for discharging the obligations with respect to Cuba imposed by the treaty of Paris on the United States, now to be assumed and undertaken by the government of Cuba.

IV. That all acts of the United States in Cuba during its military occupancy thereof are ratified and validated, and all lawful rights acquired thereunder shall be maintained and protected.

V. That the government of Cuba will execute, and as far as necessary extend, the plans already devised or other plans to be mutually agreed upon, for the sanitation of the cities of the island. . . .

VI. That the Isle of Pines shall be omitted from the proposed constitutional boundaries of Cuba, the title thereto being left to future adjustment by treaty.

VII. That to enable the United States to maintain the independence of Cuba, and to protect the people thereof, as well as for its own defense, the government of Cuba will sell or lease to the United States lands necessary for coaling or naval stations at certain specified points, to be agreed upon with the President of the United States.

VIII. That by way of further assurance the government of Cuba will embody the foregoing provisions in a permanent treaty with the United States.[18]

Reluctantly accepted by Cuba

These articles, with the exception of the fifth, which was proposed by General Leonard Wood, were carefully drafted by Elihu Root, at that time Secretary of War, discussed at length by President McKinley's Cabinet, and intrusted to Senator Platt of Connecticut, who offered them as an amendment to the army appropriation bill. In order to allay doubts expressed by members of the convention in regard to the third article, General Wood was authorized by Secretary Root to state officially that the intervention described in this article did not mean intermeddling in the affairs of the Cuban government, but formal action on the part of the United States, based upon just and substantial grounds. With this assurance the convention adopted the Platt Amendment, June 12, 1901, and added it as an appendix to the constitution.

[18] *U. S. Statutes at Large,* XXXI, 897.

Inauguration of the Cuban Republic

On May 20, 1902, Thomas Estrada Palma was inaugurated as first president of the Republic of Cuba, and General Wood handed over to him the government of the island.[19] The Americans left a substantial balance in the Cuban treasury. The total receipts for the entire period were $57,197,140.80, and the expenditures $55,405,031.28. The customs service, which furnished the principal part of the revenues during the period of military occupation, was ably administered by General Tasker H. Bliss.[20]

While the Platt Amendment determined the political relations that were to exist between Cuba and the United States, there had been no agreement on the subject of commercial relations. The sugar industry, which had been almost destroyed by the insurrection, was dependent upon the willingness of the United States to arrange for a reduction of its tariff in favor of the Cuban product. Otherwise Cuban sugar could not compete with the bounty-fed beet sugar of Europe or with the sugars of Porto Rico and Hawaii, which were now admitted to the American market free of duty. President Roosevelt had hoped to settle this question before the withdrawal of American troops, and he had urged upon Congress the expediency of providing for a substantial reduction in tariff duties on Cuban imports into the United States, but a powerful opposition, composed of the beet-sugar growers of the North and West and of the cane-sugar planters of Louisiana, succeeded in thwarting for two years the efforts of the administration to do justice to Cuba. All attempts to get a bill through Congress failed.[21]

Roosevelt recommends reduction of tariff on Cuban sugar

In the meantime a reciprocity convention was agreed

[19] *Documentary History of the Inauguration of the Cuban Government, in Annual Report of the Secretary of War*, 1902, Appendix A.

[20] *Ibid.*, Appendix B.

[21] 55 Cong., 1 Sess., Sen. Doc. Nos. 405 and 679.

upon in the ordinary diplomatic way December 11, 1902, under which Cuban products were to be admitted to the United States at a reduction of twenty per cent. As the Senate failed to act on this treaty before the 4th of March, 1903, President Roosevelt convened an extra session of the Senate which ratified the treaty with amendments, and with the very unusual provision that it should not go into effect until approved by Congress. As the House was not then in session, this meant that the treaty had to go over until the fall. The Cuban situation grew so bad that the President finally convened Congress in extra session November 9, 1903. In a special message he urged prompt action on the treaty on the ground that the Platt amendment had brought the island of Cuba within our system of international policy, and that it necessarily followed that it must also to a certain degree come within the lines of our economic policy. The House passed the bill approving the treaty November 19 by the overwhelming vote of 335 to 21, but the Senate, although it had already ratified the treaty, permitted the extra session to expire without passing the measure which was to give the treaty effect. When the new session began December 7, the Cuban treaty bill was made the special order in the Senate until December 16, when the final vote was taken and it passed. Under the reciprocity treaty commercial relations with Cuba were established on a firm basis and the volume of trade increased rapidly.

The fight for reciprocity

In August, 1906, President Palma was reëlected for another term, but the Cubans had not learned the primary lesson of democracy, submission to the will of the majority, and his opponents at once began an insurrectionary movement which had for its object the overthrow of his government. About the middle of September, President Roosevelt sent Secretary Taft to Havana for the purpose of reconciling the contending factions, but Mr. Taft's efforts proved unavailing and President Palma resigned.

Second period of American administration

When the Cuban Congress assembled, it was found impossible to command a quorum. Under these circumstances Secretary Taft assumed control of affairs on September 29 and proclaimed a provisional government for the restoration of order and the protection of life and property. A body of United States troops under command of General Franklin Bell was sent to Cuba to preserve order and to uphold the provisional government. On October 3, 1906, Secretary Taft was relieved of the duties of provisional governor in order that he might resume his duties in Washington, and Charles E. Magoon was appointed to take his place at Havana.[22] In his message to Congress December 3, 1906, President Roosevelt declared that while the United States had no desire to annex Cuba, it was "absolutely out of the question that the island should continue independent" if the "insurrectionary habit" should become "confirmed." The second period of American occupation lasted a little over two years, when the control of the government was again restored to the people of the island and the American troops were withdrawn.

Roosevelt's warning to Cuba

[22] Secretary Taft's report on the Cuban situation was sent to Congress December 17, 1906.

CHAPTER XXII

THE PANAMA CANAL

Canal postponed by Civil War

IN A previous chapter it has been shown that by the time the discordant interpretations of the Clayton-Bulwer treaty were reconciled the United States was on the verge of the Civil War, and the canal project was laid aside. During the war the Union Pacific Railroad was begun with government aid and the completion of this line, establishing direct overland communication with the Pacific, relieved the immediate necessity for a canal, but the United States government never relaxed its interest in the project.

The Nicaragua treaty of 1867

In 1867, a treaty between the United States and Nicaragua, covering the case of an interoceanic canal, was negotiated and ratified by both parties. It granted to the United States the right of transit between the Atlantic and Pacific oceans on any lines of communication, natural or artificial, by land or by water, then existing, or that might thereafter be constructed, upon equal terms with the citizens of Nicaragua, and the United States agreed to extend its protection to all such routes of communication, and "to guarantee the neutrality and innocent use of the same." The United States further agreed to employ its influence with other nations to induce them to guarantee such neutrality and protection.[1] This treaty, like the treaty with Colombia of 1846 and the Clayton-Bulwer treaty, contemplated the neutralization of the canal. It in no way infringed our engagements with

[1] *Correspondence in relation to the Proposed Inter-oceanic Canal, the Clayton-Bulwer Treaty, and the Monroe Doctrine* (Govt. Printing Office, 1885), p. 132. Referred to hereafter as "Collected Correspondence."

England under the Clayton-Bulwer treaty, but in providing for the joint guarantee of other powers, was in accord with the provisions of that treaty.

Organization of the French Panama Company

After the readjustment of 1860 the obligatory force of the Clayton-Bulwer treaty was not seriously questioned until interest in the canal was suddenly aroused anew by the concession granted by Colombia to Lieutenant Wyse in 1878, and the subsequent organization of a French construction company under the presidency of Ferdinand de Lesseps, the promoter of the Suez Canal.

The prospect of the speedy construction of a canal under French control, for which De Lesseps' name seemed a sufficient guarantee, produced a sudden and radical change of policy on the part of the United States. In a special message to Congress, March 8, 1880, President Hayes made the following statement of what he conceived to be the true policy of this country in regard to a Central American canal:

President Hayes announces new policy

> The policy of this country is a canal under American control. The United States cannot consent to the surrender of this control to any European power, or to any combination of European powers. If existing treaties between the United States and other nations, or if the rights of sovereignty or property of other nations stand in the way of this policy—a contingency which is not apprehended—suitable steps should be taken by just and liberal negotiations to promote and establish the American policy on this subject, consistently with the rights of the nations to be affected by it. . . .
>
> An interoceanic canal across the American isthmus will essentially change the geographical relations between the Atlantic and Pacific coasts of the United States, and between the United States and the rest of the world. It will be the great ocean thoroughfare between our Atlantic and our Pacific shores, and virtually a part of the coast-line of the United States.

The message was accompanied by a report from the Secretary of State, Mr. Evarts, in which he called attention to the mutual engagements entered into between the United States and Colombia by the treaty of 1846 in reference to a transit route across the isthmus and declared that the guarantee of the neutrality of the isthmus and of the sovereignty of Colombia over the same would be a very different thing when the isthmus should be opened to the interests and ambitions of the great commercial nations.[2]

Approved by President Garfield

President Garfield, in his inaugural address, approved the position taken by his predecessor on the canal question,[3] and very soon after assuming the portfolio of state, Mr. Blaine outlined the new policy to our representatives in Europe, cautioning them, however, against representing it as the development of a new policy and affirming that it was "nothing more than the pronounced adherence of the United States to principles long since enunciated by the highest authority of the government."

Secretary Blaine's dispatch

This dispatch of Mr. Blaine is remarkable for several reasons, but chiefly for the fact that it completely ignores the existence of the Clayton-Bulwer treaty, there being no allusion to that celebrated convention either open or implied. Aside from this there are three points to be noted. In the first place, Mr. Blaine calls attention to the rights and duties devolving upon the United States from the treaty with Colombia of 1846, and states that in the judgment of the President the guarantee there given by the United States requires no reënforcement, or accession, or assent from any other power; that the United States in more than one instance had been called upon to vindicate the neutrality thus guaranteed; and that there was no contingency, then foreseen or apprehended, in which such vindication would not be within the power of the nation.

Ignores Clayton-Bulwer treaty

In the second place, Mr. Blaine declared with emphasis that during any war to which the United States of America or the United States of Colombia might be a party, the passage of armed vessels of a hostile nation through the canal of Panama would be no more admissible than would

[2] *Op. cit.*, p. 313.

[3] Richardson, *Messages and Papers*, VIII, 11.

the passage of the armed forces of a hostile nation over the railway lines joining the Atlantic and Pacific shores of the United States or of Colombia. This declaration was in direct opposition to the second article of the Clayton-Bulwer treaty. Mr. Blaine then proceeded to expatiate upon the remarkable development of our Pacific slope and the importance of the canal in facilitating communication between our Atlantic and Pacific states, alluding to the canal in this connection, in the very apt phrase of President Hayes, as forming a part of the *coast-line* of the United States. It does not appear to have occurred to Mr. Blaine that the same arguments applied with equal force to Great Britain's American possessions to the north of us, which likewise extended from the Atlantic to the Pacific, and were likewise entering upon a period of unusual development.

The third point to be noted in the dispatch is the statement that the United States would object to any concerted action of the European powers for the purpose of guaranteeing the canal or determining its status.[4] This declaration was supposed to be nothing more than a reaffirmation of the Monroe Doctrine.

The British government reminds Blaine of the treaty

A copy of this document was left by Mr. Lowell at the British Foreign Office on the 12th of July, 1881. No formal notice of the dispatch was taken by the British government until November, when Lord Granville replied that, as Mr. Blaine had made the statement that the government of the United States had no intention of initiating any discussion upon this subject, he did not propose to enter into a detailed argument in reply to Mr. Blaine's observations. He wished, however, merely to point out that the position of Great Britain and the United States with reference to the canal, irrespective of the magnitude of the commercial relations of the former power, was determined by a convention signed between them at Washington on

[4]Collected Correspondence, pp. 322-326.

the 19th of April, 1850, commonly known as the Clayton-Bulwer treaty, and Her Majesty's government relied with confidence upon the observance of all the engagements of that treaty.[5]

Blaine proposes modifications

Before this reply reached Washington, Mr. Blaine had again taken up the question of the canal in a special dispatch of November 19, 1881. In this dispatch he addressed himself specifically to a consideration of the Clayton-Bulwer treaty, and urged upon the consideration of the British government modifications of such a radical character as to amount to a complete abrogation of the treaty. The grounds of objection to the treaty were stated in full. In the first place, it was declared that the treaty had been made more than thirty years before under exceptional and extraordinary conditions, which were at least temporary in their nature and had long since ceased to exist. The remarkable development of the United States on the Pacific Coast since that time had created new duties and responsibilities for the American government which required, in the judgment of the President, some essential modifications in the treaty. The objections to the perpetuity of the treaty were then stated in full. First and foremost was the objection that the treaty by forbidding the military fortification of the proposed canal practically conceded its control to Great Britain by reason of her naval superiority. The military power of the United States in any conflict on the American continent was irresistible, yet the United States was restrained from using this power for the protection of the canal, while no restrictions could be placed upon the natural advantages that England enjoyed in this regard as a great naval power. A more serious objection to the treaty, however, was urged in the statement that it embodied a misconception of the relative positions of Great Britain and the United States with respect to interests on

States objections to the treaty

[5] *Op. cit.*, p. 326.

this continent. The United States would not consent to perpetuate any treaty that impeached "our right and long-established claim to priority on the American continent."

In the third place, at the time the convention was agreed upon, Great Britain and the United States were the only nations prominent in the commerce of Central and South America. Since that time other nations not bound by the prohibitions of that treaty had become interested in Central America, and the Republic of France had become sponsor for a new canal scheme. Yet by the treaty with England the United States was prevented from asserting its rights and the privileges acquired through treaty with Colombia anterior to the Clayton-Bulwer treaty.

A canal under American control

In the fourth place, the treaty had been made with the implied understanding that British capital would be available for the construction of a canal. That expectation had never been realized, and the United States was now able to construct a canal without aid from outside resources.

In conclusion, Mr. Blaine proposed several modifications of the treaty which would leave the United States free to fortify the canal and to hold political control of it in conjunction with the country in which it might be located.[6]

Blaine's final note

A few days after the dispatch was written, Lord Granville's answer to Mr. Blaine's first dispatch reached Washington, and on the 29th of November, Mr. Blaine wrote a second dispatch equally voluminous with the one of November 19. In this he reviewed the discussions which had taken place between 1850 and 1860 in regard to the treaty with a view to showing that it had never been satisfactory to the United States and had been the cause of serious misunderstanding. He failed, however, to make mention of the settlement of 1860 and the declaration

[6] *Op. cit.*, pp. 327–332.

of President Buchanan that the United States was satisfied with that adjustment.

Lord Granville's reply

The full reply of the British government to Mr. Blaine's arguments was given in two dispatches dated respectively January 7 and 14, 1882. Lord Granville took exception to certain conclusions which Mr. Blaine had sought to establish by analogy with the conduct of Great Britain in regard to the Suez Canal. His lordship fully concurred in what Mr. Blaine had said as to the unexampled development of the United States on the Pacific Coast, but reminded him that the development of Her Majesty's possessions to the north of the United States, while less rapid, had been, nevertheless, on a scale that bore some relation even to that of the Pacific states. In the view of Her Majesty's government, the changes desired by the United States would not improve the situation as regarded the canal, while the declaration that the United States would always treat the waterway connecting the two oceans "as part of her coast-line" threatened the independence of the territory lying between that waterway and the United States.

Her Majesty's government believed that the only way to relieve the situation was to extend the invitation to all maritime states to participate in an agreement based on the stipulations of the convention of 1850.[7]

Frelinghuysen succeeds Blaine

The task of replying to Lord Granville's two dispatches fell upon Mr. Blaine's successor in the State Department, Mr. Frelinghuysen. Mr. Frelinghuysen's voluminous dispatch of May 8, 1882, reiterated in the main the arguments advanced by Mr. Blaine. He adduced evidence at great length to try to show that the Clayton-Bulwer treaty was a special contract for the accomplishment of a specific object, which had never been achieved, and was no longer binding; that Great Britain had violated the treaty by converting her *settlement* of British Honduras

[7] *Op. cit.*, pp. 340–352.

into a *possession* without ever receiving the assent of the United States, and that such act would entitle the United States to renounce the treaty. The dispatch was further characterized by a direct appeal to the Monroe Doctrine in these words:

Appeal to the Monroe Doctrine

> The President believes that the formation of a protectorate by European nations over the isthmus transit would be in conflict with a doctrine which has been for many years asserted by the United States. This sentiment is properly termed a doctrine, as it has no prescribed sanction and its assertion is left to the exigency which may invoke it. It has been repeatedly announced by the executive department of this government, and through the utterances of distinguished citizens; it is cherished by the American people, and has been approved by the government of Great Britain.

After quoting a part of President Monroe's message of December 2, 1823, and reviewing the circumstances under which it was delivered, Mr. Frelinghuysen said:

> Thus the doctrine of non-intervention by European powers in American affairs arose from complications in South America, and was announced by Mr. Monroe on the suggestion of the official representative of Great Britain.[8]

Granville's replies to Frelinghuysen

In his reply of December 30, 1882, Lord Granville proved conclusively that Article VIII of the treaty was understood by the American government during the discussions of 1850–1860 as establishing a general principle applicable to all waterways connecting the two oceans. In answer to the second point, Lord Granville adduced the notes exchanged between Mr. Clayton and Sir Henry Bulwer in July, 1850, which made it perfectly clear that, in the understanding of both governments at that time, the claims of Great Britain to Belize or British Honduras were not affected one way or the other by the treaty.[9]

In a later dispatch, August 17, 1883, Lord Granville

[8] *Op. cit.*, pp. 160–161.

[9] *Ibid.*, pp. 353–359.

briefly touched upon Mr. Frelinghuysen's appeal to the Monroe Doctrine, reminding him very pertinently that neither the American administration which negotiated the treaty nor the Senate which ratified it considered that they were precluded by the utterances of President Monroe from entering into such a treaty with one or more of the European powers.[10]

The correspondence on the treaty closed with Mr. Frelinghuysen's dispatch of November 22, 1883, in which he reiterated with no small degree of bluntness and pertinacity the arguments of his earlier dispatches.

Failure of efforts of Blaine and Frelinghuysen

The Clayton-Bulwer treaty was designed at the time of its execution to establish a permanent principle of control over interoceanic communication in Central America. No provision was made, as in most treaties, for its abrogation, and the American government could not terminate it without the consent of Great Britain for fear that she would return to her position of vantage at the time the treaty was made. For this reason, while Mr. Frelinghuysen claimed that the treaty was voidable, he did not actually declare it void.

Mr. Blaine's efforts to secure a modification were the result of the development of a new policy by the United States and the arguments presented by Mr. Blaine and Mr. Frelinghuysen in support of this policy were disingenuous and flimsy. The result was that Great Britain refused to consent to a modification of the treaty, and the United States saw before her the alternative of abiding by the terms of the treaty or ultimately resorting to war with England.

President Cleveland reverts to earlier policy

In December, 1884, Mr. Frelinghuysen negotiated a treaty with Nicaragua providing for the construction of a canal by the United States to be under the joint ownership and protection of the United States and Nicaragua. The United States also guaranteed the integrity of the

[10] *Op. cit.*, p. 364.

territory of Nicaragua. When Mr. Cleveland became President this treaty was still before the Senate for consideration. Mr. Cleveland withdrew the treaty, and in his first annual message, December 8, 1885, reverted to our traditional policy. He declared himself opposed to entangling alliances with foreign states and declared:

> Whatever highway may be constructed across the barrier dividing the two greatest maritime areas of the world, must be for the world's benefit, a trust for mankind, to be removed from the chance of domination by any single power, nor become a point of invitation for hostilities or a prize for warlike ambition.[11]

Secretary Olney on the Clayton-Bulwer treaty

The attempts of Blaine and Frelinghuysen to bring about a modification of the Clayton-Bulwer treaty were, as we have seen, unsuccessful. In fact, their only effect was to strengthen the British government for the time being in the determination to hold us more strictly to the terms of that convention. In 1896, Secretary Olney in a review of the situation declared:

> Upon every principle which governs the relations to each other, either of nations or of individuals, the United States is completely estopped from denying that the treaty is in full force and vigor. If changed conditions now make stipulations, which were once deemed advantageous, either inapplicable or injurious, the true remedy is not in ingenious attempts to deny the existence of the treaty or to explain away its provisions, but in a direct and straightforward application to Great Britain for a reconsideration of the whole matter.

The Hay-Pauncefote draft of 1900

It was precisely in this spirit that Secretary Hay undertook in 1899 to negotiate a new treaty with England. The original draft of the Hay-Pauncefote treaty, signed February 5, 1900, provided for a neutralized canal and drafted for its control rules substantially in accord with the Constantinople convention of 1888, providing for the

[11] Richardson, *Messages and Papers of the Presidents*, VIII, 327.

[12] 56 Cong., 1 Sess., Sen. Doc. No. 160.

regulation of the Suez Canal. The most important provision of the new treaty was that authorizing the United States to construct and to assume the management of an isthmian canal, either directly or through a company. The United States Senate, however, amended the treaty in three important particulars: (1) by declaring that the Clayton-Bulwer treaty was thereby superseded; (2) by providing that the restrictions in the regulations governing the use of the canal should not apply to measures which the United States might adopt for its own defense and for the maintenance of public order along the canal; and (3) by cutting out entirely the article providing for the adherence of other powers. The British government refused to accept these amendments, and a year elapsed before an agreement was finally reached.[13] The revised treaty which was ratified by the Senate December 16, 1901, was a compromise between the original draft and the Senate amendments. The new treaty abrogated in express terms the Clayton-Bulwer Convention, and provided that the United States might construct a canal under its direct auspices, to be under its exclusive management. The principle of neutralization was nominally retained, but under the sole guarantee of the United States, with power to police the canal, and the clause of the first draft forbidding fortifications was omitted.[14]

Amended by the Senate

New draft ratified

This convention removed the principal diplomatic obstacles which stood in the way of constructing a canal through the isthmus. For several years the United States had been investigating the cost of constructing a canal through Nicaragua, that route being the one which had always been considered most feasible by the great majority of American engineers. Two commissions, one in 1895 and another in 1897, had reported favorably on the practicability of that route. A third commission, headed

The choice of a canal route

[13]Moore, *Digest of Int. Law,* III, 211.
[14]*For. Rel.,* 1901, p. 245.

by Admiral John G. Walker, was appointed under act of March 3, 1899, which authorized an expenditure of $1,000,000 for the purpose of making a thorough investigation of all available routes. While the Walker commission was carrying on investigations in Nicaragua, at Panama, and along the Atrato River, the various financial interests concerned in the choice of routes were actively at work in Washington, each trying to influence Congress in favor of its particular project.

The status of the French company

The New Panama Canal Company had secured, at the time of the reorganization, an extension of its concession to October, 1904, and subsequently another concession to October, 1910, but the validity of the latter arrangement was in doubt. The company could not raise the necessary funds to continue the work at Panama and was therefore threatened with the forfeiture of its franchise and property. It concluded, therefore, that its only hope lay in transferring its concession and property to the American government. With this end in view, an active lobby was maintained at Washington for the purpose of influencing public opinion in favor of the Panama route.

The fight for the Nicaragua route

But the Panama Company had a powerful rival in the Maritime Canal Company, which held a charter from Congress and had secured a concession from Nicaragua. This company had started work at Greytown in 1890, but having been forced from lack of funds to stop work in 1893, was now urging Congress to make its enterprise a national one. It found a ready champion in Senator Morgan of Alabama, who had for years taken a lively interest in the canal question and who had strong convictions as to the superiority of the Nicaragua route. In 1900, Nicaragua declared the concession of the Maritime Canal Company null and void, and granted a new concession to a group of New York capitalists known as the Grace-Eyre-Cragin Syndicate. The Maritime Canal Company, however, refused to abandon its claims, and a contest between the two concerns was carried to the lobbies of Congress. The opposition of the transcontinental railroads to a canal at either point brought into play another set of powerful interests, usually arrayed against the plan which appeared for the time being most likely to succeed.[15]

Report of the Walker commission

On November 16, 1901, the Walker commission after a thorough investigation of the Nicaragua and Panama routes made its report. It estimated the cost of construction of the Nicaragua canal at $189,864,062, and the cost of completing the Panama Canal at $144,233,358. To this latter sum had to be added the cost of acquiring the rights and property of the French company, which had stated to the commission that it estimated its interests at $109,141,500, making the total cost of the Panama Canal $253,374,858. The commission expressed the opinion that the interests of the French company were not worth over $40,000,000. In conclusion the report stated:

> After considering all the facts developed by the investigations made by the commission and the actual situation as it now stands, and having in view the terms offered by the New Panama Company, this commission is of the opinion that the most practicable and feasible route for an isthmian canal, to be under the control, management, and ownership of the United States, is that known as the Nicaragua route.[16]

The Hepburn bill

A bill was promptly introduced into the House of Representatives by Mr. Hepburn providing for the construction of the canal through Nicaragua, and on January 9, 1902, this bill passed the House by the almost unanimous vote of 308 to 2. The report of the commission had meanwhile created great consternation among the stockholders of the New Panama Canal Company, and on January 4, 1902, a definite offer to sell out to the United States

[15]Johnson, *Four Centuries of the Panama Canal*, Chap. VIII.

[16]Report of the Isthmian Canal Commission, 57 Cong., 1 Sess., Sen. Doc. No. 54.

at $40,000,000 was made to the commission by cable. On January 18, the commission filed a supplementary report which recommended the adoption of the Panama route instead of that through Nicaragua.

The Spooner amendment

When the Hepburn bill came up for discussion in the Senate, the situation had thus been radically changed, and a long debate ensued as to the relative merits of the two routes. Senator Morgan continued to fight for Nicaragua as the traditional American route, declaring that the Panama Company could not give a valid transfer of its property and interests. But this objection was cleverly met by Senator Spooner, who offered an amendment, which was virtually a substitute, authorizing the President to acquire the rights and property of the French company at a cost not exceeding $40,000,000; to acquire from the Republic of Colombia, upon such terms as he might deem reasonable, perpetual control of a strip of land, not less than six miles in width, extending from the Caribbean Sea to the Pacific Ocean, with jurisdiction over said strip; and to proceed, as soon as these rights were acquired, to construct a canal. But should the President be unable to obtain a satisfactory title to the property of the French company and the control of the necessary strip of land from the Republic of Colombia "within a reasonable time and upon reasonable terms," then he was instructed to secure control of the necessary strip through Nicaragua and to proceed to construct a canal there.

Passage of the amended bill

The bill as amended passed the Senate June 19, 1902, by a vote of 67 to 6. The House at first refused to concur in the Spooner amendment, but after a conference it finally gave way and the measure was adopted by a vote of 260 to 8. The act was signed by President Roosevelt June 28.[17]

Attorney-General Knox was sent to Paris to make a

[17] *U. S. Statutes at Large*, XXXII, Pt. I, p. 481.

The Hay-Herran convention

thorough investigation of the affairs of the Panama Company. He reported that it could give a clear title. The next step was to secure a right-of-way through Colombia. After considerable delay Secretary Hay and Mr. Herran, the Colombian *chargé d'affaires*, signed, January 22, 1903, a canal convention, by the terms of which the United States agreed to pay Colombia $10,000,000 in cash and an annuity of $250,000 for the lease of a strip of land six miles wide across the isthmus. Objection was raised to this treaty because it failed to secure for the United States full governmental control over the canal zone, but it was considered the best that could be gotten and it was ratified by the United States Senate, March 17, 1903.

Rejected by the Colombian Senate

The Colombia Senate, however, did not regard the treaty with favor. They felt that Panama was their greatest national asset, and they knew perfectly well that in spite of threats to the contrary President Roosevelt was determined not to adopt the alternative of the Spooner amendment and go to Nicaragua. After discussing the treaty for nearly two months, they finally reiected it August 12 by the unanimous vote of the senators present.[18] They probably thought that they could get better terms from the United States and particularly that they might reserve a fuller measure of sovereignty over the isthmus. President Roosevelt declared that the action of the Colombian Senate was due to an "anti-social spirit" and to the cupidity of the government leaders, who merely wished to wait until they could confiscate the $40,000,000 worth of property belonging to the French company and then sell out to the United States. This view is not borne out by the dispatches of Mr. Beaupré, the American minister, who repeatedly warned Secretary Hay that there was a "tremendous tide of public opinion against the canal treaty," which even

[18] 58 Cong., 2 Sess., Sen. Doc. No. 51, p. 56.

the Colombian government could not ignore. The charge of bad faith against Colombia did not come in good grace from a country whose constitution also requires the ratification of treaties by the Senate.

The French company's dilemma

As soon as the Hay-Herran convention was rejected by the Colombian Senate, the advocates of the Nicaragua route began to take courage and to demand that as the "reasonable time" allowed in the Spooner act for the President to acquire the right-of-way through Panama had expired, it was now his duty to adopt the Nicaragua route. The directors of the French company were again in a state of consternation. If they could not sell to the United States they would have to sacrifice their property entirely, or sell to some other purchaser at a lower figure. It was rumored that Germany was willing to buy their interests. The directors of the company were so completely demoralized that William Nelson Cromwell, their American attorney, hastened to Paris to dissuade them from taking any rash step. The rejection of the Hay-Herran treaty was a great disappointment to the inhabitants of the isthmus, who considered this action a sacrifice of their interests, and some of the foremost citizens conferred with the American agent of the Panama Railroad Company as to the advisability of organizing a revolution. Before taking any step in this direction, it was considered advisable to send one of their number to the United States, and Doctor Amador was selected for this mission. He had conferences with William Nelson Cromwell and with Secretary Hay. The latter merely outlined what he considered the rights and duties of the United States under the treaty of 1846, but refused of course to commit the government to a definite support of the revolutionary project. Amador was somewhat discouraged at the result of his conference with Hay, but his hopes were revived by the sudden arrival of Philippe Bunau-Varilla, the former chief engineer of the French

Panama ready for revolt

company, who entered with enthusiasm into the revolutionary scheme.[19]

Roosevelt sends war ships to the isthmus

The Colombian Congress adjourned October 30 without any reconsideration of the treaty, and President Roosevelt at once ordered the *Boston*, *Dixie*, *Atlanta*, and *Nashville* to proceed within easy reach of the isthmus. Their commanders received orders to keep the transit open and to "prevent the landing of any armed force with hostile intent, either government or insurgent, at any point within fifty miles of Panama." The *Nashville* arrived off Colon November 2. It can hardly be denied that these measures created a situation very favorable to revolution.[20]

Revolution anticipated

The revolutionists had been greatly disappointed at Doctor Amador's failure to get a definite promise of support from the American government, but their spirits revived when they learned of the presence of American war vessels. Still they were slow in taking advantage of their opportunities and the government at Washington was growing impatient. At 3.40 P. M., November 3, the following dispatch was sent to the American consuls at Panama and Colon:

> Uprising on isthmus reported. Keep Department promptly and fully informed. Loomis, Acting.

At 8.15 a reply was received from the consul at Panama:

> No uprising yet. Reported will be in the night. Situation is critical.

At 9 P. M. a second dispatch was received from the same source:

> Uprising occurred to-night, 6; no bloodshed. Army and navy officials taken prisoners. Government will be organized to-night.[21]

---

[19]Johnson, *Four Centuries of the Panama Canal*, 162–171.

[20]58 Cong., 2 Sess., Sen. Doc. No. 53.

[21]58 Cong., 1 Sess. H. Doc. No. 8.

Revolution accomplished

Before the *Nashville* received the order to prevent the landing of armed forces, 450 Colombian troops arrived at Colon. The principal officers were provided with a special train to take them across the isthmus to Panama. When they arrived they were seized by the revolutionary leaders and locked up for safe-keeping, while the railroad officials saw to it that there were no trains for their troops to use. The next day Commander Hubbard landed fifty marines from the *Nashville* at Colon, and a day later the officer in charge of the Colombian forces was persuaded by a generous bribe to reëmbark his troops and leave. Events continued to follow one another with startling rapidity. On the 6th the *de facto* government was recognized and a week later Bunau-Varilla was received by President Roosevelt as envoy extraordinary and minister plenipotentiary of the Republic of Panama. Such hasty recognition of a new government was of course without precedent in the annals of American diplomacy, and it naturally confirmed the rumor that the whole affair had been prearranged. On October 10, President Roosevelt had written a personal letter to Dr. Albert Shaw, editor of the *Review of Reviews*, who was a strong advocate of the Panama route, in which he said:

Roosevelt delighted

> Privately, I freely say to you that I should be delighted if Panama were an independent state, or if it made itself so at this moment; but for me to say so publicly would amount to an instigation of a revolt, and therefore I cannot say it.[22]

This letter throws an interesting light on an article in the *Review of Reviews* for November of the same year in which Doctor Shaw discussed the question, "What if Panama should revolt?" and outlined with remarkable prophetic insight the subsequent course of events.

In his annual message of December 7, 1903, the President discussed the Panama revolution and undertook to

[22] *Literary Digest*, October 29, 1904.

justify his course under the treaty of 1846. This message failed to allay public criticism, and on January 4, 1904, he sent a special message to Congress in defense of his action. He held that Colombia was not entitled "to bar the transit of the world's traffic across the isthmus," and that the intervention of the United States was justified, (1) by our treaty rights, (2) by our international interests, and (3) by the interests of "collective civilization." The "legal" argument in this message, if we may dignify it by that name, is reported to have been prepared by Root and Knox, both at that time members of the Cabinet. Several years later, after Mr. Roosevelt had retired from the presidency, he expressed the real truth in a public speech when he said:

His attempt to allay public criticism

> If I had followed traditional conservative methods I should have submitted a dignified state paper of probably two hundred pages to the Congress and the debate would be going on yet, but I took the Canal Zone and let Congress debate, and while the debate goes on the canal does also.

The reason why the President did not wish the matter to go before Congress again was that he had decided upon the Panama route, and he knew that when Congress convened in December, the situation remaining unchanged, action would be taken to compel him to adopt the alternative of the Spooner amendment and go to the Nicaragua route. His object in the hasty recognition of the Panama revolution was therefore to make the Panama route an accomplished fact before Congress should meet. This was the attitude definitely assumed in the message of January 4, 1904, in the course of which he said:

> The only question now before us is that of the ratification of the treaty. For it is to be remembered that a failure to ratify the treaty will not undo what has been done, will not restore Panama to Colombia, and will not alter our obligation to keep the transit open across the Isthmus, and to prevent any outside power from menacing this transit.

Fait accompli

The treaty with Panama

The treaty referred to was the convention with Panama which had been signed November 18, 1903, and which was ratified by the Senate February 23, 1904, by a vote of 66 to 14. By the terms of this agreement the United States guaranteed the independence of the Panama Republic, and agreed to pay the Panama Republic a sum of $10,000,000 upon the exchange of ratifications and an annual rental of $250,000 beginning nine years thereafter. Panama on her part granted to the United States in perpetuity a zone of land ten miles wide for the construction of a canal, the United States receiving as full power and authority over this strip and the waters adjacent as if it were the sovereign of the said territory.[23] The construction of the canal was at once undertaken and the work was carried through successfully by General Goethals and a corps of army engineers. It was opened to commerce August 15, 1914, though it was not completed at that time and traffic was subsequently interrupted by landslides.

Strained relations with Colombia

The methods employed by President Roosevelt in the acquisition of the Panama Canal Zone caused indignation and alarm throughout Latin America and created strained relations with Colombia. The Colombian government refused to recognize the independence of the Republic of Panama and demanded that her claim to Panama as well as her interests in the canal should be submitted to arbitration. Colombia claimed that President Roosevelt had misinterpreted the treaty of 1846, which established mutual obligations between the United States and Colombia with reference to the isthmus, by construing its provisions as obligations to the world at large against Colombia. As the United States had always advocated the submission to arbitration of questions involving the construction of treaties, the demand of Colombia proved embarrassing, but both Secretary Hay and his successor, Secretary Root, rejected the demand for arbitration on

[23]*For. Rel.*, 1904, p. 543.

the ground that the questions involved were of a political nature.[24]

Root proposes adjustment of differences

In January, 1909, shortly before the close of the Roosevelt administration, Secretary Root undertook to reestablish friendly relations with Colombia through the negotiation in the city of Washington of three treaties, one between the United States and the Republic of Colombia, one between the United States and the Republic of Panama, and one between Colombia and Panama. In the treaty between Colombia and Panama the Republic of Colombia recognized fully the independence of Panama, and the Republic of Panama made an assignment to Colombia of the first ten installments of $250,000, the amount due annually to the Republic of Panama from the United States as rental for the canal. According to the treaty between the United States and the Republic of Panama, concluded November 18, 1903, the payment of this annual sum was to begin nine years from date. It was now agreed that the first annual payment should be regarded as due four years from the exchange of ratifications of the said treaty, so that of the $2,500,000 to be paid to Colombia, half would be paid by the United States and half by Panama. In the new treaty between the United States and Panama the necessary modification of the treaty of 1903 was made so as to permit of this assignment of the first ten installments to Colombia. In the treaty between the United States and Colombia the most important provision was as follows:

Colombia to be given special privileges in the canal

> The Republic of Colombia shall have liberty at all times to convey through the ship canal now in course of construction by the United States across the Isthmus of Panama the troops, materials for war, and ships of war of the Republic of Colombia, without paying any duty to the United States; even in the case of an international war between Colombia and another country.

[24] 62 Cong., 3 Sess., H. Doc. No. 1444, pp. 2, 3; 65 Cong., Special Sess., Sen. Doc. No. 1, pp. 47, 48.

It was further provided that the products of the soil and industry of Colombia should be admitted to the canal zone subject only to such duty as would be payable on similar products of the United States under similar conditions, and Colombian mails were to have free passage through the canal zone on payment of such duties or charges as were laid on the mails of the United States.[25]

Columbia rejects the proposed treaty

These tripartite treaties were, of course, to stand or fall together. The United States and Panama promptly ratified the agreements to which they were parties, but Colombia rejected the arrangement with indignation. In fact, when the terms of the settlement were made public, the Colombian administration that urged their acceptance was overthrown, and the Colombian envoy who participated in the negotiation of the treaties was forced to flee from the country with an indignant mob at his heels. Colombia was not to be appeased by the paltry sum of $2,500,000.

Statement of Colombia's grievances

The Taft administration made repeated efforts to placate Colombia, but without success. On September 30, 1912, Mr. Du Bois, the American minister to Colombia, submitted to Secretary Knox an interesting review of the whole question in the course of which, after referring to the friendly relations that had so long subsisted between the two countries, he said:

> Nine years ago this was changed suddenly and unexpectedly when President Roosevelt denied to Colombia the right to land her troops upon her own soil to suppress a threatened revolt and maintain a sovereignty guaranteed by treaty stipulations. The breach came and it has been growing wider since that hour. By refusing to allow Colombia to uphold her sovereign rights over a territory where she had held dominion for eighty years, the friendship of nearly a century disappeared, the indignation of every Colombian, and millions of other Latin-Americans, was aroused and is still most intensely alive. The confidence and trust in the justice and fairness of the United States, so long manifested, has completely vanished, and the maleficent

[25] *Op. cit.*, pp. 24–34.

influence of this condition is permeating public opinion in all Latin-American countries, a condition which, if remedial measures are not invoked, will work inestimable harm throughout the Western Hemisphere.[26]

An impartial summary of claims

Mr. Du Bois then proceeded to state at length Colombia's claims which he summarized as follows: "Panama Railroad annuities, $16,000,000; value of railroad, $16,446,942; Panama Canal rights, $17,500,000; cost of Costa Rican boundary arbitration, $200,000; total, $50,446,942. [The total should be $50,146,942.] Besides this sum, Colombia has lost the Province of Panama, whose value cannot be readily estimated."

In conclusion he urged the importance of a speedy adjustment of the differences with Colombia in the following words:

South America is advancing along commercial lines with giant strides. The character of the future relations of the United States with that country will be of signal importance. Friendly intercourse with all Latin America should be carefully developed and maintained, and especially is this important with Colombia, which borders the isthmus, has fine ports on both oceans, and is destined to become an influential factor in the political and commercial life of South America, especially in all countries bordering on the Caribbean sea. To approach Colombia in a conciliatory spirit and seek a renewal of her ancient friendship would not only be a wise and just move on the part of the United States, but as Colombia and all South and Central America firmly believe that the government of the United States was unjust in the Panama incident, from which has come infinite distress to Colombia, it would be a benevolent and fraternal act, and the time to move is the present, before the canal opens and while the public sentiment of both countries is in harmony with the movement.[27]

At the time that the above report on relations with Colombia was prepared by Mr. Du Bois he was in this country, having come home to confer with the Depart-

[26]*Op. cit.*, p. 35.

[27]*Ibid.*, p. 44.

Settlement proposed by the Taft administration

ment of State as to the program to be followed in the settlement of the differences with Colombia. On his return to Bogotá, Mr. Du Bois submitted the following proposals to the Colombian government: (1) ratification of the Root treaties, involving the payment to Colombia of the first ten installments of the annual rental of the canal zone amounting to $2,500,000; (2) the payment of $10,000,000 by the United States to Colombia for the right to build an interoceanic canal by the Atrato route and for the lease of the islands of Old Providence and St. Andrews as coaling stations; (3) the good offices of the United States on behalf of Colombia in bringing about an adjustment of the boundary line between Colombia and Panama; (4) the submission to arbitration of the claims of Colombia to reversionary rights in the Panama Railroad assumed by the United States under Article XXII of the treaty of 1903 between the United States and Panama, estimated by Mr. Taft's Secretary of War at over $16,000,000; and (5) the granting of preferential rights to Colombia in the use of the Panama Canal.

Colombia proposes arbitration

The Colombian government promptly rejected these proposals and in reply demanded "arbitration of the whole question of Panama or a direct proposition on the part of the United States to give Colombia compensation for all the moral, physical, and financial losses which she sustained as a result of the separation of Panama." The Colombian minister declared:

> Should Colombia grant any territorial privileges to the United States after the wrong that country has inflicted upon this republic, it would result in intense agitation and possible revolution. It seems as though your people have never fully realized the enormity of the wrong the United States has perpetrated against the Colombian people.

Mr. Du Bois then asked whether Colombia would accept $10,000,000, the good offices of the United States in settling the differences with Panama, arbitration of the reversionary rights in the Panama Railroad, and preferential rights in the canal, without granting to the United States any privileges or concessions whatever. Receiving a negative reply to this proposal, Mr. Du Bois, acting on his own responsibility, then inquired informally whether $25,000,000 without options of any kind would satisfy Colombia. The answer was that Colombia would accept nothing but the arbitration of the whole Panama question. Mr. Du Bois was instructed February 20, 1913, to stop negotiations. In reporting the matter to the President, Secretary Knox said that Colombia seemed determined to treat with the incoming Democratic administration.[28]

Colombia expects better terms from Wilson

The Bryan treaty

When the Wilson administration came in, Secretary Bryan took up the negotiations with Colombia where Knox dropped them, and concluded a treaty according to the terms of which the United States was to express "sincere regret that anything should have occurred to interrupt or to mar the relations of cordial friendship that had so long subsisted between the two nations," and to pay Colombia $25,000,000. The treaty further granted Colombia the same preferential rights in the use of the canal which the Taft administration had proposed, and in return Colombia agreed to recognize the independence of Panama and to accept a boundary line laid down in the treaty. This treaty was submitted to the Senate June 16, 1914. As soon as its terms were made public ex-President Roosevelt denounced it as blackmail, and wrote a letter to the chairman of the Senate Committee on Foreign Affairs requesting to be heard before any action was taken on the treaty. On April 20, 1921, a few weeks after the beginning of the Harding administration, the treaty was ratified by the Senate with certain amendments. The principal one was

[28] *Op. cit.*, pp. 53–79.

Held up by the Senate until the Harding administration

the omission of the clause expressing regret and the substitution of the statement that the object of the treaty was the desire on the part of both governments "to remove all the misunderstandings growing out of the political events in Panama in November, 1903.' The revised treaty also provided that the $25,000,000, instead of being paid in cash, should be paid in five annual instalments. The treaty as revised was ratified by Colombia, March 1, 1922, and proclaimed March 30.[29] American oil interests apparently found it difficult to do business in Colombia in the existing state of strained relations, and used their influence to get the treaty ratified. Roosevelt was dead and his friends, including Henry Cabot Lodge, who had held the treaty up for years, now voted for ratification.

[29] *Treaties and Conventions,* III, 2538.

CHAPTER XXIII

THE CARIBBEAN POLICIES

The advance of the United States into the Caribbean

As a result of the Spanish War the United States acquired Porto Rico and a protectorate over Cuba. Thus began the long-delayed advance into the Caribbean, which made rapid strides during the next two decades. But the real turning point in the recent history of the West Indies was the Hay-Pauncefote Treaty of 1901, under the terms of which Great Britain relinquished her claim to an equal voice with the United States in the control of an isthmian canal on which she had insisted for half a century. While the Hay-Pauncefote Treaty was limited in terms to the canal question, it was in reality of much wider significance. It amounted in effect to the transference of naval supremacy in the West Indies to the United States, for since its signature Great Britain has withdrawn her squadron from this important strategic area. So marked was Great Britain's change of attitude toward the United States at this time that some writers concluded that a secret treaty of alliance was made between the two countries in 1897. The absurdity of such a statement was pointed out at the time by Senator Lodge.

Britain's change of attitude

England's change of attitude is not difficult to understand. For one hundred years after the battle of Trafalgar she had pursued the policy of maintaining a navy large enough to meet all comers. With the rapid growth of the navies of Russia, Japan, and Germany during the closing years of the nineteenth century, England realized that she could no longer pursue a policy of isolation. Our acquisition of the Philippines, the Hawaiian

Islands, and Porto Rico and our determination to build an isthmian canal made a large American navy inevitable. Great Britain realized, therefore, that she would have to cast about for future allies. It was on considerations of this kind that she signed the Hay-Pauncefote Treaty with the United States in 1901, and the defensive alliance with Japan in 1902. In view of the fact that the United States was bent on carrying out the long-deferred canal scheme, Great Britain realized that a further insistence on her rights under the Clayton-Bulwer treaty would lead to friction and possible conflict. She wisely decided, therefore, to recede from the position which she had held for half a century and to give us a free hand in the acquisition and control of the canal at whatever point we might choose to build it. In signing the Hay-Pauncefote Treaty she gracefully recognized the fact that the United States had paramount interests in the Caribbean which it was unwise for her to contest. Since the signature of that treaty American supremacy in this area has not been seriously questioned.

Formation of new policies

The determination to build a canal not only rendered inevitable the adoption of a policy of naval supremacy in the Caribbean Sea, but led to the formulation of new political policies to be applied in the zone of the Caribbean—what Admiral Chester calls the larger Panama Canal Zone—that is, the West Indies, Mexico and Central America, Colombia, and Venezuela. The policies referred to included the establishment of protectorates, the supervision of finances, the control of all canal routes, the acquisition of naval stations, and the policing and administration of disorderly countries.

The extent of American power and influence

The advance of the United States in the Caribbean since the Spanish War has been rapid. The acquisition of Porto Rico and the establishment of a protectorate over Cuba were the natural outcome of that struggle. In 1904, we acquired the canal zone under circumstances already described. The following year President Roosevelt established financial supervision over the Dominican Republic. In 1915, the United States landed marines in Haiti and a treaty was soon drafted under which we assumed financial supervision and administrative control over the affairs of that country. In 1916, we acquired by treaty from Nicaragua an exclusive right-of-way for a canal through her territory and the lease of a naval station on Fonseca Bay, and in 1917 we acquired by treaty from Denmark her holdings in the West Indies known as the Virgin Islands.

In 1904, President Roosevelt made a radical departure from the traditional policy of the United States in proposing that we should assume the financial administration of the Dominican Republic in order to prevent certain European powers from resorting to the forcible collection of debts due their subjects. On September 12, 1904, Minister Dawson reported to the State Department that the debt of Santo Domingo was $32,280,000, the estimated revenues from customs receipts $1,850,000, and the proposed budget for current expenses $1,300,000, leaving only $550,000 with which to meet payments of interest, then accruing and in arrears, amounting to $2,600,000. About $22,000,000 of this debt was due to European creditors. Most of this indebtedness had been incurred by revolutionary leaders who had at various times taken forcible possession of the government and hastened to raise all the money they could by the sale of bonds, leaving the responsibility with their successors. The European creditors of Santo Domingo were pressing for the recognition of their claims. Germany seemed especially determined to force a settlement of her demands, and it was well known that Germany had for years regarded the Monroe Doctrine as the main hindrance in the way of her acquiring a foothold in Latin America. The only effective method of collecting the interest on the foreign debt ap-

The Dominican Republic in state of bankruptcy

peared to be the seizure and administration of the Dominican custom houses by some foreign power or group of foreign powers. President Roosevelt foresaw that such an occupation of the custom houses would, in view of the large debt, constitute the occupation of American territory by European powers for an indefinite period of time, and would therefore be a violation of the Monroe Doctrine. He had before him also the results of a somewhat similar financial administration of Egypt undertaken jointly by England and France in 1878, and after Arabi's revolt continued by England alone, with the result that Egypt soon came under the control of the British Crown to almost as great a degree as if it had been formally annexed. President Roosevelt concluded, therefore, that where it was necessary to place a bankrupt American republic in the hands of a receiver, the United States must undertake to act as receiver and take over the administration of its finances.

Financial supervision necessary

The policy that he was about to adopt was stated as follows in his annual message of December 6, 1904:

Roosevelt's warning to disorderly states

> Any country whose people conduct themselves well can count upon our hearty friendship. If a nation shows that it knows how to act with reasonable efficiency and decency in social and political matters, if it keeps order and pays its obligations, it need fear no interference from the United States. Chronic wrongdoing, or an impotence which results in a general loosening of the ties of civilized society, may in America, as elsewhere, ultimately require intervention by some civilized nation, and in the Western Hemisphere, the adherence of the United States to the Monroe Doctrine may force the United States, however reluctantly, in flagrant cases of such wrongdoing or impotence, to the exercise of an international police power.

About the same time Minister Dawson was directed by Secretary Hay to suggest to the Dominican government that it request the United States to take charge of its customs. As the Dominican government saw no other way out of its difficulties, it responded to this suggestion, and on February 4, 1905, a protocol was signed by Mr. Dawson and the Dominican foreign minister which provided that the United States should guarantee the territorial integrity of the Dominican Republic, take charge of its custom houses, administer its finances, and settle its obligations, foreign as well as domestic. In calling the new agreement a "protocol" instead of a "treaty," the President had probably not intended to submit it to the Senate, but the proposal to depart so radically from our past policy created so much criticism that the Senate was finally asked to ratify the protocol in regular form. This they failed to do, but the President did not propose to be thwarted in this way. As the Senate would not sanction his appointment of a receiver of customs for Santo Domingo, he drafted a *modus vivendi*, under the terms of which the President of the Dominican Republic appointed a receiver of customs named unofficially by President Roosevelt, who proceeded to administer the affairs of the republic under the protection of the United States navy, whose ships the President could as commander-in-chief order wherever he pleased. The President's course met with determined opposition both in and out of Congress, but as he was bent on having his way and continued to carry out his policy without the sanction of the Senate, that body finally decided that it would be best to give the arrangement a definite legal status. On February 25, 1907, the Senate agreed to the ratification of a revised treaty which omitted the territorial-guarantee clause, but provided that the President of the United States should appoint a general receiver of Dominican customs and such assistants as he might deem necessary; that the government of the United States should afford them such protection as might be necessary for the performance of their duties; and that until the bonded debt should be paid in full, the Dominican govern-

The Senate withholds consent from Roosevelt's proposed receivership

The policy carried out under *modus vivendi*

ment would not increase its debt except with the consent of the United States. In the meantime, under the *interim* arrangement, conditions in Santo Domingo had greatly improved, the customs receipts had nearly doubled, and the creditors had agreed to compromise their claims, so that the total debt at the time the above treaty was ratified amounted to not more than $17,000,000.[1]

New Dominican fiscal convention

In 1924 a new fiscal convention superseding that of 1907 was signed, authorizing the Dominican government to borrow not more than $25,000,000. The President of the United States by the terms of this convention appointed a General Receiver of Customs to collect the customs duties, apply them to the service of foreign bond issues, and pay over the balance to the Dominican Republic. Whenever the annual customs revenues exceeded $4,000,000, ten per cent of the excess was to be applied to the redemption of outstanding bonds. The General Receiver was to continue to collect the customs duties "until the payment or retirement of any and all bonds issued by the Dominican Republic." Several months before the signing of the new fiscal convention we began the withdrawal of our marines. On September 18, 1924, the removal was complete, and on September 29 the Dominican Republic was admitted to membership in the League of Nations.

Taft attempts to apply same policy to Nicaragua and Honduras

In spite of the criticism that President Roosevelt's policy encountered, the Taft administration not only continued it in Santo Domingo, but tried to extend it to Nicaragua and Honduras. The five republics of Central America had been for years in a state of political and economic disorder as the result of wars and revolutions. In 1906 there was a war between Guatemala and Salvador. President Roosevelt invited President Diaz of Mexico to unite with him in an offer of mediation, which resulted in a peace con-

[1]*For. Rel.*, 1905, p. 298; Moore, *Digest of Int. Law*, VI, 518–529; *Am. Journal of Int. Law*, I, 287, and Documentary Supplement, p. 231.

GULF OF MEXICO
Key West
Miami
Nassau
NEW PROVIDENCE
ANDROS I.
Havana New York 1197 Miles
Havana
CUBA
Cienfuegos
Camaguey
Havana Santiago 635 Miles
Havana San Juan 975 Miles
Guantanamo
Santiago de Cuba
Merida
Yucatan
MEXICO
San Miguel
COZUMEL I.
Vera Cruz - Pt.au Prince 1383 Miles
Vera Cruz - Kingston 1170 Miles
JAMAICA
Kingston
Belize - Kingston 665 Miles
Belize
BR. HOND.
GUATEMALA
Tela
HONDURAS
New Orleans - Colón 1380 Miles
CARI
Limón - Kingston 610 Miles
Colón - Kingston 555 Miles
Colón - New York 1975 Miles
SALVADOR
San Salvador
San Lorenzo
Wanks R.
Libertad
NICARAGUA
Lake Nicaragua
Managua
San Juan del Sur
COSTA RICA
Punta Arenas
Limón
San José
Cartagena
Colón (Cristobal)
PANAMA
Panama City
Balboa (U.S.)
David
Turbo
COL
PACIFIC OCEAN
GENERAL DRAFTING CO. INC., N.Y.

5. T

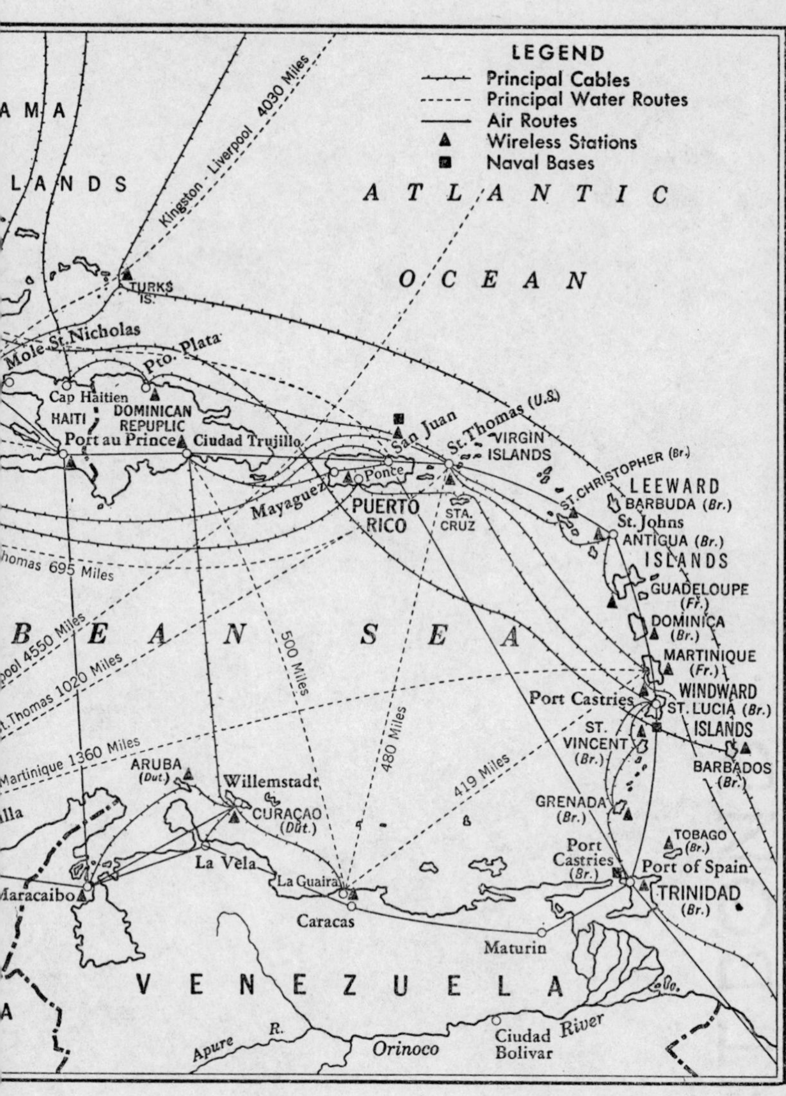

LEGEND
Principal Cables
Principal Water Routes
Air Routes
Wireless Stations
Naval Bases
A T L A N T I C
O C E A N
AMA
LANDS
Kingston - Liverpool 4030 Miles
TURKS IS.
Mole St. Nicholas
Pto. Plata
Cap Haitien
HAITI
DOMINICAN REPUPLIC
Port au Prince
Ciudad Trujillo
San Juan
St. Thomas (U.S.)
VIRGIN ISLANDS
ST. CHRISTOPHER (Br.)
LEEWARD
BARBUDA (Br.)
St. Johns
ANTIGUA (Br.)
ISLANDS
Mayaguez
Ponce
PUERTO RICO
STA. CRUZ
GUADELOUPE (Fr.)
DOMINICA (Br.)
MARTINIQUE (Fr.)
WINDWARD
ST. LUCIA (Br.)
ISLANDS
Port Castries
ST. VINCENT (Br.)
BARBADOS (Br.)
GRENADA (Br.)
TOBAGO (Br.)
Port Castries (Br.)
Port of Spain
TRINIDAD (Br.)
homas 695 Miles
B E A N S E A
ool 4550 Miles
t. Thomas 1020 Miles
500 Miles
480 Miles
419 Miles
Martinique 1360 Miles
ARUBA (Dut.)
Willemstadt
CURAÇAO (Dut.)
lla
La Vela
La Guaira
aracaibo
Caracas
Maturin
V E N E Z U E L A
Apure R.
Orinoco River
Ciudad Bolivar
A

BEAN

ference held aboard the U. S. S. *Marblehead.* At this conference the belligerents agreed to suspend hostilities and to attend another conference for the purpose of drafting a general treaty of peace. The second conference was held at San José, Costa Rica, but President Zelaya of Nicaragua declined to send a representative because he was unwilling to recognize the right of the United States to intervene in Central American affairs. At this time Zelaya was systematically interfering in the internal affairs of the other Central American states, and exercised such complete control over the government of Honduras that Guatemala and Salvador were endeavoring to stir up revolutions against him in that state and in Nicaragua. War was about to break out in the summer of 1907 when President Roosevelt and President Diaz again intervened diplomatically and persuaded the Central American governments to suspend warlike preparations and to attend a conference in the city of Washington. In November, the delegates of the five Central American states met in the Bureau of American Republics and were addressed by Secretary Root and the Mexican ambassador. The delegates adopted a general treaty of peace, providing for the settlement of existing differences and for the establishment of a Central American court of justice composed of five judges, one to be elected by the legislature of each state. The five republics agreed to submit to this tribunal all controversies, of whatever nature, that might arise between them which could not be settled through ordinary diplomatic channels.

Review of disorders in Central America

Zelaya stirs up strife in neighboring republics

But President Zelaya of Nicaragua, who still controlled Honduras, continued his interference in the affairs of the other republics by encouraging revolutionary movements and sending out filibustering expeditions. He was also hostile to the Central American court of justice, and it became evident that there was little chance of permanent peace as long as Zelaya remained in power. When, therefore, in October, 1909, members of the conservative party started a revolution at Bluefields against Zelaya's government, the movement was regarded with sympathy in the other Central American republics and in Washington. Conditions became so intolerable that many people in Nicaragua and Honduras appealed to the United States to intervene for the purpose of restoring order. President Diaz of Mexico was friendly to Zelaya and informed the United States that he did not care to take any further action. This brought to an end the coöperative efforts of the two governments and thereafter the United States had to act alone. Nothing was done, however, until two Americans were executed by Zelaya's order in November, 1909. As a result of these executions, which were without legal excuse and attended by barbarous cruelties, President Taft promptly severed diplomatic relations with Zelaya's government. In a dispatch to the Nicaraguan *chargé*, December 1, 1909, Secretary Knox said:

Denounced by Secretary Knox

> Since the Washington conventions of 1907, it is notorious that President Zelaya has almost continuously kept Central America in tension or turmoil; that he has repeatedly and flagrantly violated the provisions of the conventions, and, by a baleful influence upon Honduras, whose neutrality the conventions were to assure, has sought to discredit those sacred international obligations, to the great detriment of Costa Rica, El Salvador, and Guatemala, whose governments meanwhile appear to have been able patiently to strive for the loyal support of the engagements so solemnly undertaken at Washington under the auspices of the United States and Mexico.

He added that under the régime of President Zelaya republican institutions had ceased to exist in Nicaragua except in name, that public opinion and the press had been throttled, and that prison had been the reward of any tendency to real patriotism. The government of the United States was convinced, he said, "that the revolution represents the ideals and the will of a majority of the

Nicaraguan people more faithfully than does the government of President Zelaya."[2]

Downfall of Zelaya's government

This note caused the speedy downfall of Zelaya's government. He tried to perpetuate his party in power by resigning the presidency to Doctor Madriz, but President Taft refused to recognize the Madriz government, and a few months later it was overthrown and the revolutionary party came into power, first under the presidency of Estrada and then under that of Adolfo Diaz.

Treaties with Honduras and Nicaragua rejected by the Senate

The revolution had paralyzed agriculture and commerce and thrown the country into financial chaos. In October, 1910, the United States government sent Thomas C. Dawson to Managua to investigate conditions and to straighten out the political and financial affairs of Nicaragua. While he was engaged in this task, Secretary Knox negotiated at Washington two treaties, one between the United States and Honduras, signed January 10, 1911, and a similar treaty between the United States and Nicaragua, signed June 6. These treaties were intended to place the two countries concerned under the financial supervision of the United States. They provided for the appointment in each case of a collector of customs approved by the President of the United States, and made the customs receipts responsible for loans to be advanced by American bankers. The collectorship of customs was immediately established in Nicaragua without waiting for the ratification of the treaty by the Senate, and through the efforts of the State Department American bankers made preliminary loans to the Nicaraguan government. When the Senate rejected the treaty, the bankers refused to make further loans, and the situation was almost as bad as ever. In October, 1911, General Mena, Minister of War and head of a faction of his own, was elected president of the republic by the Assembly, but as this was contrary to an agreement which had been made with

[2] *For. Rel.*, 1909, p. 455.

Dawson, it did not meet with the approval of the United States, and President Diaz removed Mena from office and forced him to flee from the capital. Shortly afterward Mena was taken seriously ill, and the opposition to President Diaz fell again under the control of Zelaya's followers. As President Diaz was unable to guarantee protection to the life and property of foreigners, he asked the United States for assistance. In answer to this request American marines were landed at Corinto and assumed control of the national railway which connected that port with the capital and the principal cities. The American minister made a public announcement to the effect that the United States intended to keep open the routes of communication and to protect American life and property. This announcement was a great blow to the revolutionists. Some of their leaders surrendered voluntarily to the American marines, while others were attacked and forced to surrender positions along the railroad which they insisted upon holding. In these operations seven American marines lost their lives. From 1911 to 1925 a legation guard of one hundred marines was maintained at the capital of Nicaragua and a warship was stationed at Corinto. The marines were withdrawn in August, 1925.

American marines landed in Nicaragua

Second Knox treaty with Nicaragua unratified

After the revolutionary movement was thus overthrown, Secretary Knox negotiated a new treaty for the purpose of helping the Nicaraguan government out of the financial straits in which it found itself. Great Britain was threatening to force the payment of its claims and certain German interests, which were operating banana plantations in Costa Rica, were trying to secure from the Nicaraguan government a concession for the construction of a canal from the Great Lake to the Atlantic along the San Juan River. According to the terms of the Knox treaty the United States was to pay Nicaragua $3,000,000 in return for an exclusive right-of-way for a canal through her territory, a naval base on the Gulf of Fonseca, and the lease for ninety-nine years of the Great Corn and Little Corn Islands in the Caribbean. This treaty was submitted to the Senate February 26, 1913, but the close of the Taft administration was then at hand, and no action was taken.

The first Bryan treaty not approved by the Senate

The Wilson administration followed the same policy, however, and in July, 1913, Secretary Bryan submitted a third treaty with Nicaragua containing the provisions of the second Knox treaty and in addition certain provisions of the Platt Amendment which defines our protectorate over Cuba. This treaty aroused strong opposition in the other Central American States, and Costa Rica, Salvador, and Honduras filed formal protests with the United States government against its ratification on the ground that it would convert Nicaragua into a protectorate of the United States and thus defeat the long-cherished plan for a union of the Central American republics. They also claimed that the treaty infringed their own rights. In 1858, Costa Rica had been granted perpetual rights of free navigation in the lower part of the San Juan River, and Nicaragua had agreed to consult her before granting any concessions for the construction of an interoceanic canal. Salvador and Honduras objected to the establishment of a naval base in the Gulf of Fonseca, in close proximity to their coasts. They also asserted proprietary rights in the Gulf of Fonseca, claiming that Salvador, Honduras, and Nicaragua, as successors of the old Central American Federation, exercised joint ownership over the gulf. Efforts were made by the United States to arrive at a settlement with Costa Rica and Salvador on the basis of a money payment, but without success. Moreover, the Senate of the United States objected to the protectorate feature of the treaty and refused to ratify it, but the negotiations were renewed, and on August 5, 1914, a new treaty, which omits the provisions of the Platt Amendment, was signed at Washington.[3] This treaty,

[3] *Treaties and Conventions*, III, 2740.

Revised treaty ratified

which was finally ratified by the Senate, February 18, 1916, granted to the United States in perpetuity the exclusive right to construct a canal by way of the San Juan River and Lake Nicaragua, and leased to the United States for ninety-nine years a naval base on the Gulf of Fonseca, and also the Great Corn and Little Corn Islands as coaling stations. The consideration for these favors was the sum of $3,000,000 to be expended, with the approval of the Secretary of State of the United States, in paying the public debt of Nicaragua, and for other purposes to be agreed on by the two contracting parties.

In consenting to the ratification of the treaty the Senate, in order to meet the objections raised by Costa Rica, Salvador, and Honduras, attached to their resolution of ratification the proviso "that nothing in said convention is intended to affect any existing right of any of the said states." This reservation did not satisfy Costa Rica and Salvador, who took their cases to the Central American Court of Justice, requesting that Nicaragua be enjoined from carrying out the provisions of the treaty. Nicaragua refused to be a party to the action, but the court nevertheless assumed jurisdiction. Its decision in the case of Costa Rica was announced September 30, 1916. It declared that Nicaragua had violated Costa Rica's rights, but, as the court had no jurisdiction over the United States, it declined to declare the treaty void. A similar decision in the case of Salvador was handed down on March 2, 1917.[4]

Nicaragua's neighbors appeal to Central American Court

Neither Nicaragua nor the United States has paid any attention to the decision of the Central American Court of Justice, which was set up under such favorable auspices by the Washington conventions. As a matter of fact, the court had not fulfilled the expectations of those who had been interested in its establishment, but it was unfortunate that it should have received its *coup de grâce* from the

Criticism of American policy

[4]D. G. Munro, *The Five Republics of Central America*, 257.

United States. Furthermore, it was charged that the State Department, under the Knox régime, exploited the situation in Central America for the benefit of American capitalists, and that the Wilson administration maintained for years a minority party in power in Nicaragua through the presence of marines at the capital and a warship at Corinto.

Coolidge follows policy of previous administrations

The Coolidge administration continued to follow the policy of the previous administrations. Soon after the withdrawal of the United States Marines in August, 1925, the struggles of the opposing factions to obtain control of the Nicaraguan government, resulting in disorder and endangering the lives and property of foreigners, prompted the Washington-supported President Adolfo Diaz to appeal to the United States for help in restoring order. Great Britain, Italy, and Belgium requested our government to protect their nationals, a request which was interpreted as a recognition of our special position in Nicaragua. In a special message to Congress, January 10, 1927, President Coolidge stated the reasons for ordering American marines to Nicaragua: (1) protection of life and property; (2) enforcement of the Central American Treaty of 1923;[5] (3) protection of the rights of the United States in the Panama and proposed Nicaraguan canals; and (4) jeopardy of American interests by outside influences or by any foreign power.

The strength and success of the Liberal revolutionaries necessitated additional American forces to support the Conservative Diaz. It became clear that the encouragement given to Diaz by our government in the way of recognition, rifles, machine guns, and ammunition offered no solution to the difficulties. In April, 1927, Colonel Henry L. Stimson went to Nicaragua as the personal representative of President Coolidge to settle the difficulties.

[5]Although the United States is not a party to this treaty, it has felt a moral obligation to apply the treaty principles. See below p. 561.

United States supervises election

He found that the evil of government domination of elections was the root of the Nicaraguan problem. The party in power controlled the voting to such a point that free elections were impossible. Accordingly, Colonel Stimson proposed to the warring factions supervision of the 1928 election by the United States, retention of Diaz in office until the election, disarmament of contending armies, a constabulary organized and trained by United States officers, and a temporary continuance of American forces.[6] The proposals were accepted. Since 1928 two presidential elections and one congressional election have been held under the supervision of the constabulary trained by American officers. On January 2, 1933, complete evacuation of all American troops from Nicaragua was effected. If the supervised elections can not be said to have transformed the political habits of the people, they have at least, in the language of Professor H. W. Dodds, who was technical adviser to the United States Electoral Mission in Nicaragua, "provided a physical exhibition of a new method of changing governments and should form a useful precedent for those Nicaraguans who regret the bitterness and irrationality of the traditional party struggles and who wish to eliminate the unhappy cycle of destructive revolutions."[7]

Haiti lapsing into barbarism

The treaty with the Negro republic of Haiti, ratified by the Senate February 28, 1916, carried the Caribbean policies of the United States to the farthest limits short of actual annexation. Shortly before the outbreak of the European war, Haitian finances were in such bad shape as the result of internal disorders that there was grave danger of European intervention, and the United States was considering the question of acquiring supervision over the finances of the republic. In June, 1915, a

---

[6]See H. W. Dodds, "American Supervision of the Nicaraguan Election," *Foreign Affairs*, April, 1929.

[7]*Op. cit.*, p. 496.

crisis in the internal affairs of Haiti seemed imminent and, at the request of the State Department, Rear-Admiral Caperton was ordered to Haitian waters. Towards the latter part of July the government of President Guillaume was overthrown, and he and members of his cabinet took refuge in the French and Dominican legations. These buildings were entered by a mob, President Guillaume was slain at the gate of the French legation, his body cut in pieces, and dragged about the town. Admiral Caperton at once landed a force of marines at Port au Prince in order to protect the lives and property of foreigners. An additional force was brought from Guantanamo and the total number raised to two thousand and placed under the command of Colonel Waller. There was but slight resistance to the landing of the marines, but a few days later a conflict occurred in which two Americans and an unknown number of Haitians were killed.[8] On August 12, a new president was elected who coöperated with the American forces in their efforts to establish peace and order, and on September 16 a treaty with the United States was signed at Port au Prince. This treaty provided for the establishment of a receivership of Haitian customs under the control of the United States similar in most respects to that established over the Dominican Republic. It also provided for the appointment, on the nomination of the President of the United States, of a financial adviser, who was to assist in the settlement of the foreign debt and direct expenditures of the surplus for the development of the agricultural, mineral, and commercial resources of the republic. It provided further for a native constabulary under American officers appointed by the President of Haiti upon nomination of the President of the United States. And it extended to Haiti the main provisions of the Platt Amendment.[9] By controlling the

Landing of American marines

Supervision of Haitian finances and police

[8]Secretary of the Navy, Annual Report, 1915, pp. 15–17.

[9]*Treaties and Conventions*, III, 2673.

internal financial administration of the government the United States hoped to remove all incentives for those revolutions which have in the past had for their object a raid on the public treasury, and by controlling the customs and maintaining order the United States hoped to avoid all possibility of foreign intervention. The treaty was to remain in force for a period of ten years and for another period of ten years if either party should present specific reasons for continuing it on the ground that its purpose had not been fully accomplished.

When the first ten-year period was up, the hoped-for progress in preparing the Haitians for the control of their own national existence was not realized.[10] Continued intervention gave rise to fear on the part of many Haitians as well as on the part of some Latin-American states that the United States intended permanent control. To allay this fear Secretary Hughes declared at Havana:

> We would leave Haiti at any time that we had reasonable expectations of stability, and could be assured that the withdrawal would not be the occasion for a recurrence of bloodshed. Meanwhile we are endeavoring in every important direction to assist in the establishment of conditions for stability and prosperity, not that we may stay in Haiti, but that we may get out at the earliest opportunity.[11]

Control extended to 1936

The seething discontent of the Haitians which culminated in strikes and bloodshed moved several Senators to protest against the policy the State Department was pursuing in Haiti. As a result, President Hoover on February 8, 1932, sent the Forbes Commission to investigate when and how "we are to withdraw from Haiti" and to determine what policy we should pursue in the meantime. When the Commission reached Haiti it found popular feeling against President Borno running so high that it requested wider powers from President Hoover. The

[10]See A. C. Millspaugh, "Our Haitian Problem," *Foreign Affairs,* July, 1929.

[11]From a speech delivered before the American Chamber of Commerce, January 21, 1928.

Commission laid the basis for the reconstitution of Haitian autonomy scheduled to take place in 1936.[12]

That the Haitians have benefited materially from American intervention can hardly be questioned. Will these benefits survive after the withdrawal of American forces? Or will Haiti lapse into a state of barbarism which existed prior to our intervention? The inclination of the State Department under the Franklin D. Roosevelt Administration to withdraw American forces at a date earlier than that suggested by the Forbes Commission indicated perhaps that the Haitians were ready to take over the responsibilities of self-government.

Efforts to acquire Danish West Indies finally successful

The latest acquisition of the United States in the Caribbean is that of the Danish West Indies, or Virgin Islands. Reference has already been made to the treaty negotiated by Secretary Seward in 1867 for the purchase of these islands, which was unfortunately rejected by the Senate. Another attempt at purchase was made by President Roosevelt in 1902. A treaty providing for the cession of the group to the United States was signed at Washington on January 24 of that year and approved by the Senate February 17, but this time the Danish Rigsdag refused to give its approval. President Roosevelt was moved by the consideration that the Danish Islands were of great strategic importance in connection with the problem of guarding the approaches to the Panama Canal. The commercial value of the islands was also great. Moreover, the United States was confronted by the possibility of their falling under the control of Germany or some other European power, which might use them as a naval base. Had Germany been successful in the recent war,

[12]On September 3, 1932, a Treaty of Friendship between the United States and Haiti was signed, and on September 15th the Haitian National Assembly rejected it. The treaty *inter alia* called for the Haitianization of the *Garde* by December 31, 1934, instead of May 3, 1936, and the naming by the United States of a fiscal representative to control the finances of Haiti until the amortization of the loan of 1922 on or before October 1, 1952. See *infra*, pp. 848 f.

she might have forced Denmark to sell or cede the islands to her. In view of this possibility, negotiations were taken up again with Denmark in 1916, and on August 4, Secretary Lansing concluded a treaty by which the United States acquired the islands of St. Thomas, St. John, and St. Croix, together with some adjacent small islands and rocks, for the sum of $25,000,000. This treaty was duly ratified by the Senate and the ratifications were exchanged January 17, 1917.[13]

Charges of imperialism

The rapid advance of the United States in the Caribbean, described in the preceding pages, naturally aroused the fears of the smaller Latin-American states and lent color to the charge that the United States had converted the Monroe Doctrine from a policy of benevolent protection to one of imperialistic aggression. While the United States had undertaken to prevent the encroachment of European powers in Latin America, it had never admitted any limitation upon the possibility of its own expansion in this region. The silence of the Monroe Doctrine on this question was remedied to some extent by President Wilson, who, at the outset of his administration, gave the assurance that "the United States will never again seek one additional foot of territory by conquest." This declaration, followed by his refusal to be forced into war with Mexico, did much to remove the suspicion with which the policies in the Caribbean were regarded by our southern neighbors. His sincerity was further attested by his ready acceptance of the proffered mediation of the A B C powers in the Mexican embroglio and by the encouragement which he gave to the Pan-American movement.

Diplomatic recognition used to discourage revolution

With respect to the five Central American countries, the United States has used the instrument of diplomatic recognition as a weapon to discourage and suppress revolutions. The principle of this policy was first explicitly agreed to by the five Central American countries them-

[13] *Treaties and Conventions*, III, 2558.

selves and written into the Additional Convention to the General Treaty of Peace and Amity signed at the Central American Conference held in Washington in 1907. These five agreed amongst themselves not to recognize any other government which may come into power in any of the five Republics as a consequence of a *coup d'état* or of a revolution against the recognized government, so long as the freely elected representatives of the people have not constitutionally reorganized the country. At the 1923 Central American Conference the five Republics strengthened and widened the prohibition against the recognition of governments coming into power as a consequence of a revolution or *coup d'état.* To these agreements the United States has never become a signatory; yet she has applied and interpreted the principles of these conventions whenever recognition of a Central American government was involved. This policy which the United States has followed with respect to the five Central American Republics substitutes the *de jure* for the *de facto* principle of recognition. It was contrary to the recognition policy which, with a few exceptions, the United States has followed since Jefferson.

Criticism of American policy of withholding recognition

Our departure from the traditional policy of recognition was attacked and defended. The critics contended that the *de jure* principle made the United States the virtual arbiter of the eligibility of presidential candidates, a task which embroiled her in the local politics of the country concerned and exposed her to the accusation of favoring one faction over another. It was contended further that by discouraging revolution the United States was lending her support in helping to keep corrupt and oppressive governments in office. In Central America, where free and fair elections are the exceptions, revolution is resorted to as a means of changing administrations, and our special policy of recognition, it was charged, deprived the Central Americas of the right to revolution, a legitimate instrument of a free people.

Defense of the policy

The defenders of the policy contended that the Central American countries adopted it themselves in order to mitigate and if possible to terminate the incessant revolutionary attacks "instigated either by factions of its own citizens or by the machinations of another one of the five republics."[14] The frequent revolutions, the resulting disorder, and the danger to lives and property of foreign nationals involved the risk of intervention from some European nation in a region adjacent to the Canal Zone. By discouraging revolution through non-recognition, the United States was seeking to establish stability and contribute to the orderly processes of government.

---

[14]See Secretary Stimson, "The United States and the Other American Republics," *Foreign Affairs*, Special Supplement, April, 1931.

CHAPTER XXIV

WORLD POLITICS IN THE PACIFIC

A new world order

HALF a century after Commodore Perry forced Japan to open her ports to foreign commerce and the influences of Western civilization, that power, having undergone one of the most remarkable transformations recorded in history, went to war with and defeated the largest country in Europe. The principal battles were fought in the territory of China, and the treaty of peace was signed at Portsmouth, New Hampshire, under the dominating influence of the President of the United States. Surely no series of events could be cited that would illustrate in a more dramatic way the fact that the old world order had passed away and that the system known as the balance of power in Europe, which had hitherto dominated the affairs of this globe, had been superseded by a new world order in which the United States and Japan had taken their inevitable places. In fact, the emergence of Japan as a first-class world power, conscious of achievement and eager to contest with the United States the mastery of the Pacific, as well as to challenge the position and influence of the powers of Europe in China, has been the most revolutionary factor that has entered into world politics during the memory of men now living.

Significance of the rise of Japan

For a hundred years prior to the rise of Japan, we had the European balance with the United States as the only detached power. Such a world system was in every way advantageous to the United States. We were enabled to maintain the Monroe Doctrine, which Bismarck described as an international impertinence, without the necessity of maintaining a great army or a great navy. No European power dared attack us for fear of being attacked in the rear by some other European power. The rise of Japan, however, completely changed this situation. In addition to the European balance there were now two detached powers, and Japan had no tradition of isolation to embarrass her in the game of world politics. On the contrary, she has been eager to make her influence felt in all questions of general international concern. But to-day she has withdrawn from Geneva where she had enjoyed intimate relations with the great powers.[1]

Japan deprived of fruits of victory over China

Ten years before the Russo-Japanese War Japan had won a victory over China which set in motion a new and startling series of events. The defeat of a vast continental empire like China, with an estimated population of 400,000,000, by a little insular power like Japan amazed the world. Notwithstanding her decisive military victory, Japan suffered a diplomatic defeat. China had agreed to cede to Japan: Formosa, the Pescadores Islands, and the Liao-tung Peninsula, when Russia, backed by Germany and France, made what was termed "a friendly representation" to Japan and informed her, practically under a threat of war, that she would not be permitted to retain the Liao-tung Peninsula. Japan was thus deprived of the full fruits of her victory.[2] Russia's motives were soon apparent. In less than three years she took possession of Port Arthur, and under concession from China soon extended her influence throughout the whole of the Liao-tung Peninsula. The seeds of the Russo-Japanese War were thus sown. The war with China was followed by the complete enfranchisement of Japan. The powers agreed to release her from all restrictions imposed by the early treaties. Since 1899 she has had full control over her tariffs and has had the

---

[1]See Chap. XXXIII.

[2]MacMurray, *Treaties and Agreements with and Concerning China*, 1, 18, 50–53

same jurisdiction over resident aliens that other civilized nations exercise.

Threatened partition of China

After her defeat by Japan, China lay at the mercy of the great powers, and they were quick to take advantage of the situation. Russia, as already stated, had secured a lease of Port Arthur with extensive concessions to the north; Germany established herself on Kiao-chau Bay and secured concessions in Shantung; while England, in self-defense, leased Wei-hai-wei "for so long a period as Port Arthur shall remain in the occupation of Russia"; and France, secured a less important lease.[2] It is a significant fact that the partition of China took place just as the United States was going to war with Spain, while the eyes of the world were fastened on Cuba. In the autumn of 1897, when war between the United States and Spain appeared imminent, Germany and Russia made all their preparations to close in on China. Germany sent a fleet to Kiao-chau Bay nominally to exact reparation for the murder of two German missionaries, while Russia, in order to have her fleet in warm water ready for action and not ice-bound in Vladivostok, announced that, by agreement with China, it would winter at Port Arthur.

American attention riveted on Cuba

The *Maine* blew up in Havana harbor February 15, 1898, and war was no longer a matter of doubt. Within six weeks Germany and Russia had forced China to sign the treaties granting them the leases and concessions mentioned above. The United States did not regard itself as a world power, but Germany and Russia did not care to act until our back was turned. Public attention in the United States was so riveted on Cuba that the question of the leases was scarcely noticed in the press and their significance not grasped by anyone. When the war was over and the people of the United States had time to

[2] *Op. cit.*, 1, 112, 119, 124, 152; *For. Rel.*, 1898, p. 187; 1899, pp. 128. 131; 1900, p. 383; *Parl. Papers*, 1898, China No. 1; Willoughby, *Foreign Rights and Interests in China*, Chap. X.

turn around, the European powers were firmly intrenched in China. What could the United States do? The situation had an important bearing on the fate of the Philippines, which had just come within our grasp.

A naval base in the Philippines

Various explanations have been given of President McKinley's decision to retain the Philippine group, but the whole truth has in all probability not yet been fully revealed. American commerce with China was at this time second to that of England alone, and the concessions which were being wrung from China by the European powers in such rapid succession presented a bad outlook for us. The United States could not follow the example of the powers of Europe, for the seizure of a sphere of influence in China would not have been supported by the Senate or upheld by public opinion. It is probable that President McKinley thought that the Philippine Islands would not only provide a market for American goods which owing to the Dingley tariff were beginning to face retaliatory legislation abroad, but that they would provide a naval base which would be of great assistance in upholding our interests in China.

German designs thwarted

Talcott Williams made public some years later another explanation of President McKinley's decision which is interesting and appears to be well vouched for. He was informed by a member of McKinley's Cabinet that while the President's mind was not yet made up on the question, a personal communication was received from Lord Salisbury who warned the President that Germany was preparing to take over the Philippine Islands in case the United States should withdraw; that such a step would probably precipitate a world war and that in the interests of peace and harmony it would be best for the United States to retain the entire group. The unexplained conduct of the German Admiral Diederichs toward Dewey in Manila Bay confirms the idea that Germany had designs on the Philippines.

Meanwhile another important step in American expansion in the Pacific had been taken in the annexation of the Hawaiian Islands. This was an old project which antedated the Civil War, but it was not until 1893 that any very serious effort was made to acquire the islands. In that year the reigning queen was dethroned by a revolution which was organized by the descendants of American missionaries and traders, who had grown wealthy and influential and who favored annexation to the United States. They were aided by the American minister and by a body of United States Marines. A provisional government was set up and an annexation treaty was soon signed and submitted by President Harrison to the Senate. Before a vote was taken President Cleveland came into office and sent a commissioner to Honolulu to conduct an investigation. As a result of the report of the commissioner the flag of the United States was hauled down and the marines were withdrawn. The provisional government was strong enough, however, to prevent the restoration of the queen and in 1894 President Cleveland recognized the Republic of Hawaii. In 1897, a second treaty of annexation was negotiated and submitted to the Senate by President McKinley. It was found impossible to get the necessary two-thirds' vote for ratification, but under the pressure of Dewey's critical position in Manila Bay, following his victory of May 1, the advocates of annexation attained their end by a joint resolution, which passed the House June 15 and the Senate July 6. Immediately after the signing of the treaty the Japanese government made a formal protest against the annexation of the Hawaiian Islands to the United States on the ground (1) that it would disturb the good understanding of the powers having interests in the Pacific and (2) that it would endanger the rights of Japanese subjects in the islands and might result in postponing the settlement of pending claims of Japan against Hawaii based on the

Attempts to annex Hawaiian Islands by treaty

Final resort to joint resolution

The Japanese protest

violation of treaty stipulations. To this protest the American government replied that annexation would not extinguish any "vested rights," and that during the long period in which annexation had been discussed and foreshadowed, no power having interests in the Pacific had raised any objection.[3]

Hay's effort to preserve the open door in China

After the war with Spain was ended the United States turned its attention to China and was much concerned at the rapid encroachments of the powers of Europe. In September, 1899, John Hay sent to the principal powers of Europe and to Japan his famous note on the subject of the open door in China. He requested each of the powers addressed to make a declaration to the following effect: (1) that it would not interfere with any treaty port or vested interests in its so-called sphere of influence; (2) that it would permit the Chinese tariff to continue in force and to be collected by Chinese officials; and (3) that it would not discriminate against other foreigners in the matter of port dues or railroad rates. Great Britain alone expressed her willingness to sign such a declaration. The other powers, while professing general accord with Mr. Hay's proposals, were somewhat evasive in their replies. The Russian reply was the least satisfactory, and in fact contained serious reservations. Mr. Hay made a skilful move, however, to clinch matters by informing each of the powers addressed that in view of the favorable replies received from the others, its acceptance of the proposals of the United States was regarded "as final and definitive."[4]

Americans generally are under the impression that John Hay originated the open-door policy and that it was

[3]Sen. Com. on For. Rel., *Compilation of Reports,* VII, 214–306; *U. S. Statutes at Large,* XXX, 750. For Japanese protest, see Moore, *Dig. of Int. Laws,* I, 504.

[4]*For. Rel.,* 1899, pp. 128–142. The evasive French reply and a later British note of April 5, 1900, are omitted from the *Foreign Relations,* but appear in *Parl. Papers,* 1900, China, No. 2. See also *Treaties and Conventions of the United States,* I, 244—260.

successfully upheld by the United States. Neither of these impressions is correct. A few months before John Hay formulated his famous note, Lord Charles Beresford came through America on his return from China and addressed the leading chambers of commerce from San Francisco to New York, telling Americans what was actually taking place in China and urging this country to unite with England and Japan in an effort to maintain the open door. The origin of the note on which Hay's reputation as Secretary of State so largely rests has been a matter of frequent conjecture. Neither Thayer's *Life of Hay* nor the three-volume collection of Hay's letters privately printed by Mrs. Hay throws any light on the subject. It appears, however, from a memorandum on file in the Department of State that W. W. Rockhill is entitled to the credit of formulating the policy announced by Hay. The memorandum, dated August 28, 1899, prepared at Hay's request, reviews with great ability the situation in China, refers to Lord Charles Beresford's speeches in the United States, and then proceeds to draft the statement of American policy which was embodied without change by Hay in his note of September 6.

The Rockhill memorandum

Like the Monroe Doctrine, the open-door policy was thus Anglo-American in origin. There is little doubt that England and Japan were willing to form an alliance with the United States for the purpose of maintaining the open door in China, but our traditional policy of isolation prevented our committing ourselves to the employment of force. President McKinley, following the example of President Monroe, preferred announcing our policy independently and requesting the other powers to consent to it. Had John Hay been able to carry out the plan which he favored of an alliance with England and Japan, the mere announcement of the fact would have been sufficient to check the aggressions of the powers on China. Instead of such an alliance, however, we let it be known

Anglo-American in origin

that while we favored the open door we would not fight for it under any conditions.

The Boxer movement

The exploitation of China which continued at a rapid rate naturally aroused an intense anti-foreign sentiment and led to the Boxer Uprising. Events moved with startling rapidity and United States troops took a prominent part with those of England, France, Russia, and Japan in the march to Peking for the relief of the legations. In a note to the powers July 3, 1900, Secretary Hay, in defining the attitude of the United States on the Chinese question, said: "The policy of the Government of the United States is to seek a solution which may bring about permanent safety and peace to China, preserve Chinese territorial and administrative entity, protect all rights guaranteed to friendly powers by treaty and international law, and safeguard for the world the principle of equal and impartial trade with all parts of the Chinese Empire."[5] Mr. Hay's notes were skilfully worded and had some influence in helping to formulate public opinion on the Chinese question both in this country and abroad, but we know now from his private letters, which have been made public since his death, that he realized only too fully the utter futility of his efforts to stay the course of events.

During the exciting days of June, 1900, when the foreign legations at Peking were in a state of siege, Mr. Hay wrote to John W. Foster as follows:

Hay's diplomacy thwarted by politics

> What can be done in the present diseased state of the public mind? There is such a mad-dog hatred of England prevalent among newspapers and politicians that anything we should now do in China to take care of our imperiled interests would be set down to "subservience to Great Britain". . . . Every Senator I see says, "For God's sake, don't let it appear we have any understanding with England." How can I make bricks without straw? That we should be compelled to refuse the assistance of the greatest power in the world, in carrying out our

[5] *For. Rel.*, 1900, p. 345.

own policy, because all Irishmen are Democrats and some Germans are fools—is enough to drive a man mad. Yet we shall do what we can.[6]

A little later, September 20, 1900, in a confidential letter to Henry Adams, he exclaimed:

The handicap of isolation

About China, it is the devil's own mess. We cannot possibly publish all the facts without breaking off relations with several Powers. We shall have to do the best we can, and take the consequences, which will be pretty serious, I do not doubt. "Give and take"—the axiom of diplomacy to the rest of the world—is positively forbidden to us, by both the Senate and public opinion. We must take what we can and give nothing —which greatly narrows our possibilities.

I take it, you agree with us that we are to limit as far as possible our military operations in China, to withdraw our troops at the earliest day consistent with our obligations, and in the final adjustment to do everything we can for the integrity and reform of China, and to hold on like grim death to the Open Door.[7]

Again, November 21, 1900:

Denunciation of Germany

What a business this has been in China! So far we have got on by being honest and naïf. . . . At least we are spared the infamy of an alliance with Germany. I would rather, I think, be the dupe of China, than the chum of the Kaiser. Have you noticed how the world will take anything nowadays from a German? Bülow said yesterday in substance —"We have demanded of China everything we can think of. If we think of anything else we will demand that, and be d—d to you"—and not a man in the world kicks."[8]

The Chinese indemnity

During the long negotiations with China leading to the Protocol of 1901[9] the United States urged a policy of moderation, declaring that the only hope for the future lay in a strong, independent, responsible Chinese Government. The powers, nevertheless, imposed a very heavy indemnity on China, the amount assigned to the United

[6]Thayer, *Life of John Hay*, II, 234–235.

[7]*Ibid.*, p. 247.

[8]*Ibid.*, p. 248.

[9]MacMurray, I, 310; *Treaties and Agreements*, II, 2006.

States being over $24,000,000. This was greatly in excess of the losses sustained by American citizens during the Boxer disturbances and the cost of the expeditionary force, which together amounted to about $11,000,000. Upon recommendation of President Roosevelt, Congress authorized the return of the indemnity in excess of what we were actually entitled to, and China set this sum aside as an educational fund to be used in sending Chinese students to American universities.[10]

Anglo-Japanese alliance

In violation of the terms of the protocol, Russia retained in Manchuria the troops concentrated there during the Boxer movement with the intention of exacting further concessions from China. The open-door policy was again ignored. The seriousness of the situation led England and Japan to sign a defensive alliance January 30, 1902, recognizing England's interest in China and Japan's interest in Korea, and providing that if either party should be attacked in its sphere by a single power the other would remain neutral, but if attacked by more than one, the other would come immediately to its assistance.[11]

The Russo-Japanese War

With this assurance of fair play in case of war, Japan determined to use force where Secretary Hay's diplomacy had failed. The presence of Russian troops on the soil she had conquered in 1895 and returned to China was a thorn in her side. After a series of futile negotiations the Japanese Government finally presented an ultimatum to Russia, January 16, 1904, in which it was stipulated: (1) that Japan would recognize Manchuria as being outside her sphere of interest, provided Russia would respect the territorial integrity of China in Manchuria; (2) that Russia would not impede Japan or other powers in the enjoyment of rights and privileges acquired by them in Manchuria under existing treaties with China; and

---

[10] *Am. Journal of Int. Law.*, II, 160, III, 165, 451, VII, 337; MacMurray, I, 311–320.

[11] MacMurray, I, 324.

(3) that Russia would recognize Korea as being outside her sphere of interest. Not receiving a reply within the time specified, Japan withdrew her minister from St. Petersburg and a few days later formally declared war.[12]

Intervention of Roosevelt

After a series of notable victories on land and sea Japan was fast approaching the end of her resources when President Roosevelt intervened diplomatically and paved the way for peace. It is now known that he acted in response to a direct appeal from the Emperor of Japan.[13] The Russian and Japanese commissioners met at Portsmouth, New Hampshire, in August, 1905. During the war public sentiment in the United States had been strongly pro-Japanese. But during the peace negotiations it veered to the side of Russia, largely as a result of the very striking personality of Count Witte, who gave out interesting interviews, while the Japanese commissioners kept themselves in seclusion and rarely gave anything to the press. The result of the negotiations was a keen disappointment to the Japanese. Their commissioners had been instructed among other things to demand an indemnity of $600,000,000. This they had to forego. The most important provisions of the Treaty of Portsmouth were those relating to Manchuria. The Russian leases of Port Arthur, Talienwan, and adjacent territories and territorial waters were transferred to Japan; the South Manchuria Railway was also transferred to Japan, while the Eastern Railway in northern Manchuria was retained by Russia.[14] So great was the disappointment of the Japanese people at not getting an indemnity that the Treaty of Portsmouth was received with denunciations and the commissioners tried to shift the blame to President Roosevelt, who had kept in close touch with the negotiations, and who had advised them to abandon the claim to indemnity. This

The Treaty of Portsmouth

---

[12] *For. Rel.*, 1904, pp. 410–413.

[13] Dennett, *Roosevelt and the Russo-Japanese War*. Chaps. VIII and IX.

[14] *Ibid.*, Chap. X; MacMurray, I, 522.

advice was probably sound, for the opinion was expressed by many of the foreign military observers that if the war had continued six weeks longer the tide would have turned in favor of Russia. Japan was getting farther and farther away from her base of supplies every day and Russia was drawing nearer to hers. The Japanese authorities knew that they were nearing the end of their resources, but they did not care to admit it. To the Japanese people it appeared that a great military triumph had again, as in 1895, been followed by a diplomatic defeat and for this defeat they held President Roosevelt responsible.

Japanese negotiators lay blame on Roosevelt

Defeat of Russia upsets European balance

The real significance of Roosevelt's intervention in the Russo-Japanese War was not seen or even suspected at the time by anybody outside his immediate circle of friends and advisers, and it was not until the recent publication of some of Roosevelt's papers that the connection between his action in the East and his participation in the Algeciras conference was understood. Roosevelt had been in close touch with the political situation in Europe as well as in the Far East. He was quick to realize that Japan's defeat of Russia had upset the European balance and was in danger of precipitating a world war. Immediately after the defeat of the Russian armies at Mukden in March, 1905, the German Kaiser took advantage of France's temporary isolation to interfere in Morocco, a French sphere of influence.[15] At the same time, the Kaiser was seriously considering interfering in the Russo-Japanese War. He hoped to prevent Japan from reaping the fruits of victory and to continue the partition of China, Germany receiving compensation in the Near East and in Africa.

Roosevelt's adventure in world politics

At this point Roosevelt appeared on the scene. He had just been elected President of the United States by an overwhelming majority. As he said, he was no longer a political accident. With the confidence derived from a great political victory he threw precedents to the winds

[15]Dennett, 84.

and boldly plunged into the two storm centers of world politics, China and Morocco. In his efforts to prevent war he used personal contacts instead of the machinery of the Department of State. Although Elihu Root was at the time Secretary of State, he appears to have had very little to do with Roosevelt's great adventure in world politics. In fact, George von L. Meyer, ambassador at St. Petersburg, was the only American official in the diplomatic service who knew what the President had in mind or who was of any particular use to him. Roosevelt worked through Cecil Spring-Rice, who represented Great Britain in Russia, and through the French and German ambassadors at Washington, Jusserand and Von Sternberg. The first thing that Roosevelt did was to warn Germany and France that if either one of them interfered on the side of Russia, he would come in on the side of Japan.[16] This was a remarkable declaration for a constitutional President with a Congress in his rear which was supposed to have the sole right to declare war. Roosevelt did not even consult the Senate, although he had once remarked to John Hay that the more he saw of the Kaiser and the Czar the better opinion he had of United States senators, to which Hay replied, that he was unable to draw such nice distinctions. Roosevelt then came to an understanding with England.[17] He persuaded Japan and Russia to send peace commissioners to the United States, and after their arrival in this country he kept in close touch with them, several times preventing an open rupture, and finally persuading them to sign the Peace of Portsmouth. At the same time, he grappled with France and Germany, and persuaded them to come into a conference with the other powers on the Moroccan situation. This conference met at Algeciras, Spain, and the United States was represented by two delegates. Henry White, chief

His warning to France and Germany

His part in the conferences of Portsmouth and Algeciras

[16] *Op. cit.*, p. 30.

[17] *Ibid.*, p. 43 ff.

American delegate, played an important part in this conference, and the influence of the United States was exerted on the side of France, much to the chagrin of the German Kaiser, who suffered a diplomatic defeat.[18] When the United States Senate learned what Roosevelt had done, it ratified the Treaty of Algeciras with a reservation which declared that the participation of the United States in the conference had been solely for the purpose of preserving its rights under the treaty of 1880, and was "without purpose to depart from the traditional American foreign policy which forbids participation by the United States in the settlement of political questions which are entirely European in their scope."[19]

The Senate asserts its authority through a solemn reservation

Material for the future historian

Unfortunately the foregoing account of Roosevelt's excursion into the field of world politics rests largely upon his own statements of what he did, supported it is true by notes of a personal nature which passed between him and Cecil Spring-Rice, Jusserand, and Sternberg. The story was first made public in Bishop's *Theodore Roosevelt and His Time*, published in 1920. Two chapters of this book are devoted to the "Secret History of the Algeciras Conference." These chapters consist of a long letter written by Roosevelt to Whitelaw Reid, April 28, 1906. No one can read this narrative without feeling that it is a highly self-conscious document, written not for Whitelaw Reid, but for posterity. Copies of it were also sent to Meyer and White. That Roosevelt was eager to play a great part in world affairs does not admit of doubt. It is also clear that in his efforts to straighten out the European tangle he was compelled in the main to act informally through foreign diplomats, with whom he had close personal relations, rather than through his own representatives abroad,[20] for two reasons:

---

[18]Bishop, *Theodore Roosevelt and His Time.*

[19]*Treaties and Conventions,* II, 2183.

[20]Dennett, Chap. II.

in the first place, because the latter had neither the knowledge nor the experience of European affairs to be intrusted with such delicate issues, and secondly because the President wished to have no record in the Department of State which might prove embarrassing in case the Senate should try to interfere.

It is impossible at present properly to appraise Roosevelt's influence. The claim so often advanced by his friends in recent years, that he averted a world war in 1905, has recently received a damaging blow from Viscount Grey's *Twenty-five Years*. This book at least makes one suspect that Roosevelt overestimated his own influence. In a note at the end of the chapter in which he describes the Moroccan crisis, Lord Grey says:

Viscount Grey's footnote

> In 1910, four years after the Algeciras Conference, I had a long talk in England, on various matters of interest, with Theodore Roosevelt. In the course of our talk he introduced the subject of the Algeciras Conference, and told me that he believed his own action had had great if not decisive influence in making Germany give way about the port of Casablanca. What he told me of his communications with the German Emperor supported this view. I do not know what record he kept of those communications or even whether they still exist, and I shall not therefore say more about them. The fact, however, that Roosevelt believed, and from what he told me had reason to believe, that the part he took influenced a peaceful solution should be on record and is of interest.[21]

Discrimination against Japanese in California

Roosevelt's intervention in the Russo-Japanese War was followed, as we have seen, by irritation and bad feeling in Japan resulting from Roosevelt's supposed responsibility for what was generally considered another diplomatic defeat. The following year the action of the San Francisco school authorities in excluding Japanese subjects from the schools attended by American children and children of European nationality, and assigning them to a special

[21] Viscount Grey, *Twenty-five Years*, I, 118.

Oriental school, increased the bad feeling in Japan.[22] The school question was adjusted for the time being by the intervention of President Roosevelt, but it proved to be a mere incident in the development of a strong opposition in California and the other Pacific States to further Japanese immigration. Japan declared that it was not the practice of her government to issue passports to laborers to come to the United States, though passports were issued for Hawaii, Canada, and Mexico, the holders of which in many cases entered this country. Japan expressed her intention of continuing this policy, and relying on this "gentlemen's agreement," Congress inserted in the Immigration Act of 1907 a clause authorizing the President to exclude from the continental territory of the United States holders of passports issued by any foreign government to its citizens to go to any country other than the United States.[23] The Japanese feel that they have made good as a nation and are entitled to full recognition as a civilized people, while the laws of the United States admit to naturalization only white persons and persons of African descent or nativity. The anti-Japanese sentiment in the Coast States is so strong that Congress is not likely to modify our laws in favor of the Japanese. Japanese resentment of the school incident was so great and President Roosevelt was so annoyed at the attitude of Japan that in the autumn of 1907 he decided to send a great American fleet on a voyage around the world, and to have it visit Japanese waters. The fleet was received with marked courtesy by the Japanese government and returned to America without any untoward incident.

The "gentlemen's agreement"

The American fleet visits Japan

The Treaty of Portsmouth, as we have seen, transferred Russia's lease of the Liao-tung Peninsula and Russia's

[22] Root, "The Real Question Under the Japanese Treaty and the San Francisco School Board Resolution," in *Am. Journal of Int. Law,* I, 273.

[23] *Am. Journal of Int. Law,* I, 450.

railway and other rights in southern Manchuria to Japan. By a secret arrangement, of which the United States and other powers were not aware, Russia agreed to hand over to Japan various secret agreements which she had made with China. Relying upon these, Japan later claimed "absolute and exclusive right of administration in the territories attached to the railway," in utter disregard of the open-door policy. It was soon apparent that Japan had ambitions in Manchuria which went far beyond the Portsmouth Treaty and were in fact in conflict with its provisions. By a treaty signed in December, 1905, China not only agreed to the transfers made by Russia to Japan, but agreed further not to construct any line parallel with the South Manchuria Railway.[24] In 1907, Russia and Japan came to an understanding and agreed to support each other in their respective spheres in Manchuria.[25] All the while Japan was professing to the outside world her adherence to the open door. In order to quiet the apprehensions of the United States, the Root-Takahira agreement was signed in November, 1908, by which Japan confirmed "the principle of equal opportunity for commerce and industry in China" and agreed to support the "independence and integrity" of that Empire. The agreement also bound both parties to maintain "the existing *status quo*." Did this refer to the open door or to the *status quo* established by the secret arrangements with Russia and China? It could be easily interpreted by Japan to mean the latter.[26]

Japanese ambitions in Manchuria

The Root-Takahira agreement

Under the various agreements China had reserved the right to purchase, after a certain period, the railways in Manchuria. In December, 1909, Secretary Knox came forward with a plan to hasten this prospective purchase through the means of an international loan to China, the

Proposed "neutralization" of railroads in in Manchuria

---

[24] MacMurray, I, 549.

[25] *Ibid.*, p. 657.

[26] *Ibid.*, p. 769.

railroads to be administered by a joint commission of the powers advancing the money. This plan to "neutralize" the railroads of Manchuria met with the emphatic opposition of both Russia and Japan and was dropped.[27]

The Chinese Republic

The overthrow of the Chinese monarchy and the proclamation of a republic in 1911 were viewed with great satisfaction in the United States. It was felt that the awakening of China was due in no small part to American influence. American missionaries and those who supported them were in full sympathy with the political and social revolution that held out such large promises for the future. The new government needed money and American bankers united with British, French, German, Russian, and Japanese bankers in what was known as the Six-Power Consortium. This group was contemplating a loan of $125,000,000 to China when the American bankers withdrew. It appears from the announcement made at the time that the American group had been requested by the Taft Administration to go into the Consortium. When the Wilson Administration came in, the bankers declined to go on with the loan unless expressly requested to do so by the new Administration. In a public announcement issued March 18, 1913, President Wilson said: "The Administration has declined to make such request, because it did not approve the conditions of the loan or the implications of responsibility on its own part, which it was plainly told would be involved in the request."[28] American bankers have, however, taken the lead in forming the new consortium, arranged in 1920, with the full backing of the Government. Japan reluctantly came into the arrangement, which, it was hoped by some, would serve to check in some measure her exploitation of China.[29]

The question of loans to China

[27] Willoughby, *Foreign Rights and Interests in China*, 316.
[28] *Ibid.*, pp. 499–502.
[29] *Treaties and Conventions*, III, 3822.

PART VI

INTERVENTION IN EUROPE

CHAPTER XXV

THE WORLD WAR AND THE FAILURE OF NEUTRALITY

IN WASHINGTON'S day the United States was an experiment in democracy. The vital question was not our duty to the rest of the world, but whether the rest of the world would let us live. The policy of wisdom was to keep aloof from world politics and give as little cause for offense as possible to the great powers of Europe. Washington pointed out that "our detached and distant situation" rendered such a course possible. This policy was justified by events. We were enabled to follow unhindered the bent of our own political genius, to extend our institutions over a vast continent, and to attain a position of great prosperity and power in the economic world. While we are still a young country, our government is, with the possible exception of that of Great Britain, the oldest and most stable in the world, and since we declared ourselves a nation and adopted our present constitution the British government has undergone radical changes of a democratic character. By age and stability we have long been entitled to a voice and influence in the world, and yet we have been singularly indifferent to our responsibilities as a member of the community of nations. We have been in the world, but not of it.

Washington's advice to his generation

Our policy of isolation corresponded with the situation as it existed a hundred years ago, but not with the situation as it exists to-day and as it has existed for some years past. We no longer occupy a "detached and distant situation." Steam and electricity, the cable and wireless

Isolation outgrown

telegraphy have overcome the intervening space and made us the close neighbors of Europe. The whole world has been drawn together in a way that our forefathers never dreamed of, and our commercial, financial, and social relations with the rest of the world are intimate. Under such circumstances political isolation is an impossibility. It has for years been nothing more than a tradition, but a tradition which has tied the hands of American diplomats and caused the American public to ignore what was actually going on in the world. The Spanish War and the acquisition of the Philippines brought us into the full current of world politics, and yet we refused to recognize the changes that inevitably followed.

Wilson's proclamation of neutrality

It took a world war to dispel the popular illusion of isolation and to arouse us to a temporary sense of our international interests and responsibilities. When the war began the President, following the traditions of a hundred years, issued, as a matter of course, a proclamation of neutrality,[1] and he thought that the more scrupulously it was observed the greater would be the opportunity for the United States to act as impartial mediator in the final adjustment of peace terms. As the fierceness of the conflict grew it became evident that the rôle of neutral would not be an easy one to play and that the vital interests of the United States would be involved to a far greater extent than any one had foreseen.

America the champion of neutral rights

Neutrality in the modern sense is essentially an American doctrine and the result of our policy of isolation. If we were to keep out of European conflicts, it was necessary for us to pursue a course of rigid impartiality in wars between European powers. In the Napoleonic wars we insisted that neutrals had certain rights which belligerents were bound to respect and we fought the War of 1812 with England in order to establish that principle. Half a century later, in the American Civil War, we insisted

[1] *U. S. Statutes*, XXXVIII, 1999.

that neutrals had certain duties which every belligerent had a right to expect them to perform, and we forced Great Britain in the settlement of the *Alabama* Claims to pay us damages to the extent of $15,500,000 for having failed to perform what we considered her neutral obligations. We have thus been the leading champion of the rights and duties of neutrals, and the principles for which we have contended have been written into the modern law of nations. When two or three nations are engaged in war and the rest of the world is neutral, there is usually very little difficulty in enforcing neutral rights, but when a majority of the great powers are at war, it is impossible for the remaining great powers, much less for the smaller neutrals, to maintain their rights. This was true in the Napoleonic wars, but at that time the law of neutrality was in its infancy and had never been fully recognized by the powers at war. The failure of neutrality in the Great War was far more serious, for the rights of neutrals had been more clearly defined.

Neutrality a legal status

Notwithstanding the large German population in this country and the propaganda which the German government had systematically carried on for years in our very midst, the invasion of Belgium and the atrocities reported as committed by the Germans soon arrayed opinion on the side of the Allies. This was not a departure from neutrality, for neutrality is not an attitude of mind, but a legal status. As long as our Government fulfilled its obligations as defined by the law of nations, no charge of a violation of neutrality could be justly made. To deny to the citizens of a neutral country the right to express their moral judgments would be to deny that the world can ever be governed by public opinion. The effort of the German propagandists to draw a distinction between so-called ethical and legal neutrality was plausible, but without real force. While neutrality is based on the general principle of impartiality, this principle has been embodied in a fairly well-defined set of rules which may, and frequently do, in any given war, work to the advantage of one belligerent and to the disadvantage of the other. In the Great War this result was brought about by the naval superiority of Great Britain. So far as our legal obligations to Germany were concerned she had no cause for complaint. If, on the other hand, our conduct had been determined solely by ethical considerations, we would have joined the Allies long before we did.

The naval superiority of Great Britain made it comparatively easy for her to stop all direct trade with the enemy in articles contraband of war, but this was of little avail so long as Germany could import these articles through the neutral ports of Italy, Holland, and the Scandinavian countries. Under these circumstances an ordinary blockade of the German coast would have had little effect. Therefore, no such blockade was proclaimed by Great Britain. She adopted other methods of cutting off overseas supplies from Germany. She enlarged the lists of both absolute and conditional contraband and under the doctrine of continuous voyage seized articles on both lists bound for Germany through neutral countries.[2]

The doctrine of continuous voyage

Absolute and conditional contraband

As to the right of a belligerent to enlarge the contraband lists there can be no doubt. Even the Declaration of London, which undertook for the first time to establish an international classification of contraband, provided in Article 23 that "articles and materials which are exclusively used for war may be added to the list of absolute contraband by means of a notified declaration," and Article 25 provided that the list of conditional contraband might be enlarged in the same manner. Under modern conditions of warfare it would seem impossible to deter-

[2]Dept. of State, *Dip. Cor. with Belligerent Governments,* No. 1, p. 65 and No. 3, pp. 89–113.

mine in advance what articles are to be treated as contraband. During the Great War many articles regarded in previous wars as innocent became indispensable to the carrying on of the war.

American protest against British policy

Great Britain's application of the doctrine of continuous voyage was more open to dispute. She assumed that contraband articles shipped to neutral countries adjacent to Germany and Austria were intended for them unless proof to the contrary was forthcoming, and she failed to draw any distinction between absolute and conditional contraband. The United States protested vigorously against this policy, but the force of its protest was weakened by the fact that during the Civil War the American government had pursued substantially the same policy in regard to goods shipped by neutrals to Nassau, Havana, Matamoros, and other ports adjacent to the Confederacy.[3]

Floating mines and war zones

Soon after the outbreak of hostilities Germany began scattering floating mines in the path of British commerce, and on November 3, 1914, the British government, as an act of retaliation, declared the North Sea a "war area" and warned neutral vessels not to enter without receiving sailing directions from the British squadron.[4] Under the pressure of what amounted to a stringent blockade, the German naval authorities decided to employ their large submarine flotilla, which had been unable to inflict any serious damage on the British navy, in an attack on British commerce. On February 4, 1915, Germany proclaimed a war zone around the British Isles, including the whole of the Channel, declared that all enemy merchant vessels encountered in these waters after the 18th would be destroyed, even though it might not be possible to save the passengers and crews, and added the warning

---

[3] *Op. cit.*, No. 3, p. 22 ff. Comparison of British practice with that of United States during the Civil War.

[4] *Ibid.*, No. 4, p. 29.

that neutral vessels could not always be prevented from suffering from the attacks intended for enemy ships.[5]

Against this decree the United States at once protested and warned the German government that it would be held to a "strict accountability" for the destruction of American ships or the loss of American lives.[6] The submarine policy was nevertheless inaugurated on the date set, and within a few weeks two Standard Oil tankers bearing the American flag had been torpedoed and several American citizens had lost their lives. Before the American government had decided what action to take the whole world was startled by the deliberate torpedoing, without warning, off the southern point of Ireland, of the great ocean liner *Lusitania*, May 7, 1915. She was bound from New York for Liverpool, and had 1,917 souls on board. Of this number 1,153 perished, including 114 American men, women, and children.

German submarine policy

The sinking of the *Lusitania*

The German press hailed the sinking of the *Lusitania* as a triumph of the submarine policy. In America it was defended only by the extreme pro-Germans. The press of the country denounced it as an act of barbarism, and it was generally believed that the German ambassador would be given his passports as soon as the press reports of the disaster were officially confirmed. President Wilson, however, decided to exhaust the resources of diplomacy before breaking off relations with Germany, and in a calm and dignified note to the German government he reasserted the right of Americans to travel on the high seas, denounced the illegality of submarine warfare, and called on Germany for a disavowal of the act and for reparation, so far as reparation was possible.[7] The German reply was unsatisfactory. It claimed that the *Lusitania* was armed and therefore not entitled to be

President Wilson demands disavowal and reparation

---

[5] *Op. cit.*, No. 1, p. 52.
[6] *Ibid.*, p. 55.
[7] *Ibid.*, p. 75.

treated as an ordinary merchantman, and that the destruction of a ship bearing ammunition to the enemy was an act of "just self-defense."[8]

Resignation of Bryan

President Wilson was on the point of dispatching a second note to Germany when Secretary of State Bryan tendered his resignation, stating as his reason that the new note meant war, and that therefore he could not sign it. Robert Lansing of New York, a well-known authority on international law and counselor for the Department of State, was appointed to succeed him, and the note was dispatched over his signature.[9]

The case of the *Arabic*

While the *Lusitania* correspondence was still in progress, matters were brought to a crisis in August, 1915, by the torpedoing of the White Star liner *Arabic*, involving the loss of two American citizens. Count Bernstorff realized fully the seriousness of the situation, and without waiting for the American government to act, promptly assured Secretary Lansing that if it should prove true that American lives were lost on the *Arabic*, it was contrary to the intention of his government.[10] This announcement indicated a change of policy on the part of Germany, and paved the way for further negotiation. The submarine campaign had not seriously interfered with British commerce, and it had brought Germany to the verge of war with the United States. On September 1, Count Bernstorff gave assurances that henceforth liners would not be sunk by submarines without warning and without saving the lives of noncombatants, provided they would not attempt to escape or offer resistance.[11]

German pledge violated in attack on the *Sussex*

This pledge, solemnly given in order to avert a crisis, was not kept in good faith. The German submarines continued their unlawful attacks and matters were again

[8] *Op. cit.*, No. 2, p. 169.

[9] *Ibid.*, p. 171.

[10] *Ibid.*, No. 3, p. 203.

[11] *Ibid.*, p. 159.

brought to a crisis in March, 1916, when the *Sussex*, an unarmed passenger steamer, was torpedoed without warning in the English Channel. About eighty passengers, including several citizens of the United States, were killed or injured. The German government at first denied responsibility for the disaster, but conclusive evidence was finally adduced, showing that the vessel was attacked by a German submarine, and on April 18 Secretary Lansing drew up an ultimatum declaring that unless the German government should immediately abandon its methods of submarine warfare against passenger and freight vessels, the United States would have "no choice but to sever diplomatic relations with the German Empire altogether."[12] In reply the German government stated that its naval forces had received orders not to sink merchant vessels without warning and without saving human lives unless the vessels should attempt to escape or to offer resistance.[13] The United States accepted this assurance as an abandonment of the submarine policy announced on February 4, 1915, and for some months there was a marked cessation of submarine activity.

Temporary abandonment of submarine policy

Germany had sought to justify her submarine policy on the ground (1) that the American manufacture and sale of munitions of war was one-sided and therefore unneutral, and (2) that the United States had practically acquiesced in what she considered the unlawful efforts of Great Britain to cut off the food supply of Germany. The subject of the munitions trade was brought to the attention of the United States by Germany in a note of April 4, 1915. While not denying the legality of the trade in munitions under ordinary circumstances the contentions of the German government were that the situation in the present war differed from that of any previous war; that the recognition of the trade in the past had sprung from

Germany protests against the munitions trade

[12] *Op. cit.*, No. 3, p. 241.

[13] *Ibid.*, p. 302.

the necessity of protecting existing industries, while in the present war an entirely new industry had been created in the United States; and it concluded with the following statement which was the real point of the note:

> This industry is actually delivering goods to the enemies of Germany. The theoretical willingness to supply Germany also, if shipments were possible, does not alter the case. If it is the will of the American people that there should be a true neutrality, the United States will find means of preventing this one-sided supply of arms or at least of utilizing it to protect legitimate trade with Germany, especially that in food stuffs.

To this note Secretary Bryan replied:

Bryan's reply

> Any change in its own laws of neutrality during the progress of the war which would affect unequally the relations of the United States with the nations at war would be an unjustifiable departure from the principle of strict neutrality.[14]

Austria renews the discussion

Two months later the discussion was renewed by the Austro-Hungarian government.[15] The Austrian note did not question the intention of the United States to conform to the letter of the law, but complained that we were not carrying out its spirit, and suggested that a threat to withhold food stuffs and raw materials from the Allies would be sufficient to protect legitimate commerce between the United States and the Central Powers. To this note Secretary Lansing replied at length. He held: (1) that the United States was under no obligation to change or modify the rules of international usage on account of special conditions. (2) He rejected what he construed to be the contention of the Austrian government that "the advantages gained to a belligerent by its superiority on the sea should be equalized by the neutral powers by the establishment of a system of non-intercourse with the victor." (3) He called attention to the fact that Austria-Hungary and Germany had during the years preceding the

[14] *Op. cit.*, No. 1, p. 73.
[15] *Ibid.*, No. 2. p. 193.

present European war produced a "great surplus of arms and ammunition which they sold throughout the world and especially to belligerents. Never during that period did either of them suggest or apply the principle now advocated by the Imperial and Royal Government."

Defense of American position

(4) But, in addition to the question of principle, there is a practical and substantial reason why the government of the United States has from the foundation of the republic to the present time advocated and practised unrestricted trade in arms and military supplies. It has never been the policy of this country to maintain in time of peace a large military establishment or stores of arms and ammunition sufficient to repel invasion by a well-equipped and powerful enemy. It has desired to remain at peace with all nations and to avoid any appearance of menacing such peace by the threat of its armies and navies. In consequence of this standing policy the United States would, in the event of attack by a foreign power, be at the outset of the war seriously, if not fatally, embarrassed by the lack of arms and ammunition and by the means to produce them in sufficient quantities to supply the requirements of national defense. The United States has always depended upon the right and power to purchase arms and ammunition from neutral nations in case of foreign attack. This right, which it claims for itself, it cannot deny to others.[16]

The German and Austrian authorities were fully aware that their arguments had no basis in international law or practice. Indeed, their notes were probably designed to influence public opinion and help the German propagandists in this country who were making a desperate effort to get Congress to place an embargo on the export of munitions. Having failed in this attempt, an extensive conspiracy was formed to break up the trade in munitions by a resort to criminal methods. Numerous explosions occurred in munition plants destroying many lives and millions of dollars' worth of property, and bombs were placed in a number of ships engaged in carrying supplies to the Allies. The Austrian ambassador and the German military and naval attachés at Washington were involved

Efforts to destroy munition plants

[16] *Op. cit.*, No. 2, p. 194.

in these activities and their recall was promptly demanded by Secretary Lansing.[17]

Colonel House's peace mission

In January and February, 1916, while the armies were deadlocked on the western front, Colonel House visited London, Paris, and Berlin for the purpose of laying before the principal belligerent powers a proposal from President Wilson to act as mediator and call a peace conference. The significant part of the plan as stated by Colonel House and recorded by Lord Grey in a memorandum, dated February 22, 1916, was as follows:

> Colonel House told me that President Wilson was ready, on hearing from France and England that the moment was opportune, to propose that a conference should be summoned to put an end to the war. Should the Allies accept this proposal, and should Germany refuse it, the United States would probably enter the war against Germany.[18]

In conversations with Grey, Asquith, Balfour, Lloyd George, and Reading, House expressed the conviction that Germany would decline to go into a conference on any reasonable terms, and that if it failed the United States would leave such a conference as a belligerent on the side of the Allies. The English leaders were impressed with the plan, but deferred action for various reasons. If they deliberately rejected the opportunity to bring the United States into the war at that date for selfish national reasons, as Colonel House appears to believe, they assumed a terrible responsibility. At the time the plan was proposed Russia was still holding out and their prospects were good. They hoped either to starve Germany, in which case they would not need the aid of the United States, or to force Germany to renew her submarine campaign, in which case the United States would enter the war as another belligerent and not in the high and dominat-

England not ready for a peace conference

[17]*Op. cit.*, No. 3., pp. 325–327.

[18]Viscount Grey, *Twenty-Five Years*, II, 127; Seymour, *The Intimate Papers of Colonel House*, II, 201–204.

ing rôle of mediator. The Allies had war aims of their own which they feared they could not attain with President Wilson as mediator. Moreover, they did not then need men as much as supplies, and they were already getting these in abundance from the United States.

Reasons for declining the overture

But possibly the Allies stumbled at the word "probably" and doubted the willingness or ability of President Wilson to bring the United States into the war in case the conference failed. It should also be remembered that the fighting spirit had become dominant in all belligerent countries, and that any cabinet which should have proposed or accepted a peace offer would probably have gone down in defeat.

The British blacklist arouses indignation

Following the failure of the Allies to accept the American plan, Great Britain published her famous blacklist. This measure, together with the conviction that the unwillingness of the Allies to accept the offer of mediation was due to their selfish war aims, greatly aroused the President. Counsellor Polk of the State Department suggested that the President be given by Congress power to retaliate as a club for Great Britain. In September, Congress voted the largest naval appropriation ever granted by the legislative body of a country not actually at war, and also gave the President power to take drastic retaliatory measures. If the Allies did not want the United States in the war on its own terms, the President was determined to look after our interests and to inforce our rights as neutrals.[19]

In the early spring Germany began her stupendous attack on Verdun, but the French held on with unparalleled tenacity, and the end of the summer campaign saw the armies still at a deadlock. In the east the Germans made a successful drive into Rumania, and on December 6 occupied the capital city, Bucharest. Six days later the German government announced to the Entente Powers

[19]The *House Papers*, II, 315–316.

through President Wilson its willingness "to forthwith open negotiations for peace."[20] The President transmitted the German note to England and France without comment. The Allies rejected the proposal as indefinite and insincere.[21] On the 18th, President Wilson addressed an identic note to the governments of all nations at war requesting them to state definitely the terms on which they would deem it possible to make peace.[22]

The German peace move of December, 1916

This note was for a time regarded in England and France as unwarranted meddling and as an indorsement, in a way, of the German proposal, but when the replies of the warring nations were made public, the first impressions of the President's move were modified. The Central Powers merely replied that they were ready to enter into negotiations and tried to fasten on their enemies the responsibility for continuing the war. The Entente Powers, on the other hand, stated fairly definitely the measure of reparation and restitution and the guarantees which they considered indispensable conditions of a permanent peace.[23]

Statement of war aims in reply to Wilson's note

Meanwhile it was rumored that Germany was constructing ocean-going submarines of a new and larger type and that she intended to resume unrestricted submarine warfare on a more extensive scale than ever. On January 22, 1917, President Wilson delivered a notable address to the Senate, in which he outlined the principle on which the United States would be willing to enter into a League for Peace, hoping that if a satisfactory basis for the future peace of the world could be established, the war might be brought to a close. On January 31, however, the German ambassador handed Secretary Lansing a formal note announcing a new zone around Great Britain

Resumption of German submarine activity

[20]Dept. of State, *Dip. Cor. with Belligerent Governments,* No. 4, p. 305.

[21]*Ibid.,* p. 311.

[22]*Ibid.,* p. 321.

[23]*Ibid.,* pp. 327–346.

and France and warning him that all ships, those of neutrals included, found within the zone after February 1 would be sunk.[24]

The dismissal of Bernstorff

The eyes of the country were again focused on the President with an intensity of interest which had not been felt since the sinking of the *Lusitania.* On February 3, he appeared before Congress and in calm and measured tones announced that Count Bernstorff had that day been given his passports and that all diplomatic intercourse with Germany was at an end.[25] This announcement was enthusiastically received by the great majority of the American people, who were soon in a state of hourly expectation of the "overt act" which the President said he would await before recommending further action.

Wilson seeks authority to arm merchantmen

During the next three weeks two American ships were sunk by German submarines, but without loss of life. Shipowners were, however, unwilling to send their vessels to sea, and American commerce was tied up in American ports under a practical embargo laid by decree of the German government. Under these circumstances President Wilson again appeared before Congress, February 26, and asked for authority to arm American merchantmen, in order that they might protect themselves in passing through the danger zone.[26] The House voted overwhelmingly for the resolution giving the President the necessary authority, but under the rules of the Senate permitting unlimited debate, a small group of eleven senators, led by La Follette of Wisconsin and Vardaman of Mississippi, prevented a vote being taken, and Congress adjourned March 4 without action by the Senate.

The "Zimmermann Note"

Popular indignation against the recalcitrant senators was raised to a fever heat by the disclosure, on March 1, of the famous "Zimmermann Note," in which the German

[24]*Op. cit.*, No. 4, p. 403.

[25]*Ibid.*, p. 410.

[26]*Messages and Papers of Woodrow Wilson* (Edited by Albert Shaw), I, 363.

foreign secretary invited Mexico to unite with Germany and Japan in a war against the United States. The dispatch was addressed to the German minister in Mexico and was transmitted through Count Bernstorff at Washington, but was intercepted by the British and came into the possession of the State Department. Both Mexico and Japan indignantly denied any knowledge of the note or any possibility of their being led into such a scheme.[27]

Revision of Senate rules

The failure of the Senate to act on the resolution giving the President authority to arm merchantmen made it necessary for him to call an extra session of Congress, which convened April 2. The Senate had already convened in extra session on March 5, and in response to the demands of public opinion had revised its rules, placing reasonable limits on debate and making it impossible for a small group to delay action indefinitely.

Meanwhile the President had been forced to the conclusion that the arming of merchantmen would not be a sufficiently effective means of dealing with the submarine terror. On April 2, he appeared before a joint session of the two Houses and urged "that the Congress declare the recent course of the German government to be in fact nothing less than war against the government and people of the United States; that it formally accept the status of belligerent which has thus been thrust upon it; and that it take immediate steps not only to put the country in a more thorough state of defense, but also to exert all its power and employ all its resources to bring the government of the German Empire to terms and end the war."[28]

Wilson's war address

The declaration of war

On April 6, after discussion lasting several days as to the form the resolution should take, Congress finally declared that a state of war existed between Germany and the United States. A few days later the vast sum of $7,000,000,000 was appropriated for carrying on the

[27] Hendrick, *Life and Letters of Walter Hines Page,* III, 324–364.

[28] *Messages and Papers of Woodrow Wilson,* I, 372.

war. This was the largest single appropriation made by any legislative body in the history of the world. Nearly half of it was to be used in loans to foreign governments. The foreign loan was to be raised by bond issues, but the President urged that our own expenditures for the war be raised as far as possible by increased taxation. Congress at once undertook the task of providing for a great army to be raised by selective draft and of framing new revenue laws.

British and French missions visit America

Five days after the war was declared a British mission headed by Arthur J. Balfour, Secretary for Foreign Affairs, sailed for the United States. The party landed at Halifax April 20, and proceeded at once to Washington. A few days later a French mission, with former Premier Viviani and General Joffre at its head, arrived in Hampton Roads, where they were received aboard the *Mayflower* and taken to Washington. Missions from other European governments at war with Germany arrived later.

Although our historic policy of isolation precluded the idea of a formal alliance even with England and France, it was manifest that the closest coöperation would be necessary in order to win the war. The British and French missions came over in the first place to negotiate loans, secondly to urge upon the United States the importance of sending large bodies of troops to Europe, and thirdly, to give us the benefit of their three years' military and naval experience. For this purpose they brought with them a number of military and naval experts.

Loans to the Allies

England and France had hitherto been largely financing their weaker allies and had nearly reached the limit of their financial resources. Of the $7,000,000,000 appropriated by Congress on April 24, $3,000,000,000 was voted for loans to foreign governments. Great Britain, France, Italy, Belgium, and Rumania each came in for a share, and as the war progressed new loans were made amounting in all to nearly $10,000,000,000. These loans were not advanced in gold, but in credits in American banks with which our associates in the war purchased supplies in America.

In his war address President Wilson said:

The failure of neutrality

> Neutrality is no longer feasible or desirable where the peace of the world is involved and the freedom of its peoples, and the menace to that peace and freedom lies in the existence of autocratic governments backed by organized force which is controlled wholly by their will, not by the will of their people. We have seen the last of neutrality in such circumstances.

Having once abandoned neutrality we are not likely to remain neutral again in any war which involves the balance of power in the world or the destinies of the major portion of mankind. Neutrality and isolation were correlative. They were both based on the view that we were a remote and distant people and had no intimate concern with what was going on in the great world across the seas.

The failure of neutrality and the entrance of the United States into the war marked a radical, though inevitable, change in our attitude toward world politics. President Wilson did not propose, however, to abandon the great principles for which we as a nation had stood, but rather to extend them and give them a world-wide application. In his address to the Senate on January 22, 1917, he said:

Internationalizing the Monroe Doctrine

> I am proposing, as it were, that the nations should with one accord adopt the doctrine of President Monroe as the doctrine of the world; that no nation should seek to extend its polity over any other nation or people, but that every people should be left free to determine its own polity, its own way of development, unhindered, unthreatened, unafraid, the little along with the great and powerful.
>
> I am proposing that all nations henceforth avoid entangling alliances which would draw them into competitions of power, catch them in a net of intrigue and selfish rivalry, and disturb their own affairs with influences intruded from without. There is no entangling alliance in a concert of power.[29]

[29] *Messages and Papers of Woodrow Wilson*, I, 355–356.

In other words, the Monroe Doctrine, stripped of its imperialistic tendencies, was to be internationalized, and the American policy of isolation, in the sense of avoiding secret alliances, was to become a fundamental principle of the new international order.

CHAPTER XXVI

WOODROW WILSON AND THE FOURTEEN POINTS

World-wide influence of America

THE advent of the United States into the family of nations nearly a century and a half ago was an event of world-wide significance. Our revolutionary ancestors set up a government founded on the principle that governments derive their just powers from the consent of the governed. This principle threatened, although remotely, the existence of the autocratic governments of the Old World which were still based on the doctrine of divine right. The entrance of the United States into the World War was an event of equal significance because it gave an American President, who was thoroughly grounded in the political philosophy of the Virginia Bill of Rights, the Declaration of Independence, and the writings of the founders of the Republic, an opportunity to proclaim to the world the things for which America has always stood. In this connection H. W. V. Temperley, editor of the principal history of the Peace Conference,[1] says:

Wilson's political philosophy

The utterances of President Wilson have a unique significance, not only because they were taken as the legal basis of the peace negotiations, but because they form a definite and coherent body of political doctrine. This doctrine, though developed and expanded in view of the tremendous changes produced by the war, was not formed or even altered by them. His ideas, like those of no other great statesman of the war, are capable of being worked out as a complete political philosophy. A peculiar interest, therefore, attaches to his pre-war speeches, for they contain the germs of his political faith and were not

[1] *A History of the Peace Conference of Paris,* edited by H. W. V. Temperley under the auspices of the Institute of International Affairs, 6 vols., London, 1920-1924, Vol. I, 173.

influenced by the terrifying portents of to-day. The tenets in themselves were few and simple, but their consequences, when developed by the war, were such as to produce the most far-reaching results. It is not possible or necessary to discuss how far these tenets were accepted by the American people as a whole, for, as the utterances of their legal representative at a supreme moment of world history, they will always retain their value.

His Latin-American policy

The principal features of Wilson's political philosophy were revealed in his policy toward Latin America before he had any idea of intervening in the European situation. At the outset of his administration he declared that the United States would "never again seek one additional foot of territory by conquest." In December, 1915, he declared: "From the first we have made common cause with all partisans of liberty on this side of the sea and . . . have set America aside as a whole for the uses of independent nations and political freemen." A few weeks later he proposed that the nations of America should unite "in guaranteeing to each other absolute political independence and territorial integrity." This proposal was actually embodied in a treaty, but this plan for an American league of nations did not meet with the approval of the other states, who probably feared that the United States would occupy too dominant a position in such a league.[2] President Wilson's refusal to recognize the despotic power of Huerta, while expressing sympathy for the people of Mexico, was the first application of the policy which later so successfully drove a wedge in between the Kaiser and the German people. His refusal to invade Mexico and his determination to give the people of that country a chance to work out their own salvation gave evidence to the world of the unselfishness and sincerity of his policies, and paved the way for the moral leadership which he later exercised over the peoples of Europe.[3]

[2]Post, p. 665.

[3]Robinson and West, *The Foreign Policy of Woodrow Wilson*, 30–43; Temperley, *History of the Peace Conference of Paris*, I, 176.

President Wilson's insistence on neutrality in "thought, word, and deed," the expression "too proud to fight," and his statement in regard to the war, May 27, 1916, that "with its causes and objects we are not concerned," caused deep offense to many of his countrymen and were received with ridicule by others at home and abroad. His reasons for remaining neutral were best stated in the speech accepting his second nomination for the presidency September 2, 1916:

Reasons for neutrality

> We have been neutral not only because it was the fixed and traditional policy of the United States to stand aloof from the politics of Europe and because we had had no part either of action or of policy in the influences which brought on the present war, but also because it was manifestly our duty to prevent, if it were possible, the indefinite extension of the fires of hate and desolation kindled by that terrible conflict and seek to serve mankind by reserving our strength and our resources for the anxious and difficult days of restoration and healing which must follow, when peace will have to build its house anew.[4]

Other speeches made during the year 1916 show, however, that he was being gradually forced to the conclusion that "peace is not always within the choice of the nation" and that we must be "ready to fight for our rights when those rights are coincident with the rights of man and humanity."

Belligerents asked to state aims

After the German peace proposals of December 12, 1916, President Wilson called on all the belligerents to state publicly what they were fighting for. In formulating their replies the Allies were somewhat embarrassed by the secret treaties relating to Russia and Italy, which were later made public by the Bolsheviki.[5] In March, 1915, England and France had made an agreement with Russia by which she was to get Constantinople, the aim of her policy since the days of Peter the Great. By the secret Treaty of London, signed April 26, 1915, England,

[4] *Op. cit.*, I, 342.

[5] Baker, *Woodrow Wilson and World Settlement*, I, 47–63.

France, and Russia had promised Italy that she should receive the Trentino and Southern Tyrol, including in its population more than 250,000 Germans. Italy was also promised Trieste and the Istrian peninsula, the boundary running just west of Fiume, over which city, it should be remembered, she acquired no claim under this treaty. Italy was also to receive about half of Dalmatia, including towns over half of whose population were Jugo-Slavs.

Replies

To President Wilson's note the Allies had to reply, therefore, in somewhat general terms. Their territorial demands were: "The restitution of provinces formerly torn from the Allies by force or against the wish of their inhabitants; the liberation of the Italians, as also of the Slavs, Roumanes, and Czecho-Slovaks from foreign domination, the setting free of the populations subject to the bloody tyranny of the Turks; and the turning out of Europe of the Ottoman Empire, as decidedly foreign to Western civilization." The German reply contained no statement of territorial claims and gave no pledge even as to the future status of Belgium.[6]

A league for peace

In reporting the results of this interchange of views to the Senate, January 22, 1917, President Wilson delivered the first of that series of addresses on the essentials of a just and lasting peace which made him the recognized spokesman of the liberal element in all countries and gained for him a moral leadership that was without parallel in the history of the world. "In every discussion of the peace that must end this war," he declared, "it is taken for granted that that peace must be followed by some definite concert of power which will make it virtually impossible that any such catastrophe should ever overwhelm us again. Every lover of mankind, every sane and thoughtful man must take that for granted." In fact, there was no dissent from this statement. Most of our leading men, including Taft, Roosevelt, and Lodge, were

[6]Dept. of State, *Dip. Cor. with Belligerent Governments.* No. 4. pp. 305—317.

committed to the idea of a league of nations for the maintenance of law and international peace. The League to Enforce Peace, which had branches in all the Allied countries, had done a great work in popularizing this idea. The President came before the Senate, he said, "as the council associated with me in the final determination of our international obligations," to formulate the conditions upon which he would feel justified in asking the American people to give "formal and solemn adherence to a League for Peace." He disclaimed any right to a voice in determining what the terms of peace should be, but he did claim a right to "have a voice in determining whether they shall be made lasting or not by the guarantees of a universal covenant." First of all, the peace must be a "peace without victory," for "only a peace between equals can last." And, he added, "there is a deeper thing involved than even equality of right among organized nations. No peace can last, or ought to last, which does not recognize and accept the principle that governments derive all their just powers from the consent of the governed, and that no right anywhere exists to hand peoples about from sovereignty to sovereignty as if they were property." He cited Poland as an example, declaring that statesmen everywhere were agreed that she should be "united, independent, and autonomous."

"Peace without victory"

He declared that every great people "should be assured a direct outlet to the sea," and that "no nation should be shut away from free access to the open paths of the world's commerce." He added: "The freedom of the seas is the *sine qua non* of peace, equality, and cooperation." This problem, he said, was closely connected with the limitation of naval armaments. "The question of armaments, whether on land or sea, is the most immediately and intensely practical question connected with the future fortunes of nations and of mankind."[7]

Freedom of the seas

[7]Robinson and West, 362.

The Russian revolution

The Russian revolution, which came in March, 1917, and resulted in the overthrow of the Czar's government, cleared the political atmosphere for the time being, and enabled President Wilson in his address to Congress on April 2 to proclaim a war of democracy against autocracy. The new Russian government repudiated all imperialistic aims and adopted the formula: "Self-determination, no annexations, no indemnities." Poland was given her freedom and the demand for Constantinople was abandoned. The Allies were thus relieved from one of their most embarrassing secret treaties.[8]

Even after America entered the war, President Wilson continued to advance the same ideas as to the ultimate conditions of peace. His attitude remained essentially different from that of the Allies, who were hampered by secret treaties wholly at variance with the President's aims. In his war address, he declared that we had "no quarrel with the German people. We have no feeling toward them but one of sympathy and friendship. It was not upon their impulse that their government acted in entering this war." Prussian autocracy was the object of his attack.

Distinction between German government and German people

> We are now about to accept gauge of battle with this natural foe to liberty and shall, if necessary, spend the whole force of the nation to check and nullify its pretensions and its power. We are glad, now that we see the facts with no veil of false pretense about them, to fight thus for the ultimate peace of the world and for the liberation of its peoples, the German peoples included: for the rights of nations great and small and the privilege of men everywhere to choose their way of life and of obedience. The world must be made safe for democracy. Its peace must be planted upon the tested foundations of political liberty. We have no selfish ends to serve. We desire no conquest, no dominion. We seek no indemnities for ourselves, no material compensation for the sacrifices we shall freely make. We are but one of the champions of the rights of mankind. We shall be satisfied when those rights have been

[8]Temperley, I, 183.

made as secure as the faith and the freedom of nations can make them.[9]

About the time that the United States declared war, Austria and Germany began another so-called "peace offensive." Overtures were made by Austria to France in March, and in August the Pope made a direct appeal to the powers. This move was unmasked by President Wilson in a public address at the Washington Monument, June 14, 1917:

The Austrian peace move

The military masters under whom Germany is bleeding, [he declared] see very clearly to what point fate has brought them: if they fall back or are forced back an inch, their power abroad and at home will fall to pieces. It is their power at home of which they are thinking now more than of their power abroad. It is that power which is trembling under their very feet. Deep fear has entered their hearts. They have but one chance to perpetuate their military power, or even their controlling political influence. If they can secure peace now, with the immense advantage still in their hands, they will have justified themselves before the German people. They will have gained by force what they promised to gain by it—an immense expansion of German power and an immense enlargement of German industrial and commercial opportunities. Their prestige will be secure, and with their prestige their political power. If they fail, their people will thrust them aside. A government accountable to the people themselves will be set up in Germany, as has been the case in England, the United States, and France —in all great countries of modern times except Germany. If they succeed they are safe, and Germany and the world are undone. If they fail, Germany is saved and the world will be at peace. If they succeed, America will fall within the menace, and we, and all the rest of the world, must remain armed, as they will remain, and must make ready for the next step in their aggression. If they fail, the world may unite for peace and Germany may be of the union.[10]

Insincerity of the military masters of Germany

The task of replying to the Pope was left by the Allied governments to Wilson, who was not hampered by secret treaties. In this remarkable document he drove still

[9]Robinson and West, 382.

[10]*Ibid.*, p. 400.

further the wedge between the German people and the Kaiser:

Reply to the Pope

> The American people have suffered intolerable wrongs at the hands of the Imperial German government, but they desire no reprisal upon the German people who have themselves suffered all things in this war which they did not choose. They believe that peace should rest upon the rights of peoples, not the rights of governments—the rights of peoples great or small, weak or powerful—their equal right to freedom and security and self-government and to a participation upon fair terms in the economic opportunities of the world, the German people of course included if they will accept equality and not seek domination.

In conclusion he said:

Present rulers of Germany not trusted

> We cannot take the word of the present rulers of Germany as a guarantee of anything that is to endure, unless explicitly supported by such conclusive evidence of the will and purpose of the German people themselves as the other peoples of the world would be justified in accepting. Without such guarantees, treaties of settlement, agreements for disarmament, covenants to set up arbitration in the place of force, territorial adjustments, reconstitutions of small nations, if made with the German government, no man, no nation could now depend on. We must await some new evidence of the purposes of the great peoples of the Central Powers. God grant it may be given soon and in a way to restore the confidence of all peoples everywhere in the faith of nations and the possibility of covenanted peace.[11]

Peace proposals of the Bolsheviki

Early in November, 1917, the Kerensky government was overthrown in Russia and the Bolsheviki came into power. They at once proposed a general armistice and called upon all the belligerents to enter into peace negotiations. The Central Powers accepted the invitation, and early in December negotiations began at Brest-Litovsk. The Russian peace proposals were: the evacuation of occupied territories, self-determination for nationalities not hitherto independent, no war indemnities or economic boycotts, and the settlement of colonial questions in ac-

[11] *Op. cit.*, p. 408.

cordance with the above principles. The Austrian minister, Count Czernin, replied for the Central Powers, accepting more of the Russian program than had been expected, but rejecting the principle of a free plebiscite for national groups not hitherto independent, and conditioning the whole on the acceptance by the Allies of the offer of general peace.[12] The conference called on the Allies for an answer by January 4. No direct reply was made to this demand, but the Russian proposals had made a profound impression on the laboring classes in all countries, and both Lloyd George and President Wilson felt called on to define more clearly the war aims of the Allies.

Statement of British war aims

In a speech delivered January 5, 1918, Lloyd George made the first comprehensive and authoritative statement of British war aims. He had consulted the labor leaders and Viscount Grey and Mr. Asquith, as well as some of the representatives of the overseas dominions, and he was speaking, he said, for "the nation and the Empire as a whole." He explained first what the British were not fighting for. He disclaimed any idea of overthrowing the German government, although he considered military autocracy "a dangerous anachronism"; they were not fighting to destroy Austria-Hungary, but genuine self-government must be granted to "those Austro-Hungarian nationalities who have long desired it"; they were not fighting "to deprive Turkey of its capital or of the rich and renowned lands of Thrace, which are predominantly Turkish in race," but the passage between the Mediterranean and the Black Sea must be "internationalized and neutralized." The positive statement of aims included the complete restoration of Belgium; the return of Alsace-Lorraine to France; rectification of the Italian boundary; the independence of Poland; the restoration of Serbia, Montenegro, and the occupied parts of France, Italy, and Rumania; and a disposition of the German

[12]Temperley, I, 221 ff.

colonies with "primary regard to the wishes and interests of the native inhabitants of such colonies." He insisted on reparation for injuries done in violation of international law, but disclaimed a demand for war indemnity. In conclusion he declared the following conditions to be essential to a lasting peace:

Essentials of lasting peace

> First, the sanctity of treaties must be reëstablished; secondly, a territorial settlement must be secured, based on the right of self-determination or the consent of the governed; and lastly, we must seek, by the creation of some international organization, to limit the burden of armaments and diminish the probability of war.

In this speech Lloyd George adopted the principles which Wilson had long been advocating and a cablegram from Balfour, informing the President of the fact, urged him to make a statement of his own views for the purpose of counteracting the effect of the appeal made to the peoples of the world by the Bolsheviki.[13]

Wilson announces the Fourteen Points

On January 8, 1918, three days after Lloyd George's speech, President Wilson, acting on Balfour's suggestion, appeared before both Houses of Congress and delivered the most important of all his addresses on war aims. It contained the famous Fourteen Points:

Open diplomacy

> I. Open covenants of peace, openly arrived at, after which there shall be no private international understandings of any kind, but diplomacy shall proceed always frankly and in the public view.

Freedom of the seas

> II. Absolute freedom of navigation upon the seas, outside territorial waters, alike in peace and in war, except as the seas may be closed in whole or in part by international action for the enforcement of international covenants.

Removal of economic barriers

> III. The removal, so far as possible, of all economic barriers and the establishment of an equality of trade conditions among all the nations consenting to the peace and associating themselves for its maintenance.

Reduction of armaments

> IV. Adequate guarantees given and taken that national armaments will be reduced to the lowest point consistent with domestic safety.

[13] Baker, *Woodrow Wilson and World Settlement*, I, 40.

V. A free, open-minded and absolutely impartial adjustment of all colonial claims, based upon a strict observance of the principle that in determining all such questions of sovereignty the interests of the populations concerned must have equal weight with the equitable claims of the Government whose title is to be determined.

Adjustment of colonial claims

VI. The evacuation of all Russian territory and such a settlement of all questions affecting Russia as will secure the best and freest coöperation of the other nations of the world in obtaining for her an unhampered and unembarrassed opportunity for the independent determination of her own political development and national policy and assure her of a sincere welcome into the society of free nations under institutions of her own choosing; and, more than a welcome, assistance also of every kind that she may need and may herself desire. The treatment accorded Russia by her sister nations will be the acid test of their good will, of their comprehension of her needs as distinguished from their own interests and of their intelligent and unselfish sympathy.

Russia

VII. Belgium, the whole world will agree, must be evacuated and restored, without any attempt to limit the sovereignty which she enjoys in common with all other free nations. No other single act will serve as this will serve to restore confidence among the nations in the laws which they have themselves set and determined for the government of their relations with one another. Without this healing act the whole structure and validity of international law is forever impaired.

Belgium

VIII. All French territory should be freed and the invaded portions restored, and the wrong done to France by Prussia in 1871 in the matter of Alsace-Lorraine, which has unsettled the peace of the world for nearly fifty years, should be righted, in order that peace may once more be made secure in the interest of all.

Alsace-Lorraine

IX. A readjustment of the frontiers of Italy should be effected along clearly recognizable lines of nationality.

Italian frontiers

X. The peoples of Austria-Hungary, whose place among the nations we wish to see safeguarded and assured, should be accorded the freest opportunity of autonomous development.

Austria-Hungary

XI. Rumania, Serbia, and Montenegro should be evacuated: occupied territories restored; Serbia accorded free and secure access to the sea; and the relations of the several Balkan states to one another determined by friendly counsel along historically established lines of allegiance and nationality; and international guarantees of the political and economic independence and territorial integrity of the several Balkan states should be entered into.

The Balkans

Turkey

XII. The Turkish portions of the present Ottoman Empire should be assured a secure sovereignty, but the other nationalities which are now under Turkish rule should be assured an undoubted security of life and an absolutely unmolested opportunity of autonomous development, and the Dardanelles should be permanently opened as a free passage to the ships and commerce of all nations under international guarantees.

Poland

XIII. An independent Polish state should be erécted which should include the territories inhabited by indisputably Polish populations, which should be assured a free and secure access to the sea, and whose political and economic independence and territorial integrity should be guaranteed by international covenant.

Association of nations

XIV. A general association of nations must be formed under specific covenants for the purpose of affording mutual guarantees of political independence and territorial integrity to great and small states alike.[14]

Cheap triumph of Germany in the East

In February, negotiations at Brest-Litovsk were broken off as a result of the excessive demands of the Germans and the Armistice was declared at an end. The Germans quickly overran Poland and the Baltic provinces and occupied Ukraine under a treaty which virtually placed the material resources of that country at the disposal of the Central Powers. In an address at Baltimore, April 6, the anniversary of our entrance into the war, President Wilson denounced the insincerity and perfidy of the German rulers, who, he said, were "enjoying in Russia a cheap triumph in which no brave or gallant nation can long take pride." He concluded with these strong words:

"Force to the utmost"

Germany has once more said that force, and force alone, shall decide whether justice and peace shall reign in the affairs of men, whether right as America conceives it or dominion as she conceives it shall determine the destinies of mankind. There is, therefore, but one response possible from us: Force, force to the utmost, force without stint or limit, the righteous and triumphant force which shall make right the law of the world and cast every selfish dominion down in the dust.[15]

[14]Albert Shaw, editor, *Messages and Papers of Woodrow Wilson,* I, 464; Temperley, I, 431.

[15]*Messages and Papers of Woodrow Wilson,* I. 479.

Elaboration of the Fourteen Points

Between the addresses of January 8 and the Armistice, the President delivered other addresses in which he elaborated some of the principles of the Fourteen Points. Of special significance were his speeches of February 11, July 4, and September 27. In the last his mind centered on the League of Nations. "There can be no leagues or alliances or special covenants and understandings within the general and common family of the League of Nations," he declared, and "there can be no special selfish economic combinations within the League, and no employment of any form of economic boycott or exclusion, except as the power of economic penalty, by exclusion from the markets of the world, may be vested in the League of Nations itself as a means of discipline and control." In conclusion he said that the United States was prepared "to assume its full share of responsibility for the maintenance of the common covenants and understandings upon which peace must henceforth rest."[16]

Impression made on the peoples of Central Europe

We now know from the published memoirs of German and Austrian statesmen that President Wilson's speeches made a profound impression on the peoples of Central Europe. His utterances in behalf of the oppressed nationalities, not only Belgium, Serbia, and Poland, but also the Czecho-Slovaks and the Jugo-Slavs, became stronger and more frequent during the spring and summer of 1918, and solidified the opposition to Germany at a critical period of the war. On September 3, he recognized the Czecho-Slovak National Council as a belligerent government.[17] This meant the break-up of the Austro-Hungarian Empire, which had not been contemplated at an earlier period, but, as he stated in his reply to the Austrian request for an armistice in October, conditions had changed since the announcement of the Fourteen Points, and these peoples would no longer be satisfied with mere autonomy.

[16] *Op. cit.*, I, 472, 502, 520.

[17] Temperley, I, 199.

Germany asks for peace on the Wilson program

As a result of the Russian collapse and the negotiations at Brest-Litovsk, the Germans withdrew their divisions from the eastern front and staked everything on the great western drive of March, 1918. When this movement was finally checked and the Allied advance began, the German military leaders knew that the game was up, but they did not have the courage to face the facts, for an acknowledgment of defeat meant the overthrow of the old system of government based on military success. They waited in vain for some military advantage which would give them an opportunity to open negotiations without openly acknowledging defeat. Finally the state of demoralization at Headquarters became so complete that there was no alternative but to ask for an immediate armistice. In order to pave the way for this step, the ministry resigned October 1, and Prince Max of Baden was called on to form a new government. On the 4th, he dispatched a note to President Wilson through the Swiss government, requesting him to call a peace conference and stating that the German government "accepts the program set forth by the President of the United States in his message to Congress of the 8th January, 1918, and in his later pronouncements, especially his speech of the 27th September, as a basis for peace negotiations."[18]

The President demands assurances

In reply the President asked for a clearer understanding on three points: (1) Did the Imperial Chancellor mean that the German government accepted the terms laid down in the President's addresses referred to, and "that its object in entering into discussion would be only to agree upon the practical details of their application?" (2) The President would not feel at liberty to propose a cessation of arms to the Allied governments so long as the armies of the Central Powers were upon their soil.

[18]The notes relating to the Armistice are printed in *The Messages and Papers, of Woodrow Wilson*, I, 533–556, and in Temperley, I, Appendix IV, pp. 448–458.

(3) The President asked whether the Chancellor was speaking for the constituted authorites of the Empire who had so far conducted the war.

The German reply of October 12 was satisfactory on the first point. With respect to the withdrawal of their troops from occupied territory they proposed a mixed commission to arrange the details. On the third point it was stated that the new government had been formed in agreement with the great majority of the Reichstag. Having accomplished this much, the President's next step was skilfully taken. He replied that the process of evacuation and the conditions of an armistice were matters which must be left to the judgment of the military advisers of the United States and the Allied governments, but that he would not agree to any arrangement which did not provide "absolutely satisfactory safeguards and guarantees of the maintenance of the present military supremacy of the armies of the United States and of the Allies in the field." Referring next to submarine warfare, he declared that the United States and the Allied governments could not consider an armistice "so long as the armed forces of Germany continue the illegal and inhumane practices which they persist in." In conclusion he referred to a clause contained in his speech of July 4, now accepted by the German government as one of the conditions of peace, namely, "The destruction of every arbitrary power anywhere that can separately, secretly, and of its single choice disturb the peace of the world." He added: "The power which has hitherto controlled the German nation is of the sort here described. It is within the choice of the German nation to alter it." He demanded that the United States and the Allied governments "should know beyond a peradventure" with whom they were dealing.

Conditions of armistice left to military advisers

Changes in the German government demanded

In reply the Chancellor assured the President that a bill had been introduced in the Reichstag to alter the constitution of the Empire so as to give the representatives of the people the right to decide for war or peace, but the President was not satisfied that there had been any real change. "It may be that future wars have been brought under the control of the German people, but the present war has not been; and it is with the present war that we are dealing." He was not willing to accept any armistice which did not make a renewal of hostilities on the part of Germany impossible. If, he concluded, the United States "must deal with the military masters and the monarchical autocrats of Germany now, or if it is likely to have to deal with them later in regard to the international obligations of the German Empire, it must demand not peace negotiations but surrender. Nothing can be gained by leaving this essential thing unsaid." This note was written October 23. Four days later the Chancellor replied:

Assurances of change given

> The President knows the deep-rooted changes which have taken place and are still taking place in German constitutional life. The peace negotiations will be conducted by a people's government, in whose hands the decisive legal power rests in accordance with the constitution, and to which the military power will also be subject. The German government now awaits the proposals for an armistice which will introduce a peace of justice such as the President in his manifestations has described.

Terms of the Armistice

The terms of the Armistice were drawn up by the Interallied Council at Versailles and completed by November 5.[19] They were much more severe than the public had expected them to be. Germany was required immediately to evacuate Belgium, France, Alsace-Lorraine, and Luxemburg; to withdraw her armies from the entire territory on the left bank of the Rhine, and from Russia, Austria-Hungary, Rumania, and Turkey; she was to surrender enormous quantities of heavy artillery and air-

[19]Temperley, I, 459; *Treaties and Conventions of the United States*, III, 3307.

planes, all her submarines, and most of her battleships, cruisers, and destroyers. This was practically unconditional surrender. Contrary to the general belief at the time, it is now known that Foch and Haig considered these terms too severe and feared that Germany would not accept them. They wanted an armistice that Germany would accept. General Bliss, on the other hand, wanted to demand "the complete disarmament and demobilization of the military and naval forces of the enemy."[20] In America there was much criticism of the President for being willing to negotiate with Germany at all. "On to Berlin!" was a popular cry, and it was thought that the President was preventing a complete military triumph. On October 10, Senator Lodge declared in the Senate: "The Republican party stands for unconditional surrender and complete victory, just as Grant stood. My own belief is that the American people mean to have an unconditional surrender. They mean to have a dictated, not a negotiated peace."

Wilson criticized for stopping the war

After reviewing the Armistice negotiations André Tardieu, a member of the French Cabinet and delegate to the Peace Conference, says:

> What remains of the fiction, believed by so many, of an armistice secretly determined upon by an American dictator; submitted to by the European governments; imposed by their weakness upon the victorious armies, despite the opposition of the generals? The Armistice was discussed in the open light of day. President Wilson only consented to communicate it to his associates on the triple condition that its principle be approved by the military authorities and its clauses would be drawn up by them; that it be imposed upon the enemy and not discussed with him; that it be such as to prevent all resumption of hostilities and assure the submission of the vanquished to the terms of peace. So it was that the discussion went on with Berlin till October 23, and in Paris from that date till November 5. It was to the Commander-in-Chief [Foch] that final decision was left not only on the principle of the Armistice but

The fiction of an American dictator

[20] André Tardieu, *The Truth About the Treaty*, 65–71.

upon its application. He it was who drew up the text. And it was his draft that was adopted. The action of the governments was limited to endorsing it and making it more severe. That is the truth:—it is perhaps less picturesque but certainly more in accord with common sense.[21]

Collapse of Austria and Germany

The terms of the Armistice were delivered to the Germans by Marshal Foch November 7, and they were given seventy-two hours to accept or reject them. Meanwhile, Germany's allies were rapidly deserting her. Bulgaria surrendered September 30, and on October 30 Turkey signed an armistice. Finally, on November 4, the rapidly disintegrating Austro-Hungarian Monarchy also signed an armistice. On October 28, there had been a naval mutiny at Kiel which spread rapidly to the other ports. On the 31st, the Emperor departed for Army Headquarters, leaving Berlin on the verge of revolution. On the 7th of November the Social Democrats demanded the abdication of the Emperor and the Crown Prince. On the 9th, Prince Max resigned the chancellorship, and the Kaiser abdicated and ignominiously fled across the border into Holland. On the 11th, at 5 A. M., the Armistice was signed by the German delegates and Marshal Foch, and it went into effect at 11 o'clock that day.

In two particulars the Wilson principles had been modified by the Allies. In the American note to Germany of November 5 Secretary Lansing stated that the President had submitted his correspondence with the German authorities to the Allied governments and that he had received in reply the following memorandum:

Modification of the Wilson principles by the Allies

The Allied Governments have given careful consideration to the correspondence which has passed between the President of the United States and the German government. Subject to the qualifications which follow, they declare their willingness to make peace with the Government of Germany on the terms of peace laid down in the President's Address to Congress of

[21] *Op. cit.*, p. 74.

January 8, 1918, and the principles of settlement enunciated in his subsequent Addresses. They must point out, however, that Clause 2, relating to what is usually described as the freedom of the seas, is open to various interpretations, some of which they could not accept. They must therefore reserve to themselves complete freedom on this subject when they enter the peace conference. Further, in the conditions of peace laid down in his address to Congress of January 8, 1918, the President declared that the invaded territories must be restored as well as evacuated and freed, and the Allied Governments feel that no doubt ought to be allowed to exist as to what this provision implies. By it they understand that compensation will be made by Germany for all damage done to the civilian population of the Allies and their property by the aggression of Germany by land, by sea, and from the air."

The legal basis of the peace negotiations

In transmitting this memorandum Secretary Lansing stated that he was instructed by the President to say that he agreed with this interpretation.

With these modifications the Wilson principles were accepted by all parties as the legal basis of the peace negotiations.[22]

[22]Temperley, I. 457.

CHAPTER XXVII

AMERICA AND THE LEAGUE OF NATIONS

Wilson decides to go to Paris

IT WAS agreed that the peace conference should meet at Paris, and President Wilson considered the issues involved of such magnitude that he decided to head the American delegation himself. Great Britain, France, and Italy were to be represented by their premiers, and it was fitting that the United States should be represented by its most responsible leader, who, furthermore, had been the chief spokesman of the Allies and had formulated the principles upon which the peace was to be made. But the decision of the President to go to Paris was without precedent in our history and, therefore, it met with criticism and opposition. When he announced the names of the other members of the delegation, the criticism became even more outspoken and severe. They were Secretary of State Lansing, Henry White, former ambassador to France, Colonel Edward M. House, and General Tasker H. Bliss. There had been a widespread demand for a non-partisan peace commission, and many people thought that the President should have taken Root, or Roosevelt, or Taft. Mr. White was a Republican but he had never been active in party affairs or in any sense a leader. In the Senate there was deep resentment that the President had not selected any members of that body to accompany him. President McKinley had appointed three senators as members of the commission of five that negotiated the treaty of peace at the close of the Spanish War. With that exception, senators had never taken part directly

Criticism of the American delegation

in the negotiation of a treaty. The delegation was attended by a large group of experts on military, economic, geographical, ethnological, and legal matters, some of whom were men of great ability, and in their selection no party lines were drawn.

But just before the signing of the Armistice, the President had suffered a serious political defeat at home. There had been severe criticism of Democratic leadership in Congress and growing dissatisfaction with some of the members of the Cabinet. In response to the appeals of Democratic Congressmen, the President issued a statement from the White House on October 25, asking the people, if they approved of his leadership and wished him to continue to be their "unembarrassed spokesman in affairs at home and abroad," to vote for the Democratic candidates for Congress. He acknowledged that the Republicans in Congress had loyally supported his war measures, but he declared that they were hostile to the administration and that the time was too critical for divided leadership.[1] This statement created a storm of criticism, and did more than any other act in his administration to turn the tide of public opinion against the President. The elections resulted in a Republican majority of thirty-nine in the House and two in the Senate. The President had followed the practice of European premiers in appealing to the people, but under our constitutional system he could not very well resign. Had he not issued his appeal, the election would have been regarded as a repudiation of the Democratic Congress, but not necessarily as a repudiation of the President. The situation was most unfortunate, but the President made no comments and soon after announced his intention of going to Paris. In December, Lloyd George went to the country, and on pledging himself to make Germany pay for the war and to hang the Kaiser, he was returned by a substantial

Wilson's appeal to the country meets with a rebuff

Lloyd George strengthened

[1]*Messages and Papers of Woodrow Wilson,* I, 557.

majority. These pledges were unnecessary and had a most unfortunate influence on the subsequent negotiations at Paris.

Wilson leaves a divided country behind him

The President sailed for France December 4, leaving a divided country behind him. His enemies promptly seized the opportunity to assail him. Senator Sherman introduced a resolution declaring the presidency vacant because the President had left the territory of the United States, and Senator Knox offered another resolution declaring that the Conference should confine itself solely to the restoration of peace, and that the proposed league of nations should be reserved for consideration at some future time.

His reception abroad

While his enemies in the Senate were busily organizing all the forces of opposition against him, the President was welcomed by the war-weary peoples of Europe with demonstrations of genuine enthusiasm such as it had been the lot of few men in history to receive. Sovereigns and heads of states bestowed the highest honors upon him, while great crowds of working men gathered at the railroad stations in order to get a glimpse of the man who had led the crusade for a peace that would end war and establish justice as the rule of conduct between the nations of the world, great and small nations alike.

The hopes of the world centered in him

No mortal man could have fulfilled the hopes and expectations that centered in Wilson when he landed on the shores of France in December, 1918. The Armistice had been signed on the basis of his ideals, and the peoples of Europe confidently expected to see those ideals embodied in the treaty of peace.[2] He still held the moral leadership of the world, but the war was over, the German menace ended, and national rivalries and jealousies were beginning to reappear, even among those nations that had so recently fought and bled side by side. This change was to be revealed when the Conference met. There was no

[2] Baker, *Woodrow Wilson and World Settlement*, I. chap. i.

sign of it in the plaudits of the multitudes that welcomed the President in France, in England, and in Italy. He returned on January 7, 1919, from Italy to Paris, where delegates to the Conference from all the countries that had been at war with Germany were gathering.

Organization of the Peace Conference

The first session of the Peace Conference was held January 18. The main work of the Conference was carried on by the Supreme Council, constituted at this meeting and composed of the two ranking delegates of each of the Five Great Powers, Great Britain, France, Italy, the United States, and Japan. The decisions which this Council arrived at, with the aid of the large groups of technical advisers which accompanied the delegations of the great powers, were reported to the Conference in plenary session from time to time and ratified. The Supreme Council was, however, gradually superseded by the "Big Four," Wilson, Lloyd George, Clemenceau, and Orlando, while the "Five," composed of ministers of foreign affairs, handled much of the routine business, and made some important decisions, subject to the approval of the "Four." According to statistics compiled by Tardieu, the Council of Ten held seventy-two sessions, the "Five" held thirty-nine, and the "Four" held one hundred and forty-five. As one of the American experts puts it: "The 'Ten' fell into the background, the 'Five' never emerged from obscurity, the 'Four' ruled the Conference in the culminating period when its decisions took shape."[3]

Wilson presents the Covenant of the League

At the plenary session of January 25, President Wilson made a notable speech in which he proposed the creation of a league of nations, and a resolution to organize such a league and make it an integral part of the general treaty was unanimously adopted. A commission to draft a constitution for the League was appointed with Presi-

[3]House and Seymour, *What Really Happened at Paris,* 33; Temperley, *History of the Peace Conference at Paris,* I, 247–267, 497–504.

dent Wilson as chairman. On February 14, the first draft of the Covenant of the League was presented by him to the Conference,[4] and on the following day he sailed for the United States in order to consider the bills passed by Congress before the expiration of the session on March 4. The first draft of the Covenant was hastily prepared, and it went back to the commission for revision. As soon as the text was made known in the United States, opposition to the Covenant was expressed in the Senate. During the President's brief visit to Washington, he gave a dinner at the White House to members of the Senate Committee on Foreign Relations and of the House Committee on Foreign Affairs for the purpose of explaining to them the terms of the Covenant.[5] There was no official report of what occurred at this dinner, but it was stated that some of the senators objected to the Covenant on the ground that it was contrary to our traditional policies and inconsistent with our Constitution and form of government. On March 4, the day before the President left New York to resume his duties at the Conference, Senators Lodge and Knox issued a round robin, signed by thirty-seven senators, declaring that they would not vote for the Covenant in the form proposed, and that consideration of the League of Nations should be postponed until peace had been concluded with Germany.[6] That same night the President made a speech at the Metropolitan Opera House in New York City in which, after explaining and defining the Covenant, he said:

The President's hurried visit home

Opposition in the Senate

When that treaty comes back gentlemen on this side will find the Covenant not only in it, but so many threads of the treaty tied to the Covenant that you cannot dissect the Covenant from the treaty without destroying the whole vital structure.

---

[4]Baker, I, 213–249, 276, 292.

[5]New York *Times*, February 27, 1919.

[6]*Cong. Record*, March 4, 1919, p. 4974.

In this same address he also said:

> The first thing I am going to tell the people on the other side of the water is that an overwhelming majority of the American people is in favor of the League of Nations. I know that this is true. I have had unmistakable intimations of it from all parts of the country, and the voice rings true in every case.[7]

The President was evidently quite confident that public sentiment would compel the Senate to ratify the peace treaty, including the Covenant of the League. A nation-wide propaganda was being carried on by the League to Enforce Peace and other organizations, and public sentiment for the League appeared to be overwhelming. The President took back to Paris with him various suggestions of changes in the Covenant, and later, ex-President Taft, Elihu Root, and President Lowell of Harvard proposed amendments which were forwarded to him and carefully considered by the commission.[8] Some of these suggestions, such as the reservation of the Monroe Doctrine and the right of withdrawal from the League, were embodied in the final draft.

Changes in the Covenant

When the President returned to Paris he found that the League had been sidetracked and that Lansing and House, possibly without realizing what was being "put over" on them, had given way. The general belief in Paris was that the League was dead, and reports to that effect were cabled to the American papers. On the day after his arrival in Paris, Wilson issued a statement to the press in which he declared he would stand by the resolution of the Conference of January 25 making the Covenent an integral part of the treaty of peace.[9] The final adoption of the Covenant was delayed, however, by the demand of Japan that a clause be inserted establishing "the principle

Wilson prevents sidetracking of the League

Delay in the adoption of the Covenant

---

[7]*Messages and Papers of Woodrow Wilson,* II, 647.

[8]Baker, I, 323.

[9]*Ibid.,* 295–313.

of equality of nations and just treatment of their nationals," which would have brought within the jurisdiction of the League the status of Japan's subjects in California and in the British dominions. France urged the inclusion of a provision creating a permanent General Staff to direct the military operations of the League, and Belgium insisted that Brussels rather than Geneva should be the seat of the League. Meanwhile other national aspirations were also brought forward which delayed the general treaty of peace. France wanted the entire left bank of the Rhine; Italy put forth a claim to Fiume; and Japan, relying on secret agreements with England, France, and Italy, insisted on her claims to Shantung. No economic settlement had as yet been agreed upon, and the question of reparations was threatening the disruption of the Conference.[10]

The Franco-German frontier

The most difficult problem that the Conference had to solve was the establishment of a new Franco-German frontier. There was no question about Alsace-Lorraine. That had been disposed of by the Fourteen Points, and Germany had acquiesced in its return to France in the pre-Armistice agreement. But no sooner was the Armistice signed than Foch addressed a note to Clemenceau, setting forth the necessity of making the Rhine the western frontier of Germany. The Left Bank, extending from Alsace-Lorraine to the Dutch frontier, embraced about 10,000 square miles and 5,500,000 people. The debate on this question continued at intervals for six months and at times became very acrimonious. The French representatives did not demand the direct annexation of the Left Bank, but they proposed an independent or autonomous Rhineland and French, or inter-Allied, occupation of the Rhine for an indefinite period, or at least until the full execution by Germany of the financial clauses of the treaty. Both the British and

[10]*Op. cit.*, Vol. II.

American delegates opposed the French proposals. Lloyd George repeatedly said: "We must not create another Alsace-Lorraine." He also remarked on one occasion: "The strongest impression made upon me by my first visit to Paris was the statue of Strasburg veiled in mourning. Do not let us make it possible for Germany to erect a similar statue."[11]

The proposed guarantee treaties

This discussion was being carried on with great earnestness and intensity of feeling when Wilson returned to Paris March 14. That very afternoon he met Lloyd George and Clemenceau. The French argument was set forth again at length and with great skill. The fact was again pointed out that the destruction of the German fleet had relieved England from all fear of German invasion, and that the Atlantic Ocean lay between Germany and the United States, while France, which had suffered two German invasions in half a century, had no safeguard but the League of Nations, which she did not deem as good a guarantee as the Rhine bridges. Finally Wilson and Lloyd George offered the guarantee treaties, and Clemenceau agreed to take the proposal under consideration. Three days later he came back with a counter proposition and a compromise was reached. France gave up her demand for a separate Rhineland, but secured occupation of the Left Bank, including the bridge-heads, for a period of fifteen years as a guarantee of the execution of the treaty. In return the United States and Great Britain pledged themselves to come to the immediate aid of France, in case of an unprovoked attack, by an agreement which was to be binding only if ratified by both countries. This treaty the United States Senate refused to ratify. Foch was opposed to this compromise, and adopted a course of action which was very embarrassing to Clemenceau. Fierce attacks on the French govern-

Foch opposed to compromise

[11]Haskins and Lord, *Some Problems of the Peace Conference;* Baker, Vol. II, part V.

ment and on the representatives of Great Britain and the United States, inspired by him, appeared in the papers. When the treaty was finally completed, he even went so far as to refuse to transmit the note summoning the German delegates to Versailles to receive it. Wilson and Lloyd George finally protested so vigorously to Clemenceau that Foch had to give way.[12]

German reparations

In view of the promises of Clemenceau and Lloyd George that Germany should pay the cost of the war, the question of reparations was an exceedingly difficult one to adjust. President Wilson stoutly opposed the inclusion of war costs as contrary to the pre-Armistice agreement, and Lloyd George and Clemenceau finally had to give in. The entire American delegation and their corps of experts endeavored to limit the charges imposed on Germany rigidly to reparation for damage done to civilians in the occupied areas and on land and sea. Lloyd George, remembering the promises which he had made prior to the December elections, insisted that pensions paid by the Allied governments should be included as damage done to the civilian population. This claim was utterly illogical, for pensions fall properly into the category of military expenses, but it was pressed with such skill and determination by Lloyd George and General Smuts that President Wilson finally gave his assent.

The amount left indefinite

From the first the American delegates and experts were in favor of fixing definitely the amount that Germany was to pay in the way of reparations and settling this question once for all. They hoped to agree upon a sum, which it was within Germany's power to pay. But Clemenceau and Lloyd George had made such extravagant promises to their people that they were afraid to announce at this time a sum which would necessarily be much less than the people expected. They, therefore, insisted that the question should be left open to be determined later by a Repa-

[12]Tardieu, *The Truth About the Treaty,* 187–195.

rations Commission. They declared that any other course would mean the immediate overthrow of their governments and the reorganization of the British and French delegations. President Wilson did not care to put himself in the position of appearing to precipitate a political crisis in either country, so he finally gave way on this point also. These concessions proved to be the most serious mistakes that he made at Paris, for they did more than anything else to undermine the faith of liberals everywhere in him.[13]

The Italian claim to Fiume

The Italian delegation advanced a claim to Fiume which was inconsistent both with the Treaty of London and the Fourteen Points. When disagreement over this question had been delaying for weeks the settlement of other matters, President Wilson finally made a public statement of his position which was virtually an appeal to the Italian people over the heads of their delegation. The entire delegation withdrew from the Conference and went home, but Premier Orlando received an almost unanimous vote of confidence from his parliament, and he was supported by an overwhelming tide of public sentiment throughout Italy. This was the first indication of Wilson's loss of prestige with the peoples of Europe.[14]

The status of Shantung

As already stated, the Japanese had insisted on the insertion in the Covenant of the League of the principle of racial equality. It is very doubtful whether they ever expected to succeed in this. The probability is that they advanced this principle in order to compel concessions on other points. Japan's main demand was that the German leases and concessions in the Chinese province of Shantung should be definitely confirmed to her by the treaty. Two weeks after the outbreak of the World War, Japan had addressed an ultimatum to Germany to

---

[13]Temperley, II, 60–90; Baker, II, part VIII; Baruch, *The Making of the Reparation and Economic Sections of the Treaty.*

[14]Baker, II, 127–204.

the effect that she immediately withdraw all German vessels from Chinese and Japanese waters and deliver not later than September 15 "to the Imperial Japanese authorities without condition or compensation the entire leased territory of Kiao-chau with a view to the eventual restoration of the same to China." In a statement issued to the press Count Okuma said:

> As Premier of Japan, I have stated and I now again state to the people of America and all the world that Japan has no ulterior motive or desire to secure more territory, no thought of depriving China or any other peoples of anything which they now possess.

The Germans had spent about $100,000,000 in improving Tsing-tau, the principal city of Kiao-chau, and they had no intention of surrendering. After a siege of two months the city was captured by the Japanese army and navy, assisted by a small force of British troops. This was the first act in the drama. On January 8, 1915, Japan suddenly presented to the Chinese government the now famous Twenty-one Demands, deliberately misrepresenting to the United States and other powers the nature of these demands. Among other things, Japan demanded not only that China should assent to any agreement in regard to Shantung that Japan and Germany might reach at the conclusion of the war, but that she should also grant to her greater rights and concessions in Shantung than Germany had enjoyed. China was finally forced to agree to fifteen of these demands.[15]

The Twenty-One Demands of Japan

Japan's next step was to acquire from the Allies the assurance that they would support her claims to Shantung and to the German islands in the Pacific north of the equator at the end of the war. This she did in secret agreements signed in February and March, 1917, with England, France, Italy, and Russia. England agreed to support Japan's

The secret treaties with Japan

[15]MacMurray, II, 1231.

claim on condition that Japan would support her claims to the Pacific islands south of the equator. France signed on condition that Japan would use her influence on China to break relations with Germany and place at the disposal of the Allies the German ships interned in Chinese ports. The Allies were evidently uneasy about Japan, and were willing to do anything that was necessary to satisfy her. This uncertainty about Japan may also be the explanation of the Lansing-Ishii agreement signed November 2, 1917, in which the United States recognized the "special interests" of Japan in China.[16]

An embarrassment to Wilson

The secret treaties of the Allies relating to the Japanese claims were not revealed until the disposition of the German islands in the Pacific was under discussion at the Peace Conference. When informed by Baron Makino that the islands north of the equator had been pledged to Japan by agreements signed two years before, President Wilson inquired whether there were other secret agreements, and was informed that the German rights in Shantung had also been promised to Japan. As the other powers were pledged to support Japan's claims, President Wilson found himself in a very embarrassing situation, especially as he had also to oppose Japan's demand that a clause recognizing racial equality be inserted in the Covenant of the League. This was a moral claim that Japan urged with great strategic effect. In pushing her claims to Shantung she ignored all moral considerations and relied entirely upon her legal status, secured (1) by the secret treaties with the Allies, (2) by the treaty of 1915 with China, and (3) by right of conquest. When charged with having coerced China into signing the treaty of 1915, Japan replied with truth that most of the important treaties with China had been extorted by force. Japan declared, however, that she had no intention of holding Shantung permanently, but that she would restore

[16]MacMurray, II, 1167–1169, 1394.

the province in full sovereignty to China, retaining only the economic privileges transferred from Germany. In view of this oral promise, President Wilson finally acquiesced in the recognition of Japan's legal status in Shantung.[17]

Signing of the Treaty of Versailles

On May 7 the completed treaty was presented to the German delegates who had been summoned to Versailles to receive it. When the text was made public in Berlin there was an indignant outcry against the alleged injustice of certain provisions which were held to be inconsistent with the pledges given by President Wilson in the pre-Armistice negotiations, and the Germans made repeated efforts to draw the Allies into a general discussion of principles. They were, however, finally given to understand that they must accept or reject the treaty as it stood, and on June 28 it was signed in the Hall of Mirrors at Versailles—the same hall in which William I had been crowned German Emperor forty-eight years before.[18]

The treaty submitted to the Senate

The next day President Wilson sailed for the United States, and on July 10 personally presented the treaty to the Senate with an earnest appeal for prompt ratification. The Committee on Foreign Relations, to which the treaty was referred, proceeded with great deliberation, and on July 31 began a series of public hearings which lasted until September 12.[19] The Committee called before it Secretary Lansing and several of the technical advisers to the American delegation, including B. M. Baruch, economic adviser, Norman H. Davis, financial adviser, and David Hunter Miller, legal adviser. The Committee also called before it a number of American citizens who had had no official connection with the negotiations but who wished to speak in behalf of foreign groups, including

Hearings of the Committee on Foreign Relations

---

[17]Baker, II, 223–267.

[18]*Ibid.*, pp. 491–522; Temperley, II, 1–20.

[19]Hearings before the Committee on Foreign Relations of the United States Senate, 66 Cong., 1 Sess., Sen. Doc. No. 106.

Thomas F. Millard for China, Joseph W. Folk for Egypt, Dudley Field Malone for India, and a large delegation of Americans of Irish descent who opposed the League of Nations on the ground that it would stand in the way of Ireland's aspiration for independence. The rival claims of Jugo-Slavs and Italians to Fiume, the demand of Albania for self-determination, the claims of Greece to Thrace, and arguments for and against the separation of Austria and Hungary were all presented at great length to the Committee. On August 19, the President received the Committee at the White House, and after submitting a written statement on certain features of the Covenant, he was questioned by members of the Committee and a general discussion followed.[20]

The debate on the treaty

Meanwhile, the treaty was being openly debated in the Senate. The President had been an advocate of publicity in diplomacy as well as in other things, and the Senate now undertook to use his own weapon against him by a public attack on the treaty. Although the opposition to the treaty was started in the Senate by Lodge, Borah, Johnson, Sherman, Reed, and Poindexter, it was not confined to that body. Throughout the country there were persons of liberal views who favored the League of Nations but objected to the severe terms imposed on Germany, and charged the President with having proved false to the principles of the Fourteen Points. There were others who did not object to a severe peace, but who were bound fast by the tradition of isolation and thought membership in the League of Nations would involve the sacrifice of national sovereignty. The main object of attack was Article X, which guaranteed the territorial integrity and political independence of all the members of the League. President Wilson stated to the Senate Committee that he regarded Article X as "the very backbone of the whole Covenant," and that "without it the League would be

[20]Lodge, *The Senate and the League of Nations*, 297–379.

hardly more than an influential debating society."[21] The opponents of the League declared that this article would embroil the United States in the internal affairs of Europe, and that it deprived Congress of its constitutional right to declare war.

Senatorial groups

In the Senate there were three groups: the small number of "irreconcilables," who opposed the ratification of the treaty in any form; a larger group, who favored ratification without amendments, but who finally expressed their willingness to accept "interpretative reservations"; and a large group composed mainly of Republicans, who favored the ratification of the treaty only on condition that there should be attached to it reservations safeguarding what they declared to be the fundamental rights and interests of the United States. This group differed among themselves as to the character of the reservations that were necessary, and some of them became known as "mild reservationists."[22]

It is probable that at the outset only the small group of "irreconcilables" hoped or intended to bring about the defeat of the treaty, but as the debate proceeded and the opposition to the treaty received more and more popular support, the reservationists determined to defeat the treaty altogether rather than accept any compromise.

The partisan attack on Wilson

The Republican leaders were quick to realize that the tide of public opinion had turned and was now running strongly against the President. They determined, therefore, to ruin him at all hazards, and thus to bring about the election of a Republican president.

When President Wilson realized that the treaty was really in danger of defeat, he determined to go on an extended tour of the country for the purpose of explaining the treaty to the people and bringing pressure to bear on

---

[21]66 Cong., 1 Sess., Sen. Doc. No. 106, p. 500.

[22]Finch, "The Treaty of Peace with Germany in the United States Senate," in *Am. Journal of Int. Law*, XIV, 164.

the Senate. Beginning at Columbus, Ohio, on September 4, he proceeded through the northern tier of states to the Pacific Coast, then visited California and returned through Colorado. He addressed large audiences who received him with great enthusiasm. He was "trailed" by Senator Hiram Johnson, who was sent out by the opposition in the Senate to present the other side. Johnson also attracted large crowds. On the return trip, after delivering an address at Pueblo, Colorado, and while on the train bound for Wichita, Kansas, September 26, the President showed signs of a nervous breakdown and returned immediately to Washington.[23] He was able to walk from the train to his automobile, but a few days later he was partially paralyzed. The full extent and the seriousness of his illness were carefully concealed from the public. He was confined to the White House for five months, and had to abandon all efforts in behalf of the treaty.

The President's tour of the West

His illness

On September 10, the Committee on Foreign Relations reported the treaty to the Senate with a number of amendments and reservations. The Committee declared that the League was an alliance, and that it would "breed wars instead of securing peace." They also declared that the Covenant demanded "sacrifices of American independence and sovereignty which would in no way promote the world's peace," and that the amendments and reservations which they proposed were intended "to guard American rights and American sovereignty." The following day the minority members of the Committee submitted a report opposing both amendments and reservations. A few days later Senator McCumber presented a third report representing the views of the "mild reservationists." It objected to the phraseology of the Committee's reservations as unnecessarily severe and recommended substitute reservations. The treaty then became the regular

The treaty reported to the Senate

[23]His addresses on the western tour are published in *The Messages and Papers of Woodrow Wilson* (Shaw, Editor), II, 727–1130.

order in the Senate and was read section by section and debated each day for over two months. The amendments of the text of the treaty were all rejected by substantial majorities for the reason that their adoption would have made it necessary to resubmit the treaty not only to the Allies but also to Germany. The majority of the senators were opposed to such a course. The Committee, therefore, decided to substitute reservations for amendments, and Senator Lodge finally submitted, on behalf of the Committee, fourteen reservations preceded by a preamble, which declared that the ratification of the treaty was not to take effect or bind the United States until these reservations had been accepted as a condition of ratification by at least three of the four principal Allied and associated powers, namely, Great Britain, France, Italy, and Japan.[24]

Fourteen reservations adopted

The first reservation provided that in case of withdrawal from the League the United States should be the sole judge as to whether its international obligations under the Covenant had been fulfilled. This reservation was adopted by a vote of 50 to 35.

The second reservation declared that the United States assumed no obligation to preserve the territorial integrity or political independence of any other country, or to interfere in controversies between nations under the provisions of Article X, "or to employ the military or naval forces of the United States under any article of the treaty for any purpose, unless in any particular case the Congress which, under the Constitution, has the sole power to declare war or authorize the employment of the military or naval forces of the United States, shall by act or joint resolution so provide." This reservation was adopted by a vote of 46 to 33.

Article X

Reservation Number 3, providing that no mandate under

[24]Finch, "The Treaty of Peace with Germany in the United States Senate," *Am. Journal of International Law,* XIV, 165–174.

the treaty should be accepted by the United States except by action of Congress, was adopted by a vote of 52 to 31.

Number 4, excluding domestic questions from consideration by the Council or the Assembly of the League, was adopted by a vote of 59 to 36.

The Monroe Doctrine

Number 5, declaring the Monroe Doctrine "to be wholly outside the jurisdiction of said League of Nations and entirely unaffected by any provision contained in said treaty of peace with Germany," and reserving to the United States the sole right to interpret the Monroe Doctrine, was adopted by a vote of 55 to 34.

Number 6, withholding the assent of the United States from the provisions of the treaty relating to Shantung and reserving full liberty of action with respect to any controversy which might arise under said article between China and Japan, was adopted by a vote of 53 to 41.

Number 7, reserving to Congress the right to provide by law for the appointment of the representatives of the United States in the Assembly and Council of the League, and members of commissions, committees, or courts under the League, and requiring the confirmation of all by the Senate, was adopted by a vote of 53 to 40.

Number 8, declaring that the Reparations Commission should not be understood as having the right to regulate or interfere with exports from the United States to Germany or from Germany to the United States without an act or joint resolution of Congress, was adopted by a vote of 54 to 40.

Number 9, declaring that the United States should not be under any obligation to contribute to any of the expenses of the League without an act of Congress, was adopted by a vote of 56 to 39.

Number 10, providing that if the United States should at any time adopt any plan for the limitation of armaments proposed by the Council of the League, it reserved "the right to increase such armaments without the consent of the Council whenever the United States is threatened with invasion or engaged in war," was adopted by a vote of 56 to 39.

Number 11, reserving the right of the United States to permit the nationals of a Covenant-breaking state residing within the United States to continue their commercial, financial, and personal relations with the nationals of the United States, was adopted by a vote of 53 to 41.

Number 12, relating to the very complicated question of private debts, property rights and interests of American citizens, was adopted by a vote of 52 to 41.

Number 13, withholding the assent of the United States from the entire section of the treaty relating to international labor organization until Congress should decide to participate, was adopted by a vote of 54 to 35.

Restrictions on the votes of dominions or colonies

Number 14 declared that the United States would not be bound by any action of the Council or Assembly in which any member of the League and its self-governing dominions or colonies should cast in the aggregate more than one vote. This reservation was adopted by a vote of 55 to 38.[25]

A number of other reservations were offered and rejected. Under the rules of the Senate, amendments and reservations to a treaty may be adopted by a majority vote, while a treaty can be ratified only by a two-thirds vote. A number of senators who were opposed to the treaty voted for the Lodge reservations in order to insure its defeat.

The Senate unable to reach an agreement

When the vote on the treaty with the reservations was taken November 19, it stood 39 for and 55 against. A motion to reconsider the vote was then adopted, and Senator Hitchcock, the Democratic leader, proposed five reservations covering the right of withdrawal, domestic questions, the Monroe Doctrine, the right of Congress to decide on the employment of the naval and military forces of the United States in any case arising

[25] *Op. cit.*, p. 203.

under Article X, and restrictions on the voting powers of self-governing colonies or dominions. These reservations were rejected, the vote being 41 to 50. Another vote was then taken on the treaty with the Lodge reservations, the result being 41 for and 51 against. Senator Underwood then offered a resolution to ratify the treaty without reservations of any kind. The vote on this resolution was 38 for and 53 against.[26]

It was now evident that there was little prospect of securing the ratification of the treaty without compromise. On January 8, 1920, a letter from the President was read at the Jackson Day dinner in Washington, in which he refused to accept the decision of the Senate as final and said:

Wilson's Jackson Day letter

> There can be no reasonable objection to interpretations accompanying the act of ratification itself. But when the treaty is acted upon, I must know whether it means that we have ratified or rejected it. We cannot rewrite this treaty. We must take it without changes which alter its meaning, or leave it, and then, after the rest of the world has signed it, we must face the unthinkable task of making another and separate kind of treaty with Germany.

In conclusion he declared:

> If there is any doubt as to what the people of the country think on this vital matter, the clear and single way out is to submit it for determination at the next election to the voters of the nation, to give the next election the form of a great and solemn referendum, a referendum as to the part the United States is to play in completing the settlements of the war and in the prevention in the future of such outrages as Germany attempted to perpetrate.[27]

Futile attempt at compromise

During the last week of January a compromise was discussed by an informal bi-partisan committee, and the President wrote a letter saying he would accept the Hitchcock reservations, but Lodge refused to accept any

[26] *Op. cit.*, p. 204.

[27] *Messages and Papers of Woodrow Wilson*, II, 1161.

compromise.[28] On February 9, the Senate again referred the treaty to the Committee on Foreign Relations with instructions to report it back immediately with the reservations previously adopted. After several weeks of fruitless debate a fifteenth reservation, expressing sympathy for Ireland, was added to the others, by a vote of 38 to 36. It was as follows:

> In consenting to the ratification of the treaty with Germany the United States adheres to the principle of self-determination and to the resolution of sympathy with the aspirations of the Irish people for a government of their own choice adopted by the Senate June 6, 1919, and declares that when such government is obtained by Ireland, a consummation it is hoped is at hand, it should promptly be admitted as a member of the League of Nations.

Final vote and return of treaty to the President

With a few changes in the resolutions previously adopted and an important change in the preamble, the ratifying resolution was finally put to the vote March 19, 1920. The result was 49 votes for and 35 against. On the following day the secretary of the Senate was instructed by a formal resolution to return the treaty to the President and to inform him that the Senate had failed to ratify it.[29]

The "referendum" of 1920

The treaty thus became the leading issue in the Presidential campaign, but unfortunately it was not the only issue. The election proved to be a referendum on the Wilson administration as a whole rather than on the treaty. The Republican candidate, Senator Harding, attacked the Wilson administration for its arbitrary and unconstitutional methods and advocated a return to "normalcy." He denounced the Wilson League as an attempt to set up a super-government, but said he favored an association of nations and an international court. Governor Cox, the Democratic candidate, came out strongly for the treaty, particularly during the latter

[28] *Op. cit.*, p. 1166.

[29] *Cong. Record*, March 19, 1920, p. 4599.

part of his campaign. The result was an overwhelming victory for Harding. President Wilson had been too ill to take any part in the campaign. His administration had been the chief issue, and the people had, certainly for the time being, repudiated it. He accepted the result philosophically and refrained from comments, content, apparently, to leave the part he had played in world affairs to the verdict of history. In December, 1920, the Nobel Peace Prize was awarded to him as a foreign recognition of the services he had rendered to humanity, and after his death, which occurred February 3, 1924, a bronze tablet, with his head in bas-relief, was set up at Geneva, bearing the simple inscription: "Woodrow Wilson, Founder of the League of Nations."

Death of Wilson

PART VII

THE UNITED STATES IN THE POST-WAR PERIOD

CHAPTER XXVIII

PAN AMERICANISM

Fundamental changes

ALTHOUGH Latin America played a relatively insignificant part in the World War, its economic and financial relations with Europe and the United States were profoundly affected and are still in process of readjustment. Furthermore, the changes produced by the war were not merely economic and financial, but political as well, for the membership of most of the Latin-American states in the League of Nations has raised delicate questions affecting the Monroe Doctrine and relations with the United States. Thus while the war brought these countries into closer commercial and financial relations with North America, it also brought them into closer political relations with Europe.

Pan Americanism *versus* *Hispano Americanismo*

The failure of President Wilson to bring about American solidarity in face of the cataclysm that overwhelmed Europe in 1914 was due to psychological, racial, and political conditions in the Southern Hemisphere that require some description. His hopes were based on Pan Americanism, a movement which during the preceding quarter of a century had made what appeared to be substantial progress, but this movement was counteracted to a considerable extent by an opposing force of more recent origin and little noticed in the United States, namely Pan Hispanism, or to use the Spanish term *Hispano Americanismo*.

The Pan American movement, which has for its object the promotion of closer social, economic, financial, and

The Pan-American movement

political relations between the independent republics of the Western Hemisphere, dates back to the Panama Congress called by Simón Bolívar in 1826. This congress was a failure largely because the delegates of the United States, whose departure from Washington was delayed for several months by the debate in the Senate over their confirmation, did not reach Panama until the congress had adjourned. This was a keen disappointment to Henry Clay, then Secretary of State, who was our first Pan Americanist. The idea did not die, however, and various other attempts to convene the several republics in conference were made during the next half century, but these gatherings were not widely representative and accomplished little.[1]

The work of James G. Blaine

The modern Pan-American movement is identified with the name of James G. Blaine. On November 29, 1881, as Secretary of State he extended "to all the independent countries of North and South America an earnest invitation to participate in a general congress, to be held in the City of Washington on the 24th day of November, 1882, for the purpose of considering and discussing the methods of preventing war between the nations of America." He expressed the desire that the attention of the congress should be strictly confined to this one great object, and he expressed the hope that in setting a day for the assembling of the congress so far ahead, the war that was then in progress on the South Pacific coast would be ended, and the nations engaged would be able to take part in the proceedings.[2] In this expectation Mr. Blaine was disappointed. The war between Chile and Peru continued, and the invitations to the conference were withdrawn.[3]

Toward the close of President Cleveland's first adminis-

[1]*International American Conference,* IV (Historical Appendix). Washington: Govt. Printing Office, 1890.

[2]*Ibid.,* p. 255.

[3]*Ibid.,* p. 272.

tration, the Congress of the United States passed an act authorizing the President to invite the republics of Mexico, Central and South America, Haiti, Santo Domingo, and the Empire of Brazil, to join the United States in a conference at Washington on October 2, 1889.[4] Among the subjects proposed for discussion were the adoption of a customs union, the improvement of the means of communication between the various countries, uniform customs regulations, a uniform system of weights and measures, laws for the protection of patents and copyrights, extradition, the adoption of a common silver coin, and the formulation of a definite plan for the arbitration of international disputes of every character. When the conference assembled, Mr. Blaine was again Secretary of State, and presided over its opening sessions. The conference formulated a plan for international arbitration and declared that this means of settling disputes was "a principle of American international law." Unfortunately this treaty was not ratified by the governments whose representatives adopted it. The most lasting achievement of the conference was the establishment of the Bureau of American Republics in Washington. While the conference was in session Brazil went through a bloodless revolution, which converted the empire into a republic. Thus disappeared the only independent monarchy of European origin which existed on American soil.

The first International American Conference

The Bureau of American Republics

Scarcely had the Washington conference adjourned, when the United States and Chile got into an ugly wrangle and were brought to the verge of war over an attack on American sailors on shore leave at Valparaiso. During the civil war between President Balmaceda and the Congressional party, the American minister, Mr. Egan, admitted to the American legation certain adherents of the President. The people of Chile resented the action of the American minister, and were further aroused against

Chile and the United States on the verge of war

[4] *Op. cit.*, p. 375.

the United States by the case of the *Itata*, a vessel which left a California port with a cargo of arms for the Congressional party. She was followed to Iquique by two American war vessels and brought back to the United States, but eventually released by a court decision. The United States Cruiser *Baltimore* was lying in the harbor of Valparaiso when news of the seizure of the *Itata* was received. Members of the *Baltimore's* crew on shore leave were attacked by the populace. One American sailor was killed and several severely wounded. An apology was immediately demanded, but refused. After considerable delay, President Harrison had just laid the matter before Congress when a belated apology from Chile arrived, and war was fortunately averted. The charge that the United States had interfered in behalf of one of the parties in a civil strife created an unfavorable impression throughout Latin America and counteracted, to a considerable extent, the good effects of the Washington conference.[5]

The Second International American Conference

The Second International American Conference was held in the city of Mexico 1901-02. This conference arranged for all Latin-American states to become parties to the Hague Convention of 1899 for the pacific settlement of international disputes, and drafted a treaty for the compulsory arbitration of pecuniary claims, the first article of which was as follows:

> The High Contracting Parties agree to submit to arbitration all claims for pecuniary loss or damage which may be presented by their respective citizens, and which cannot be amicably adjusted through diplomatic channels and when said claims are of sufficient importance to warrant the expenses of arbitration.

This treaty was signed by the delegates of seventeen states, including the United States of America.[6]

The Third International American Conference was held

[5]Moore, *Dig. of Int. Law*, VI, 854–864.

[6]*Second International American Conference*, English text (Mexico, Government Printing Office, 1902), p. 309.

at Rio de Janeiro in 1906. Among other things it extended the pecuniary claims convention drafted by the previous conference for another period of five years, and recommended to the governments represented that they invite the Second Hague Conference, which had been called for 1907, "to examine the question of the compulsory collection of public debts, and, in general, means tending to diminish between nations conflicts having an exclusively pecuniary origin."[7] Added significance was given to the Rio conference by the presence of Secretary Root who, although not a delegate, made it the occasion of a special mission to South America. The series of notable addresses which he delivered on this mission gave a new impetus to the Pan-American movement.

The Third Conference

The Fourth International American Conference was held at Buenos Aires in 1910. It drafted treaties relating to patents, trade-marks, and copyrights. It extended the pecuniary claims convention for an indefinite period. And finally, it enlarged the scope of the Bureau of American Republics and changed its name to the Pan-American Union.[8] A fifth conference was called to meet at Santiago, Chile, in 1914, but was postponed on account of the European war. It finally met in the spring of 1923.

The Fourth Conference

The conferences above described were political or diplomatic in character. Besides these there have been several Pan-American scientific and financial conferences. These conferences have accomplished a great deal in the way of promoting friendly feeling and the advancement of science and commerce among the republics of the Western Hemisphere. The First Financial Conference held in Washington in May, 1915, recommended the establishment of an International High Commission, to be composed of not more than nine members resident in each

Scientific and financial conferences

[7] *Third International American Conference, Minutes, Resolutions. Documents* (Rio de Janeiro, Imprensa Nacional, 1907), p. 605.

[8] Bulletin of the Pan American Union, Vol. 31, p. 796.

country appointed by the Minister of Finance of such country for the purpose of carrying on the work of the conference. This recommendation was adopted by the various countries, and the Congress of the United States, by act of February 7, 1916, authorized the establishment of a section in this country. The International High Commission carries on its labors largely through the various national sections. Its first general meeting was held at Buenos Aires in April, 1916.

The American Institute of International Law

The American Institute of International Law, organized at Washington in October, 1912, is a body which is likely to have great influence in promoting the peace and welfare of this hemisphere. The Institute is composed of five representatives from the national society of international law in each of the twenty-one American republics. At a session held in Washington January 6, 1916, the Institute adopted a Declaration of the Rights and Duties of Nations which emphasized the favorite Pan-American doctrine of the equality of States in international law.[9] On the same day that the above Declaration was made public, President Wilson delivered a notable address before the Second Pan-American Scientific Conference then in session at Washington. In the course of this address he said:

Wilson's views on the Monroe Doctrine

> The Monroe Doctrine was proclaimed by the United States on her own authority. It has always been maintained, and always will be maintained, upon her own responsibility. But the Monroe Doctrine demanded merely that European governments should not attempt to extend their political systems to this side of the Atlantic. It did not disclose the use which the United States intended to make of her power on this side of the Atlantic. It was a hand held up in warning, but there was no promise in it of what America was going to do with the implied and partial protectorate which she apparently was trying to set up on this side of the water, and I believe you will sustain me in the statement that it has been fears and sus-

[9] *Am. Journal of Int. Law*, X, 212.

picions on this score which have hitherto prevented the greater intimacy and confidence and trust between the Americas. The states of America have not been certain what the United States would do with her power. That doubt must be removed. And latterly there has been a very frank interchange of views between the authorities in Washington and those who represent the other states of this hemisphere, an interchange of views charming and hopeful, because based upon an increasingly sure appreciation of the spirit in which they were undertaken. These gentlemen have seen that, if America is to come into her own, into her legitimate own, in a world of peace and order, she must establish the foundations of amity, so that no one will hereafter doubt them. I hope and I believe that this can be accomplished. These conferences have enabled me to foresee how it will be accomplished. It will be accomplished, in the first place, by the states of America uniting in guaranteeing to each other absolute political independence and territorial integrity. In the second place, and as a necessary corollary to that, guaranteeing the agreement to settle all pending boundary disputes as soon as possible and by amicable process; by agreeing that all disputes among themselves, should they unhappily arise, will be handled by patient, impartial investigation and settled by arbitration; and the agreement necessary to the peace of the Americas, that no state of either continent will permit revolutionary expeditions against another state to be fitted out in its territory, and that they will prohibit the exportation of the munitions of war for the purpose of supplying revolutionists against neighboring governments.[10]

The proposed Pan-American Pact

Rejected through fear of United States

President Wilson's Pan Americanism went further than some of the Latin-American states were willing to go. A treaty embodying the above proposals was actually drafted, but some of the states held back through the fear that, though equal in terms, it would in fact give the United States a plausible pretext for supervising the affairs of weaker states.[11] The main opposition came from Chile, and her attitude was probably due to the fear that under such a treaty she might be compelled to arbitrate the Tacna-Arica dispute.[12]

[10]World Peace Foundation, "The New Pan Americanism," Part II, p. 107.

[11]Moore, *Principles of American Diplomacy*, 407–408.

[12]Seymour, *Intimate Papers of Colonel House*, I, 221, 231.

Pan Americanism different from pan-national movements

Pan Americanism differs from the various pan-national movements, such as Pan Germanism and Pan Slavism, in being a continental and not a racial movement, for it embraces nations of such diverse race and culture as the United States on the one hand and the various countries of Hispanic origin on the other. Some Latin-American writers and at least one American writer[13] have tried to represent it as an imperialistic movement of the United States, differing little from the extreme militaristic type of Pan Germanism which aimed at the subjection of other peoples. The main force opposed to Pan Americanism in later years has been the pan-national movement known as Pan Hispanism or *Hispano Americanismo*.

Opposed by Pan Hispanism

This movement, which has for its object the racial, cultural, economic, and political solidarity of the Latin-American races, came into existence in the years following the Spanish War and kept pace with the advance of the United States in the Caribbean area. It is an appeal to the racial consciousness of the Hispanic peoples against Anglo-Saxon domination. It is based largely on Yankeephobia, and during the period of the World War was stimulated to some extent by German propaganda in Mexico and certain states of South America.

Manuel Ugarte

The chief apostle of Pan Hispanism was Manuel Ugarte, a native of the Argentine, who went to Paris as a young man to complete his education and spent many years abroad. He visited the United States in 1900 and spent some time in Mexico before returning to Europe. He was so impressed by the material progress and extraordinary vigor of the American people that he became convinced that they were destined to extend their sway, either through conquest or economic imperialism, over the less enterprising and aggressive peoples of Latin America, unless the latter could be aroused to a full realization of the danger. He returned to Europe with the determina-

[13] Usher, *Pan Americanism.*

tion to devote his literary skill to the task of warning his kindred of Hispanic blood against the "Yankee Peril." In 1910, he set forth his views in a book published at Valencia entitled *El Porvenir de la América Latina* (The Future of Latin America). In 1910 and 1911 he lectured in Barcelona and at the Sorbonne and then set out on a tour of America. During 1912 and 1913 he carried his message to the capitals of all the Latin-American countries and again visited the United States. In most of the Latin-American capitals he was received with popular enthusiasm but encountered official opposition and in some countries was not allowed to speak. He attributed the opposition to the official subservience to the United States, but it was probably due at least in equal measure to the fact that he was known to be a pronounced socialist. In 1917, he returned to Mexico at the invitation of President Carranza and later proceeded to his native city of Buenos Aires where he remained until the close of the World War. In 1923, he published at Madrid another book *El Destino de un Continente*.[14]

His tour of Latin America

Ugarte professed great admiration for the national characteristics which have made the United States great, but he blamed the people of his own race for not developing similar characteristics. He stated:

Warning against suicidal dissensions

> I have never blamed Cæsar for dividing Gaul against itself in order to subdue it. Cæsar's manœuvre was a sign of his superiority. But it is legitimate to deplore the fact that the Gauls were not astute enough to frustrate it. . . . My object has been to call the attention of the Aztecs and Gauls of my time and my family of nations to the possibility of avoiding suicidal dissensions, in order to develop a vigorous power, increase the health of their community, and co-ordinate it, in view of what is the supreme aspiration of every living species: development and survival. The United States have done and will continue to do what all the strong peoples in history have done, and

[14]This book has been translated into English by Catherine A. Phillips and edited with an introduction by J. Fred Rippy under the title *The Destiny of a Continent*, New York, 1925.

nothing can be more futile than the arguments used against this policy in Latin America. To invoke ethics in international affairs is almost always a confession of defeat.[15]

Ugarte's description of American imperialism would be flattering if it were true. He says:

Description of American imperialism

Never in all history has such an irresistible or marvellously concerted force been developed as that which the United States are bringing to bear upon the peoples which are geographically or politically within its reach in the south of the Continent or on the shores of the sea. Rome applied a uniform procedure. Spain persisted in a policy of ostentation and glittering show. Even in the present day, England and France strive to dominate rather than absorb. Only the United States have understood how to modify the mechanism of expansion in accordance with the tendencies of the age, employing different tactics in each case, and shaking off the trammels of whatever may prove an impediment or a useless burden in the achievement of its aspirations. . . . At times imperious, at other times suave, in certain cases apparently disinterested, in others implacable in its greed, pondering like a chess-player who foresees every possible move, with a breadth of vision embracing many centuries, better informed and more resolute than any, without fits of passion, without forgetfulness, without fine sensibilities, without fear, carrying out a world activity in which everything is foreseen—North American imperialism is the most perfect instrument of domination which has been known throughout the ages.[16]

His view of the Pan-American Union

Pan Americanism was regarded by Ugarte as "a skilful move in the expansionist policy of the North, and a suicidal tendency of the simple-minded South."[17] The Pan-American Union raised in his mind this question: "Can the existence at Washington of a department for the Spanish-American republics, organized like a Ministry for the Colonies, be reconciled with the full autonomy of our countries?"[18]

Ugarte's writings had a wide appeal and he had a large

[15]*The Destiny of a Continent,* 125.

[16]*Ibid.,* pp. 139–140.

[17]*Ibid.,* p. 288

[18]*Ibid.,* p. 6.

following particularly among university students. Many of his statements were rash, or exaggerated, and in general unsupported by documentary evidence. Some advocates of Pan Hispanism went even further than he did. Francisco Silva, for instance, another Argentine, lamented the fact that the Spanish colonies, influenced by the example of the United States, severed their relations with the mother country, and he advocated the organization of a vast imperial federation, including Spain and Portugal as well as the countries of Latin America, as the only means of resisting Anglo-Saxon absorption.[19]

Pan-Hispanic federation

The Pan-Hispanic movement received great encouragement in Spain, whose relations with Spanish America grew much closer after the liberation of Cuba. Since the beginning of the century historical, literary, and scientific congresses of Hispanic peoples have been held at Madrid, Barcelona, and Seville; permanent centers of Hispanic-American culture were established in the above-named cities and in Cadiz; and there were frequent interchanges of students and professors between the universities of Spain and South America.[20]

Pan-Hispanic movement encouraged by Spain

When President Wilson came into office he announced a new Latin-American policy. He not only declared that the United States would never seek another foot of territory by conquest, but he warned the Latin-American states against concessions to foreign capitalists and urged them to seek "emancipation from the subordination which has been inevitable to foreign enterprise."[21] He was soon embroiled much against his will with Mexico, and during the early years of the European War deemed it expedient to land marines in Haiti and Santo Domingo. These apparent departures from the principles of his announced

Sincerity of Wilson's policy questioned

[19]Silva, *Reparto de América Español y Pan-Hispanismo*, Madrid, 1918.
[20]Rippy, "Pan-Hispanic Propaganda in Hispanic America," in *Pol. Sci. Quarterly*, XXXVII, 389.
[21]*Messages and Papers of Woodrow Wilson*, I, 18, 32.

policy were eagerly seized by the Pan Hispanists and used for propaganda. They refused to believe in his sincerity and declared that his actions did not correspond with his words. Fortunately this view was taken only by the extremists, for Wilson's Mexican policy finally won general approval in Latin America. That policy was the acid test of his sincerity.

The Mexican situation

His handling of the Mexican situation, although denounced at the time as weak and vacillating, was in full accord with his new Latin-American policy. On February 18, 1913, Francisco Madero, who had overthrown the Diaz régime in 1911, was seized and imprisoned as the result of a conspiracy formed by one of his generals, Victoriano Huerta, who forthwith proclaimed himself dictator. Four days later Madero was murdered while in the custody of Huerta's troops. Henry Lane Wilson, the American ambassador, promptly urged his government to recognize Huerta, but President Taft, whose term was rapidly drawing to a close, took no action and left the question to his successor.

Refusal to recognize Huerta

President Wilson thus had a very disagreeable situation to face when he assumed control of affairs at Washington. He refused to recognize Huerta, whose authority was contested by insurrectionary chiefs in various parts of the country. It was claimed by the critics of the administration that the refusal to recognize Huerta was a direct violation of the well-known American policy of recognizing *de facto* governments without undertaking to pass upon the rights involved. It was perfectly true that the United States had consistently followed the policy of recognizing *de facto* governments as soon as it was evident in each case that the new government rested on popular approval and was likely to be permanent. This doctrine of recognition was distinctively an American doctrine. It was first laid down by Thomas Jefferson when he was Secretary of State as an offset to the European doctrine of divine right, and it was the natural outgrowth of that other Jeffersonian doctrine that all governments derive their just powers from the consent of the governed. Huerta could lay no claim to authority derived from a majority or anything like a majority of the Mexican people. He was a self-constituted dictator whose authority rested solely on military force. President Wilson and Secretary Bryan were fully justified in refusing to recognize his usurpation of power as long as there was armed opposition in Mexico, though they probably made a mistake in announcing that they would never recognize him and in demanding his elimination from the presidential contest. This announcement made him deaf to advice from Washington and utterly indifferent to the destruction of American life and property.

A self-constituted dictator

In dealing with the Mexican situation the administration was embarrassed by the fact that the British Minister in Mexico, Sir Lionel Carden, was an advocate of Huerta and was supposed to represent the oil interests of Lord Cowdray, the head of Pearson and Son of London. Lord Cowdray also had large oil concessions in Nicaragua and had just arranged the terms of a still more extensive concession in Colombia. His contracts ran counter to President Wilson's warning to Latin America against concessions that might imperil a country's autonomy. One of Ambassador Page's first delicate tasks was to win British support for the President's new Latin-American policy, and in particular for his Mexican policy.

British oil interests support Huerta

But the situation was further complicated by the dispute with Great Britain over the Panama Tolls Act which had exempted American ships engaged in the coast-wise trade from the payment of tolls. Great Britain claimed that this act was in violation of the Hay-Pauncefote treaty and this contention was supported by Elihu Root and many of the ablest international lawyers in America. Great Britain took a determined stand on this question,

Wilson embarrassed by the Panama Tolls Act

which involved the sanctity of a treaty obligation, and Page felt that it was hopeless to ask British support for American policy in Mexico until this matter was settled. He explained to Sir Edward Grey the difficulties that the President would encounter in persuading Congress to reverse its action and he pleaded for patience, promising that the President would take the matter up in due time. The British government in the meantime compelled Lord Cowdray to abandon his concession still pending before the Colombian congress and recalled Sir Lionel Carden from Mexico. On March 5, 1914, after conference with the Senate Committee on Foreign Relations, President Wilson appeared before the two Houses of Congress and in a short address urged the repeal of the exemption clause of the Tolls Act. He made the following extraordinary appeal:

His extraordinary appeal to Congress

> I ask this of you in support of the foreign policy of the Administration. I shall not know how to deal with other matters of even greater delicacy and nearer consequence if you do not grant it to me in ungrudging measure.

This mysterious reference was the subject of much conjecture in the press. Some interpreted it as referring to Japan and the Anglo-Japanese alliance, but none hit upon the true explanation—the understanding which Page had arranged with Great Britain and the elimination of Huerta. The President's appeal precipitated an intemperate debate, which lasted for three months and in which anti-British feeling was conspicuous, but the repeal measure was in the end adopted.[22]

Occupation of Vera Cruz

The next step in the President's course with reference to Mexico was the occupation of Vera Cruz. On April 20, 1914, he asked Congress for authority to employ the armed forces of the United States in demanding redress for the arbitrary arrest of American marines at Tampico

[22]Seymour, *Intimate Papers of Colonel House*, I, 194–206; Hendrick, *Life and Letters of Walter H. Page*, I, 175–269.

and the next day Admiral Fletcher was ordered to seize the custom house at Vera Cruz. This he did after a sharp fight with Huerta's troops in which nineteen Americans were killed and seventy wounded. The American *chargé d'affaires*, Nelson O'Shaughnessy, was at once handed his passports, and all diplomatic relations between the United States and Mexico were severed.

Mediation of the A B C Powers

A few days later the representatives of the so-called A B C Powers, Argentina, Brazil, and Chile, tendered their good offices for a peaceful settlement of the conflict and President Wilson promptly accepted their mediation. The resulting conference at Niagara, May 20, was not successful in its immediate object, but it was followed by the elimination of Huerta who resigned July 15, 1914. On August 20, General Venustiano Carranza, head of one of the revolutionary factions, assumed control of affairs at the capital, but his authority was disputed by General Francisco Villa, another insurrectionary chief. On Carranza's promise to respect the lives and property of American citizens the United States forces were withdrawn from Vera Cruz in November, 1914.

Recognition of Carranza

In August, 1915, at the request of President Wilson the six ranking representatives of Latin America at Washington made an unsuccessful effort to reconcile the contending factions of Mexico. On their advice, however, President Wilson decided in October to recognize the government of Carranza, who now controlled three-fourths of the territory of Mexico. As a result of this action Villa began a series of attacks on American citizens and raids across the border, which in March, 1916, compelled the President to send a punitive expedition into Mexico and later to dispatch most of the regular army and large bodies of militia to the border.[23]

[23] "Affairs in Mexico," 64 Cong., 1 Sess., Sen. Doc. No. 324. The World Peace Foundation has issued two pamphlets containing documents on Mexico under the title of "The New Pan Americanism," Parts I and II (February and April, 1916).

"Watchful waiting"

The raids of Villa created a very awkward situation. Carranza not only made no real effort to suppress Villa but he vigorously opposed the steps taken by the United States to protect her own citizens along the border, and even assumed a threatening attitude. There was a loud and persistent demand in the United States for war against Mexico. American investments in land, mines, rubber plantations, and other enterprises were very large, and these financial interests were particularly outraged at the President's policy of "watchful waiting." The President remained deaf to this clamor. No country had been so shamelessly exploited by foreign capital as Mexico. Furthermore, it was suspected and very generally believed that the recent revolutions had been financed by American capital. President Wilson was determined to give the Mexican people an opportunity to reorganize their national life on a better basis and to lend them every assistance in the task. War with Mexico would have been a very serious undertaking and even a successful war would have meant the military occupation of Mexico for an indefinite period. President Wilson's refusal to become involved in war with Mexico convinced the world of his sincerity and gave him a hearing during the Great War such as no political leader of any nation ever before commanded. His acceptance of the mediation of the A B C Powers and his subsequent consultation with the leading representatives of Latin America gave new life and meaning to Pan Americanism and tended to refute the charges of the Pan Hispanists. Mr. Fletcher, the United States minister in Chile, wrote enthusiastically to Colonel House of "the President's success in the Mexican difficulties—turning, as he did, a situation fraught with difficulties and danger to our American relations into a triumph of Pan Americanism."[24]

Moral effect of Wilson's policy

The loyalty of the Latin-American states to the prin-

[24]Seymour, *Intimate Papers of Colonel House,* I, 207.

ciples of Pan Americanism was put to a severe test when the United States entered the Great War. When President Wilson announced to Congress the severance of relations with Germany and declared his intention of protecting our commerce on the high seas, he expressed the confident hope that all neutral governments would pursue the same course. He probably had especially in mind our Latin-American neighbors, but if so, his expectation was not fully realized. Only eight of the twenty Latin-American republics eventually entered the war: Brazil, Costa Rica, Cuba, Guatemala, Haiti, Honduras, Nicaragua, and Panama. Five others broke off relations with Germany: Bolivia, Peru, the Dominican Republic, Ecuador, and Uruguay. Seven remained neutral: Argentina, Chile, Colombia, Mexico, Salvador, Venezuela, and Paraguay.[25]

Pan Americanism tested by the War

Only two Latin-American states, Brazil and Cuba, took an active part in the war. At the request of the British government in December, 1917, Brazil sent two cruisers and four destroyers to European waters to coöperate with the British navy, and a few months later a group of Brazilian aviators took their place on the Western front. A number of physicians and several Red Cross units from Brazil also coöperated with the Allies. Cuba turned over to the United States several German steamships interned in her waters. A compulsory military service law was passed and a number of training camps established. In October, 1918, the Cuban government announced that it had 25,000 troops ready to send to France, but the Armistice was signed before arrangements could be made for their transportation. The only active service rendered by Cubans was in the field of aviation, where several individuals won high distinction.[26]

Brazil and Cuba take part

Of the A B C Powers Argentina and Chile remained neutral. So also did Mexico. Brazil was thus the only one

[25]Percy A. Martin, *Latin America and the War*, Introd., p. 1.

[26]*Ibid.*, chap. ii.

Brazil in full sympathy with the United States

of the larger states that actually entered the war. The relations between Brazil and the United States have almost always been peculiarly close and friendly. From the outbreak of the European War strong sympathy for the allied cause was manifested in Brazil, and a league for aiding the Allies through the agency of the Red Cross was organized under the presidency of Ruy Barbosa, the most distinguished statesman of Brazil and one of the most brilliant orators of Latin America. Brazil's experience during the period of neutrality was very similar to that of the United States. Her commerce was interfered with and her ships were sunk by German submarines. A few weeks after the United States entered the war, Brazil severed relations with Germany and seized the forty-six German ships interned in Brazilian harbors. In a circular note of June 2 the Brazilian government declared to the world that it had taken this step because the Republic of Brazil was bound to the United States "by a traditional friendship and by a similarity of political opinion in the defense of the vital interests of America and the principles accepted by international law," and because it wished to give to its foreign policy, in this critical moment of the world's history, "a practical form of continental solidarity—a policy indeed which was that of the old régime on every occasion on which any of the other friendly sister nations of the American continent were in jeopardy." President Wilson's reply to this note expressed the deep appreciation of the United States and the hope that the act of the Brazilian Congress was "the forerunner of the attitude to be assumed by the rest of the American states."

Declares war

On October 26, 1917, on the receipt of the news of the torpedoing of another Brazilian ship by a German submarine, a resolution recognizing "the state of war initiated by the German Empire against Brazil" was adopted by the unanimous vote of the Brazilian Senate and by a vote of 149 to 1 in the Chamber of Deputies. Brazil's enthusiastic support of the United States and of the allied cause was recognized by those powers by giving her representation on the Council of the League of Nations. In fact, at the first meeting of the Council in London in February, 1920, Brazil was the sole American power represented.[27]

Pro-Ally sentiment in the Argentine

Argentina, the largest and most important of the states of Spanish origin, remained neutral throughout the war, notwithstanding the fact that a large part of the population and some of the leading newspapers were strongly pro-Ally. When the United States declared war, Señor Drago, the former Minister of Foreign Affairs and author of the doctrine that bears his name, issued a statement in which he said:

> The war between Germany and America is a struggle of democracy *versus* absolutism, and no American nation can remain neutral without denying its past and compromising its future.

President Irigoyen persists in neutral course

About the same time a note was sent through Ambassador Naón stating that "in view of the causes which have prompted the United States to declare war against the government of the German Empire," the Argentine government recognizes "the justice of that decision." But German propaganda, which had its headquarters in Buenos Aires, and the attitude of President Irigoyen kept the country out of the war. Popular indignation was aroused by the Luxburg disclosures, which revealed the fact that the German representative, after coming to an understanding with the President, had advised his government that two Argentine ships then approaching the French coast "be spared if possible, or else sunk without a trace being left" (*spurlos versenkt*). The Senate and Chamber of Deputies passed by large majorities a resolution severing relations with Germany, but to the surprise of everybody President Irigoyen expressed himself as

[27] *Op. cit.*, chap. 1.

satisfied with Germany's disavowal of Luxburg's conduct and continued his policy of neutrality.[28]

Division of public sentiment in Chile

Chile was so far removed from the scene of the war in Europe and had so few ships engaged in European trade that her government did not have the same provocation that others had. Furthermore, German propaganda had made great headway in Chile and the Chilean army, trained by German officers, was strongly pro-German. In the navy, on the other hand, sentiment was strongly in favor of the Allies. This was a matter of tradition, for since the days of Lord Cochrane the Chilean navy has followed English ideals. Under these circumstances Chile remained neutral, though before the end of the war public sentiment had shifted to the side of the Allies.[29]

The remaining states

Peru, Ecuador, Bolivia, and Uruguay in severing relations with Germany proclaimed their adherence to the principle of American solidarity. Paraguay's neutrality was due to her isolation. Colombia, still smarting under the loss of the Isthmus, was not disposed to take sides with the United States. In Venezuela most of the government officials were under German influence. Panama and four of the five Central American republics declared war on Germany, Salvador alone remaining neutral. Cuba and Haiti also declared war on Germany, while the Dominican Republic severed consular relations. Mexico proclaimed its neutrality, but permitted its soil to become a hot-bed of German intrigue, and President Carranza exhibited at times a spirit of hostility to the United States which tended to increase the tension that already existed between the two countries.[30]

Of the thirteen Latin-American republics which severed relations with Germany eleven were represented at the Peace Conference at Paris and signed the Treaty of

---

[28] *Op. cit.*, chap. iii.

[29] Enrique Rocuant, *The Neutrality of Chile and the Grounds That Prompted and Justified It* (Valparaiso, 1919); Martin, chap. iv.

[30] Martin, chaps. v–x.

Versailles. Of those who signed the treaty all except Ecuador ratified it and thus became members of the League of Nations. Most of the remaining Latin-American states joined at the first opportunity. But with the declining prestige of the League many of the South American countries have withdrawn or have given notice of their intention to withdraw. Most of the member states have accepted the protocol establishing the Permanent Court of International Justice and twelve of them[31] have signed the additional protocol accepting the compulsory jurisdiction of the Court.[32] In view of the membership of these American republics, not to mention Canada, in the League, that body could not properly be referred to, as it so often was by high officials in the United States, as a European League. The Latin-American states took a prominent part in the work of the League, and in the early years of the Geneva institution gave it full-hearted and warm support. Brazil became a member of the Council when that body was first created, and though a temporary member, she was annually reëlected. Her refusal at the meeting of the League in March, 1926, to agree to the enlargement of the permanent membership of the Council except on the condition that she be given a permanent seat, made it necessary to postpone the admission of Germany to the League and to defer the operation of the Locarno treaties upon which the hope of European peace was based. Brazil's position was the subject of much criticism and she failed to receive the support of what is sometimes referred to as the Latin-American block. When she was refused a permanent Council seat, she resigned from the League, June 12, 1928.

Latin-American members of the League

Brazil's prominence

Brazil has also contributed two judges to the World

[31]They are Bolivia, Brazil, Colombia, Haiti, Panama, Peru, Salvador, Uruguay, Dominican Republic, Costa Rica, Guatemala, Nicaragua.

[32]League of Nations, A6, 1939, Annex 1, pp. 10–15.

Latin-American judges on the World Court

Court: Ruy Barbosa and after his death Judge Pessoa. Cuba has contributed Judge Bustamante, the author of an admirable book on the history and work of the Court. Agustin Edwards of Chile was elected president of the Third Assembly in 1922 and Cosme de la Torriente of Cuba was elected to the same position by the Fourth Assembly in 1923. Americans have seven times been honored with the presidency of the Assembly of the League.

Failure of United States to join the League regarded with suspicion

Article X of the Covenant guaranteeing the territorial integrity and political independence of all members of the League was regarded with enthusiasm by Latin-Americans as a fulfilment of President Wilson's proposal to internationalize the Monroe Doctrine, but the subsequent reservation of "regional understandings like the Monroe Doctrine" in Article XXI was regarded with disfavor and suspicion. The fact that the United States Senate did not regard this reservation as sufficient and the final refusal to ratify the Covenant were interpreted as evidence of an intention on the part of the United States to retain the Monroe Doctrine as a cloak for American imperialism. This view was confirmed later by the action of the United States at the Fifth Pan-American Conference at Santiago in 1923. President Brum of Uruguay presented to the conference a plan for the organization of an American League, based on the absolute equality of states, as a subsidiary of the League of Nations. This scheme, which was not unlike President Wilson's proposed Pan-American Pact, would have converted the Monroe Doctrine into a Pan-American doctrine. Through the opposition of the United States delegation President Brum's proposal was not allowed to come to a vote.[33]

In March, 1921, while the Council of the League was in session at Paris news was received through the press that Panama and Costa Rica were on the point of going to

[33] Martin, *Latin America and the War,* 570.

war over a boundary dispute. As both states were members of the League, the Council directed the Secretary-General to send the following cablegram to the secretaries of foreign affairs of Panama and Costa Rica:

Council of League takes cognizance of American dispute

> Council of League of Nations now sitting in Paris has had brought to its notice certain reports from which it would appear that a state of tension exists between the Governments of Costa Rica and Panama. The members of Council feel it incumbent upon them to bring these reports to the attention of the Governments of Costa Rica and Panama, states members of the League, who have solemnly and publicly subscribed to the high principle and obligations of the Covenant and to request information as to the facts.[34]

Both states replied promptly, each giving its side of the controversy.

Secretary Hughes intervenes

At this point Secretary Hughes intervened and reminded the parties that under the Panama-Costa Rica treaty of 1915 they had agreed to submit disputes to the mediation of the United States. In a note to Panama he informed her that unless she turned over at once to Costa Rica the territory in dispute the United States would feel compelled to take the necessary steps to inforce the award of President Loubet of France, which defined the boundary on the Pacific side, and the award of Chief Justice White, which defined the boundary on the Atlantic side. Both states accepted the good offices of the United States and the dispute was settled without further action by the League.[35]

Bolivia's appeal to the League

In September, 1921, Bolivia appealed to the Assembly of the League for a revision of her treaty of 1904 with Chile, by which she had surrendered her title to the former Bolivian province of Antofagasta, on the ground that the treaty had been imposed on her by force. The Bolivian demand was stoutly opposed by the Chilean delegation and gave rise to a hot debate. Agustin Edwards

[34]Minutes of the Council, 12th session, 1921, pp. 42, 199.

[35]*Ibid.*, p. 201.

insisted that the League was without power to revise existing treaties and furthermore that in view of the reservation in Article XXI of "regional understandings like the Monroe Doctrine" it had no power to interfere in purely American affairs. The question was finally referred to a commission of jurists, who reported that "the demand of Bolivia was inadmissible, as the Assembly of the League of Nations cannot modify on its own accord any treaty, such modification being solely within the competency of the contracting states."[36]

The Tacna-Arica dispute

Secretary Hughes forestalled the submission of the Tacna-Arica dispute between Peru and Chile to the League of Nations by insisting that it be submitted to the arbitration of the President of the United States. These provinces had been seized by Chile in the so-called War of the Pacific which began in 1879. By the treaty of Ancon, ratified in 1884, Peru ceded the valuable nitrate province of Tarapaca to Chile and agreed to Chilean occupation and administration of the provinces of Tacna and Arica for a period of ten years, on condition that at the end of that term the future ownership of the provinces should be determined by a plebiscite. When the time came for holding the plebiscite the two powers were unable to agree upon the terms under which it should be carried out. For over thirty years the dispute over these provinces had been a sore spot in the international relations of South America. It involved legal and political questions of the most delicate nature. The provinces themselves are of little value, but the national pride involved is immense. In 1925, President Coolidge, acting as arbiter, finally decided that the Treaty of Ancon should be carried out and a plebiscite held. This decision appeared equivalent to giving the provinces to Chile, for in the now more than forty years that they have been in her possession they have been to a large extent Chileanized. General Pershing was

[36]Martin, *Latin America and the War*, 552–554.

Pershing's futile mission

sent down as chairman of a commission, which included representatives of Chile and Peru, to decide who should vote and to superintend the plebiscite. Never was a man sent on a more fruitless mission or assigned a more impossible task. If it was the intention of the President to give the provinces to Chile, as has been intimated, that object could have been accomplished by a Tammany politician better than by an honest, straightforward man like Pershing. Only a man with Hughes' lack of imagination could have deliberately put his country in such a position. If he had let the dispute go to the World Court or to the League, the result might have been equally fruitless, but the loss of prestige would have fallen on the League and not on the United States. Prior to the organization of the League of Nations the United States witnessed without objection the submission of American boundary disputes to the kings of England, Spain, and Italy, to the Czar of Russia, and to the Presidents of France and Switzerland. But Hughes' desire to boycott the League led to a change of policy. American questions, he felt, must be decided in America. This policy, however, was abandoned by the Hoover administration. In the Chaco dispute[37] between Paraguay and Bolivia and in the Leticia dispute between Colombia and Peru, the League has taken a lively part with the consent and blessing of the United States.

Hughes' desire to boycott the League

Of great importance, however, is the question of the financial dependence of the weaker Latin-American states on the United States. In this respect the World War has brought about revolutionary changes. Prior to the War there was not a single United States bank in Latin America, and capital for industrial development was supplied mainly by Europe, especially by England and Germany. Today the United States has numerous banks in South America and in the Caribbean area. The total

[37] See p. 852.

Financial interest of United States in Latin America

of North American investments in Latin America at the end of 1930 was estimated by the Department of Commerce to be between $5,150,000,000 and $5,350,000,000.[38] Some of these advances were made only after consultation with the Department of State. With the defaults that have come as the result of the world economic depression the State Department up to 1933 had taken no step to help our investors.

In order to secure loans, Peru and several of the weaker states accepted, through the good offices of the Department of State, the inevitable financial adviser. But his presence did not prevent Peru from defaulting on her foreign bonds. As a further mark of the growing influence of the United States, Peru received an American naval mission and an educational mission. Even Brazil, which since the days of Lord Cochrane had followed the traditions and models of the British navy, decided after the War to turn to the American navy, and in response to her request the United States sent down in 1922 an imposing mission including about thirty officers of all branches of the service. In matters of public health the Rockefeller Foundation has done a vast amount of highly commendable work in stamping out the hook worm, malaria, yellow fever, and other tropical diseases in Colombia, Ecuador, Peru, and Brazil.

Other influences

Whatever may be the fate of the weaker states that border on the Caribbean, South America as a whole has little to fear from the "Yankee Peril" even in the form of financial imperialism. The Monroe Doctrine has in the past been an open-door policy. It has saved South America from European domination and spheres of influence. And while the United States as a result of the War attained a position of unexpected financial and commercial influence, England and Germany recovered

[38] *A New Estimate of American Investments Abroad.* U. S. Department of Commerce, Bulletin No. 767, 1931.

lost ground, and this rivalry has stimulated the delayed industrial development of one of the most wonderful regions of the world. Brazil, Peru, Paraguay, Uruguay, Argentina, and Chile have lands and resources for an enormous population and are destined to undergo in the twentieth century a development commensurate with that of the United States in the nineteenth. With such an assured future these countries need have little fear of foreign domination.

Sixth Pan American Conference

The Sixth International Conference of American States met at Havana from January 16 to February 20, 1928. President Coolidge attended the Conference in person and delivered one address. Of the political questions discussed at this Conference the one concerning the principle of intervention was undoubtedly the most important. Our neighbors to the south contended that no state had the right to intervene in the internal affairs of another, and sought to have this provision embodied in a project relating to the codification of international law. This, Secretary Hughes, head of the American delegation, opposed with great skill, and managed to have the project postponed for future consideration. The Conference also considered the rôle and function of the Pan American Union. Considerable criticism of our dominating influence in this organization has been voiced by the other members from time to time. Mexico sought to cut down the influence of the United States over the Union by proposing that the Chairman of the Board, who has always been the Secretary of State, and the Director General, also always an American, rotate annually among the various Union members. And Mexico further proposed that the Pan American Union be prohibited from exercising political functions. A convention was drawn up continuing the Union in its present set-up but prohibiting it from exercising political functions. This convention has as yet not received the unanimous ratification necessary for its coming into force.[39]

United States relinquishes policy of intervention

Our attitude on intervention at Havana was not calculated to strengthen Pan Americanism; if anything it weakened it for the time being. Under President Hoover's administration[40] our policy towards Latin America began to move in a new orbit. The United States withdrew her marines from Nicaragua in January, 1933. When, on October 23, 1931, the Dominican Republic suspended amortization payments on its foreign debt in violation of its treaty obligation the State Department acquiesced instead of sending troops and a fiscal administrator to run the Republic and collect payments. When Salvador defaulted on her debt in February, 1932, we declined to exercise the right to establish a customs receivership. When a number of South American countries defaulted on their bonds in 1931 and 1932, our government made no move to intervene and collect.

In 1930 and 1931, there was an epidemic of revolutions in Latin America.[41] There was no hesitation on the part of our Department of State to accord recognition to these new governments. Our promptness in recognizing them demonstrated that we were neutral and that we had returned to the recognition policy announced by Jefferson in 1792, a policy which had been abandoned by President Wilson in dealing with Mexico in 1913. But with all these favorable signs the Latin American countries remained distrustful of the Monroe Doctrine[42] and the United States' policy of intervention.

---

[39]Status of the Treaties and Conventions signed at the International Conferences of American States and at other Pan American Conferences (Pan American Union, Washington, D. C., 1939).

[40]See Chapter XXIII.

[41]Cf. C. H. Haring, "Revolution in South America," *Foreign Affairs*, January, 1931.

[42]In 1930 the Dept. of State published the *Memorandum on the Monroe Doctrine* written by J. Reuben Clarke, then Undersecretary of State. This memorandum rejected the Theodore Roosevelt Corollary of the doctrine, but asserted that intervention might be justified by the necessities of self defense.

On August 12, 1933, the people of Cuba overthrew their President, Gerardo Machado y Morales, who had held office since 1925. In the early part of his administration, Machado was acclaimed as an efficient and able administrator. In his first year in office, the Cuban sugar industry collapsed. Being a one-crop country with 80 per cent of the national income dependent upon sugar, an economic crisis arose in the island. Machado attempted to meet it by embarking upon a program of agricultural and industrial diversification and a vast program of public works. The public works program doubled the public debt, and in the face of a falling sugar market the debt service became more and more burdensome as the national income diminished. Unrest and a desire for a change under such circumstances were bound to come, and President Machado's terroristic methods to exterminate it proved his undoing. With the army, the police, the legislative and judicial bodies under his control, President Machado, by invoking martial law, suspending constitutional guarantees, killing, exiling, or imprisoning his political enemies, drove the opposition underground but did not exterminate it.

The Cuban revolution

During these troubles the United States government followed the political policy of "hands off."[43] Under the Platt Amendment we exercised the power in 1930 to prohibit any further loans by American bankers to the Cuban government to prevent additions to the already staggering debt burden. Soon after Franklin D. Roosevelt became President, he sent Sumner Welles as the new American Ambassador to Cuba. His task was to bring political peace between the opposing factions. His "good offices" was intervention, but not of the military

United States maintains political policy of "hands off"

The memorandum was not issued as an official statement of the Hoover administration.

[43]Cf. Russell Porter, "Cuba Under President Machado," *Current History*, April, 1933, p. 34.

type, and it was he who set the stage for the Cubans to overthrow Machado.

The various régimes in Cuba

Carlos Manuel de Cespedes succeeded Machado. But his régime was short-lived, for on September 5, 1933, the enlisted men of the army turned him out[44] and substituted Grau San Martin. From Washington came assurances that we had no desire to intervene and that we would recognize any government representing the will of the Cuban people, and capable of maintaining law and order throughout the island. The Grau régime was also short-lived, for on January 15, 1934, Carlos Hevia succeeded to the presidency. He, in turn, was overthrown by Charles Mendietta, whose government was accorded recognition by President Franklin D. Roosevelt on January 23, 1934.

Possibility of revising the Platt Amendment

Our government indicated that it was prepared to revise the Platt Amendment stripping it of our power to intervene in the affairs of Cuba. In a statement issued on November 24, 1933, the President said:[45]

> We have been keenly desirous during all this period of showing by deed our intention of playing the part of a good neighbor to the Cuban people. We have wished to commence negotiations for a revision of the commercial convention between the two countries and for a modification of the permanent treaty between the United States and Cuba.

Seventh Pan American Conference

The Seventh Pan American Conference convened at Montevideo on December 3, 1933. This Conference marked a departure in our relations with our neighbors to the South. Secretary of State Cordell Hull, head of the United States delegation, indicated that the "New Deal" of the Roosevelt administration meant a new Latin-American policy on our part. It was with great satisfaction that the assembled delegates listened to Secretary Hull's statement that "no government need fear any

---

[44]By this time United States warships were in Cuban waters.

[45]White House, Press Release, November 25, 1933. See *infra*, pp. 847 f.

intervention on the part of the United States under the Roosevelt administration."[46] The policy of the "good neighbor" as President Roosevelt had defined the phrase, Secretary Hull declared, meant respect for one's own rights as well as the rights of others; and the corollary to this philosophy was "the absolute independence, the unimpaired sovereignty, the perfect equality, and the political integrity of each nation, large or small . . ."[47] At no previous Pan American Conference did a better spirit prevail. Our usual attitude of sitting on the lid and preventing free discussion of policies was absent at this Conference, and when the meeting adjourned our Latin-American neighbors were convinced that the "New Deal" of the Franklin D. Roosevelt administration had for one of its objectives a new policy towards Latin America.

President Roosevelt's policies

What was projected by Secretary Hull at the Seventh Pan American Conference was made even clearer by President Roosevelt in a speech before the Woodrow Wilson Foundation on December 28, 1933, when he declared

> . . . The definite policy of the United States from now on is one opposed to armed intervention.
>
> The maintenance of Constitutional government in other nations is not a sacred obligation devolving upon the United States alone. The maintenance of law and the orderly processes of government in this hemisphere is the concern of each individual nation within its own borders first of all. It is only if and when the failure of orderly processes affects the other nations of the continent that it becomes their concern; and the point to stress is that in such an event it becomes the joint concern of a whole continent in which we are all neighbors.[48]

Thoughtful students viewed President Roosevelt's declaration as discarding the unilateral method hitherto used by us to enforce the Monroe Doctrine. While we still

[46]Dept. of State, Press Release, December 20, 1933.

[47]Dept. of State, Press Release, December 15, 1934.

[48]Dept. of State, Press Release, Publication No. 541, p. 381.

reserved the right to protect the American hemisphere against external aggression his statement was interpreted as safeguarding Latin America against the United States. Thus the Theodore Roosevelt Corollary to the Monroe Doctrine by which we claimed the right to intervene in Latin America was replaced by collective intervention when the failure of orderly processes of government affects the other nations of this continent.

Collective intervention

What American policy of the future would be with respect to Latin America was then a matter of conjecture. President Franklin D. Roosevelt, writing as a private citizen in 1928, declared:

> . . . the time has come when we must accept not only certain facts but many principles of a higher law, a newer and better standard in international relations. We are exceedingly jealous of our sovereignty and it is only right that we should respect a similar feeling among other nations. The peoples of the other Republics of this Western world are just as patriotic, just as proud of their sovereignty. . . . Neither from the argument of financial gain, nor from the sounder reasoning of the Golden Rule, can our policy, or lack of policy, be approved. The time is ripe to start another chapter.[49]

As President of the United States he has made good the promise of a new chapter in Latin-American relations.[50]

---

[49] *Foreign Affairs*, July, 1928.

[50] See Chapter XXXVI.

CHAPTER XXIX

THE WASHINGTON CONFERENCE

American rights in mandated areas

AFTER the rejection of the Treaty of Versailles by the Senate, President Wilson withdrew as far as possible from participation in European affairs, and after the election of Harding he let it be known that he would do nothing to embarrass the incoming administration. The public had been led to believe that when Harding became President there would be a complete reversal of our foreign policy all along the line, but such was not to be the case. The new administration continued unchanged the Wilson policy toward Mexico and toward Russia, and before many months had passed was seeking from Congress the authority, withheld from Wilson, to appoint a member on the Reparations Commission. On the question of our rights in mandated areas, Secretary Hughes adopted in whole the arguments which had been advanced by Secretary Colby in his note to Great Britain of November 20, 1920, in regard to the oil resources of Mesopotamia. By the San Remo agreement of April 25, 1920, Great Britain and France had agreed upon a division of the oil output of Mesopotamia by which France was to be allowed twenty-five per cent and Great Britain seventy-five per cent. The British government had intimated that the United States, having declined to join the League of Nations, had no voice in the matter. On this point Secretary Colby took sharp issue in the following statement:

> Such powers as the Allied and Associated nations may enjoy or wield, in the determination of the governmental status of the mandated areas, accrued to them as a direct result of the war

Colby's note

against the Central Powers. The United States, as a participant in that conflict and as a contributor to its successful issue, cannot consider any of the Associated Powers, the smallest not less than herself, debarred from the discussion of any of its consequences, or from participation in the rights and privileges secured under the mandates provided for in the treaties of peace.[1]

The island of Yap

Japan likewise assumed that we had nothing to do with the disposition of the former German islands in the Pacific. When the Supreme Council at Paris decided to give Japan a mandate over the islands north of the equator, President Wilson reserved for future consideration the final disposition of the island of Yap, which lies between Guam and the Philippines, and is one of the most important cable stations in the Pacific. The entire question of cable communications was reserved for a special conference which met at Washington in the autumn of 1920, but this conference adjourned about the middle of December without having reached any final conclusions, and the status of Yap became the subject of a very sharp correspondence between the American and Japanese governments. When Hughes became Secretary of State, he restated the American position in a note of April 2, 1921, as follows:

Hughes' note to Japan

> It will not be questioned that the right to dispose of the overseas possessions of Germany was acquired only through the victory of the Allied and Associated Powers, and it is also believed that there is no disposition on the part of the Japanese Government to deny the participation of the United States in that victory. It would seem to follow necessarily that the right accruing to the Allied and Associated Powers through the common victory is shared by the United States and that there could be no valid or effective disposition of the overseas possessions of Germany, now under consideration, without the assent of the United States.[2]

The discussion between the two governments was still in progress when the Washington Conference convened,

[1]New York *Times*, November 26, 1920.
[2]*Ibid.*, April 7, 1921.

and at the close of the Conference it was announced that an agreement had been reached which would be embodied in a treaty. The United States recognized Japan's mandate over the islands north of the equator on the condition that the United States should have full cable rights on the island of Yap, and that its citizens should enjoy certain rights of residence on the island. The agreement also covered radio telegraphic service.

The League ignored by Harding

During the presidential campaign Harding's position on the League of Nations had been so equivocal that the public knew not what to expect, but when Hughes and Hoover were appointed members of the Cabinet, it was generally expected that the new administration would go into the League with reservations. This expectation was not to be fulfilled, however, for the President persistently ignored the existence of the League, and took no notice of the establishment of the permanent Court of International Justice provided for in Article 14 of the Covenant. Meanwhile Elihu Root, who as Secretary of State had instructed our delegates to the Hague Conference of 1907 to propose the establishment of such a court, had been invited by the Council of the League to be one of a commission of distinguished jurists to draft the statute establishing the court. This service he performed with conspicuous ability. As another evidence of Europe's unwillingness to leave us out, when the court was organized, John Bassett Moore, America's most distinguished authority on international law, was elected one of the judges.

Separate peace with Germany

Meanwhile a technical state of war with Germany existed and American troops were still on the Rhine. On July 2, 1921, Congress passed a joint resolution declaring the war at an end, but undertaking to reserve to the United States "all rights, privileges, indemnities, reparations or advantages" to which she was entitled under the terms of the Armistice, or by reason of her participation in the war, or which had been stipulated for her benefit in the Treaty of Versailles, or to which she was entitled as one of the Principal Allied and Associated Powers, or to which she was entitled by virtue of any act or acts of Congress. On August 25, the United States Government, through its commissioner to Germany, signed at Berlin a separate treaty of peace with Germany, reserving in detail the rights referred to in the joint resolution of Congress. About the same time a similar treaty was signed with Austria, and the two treaties were ratified by the Senate of the United States October 18.[3] The proclamation of peace produced no immediate results of any importance. American troops continued on the Rhine, and there was no apparent increase in trade, which had been carried on before the signing of the treaty by special licenses.

Competition in armaments

If mankind is capable of learning any lessons from history, the events leading up to the World War should have exploded the fallacy that the way to preserve peace is to prepare for war. Competition in armament, whether on land or sea, inevitably leads to war, and it can lead to nothing else. And yet, after the terrible lessons of the recent war, the race for armaments continued with increased momentum. France, Russia, and Poland maintained huge armies, while the United States and Japan entered upon the most extensive naval construction programs in the history of the world. Great Britain, burdened with debt, was making every effort to keep pace with the United States.

The Anglo-Japanese Alliance

This naval rivalry between powers which had so lately been united in the war against Germany led thoughtful people to consider the probable outcome and to ask against whom these powers were arming. We had no quarrel with England, but England was the ally of Japan, and relations between Japan and the United States in the

[3] *Treaties and Conventions*, III, 2596.

Pacific and in eastern Asia were far from reassuring. The question of the continuance of the Anglo-Japanese Alliance was discussed at the British Imperial Conference, which met at London in the early summer of 1921. In fact, it had been forced into a prominent place on the program by a significant discussion that had taken place in the Canadian parliament in April, in which strong opposition was expressed to the renewal of the Anglo-Japanese Alliance in any form. The debate took a wide range, covering the fundamental question of the internal organization of the British Empire and the right of the overseas dominions to a voice in matters of foreign policy that concerned them. It was openly asserted that as a Pacific power Canada had a right to refuse to consent to the renewal of the alliance, a right which she would very probably exercise. In the critical condition in which China had been left by the Treaty of Versailles, the sympathies of the Canadians were with China and against Japan. Above all, Canada feared the consequences of a war between the United States and Japan. If Great Britain should become involved in such a contest, it would mean the dissolution of the Empire, for Canada would not follow her and would probably side with the United States. This discussion and the subsequent action of the Canadian prime minister at the Imperial Conference in London forced the hand of the British government and paved the way for the close accord between England and the United States at the Washington Conference.[4]

Unpopular in Canada

The original purpose of the Anglo-Japanese Alliance was to check the Russian advance in Manchuria. It was renewed in revised form in 1905 against Germany, and again renewed in 1911 against Germany for a period of ten years. With the removal of the German menace, what reasons were there for Great Britain to continue the alliance? It bore too much the aspect of a combination

Regarded with suspicion in the United States

[4]Putnam Weale, *An Indiscreet Chronicle from the Pacific*, 41 ff.

against the United States, and was of course the main reason for the naval program which we had adopted. So long as there were only three navies of importance in the world and two of them united in a defensive alliance, it behooved us to safeguard our position as a sea power.

Limitation of armament adopted as policy by Harding

One of the main objects of the formation of the League of Nations was to bring about a limitation of armaments on land and sea, and a commission was organized under the League to consider this question, but this commission could not take any steps toward the limitation of navies so long as a great naval power like the United States refused to coöperate with the League of Nations or even to recognize its existence. As President Harding had promised the American people some substitute for the League of Nations, he decided, soon after coming into office, to convene an international conference to consider the limitation of armament on land and sea. By the time the Conference convened it was evident that no agreement was possible on the subject of land armament. It was recognized from the first that the mere proposal to limit navies would be utterly futile unless effective steps could be taken to remove some of the causes of international conflict which make navies necessary. Therefore the formal invitation to the Conference extended to the governments of Great Britain, France, Italy, and Japan, August 11, 1921, linked the subject of Limitation of Armament with Pacific and Far Eastern Questions.[5] The European powers accepted the invitation without much enthusiasm, but Japan's answer was held back for some time. She was reluctant to have the powers review the course she had pursued in China and Siberia while they were at war with Germany. After agreeing to attend the Conference, Japan endeavored to confine the program to as narrow limits as possible, and she soon entered into

Washington Conference called

[5] *Conference on the Limitation of Armament* (Washington, Govt. Printing Office, 1922), 5. Referred to hereafter as *Proceedings*.

negotations with China over the Shantung question with the hope of arriving at a settlement which would prevent that question from coming before the Conference. Invitations to the Conference were later sent to the governments of Belgium, the Netherlands, Portugal, and China. Portugal was interested because of her settlement at Macao, the oldest European settlement in China. Holland of course is one of the great colonial powers of the Pacific. While Belgium has no territorial interests in the Orient, she has for years been interested in Chinese financial matters.

Smaller powers included

The Washington Conference convened in plenary session November 12, 1921, in Memorial Continental Hall.[6] Seats were reserved on the main floor for press representatives, and the galleries were reserved for officials and those individuals who were fortunate enough to secure tickets of admission. The question of open diplomacy which had been much discussed was settled at the first session by Secretary Hughes, who, in his introductory speech, boldly laid the American proposals for the limitation of navies before the Conference. There were in all seven plenary sessions, but the subsequent sessions did little more than confirm agreements that had already been reached in committee. The real work of the Conference was carried on by committees, and from the meetings of these committees the public and press representatives were as a matter of course excluded. There were two principal committees, one on the Limitation of Armament and the other on Pacific and Far Eastern Questions. There were various sub-committees, in the work of which technical delegates participated. Minutes were kept of the meetings of the two principal committees, and after each meeting a communiqué was prepared for the

Organization of the Conference

Publicity

[6]This chapter is based largely on information gathered by the author during the Conference. He had press privileges and attended some of the plenary sessions as well as many of the daily interviews given by Secretary Hughes and the British and Japanese delegates to the press correspondents.

press. In fact, the demand for publicity defeated to a large extent its own ends. So much matter was given to the press that when it was published in full very few people had time to read it. As a general rule, the less real information there was to give out, the longer were the communiqués. Experienced correspondents maintained that decisions on delicate questions were made with as much secrecy in Washington as at Paris.

The plan proposed by the United States

The plan of the United States for the limitation of armament presented by Secretary Hughes at the first session proposed (1) that all programs for the construction of capital ships, either actual or projected, be abandoned; (2) that a large number of battleships of older types still in commission be scrapped; and (3) that the allowance of auxiliary combatant craft, such as cruisers, destroyers, submarines, and airplane carriers, be in proportion to the tonnage of capital ships. These proposals, it was claimed, would leave the powers under consideration in the same relative positions. Under this plan the United States would be allowed 500,000 tons of capital ships, Great Britain 500,000 tons, and Japan 300,000 tons.[7]

The 5–5–3 ratio

Japan objected to the 5–5–3 ratio proposed by Secretary Hughes, and urged a 10–10–7 ratio as more in accord with existing strength. The American proposal included the scrapping of the *Mutsu*, the pride of the Japanese navy, which had been launched but not quite completed. The sacrifices voluntarily proposed by the United States for its navy were much greater than those which England or Japan were called upon to make, and in this lay the strength of the American position. The Japanese refused, however, to give up the *Mutsu*, and they were finally permitted to retain it, but in order to preserve the 5–5–3 ratio, it was necessary to increase the tonnage allowance of the United States and Great Britain. In the treaty as finally agreed upon, Japan was allowed 315,000 tons

[7] *Proceedings*, 60–65.

of capital ships and the United States and Great Britain each 525,000 tons.

In his address at the opening session, Secretary Hughes said·

French and Italian ratios considered last

> In view of the extraordinary conditions due to the World War affecting the existing strength of the navies of France and Italy, it is not thought to be necessary to discuss at this stage of the proceedings the tonnage allowance of these nations, but the United States proposes that this subject be reserved for the later consideration of the Conference.[8]

This somewhat blunt, matter-of-fact way of stating the case gave unexpected offence to the French delegation. During the next four or five weeks, while Great Britain, the United States, and Japan were discussing the case of the *Mutsu* and the question of fortifications in the Pacific, the French delegates were cherishing their resentment at being treated as the representatives of a second-class power. Hughes' failure to regard the susceptibilities of a great nation like France undoubtedly had a good deal to do with the upsetting of that part of the naval program relating to subsidiary craft and submarines.

The program upset by the French

When, after the agreement on the 5–5–3 ratio, the question of the allowance of capital ship tonnage for France and Italy was taken up in committee, the other powers were wholly unprepared for France's demand of 350,000 tons of capital ships. According to Hughes' figures based on existing strength, she was entitled to 175,000 tons. It is not probable that the French delegates intended to insist on such a large tonnage. It is more likely that they put forth this proposal in the committee in order to give the other delegates to understand that France could not be ignored or dictated to with impunity and in order to pave the way for their submarine proposal. Unfortunately the French demands were given to the

[8] *Op. cit.*, p. 60.

press through some misunderstanding and caused an outburst of criticism in the British and American papers. In the committee the relations between the British and French delegates became very bitter over the refusal of the latter to abandon the submarine, or even agree to a moderate proposal as to submarine tonnage. On December 16, Secretary Hughes cabled an appeal, over the heads of the French delegation, to Briand, who had returned to Paris. As a result, the French finally agreed to accept the 1.75 ratio for capital ships, but refused to place any reasonable limits upon cruisers, destroyers, submarines, or aircraft. Italy accepted the same ratio as France.[9]

Only capital ships limited

Thus an important part of the Hughes program failed. As a result, the treaty left the contracting parties free to direct their energies, if they so desired, to the comparatively new fields of submarine and aerial warfare. As is well known, many eminent naval authorities, such as Sir Percy Scott in England and Admiral Sims in this country, expressed the view that the capital ship is an obsolete type, and that the warfare of the future would be carried on by submarines, aircraft, and lighter surface ships. The unfortunate feature of the situation created by the naval treaty was, therefore, that those who regarded the capital ship as obsolete would now have an opportunity to bring forward and press their submarine and aircraft programs. There was no limitation upon the building of cruisers, provided they did not exceed 10,000 tons displacement or carry guns with a caliber exceeding eight inches.

***Status quo* in the Pacific**

By Article 19 of the naval treaty the United States, Great Britain, and Japan agreed to maintain the *status quo* as regards fortifications and naval bases in the islands of the Pacific with certain exceptions, notably the Hawaiian Islands, Australia, and New Zealand.[10] This agreement relieved Japan of all fear of attack from us, and it was

[9] *Op. cit.*, pp. 454–460.

[10] *Treaties and Conventions*, III, 3105.

hoped it would prove as beneficent and as enduring as the agreement of 1817 between the United States and Great Britian for disarmament on the Great Lakes.

Navies put on defensive footing

The 5–5–3 ratio placed the navies of Great Britain, the United States, and Japan, for the present, at least, on a strictly defensive basis. Each navy was left strong enough to defend its home territory, but no one of them would be able to attack the home territory of the others. Of course it was possible that the development of aircraft and submarines, together with cruisers and other surface craft, would eventually alter the situation. Hitherto navies existed for two purposes: national defense and the enforcement of foreign policies. The new treaty meant that as long as it lasted the navies of the ratifying powers could be used for defense only and not for the enforcement of their policies in distant quarters of the globe. In other words, when disputes arise, British policies will prevail in the British area, American policies in the American area, and Japanese policies in the Japanese area. Having agreed to place ourselves in a position in which we could not attack Japan, the only pressure we could bring to bear upon her in China or elsewhere would be moral pressure. Through what was considered by some a grave strategical error, the naval treaty was completed before any settlement of the Chinese and Siberian question had been reached.

Attempt to limit use of submarines

The French insistence on the practically unlimited right to build submarines caused much hard feeling in England. The British delegates had proposed the total abolition of submarines, and this proposal had been ably supported by the arguments of Mr. Balfour and Lord Lee. Unfortunately the United States delegation stood for the submarine, proposing merely certain limits upon its use. The five naval powers finally signed a treaty reaffirming the old rules of international law in regard to the search and seizure of merchant vessels, and declaring that

> . . . any person in the service of any Power who shall violate any of those rules, whether or not such person is under orders of a governmental superior, shall be deemed to have violated the laws of war and shall be liable to trial and punishment as if for an act of piracy and may be brought to trial before the civil or military authorities of any Power within the jurisdiction of which he may be found.[11]

By the same treaty the signatory powers solemnly bound themselves to prohibit the use in war of poisonous gases.

Futility of the action taken

The attempt to limit by treaty the use of the submarine and to prohibit altogether the use of gases appeared to many to be utterly futile. After the experience of the late war, no nation would readily trust the good faith of another in these matters. Each party to a war would probably feel justified in being prepared to use the submarine and poison gases, contrary to law, in case the other party should do so. We would thus have the same old dispute as in the late war in regard to floating mines as to which party first resorted to the outlawed practice. What was the use in solemnly declaring that a submarine shall not attack a merchant vessel, and that the commander of a submarine who violates this law shall be treated as a pirate, when the contracting parties found it utterly impossible to agree among themselves upon a definition of a merchant vessel?

But the reader may ask, what is the use in signing any treaty if nations are so devoid of good faith? The answer is that the vast majority of treaties are faithfully kept in time of peace, but that very few treaties are fully observed in time of war. Had these five powers signed a treaty pledging themselves not to build or maintain submarines of any kind or description, we would have every reason to expect them to live up to it. But when a nation is engaged in war and has a large flotilla of submarines which it has agreed to use only for certain purposes, there is apt to come

Building of submarines not prohibited

[11] *Op. cit.*, III, 3118.

a time when the temptation to use them for wholly different purposes will be overwhelming.

Rapid growth of Japanese power

The Committee on Pacific and Far Eastern Questions held its first meeting November 16. This committee was primarily concerned with the very delicate situation created by the aggressive action and expansion of Japan during the past twenty years. In 1905, by the Treaty of Portsmouth, Japan succeeded to the Russian rights in southern Manchuria; in 1910, she annexed Korea; in 1911, during the Chinese Revolution, she stationed troops at Hankow and later constructed permanent barracks; in 1914, after the defeat of the Germans at Kiao-chau, she took over all the German interests in the Shantung peninsula; in 1915, she presented the Twenty-one Demands to China and coerced that power into granting most of them; and in 1918, in conjunction with the United States, Great Britain, and France, she landed a military force in the Maritime Province of Siberia for the definite purpose of rescuing the Czecho-Slovak troops who had made their way to that province and of guarding the military stores at Vladivostok. The other powers had all withdrawn their contingents, but Japan had increased her force from one division to more than 70,000 troops. The eastern coast of Asia was thus in the firm grip of Japan, and she had secured concessions from China which seriously impaired the independence of that country.

Eastern Asia in her grip

It was commonly supposed that the United States delegation had prepared a program on the Far Eastern question, and that this would be presented in the same way that Hughes had presented the naval program. If this was the intention there was a sudden change of plan, for between one and two o'clock at night the Chinese delegates were aroused from their slumbers and informed that there would be an opportunity for them to present China's case before the committee at eleven o'clock that morning. They at once went to work with their advisers,

The Chinese case presented

and a few minutes before the appointed hour they completed the drafting of the Ten Points, which Minister Sze read before the committee.[12] These Points constituted a Chinese declaration of independence, and set forth a series of general principles to be applied in the determination of questions relating to China. Several days later the committee adopted four resolutions, presented by Mr. Root, covering in part some of the Chinese principles.[13] By these resolutions the powers agreed to respect the independence and territorial integrity of China, to give China the fullest opportunity to develop and maintain an effective and stable government, to recognize the principle of equality for the commerce and industry of all nations throughout the territory of China, and to refrain from taking advantage of present conditions in order to seek special rights or privileges. This somewhat vague and general declaration of principles appeared to be all that China was likely to get. Had Mr. Hughes presented a Far Eastern program and gotten nothing more than this, it would have been a serious blow to the prestige of the United States. That was probably why he decided at the last moment to let China present her own case.

The Root resolutions

The Four-Power Treaty

At the fourth plenary session of the Conference the treaty relating to the Pacific islands, generally known as the Four-Power Treaty, was presented by Senator Lodge. By the terms of this treaty, the United States, Great Britain, France, and Japan agreed "to respect their rights in relation to their insular possessions and insular dominions in the region of the Pacific Ocean," and in case of any dispute arising out of any Pacific question to refer the matter to a joint conference for consideration and adjustment. This article appeared harmless enough, but Article 2 seemed to lay the foundations of an alliance between these powers. It was as follows:

[12]Willoughby, *China at the Conference*, pp. 32–36.

[13]*Ibid.*, pp. 36–44.

> If the said rights are threatened by the aggressive action of any other Power, the High Contracting Parties shall communicate with one another fully and frankly in order to arrive at an understanding as to the most efficient measures to be taken, jointly or separately, to meet the exigencies of the particular situation.[14]

This treaty was to remain in force for ten years, after which it could be terminated by any of the High Contracting Parties on twelve months' notice. It superseded the Anglo-Japanese Alliance which, it expressly provided, should terminate on the exchange of ratifications.

Its "baffling brevity"

In presenting the treaty, Senator Lodge assured his hearers that "no military or naval sanction lurks anywhere in the background or under cover of these plain and direct clauses," and Secretary Hughes in closing the discussion declared that it would probably not be possible to find in all history "an international document couched in more simple or even briefer terms," but he added, "we are again reminded that the great things are the simple ones." In view of these statements the members of the Conference and the public generally were bewildered and amazed some days later when Secretary Hughes and the President gave out contradictory statements as to whether the treaty included the Japanese homeland. Hughes stated to the correspondents that it did, the President said it did not. Whereupon some wag remarked that at Paris President Wilson did not let the American delegation know what he did, while at Washington the delegates did not let President Harding know what they were doing. In deference to the President's views and to criticisms of the treaty in the Japanese press a supplementary treaty was later signed expressly declaring that the term "insular possessions and insular dominions" did not include the Japanese homeland.[15]

The President at odds with his commissioners

[14] *Treaties and Conventions*, III, 3095.

[15] *Ibid.*, p. 3098.

The Shantung question

Meanwhile the Shantung question was being discussed by China and Japan outside of the Conference, but with representatives of the British and American governments sitting as observers ready to use their good offices if called on. The reason for not bringing the question before the Conference was that Great Britain, France, and Italy were parties to the Treaty of Versailles, which gave Japan a legal title to the German leases in Shantung. The restoration of the province to China was vital to a satisfactory adjustment of Chinese affairs generally. Japan, however, was in no hurry to reach an agreement with China, wishing for strategical purposes to keep the matter in suspense to the last, if not to avoid a settlement until after the adjournment of the Conference and continue negotiations under more favorable conditions at Peking or Tokio.

An apparent deadlock

By Christmas it seemed that the Conference had accomplished about all that was possible, and that it would adjourn as soon as the agreements already reached could be put into treaty form and signed. At the end of the first week in January it looked as if the Chinese and Japanese had reached a deadlock, and that the Conference would adjourn without a satisfactory adjustment of any of the Chinese problems. Mr. Balfour and other important delegates had engaged return passage, and all indications pointed to an early dissolution of the Conference. But the unexpected happened. At an informal gathering of Administration leaders at the White House on Saturday night, January 7, stock was taken of the work of the Conference, and some of the senators present expressed the opinion that if it adjourned without doing more for China, there would be little hope of getting the treaties ratified. As a result Secretary Hughes persuaded the British and Japanese delegates to cancel their sailings, and with characteristic energy and determination took personal charge of the Far Eastern situation, which

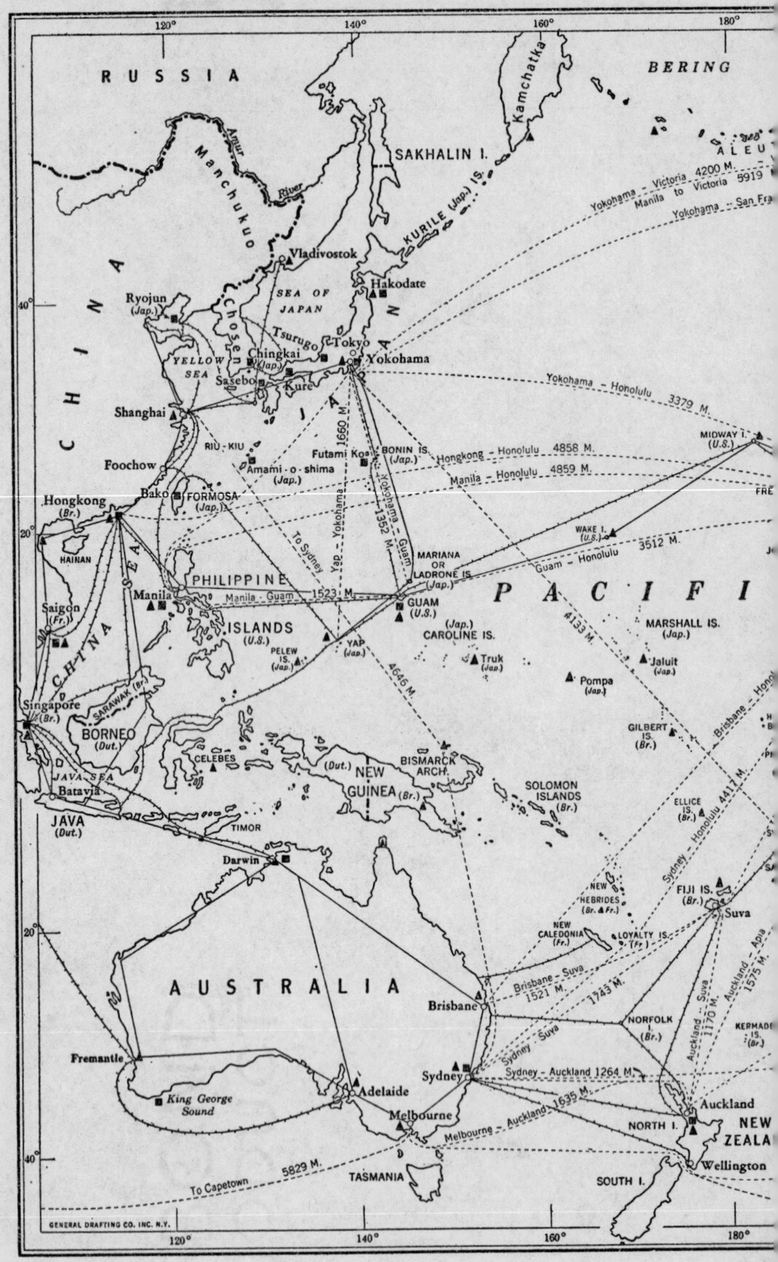
RUSSIA
BERING
Kamchatka
SAKHALIN I.
ALEU
Amur River
Manchukuo
CHINA
KURILE (Jap.) IS.
Yokohama - Victoria 4200 M.
Manila to Victoria 5919
Yokohama - San Fra
Vladivostok
Hakodate
SEA OF JAPAN
Ryojun (Jap.)
Chosen
Tsurugo
Tokyo
Yokohama
Chingkai (Jap.)
YELLOW SEA
Sasebo
Kure
JAPAN
Shanghai
Yokohama - Honolulu 3379 M.
MIDWAY I. (U.S.)
1660 M.
RIU-KIU
Amami-o-shima (Jap.)
Futami Ko
BONIN IS. (Jap.)
Hongkong - Honolulu 4858 M.
Manila - Honolulu 4859 M.
Foochow
Bako
FORMOSA (Jap.)
Hongkong (Br.)
HAINAN
To Sydney
Yap - Yokohama
Yokohama - Guam 1352 M.
WAKE I. (U.S.)
Guam - Honolulu 3512 M.
MARIANA OR LADRONE IS. (Jap.)
PACIFI
PHILIPPINE ISLANDS (U.S.)
Manila
Manila - Guam 1523 M.
GUAM (U.S.)
Saigon (Fr.)
SOUTH CHINA SEA
4133 M.
MARSHALL IS. (Jap.)
YAP (Jap.)
PELEW IS. (Jap.)
(Jap.) CAROLINE IS.
Truk (Jap.)
Jaluit (Jap.)
4646 M.
Pompa (Jap.)
Singapore (Br.)
SARAWAK (Br.)
BORNEO (Dut.)
GILBERT IS. (Br.)
Brisbane - Hono
CELEBES
(Dut.) NEW GUINEA (Br.)
BISMARCK ARCH.
SOLOMON ISLANDS (Br.)
JAVA SEA
Batavia
JAVA (Dut.)
TIMOR
ELLICE IS. (Br.)
Sydney - Honolulu 4417 M.
Darwin
NEW HEBRIDES (Br. & Fr.)
FIJI IS. (Br.)
Suva
NEW CALEDONIA (Fr.)
LOYALTY IS. (Fr.)
AUSTRALIA
Brisbane - Suva 1521 M.
1743 M.
Auckland - Apia 1575 M.
Brisbane
NORFOLK I. (Br.)
Auckland - Suva 1170 M.
KERMADEC IS. (Br.)
Sydney - Suva
Fremantle
Sydney
Sydney - Auckland 1264 M.
King George Sound
Adelaide
Melbourne
Melbourne - Auckland 1635 M.
Auckland
NORTH I.
NEW ZEALA
Wellington
To Capetown 5829 M.
TASMANIA
SOUTH I.
120°
140°
160°
180°
40°
20°
GENERAL DRAFTING CO. INC. N.Y.

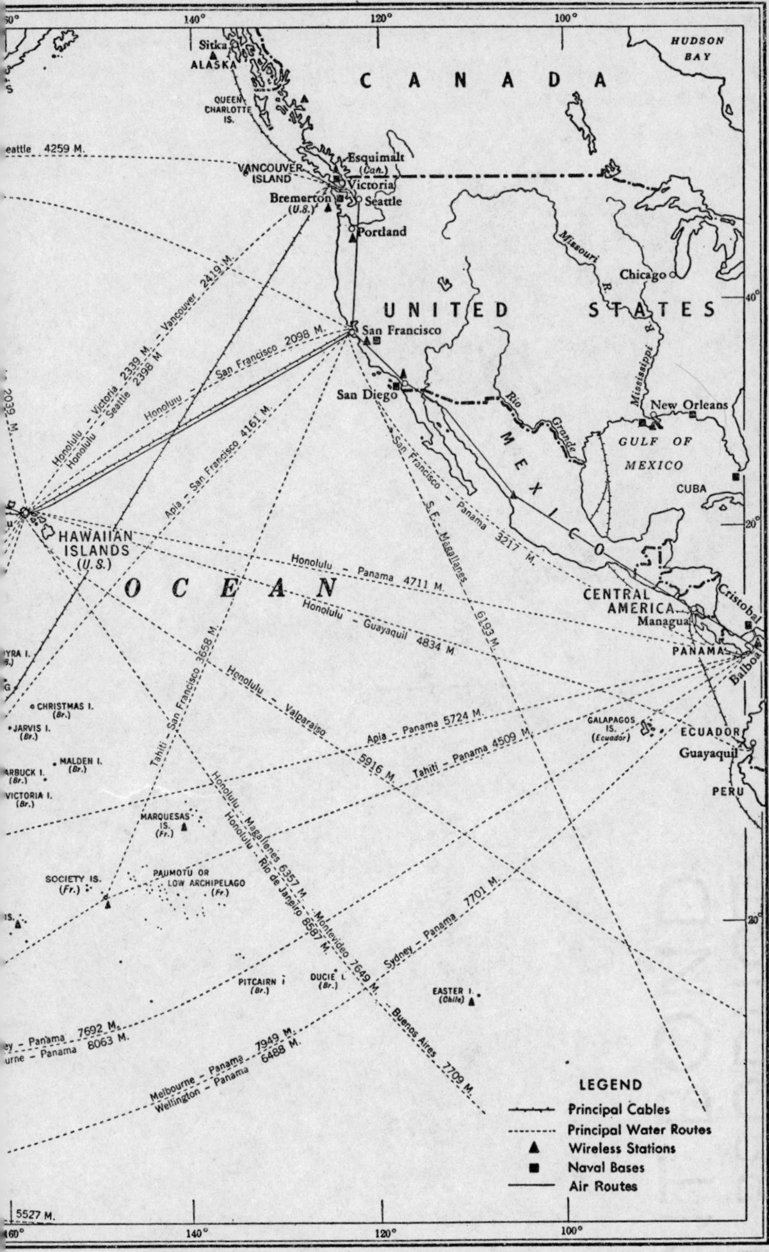
HUDSON BAY
CANADA
Sitka
ALASKA
QUEEN CHARLOTTE IS.
Seattle 4259 M.
Esquimalt (Can.)
VANCOUVER ISLAND
Victoria
Bremerton (U.S.)
Seattle
Portland
Missouri R.
Chicago
UNITED STATES
San Francisco
San Diego
Mississippi R.
New Orleans
Rio Grande
MEXICO
GULF OF MEXICO
CUBA
CENTRAL AMERICA
Managua
Cristobal
PANAMA
Balboa
GALAPAGOS IS. (Ecuador)
ECUADOR
Guayaquil
PERU
HAWAIIAN ISLANDS (U.S.)
OCEAN
Honolulu - Vancouver 2419 M.
Honolulu - Victoria 2339 M.
Honolulu - Seattle 2398 M.
Honolulu - San Francisco 2098 M.
Apia - San Francisco 4161 M.
San Francisco - Panama 3217 M.
S.F. - Magallanes 6193 M.
Honolulu - Panama 4711 M.
Honolulu - Guayaquil 4834 M.
Honolulu - Valparaiso 5916 M.
Tahiti - San Francisco 3658 M.
Apia - Panama 5724 M.
Tahiti - Panama 4509 M.
Honolulu - Magallenes 6357 M.
Honolulu - Rio de Janeiro 8587 M.
Montevideo 7649 M.
Buenos Aires 7709 M.
Sydney - Panama 7701 M.
Sydney - Panama 7692 M.
Melbourne - Panama 8063 M.
Melbourne - Panama 7949 M.
Wellington - Panama 6488 M.
2039 M.
5527 M.
CHRISTMAS I. (Br.)
JARVIS I. (Br.)
MALDEN I. (Br.)
VICTORIA I. (Br.)
MARQUESAS IS. (Fr.)
SOCIETY IS. (Fr.)
PAUMOTU OR LOW ARCHIPELAGO (Fr.)
PITCAIRN I. (Br.)
DUCIE I. (Br.)
EASTER I. (Chile)
LEGEND
Principal Cables
Principal Water Routes
Wireless Stations
Naval Bases
Air Routes
140°
120°
100°
40°
20°

IC

Final settlement

up to this time had been left mainly to Mr. Root. After a little pressure had been brought to bear on the Chinese by President Harding, and probably on the Japanese by Mr. Balfour, Secretary Hughes was finally able to announce at the plenary session of February 1 that China and Japan had reached an agreement as to the terms on which Shantung was to be restored.[16] At the same session the agreements in regard to China reached by the Committee on Far Eastern Affairs were announced. These agreements were finally embodied in two treaties, one dealing with the tariff and the other with the open door, and a series of ten resolutions.[17]

The Chinese tariff

Since the middle of the last century Chinese tariffs have been regulated by treaties with foreign powers, the customs service organized and administered by foreigners, and the receipts mortgaged to meet the interest on foreign loans. China has never been permitted to levy duties in excess of five per cent, and, in fact, as a result of the methods of valuation the duties had not averaged above three and one half per cent. This had been an unjust state of affairs, and had deprived the Chinese government of what would naturally be one of its main sources of revenue. By the new agreement there was to be an immediate revision of tariff valuations so as to make the five per cent effective. China was also to be allowed to levy a surtax on certain articles, mainly luxuries, which would yield an additional revenue. It was estimated that the total annual increase in revenue derived from maritime customs would be about $150,000,000 silver. It was claimed by some, with a certain degree of truth, that any increase in Chinese customs duties would be immediately covered by liens to secure new loans, and that putting money into the Chinese treasury just then was like pouring it into a rat hole. As soon as China is able to establish a stable and honest

[16] *Proceedings*, p. 200 ff.; Willoughby, *China at the Conference*, chap. xxiii.

[17] *Treaties and Conventions*, III, 3120–3140.

government, she should, without question, be relieved of all treaty restrictions on her tariffs.

Other questions

The Conference also took certain steps to restore to China other sovereign rights long impaired by the encroachments of foreign powers. A commission was to be appointed to investigate the administration of justice with a view to the ultimate extinction of extraterritorial rights now enjoyed by foreigners. The powers also agreed to abandon not later than January 1, 1923, their existing postal agencies in China, provided an efficient Chinese postal service be maintained. The system of foreign post offices in China was the subject of great abuses, as through these agencies goods of various kinds, including opium and other drugs, were smuggled into China. The powers further made a general promise to aid the Chinese government in the unification of railways into a general system under Chinese control. They also agreed to restore to China all radio stations other than those regulated by treaty or maintained by foreign governments within their legation limits.

In the treaty relating to the open door, the Contracting Powers other than China pledged themselves to the following principles:

The open door pledged by treaty

(1) To respect the sovereignty, the independence, and the territorial and administrative integrity of China;

(2) To provide the fullest and most unembarrassed opportunity to China to develop and maintain for herself an effective and stable government;

(3) To use their influence for the purpose of effectually establishing and maintaining the principle of equal opportunity for the commerce and industry of all nations throughout the territory of China;

(4) To refrain from taking advantage of conditions in China in order to seek special rights or privileges which would abridge the rights of subjects or citizens of friendly States, and from countenancing action inimical to the security of such States.[18]

[18]*Op. cit.*, III, 3122.

Now an international policy

China on her part accepted fully the principle of the open door, and pledged herself for the first time to respect it. Pledges to respect the open door in China have been made by foreign powers upon various occasions in the past and broken as often as made. The expression "equal opportunity for the commerce and industry of all nations" was not new. It occurred in the Anglo-Japanese Alliance of 1902, in the Root-Takahira agreement of 1908, and in numerous other documents. Up to that time, however, the United States was the only power which had tried to preserve the open door in China. Most of the other powers have regarded the Chinese situation as hopeless, and have believed that the only solution was to let foreign powers come in and divide and rule the territory of the empire. In view of the new treaty the open door was no longer merely an American policy, but an international policy, and responsibility for its enforcement was to rest not on the United States alone but on all nine parties to the treaty.

Prior commitments

The agenda or program of the Conference offered as one of the subjects to be considered the status of existing commitments in China. When Secretary Hughes brought this subject up before the Far Eastern Committee, Japan entered an emphatic objection to its consideration, and the matter was dropped immediately without argument. The treaty, therefore, was not retroactive, for it recognized the *status quo* in Manchuria and to a less extent in other parts of China. The saving clause of the new agreement was, however, a resolution providing for the establishment of an international board of reference, to which questions arising in regard to the open door may be referred.

When the treaties drafted by the Conference were submitted by the President to the Senate, they encountered serious opposition, but were finally ratified. The Republican leaders, particularly Senator Lodge, were twitted with charges of inconsistency in advocating cer-

The treaties attacked but ratified

tain features of these treaties when they had violently opposed the League of Nations. The Four-Power Treaty was much more of an entangling alliance than the Covenant of the League, and the Naval Treaty deprived Congress for a period of fifteen years of its constitutional right to determine the size of the navy and to provide for the defense of Guam and the Philippines. In fact, there were very few objections raised to the League of Nations which could not with equal force be applied to the Four-Power and Naval Treaties. The Four-Power Treaty was the main object of attack, and Senators Lodge and Underwood were greatly embarrassed in attempting to explain its meaning. Its "baffling brevity" demanded explanations, but no satisfactory explanations were forthcoming. They talked in general terms about the tremendous importance of the treaty, but they dared not state the real fact that the treaty was drafted by Mr. Balfour and Baron Kato as the most convenient method of terminating the Anglo-Japanese Alliance without making it appear to the Japanese public that their government had surrendered the alliance without due compensation. According to an Associated Press Dispatch from Tokio, January 31, 1922, Baron Uchida, the Japanese Minister of Foreign Affairs, replying to interpolations in the House of Peers, said: "The Four-Power Treaty was not intended to abrogate the Anglo-Japanese Alliance, but rather to widen and extend it." The real *quid pro quo* for the termination of the Anglo-Japanese Alliance was the agreement of the United States not to construct naval bases or new fortifications in Guam and the Philippines, and the clause terminating the Anglo-Japanese Alliance might just as well have been attached to the Naval Treaty, but this would not have satisfied Japanese public opinion. Great Britain and Japan were permitted to terminate their alliance in any way that they might deem best. After the Four-Power Treaty was accepted by the Ameri-

The American Commissioners conceal the real facts

The Anglo-Japanese Alliance ended

can delegates, they feared that it would look too much as if the United States had merely been drawn into the Anglo-Japanese Alliance. It was decided, therefore, at the eleventh hour to give the agreement a more general character by inviting France to adhere to it. France agreed to sign, although she resented not having been consulted during the negotiation of the treaty.

Anglo-American accord

The achievements of the Conference, although falling far short of the extravagant claims made by the President and the American delegates, were undoubtedly of great importance. The actual scrapping of millions of dollars' worth of ships in commission or in process of construction gave the world an object lesson such as it had never had before. One of the most significant results of the Conference was the development of a complete accord between England and the United States, made possible by the settlement of the Irish question and furthered by the tact and gracious bearing of Mr. Balfour. One of the unfortunate results was the increased isolation of France, due to the failure of her delegates to grasp the essential elements of the situation and to play any but a negative rôle. The success of the Conference was due largely to Secretary Hughes, who, though handicapped at every point by fear of the Senate, and by the unfortunate commitments of President Harding during the presidential campaign, may be said on the whole to have played his hand reasonably well.

CHAPTER XXX

DISARMAMENT AFTER THE WASHINGTON CONFERENCE

Great Britain acceded naval equality to United States

THE Washington Conference of 1921–22[1] marked a distinct turning point in the history of our naval policy. While the Spanish-American War of 1898 served to focus public interest on the navy and thereby made possible relatively generous appropriations for its upbuilding, this interest was not a vital one. Not until our neutral trade was interfered with in the World War did we give serious attention to the problems of the sea. Such was the extreme irritation at the disregard of our neutral rights by the belligerents that President Wilson, in his St. Louis speech of February 3, 1916, came out for "incomparably the most adequate navy in the world." Congress was quick to respond and in August of that year voted the largest naval appropriation in its history. And long before the 1916 program was completed, the General Board of the navy was asking for more ships and in September, 1920, advocated "a navy equal to the most powerful maintained by any other nation in the world." The Washington Conference was a triumph for those who advocated an American navy equal to the most powerful, for Great Britain, fearing that we might outstrip her in battleship construction, acceded naval equality to us. This sharing of dominion over the seas was a victory won without war. The nation's *amour propre* was gratified, for it was felt that the recognition of the political principle of naval equality with the strongest maritime power was

[1]For an account of the Washington Conference, see Chapter XXIX.

one which comported with our wealth and station in the post-war international society.

Naval competition continued in auxiliary types of vessels

But even though the Washington Conference accorded equality of naval strength to the United States through the ratio symbol of 5:5 for capital ships and aircraft carriers, and arrested competition in these types, competition in cruisers, destroyers, and submarines among the five leading naval powers, Great Britain, the United States, France, Italy, and Japan, was not eliminated. Almost from the moment of ratification, some of the powers signatory to the naval treaty began laying down keels in the unlimited categories. The dangers which had appeared in the competition of capital ship construction before the Washington Conference now shifted to competition in auxiliary types. Yet between the Washington Conference of 1921–22 and the Three-Power Naval Conference at Geneva in 1927 there were no indications that the American government had made any formal efforts to persuade the great naval powers to consider another conference for the purpose of extending the Washington naval limitation principles to other categories of warships. There were reasons to believe that if such an invitation had been extended, it would not have been accepted. With the exception of Great Britain, European nations are more interested in land armaments than they are in naval armaments. They preferred to deal with the problem as a whole and not piecemeal because they felt that, in all their schemes of military preparation, land, sea, and air armaments were interdependent and should be dealt with together in one limitation agreement. The political factors underlying the half success of the Washington naval agreement, moreover, were not fully appreciated by our government. The limitation of cruisers, destroyers, and submarines would have raised political problems in the Mediterranean for Great Britain, France, and Italy. But with European politics the United States

Land, sea, and air armaments considered interdependent

Political involvements

would have nothing to do; the attempts therefore to include these categories in the naval treaty were accordingly abandoned.

The League's attempts to deal with the problem

While the Washington Conference confined its task to naval armaments, the League of Nations endeavored to deal with the disarmament problem as a whole. Its efforts to evolve a disarmament agreement arose out of the recognition expressed in Article 8 of the Covenant which reads in part as follows:

> The members of the League recognize that the maintenance of peace requires the reduction of national armaments to the lowest point consistent with national safety and the enforcement by common action of international obligations.
>
> The Council, taking account of the geographical situation and circumstances of each State, shall formulate plans for such reduction for the consideration and action of the several Governments.

The Temporary Mixed Commission

From its very beginning the League attempted to carry out the purposes expressed in this Article. The Council, on the recommendation made to it by the First Assembly, in 1921, appointed a special Preparatory Committee, better known as the Temporary Mixed Commission, to examine the whole problem and to draft reports and proposals for the reduction of armaments. Under the leadership of Viscount Cecil, this Commission prepared the Draft Treaty of Mutual Assistance upon which the principles of the stillborn Geneva Protocol were founded.[2] The support for the Temporary Mixed Commission work was not sufficient to justify attacking the problem along the lines laid down by it.[3] In 1925, the Sixth Assembly of the League recommended the creation of a preparatory disarmament commission to deal with the technical questions of armaments. This commission was to be composed of experts, who would study the technical aspects of the disarmament problem and thus pave the way for a political conference. The Council of the League in-

[2]See Denys P. Myers, *World Disarmament*, pp. 110–112.

[3]League of Nations, Official Journal, III, pp. 403, 982, 1432; V, p. 1605.

vited the United States to participate in the work of this Preparatory Commission. The United States accepted the League invitation.[4]

The Preparatory Disarmament Commission

The Preparatory Commission held its first session at Geneva in May, 1926. The long and dreary discussions of the Commission on the technical aspects of the disarmament problem brought out the conflicting and divergent points of view of the various experts. Such opinion was, of course, national opinion, and national opinion was based on the political policies of the state the expert represented. The early discussions at Geneva nevertheless served a useful purpose: they revealed the attitudes of the various nations on matters of high policy and brought to the surface the political alignments of Europe.

Proposal of Great Britain, Japan, and the United States

When the Preparatory Commission came to a consideration of naval armaments there was a clear division of opinion among the five principal naval powers. Great Britain, Japan, and the United States proposed that in each class of warship, *viz.*, battleships, cruisers, submarines, destroyers, etc., a limit should be placed on the size of the individual ship, the number of ships in the class, and on the calibre of the guns carried. France and Italy contended that limitation be only as to total tonnage of the whole fleet and that within that total each nation should be free to build whatever kind of ship best suited her needs. At this stage of the Commission's work, President Coolidge felt that the five naval powers would make better progress if the naval disarmament question was dealt with in a separate conference. In his message to Congress of February 10, 1927, and in a memorandum of the same day to Great Britain, Japan, France, and Italy, the President suggested that these nations "empower their delegates at the forthcoming meeting of the Preparatory Commission [meeting of March–April, 1927] to negotiate and conclude at an early date an agreement further lim-

Proposal of France and Italy

[4]See Chapter XXXVIII.

iting naval armament, supplementing the Washington Treaty in that subject, and covering the classes of vessels not covered by that Treaty."[5] Our government wanted the 5:5:3 ratio which had been adopted for capital ships applied to auxiliary craft. What prompted President Coolidge to call for a conference was that naval competition in the new 10,000-ton cruiser class, which the Washington Conference had popularized, was in the offing.[6] Our government could well afford this naval luxury, but did not desire the international political consequences which invariably accompany naval competition. The American invitation was accepted by Great Britain and Japan, and declined by France and Italy. The latter two refused on the grounds that land and sea armaments are interdependent and must be dealt with as a whole; in addition, the French claimed that a separate naval conference outside the portals of the League of Nations would tend to weaken the authority of that organization with respect to the disarmament problem. In this way a naval conference of five powers dwindled down to one of three.

President Coolidge proposed special conference of the five nations

Great Britain and Japan accepted, France and Italy declined, invitation

The Geneva Three-Power Naval Conference was a failure, and two important matters contributed to its failure: first, the American approach to the limitation of armament as though it were a problem in arithmetic; second, the British insistence on the doctrine of "absolute requirements," which were set at an irreducible minimum of 70 cruisers. Our delegates proposed a maximum total tonnage for auxiliary craft of 640,000 tons,[7] of which 300,000 tons were allocated for cruisers. This meant a cruiser strength of some forty vessels, the exact number

[5]New York *Times*, February 11, 1927.

[6]Japan forced the pace in this type of naval expansion soon after the Washington Conference. In 1922–23, Japan laid down six cruisers, fifteen destroyers, and eleven submarines; Great Britain, one cruiser; the United States, no ships whatever; France, three cruisers, eighteen destroyers, and eleven submarines; Italy, four destroyers.

[7]Records of the Conference for the Limitation of Naval Armament, Geneva, 1927, 70th Congress, 1st session, Senate Document No. 55, p. 27.

depending upon the size of each ship. The British counter-proposal was for 875,000 tons, later reduced to 737,000 tons, and at the same time they insisted on a minimum of seventy cruisers. The British figures would have meant a cruiser-building program for us of thirty new ships, not counting those already in service and authorized, at a cost of some $500,000,000 to our taxpayers, a high price for parity with Great Britain. There were other proposals and counter-proposals, but the British demand for seventy cruisers and our insistence upon arming large or small cruisers with eight-inch guns finally led to the failure of the Conference.[8]

Reasons for failure of Geneva Three-Power Naval Conference

Behind the maze of figures there were, of course, the national policies of the negotiators, which were not publicly discussed but which were in their minds throughout the Conference. The real but unexpressed issue which separated the British and American delegates was what is known as "the freedom of the seas,"[9] and the naval demands were in good measure premised on a future war in which the United States would be neutral and would attempt to keep the "seas free," with Great Britain, as a belligerent, interfering with our neutral trade as she did in the first three years of the World War. The Conference could not rise above the discussion of tons and guns to consider the political realities underlying the demands of each. By President Coolidge's invitation to the Conference, the basis of discussion was limited to an extension of the 5:5:3 ratio to vessels not covered by the Washington Treaty,[10] and our delegation was prevented from lifting the discussions from naval figures to the realm of politics.

Hidden political considerations

---

[8]The Japanese wanted an agreement that would relieve them of the necessity of large additional construction.

[9]Mr. Bridgeman, the British delegate to the Conference, declared, "I will never be a party to a policy which leaves us in any anxiety as to whether we are able to maintain the freedom of the seas." See the *Times* (London), March 26, 1927, p. 14.

[10]Records of the Conference for the Limitation of Naval Armament, Geneva, 1927, 70th Congress, 1st session, Senate Document No. 55, p. 25.

American reaction to failure of Geneva Conference

The failure of the Geneva Naval Conference produced an unfortunate reaction in this country. In some quarters it was interpreted as a refusal on the part of Great Britain to implement the principle of naval equality accorded to us in 1922. The "Big Navy" group took advantage of the situation, and on December 14, 1927, Congressman Butler, Chairman of the Committee on Naval Affairs, introduced in the House a bill calling for the construction of 71 vessels at a cost of $725,000,000. The bill had the approval of President Coolidge and Secretary of the Navy Wilbur. Those who were angered by the Geneva outcome regarded the proposed program as a proper retort to British behavior at the Naval Conference. By others, it was looked upon as "sheer madness" which would inevitably lead to war. The [London] *Times*,[11] in an editorial, declared that the "Government of the United States . . . is now definitely embarked on an armaments program that is in fact competitive, is by implication provocative, and, to judge by the number of hints, pointers, and allusions, is at least designed partly with the object of making a strong impression on British public opinion."

In the light of our geographical position and the sense of security which it gives us, the Butler bill contemplated an extravagant building program. Public opinion was aroused to the dangers of a naval race with a friendly nation, and began to bring pressure on the Administration. In place of the Butler bill, another was introduced providing for the construction of fifteen ten-thousand-ton cruisers and one aircraft carrier at a total cost of $274,000,000. Under this bill the President was authorized to suspend naval construction in the event of an international agreement for the limitation of naval armaments to which the United States might become a signatory. The debate in the Senate revealed that the majority of Senators were either for cruisers or for naval

[11]December 17, 1927.

limitation conferences; the issue was as to which should come first. Senators recalled that when the United States was forging ahead of Great Britain in battleships the latter agreed to limit them. And the way to compel a cruiser agreement was to match if not outdo Great Britain's cruiser strength; for the failure of the Geneva Conference and the ill-fated Anglo-French naval "compromise"[12] meant to these Senators that equality was possible only to those who have the wealth to claim it. The modified bill calling for the construction of fifteen cruisers and one aircraft carrier became law when President Coolidge signed it on February 13, 1929.

Bill introduced to build fifteen cruisers, one aircraft carrier.

Signed by President Coolidge

A quarrel between the two greatest naval powers controlling more than half of the world's naval armaments was not to be settled by competitive building. President Hoover in his inaugural address declared that "peace can be promoted by the limitation of arms and by the creation of the instrumentalities for the peaceful settlement of controversies. I covet for this administration a record of having further contributed to advance the cause of peace." In the League of Nations Preparatory Commission at Geneva in April, 1929, Mr. Hugh Gibson, on behalf of the President, opened the way for new negotiations, primarily with Great Britain, by urging that an agreement should not be predicated on an "exact balance of ships and guns, which can be based only on the idea of conflict; what is really wanted is a common-sense agreement based on the idea that we are going to be friends and settle our problems by peaceful means."[13] This declaration made a favorable

[12]Opposition to the cruiser bill was weakened by the publication of the so-called Anglo-French naval "compromise" on October 22, 1928, the gist of which was French support for the British desire to limit cruisers above 7,500 tons armed with 8-inch guns, the type of ships demanded by our naval experts at the Geneva Naval Conference of 1927. In return for this support Great Britain promised to offer no further resistance to the French contention that "trained reserves" be left out of the reckoning. Our government promptly rejected the idea. For a detailed discussion, see C. P. Howland, ed., *Survey of American Foreign Relations,* 1930, pp. 356–371.

[13]League of Nations, C. 195, M. 74, 1929, IX, p. 56.

impression upon the world, for it was the first concrete indication as to the kind of disarmament policy the new President would pursue.[14]

Negotiations, primarily with Great Britain, reopened by President Hoover

The time for a fresh start was propitious. In Great Britain, a Labor Government had come into power and was eager for success in foreign affairs. Through Mr. Gibson, President Hoover had dispelled the gloom hanging over the deadlocked Preparatory Commission. It was agreed that no progress in the reduction of the naval armaments of the five principal nations could be made until Great Britain and the United States had solved their differences. Accordingly Anglo-American negotiations were begun by General Charles G. Dawes, Ambassador to Great Britain, and Prime Minister Ramsay MacDonald. The starting point of their conversations was equality between the two fleets, category by category. The main difficulty in these exchanges was, as at the Geneva Naval Conference, the cruiser. Within three months the two governments were able to announce that they had reached an accord and had reduced their differences to the type of gun to be placed on three 10,000-ton cruisers. It was at this juncture of the negotiations that Prime Minister MacDonald set sail for the United States. The object of his visit was to establish by personal contact "a relationship based upon mutual understanding, not only of common objects to be pursued, but of natural differences to be respected."[15] His visit signalized to the world the accord reached by the two great English-speaking peoples as well as the readiness of their governments to enter a five-power naval conference. It was also a recognition that Great Britain was prepared to share with us equality of naval strength in all classes of warships.

Prime Minister MacDonald visits President Hoover

[14]The United States consistently maintained that "trained reserves" should be taken into account in measuring the strength of land armies. At this meeting of the Commission, however, Mr. Gibson announced that our government was disposed "to defer to the views of the majority of those countries [the conscriptionist powers] whose land forces constitute their chief military interest, and . . . accept their ideas in the matter of trained reserves." League of Na-

Hoover-MacDonald conversations

The fruits of the Hoover-MacDonald conversations were summarized by them in a joint statement on October 9, 1929. "Both our governments," the statement read, "resolve to accept the peace pact [the Kellogg-Briand Pact] not only as a declaration of good intentions, but as a positive obligation to direct national policy in accordance with its pledge. . . . Therefore, in a new and reinforced sense, the two Governments not only declare that war between them is unthinkable but distrusts and suspicion arising from doubts and fears which may have been justified before the peace pact must now cease to influence national policy." Both men felt they had to tread warily; one had an ever suspicious Senate to appease and the other a neighbor across the Channel who feared that the two greatest naval powers were planning to impose a *fait accompli* upon the others. The joint authors therefore made it clear that the part each of their governments would play in the promotion of peace would be different, "as one will never consent to become entangled in European diplomacy and the other is resolved to pursue a policy of active coöperation with its European neighbors." Historic problems, such as belligerent rights and freedom of the seas, Mr. MacDonald later told the House of Commons,[16] were discussed; but owing to the inflammable nature of these topics, it was agreed that they had better be left alone.

Great Britain and the United States reach an understanding

It took a fruitless Geneva Naval Conference of 1927 as well as three months of strenuous negotiating between Ambassador Dawes and Prime Minister MacDonald before an understanding on cruisers was reached. The task of fitting the Japanese, French, and Italian naval programs into the Anglo-American program however still

tions, C. 195, M. 74, 1929, IX, p. 114. In deferring to the views of the conscriptionist powers, our government joined Great Britain in withdrawing opposition to the military reservist question. See note (12) on page 705.

[15]The *Times* (London), November 6, 1929.

[16]*Op. cit.*

remained, for no effective agreement was possible unless these three were included. Between October, 1929, and January 21, 1930, the date set for a naval conference which was to meet at London, France, Italy, and Japan disclosed the policies they would pursue.

Attitude of France

France's attitude was a familiar one. The history of her disarmament policy in the post-war period was characterized by a quest for security within and without the League system in a Europe whose peace rested upon the frail structure of Versailles.[17] Her thesis at Geneva was that the possibility of war necessitates the maintenance of large armaments. In the absence of a well organized international machinery to maintain the peace, nations must rely upon their own military forces for security. The problem of disarmament, in French eyes, rested on the creation of those political conditions which would make large armaments unnecessary. As the price of reducing her military strength France demanded guarantees of political security, i.e., pledges of mutual assistance in case of aggression, and only in proportion to such assistance as she could rely upon from without was she prepared to reduce armaments materially. The memorandum[18] which France sent to the nations invited to the London Naval Conference set forth this thesis in unmistakable terms and reminded the powers that in accepting the London invitation she was not abandoning the political considerations underlying her disarmament policy.

Attitude of Italy

Prior to the Conference the Franco-Italian negotiations centered around the problem of naval equality. Ever since the Washington Conference of 1921–22, when Italy and France were bracketed together in capital ship equality, it was the aim of the Italian government to obtain equality in all other categories of vessels. France

[17]See *supra*, pp. 623–624, for the account of the unratified three-power treaty of guarantee. The French contention was that the ratification of this treaty would have given them the security they tried to maintain by arms.

[18]This was issued on December 20, 1929.

steadfastly resisted this aim. Privately the Italians admitted that they had to have equality for home consumption. If Mussolini's Socialist predecessors brought home equality in capital ships with France, how could the Fascist dictator take less in auxiliary crafts? Here was a problem of prestige *par excellence.* After negotiations lasting over a period of three months Franco-Italian attitudes had hardened considerably, and on the eve of the London Naval Conference their naval quarrel was still in an insoluble form.

Attitude of Japan

Japan's naval policy after the Washington Conference was characterized as one of defensive parity which she defined as the possession of a fleet capable of meeting any hostile fleet that might be sent against her. This thesis presupposed a naval strength which would vary with the size of other great fleets, i.e., those of the United States and Great Britain. The policy was aimed at insuring safety and security; it resulted in Japanese naval mastery of Far Eastern waters. In battleship strength the Tokio government announced that it would abide by the 3:5 ratio agreed to at the Washington Conference; in cruisers, it would demand a 7:10 ratio.

London Naval Conference

The London Naval Conference to which the five leading naval powers, Great Britain, the United States,[19] France, Japan, and Italy, sent delegates opened on January 21, 1930. Its object was an agreement among the five powers to limit the size and number of those ships left unlimited by the Washington Conference. Our delegation proposed to the British *immediate parity* in every type of ship; to the Japanese, it proposed the 5:5:3 ratio in all categories. No proposal was made to the French nor to the Italians, but Secretary Stimson, the head of our delegation, suggested informally that these two nations agree to a pro-

5:5:3 ratio for Great Britain, the United States, and Japan

[19]The American delegation was composed of Secretary of State Henry L. Stimson, Secretary of the Navy Charles Francis Adams, Ambassador Dawes, Ambassador Gibson, Senator Reed, Senator Robinson, and Dwight Morrow.

gram that would enable them to build what each wanted for a period of years and thus avoid the difficult problem of Franco-Italian parity. The suggestion was turned down by both.

Franco-Italian parity

Demands of France

The figures[20] named by France called for a navy of 724,479 tons by 1936. This strength was based on her absolute needs, and contemplated the construction of 240,000 tons over the next six years. The figures were pitched high in order to maintain a clear superiority over Italy on the one hand and leave a sufficient margin with which to bargain for a security pact with the British on the other. "Absolute needs," as M. Tardieu, head of the French delegation, made clear, would be transformed into "relative needs" as the price of a treaty of mutual guaranty by Great Britain. The British government was disturbed because the French claim was a distinct threat to her two-power standard, i. e., a British fleet equal to any two fleets in Europe. If the French figure was incorporated in a naval agreement, Great Britain would be compelled to raise the level of Anglo-American parity figures in order to maintain her relative strength over France. With the British press carrying on an intensive campaign warning the government against any further military commitments on the Continent, Great Britain had to tread warily.

Effect of French demands upon Great Britain

Desire of France for mandatory financial and economic boycott as defensive measure

The hope of a five-power limitation treaty depended upon a solution of the Franco-Italian parity problem and a political agreement contributing to the organization of security as France understood it. What France wanted from Great Britain was an agreement to revise Article 16 of the League Covenant making it mandatory upon League members to carry out the financial and economic boycott measures[21] determined upon by the League

[20]The Italian statement was the old refrain of equality with France. The Japanese repeated their stand for a 7:10 ratio in auxiliary craft.

[21]See Charles P. Howland, ed., *Survey of American Foreign Relations*, 1931, pp. 356–364.

Council. British policy in this respect was largely influenced by the American position towards neutrality. Our remaining outside the League of Nations deterred Great Britain from committing herself to France beyond the pledges contained in the League Covenant and the Locarno treaties. A British blockade in pursuance of such a pledge as the French had in mind involved the risk of a head-on collision with the United States who might insist as a neutral upon carrying on trade with the Covenant-breaking state. Great Britain would not give such a pledge as a condition precedent to French adherence to a naval pact without first knowing what position America would assume with respect to neutrality. Secretary Stimson, knowing well what the Senate's reaction would be to a commitment fettering our freedom of action, gave the British our traditional answer.

French withdrawal from Conference

The fall of the Tardieu Cabinet on February 17, 1930, temporarily withdrew the French from participation in the discussions, and enabled the three "oceanic" powers—Great Britain, the United States, and Japan—to lay the basis of a tri-partite agreement. The London Naval Treaty, which finally emanated from the Conference in the form of a three-power pact, which could be expanded to include France and Italy, marked a milestone along the road of the disarmament movement. It was the first naval treaty of its kind in the history of the modern world. By it the navies of the three largest naval powers were stabilized and competition in all categories terminated.[22] The Anglo-American problem of cruiser parity was solved

London Naval Treaty

[22]The figures, in tons, taken from Article XVI of the Treaty are as follows:

	United States	*British Commonwealth of Nations*	*Japan*
Cruisers			
a. With guns of more than 6.1-inch caliber	180,000	146,800	108,400
b. With guns of 6.1-inch	143,500	192,200	100,450
Destroyers	150,000	150,000	105,500
Submarines	52,700	52,700	52,700
Total	526,200	541,700	367,050

and the Japanese demand for a 70 per cent cruiser ratio resulted in a compromise. Japan accepted a ratio of 6:10 in the large class of cruisers, a 7:10 ratio in the small class, 7:10 in destroyers, and equality in submarines. The British fear of a threat to her two-power standard was solved by inserting a safeguarding clause[23] which provided that if the national security of any signatory was materially affected by new construction of any nation [meaning, of course, France or Italy] not a party to that section of the agreement limiting cruisers, destroyers, and submarines, that signatory should have the right to make whatever increases it saw fit.

France and Italy not parties to Treaty

Final work of League's Preparatory Commission

The London Naval Treaty of 1930 was a contribution to the labors of the League of Nations Preparatory Commission. With the Anglo-American cruiser controversy solved, hitherto one of the stumbling blocks to armament limitation, the way was cleared for the Preparatory Commission to wind up its protracted deliberations. It did so by drawing up a skeleton draft convention for the reduction and limitation of armaments as a working basis for a world disarmament conference. When the Preparatory Commission met on November 9, 1930, it proceeded with the final reading of the draft convention and wound up its labors on December 9. It presented to the World Disarmament Conference a framework[24] containing no figures, but yet proposing principles[25] for the limitation or reduction of all forms of armament.

The long-awaited World Disarmament Conference met at Geneva on February 2, 1932. Sixty-odd nations

[23]Article XXI of the Treaty—the "escalator clause."

[24]The draft was divided into six parts as follows: personnel, material (land, naval, and air), budgetary expenditure, chemical arms, exchange of information, and the miscellaneous provisions for a permanent disarmament commission, procedure regarding complaints and temporary derogation under certain conditions from the agreed terms. The text of the draft is given in League of Nations, C. 687, M. 288, 1931, IX, 8.

[25]There was hardly an important article in the draft that was not excepted to by one or more of the 27 governments which participated in its making.

gathered there to deliberate on one of the most difficult problems Western civilization has yet faced. The task of the Conference was stated by its president, Mr. Arthur Henderson, former British Secretary of State for Foreign Affairs, to be "to arrive at a collective agreement on an effective program of practical proposals, speedily to secure a substantial reduction and limitation of all national armaments."[26] At the end of the first phase of the deliberations—a phase devoted to the organization of the Conference and to the exposition of the national attitudes of the nations represented—there were nearly as many proposals for disarmament as there were nations participating. All expressed the need in general for the limitation and reduction of armaments; the same purpose animated all participants—it was to strengthen one's own position with respect to armaments by cutting down those of the others.

World Disarmament Conference

Our government did not play a leading rôle in the first stage of the Conference. Mr. Hugh Gibson, Ambassador to Belgium, and acting head of the American delegation,[27] presented a nine-point program[28] with the hope of furthering an agreement. He proposed (1) the acceptance of the draft convention as a basis for discussion; (2) the total abolition of submarines; (3) total abolition of lethal gases and bacteriological warfare; (4) special restrictions for tanks and heavy mobile guns as arms of peculiarly aggressive character; (5) measures to protect civilian populations against aërial bombing; (6) computation of the numbers of armed forces on the basis of the effectives necessary for the maintenance of internal order plus some suitable contingent for defense; (7) budgetary limitation on material as a complementary method to direct limitation; (8) pro-

Nine-point program of the United States

[26]League of Nations, Conference for the Reduction and Limitation of Armaments, Conf. D. P. V. 1 (1), p. 2.

[27]The other members of the American delegation were: Secretary of State Stimson, Senator Claude A. Swanson, Mr. Norman H. Davis, and Dr. Mary Emma Wooley.

[28]League of Nations Publication, Official No. Conf. D. 56.

longing the Washington and the London Naval treaties; and (9) proportional reductions from the figures of these treaties as soon as they have been completed by French and Italian adherence. The thesis which Mr. Gibson set forth in introducing the American program was predicated on what he termed a "new conception of national armaments." He declared:

> Every nation has not only the right but the obligation to its own people to maintain internal order. This obviously calls for an adequate military force for internal police work. Beyond and above this there is the obligation of each government to its people to maintain a sufficient increment of military strength to defend the national territory against aggression and invasion. We therefore have this formula dividing our military forces into two parts. Beyond this reasonable supplement to the police force we have taken an implicit obligation to restrict ourselves. Our problem is, therefore, to establish by honest scrutiny and agreement the margin that now exists beyond what is essential for the maintenance of internal order and defense of our territories.[29]

Failure to recognize political implications

The American proposal—disarmament without a political price—was admirably suited to a nation that is supreme in the Western hemisphere. The formula fitted our geographical position. A nation such as ours, believing itself secure and free from the political complications of the European system, proposed a disarmament program without in any way taking into account the insecurity which haunted some European nations and prompted them to maintain large armaments. Our disarmament proposals furthermore were based on the idea that the reduction of armaments was in and of itself a guaranty of political security. This was not the faith we preached at the Washington Conference in 1921 where we recognized the need for organizing political security in the Pacific as a condition to the naval agreement.[30] Secretary Stimson, in his letter to Senator Borah of February 24, 1932, pointed

[29] League of Nations, Conf. D. P. V. 5 (1), pp. 1–4.
[30] See Chapter XXIX.

out that the Naval Treaty and the Nine-Power Treaty of the Washington Conference were "interrelated and interdependent," for, wrote Secretary Stimson, "the willingness of the American government to surrender its then commanding lead in battleship construction and to leave its positions at Guam and in the Philippines without further fortification was predicated upon, among other things, the self-denying covenants contained in the Nine-Power Treaty. . . ."[31] The Washington Naval Treaty would not have been possible without political agreements such as the Nine-Power Treaty, the Four-Power Treaty, and the non-fortification agreement.[32]

Program submitted by France

The American nine-point program was in striking contrast to the one submitted by France on February 5, 1932. It called for (1) the creation of an international police force under the authority of the League of Nations to be composed of small land and naval contingents furnished by the contracting states and supplemented by national contingents in time of need; (2) an international civil air transport service operated by organizations under League auspices; and (3) an international military air force. In this proposal, France declared, she was making "the choice between a League of Nations possessing executive authority and a League of Nations paralyzed by the uncompromising attitude of national sovereignty."[33] The establishment of an international police force, it was contended, would result in drastic reductions of national military establishments, but by what figures the French plan did not indicate. Upon presenting this plan to the Conference, M. Tardieu declared:

> I ask you . . . to heed the voice of France when she asserts that peace can never be assured until the fabric of the League has been strengthened in truth and in fact. I ask you

[31]Dept. of State, Press Release, February 27, 1932. See also p. 776.

[32]Cf. R. L. Buell, *The Washington Conference*, pp. 170–171; and P. J. Noel Baker, *Disarmament*, pp. 182–184.

[33]League of Nations, Conf. D. 99, p. 23.

also to heed her voice when, as a means to such strength, she asks you to begin by implementing the Covenant with the resources which implicitly it contains.[34]

In the absence of some plan which would contribute to French security, M. Tardieu asserted, no reduction of armaments could be effected. With this thesis, Czechoslovakia, Poland, Rumania, and Jugoslavia, allies of France, were in general agreement.

Contentions over offensive and defensive armaments

The delegates spent many weeks discussing what armaments were offensive and what defensive. The United States contended that the battleship is defensive and the submarine offensive; France and many of the small nations maintained that the battleship is a weapon of aggression and the submarine a weapon of defense. Japan maintained that aircraft carriers are offensive and the United States experts argued that they are defensive. There was hardly a weapon in the military profession that was not thus defended or challenged and the technical discussions produced deadlock after deadlock.

Second American proposal

In an endeavor to break the deadlock and give the Conference fresh impetus, President Hoover on June 22, 1932, submitted an ambitious plan[35]—the second to come from our government. This proposal again reflected our attitude in dealing with armaments as isolated phenomena bearing no relation to the political world in which they exist. Underlying it was the philosophy that reduction in armaments can be made without jeopardizing the security of any nation. Political, geographical, and economic imponderables were not taken into consideration by the President. The plan was based on the principles that the signers of the Pact of Paris in renouncing war as an instrument of national policy would use their arms solely for defense, that reduction in armaments must be carried out by increasing the relative power of defense through de-

[34]League of Nations, Conf. D. P. VI. 4, pp. 7–9.

[35]League of Nations, Conf. D. 126.

creasing the power of attack, and that proportionate reductions must be made by all states.

The method of reduction for land effectives was predicated on the dual functions of land armaments—the maintenance of internal order, and defense against foreign attack. President Hoover proposed that the size of armies for internal order may be measured by the size of a nation's population,[36] and that the size of armies for defense purposes, over and above the troops maintained for internal order, be reduced by one-third. Navies of the five naval powers were to be reduced without any distinction as to aggressive and defensive ships as follows: battleships by one-third; aircraft carriers, cruisers, and destroyers by one-fourth; submarines by one-third, no nation to possess more than 35,000 tons of this type.

Unfavorable results of this proposal

It soon became obvious to the Hoover administration that the plan as proposed was not well thought out. The enthusiasm with which Russia, Italy, and Germany greeted the Hoover plan reflected their desire for a change in the public law of Europe as established by the Treaty of Versailles. To Great Britain, France, and the Succession States, the plan was unacceptable because it contemplated a reduction of armaments which would alter the military balance of power in Europe to their detriment and in favor of the defeated powers. The American delegation was placed in the embarrassing position of heading the revisionist bloc against France and her allies. Notwithstanding that the Hoover plan was generally acceptable to a majority[37] of the representatives to the Confer-

[36] President Hoover proposed that the proportion of troops to total population allowed Germany and the other defeated powers in the peace treaties be taken as a basis. This was manifestly unsound as a formula, since the proportion conceded to Germany, 100,000 troops to a population of 65,000,000, differed from that granted to Austria, 30,000 troops to a population of some 6,000,000. Under this formula, the United States would actually be entitled to a force of 200,000 men, an increase of 62,000 men over the existing number, which was 138,000.

[37] Journal of the Conference for the Reduction and Limitation of Armaments, pp. 827–845.

ence, the American delegates held private conversations with the French and British to work out a compromise which would also win these two over to the plan. What emerged was the resolution[38] of July 23, 1932, drafted largely by France, Great Britain, and the United States, which in effect transformed the Hoover plan into a declaration of good-will, causing painful disappointment to the Russian, German, and Italian governments.

Germany withdraws from Conference

The immediate result of the July 23 resolution was the withdrawal of Germany from the Conference because it failed to make clear whether Germany would be given equality in armaments with other nations or whether she would still have the special status imposed upon her by the Treaty of Versailles. Her withdrawal created a diplomatic crisis of the first order and paralyzed the work of the Conference. A way of bringing Germany back had to be found if the Conference was not to collapse completely. On the initiative of Mr. Norman Davis, one of the American delegates to the Conference, Prime Minister MacDonald of Great Britain, Premier Herriot of France, Baron Aloisi of Italy, and Baron von Neurath of Germany met in a series of private negotiations at Geneva and on December 11, 1932, made public the formula[39] which enabled Germany to resume her place at the Conference.

Formula enabling Germany to resume place in Conference

The declaration in part read that "one of the principles that should guide the Conference on Disarmament should be the grant to Germany, and the other disarmed powers, of equality of rights in a system which would provide security for all nations. . . ." The significant thing about the quoted passage was that the recognition of the principle of German armament equality was linked with French security. In the German press generally the five-power declaration was interpreted as an acceptance of the German claim to equality, which, while still to be incor-

[38]For the text, see League of Nations Publication, Official No. Conf. D. p. 136.

[39]Dept. of State, Press Release, December 12, 1932.

porated in a general disarmament treaty, constituted nevertheless a victory for German diplomacy. The French press was divided; some papers supporting the government regarded the declaration as a basis for future discussion which safeguarded the French thesis of security, while the nationalistic journals, such as *Le Journal des Débats*, denounced it as a surrender of the traditional French position.[40]

Second French proposal

During the time when efforts were being made to bring Germany back to Geneva, Premier Herriot of France, on November 14, 1932, submitted to the Conference a new French plan[41] with a view to reconciling the French thesis of security through sanctions with the American, British, and German theses based on varying methods of direct limitation, as well as to make certain concessions to Germany regarding her armaments. The Herriot plan restated in a modified form the traditional French thesis of security by collective military and economic sanctions through the medium of an international authority. Specifically the Herriot plan envisaged a system of security based on two groups of interrelated proposals: one, an agreement of all the powers to implement the Pact of Paris; and the other, a special arrangement for Continental Europe. The proposals in group one deserve to be quoted in full because they show what rôle the United States was expected to play in the French program of security.

All the Powers taking part in the work of the Conference shall be called upon to establish in an effective manner the following principles, which are generally recognized to be a necessary consequence of the Pact for the Renunciation of War.

(a) Any war undertaken in breach of the Paris Pact is a matter of interest to all the Powers and shall be regarded as a breach of the obligations assumed towards each one of them;

[40]See the New York *Times*, December 12 and 13, 1932, where the German and French press comments are reprinted.

[41]New York *Times*, November 15, 1932.

(b) In the event of a breach or threat of breach of the Paris Pact, the said Powers shall concert together as promptly as possible with a view to appealing to public opinion and agreeing upon the steps to be taken;

(c) In application of the Pact of Paris outlawing war, any breach of the Pact shall involve the prohibition of direct or indirect economic or financial relations with the aggressor country. The Powers shall undertake to adopt the necessary measures to make that prohibition immediately effective; and

(d) The said Powers shall declare their determination not to recognize any *de facto* situation brought about in consequence of the violation of an international undertaking.[42]

The French plan and the United States

The aim of the French in having these four principles embodied in a treaty was to insure a coöperative policy on the part of non-members of the League and non-European nations whenever the need for applying sanctions on the European continent arose. From the speeches of Secretary of State Stimson the French assumed that the United States would join in a consultative pact and agree not to aid an aggressor. While Secretary Stimson did declare that consultation was inherent in the Pact of Paris and that the Pact had altered the old concept of neutral rights and obligations,[43] the Hoover administration was not prepared to embody these ideas in a treaty which it was certain would meet with Senatorial opposition.

The French plan applied to Europe

The proposals in the second group applied to Europe and were more far-reaching. Briefly summarized they provided a method for defining and detecting the aggressor and guaranteeing assistance to a state whose territory was attacked or invaded by foreign forces. To the Council of the League was given the authority to determine by majority vote the assistance to be given after it had ascertained that an attack or invasion had taken place. To facilitate ascertaining the facts in any given dispute, a permanent commission of diplomatic and military representatives ap-

[42]League of Nations, Conf. D. No. 146.

[43]See Chapter XXXII. Cf. Philip Jessup, "The Birth, Death and Reincarnation of Neutrality," *Am. Journal of Int. Law,* vol. 26, p. 792.

pointed by the League Council would be set up in each of the signatory states. All European nations subscribing to this plan would be required to adhere to the General Act of Arbitration[44] providing for pacific settlement of all disputes and sanctions in case a signatory refused to conform to its obligations or failed to carry out an award.

Restrictions upon land armaments

The plan further proposed that the armies of Continental Europe should be reduced to a uniform general type, that of a national short-service army, with limited effectives not adapted to a sudden offensive. All powerful mobile material, especially such as would facilitate an attack on permanent fortifications (powerful artillery and powerful tanks), would be prohibited to the armies of the European states. Each of the contracting powers would place at the disposal of the League of Nations as a contingent for joint action a small number of specialized units consisting of troops serving a relatively long term and equipped with the powerful materials prohibited to the national armies. Air forces would be internationalized and placed at the disposal of the League, and civil aviation would be entrusted to a European air transport union to safeguard against the use of civil aircraft for military purposes.[45]

Difficult involvements facing the United States and Great Britain

The Herriot plan marked a distinct advance in French disarmament policy. An international army on a world scale—this was one of the aims of the Tardieu plan submitted in February, 1932—was abandoned in favor of a small number of professional troops to be furnished by European states and held at the disposal of the League. Such a plan as this would have resulted in placing all continental armies, including the German army, on the same footing—a distinct concession to Germany's desire for equality. The outlook for the plan was not bright not-

[44]League of Nations, Pacific Settlement of International Disputes, Non-Aggression and Mutual Assistance, C. 536. M. 163. 1928, IX.

[45]A Mediterranean pact between Great Britain, France, and Italy providing for the coöperation of their naval fleets against an aggressor was also included.

withstanding that it contained many original suggestions and offered a basis for fruitful discussion. To the United States the plan was inconceivable because it involved the use of military sanctions; and to England it meant adding to her burden of responsibility which she felt was already too large under the Covenant and the Locarno treaties. Without the support of the United States and Great Britain, the Herriot plan was destined to fail.

The "security school" and military sanctions

A year of the Conference revealed how infinitely complex was the problem of disarmament. The conflict in general revolved about the two basic methods of organizing the world for peace. The "security school" with France as its major protagonist conditioned disarmament upon security through military sanctions. The League of Nations Covenant, the Kellogg-Briand Pact, the Locarno Treaties—these had not instilled in her a sense of security. Her disarmament policy pointed to one of two ways by which the security complex might be satisfied: permanent military superiority over her potential enemies—a situation which, in the light of the history of post-war Europe, was fraught with great danger; or, a water-tight system calling for collective international action against the disturber of the peace. In opposition to the "security school" stood the "disarmament school" of which the United States was the guiding spirit and which sought the reduction of armaments as a way to security without political equivalents as a substitute. If an agreement on a general treaty were to have been reached the Disarmament Conference would have had to reconcile these two major conceptions of the organization of peace.

The "disarmament school"

The disarmament problem was further complicated by the advent to power in Germany of Adolf Hitler, who demanded, in effect, that the former Allies either disarm to Germany's level or release Germany from the disarmament restrictions of the Versailles Treaty.

CHAPTER XXXI

THE UNITED STATES AND THE PERMANENT COURT OF INTERNATIONAL JUSTICE

It is one of the ironies of our foreign policy that the United States, which has been a pioneer and leader in the movement of settling international disputes by arbitration and judicial settlement, should today be one of the great nations of the world not a member of the Permanent Court of International Justice at the Hague.[1] When the first Hague Conference met in 1899, there was no tribunal of a permanent nature to which nations might resort for the settlement of international disputes.[2] It was the American delegation to the 1899 Hague Conference that urged the creation of a permanent court of international justice. The other delegations, particularly those of the great European powers, however, were not prepared to follow the lead of the United States. While not establishing a court of international justice, the Hague Conference of 1899 did succeed in establishing a Permanent Court of Arbitration. The Court which was set up and which is still in existence is made up of a panel of judges, out of which *ad hoc* tribunals may be constituted for a dispute.

Though a leader in advocating arbitration, the United States is not a member of the Permanent Court

[1]In his inaugural address in 1897, President McKinley stated that the corner stone of American foreign policy throughout its existence has been "the adjustment of difficulties by judicial methods rather than by force of arms." U. S. Foreign Relations, 1899, p. 512.

[2]The first Hague Conference was convened on May 18, 1899, on the initiative of Czar Nicholas II of Russia. The program which the Russian government furnished for the labors of this international gathering sought in part to limit the progressive increase of military and naval armaments, as well as war budgets; the revision of the laws of war; the prohibition of the use of submarines in war; the acceptance of the use of good offices, mediation and voluntary arbitration

The Permanent Court of Arbitration

Each state may appoint four members to the panel. Recourse to the Court is not obligatory; attempts to make it so were unsuccessful.[3] The business of the Court is directed by an Administrative Council made up of the diplomatic representatives, at the Hague, of parties to the convention. What the first Hague Conference created was "a court only in name—a framework for the selection of referees for each particular case,"[4] but it was nevertheless, as the American delegation expressed it in its final report, "a thoroughly practical beginning" which would "produce valuable results from the outset," and would serve as the "germ out of which a better and better system will be gradually evolved."[5] During the forty-odd years of its existence there have been numerous arbitrations before tribunals of this Court. The United States, which has been a party to five arbitrations before such tribunals, was the first to resort to the Court in 1902 in a dispute with Mexico over the Pious Fund.

First case of arbitration between the United States and Mexico

While the creation of the Permanent Court of Arbitration in 1899 was a progressive step in the direction of pacific settlement of international disputes, there was much criticism that the Hague Conference had not gone far enough. Accordingly at the second Hague Conference in 1907 the American delegates were instructed by Secretary of State Root to work for the development of the

with the purpose of preventing armed conflict between nations. The fruits of this Conference with respect to armaments were barren. It adopted a resolution saying that "the restriction of military charges, which are at present a heavy burden on the world, is extremely desirable for the increase of the material and moral welfare of mankind." [James Brown Scott, *The Hague Peace Conferences of 1899 and 1907*, I, p. 83.] This was a highly honorable sentiment which left the nations in the same position after the Conference as they were before. Texts of conventions regarding the laws and customs of war by land and by sea were also drawn up. By far the most fruitful accomplishment of this Conference was the convention for the Pacific Settlement of International Disputes in which 26 powers undertook to establish a Permanent Court of Arbitration.

[3]James Brown Scott, *The Hague Peace Conferences of 1899 and 1907*, I, p. 427.

[4]*Ibid.*

[5]U. S. Foreign Relations, 1899, p. 517.

Permanent Court of Arbitration "into a permanent tribunal composed of judges who are judicial officers and nothing else, who are paid adequate salaries, who have no other occupation, and who will devote their entire time to the trial and decision of international causes by judicial methods and under a sense of judicial responsibility."[6] The instructions moreover contemplated a plan whereby judges would be so selected from the different countries that different systems of law would be fairly represented.[7]

Effort to establish Judicial Arbitration Court fails

The Second Hague Conference of 1907 not only sought to revise the Convention of 1899 for the Pacific Settlement of International Disputes, but also to create in addition to the Permanent Court of Arbitration a new body to be known as the Judicial Arbitration Court. The draft convention provided for a court composed of "judges representing the various juridical systems of the world, and capable of insuring continuity in jurisprudence of arbitration."[8] While the Conference was ready to found such a court, it could not agree on a method of appointing the judges. The smaller states asserted that sovereignty was sovereignty, that all nations are absolutely equal, and therefore that absolute equality be preserved in the appointment of judges. As the big powers, such as Russia, Great Britain, France, and the United States, did not agree that every nation was on a par with every other—that Panama was in all respects the equal of Russia, and Switzerland the equal of Great Britain—the attempt to set up a permanent court proved abortive.[9]

Organization of an international prize court also fails

The Second Hague Conference also sought to create an international court of appeal in prize cases.[10] The practice in time of war has been for each combatant to es-

[6] *Op. cit.*, 1907, p. 1135.

[7] See William I. Hull, *The Two Hague Conferences*, p. 412.

[8] For text of draft, see Malloy's Treaties, II, p. 2380.

[9] See Joseph H. Choate, The Two Hague Conferences, pp. 77–79.

[10] See Charles Noble Gregory, The Proposed International Prize Court, Am. J. of Int. Law, vol. 2, p. 458.

tablish or resort to national prize courts of its own to pass on the validity of captures made by its forces. Prize courts passing judgment on property of neutrals who are alleged to have violated their neutrality leaned unduly towards sustaining the capture. If the validity of the capture was affirmed on appeal, and this was usually so, the neutral owner had no further legal remedy. The object of setting up an International Prize Court was to provide a court of appeal with power to review the decision of a national court of justice. Such a tribunal, it was thought, would be free from the national interests and passions of the contending parties, and would adjudge cases on the general principles of international law. The Hague Conference of 1907 drew up a convention for the establishment of an International Prize Court, consisting of fifteen judges appointed by the contracting parties named in the convention.[11] In order that this proposed Court might function effectively, for the debates at the Hague revealed differences of opinion concerning some of the most important questions in prize law, it was considered necessary to enact a code of prize law, and for this purpose the British government called a conference of the chief naval powers in London in 1908 and 1909. An agreement, known as the Declaration of London, was signed by all the powers present in February, 1909. But failure of the signatories to ratify this Declaration proved fatal to the creation of the projected International Prize Court.[12]

Code of prize law proposed

When the Paris Peace Conference assembled in January

[11]For a detailed description of the constitution of the International, Prize Court, see Articles 10–27 of Convention XII creating the Court, in J. B. Scott's *The Hague Peace Conference of 1899 and 1907*, II, pp. 479–487.

[12]The American government objected to the Convention instituting the International Prize Court on the ground that it allowed appeals from a decision of the United States Supreme Court. To meet this objection, a special protocol was concluded in September, 1910, providing that recourse to the International Prize Court should take place in the form of an action for damages on account of the injury caused by the capture. But this protocol was not ratified.

1919, it was generally hoped that a court would be set up, one that would be built along the lines suggested by Mr. Root to the American delegates to the Second Hague Conference. The establishment of such an international tribunal had been included as a provision in numerous proposals for the creation of a league of nations.[13] The Covenant of the League of Nations in its final form contained an article [Article 14] directing the Council of the League to formulate and submit to the members of the League for adoption plans for the establishment of a Permanent Court of International Justice. "The Court," the Article reads, "shall be competent to hear and determine any dispute of an international character which the parties thereto submit to it." Pursuant to this article, the Council appointed a committee of jurists to draw up plans for such a court. The committee, composed of eminent jurists, including Mr. Elihu Root, former Secretary of State, met at the Hague in June, 1920, and after five weeks of deliberation evolved a draft which, with some amendments, was adopted first by the Council, and later by the Assembly of the League.

The Permanent Court of International Justice

The difficulty of discovering a plan for the election of judges, that very difficulty which arose at the Hague Conference of 1907, was met through the suggestions of Mr. Root and Lord Phillimore, the British representative, by providing that members of the Court are to be elected by a majority vote of the Assembly and the Council, each voting separately, from a list of persons nominated by the national groups of the old Court of Arbitration, each of which may nominate four candidates. By stipulating for the election of judges in this manner the *amour propre* of the great powers represented on the Council was reconciled with the equality dogma of the small powers who are in a majority in the Assembly.

Method of electing judges

[13]See David Hunter Miller, The Drafting of the Covenant, II, where the drafts for a league are compiled.

Differences between the Hague Court and the Court of International Justice

There are fundamental differences between the Hague Court of Arbitration and the Permanent Court of International Justice. The Court of Arbitration is a panel and as such it never meets as a body; it is merely a group from which arbitrators may at any time be chosen. The Court of International Justice sits permanently as a picked body of men without the need of being specially chosen after the dispute arises. The continuity in the performance of their functions assures that degree of permanence which is lacking in the Hague Court of Arbitration. The new Court is a court of justice and not merely a court of arbitration.

The judges of the Court

The basic law governing the creation and the activities of the Permanent Court of International Justice is to be found in the Covenant of the League of Nations, the resolution of the Assembly of December 13, 1920, the Protocol of Signature, the Statute accompanying this Protocol, and the Protocol concerning the Revision of the Statute approved by the Assembly on September 14, 1929. The Statute of the Court provides for a membership of eleven judges and four deputy judges,[14] chosen "regardless of their nationality from amongst persons of high moral character, who possess the qualifications required in their respective countries for appointment to the highest judicial offices." The judges are elected for nine years and are eligible for reëlection. Article 9 of the Statute provides that the electors of the judges shall bear in mind that not only should all the candidates appointed as members of the Court possess the qualifications required, but the whole body should also represent the main forms of civilization and the principal legal systems of the world.

The law applied by the Court

What law the Court shall apply is set out in Article 38 of the Statute. It includes international conventions

[14]An amendment abolishing the office of deputy judge and increasing the number of regular judges from eleven to fifteen was adopted by the Conference of Signatory States on September 4, 1929.

establishing rules expressly recognized by the contesting states; international custom, as evidence of general practice accepted as law; the general principles of law recognized by civilized nations; and the judicial decisions and the teachings of the most highly qualified publicists of the various nations, as subsidiary means for the determination of rules of law. The Court does not entertain suits by individuals; it is strictly an interstate tribunal, open for signatures to members of the League, to states mentioned in the Annex to the Covenant,[15] and under certain conditions is also accessible to other states.[16]

Character of cases reviewed by the Court

Notwithstanding the fact that the United States has been a pioneer in the promotion of the judicial settlement of international disputes, it has thus far failed to join the Permanent Court of International Justice at the Hague. The history of this failure, and the rôle the Senate has played in it, is one of the most deplorable episodes of American post-war diplomacy.

United States not a member of the Court

On February 24, 1923, President Harding asked the Senate to give its advice and consent to the adherence on the part of the United States to the Protocol of December 16, 1920, of signature of the Statute of the Court subject to four "conditions and understandings" which the President said he had good reason to believe would be acceptable to the states already members of the Court.[17] It was the opinion of the President that the reservations suggested rendered the United States "wholly free from any legal relation to the League or assumption of obligations under the Covenant of the League." This reference to the League was designed to overcome the fear that the Administration was involving the country with the League of Nations, or that the American government was entering the League through the back door. The President's

Membership in Court urged by President Harding

[15]Those mentioned in the Annex to the Covenant which are not members of the League are Ecuador, Hedjaz, and the United States.

[16]See Article 32 of the Statute.

[17]*Congressional Record,* vol. 64, p. 4508.

request for adherence was accompanied by a letter from Secretary of State Hughes which put forward the argument that the Court was truly a World Court and not an arm of the League, and that the conditions of adherence were safeguards against any entangling relationship with the League. Mr. Hughes set forth the advantage of the system of electing judges by the majority votes of the Council and Assembly of the League. "It was this arrangement," he wrote, "which solved the difficulty, theretofore appearing almost insuperable, of providing an electoral system conserving the interests of the powers, both great and small. It would be impracticable, in my judgment, to disturb the essential features of this system." He pointed out that in electing the judges, the members of the Council and Assembly exercised that function not under the Covenant but under the Statute of the Court, a separate and independent convention.

Reservations precedent to membership proposed by Secretary Hughes

The conditions or reservations which Mr. Hughes felt would constitute safeguards against entangling relationship with the League, he set out as follows:

1. That such adhesion shall not be taken to involve any legal relation on the part of the United States to the League of Nations or the assumption of any obligations by the United States under the Covenant of the League of Nations constituting Part I of the Treaty of Versailles.

2. That the United States shall be permitted to participate through representatives designated for the purpose and upon an equality with the other States members, respectively, of the Council and Assembly of the League of Nations, in any and all proceedings of either the Council or the Assembly for the election of judges or deputy judges of the Permanent Court of International Justice, or for the filling of vacancies.

3. That the United States will pay a fair share of the expenses of the Court as determined and appropriated from time to time by the Congress of the United States.

4. That the Statute for the Permanent Court of International Justice adjoined to the Protocol shall not be amended without the consent of the United States.[18]

[18] 67th Congress, 4th Session, Senate Document No. 309.

The first reservation was directed more to allaying Senatorial fears than dispelling doubt as to the legal relation or status of the United States to the Covenant. The second reservation was a material addition to the Statute, but in view of America's position in the councils of the world, it was known to be acceptable to the other signatories. The third reservation was a mode of payment dictated by American constitutional procedure. The fourth reservation was surplusage, for since the Statute is an international convention, it could not be changed without the consent of any of its signatories.

Opponents of the League in the Senate oppose membership in the Court

The atmosphere in the Senate, with Senator Lodge as chairman of the Committee on Foreign Relations to which the Harding proposal was referred, was far from propitious. The upper House still rang with the memories of the bitter fight that was waged over the ratification of the Treaty of Versailles. The "enemies" of the League who sat in judgment when President Wilson laid the Treaty of Versailles before them were still in control of the Committee on Foreign Relations and attacked the Permanent Court as a "League court." Their resistance was not to be broken easily. Both President Harding and Secretary of State Hughes denied that the Court was tied to the League, but asserted that it was an independent judicial body, to which the United States, as a nation which believes in the judicial settlement of international disputes, should adhere. The President declared that he was firmly opposed to entering the League but that American adherence to the Court "will not be an entry into the League by the side door, by the back door, or by the cellar door." Mr. Hughes put the issue squarely when he declared: "It is not too much to say that there will be no world court if this Court cannot be made one, and whether or not it is to be in the fullest sense a world court depends upon our action." Notwithstanding what the President regarded as an impressive demonstration of substantially unified opinion on American adherence, the irreconcilable Senators would not yield. They contended that the Senate was being asked to give its advice and consent to an international engagement that would draw the United States into the League. Some Senators resisted on the ground that the Court had no compulsory jurisdiction, whereas others contended that the Court would have no law to apply for there was no international law.

Alterations in the Court proposed by President Harding

The pressure from the irreconcilables was too much for President Harding. In a speech at St. Louis, June 21, 1923, he proposed some startling alterations in the set-up of the Court. The Court, he declared, must be completely independent of the League. "This," he suggested, "could be done in one of two ways, (1) by empowering the court itself to fill any vacancy arising from the death of a member or retirement for whatever cause, without interposition from any other body; or, (2) by continuing the existing authority of the Permanent Court of Arbitration to nominate and by transferring the power to elect from the council and assembly of the league to the remaining members of the court of justice."[19] The scheme contemplated taking from the Council and Assembly the right to elect the judges thus meeting the objection on the part of some Senators to the disparity in voting strength between a unit nation and an empire such as that of Great Britain which consists of several countries each having a vote. Notwithstanding the President's declaration that this program involved no change in his position, it was clear that he was advocating a project which would remove the Court from its League structural base and by so doing destroy the Court itself. Such a project had little possibility of acceptance by those nations which had already joined the Court. To them it appeared like an attempt to cast overboard the machinery which reconciled

Complete separation of Court from the League proposed

---

[19]Cited in *Am. J. of Int. Law,* vol. 17, p. 522.

the differences between the great and small powers in the selection of judges.

President Coolidge recommended the original Hughes proposal

Calvin Coolidge, who succeeded to the Presidency upon President Harding's death, in his address to Congress, December 6, 1923, commended the original Hughes proposal. He expressed the view that the proposal presented the only practical plan upon which many nations had ever agreed. While it did not meet every desire, he felt nevertheless that the Senate should give it favorable consideration with the proposed reservations. The Senate Committee on Foreign Relations under the chairmanship of Senator Lodge rejected the President's plea. Instead, Senator Lodge brought forth his own scheme for a world court by amending the Statute so completely as to destroy it. The protests which his plan aroused insured for it a still birth. Such was the wrangling in and out of the Senate Foreign Relations Committee up to the national conventions of the summer of 1924. The Democratic party platform was clear and unequivocal. It stood for "the League of Nations and the World Court of Justice as together constituting the supreme effort of statesmanship and religious conviction of our time to organize the world for peace." The Republican party platform incorporated the views of President Coolidge. It endorsed the Permanent Court of International Justice and favored American adherence.

Democratic platform of 1924 advocated membership in League and Court

Republican platform incorporated views of President Coolidge

The overwhelming victory of President Coolidge led him once more to press upon the Senate American adherence to the Court. In his message of December 3, 1924, he again urged the Senate to consider favorably the Hughes proposal, adding, however, another condition that "our country shall not be bound by advisory opinions which may be rendered by the Court upon questions which we have not voluntarily submitted for its judgment." The Committee on Foreign Relations, this time under the chairmanship of Senator Borah, again evolved a scheme to divorce the Court from the League. But this did not reach the Senate floor. Thus on the eve of President Coolidge's inaugural as President in his own right, and after a year of wrangling between the Executive and the Senate Committee on Foreign Relations, American adherence to the Court was still a matter of the future.

President Coolidge again presses for adherence to Court

The contest for the Court was to continue under the leadership of President Coolidge. In his inaugural address of March 4, 1925, he stated that "we ought not to withhold our own sanction [to the Court] because of any small and inessential difference." Public opinion in the country favored adherence. The American Bar Association, the American Federation of Labor, the United States Chamber of Commerce, and numerous other bodies declared themselves in favor of American adherence. It was indeed a strange spectacle for a few Senators to resist successfully the desire of a nation. The day after the President delivered his inaugural address, Senator Swanson, a Democrat, reintroduced his resolution at the special session, adding to the four reservations a fifth incorporating President Coolidge's suggestion on advisory opinions in the following terms:

The Swanson Resolution

> 5. That the United States shall be in no manner bound by any advisory opinion of the Permanent Court of International Justice not rendered pursuant to a request in which it, the United States, shall expressly join in accordance with the statute for the said court adjoined to the protocol of signature of the same to which the United States shall become signatory.

By a vote of 77 yeas and 2 nays taken on March 13 the Senate agreed to consider the Swanson resolution in open executive session on December 17. By this vote the Senate took from the Foreign Relations Committee the Harding-Hughes proposal and forced it to the floor of the Senate.

In due course the Swanson resolution came up for debate. The Senate was again memorialized by hundreds of organizations throughout the country urging adherence. Public opinion on the whole seemed in favor of Senatorial approval. The American Bar Association, the American Federation of Labor, church groups, and women's organizations again petitioned the Senate for favorable action. But these expressions of popular approval intensified the position of the "bitter-enders" who accused the memorialists of being financed by persons selfishly bent on drawing the United States into closer relations with Europe. The debate centered around the position the United States would occupy with respect to advisory opinions. The argument that the Court was the back door to the League was repeated. Some Senators contended that the United States would be compelled to join the League in order to enforce the judgments of the Court, that adherence would involve us in foreign wars, and rob the American people of their sovereignty. The arguments by Senators favoring adherence were that the Court and the League were founded on different treaties, that one was not a creature of the other, and that the Assembly and the Council were merely electoral bodies for choosing the judges. The debate was of a most searching kind and led to material alterations of the Swanson Resolution—alterations which were regarded as essential by the foes as well as the friends of the Court. On January 27, 1926, the Senate, by a vote of 76 to 17, adopted the Swanson Resolution in its amended form. The reservations read as follows:

Adherence to the Court widely supported

Swanson Resolution adopted in amended form

1. That such adherence shall not be taken to involve any legal relation on the part of the United States to the League of Nations or the assumption of any obligations by the United States under the treaty of Versailles.

2. That the United States shall be permitted to participate through representatives designated for the purpose and upon equality with the other states members, respectively, of the council and assembly of the League of Nations in any and all proceedings of either the council or the assembly for the election

of judges or deputy judges of the Permanent Court of International Justice or for the filling of vacancies.

3. That the United States will pay a fair share of the expenses of the court as determined and appropriated from time to time by the Congress of the United States.

4. That the United States may at any time withdraw its adherence to the said protocol and that the statute for the Permanent Court of International Justice adjoined to the protocol shall not be amended without the consent of the United States.

5. That the court shall not render any advisory opinion except publicly after due notice to all States adhering to the court and to all interested States and after public hearing or opportunity for hearing given to any State concerned; nor shall it, without the consent of the United States, entertain any request for an advisory opinion touching any dispute or question in which the United States has or claims an interest.[20]

Reservations far-reaching in protecting United States

These reservations were far-reaching in protecting the United States against all the fears which were voiced in the Senate Chamber. The right to withdraw from the Court at any time was reserved. The Senate protected its traditional prerogative by guaranteeing to itself the right to pass upon whether a case should go before the Court. The Senate, moreover, embalmed in the resolution a provision protecting the traditional American policy of not intruding upon, interfering with, or entangling itself in the political questions of policy or internal administration of any foreign state, at the same time protecting its traditional policy toward American questions, i. e., the Monroe Doctrine.

On March 2, 1926, Secretary of State Kellogg sent a copy of the Senate resolution to the Secretary-General of

[20] 69th Congress, 1st Session, Senate Document No. 45. The Senate's attitude with respect to advisory opinions may be said to be a reflection of the American lawyers' traditional attitude that the duty of a court of law is to decide controversies between parties and not to render opinions upon questions of law. The English practice by which the judges were asked to give opinions on questions of law was never adopted by the United States Supreme Court. In 1793, President Washington sought the advice of the Supreme Court regarding the operation of treaties between France and the United States. The justices refused to give their advice, and this precedent the Court has followed ever since.

The practice of giving advisory opinions in the courts of some of the states of the Union however is a familiar one. For a discussion of this subject, see M. O. Hudson, *The Permanent Court of International Justice*, pp. 136–169.

the League of Nations[21] and to each of the signatories of the Protocol, requesting the signatories to inform him in writing "whether they will accept the conditions, reservations and understandings contained therein." The Secretary-General placed the American communication before the League Council at its meeting of March 18, 1926. To the Council the American desire to change a multilateral agreement like the Protocol by separate agreement seemed awkward. Moreover, the fifth reservation appeared not only a limitation on the jurisdiction of the Court, but on its own action as well as that of the Assembly. It accordingly resolved to call a conference of the signatory states to consider the questions raised by the American reservations. An invitation was extended to the United States to attend such a conference. Secretary Kellogg promptly and curtly declined the invitation. He stated that the Senate reservations "are plain and unequivocal, and according to their terms, they must be accepted by the exchange of notes between the United States and each one of the forty-eight States signatory to the Statute before the United States can become a party and sign the Protocol."

Reservations adopted by the Senate submitted to the League

Conference of signatory states called to consider reservations

The conference of the states parties to the Protocol met in Geneva on September 1, 1926, and sat till the 23rd of that month. The President of the Conference, Jonkheer van Eysinga, stated that the task of the Conference was to reconcile the wishes of the United States with the constitutional law of the League of Nations.[22] The Conference worked in a spirit of accommodation. The first three Senate reservations were examined and approved without any difficulty. There was considerable discussion over the fourth which raised the question whether a member of the League could withdraw from the Court at its own will

First three reservations approved

[21]League of Nations Official Journal, April, 1926, pp. 628–629.

[22]Minutes of the Conference of States Signatories of the Protocol of Signature of the Statute of the Permanent Court of International Justice, September 1–23, 1926. Publications of the League of Nations, V, Legal V, 26.

and pleasure. Some contended that signatories to the Statute ought to stand on a basis of equality and the United States should be in no better position than the rest. However, it was pointed out that a League member withdrawing from the Court still remained in the League, and would still be entitled to vote for judges by virtue of its membership in the Council or the Assembly. No such considerations, however, entered into the case of the United States, which was not a member of the League. The Final Act of the Conference nevertheless carried a stipulation with reference to the fourth reservation that each of the other contracting parties, to assure equality of treatment, acting together and by no less than a majority of two-thirds, should possess the corresponding right to withdraw their acceptance of the special conditions attached by the United States to its adherence to the Protocol.

Fourth reservation to apply to all signatories

The first part of the fifth reservation provoked no discussion; the Rules of the Court had already been revised in July, 1926, and conformed to it. The last part of the fifth reservation was the crux of the problem and the subject of much discussion. To the delegates of the Conference it was not clear what the United States meant by the phrase that the Court shall not "without the consent of the United States entertain any request for an advisory opinion touching any dispute or question in which the United States has or claims an interest." Two difficulties arose in the minds of the delegates. First, it was felt that the effect of the second part of the reservation would diminish the value of advisory opinions in connection with the functioning of the League. The Assembly and the Council would ask the Court for advisory opinions in ignorance of the attitude of our government, "because," as Mr. Elihu Root later stated before the Senate Committee on Foreign Relations, "the way for the United States to take advantage of the resolution . . . would be by going into court or sending some communication to the court, advis-

First part of fifth reservation accepted

Second part presented two difficulties

ing the court that the opinion would touch upon some dispute or question in which the United States was interested, and that the United States did not consent."[23] This would put an end to the proceeding before the Court notwithstanding that the Council and Assembly had asked for the advisory opinion beforehand in ignorance of what the United States would do. The United States would thus place herself in a position whereby she could exercise a veto on the request of the Council and Assembly—a position not only more favorable than that enjoyed by members of the Council, but one which would hinder and interfere with the proper working of the League. The second difficulty was as to the meaning of the term "interests." What scope and meaning would the United States give to the term "interests"? It might, as Mr. Root suggested,[24] mean legal interest, political interest, sentimental interest, interest in having rules of international law obeyed, interest in our neighbor republics, or a general interest held in common with the family of nations. These two difficulties raised the questions: Should the United States communicate its objection to the Court or to the League? If to the League, should it act before or after the Council or the Assembly had decided to ask the Court for an advisory opinion? The Conference concluded that it would be desirable that the manner in which the consent provided for in the second part of the fifth reservation would be given should form the subject of a supplementary agreement between the American government and the Council of the League of Nations.

Supplementary agreement requested on second part of fifth reservation

The proposal of the Conference for a supplementary agreement to clarify the issues raised under the fifth reservation was not well received by the Coolidge administration. To the President the Senate resolution was clear enough, and he would not ask it to alter its position.

President Coolidge refused to ask Senate to alter its position

[23] 71st Congress, 3rd Session, United States Senate Hearings before the Committee on Foreign Relations, January 21, 1931, p. 3.

[24] *Ibid.*

In his Armistice Day address, 1926, he declared that "unless the requirements of the Senate are met by the other interested nations, I can see no prospect of this country adhering to the Court." Senators of the pro and anti-Court camps approved the President's stand. Here the matter rested down to the closing months of the Coolidge administration. Six years had elapsed since the United States was invited to adhere to the World Court. The stumbling block was the fifth reservation. While signatories to the Court were not willing to accept that reservation without an understanding as to the procedure and manner of ascertaining America's consent to the Court's giving an advisory opinion, our government treated the refusal of the Geneva Conference of September, 1926, to accept the fifth reservation as though it were a definite rejection of the offer. This attitude the Coolidge administration maintained until very near its close.

Efforts renewed to outlaw war

In the meantime, the adoption in 1928 of the Pact for the Renunciation of War[25] as an instrument of national policy aroused fresh interest in America's adherence to the Court. The solemn undertaking not to seek a solution of any dispute except by peaceful means, an undertaking so assiduously pressed by Secretary Kellogg, made it more than ever desirable to perfect machinery for the pacific settlement of international disputes. The success of the outlawry of war movement which culminated in the signature of the Pact of Paris on August 27, 1928, must have encouraged Mr. Kellogg to reopen the question of our adherence to the Statute of the Court. Accordingly on February 19, 1929, he addressed a circular note to the Secretary-General of the League and to each signatory of the Court Protocol in which he stated that "the government of the United States desires to avoid in so far as may be possible any proposal which would interfere with or embarrass the work of the Council of the League of Na-

[25]See Chapter XXXII.

tions, doubtless often perplexing and difficult."[26] The 1926 Conference, he recalled, suggested further negotiations concerning the manner in which the consent of the United States was to be given. There were, however, some elements of uncertainty in the bases of these suggestions which, Mr. Kellogg believed, required further discussion. The fears that arose in his mind were reflected in the following passage of his note: "The powers of the Council and its modes of procedure depend upon the Covenant of the League of Nations which may be amended at any time. The ruling of the Court in the Eastern Carelia case[27] and the rules of the Court are also subject to change at any time." For these reasons he felt that the suggestions of the 1926 Conference which were embodied in the Preliminary Draft of a Protocol would not safeguard America's rights and interests, and suggested an informal exchange of views as a way of reaching an agreement. This expectation he felt was strongly supported by the fact that "there seems to be but little difference regarding the substance of these rights and interests."

Secretary Kellogg reopens question of American membership in the Court

Meanwhile, and in response to a resolution adopted by the Assembly, the Council of the League on December 13, 1928, invited a group of expert jurists to undertake an examination of the World Court Statute in the light of the preceding eight years of experience. It was considered timely to undertake such an examination, since the entire bench of the Court faced an election in 1930. Mr. Elihu Root, "the spiritual father of the Court," accepted an invitation to serve on the Committee of Jurists entrusted with the task of amending the Statute. Before leaving for Geneva, Mr. Root had privately discussed the question of American adherence with Mr. Kellogg and with certain

Root submits plan to bring Court into harmony with American reservations

[26]The text of the note appears in the Fifth Annual Report of the Permanent Court of International Justice, pp. 142–145.

[27]In this case the Permanent Court of International Justice declared that it would not pass on disputes between League members and non-League members without the consent of the non-League member.

of the members of the Senate Foreign Relations Committee.[28] When the Committee of Jurists met, Mr. Root submitted a plan to bring the provisions of the Final Acts of the 1926 Conference of Signatories to the Protocol of the Court into line with the reservations made by the United States Senate.

The "Root Plan"

The "Root Plan"[29] provided that "The Court shall not, without the consent of the United States, render an advisory opinion touching any dispute to which the United States is a party." Where the United States is not a party but claims an interest, the "Plan" stipulated that "The Court shall not, without the consent of the United States, render an advisory opinion touching any dispute to which the United States is not a party but in which it claims an interest or touching any questions other than a dispute in which the United States claims an interest." This was in effect the second part of the Senate's fifth reservation. The manner in which the United States shall make known whether it claims an interest and gives or withholds its consent was provided for as follows: "Whenever in contemplation of a request for an advisory opinion it seems to them desirable, the Council or Assembly may invite an exchange of views with the United States and such an exchange of views shall proceed with all convenient speed." If the request for an advisory opinion comes to the Court, the "Plan" provided that the Registrar of the Court "shall notify the United States thereof among other States mentioned in the now existing Article 73 of the Rules of the Court stating a reasonable time limit fixed by the President within which a written statement by the United States concerning the request will be received."

[28]Philip C. Jessup, "Mr. Root, the Senate and the World Court," Foreign Affairs, July, 1929.

[29]League of Nations, Committee of Jurists on the Statute of the Permanent Court of International Justice, Minutes of the Sessions, Geneva, March 11–19, 1929. The text of the Plan is reprinted in Philip C. Jessup's *The United States and the World Court.* World Peace Foundation Pamphlets, vol. XII, No. 4, 1929.

If the United States informed the Court that it had an interest and did not consent to the submission of the question all proceedings upon the question before the Court would be stayed to permit an exchange of views between the United States and the proponents of the request, the proponents, of course, being the Council or Assembly of the League. In addition, it was specifically provided that an objection by the United States to a request for an advisory opinion should have the same effect and force as an adverse vote by a member of the Assembly or the Council. In case the United States and the Council or the Assembly failed to reach an agreement as to whether the question affected an interest of the United States, the "Plan" provided for America's withdrawal from the Court "without any imputation of unfriendliness or unwillingness to coöperate generally for peace and goodwill."

Accepted by the Committee of Jurists

Mr. Root's project reconciled the Senate reservations and the difficulties which they raised in the minds of the signatories to the 1920 Protocol who deliberated about the reservations in 1926. The Committee of Jurists before which it was placed accepted its essential principles and incorporated them in what is known as the Draft Protocol for the Accession of the United States. In addition, the Committee of Jurists revised the World Court Statute. At a conference of signatory states on September 4, 1929, the Protocol for the Accession of the United States was unanimously adopted.[30]

Secretary Stimson requests authorization to sign for the United States

On November 18, 1929, Secretary of State Stimson addressed a letter to President Hoover requesting authorization for signature on behalf of the United States to the three Protocols providing for membership in the World Court. The Secretary of State took occasion to review

[30] On August 14, 1929, the American Minister at Berne informed the Secretary General of the League that the draft protocol effectively met the objections represented in the reservations of the United States Senate and would constitute a satisfactory basis for American adherence to the World Court. Press release, Dept. of State, September 5, 1929.

the considerations involved in American adherence. He pointed out that "by joining the Court the United States would resume its time-honored place of leadership in the great movement for the judicial settlement of international controversies, and in the future, through its representations and jurists, exercise its proper influence in the development of the kind of court which our representatives proposed to the Hague Conference more than thirty years ago." He stressed the fact that the Senate reservations had been met both by the action of the Court itself and by the new protocols.[31] In conclusion he advised the President that, in his opinion, the United States could safely adhere to the Court. On November 26, 1929, the President authorized Mr. Stimson to make the necessary arrangements for the signature of the three Protocols on behalf of the United States, and on December 9, the Protocols were signed.

The three Protocols signed

President Hoover, on December 10, 1929, transmitted the three documents to the Senate for its advice and consent urging prompt and favorable action. He stated, as he had in his inaugural address on March 4, 1929, his belief in the Court as an agency of peace. "The provisions of the protocols," he wrote, "free us from any entanglement in the diplomacy of other nations. We cannot be summoned before this Court, we can from time to time seek its services by agreement with other nations. These protocols permit our withdrawal from the Court at any time without reproach or ill will." The documents were referred to the Committee on Foreign Relations. There they remained until January 10, 1935, when the Senate Committee on Foreign Relations recommended[32] the adoption of the following resolution:

Ratification by the Senate still to be accomplished

[31]The three are: (1) Protocol of Signature of the Permanent Court of International Justice; (2) Protocol of Revision of the Statute of the Permanent Court of International Justice; (3) Protocol of Accession of the United States of America to the Protocol of Signature of the Statute of the Permanent Court of International Justice.

[32]74th Congress, First Session, Senate Executive Report No. 1.

Whereas the President, under date of December 10, 1930, transmitted to the Senate a communication, accompanied by a letter from the Secretary of State dated November 18, 1929, asking the favorable advice and consent of the Senate to adherence by the United States to the protocol of date December 16, 1920, of signature of the Statute for the Permanent Court of International Justice, the protocol of revision of the Statute of the Permanent Court of International Justice of date September 14, 1929, and the protocol of accession of the United States of America to the protocol of signature of the Statute of the Permanent Court of International Justice of date September 14, 1929, all of which are set out in the said message of the President dated December 10, 1930: Therefore be it:

Resolved (*two-thirds of the Senators present concurring*), That the Senate advise and consent to the adherence by the United States to the said three protocols, the one of date December 16, 1920, and the other two each of date September 14, 1929, (without accepting or agreeing to the optional clause for compulsory jurisdiction,) with the clear understanding of the United States that the Permanent Court of International Justice shall not, over an objection by the United States, entertain any request for an advisory opinion touching any dispute or question in which the United States has or claims an interest.

The resolution was debated in the Senate from January 14 to January 29. In a special message to the Senate on January 16, 1935, President Roosevelt urged that "consent be given in such form as not to defeat or delay the objective adherence."

The debate on the Court

There were numerous reservations, understandings, and amendments offered. The debate on the floor brought out few points which had not been made over and over again, on one side or the other, during the twelve years the issue was before the Senate. Opposition to the court was based chiefly on its connection with the League, on a fear of ratification as a step toward joining the League, on apprehension of loss of independence by the United States and of loss by the Senate of its share in the control of our foreign relations.

Opposition grew in intensity both in the Senate and over the country. Various state legislatures voted resolutions expressing opposition to adherence. The Senator from North Carolina (Reynolds) in a radio address on January 27, 1935, expressed himself as follows:[33]

> The World Court is nothing but a court of babble, ballyhoo, and bunk—a court of intrigue—the League of Nations is nothing but a league of notions designed to deceive and camouflage. If we affiliate with the World Court it perhaps means the ultimate cancellation of the war debts—the breaking down of our immigration barriers, and injection of Old World ideas of conquest into the New World's idea of peace.

The Senate rejects the Court proposal

It was in an atmosphere created by such a campaign that the resolution came to vote in the Senate on January 29, 1935. Whereas in 1926 the court resolution had been passed by 76 votes to 17, the 1935 resolution was defeated (two-thirds of the votes being required) by 52 to 36. Why had the Senate receded from the position which it took in 1926? The explanation of the shift is to be sought perhaps in events not related to the court itself. The American people resented the default by various European governments in payment of their war debts to the United States. Germany's rearmament and the growing fear that war was imminent in Europe increased isolationist sentiment. The whole pyramid of conditions, reservations, and understandings had confused the public, and that confusion was reflected in the Senate debate.[34] The exhortation of President Roosevelt to the Senate, as of every President since Harding,—"at this period in international relationships, when every act is of moment to the future of world peace, the United States has an opportunity once more to throw its weight into the scale in favor of peace"[35]—fell upon deaf ears.

---

[33]The address is printed in the *Congressional Record,* 74th Congress, First Session, pp. 1221–1222.

[34]Cf. Manley O. Hudson, "The United States and the World Court," *American Journal of International Law,* vol. 29, pp. 301–307.

[35]*Congressional Record,* 74th Congress, First Session, p. 479.

CHAPTER XXXII

THE PACT OF PARIS

On the occasion of the tenth anniversary of America's entry into the World War, April 6, 1927, M. Briand, the French Minister of Foreign Affairs, addressed a message[1] to the American people, offering to conclude a treaty "outlawing war." The memorable message, in part, read as follows:[2]

Briand's message to the American people

> If there were need of it between the two great democracies in order to give high testimony of their desire for peace and to furnish a solemn example to other peoples, France would be willing to enter into an engagement with America mutually outlawing war, to use your way of expressing it.
>
> The renunciation of war as an instrument of national policy is a conception already familiar to the signatories of the League Covenant and the Locarno treaties. Any engagement subscribed to in the same spirit by the United States toward another nation, such as France, should greatly contribute in the eyes of the world to enlarge and fortify the foundation on which the international policy of peace is being erected. Thus the two great friendly nations, equally devoted to the cause of peace, would furnish the world the best illustration of the truth that the condition immediately to be obtained is not disarmament but the practice of peace.

Nicholas Murray Butler gives it emphasis

The Briand offer seemed to have fallen on deaf ears, for a survey of the leading American journals immediately following the message shows that the press was not alive to the far-reaching implications of the offer. It was not until Nicholas Murray Butler, President of Columbia

[1]The inspiration for this message is said to have been given M. Briand by Professor James T. Shotwell of Columbia University. See David Hunter Miller, The Peace Pact of Paris, p. 7.

[2]New York *Times*, April 6, 1927.

University,[3] called attention to the importance of the Briand proposal that American public opinion awoke to its significance, and the press to its news value. There followed wide public discussion of the Briand idea. American public opinion seemed to be ahead of official sentiment at Washington. The manner in which the "offer" was communicated was not according to strict diplomatic form, and the public discussion of an idea, which was not even an invitation to the Department of State—the properly constituted authority for the conduct of foreign affairs—was indeed novel if not embarrassing to it.

Early in June, 1927, M. Briand, through the American Ambassador at Paris, sought the reaction of the State Department to the suggestion for negotiating a treaty between the United States and France for the elimination of war and the preservation of peace between the two nations. On June 11, the Department announced that M. Briand had made an informal inquiry on the subject of a possible agreement along the lines indicated by his statement on April 6. In reply to this inquiry the American Ambassador was authorized to say that the United States would be pleased to engage in diplomatic conversations on the subject.[4] On June 20, M. Briand submitted to the American government the following proposal for a treaty:[5]

Briand's proposal submitted to the American government

Article 1. The High Contracting Powers solemnly declare, in the name of the French people and the people of the United States of America, that they condemn recourse to war and renounce it respectively as an instrument of their national policy towards each other.

Article 2. The settlement or the solution of all disputes or conflicts, of whatever nature or of whatever origin they may be, which may arise between France and the United States of America, shall never be sought by either side, except by pacific means.

---

[3]See his letter in the New York *Times*, April 25, 1927.

[4]Press Release, Dept. of State, June 11, 1927. In the New York *Times* of June 9, 1927, there appeared a summary of the memorandum purported to have been handed the American Ambassador by M. Briand.

[5]The text was not given to the public until January 11, 1928. Its existence was asserted and denied in the press.

A comparison of this initial offer which M. Briand termed a "Pact of Perpetual Friendship" between the two nations with the "General Pact for the Renunciation of War" [the Kellogg-Briand Pact] of August 27, 1928, shows their striking similarity in language. Whereas the Briand proposal envisaged an agreement between two nations, the final agreement as it emerged became a multipartite contract of the civilized states. In extending the number of signatories to the treaty from two to sixty-odd nations, the relations of our government with foreign states were destined to undergo significant changes. It is in this respect that the Kellogg-Briand Pact formed a landmark in the history of American foreign policy.

Extension of Briand proposal into a multipartite compact

The American government was over six months considering the Briand proposal. During that period the State Department kept its own counsel, and maintained an air of mystery about the very existence of the proposal. Meanwhile public discussion of the idea went on apace. The notion of organizing peace through the "outlawry of war" caught the popular imagination. The Republican party which came into power in 1921 had thrown overboard the Wilson program of international coöperation. The Harding administration was hostile towards the League of Nations, but by 1927 American participation in international activities at Geneva had steadily increased. The Senate had given its advice and consent to American adherence to the World Court subject to reservations,[6] and in the League of Nations Preparatory Commission we were active in pressing for the limitation of armaments. The foreign policy of the United States in form remained "non-entanglement" but in fact it was veering, by the logic of events, towards a cautious form of international cooperation. Aside from this changing attitude the Briand offer appealed to the American sense of international

American foreign policy turning toward cautious co-operation

[6]The United States never became a member of the Court. See preceding chapter for a detailed account.

morality. The proposal was a simple vehicle, and carried none of the complicated machinery of the League of Nations Covenant. No problem of guarantees was involved, no commitments, no machinery to enforce peace, no fetters on our freedom of action! America saw in it a way of preserving peace, sympathetic to American tradition and feeling.

No problem of guarantees involved

On December 28, 1927, Mr. Kellogg replied to M. Briand's offer. He proposed that "the two Governments, instead of contenting themselves with a bilateral declaration . . . might make a more signal contribution to world peace by joining in an effort to obtain the adherence of all of the principal powers of the world to a declaration renouncing war as an instrument of national policy."[7] Mr. Kellogg felt that "such a declaration, if executed by the principal world powers, could not but be an impressive example to all the other nations of the world, and might conceivably lead such nations to subscribe in their turn to the same instrument, thus perfecting among all the powers of the world an arrangement heretofore suggested only as between France and the United States."[8] To this the French government replied that it would be advantageous for the United States and France to sign first and then to invite the other states to a multilateral treaty using the Franco-American agreement as a basis under which the parties would "renounce all wars of aggression and shall declare that for the settlement of differences of whatever nature which may arise between them they will employ all pacific means."[9] In this reply the French introduced an additional phrase—"war of aggression"—to which Mr. Kellogg objected partly on the ground that he did not

Negotiations continued

Renouncing wars of aggression

[7]The General Pact for the Renunciation of War. United States Govt. Printing Office, Washington, 1928, p. 6.

[8]*Ibid.*, p. 6. It may be that a reason for making the pact multilateral was to avoid embarrassment in accepting or declining an intimate bilateral pact with France.

[9]*Ibid.*, p. 7.

want to see the ideal of world peace qualified in any way and partly because of the difficulty of defining[10] the word "aggressor" or the phrase "wars of aggression."

France raised the question whether as a member of the League of Nations, as a party to the Locarno treaties,[11] and other treaties relating to guarantees of neutrality, she could agree with the United States and the other chief powers not to resort to war without contravening her present obligations under those treaties. Mr. Kellogg, however, allayed this French fear by pointing out that the difference between a bilateral and a multilateral form of treaty having for its object the unqualified renunciation of war was one of degree and not of substance, and that a nation which believes itself able to conclude such a bilateral treaty should be no less able to become a party to an identical multilateral treaty. For, he contended, it could hardly be presumed that members of the League of Nations were in a position to do separately something that they would not do together.

French fears allayed by making Pact multilateral

The diplomatic exchanges which followed when Mr. Kellogg on April 13, 1928, submitted his preliminary of a draft treaty to the British, German, Italian, and Japanese governments assured the success of an agreement "outlawing war." The articles, practically the same as those which M. Briand submitted to the United States the previous June, appeared in the text of the Treaty which was finally signed in Paris, August 27, 1928.

Pact of Paris signed, Aug. 27, 1928

[10]Sir Austen Chamberlain said in the House of Commons, November 24, 1927: "If you laid down, far in advance, before circumstances that you cannot foresee, rigid definitions by which the aggressor is to be determined, are you quite sure that in thus making these strict rules in circumstances which are unknown to you, you may not find when the occasion arises that by some unhappy turn in your definition you have declared to be the aggressor that party which, to the knowledge of all men at the time, is the aggressed and not the offender?"

[11]The object of the Locarno treaties was to guarantee the maintenance of the existing Franco-German frontier. The states primarily concerned were Germany and France, which agreed not to invade each other, with England and Italy as guarantors agreeing to join against the aggressor state. France was also fearful lest she be prevented from aiding her allies, Belgium, Poland, and Czechoslovakia, against German attack.

Article 1. The High Contracting Parties solemnly declare in the names of their respective peoples that they condemn recourse to war for the solution of international controversies, and renounce it as an instrument of national policy in their relations with one another.

Article 2. The High Contracting Parties agree that the settlement or solution of all disputes or conflicts of whatever nature or of whatever origin they may be, which may arise among them, shall never be sought except by pacific means.

Opinions as to the effectiveness of the Pact

What is the meaning of this far-reaching declaration embodied in a solemn international engagement? Notwithstanding the brevity and the seeming clarity of these two articles consisting of seventy-eight words lawyers and diplomats have differed widely as to their meaning. In the negotiations which led up to its signature there were "reservations," interpretations, explanations, and exceptions by the separate signatories. Had they robbed it of its fundamental purpose? Does the text of the Pact embody the full intention of the negotiators, or is it to be read in the light of the "reservations" which the signatories made but did not formally incorporate in the agreement?

Right of self-defense

During the course of the negotiations, the nations invited to give favorable consideration to the proposal raised some doubts as to the bearing of the proposal upon the right of self-defense, and the obligations they had already assumed under other treaties, such as the Covenant of the League of Nations, the Locarno treaties, and neutrality treaties. Accordingly, Mr. Kellogg, in his interpretative note of June 23, 1928, took the pains to explain at some length the considerations raised. As to self-defense, the Secretary of State wrote, nothing in the American draft restricts or impairs in any way this inalienable right. "That right is inherent in every sovereign state and is implicit in every treaty. Every nation is free at all times and regardless of treaty provisions to defend its territory from attack or invasion and it alone is competent to decide

Relation of Pact to the Covenant of the League

whether the circumstances necessitate recourse to war in self-defense."[12] The Kellogg proposal is not in conflict with the Covenant of the League of Nations which imposes no affirmative primary obligations to go to war. The obligation, Mr. Kellogg argued, is secondary and attaches only when deliberately accepted by a state. He cited an interpretative resolution on Article 10 of the Covenant submitted to the Fourth Assembly, not formally adopted because of one adverse vote, to support his contention. As for the Locarno treaties, resort to war by any state in violation of the Locarno engagement would also be a breach of the multilateral anti-war treaty. The parties to the anti-war treaty would thus as a matter of law be automatically released from their obligations and free to fulfil their Locarno commitments. Thus, if all the parties to the Locarno treaties became signatories to the anti-war treaty, the Locarno engagements would thereby be reinforced.

Relation of Pact to the Locarno treaties

The British government's attitude towards the anti-war treaty deserves special mention. It agreed with Mr. Kellogg's interpretative note of June 23, and at the same time reaffirmed its special position as an imperial power which had been explained in some detail in a previous note.[13]

Attitude of Great Britain

> There are certain regions of the world, the welfare and integrity of which constitute a special and vital interest for our peace and safety. His Majesty's Government have been at pains to make it clear in the past that interference with these regions cannot be suffered. Their protection against attack is to the British Empire a measure of self-defence. It must be clearly understood that His Majesty's Government in Great Britain accept the new treaty upon the distinct understanding that it does not prejudice their freedom of action in this respect. . . .

Britain's "Monroe Doctrine"

---

[12]The General Pact for the Renunciation of War, p. 36.

But as Professor Shotwell has pointed out, the Pact in Article 2 "defines aggression and defense without a definition," War as an Instrument of National Policy, p. 212.

[13]The General Pact for the Renunciation of War, pp. 26–29.

This statement was dubbed a "Monroe Doctrine" for the British Empire. What regions of the world were comprehended by the phrase "certain regions" was not revealed, but it was commonly understood that the qualification concerned Egypt which is strategically necessary for imperial security. Yet when Egypt and Persia adhered to the anti-war treaty, they objected to the British observations and by implication refused to be bound by them.

Exchange of notes suggested to determine exact meaning of the Pact

The effect of these pre-treaty "understandings" upon the anti-war pact was discussed by Mr. Kellogg before the Senate Committee on Foreign Relations. It was his opinion that the exchange of notes could be resorted to in determining just exactly what was meant by the treaty. But "if there was anything in these notes contrary to the provisions of the treaty, naturally the treaty would control."[14] There have been serious legal discussions as to the effect of the "interpretations," "understandings," and "constructions" which the various nations placed on record before accepting the Pact. Some have contended that the interpretative notes are just as binding and as much within the meaning of the agreement as if they were written into the text itself,[15] while others maintain that they are not a part of the treaty and hence not binding upon the signatories.[16] Whatever the right legal answer might be, the considerations by which a nation violating the treaty will be judged lie more in the field of politics and public opinion than they do in that of law.[17]

The debate in the Senate

The debate over the treaty in the Senate was revealing indeed. The utterances of individual Senators disclosed wide differences of opinion as to what this treaty stood for and what it intended to accomplish. Senator Swanson

[14]Professor P. M Brown expresses a contrary view in *Am. J. of Int. Law,* April, 1929, p. 375.

[15]See, for instance, D. H. Miller, *The Pact of Paris*, p. 119; and Professor E. M. Borchard, *Am. J. of Int. Law*, January, 1929, pp. 116–120.

[16]Secretary Kellogg and Senator Borah have expressed such views. See D. H. Miller, *The Pact of Paris*, p. 118.

[17]See Chapter XXXIII.

said it "is a friendly gesture for peace, that as a peace pact it will be found ineffective and disappointing." Senator Glass declared that he would vote for the peace pact, "but I am not willing anybody in Virginia shall think I am simple enough to suppose that it is worth a postage stamp in the direction of accomplishing permanent international peace." Senator Bruce felt that the treaty substitutes "a peace psychology for a war psychology" and strengthens "the disposition of our people to enter into closer working relations with the other peoples of the world for the preservation of international peace, and to make it easier for us than it has been in the past to devise with other peoples proper measures for that purpose." Senator Borah declared the underlying principle of the treaty to be "a solemn pledge upon the part of the nations representing now practically all the inhabitants of the earth that they will not seek other methods than peaceful methods for the settlement of their controversies. It may be said that it is not much. I think it is a stupendous fact." Before ratification could be secured Senator Borah had to lay before the Senate a report from the Committee on Foreign Relations as to what the Committee understood the treaty to mean. It was agreed beforehand that such a report should neither be adopted by the Senate nor have the effect of modifying the treaty, nor be communicated to foreign governments. With this understanding Senator Borah presented the Committee's report which contained the following important passages:[18]

Report of Committee on Foreign Relations

The treaty in brief pledges the nations bound by the same not to resort to war in the settlement of their international controversies save in bona fide self-defense, and never to seek settlement of such controversies except through pacific means. It is hoped and believed that the treaty will serve to bring about a sincere effort upon the part of the nations to put aside war and to employ peaceful methods in their dealing with each other.

Not a reservation

[18]U. S. Senate, 70th Congress, 2nd Session, Report of Committee on Foreign Relations.

The committee reports the above treaty with the understanding that the right of self-defense is in no way curtailed or impaired by the terms or conditions of the treaty. Each nation is free at all times and regardless of the treaty provisions to defend itself, and is the sole judge of what constitutes the right of self-defense and the necessity and extent of the same.

The United States regards the Monroe doctrine as a part of its national security and defense. Under the right of self-defense allowed by the treaty must necessarily be included the right to maintain the Monroe Doctrine which is part of our system of national defense. . . .

The committee further understands that the treaty does not provide sanctions, express or implied. Should any signatory to the treaty or any nation adhering to the treaty violate the terms of the same, there is no obligation or commitment, express or implied, upon the part of any other signers of the treaty to engage in punitive or coercive measures as against the nation violating the treaty. The effect of the violation of the treaty is to relieve the other signers of the treaty from any obligation under it with the nation thus violating the same.

The Senate ratifies the Pact

With this report made solely for the purpose of putting upon record what the Committee understood "to be the true interpretation of the treaty," and not in any sense an attempt to effectuate a "reservation,"[19] the Senate on January 15, 1929, gave its advice and consent to the United States government's execution of the multilateral treaty for the renunciation of war as an instrument of national policy.[20]

War as an instrument of national policy, to construe the word simply, would mean any war in the assertion or prosecution or defense of policy or of interests or of "rights." To renounce war as an instrument of national policy would be to bar any war but that waged in defense of one's territory. By this interpretation the wars of 1812, 1846, 1898, and 1917, which our nation waged, might be banned. These were not wars of territorial de-

[19]The report of the Senate Committee on Foreign Relations, in its reference to the Monroe Doctrine, is considered by some to be a device to satisfy those who were clamoring for a Monroe Doctrine "reservation."

[20]Immediately after the vote on the treaty, the Senate proceeded to consider a bill authorizing a large naval construction program.

fense, but wars to support a policy, an interest, or a "right." Under the ban might also come, for example, such wars as the three waged by Bismarck for German unity, the Crimean War, the Boer War, the Russo-Japanese War, and numerous others.[21] The question arises: Did the powers, especially the major powers, intend to give up war as they had known it and engaged in it for centuries? The answer to this question lies in the definition of the term self-defense. But neither the definition of the term nor the term itself appears in the treaty. In fact, Secretary Kellogg contended that it was not necessary to define "self-defense." In his opinion self-defense is not only an invaluable prerogative of sovereignty, but the right to define it is also such a prerogative. If his view is a correct one, doesn't war occupy the same position in the relations of states after the Pact of Paris as before?[22] How then can any nation ever violate the Pact?

What type of war would be banned by the Pact?

The term "self-defense" not used in the Pact

The anti-war pact provides no machinery to determine when a party has broken its pledge, nor for military or economic sanctions; how it is to operate is not made clear. There is no legal obligation upon us or any other signatory to the treaty to join in police action against a state which has broken its pledge. The preamble however does state that "any signatory Power which shall hereafter seek to promote its national interests by resort to war should be denied the benefits furnished by this treaty." No legal obligation rests upon the parties to take this step. The duty to deny "the benefits" is therefore a moral one only. The contention was made by some publicists[23] that while the Pact does not state what is to happen in the event a signatory violates its terms, it is inconceivable that the other signatories would stand by idly in case of a

The force of the Pact is moral rather than legal

[21]Cf. C. G. Fenwick, *Am. J. of Int. Law*, 1928, p. 827.
[22]Cf. Edwin M. Borchard, *Am. J. of Int. Law*, 1929, pp. 116–120.
[23]Cf. Professor J. L. Brierly, *British Year Book of Int. Law*, 1929, p. 208.

breach.[24] What benefits are to be denied a violator do not appear in the treaty. Presumably a state taking the law into its own hands might forfeit the friendship of the other signatories and receive no aid or comfort from them.[25] Under such circumstances, a signatory, it was contended, could not aid an aggressor without becoming an accomplice in the aggression. Morally, therefore, if the United States insisted on her neutral rights she would be giving aid and comfort to an aggressor.

Effect of Pact upon American policy of neutrality

If this is a correct implication of the Pact how then does it affect the traditional American policy of neutrality? Secretary Stimson contended that the old notions of neutrality have been affected by the existence of the Pact. He declared:

> Under the former concepts of international law when a conflict occurred, it was usually deemed the concern only of the parties to the conflict. The others could only exercise and express a strict neutrality alike towards the injured and the aggressor. If they took any action or even expressed an opinion, it was likely to be deemed a hostile act towards the nation against which it was directed. The direct individual interest which each nation has in preventing war had not yet been fully appreciated, nor had that interest been given legal recognition. But now under the covenants of the Briand-Kellogg Pact such a conflict becomes of concern to everybody connected with the

[24]Senator Borah expressed this view in an interview in the New York *Times*, March 25, 1928. "It is quite inconceivable," he is quoted as saying, "that this country would stand idly by in case of a grave breach of a multilateral treaty to which it is a party. . . . Of course, in such a crisis we would consult with the other signatories and take their judgment into account. . . . The effect of the Kellogg proposal is a solemn pledge to let all this peace machinery [i.e., the League Covenant, the World Court, etc.] work."

[25]The resolution of Senator Capper introduced in the Senate on December 8, 1927, in support of the Briand proposal of April 6 sought to renounce war as an instrument of public policy and the settlement of international disputes by pacific means. In addition, the resolution further proposed that governments engaging in such a treaty would not support their own nationals in giving aid to aggressor nations in war. The resolution defined an "aggressor nation as one which, having agreed to submit international differences to conciliation, arbitration or judicial settlement, begins hostilities without having done so." The resolution was not acted upon by Congress. The Capper resolution of February 11, 1929, imposing an arms embargo on violators of the anti-war pact, was also not acted upon by Congress.

Pact. All of the steps taken to enforce the treaty must be judged by this new situation.[26]

Thoughtful students of international law, however, do not agree with Secretary Stimson. They contend that neutrality is still a status possible in law, especially for those not members of the League of Nations,[27] and point to the numerous "neutrality treaties" negotiated by members of the League and the United States.[28]

Application of Pact invoked by United States in Sino-Russian dispute over Chinese Eastern Railway

The Kellogg-Briand Pact had not been in existence very long before its application was invoked in one of the most difficult regions in the world, Manchuria, and the signatory to invoke it was the government of the United States. The parties to the controversy were Russia and China, and the subject matter in dispute was the Chinese Eastern Railway operated under the joint control of China and Russia. The seizure of the railway by China led Russia to break off diplomatic relations[29] and there followed a concentration of troops on both sides of the frontier. Each disputant called the Pact of Paris to its aid. China announced that she was prepared to take appropriate meas-

---

[26]Dept. of State, The Pact of Paris—Three Years of Development. An address by Secretary Stimson before the Council on Foreign Relations, August 8, 1932. In another part of the address the Secretary of State said, ". . . we have made obsolete many legal precedents and have given the legal profession the task of reëxamining many of its codes and treaties."

At the conclusion of his testimony on February 9, 1933, before the House Committee on Foreign Affairs on the resolution authorizing the President to join other countries in a refusal to ship arms whenever the shipment would promote war, Secretary Stimson left a memorandum with the Committee which contained this significant passage: "The argument is made that action taken under this resolution would sacrifice American neutrality and so involve us. The fact is that the developments of the past few years show there is little or no practical danger involved and that the discussion is based on almost medieval conditions which modern experience and realities have almost wholly replaced."

[27]Cf. M. O. Hudson, "The Development of International Law Since the War," *Am. J. of Int. Law*, 1928, pp. 330, 337. Also, Philip C. Jessup, *Am. J. of Int. Law*, 1932, pp. 789–793; John Bassett Moore, "Appeal to Reason," *Foreign Affairs*, July, 1933.

[28]On January 28, 1932, the Senate gave its consent to the ratification of the Convention on Maritime Neutrality adopted by the Pan American Conference at Havana in February, 1928.

[29]Russia broke off diplomatic relations on July 18, 1929.

ures for "self-defense" under the Kellogg Pact, and Russia declared the observance of the Pact as more important than its financial stake in the railway. Each side professed its willingness to settle the controversy. China insisted that the basis of settlement be the *status quo*, while Russia wanted the restoration of the *status quo ante;* this point involved the issue of control which was the nub of the controversy.

United States assumes the rôle of defender of the Pact

The situation in the Far East appeared ominous indeed. On July 19, Secretary of State Stimson announced that he was coöperating with the diplomatic representatives of Great Britain, France, China, and Japan in an effort to avert war between Russia and China by calling attention to the principles of the Kellogg Pact. He reminded China that it was the wish of the United States and the coöperating powers that the dispute be settled under the principles of Article 2 of the Pact. A similar reminder was sent to the U. S. S. R. through the French government.[30] By this invocation the United States assumed the rôle of defender of the Kellogg-Briand Pact.

Hostilities carried on by Russia and China without declaration of war

Hostilities between the two contestants were carried on without formal declarations of war. The superior Russian forces drove the Chinese troops into a disordered retreat. On November 28, the Tokio correspondent of the New York *Times* was able to say that the Russians apparently had not occupied any Chinese towns and were back on their own territory. They had given the Chinese a severe slap, humiliated them by disarming 10,000 troops, and scared Mukden into a settlement, all by a relatively small operation which led to no entanglements.[31] While the November fighting was going on, Secretary Stimson was conferring once more with the Washington diplomatic

[30]The American government was obliged to ask the French government to transmit this reminder, for at that time it was not on speaking terms with the Soviet government.

[31]New York *Times*, November 29, 1929.

representatives of the five big powers. Another reminder was sent to China and to Russia through French diplomatic channels. In this action he was joined by Great Britain, France, Italy and thirty-eight other signatories. Japan and Germany declined to lend their support, a significant fact in itself, for it indicated that it was not to the interest of either of these nations to provoke Russian resentment.

Japan and Germany withhold support

Russia's reply to the démarche by the forty-two signatories was a justification of her conduct and a condemnation of the provocative policy of the Chinese government which she accused of violating treaties and allowing armies to make systematic attacks on her frontier villages, and robbing and violating a peaceful population. But the Russian government was not content to justify its action against China; it could not resist the temptation to rebuke the United States which had refused it recognition. There followed these significant paragraphs of the Russian reply:[32]

Russia's defense of her conduct

> The Soviet government states that the government of the United States has addressed its declaration at a moment when the Soviet and Mukden governments already had agreed to several conditions and were proceeding with direct negotiations which would make possible prompt settlement of the conflict between the Soviet Union and China.
>
> In view of this fact the above declaration cannot but be considered unjustifiable pressure on the negotiations, and cannot therefore be taken as a friendly act.
>
> The Soviet government states further that the Paris Pact does not give any single State or group of States the function of protector of this pact. The Soviet, at any rate, never expressed consent that any States themselves or by mutual consent should take upon themselves such a right. . . .
>
> In conclusion, the Soviet government cannot forbear expressing amazement that the government of the United States, which by its own will has no official relations with the Soviet, deems it possible to apply to it with advice and counsel.

Russia rebukes the United States

[32]New York *Times*, December 4, 1929.

Necessity for coöperative action

This was indeed an unexpected rebuke and brought home the difficulty of leaving the initiative of invoking the Pact to a single state, and the need for advance clarification, on the part of the United States and the other signatories, of the action they would take in case of a violation of the Pact. The test to which the Pact was put in the Sino-Russian imbroglio bore out Sir Austen Chamberlain's doubt about including certain states which were scarcely in a position to ensure the maintenance of good order and security within their territories. There was little use in asking Nanking, which was only the nominal seat of national authority, to stop hostilities in Manchuria where its authority was non-existent.

The most significant fact of the first test of the Kellogg-Briand Pact was that the United States took the initiative in enlisting the coöperation of the signatories in an effort to stop hostilities which might have developed into a first-class war. Our activity in the first test of the anti-war pact appeared to bear out the prediction made by its supporters that in giving civilization this peace machinery the United States was entering the peace system the world has been trying to organize since 1919.[33] The hopes of those who saw in the Pact an entering wedge for American participation in building a better world order were short-lived. It is not surprising that a moral declaration which depended for its sanction on world opinion alone was destined to have an unhappy fate. In an era of international anarchy the sanction of world opinion succumbed to the sanction of force.

[33]For the history of the application of the Kellogg-Briand Pact in the Sino-Japanese conflict, see Chapter XXXIII.

CHAPTER XXXIII

THE SINO-JAPANESE CONFLICT AND POST-WAR AGENCIES OF PEACE

Manchuria, a region of conflict

MANCHURIA, a territory as large as France and Germany combined, has long been known as one of the danger spots of the world. Its strategic position and its potential wealth were destined to make it a region of conflict. The need of the former Russian Empire for a warm water port in the Pacific ran counter to the economic need and the expansionist policy of the Japanese Empire.[1] This conflict brought on the Russo-Japanese War of 1904. By the Treaty of Portsmouth, signed on September 5, 1905, terminating the war, Russia with the consent of China relinquished to Japan a part of her exceptional rights in South Manchuria. The most important of these rights was the possession of the warm water port at Dalny, rechristened Dairen by the Japanese. Dairen is the terminal of the railway system which Russia had built in Manchuria for the purpose of leading her from the bleak north to warm Pacific waters. The road was in the form of a T. The lateral was part of the Moscow–Vladivostok trunk system. It was the branch from the lateral on which the Japanese had their eyes. Under the Portsmouth Treaty, therefore, this branch was cut at Changchun (now Hsinking, capital of Manchukuo), which became the new terminal for the Russian railway, and the line from Changchun to Dairen became Japanese, being renamed the South Manchuria Railway. This line

[1]Cf. Chapter XXIV.

passed through Mukden, the former Chinese capital of Manchuria. With collateral lines, the railroad was about 700 miles long.

China's sovereignty over Manchuria

The Treaty of Portsmouth reaffirmed China's sovereignty over Manchuria, but unlike Russia and Japan, China did little to further its economic development, save to allow the migration of her people to the new lands. To-day, of a total population of 30,000,000 there are 28,000,000 Chinese or assimilated Manchus in Manchuria. While millions of Chinese farmers continued to enter Manchuria, Russia and Japan engaged in consolidating their respective spheres of influence.

Japan's special privileges

The special privileges which Japan acquired in South Manchuria gave her an exceptional political, economic, and legal position in Manchuria. The Japanese have grown to refer to this territory as the "life-line" of Japan. Since the advent of Communism and the first Five-Year Plan in Russia, the strategic position of Manchuria assumed an even more vital importance in Japan's national existence. Finally, there was a strong sentimental attachment arising from the sacrifice that Japan made on Manchurian soil in the Russo-Japanese War.

> Patriotic sentiment, the paramount need for military defense and the exceptional treaty rights all combine to create the claim to a "special position" in Manchuria. The Japanese conception of this "special position" is not limited to what is legally defined in treaties and agreements either with China or with other States. Feelings and historical association which are the heritage of the Russo-Japanese War, and pride in the achievements of Japanese enterprise in Manchuria for the last quarter century, are an indefinable but real part of the Japanese claim to a "special position."[2]

The principles which have guided our foreign policy towards China were restated formally by John Hay in

[2]Appeal by the Chinese government, Report of the Commission of Enquiry, League of Nations Publication, Official No. C. 663. M. 320, 1932. Hereafter referred to as the Lytton Report.

Our policy towards China

1899[3] and crystallized in the Nine-Power Treaty of the Washington Conference of 1921–22. The agreement among the powers most interested in the Pacific, wrote Secretary Stimson to Senator Borah in 1932, "represents a carefully developed and matured international policy intended, on the one hand, to assure to all of the contracting parties their rights and interests in and with regard to China, and, on the other hand, to assure to the people of China the fullest opportunity to develop without molestation their sovereignty and independence according to the modern and enlightened standards believed to maintain among the peoples of this earth."[4] Thus, the principles of the open door and the territorial integrity of China which rested in informal commitments were formally embodied in the Nine-Power Treaty.

Japan's obligations to China under the Nine-Power Treaty

The signatories of the Nine-Power Treaty of the Washington Conference, of February 6, 1922, undertook to respect the sovereignty, the independence, and the territorial and administrative integrity of China, to maintain equality of opportunity in China for the trade and industry of all nations, and to refrain from taking advantage of conditions to seek special rights or privileges.[5] This agreement to which Japan is a party denied the right of any signatory to seek a "special position" or to "special rights and interests" in any part of China, including Manchuria. The acceptance of this treaty by Japan, however, did not bring about a change of attitude toward Manchuria, which in Japanese minds was regarded as distinct from the rest of China. From the Washington Conference down to the invasion of Manchuria in 1931 Japan pursued either the "friendship policy" which rested "on the basis of good will and neighborliness" or the

[3]See *infra*, p. 564.

[4]Dept. of State, Text of Letter from Secretary Stimson to Senator Borah, February 23, 1932.

[5]The nine signatories at that time were the United States, Belgium, Great Britain, China, France, Japan, Italy, the Netherlands, and Portugal.

Manchuria considered distinct from China by Japan

"positive policy"[6] which rested upon military force, the one or the other depending upon the party complexion of the government of the day. The general aims of both of these policies,[7] however, were directed at the same objective: to secure and maintain Japan's vested interests, to protect Japanese lives and property, and to encourage expansion of Japanese enterprise in Manchuria.

Japan's invasion of Manchuria and Jehol

The conflict which broke out in Manchuria on September 18, 1931, between Chinese and Japanese troops[8] and which led rapidly to the Japanese military occupation of Manchuria, and later to the invasion and occupation of Jehol province as well, has had world-wide repercussions. The incident which led to the invasion of Manchuria by Japanese forces was an explosion which damaged the Japanese-concessioned South Manchuria railroad just a few miles north of Mukden, the capital of Manchuria. The Japanese version as to what happened that eventful night differed from the Chinese. The Commission of Enquiry appointed by the League of Nations found that "an explosion undoubtedly occurred on or near the railroad between 10:00 and 10:30 P. M. on September 18th, but the damage, if any, to the railroad did not in fact prevent the punctual arrival of the southbound train from Changchun, and was not in itself sufficient to justify military action. The military operations of the Japanese troops during the night . . . cannot be regarded as measures of legitimate self-defense."[9]

The Japanese drive in China was as startling to the

[6]Cf. Lytton Report, p. 40.

[7]The "positive policy" of the Tanaka Cabinet carried with it the statement that Japan would preserve peace and order in Manchuria and would defend her "special position" there no matter where the menace came from.

[8]Under agreements with China, Japan and Russia were accorded the right to maintain a fixed number of railway guards to protect their respective properties in Manchuria. This accounts for the presence of Japanese troops on Chinese soil. Cf. John V. A. MacMurray, *Treaties and Agreements with and Concerning China*, I, p. 522; and C. W. Young, *The International Relations of Manchuria*, p. 55.

[9]Lytton Report, p. 71.

world as it was unexpected. The rapidity with which the Japanese troops occupied the strategic points in Manchuria was indeed ominous, for it suggested a military plan well conceived and only too rapidly carried out. There were indications that the military move was taken without the knowledge of the Japanese Foreign Office, and that a cleavage had developed between the civil and military authorities. Secretary Stimson was desirous of pursuing a conciliatory course which would strengthen the position of Baron Shidehara, Japanese Foreign Minister, who, it was understood, disapproved of what the military had done. Our government viewed the events in the Far East with surprise and dismay and four days after the initial outbreak handed the Japanese Ambassador at Washington a memorandum[10] stating that the events in Manchuria were of "concern, morally, legally, and politically to a considerable number of nations. . . . It [the occupation by Japanese troops] brings into question at once the meaning of certain provisions of agreements, such as the Nine-Power Treaty of February 6, 1922, and the Kellogg-Briand Pact." The memorandum went on to say that "the responsibility for determining the course of events with regard to the liquidating of this situation rests largely upon Japan, for the simple reason that Japanese armed forces have seized and are exercising *de facto* control in South Manchuria."[11]

Secretary Stimson pursues a conciliatory course

Reminds Japan of her obligations under the Nine-Power Treaty and the Pact of Paris

Meanwhile China as a member of the League of Nations officially brought the crisis to the League's attention and requested that by virtue of Article 11[12] of the Covenant a meeting of the Council be summoned to consider such action as it might deem wise and necessary to safeguard the peace of nations. The Council acted with dispatch and cabled the Tokio and Nanking governments "to re-

China appeals to the League

[10]Conditions in Manchuria, Senate Document No. 55, 72nd Congress, 1st Session, p. 4.

[11]*Op. cit.*, p. 5.

[12]*Ibid.*, p. 4.

frain from any act which might aggravate the situation or prejudice the peaceful settlement of the problem," and "to endeavor in consultation with the Chinese and Japanese representatives to find adequate means of enabling the two countries to withdraw their troops forthwith without the safety of their nationals and their property being endangered. . . ."[13] The Council, moreover, informed the parties that it decided to keep the American government informed by forwarding the minutes of all its meetings and documents relating to the dispute. Our response to the Council's decision to keep us informed was friendly and coöperative, and was received at Geneva with great relief. Secretary Stimson's note to the Secretary-General of the League said: "I assure you that the Government of the United States is in whole-hearted sympathy with the attitude of the League of Nations as expressed in the Council's resolution and will dispatch to Japan and China notes along similar lines."[14] This assurance, for the time being at least, found the United States and the League united in seeking a peaceful settlement of the Sino-Japanese controversy.[15] While there was unofficial contact between our government and the League of Nations through the American Minister at Berne, Mr. Hugh Wilson, and the American Consul-General at Geneva, Mr. Prentiss Gilbert, coöperation through written communications left much to be desired. Yet the question, what would the United States do if the League were confronted with the grave issue of war or peace, a question which Europe had been asking us since 1919, was in part answered by Secretary Stimson's memorandum of October 5, 1931, communicated to the Council of the League. The Secretary wrote:

United States expresses sympathy with the attitude of the League

[13] *Op. cit.*, p. 4.

[14] *Ibid.*, p. 5.

[15] On September 24, 1931, the American government sent an identical note to the Chinese and Japanese governments expressing hope of an amicable adjustment.

The American government, acting independently through its diplomatic representatives, will endeavor to reinforce what the league does and will make clear that it has a keen interest in the matter and is not oblivious to the obligations which the disputants have assumed to their fellow signatories in the pact of Paris as well as in the nine-power pact should a time arise when it would seem advisable to bring forward those obligations. By this course we avoid any danger of embarrassing the league in the course to which it is now committed.[16]

Japanese and Chinese representatives make pledges of peace

When the Council of the League adjourned on September 30, both the Japanese and Chinese representatives had made pledges of peace. Japan assured the world that she had no territorial designs in Manchuria, and that she would withdraw her troops as rapidly as possible into the railway zone. Both governments declared that they would take all necessary steps to prevent any extension of the scope of the incident or any aggravation of the situation.[17] To our own government Japan stated that she had caused her "military forces in Manchuria to refrain from any further acts of hostility . . ." and would "avoid any action that is calculated to prejudice an amicable settlement of the differences between Japan and China."[18]

Japan's pledges broken

The assurances given by the Japanese government which were embodied in the resolution by the League of Nations on September 30 vanished in thin air when the world learned that Japanese military planes on October 8 had flown over the unfortified city of Chinchow, some fifty miles from the Japanese railway zone, and had dropped bombs causing the death of a considerable number of civilians. Our government lodged a strong protest with the Japanese Minister of Foreign Affairs over the bombing of Chinchow. It read:

[16]Conditions in Manchuria, Senate Document No. 55, 72nd Congress, 1st Session, p. 14.

[17]League of Nations, C. 648, 1931, VII.

[18]Conditions in Manchuria, Senate Document No. 55, 72nd Congress, 1st Session, p. 11.

Protest of the United States

The Secretary of State cannot understand how the bombing of Chinchow can be minimized or how it can be said to be of no importance. The explanation given by the Japanese military authorities seems quite inadequate. Chinchow is more than 50 miles from the Japanese railway zone and is situated in territory where the Chinese have an entire right to maintain troops. The Secretary of State is at a loss to see what right Japanese military planes had to fly over the town, thereby provoking attack, and to drop bombs. . . . Bombing of an unfortified and unwarned town is one of the most extreme of military actions, deprecated even in time of war.

. . . this attack would appear quite at variance with the commitments undertaken by the Japanese Government in respect to the resolution of September 30 of the Council of the League of Nations.[19]

American representative invited, over protest of Japan, to sit with League Council

The consequence of these events brought the United States and the League into closer association. Our government, it was understood, was prepared to go further and send a representative to sit with the Council to consider and discuss with that body the application of the Kellogg-Briand Pact. When the Council reassembled on October 13, the question of extending an invitation to the United States overshadowed for a time the Sino-Japanese dispute itself. Of the fourteen nations represented, thirteen desired to extend the invitation and one—Japan—objected. At a public debate on the question of sending an invitation, which the Council had already settled in private session, the Japanese delegate voiced his objections. He contended that the proposal to invite a non-member State to take part in Council discussions raised constitutional and legal questions of the utmost importance for the League.[20] The Council placed on record the objections of the Japanese delegate for future determination and issued an invitation to the United States on October 16,

[19] *Op. cit.*, p. 17.

[20] The legal point raised by the Japanese delegate was whether the invitation by the Council involved a question of principle or merely procedure. If the question was one of principle, the invitation had to be unanimous and Japan could veto it; if it was one of procedure the Council could issue the invitation by majority vote, and thus override Japan.

1931, "to send a representative to sit at the Council table so as to be in a position to express an opinion as to how, either in view of the present situation or of its future development, effect can best be given to the provisions of the pact."[21]

Japan's objections recorded for later consideration

Our acceptance of the invitation and the designation of Prentiss Gilbert, American Consul-General at Geneva, to sit with the Council of the League of Nations was a significant historical fact. A Republican administration—that party which a decade earlier turned away from the League—by accepting the invitation was officially giving recognition of and its stamp of approval to that body. This action of the administration was, in general, favorably received. For the first time in the League's history the United States manifested her desire to coöperate with the Council in an effort to prevent war. It was a dramatic recognition of the fact that we cannot remain aloof from a permanent international conference dealing with matters which affect our interests.[22] The extent of our coöperation was set out in the State Department's carefully worded instructions:

United States accepts the League's invitation

> You are authorized to participate in the discussions of the Council when it relates to possible obligations of the Briand-Kellogg Pact to which the United States is a party. You are expected to report the result of such discussion to the Department for its determination as to possible action. If you are present at a discussion on any other aspect of the Chinese-Japanese dispute, it must be only as an observer and auditor.

American representation made ineffective by the instructions imposed

Our coöperation was more complete in form than it was in substance, for the limitations imposed upon Mr. Gilbert by these instructions were so severe that he was relegated to the rôle of a listener.

The Council with an American representative sitting

[21]Conditions in Manchuria, Senate Document No. 55, 72nd Congress, 1st Session, p. 17.

[22]Cf. Clarence A. Berdahl, *The Policy of the United States with Respect to the League of Nations*, Chapter V.

The Council invokes the Pact of Paris

at its table made the important decision to invoke the Pact of Paris. France, Great Britain, Germany, Italy, Spain, and Norway sent identic notes to China and Japan calling the attention of these two governments to the obligations they had undertaken under Article 2 of the Pact. Our government joined in the reminder on October 20, and at the same time instructed Mr. Gilbert to stay away from the secret meetings of the Council and appear at the public sessions when matters arising out of the Pact were to be discussed.[23]

Japanese aggression continues in Manchuria

While the Council was anxiously searching for a formula acceptable to both disputants, the Japanese armies were extending the area of conflict, compelling the Chinese to retire within the Great Wall and thus leaving all Manchurian territory under the control of officials subject to Japan's sovereignty or domination. The Japanese representative to the League continued to repeat the thesis that "the whole Manchurian affair was occasioned solely by a violent and provocative attack launched by the Chinese Army on the railway zone."[24] It was becoming evident as the debate progressed that the Japanese adventure in Manchuria was not, as her spokesman alleged, an intervention to quell a local disorder. M. Briand, French Foreign Minister and President of the Council, offered a resolution, *inter alia*, calling upon the Japanese government to withdraw its troops into the railway zone "so that the total withdrawal may be effected before the date fixed for the next meeting of the Council," which it was proposed should be November 16. The onus was

[23]The Hoover-Stimson policy towards the League was attacked and defended in the American press. The *Literary Digest* of October 24, 1931, summed it up by stating that the applause for the Hoover-Stimson policy seemed to be louder and more wide-spread than the booing and hissing. A survey of American newspaper opinion by the League of Nations Association showed that 75 per cent of the newspapers in the country as a whole and almost 90 per cent in the Middle West approved of the coöperation with the Council.

[24]Conditions in Manchuria, Senate Document No. 55, 72nd Congress, 1st Session, p. 24.

thus thrust on the Japanese delegate to agree to the withdrawal of troops quickly or to explain definitely why it could not be done. He stated that there were several "fundamental principles" on which an understanding was indispensable before the troops could be withdrawn into the railway zone. What these "fundamental principles" were the Japanese delegate said he had no authority to divulge. It became clear to the Council, however, that the most important principle, in the mysterious rubric of "fundamental principles" which Japan was demanding as a condition of withdrawing her forces, was a recognition by China of Japanese treaty rights in Manchuria, particularly the right which China contracted away not to construct any line parallel to the South Manchuria Railway. China, of course, disputed the validity of the treaty.[25] To the Council this was clearly the use of military force to command respect for treaties the validity of which was in dispute. As such it was felt that the Japanese action was a resort to war as an instrument of national policy, and hence a violation of the Kellogg-Briand Pact. Our own government, judging from events which were to follow, took the same view.[26] On October 24, the Council put to a vote the resolution calling upon Japan to begin immediately the withdrawal of troops into the railway zone, this withdrawal to be effected before the date fixed for the next Council meeting, November 16, and recommended that China and Japan begin direct negotiations on outstanding issues as soon as the evacuation was completed. But the Japanese representative defeated the resolution with his negative vote.

Resolution framed demanding withdrawal of Japanese troops

Demands of Japan

Violation of Pact of Paris

Resolution defeated by Japan's negative vote

Not being a member of the League, the United States did not vote on the resolution. While no public statement was made by the Department of State concerning the

[25]Cf. p. 575.

[26]Cf. Dept. of State, text of Letter from Secretary of State Stimson to Senator Borah, February 23, 1932.

wisdom of the Council's attempt to fix a definite date for the withdrawal of troops, Secretary Stimson did not consider the action well advised. The developing events in Manchuria and the widening occupation by Japanese troops led our government to restate its views to Japan.[27] The situation created by Japan's desire "to protect the South Manchuria Railway and the lives and property of Japanese subjects against attack . . . has, temporarily, at least, destroyed the administrative integrity of China in this region." According to our government's view there were two separate and distinct points to be considered—first, the peaceful solution of the existing situation in Manchuria, and second, a solution through direct negotiations of the issues arising out of misunderstandings as to the respective Chinese and Japanese rights under various treaties. With regard to the first point Secretary Stimson wrote that effective withdrawal of the Japanese troops would destroy the idea that Japan was using military pressure to bring about a settlement of the broader treaty issues; the second point could not be appropriately settled until the first had been disposed of.

The United States restates its views to Japan

When the special session of the Council met in Paris on November 16, Japan had not only disregarded the appeals by the League and the American government, but had extended her occupation of Manchuria. The precedent of "direct participation," i. e., of an American representative sitting with the Council established at the October session, was abandoned in favor of "independent coöperation" at the November session. General Charles G. Dawes, American Ambassador to London, was instructed to be present in Paris during the session in order to be available for conference but not to sit with the Council.[28] With our government's approval, the negotiations in Paris

Japan disregards appeals of the League and the United States

[27]Conditions in Manchuria, Senate Document No. 55, 72nd Congress, 1st Session, p. 31.

[28]Secretary Stimson apparently had become sensitive to the accusation that he was drawing the United States deeper into the League's affairs.

finally culminated on December 10 in the creation of a neutral commission of five[29] [later known as the Lytton Commission] to study on the spot and report to the Council the circumstances affecting the relations between China and Japan. Once more the Council called upon the disputants for immediate cessation of hostilities, and reminded Japan of her solemn pledge to withdraw her troops within the railway zone as speedily as possible, instead of at a fixed date such as it had attempted to set in the resolution of October 24.

Neutral commission of five appointed to study question and report to the Council

This was the third attempt by the Council to put an end to the military aggression of Japan in China. Our government "by means of parallel and incessant activities" within the limits determined by our relation to the League assisted the Council in its work. President Hoover in his message to Congress on December 10 reminded the country of our responsibility for maintaining the integrity of China and stated that he deemed it "wise and appropriate rather to aid and advise with the League, and thus have unity of effort to maintain peace, than to take independent action." But to allay the fears of those who felt that the United States was drawing herself into the League through the "back door," the President went on to say that "in all the negotiations the Department of State has maintained complete freedom of judgment and action as to participation in any measures which might finally be determined upon."[30]

President Hoover advises cooperation with the League

On January 3, 1932, the Japanese forces marched into Chinchow driving the Chinese forces within the Great Wall, leaving Manchuria under the control of the Japanese. With the occupation of Manchuria completed, Secretary Stimson on January 7, 1932, sent an identic note to the governments of China and Japan—handing it

Japan in complete control of Manchuria

[29]The members of the Commission were: Lord Lytton (British); Count Aldrovand, (Italian); General Henri Claudel (French); Dr. Heinrich Schnee (German); and, Major-General Frank Ross McCoy (American).

[30]New York *Times*, December 11, 1931.

simultaneously to the diplomatic representatives in Washington of the other signatories of the Nine-Power Treaty of 1922—setting forth the intention of the American government not to recognize "any situation, treaty or agreement which may be brought about by means contrary to the covenants and obligations of the Pact of Paris." It was the strongest move yet made by a neutral power in the crisis, bringing forward a policy of negative sanction to support the moral obligation of the Pact. The full text of the note follows:[31]

Secretary Stimson declares the United States will not recognize any situation, treaty, or agreement brought about by means contrary to the Pact of Paris

With the recent military operations about Chinchow, the last remaining administrative authority of the Government of the Chinese Republic in South Manchuria, as it existed prior to September 18, 1931, has been destroyed. The American Government continues confident that the work of the neutral commission recently authorized by the Council of the League of Nations will facilitate an ultimate solution of the difficulties now existing between China and Japan. But in view of the present situation and of its own rights and obligations therein, the American Government deems it to be its duty to notify both the Government of the Chinese Republic and the Imperial Japanese Government that it can not admit the legality of any situation *de facto* nor does it intend to recognize any treaty or agreement entered into between those governments, or agents thereof, which may impair the treaty rights of the United States or its citizens in China, including those which relate to the sovereignty, the independence, or the territorial and administrative integrity of the Republic of China, or to the international policy relative to China, commonly known as the open-door policy; and that it does not intend to recognize any situation, treaty, or agreement which may be brought about by means contrary to the covenants and obligations of the pact of Paris of August 27, 1928, to which treaty both China and Japan, as well as the United States, are parties.[32]

---

[31]Conditions in Manchuria, Senate Document No. 55, 72nd Congress, 1st Session, pp. 53–54.

[32]The League of Nations Assembly on March 11, 1932, Japan alone refraining from voting, indorsed the Stimson Doctrine in a resolution declaring that "it is incumbent upon the Members of the League of Nations not to recognize any situation, treaty or agreement which may be brought about by means contrary to the Covenant of the League of Nations or to the Pact of Paris."

Opinions on the doctrine of non-recognition

The doctrine of non-recognition was hailed by some as "the corner stone of the world's policy toward the Far East,"[33] and if made effective would in due course revolutionize international law, for "violence and war would cease to have value in advancing the legal position of states."[34] By others the doctrine was criticized because it is not supported by material sanctions. President Lowell expressed the view that any interpretation of the Briand-Kellogg Pact whereby "the signatories are under no obligation to prevent war, yet are at liberty to disregard its results, might create more causes of strife than it would allay. . . . Now the object of international law is to make the rights of nations certain, not to unsettle them; if a wrong has been done to correct it at once, not to leave it as a festering sore for any nation to probe thereafter, or as an excuse for action that would otherwise be without justification."[35]

Japan maintains that conditions in China modified application of treaties

The Japanese in reply pointed out that treaties relating to China must be applied with due regard to the state of affairs existing in China from time to time, and that the unsettled and distracted state now existing in China is not what the signatories to the Nine-Power Pact of the Washington Conference of 1921–22 contemplated. The Japanese government explained that the chaos in China cannot affect the binding character of the treaties, "but it may in material respects modify their application, since they must necessarily be applied with reference to the state of facts as they exist."[36] There was no direct rejoinder by our government to the Japanese reply.

In the short period of three months we sent nine notes to the Tokyo government, all of which had no effect in

---

[33]Walter Lippmann, in the New York *Herald-Tribune*, January 12, 1933.

[34]Cf. Professor Quincy Wright, *Am. J. of Int. Law*, April, 1932, p. 348.

[35]"Manchuria and the League," *Foreign Affairs*, April, 1932.

[36]Conditions in Manchuria, Senate Document No. 55, 72nd Congress, 1st Session, p. 56.

Nine notes sent to Japan, all without effect

stopping the military operations in Manchuria. Our government even concentrated the entire fleet in the Pacific for the alleged purpose of effecting economy. In an open and important letter to Senator Borah, Chairman of the Senate Committee on Foreign Relations, dated February 23, 1932, Secretary Stimson restated and clarified our Far Eastern policy and at the same time answered the points raised by the last Japanese reply. The Nine-Power Pact, the Secretary pointed out, was one of several treaties and agreements entered into at the Washington Conference all of which were interrelated and interdependent.

> No one of these treaties can be disregarded without disturbing the general understanding and equilibrium which were intended to be accomplished and effected by the group of agreements arrived at in their entirety. . . . The willingness of the American government to surrender its then commanding lead in battleship construction and to leave its positions at Guam and in the Philippines without further fortification, was predicated upon, among other things, self-denying covenants contained in the Nine-Power Treaty, which assured the nations of the world not only of equal opportunity for their Eastern trade but also against the military aggrandizement of any other power at the expense of China. One cannot discuss the possibility of modifying or abrogating those provisions of the Nine-Power Treaty without considering at the same time the other promises upon which they were really dependent.[37]

The Secretary of State, in his letter to Senator Borah, also declared that, if the non-recognition doctrine were generally adopted, "a caveat will be placed upon such action in violation of the Anti-War Pact which will effectively bar the legality hereafter of any title or right sought to be obtained by pressure or treaty violation, and which, as has been shown by history in the past, will eventually lead to the restoration to China of rights and titles of which she may have been deprived."

[37]While the Japanese armies were invading Manchuria, Congress on January 17, 1933, over President Hoover's veto, enacted the Hawes-Cutting bill for Philippine independence. See *infra*, pp. 906 ff.

Mr. Stimson went further by stating that "it is clear beyond peradventure that a situation has developed which cannot, under any circumstances, be reconciled with the obligations of the covenants of these two treaties, and that if the treaties had been faithfully observed such a situation could not have arisen." The Secretary clearly implied by these words that Japan had violated the Nine-Power Treaty and the Kellogg-Briand Pact.[38]

Secretary Stimson implies Japan violated Nine-Power Treaty and Pact of Paris

The Japanese contention that her use of force in Manchuria was justified on grounds of self-defense, which by our own government was admitted to be an exception to the Kellogg-Briand Pact,[39] led the Hoover administration to a new interpretation of that instrument. In so doing it cast overboard the construction given to the Pact by Secretary Kellogg and the Senate in 1928 and 1929 on which Japan relied. In an address before the Council on Foreign Relations, August 8, 1932, Secretary Stimson emphatically stated that the limits of self-defense have been clearly defined by countless precedents and "a nation which sought to mask imperialistic policy under the guise of the defense of its nationals would soon be unmasked."[40] Again on October 26, 1932, he declared that there was nothing in the Treaty to warrant "such destructive interpretation" that "each signatory was to be the sole judge of its own behavior."[41] Whether the exposition of the Kellogg-Briand Pact given by Secretary Stimson was a sound one or not, there is no principle of international law which obliges one nation to accept another nation's view as to the meaning of a treaty. Were the United States a member of the Permanent Court of International

Japan justifies action on grounds of self-defense

[38]The Japanese Foreign Office indicated that it would press for equality in naval strength with Great Britain and the United States at the naval conference scheduled to take place in 1935. See *infra*, pp. 892 ff.

[39]See Chapter XXXII on the Pact of Paris.

[40]Dept. of State, The Pact of Paris; Three Years of Development, 1932. On the revitalizing of the Pact of Paris, see Yuen-Li Liang, The Pact of Paris as Envisaged by Mr. Stimson; Its Significance in International Law.

[41]Dept. of State, Press Release, October 25, 1932.

Justice, or had she associated herself with it, she could have urged Japan to submit the issue of what constitutes self-defense to this tribunal.

Chinese boycott of Japanese goods tightened

When the Japanese started their military campaign in Manchuria, the Chinese tightened their boycott against Japan which they had launched in July, 1931, because of the killing of several hundred Chinese in Korea. There followed a series of incidents in and around the International Settlement of Shanghai which culminated in the bombing of the suburb of Chapei by Japanese airplanes on January 28, 1932. The Japanese army met with unexpected resistance by the Chinese; heavy reinforcements on both land and sea were necessary before Japan attained her objective in Shanghai. The Japanese troops evacuated on May 31, 1932. The loss of life and property was enormous. The representations of the American, British, French, and Italian governments to Japan before the fighting began to the effect that there should be no military operations in the International Settlement, were unavailing. The Japanese bombardment created a tense situation. Our State Department was extremely concerned for a time by this threat of war.

Japanese bombardment of Chapei

Mukden was attacked on September 18, 1931, and immediately thereafter the Japanese military authorities began organizing the civil administration, which was completely demoralized by the flight of the panic-stricken Chinese population. The zeal with which the Japanese took control of the banks, railroads, and public utility services indicated that "objects more permanent than the requirements of a temporary military occupation were being pursued."[42] Japanese were appointed as advisers and experts to officials and no single source of revenue was left free from their supervision. The independence movement of Manchuria inspired, fostered, and controlled

Japanese take control of banks, railroads, and public utilities of Manchuria

[42] Lytton Report, p. 96.

by Japanese officials culminated in a declaration of independence on February 18, 1932. The former Emperor Hsuan Tung, better known as Mr. Henry Pu-yi, was installed on March 9 as Regent of "Manchukuo." On September 15, 1932, two weeks before the publication of the Lytton Commission Report, and in anticipation that the finding would be adverse, Japan accorded not only formal recognition to the newly styled state of "Manchukuo," but also signed a treaty of alliance with it, steps which were calculated to prejudice the settlement of the dispute. Thus, with the recognition of "Manchukuo" by Japan, a year after the initial outbreak of an undeclared war, one phase of the Far Eastern drama came to a close.

Henry Pu-yi made Regent of Manchukuo

With the publication of the Report of the Commission of Enquiry [the Lytton Report] on October 1, 1932, the Far Eastern crisis entered a new phase. The Commission's findings of fact have been indicated throughout this chapter. The broad principles it suggested for a settlement of the dispute may now be summarized. A mere restoration of the *status quo ante*, i. e., the status of Manchuria prior to September 18, 1931, would be no solution. To return to conditions as they were would merely be to risk a repetition of the trouble. "Manchukuo," a bogus government created and supported by Japan, constitutes a violation of the League Covenant, the Nine-Power Treaty, and the Pact of Paris. In passing judgment on this new political creation the Commission declared that the most effective factors without which "the new State could not have been formed, were the presence of Japanese troops and the activities of Japanese officials, both civil and military."[43] Accordingly it concluded that "the present régime cannot be considered to have been called into existence by a genuine and spontaneous independence movement."[44] The finding in this re-

The Lytton Report, published

Report denies that there was a genuine movement for independence in Manchuria as claimed by Japan

[43]*Op. cit.*, p. 97.

[44]*Ibid.*, p. 97.

spect contradicted the assertion of the Japanese that the population of Manchuria had spontaneously asserted its independence, established its own government, and severed all connection with China. In a solution of the controversy, the Commission suggested that the government of Manchuria be modified in a way to harmonize the sovereignty and administrative integrity of China with a large measure of autonomy to meet the local conditions and the conflicting interests of Japan and Russia. Japan's special position in that region was a fact which had to be recognized in new treaty relations with China. The rights of the Union of Soviet Socialist Republics in the Far East also had to be considered in the interests of peace. The political instability of China and the need for a strong central government necessitate international coöperation in the internal reconstruction of China.

Recommendations of the Report

The Lytton Report was on the whole a statesmanlike document. The findings of fact and the recommendations it contained were universally applauded, save by the Japanese, whose reaction foreshadowed the line that the government would take when the discussion of it would come up before the Council of the League. In the United States it was generally approved but official opinion was discreetly silent. With the report in the League's hands there followed three months of patient and trying negotiations between the League's Committee of Nineteen and the disputants. China accepted the recommendations of the Lytton Commission as a basis of settlement, but Japan submitted proposal after proposal in an endeavor to prolong the discussion—proposals which showed how wide the gulf was between the recommendations of the Commission and Japanese ambitions in Manchuria.

Report generally approved

On February 17, 1933, the League in a ten-hour radio broadcast to the world released the findings[45] of the Committee of Nineteen, under Article XV, paragraph 4, of the

[45]The text appeared in the New York *Times*, February 18, 1933.

Covenant, condemning Japan and absolving China. It was the gravest statement drawn up in the League's history. Confirming the findings of the Lytton Commission and branding "Manchukuo" as a Japanese puppet, the report proclaimed unequivocally that "sovereignty over Manchuria belongs to China." The maintenance and recognition of "Manchukuo" by Japan and the presence of Japanese troops in this territory were found to be "incompatible" with the League Covenant, the Nine-Power Treaty, and the Kellogg-Briand Pact. The Committee of Nineteen recommended that Japan withdraw her troops and that China establish an autonomous Manchuria, taking into account the special interests of Japan in that territory, and that China and Japan settle their dispute on the Lytton Report principles through a League committee in which the United States and Soviet Russia should be invited to participate.

League confirms findings of Lytton Commission

One week later, February 24, 1933, the Assembly of the League of Nations—with Japan casting a negative vote—adopted the report of the Committee of Nineteen.[46] The action of the League Assembly was a landmark in the history of that international organization. It was the first instance in its history of the world passing judgment upon a great international dispute.

Assembly of League adopts the Report

Our government in a note[47] to the League declared that "the findings of fact arrived at by the League and the understanding of the facts derived by the American government from reports made to it by its own representatives are in substantial accord." The principles of settlement recommended by the League were likewise endorsed by our government. Thus the Assembly's action and our endorsement of it, the policy of the members of the League and that of the United States, became identical and ended

Settlement recommended by League endorsed by United States

[46]The Japanese delegation, following the vote, walked out of the Assembly. On March 27, 1933, Japan gave formal notification of her withdrawal from the League of Nations.

[47]New York *Times*, February 26, 1933.

another effort to settle the Sino-Japanese dispute by pacific means.[48]

Failure of efforts to settle conflict

The efforts of the League of Nations and the American government to resolve the Sino-Japanese conflict in Manchuria failed. A member of the community of nations took the law into her own hands and gained an advantage at the expense of another by means contrary to her treaty engagements at a time when the world was engaged in combating an economic depression of an unprecedented nature. To what extent the undeclared war in the Far East affected the Disarmament Conference[49] it is difficult to measure, but that it led to a diminished faith in the post-war agencies of peace and an increased faith in armaments cannot be denied. The Far Eastern crisis revealed defects in the world's peace machinery. The League Covenant operated in a cumbersome and time-consuming fashion. The fact-finding agency, at first objected to by the United States, had to be created *ad hoc* and it was not until a year after the initial outbreak of hostilities that it brought in its report. The League's lack of universal support—with Russia and the United States not members and vitally concerned in the region of conflict—made for uncertainty, hesitation, and reluctance on the part of those who would be obliged to bear the brunt of League sanctions. At best the League served to create and crystallize world opinion against Japan, an opinion which failed to bring about a settlement of the Sino-Japanese conflict over Manchuria.

League lacked universal support

[48]The Assembly of the League on February 24, 1933, appointed an advisory committee to follow the Sino-Japanese controversy, and at the same time aid members of the League in concerting their action among themselves and with non-member states. Russia and the United States were invited to coöperate in the committee's work.

[49]See Chapters XXX and XXXVIII.

CHAPTER XXXIV

WAR DEBTS AND REPARATIONS

By the time the United States entered the war on April 6, 1917, the Allied governments had about reached the end of their financial resources. Franklin K. Lane, a member of President Wilson's Cabinet, in a letter to his brother wrote, "On all sides they are frank in telling of their distress. We did not come in a minute too soon. England and France, I believe, were gone if we had not come in."[1] Prior to our entry, Great Britain acted as banker to the Allies. Of the total amount of inter-Allied borrowing of approximately $8,000,000,000 between 1914 and 1917, Great Britain loaned nearly $6,000,000,000[2] to France, Italy, Russia, the Dominions, Rumania, Montenegro, Serbia, Greece, and Portugal. Upon our entry into the war it became apparent that America's immediate contribution would have to be a financial one because of our comparative military unpreparedness. In his message to Congress in April, 1917, President Wilson called for "the organization and mobilization of all the material resources of the country to supply the materials of war," and "the extension to these governments of the most liberal credit in order that our resources may so far as possible be added to theirs." Between April, 1917, and November, 1920, our government loaned to twenty different nations a total of over ten billion dollars. The following table shows the amounts of pre-armistice and

Allies' finances at low ebb in 1917

America's immediate aid financial

[1]A. W. Lane and A. W. Wall, Letter of Franklin K. Lane, p. 250; J. M. Keynes in his book *The Economic Consequences of the Peace* states that "Without the assistance of the United States, the Allies could never have won the war."

[2]H. E. Fisk, *Inter-Ally Debts.*

Country	Pre-Armistice cash loans	Post-Armistice Cash loans	Post-Armistice War supplies and relief supplies	Total Indebtedness
Armenia	$	$	$ 11,959,917.49	$ 11,959,917.49
Austria	....	....	24,055,708.92	24,055,708.92
Belgium	171,780,000	177,434,467.89	29,872,732.54	339,087,200.43
Cuba	10,000,000	....	....	10,000,000.00
Czechoslovakia	....	61,974,041.10	29,905,629.93	91,879,671.03
Estonia	....	....	13,999,145.60	13,999,145.60
Finland	....	....	8,281,926.17	8,281,926.17
France	1,970,000,000	1,027,477,800.00	407,341,145.01	3,404,818,945.01
Great Britain	3,696,000,000	581,000,000.00	....	4,277,000,000.00
Greece	....	27,167,000.00[1]	....	27,167,000.00
Hungary	....	....	1,685,835.61	1,685,835.61
Italy	1,031,000,000	617,034,050.90	....	1,648,034,050.90
Latvia	....	....	5,132,287.14	5,132,287.14
Liberia	....	26,000.00	....	26,000.00
Lithuania	....	....	4,981,628.03	4,981,628.03
Nicaragua	....	....	431,849.14	431,849.14
Poland	....	....	159,666,972.39[2]	159,666,972.39
Rumania	....	25,000,000.00	12,911,152.92	37,911,152.92
Russia	187,729,750[3]	....	4,871,547.37	192,601,297.37
Yugoslavia	10,605,000	16,175,465.56	24,978,020.99	51,758,486.55
	$7,077,114,750	$2,533,288,825.45	$740,075,499.25	$10,350,479,074.70

[1]Includes $12,167,000 authorized under act of February 14, 1929.
[2]Includes $3,736,628.42 acquired by the United States Shipping Board Emergency Fleet Corporation, for services rendered.
[3]Exclusive of $5,000,000 conditional advance not availed of and returned.

post-armistice indebtedness of foreign governments to the United States.[3]

Most of the money loaned spent in the United States

Very little of the money lent to the Allies went out of the United States. Most of it was spent in America to purchase war materials and foodstuffs. The following table indicates the supplies on which the advances were used:[4]

Munitions, including remounts	$ 2,493,610,000
Munitions for other governments	205,495,000
Exchange and cotton purchases	2,644,783,000
Cereals	1,422,476,000
Other foods	1,629,726,000
Tobacco	145,100,000
Other supplies	613,107,000
Transportation	136,083,000
Shipping	173,397,000
Interest	730,504,000
Maturities	648,246,000
Relief	538,188,000
Silver	267,943,000
Food for Northern Russia	7,029,000
Purchases from neutrals	18,718,000
Special for U. S. war purchases in Italy	25,000,000
Miscellaneous	168,530,000
	$11,867,935,000

Problem of liquidation and readjustment

Soon after hostilities ceased the problem of liquidating and readjusting the war loans came to the fore. The French and the British desired a general settlement of accounts to be made simultaneously with the Peace Conference in which the respective positions of each of the interested governments[5] toward the others would be taken into consideration. To the Allies, particularly France, the object of a simultaneous discussion was to link inter-

[3]Memorandum Covering the Indebtedness of Foreign Governments to the United States . . ., Treasury Department, February 20, 1933, p. 16.

[4]These figures are taken from U. S. Treasury Dept., *Ann. Report on State of Finances*, 1919–1920, p. 340.

[5]See Harold G. Moulton and Leo Pasvolsky, *War Debts and World Prosperity*, pp. 54–55; and Combined Annual Reports of the World War Foreign Debt Commission, pp. 64–71 (hereafter referred to as Combined Annual Reports).

Inter-Allied debts linked with reparations by France

Allied debts with the problem of German reparations. The American government objected to discussing repayment of war debts in Paris in conjunction with the Peace Conference and succeeded in keeping the subject off the agenda in spite of the persistent efforts of some of the Allies to have it included.

Attempts made to have United States cancel war debts

Subsequent to the signing of the Treaty of Versailles, various attempts were made to have the United States agree to a general cancellation of the war debts. The initiative in this direction came from the British government which, on February 9, 1920, informed our government that it would "welcome a general cancellation of intergovernmental war debts." The communication went on to say that "the existence of these intergovernmental debts deters neutrals from giving assistance, checks private credits, and will . . . prove a disturbing effect in future international relations."[6] Secretary of the Treasury Houston replying on March 1, 1920, to this bid for cancellation stated that neither the American people nor Congress would look with favor upon such a proposal. Cancellation all around would not mean mutual sacrifices on the part of all the nations concerned; it would simply involve a contribution mainly[7] by the United States, he contended. The proposal, he went on to say, would throw upon the American people the exclusive burden of meeting interest charges and of ultimately extinguishing the principal of our loans to the Allied governments. Secretary Houston wrote:

Cancellation proposals refused

> This nation has neither sought nor received substantial benefits from the war. On the other hand, the Allies, although having suffered greatly in loss of lives and property, acquired very considerable accessions of territories, populations, economic and other advantages. It would, therefore, seem that if a full account were taken of these and of the whole situation there would be no desire nor reason to call upon the government of this country for further contributions.

[6] Combined Annual Reports, p. 68.
[7] *Op. cit.*, pp. 68–70.

The attitude taken by Secretary Houston was destined to become the American policy on the cancellation of war debts.

Refusal to cancel becomes American policy

After Great Britain and France joined together at the Hythe Conference in May, 1920, to urge a parallel liquida tion of debts and German reparations, Lloyd George, the British Prime Minister, on August 4, 1920, addressed a letter to President Wilson setting forth the British dilemma. "The British government," he wrote, "has stood steadily by the view that it was vital that Germany's liabilities should be fixed at a figure which it was within the reasonable capacity of Germany to pay, and that this figure[8] should be fixed without delay because the reconstruction of Central Europe could not begin until this uncertainty was removed. France, he went on to state, accepted this view, but would not agree to abate one farthing of her rights under the Treaty unless her debts to her Allies and Associates were treated in the same way. Great Britain, he declared, was prepared to agree to any equitable arrangement for the reduction or cancellation of inter-Allied indebtedness if the debts to the United States formed a part of such a settlement. The President in his reply restated the views of the Treasury Department, rejected the European view that there was any connection between German reparations and inter-governmental debts, and called upon the European debtors to initiate debt-funding negotiations with Washington.

President Wilson denied that any connection existed between debts and reparations

Soon after President Harding assumed office, his Secretary of the Treasury, Andrew W. Mellon, asked Congress to grant him broad powers to negotiate debt-funding agreements. Congress refused the Treasury's request for full powers, but instead set up a body called the World War Foreign Debt Commission whose members were to be appointed by the President with the advice and consent

War Debt Commission set up by Congress

[8]The Treaty of Versailles condemned Germany to pay reparations, but did not stipulate the amount. This task was left to the Reparations Commission.

of the Senate and stipulated that the Secretary of the Treasury should serve as chairman.[9]

The debt-funding act originally authorized the Commission to refund or convert the obligations of foreign governments arising from the World War on not longer than a 25-year basis and at not less than four and one-quarter per cent interest which was the maximum rate borne by our Liberty Bonds.[10] Not even England could meet these conditions, and when, in December, 1922, Mr. Stanley Baldwin, then British Chancellor of the Exchequer and later Prime Minister, was sent over to arrange for funding the British debt, he succeeded in getting more favorable terms. An agreement between him and the World War Foreign Debt Commission was reached in February, 1923, and accepted by Congress in March.[11] It provided that the British debt of $4,600,000,000—the total amount of the loans—should be paid in sixty-two annual instalments with interest at the rate of three per cent during the first ten years and three and one-half per cent during the remaining fifty-two years, a cut from the five per cent of the original obligation. The amortization payments were small to begin with but gradually increased so that toward the close of the period they would become very heavy.

Agreement reached with Great Britain

This settlement was not popular in Britain. The immediate post-war feeling that "Germany should pay to the last pfennig" had changed to the feeling that Britain would be better served by all-round cancellation of both

Settlement unpopular in England

[9]The debt-funding bill was approved by President Harding on February 9, 1922. The text of the act is to be found in Combined Annual Reports, pp. 6–7.

[10]The original members of the Commission were Secretary of the Treasury, A. W. Mellon; Secretary of State, Charles Evans Hughes; Secretary of Commerce, Herbert C. Hoover; Senator Reed Smoot, and Representative Theodore E. Burton. The three members added to the Commission in 1923 were Representatives Charles E. Crisp, Richard Olney, and Edward N. Hurley.

[11]By the Act of February 28, 1923, amending the Act of February 9, 1922, Congress, *inter alia*, authorized the Commission to settle with governments indebted to the United States on terms such as the Commission believed to be just. Each settlement, of course, had to receive the approval of Congress.

debts and reparations. The British policy with respect to debt-funding was set forth by Arthur Balfour, British Secretary of State for Foreign Affairs, in a note[12] August 1, 1922. After stating that Great Britain favored surrendering her share of German reparations, and writing off, through "one great transaction," the whole body of inter-Allied indebtedness, the note went on to say that in no circumstances would the British government "ask more from our debtors than is necessary to pay our creditors. And, while we do not ask for more, all will admit that we can hardly be content with less." The policy thus enunciated became, on the whole, the guiding principle in Great Britain's negotiations with her war debtors. She was criticized on the Continent on the ground that in undertaking separate negotiations with the American government she had weakened the bargaining power of her Allies.

Great Britain determined to ask no more of her debtors than was needed to pay her creditors

The other countries were reluctant to enter into negotiations with the United States because of the onerous terms prescribed by Congress, but they needed American capital which, according to a statement issued by President Harding, should not be lent to any country which failed to enter into a refunding agreement. One after another the debtor nations sent over missions to make what terms they could. With the Yugoslavian debt funded and signed on May 3, 1926, the work of the Commission was practically completed. The settlements all cover a period of sixty-two years and contain amortization features providing for a progressive increase of capital payments. The thirteen debt settlements negotiated by the Commission represented more than ninety-seven per cent of the total principal amount due at the time the Commission was created. The next table shows for each government the amount of the debt as funded, the total

Need of loans compels other governments to seek settlements

Thirteen settlements negotiated

[12]The text of the note is quoted in Moulton and Pasvolsky, *War Debts and World Prosperity*, pp. 111–112, 113.

Country	Date of agreement	Funded principal	Interest to be received	Total	Interest[1] per cent
Belgium	Aug. 18, 1925	$417,780,000.00	$310,050,500.00	$727,830,500.00	1.8
Czechoslovakia	Oct. 13, 1925	115,000,000.00	197,811,433.88[2]	312,811,433.88	3.3
Estonia	Oct. 28, 1925	13,830,000.00	19,501,140.00	33,331,140.00	3.3
Finland	May 1, 1923	9,000,000.00	12,695,055.00	21,695,055.00	3.3
France	Apr. 29, 1926	4,025,000,000.00	2,822,674,104.17	6,847,674,104.17	1.6
Great Britain	June 19, 1923	4,600,000,000.00	6,505,965,000.00	11,105,965,000.00	3.3
Hungary	Apr. 25, 1924	1,939,000.00	2,754,240.00	4,693,240.00	3.3
Italy	Nov. 14, 1925	2,042,000,000.00	365,677,500.00	2,407,677,500.00	0.4
Latvia	Sept. 24, 1925	5,775,000.00	8,183,635.00	13,958,635.00	3.3
Lithuania	Sept. 22, 1924	6,030,000.00	8,501,940.00	14,531,940.00	3.3
Poland	Nov. 14, 1924	178,560,000.00	257,127,550.00	435,687,550.00	3.3
Rumania	Dec. 4, 1925	44,590,000.00	77,916,260.00[2]	122,506,260.05	3.3
Yugoslavia	May 3, 1926	62,850,000.00	32,327,635.00	95,177,635.00	1.0
Total		$11,522,354,000.00	$10,621,185,993.10	$22,143,539,993.10	

[1]Average interest rate approximate over the whole period of payments.
[2]Includes deferred payments which will be funded into principal.

amount the United States is scheduled to receive over the funding period on account of interest and principal, and the average interest for each debtor nation.[13]

Capacity to pay used to measure debt

Capacity to pay was the yardstick used by the World War Foreign Debt Commission. It was first evidenced in the settlement with Great Britain in 1923. On October 1, 1925, the American Commission restated the principle in the following terms:[14]

> We believe it is fully recognized by the commissions that the only basis of negotiations fair to both peoples is the principle of the capacity of France to pay. The nub of the difficulty of the two commissions arises from a difference in judgment as to the future capacity of France to pay without, as we have stated, undermining her economic and social fabric; and this difficulty narrows itself to the future rather than the present, for we are prepared to accept the views of the French Commission as to the immediate difficulties of France.

But "capacity" was a rough-and-ready formula. This is plainly seen in the way the Commission prescribed for eight other debtors[15] substantially the same terms it had accorded to Great Britain. Mountains of data were accumulated in an effort to discover whether the relative paying capacity of these eight debtors differed in any way from that of Great Britain. But a seer, not a statistician, was required to find out how the future would deal with "capacity." How could the negotiators predict in advance the economic fortunes of a country for sixty-two years? The fact was that the American negotiators as well as the debtor representatives sought to obtain for their respective principals the greatest possible advantages in the war-debts settlement. Secretary Mellon's words

[13]See Combined Annual Reports, p. 449.

[14]In the Italian debt-funding agreement in November, 1925, the capacity-to-pay principle was applied with an intelligent appreciation of the economic factors involved.

[15]These were: Hungary, Lithuania, Poland, Belgium, Latvia, Czechoslovakia, Rumania, and Estonia.

bear testimony to that. "We," he reported, "have made for the United States the most favorable settlements that could be obtained short of force."[16]

Few economists believed debts would be paid

When these debt agreements were made there was much discussion as to whether the United States had pursued a wise and expedient policy. Few economists believed that these debts could or would ever be paid in full. Debt payments across frontiers in the last analysis can only be made through the delivery of goods or the rendering of services, or both, to the creditors—unless the creditors intended to pursue the quixotic policy of financing payments to themselves. Some economists contended that if the United States was to receive war-debt payments from her European debtors, the latter would have to create an export surplus by selling goods to the United States. But the American trade policy of protective tariffs was intended to restrict imports from abroad in all competitive lines and this, along with an aggressive policy for the promoting of export trade in every field, would combine to prevent a favorable balance of trade on the part of her debtors. So far as the rendering of services in the form of shipping, insurance, banking, and the like, the policy of the United States was equally obstructive in that she performed these services for herself as far as she could by subsidizing shipping and discouraging the operation here of foreign banks, insurance companies, *et cetera*.

American trade policy made payment of debts in money impossible

Determining amount of German reparations

By the time the World War Foreign Debt Commission had completed its work, the problem of German reparations had gone through a long and tortuous evolution. The reparations obligation rested on the acceptance by Germany of the full responsibility "for causing all the loss and damage to which the Allied and Associated governments and their nationals have been subjected as a

[16]Combined Annual Reports, p. 302.

consequence of the war imposed upon them by the aggression of Germany and her allies."[17] What the size of the reparations bill was to be remained for the Reparations Commission to fix. It determined the amount to be 132 billion gold marks, or approximately 33 billion dollars. Following an ultimatum by the Supreme Council of the Allies on May 5, 1921, Germany accepted the terms which the Reparations Commission had laid down.

Germany unable to meet schedule of payments

Germany's inability to comply with the schedule of payments soon became evident and the Commission was obliged to make modifications from the very start. How far German economy, already disorganized, could withstand the strain imposed upon it by the reparations schedule became an issue between France and Great Britain, the two chief reparations creditors. France viewed Germany's delays and postponements as a lack of willingness to discharge her obligations faithfully, while Great Britain interpreted Germany's failure to meet the reparations schedule as evidence of economic inability and proposed a drastic reduction of the reparations bill. Under the stress of creditors' demands, the German government not only lost the will to pay but the capacity as well, and in November, 1922, she declared her inability to continue reparations payments on the 1921 schedule. To France this was clearly an attempt to sabotage the Treaty. And when the Reparations Commission on January 9, 1923, adopted a resolution[18] declaring Germany in willful default, the French and Belgian armies marched into the Ruhr, which is Germany's chief industrial area. With the occupation of the Ruhr, the disintegration of German economy was hastened. Between June and October, 1923, the German mark dropped from 100,000 to the dollar to the fantastic figure of 1,000,000,000. Not until Germany's economic life almost came to a standstill

Germany declared in willful default

[17] Article 231 of the Treaty of Versailles.

[18] The French, Belgian, and Italian representatives on the Commission voted for the resolution and the British against it.

did the French realize the folly of trying to collect reparations payments by force of arms.

Secretary Hughes suggests a commission to study Germany's ability to pay

Shortly before the French and Belgian occupation of the Ruhr, Secretary of State Hughes, on December 20, 1922, delivered a speech at New Haven suggesting the appointment of a committee of experts to study Germany's capacity to pay and to devise a plan under which such payments would be made. His speech disclosed our government's concern about the critical trend of affairs in Europe, and our desire to help in the liquidation of some of the post-war problems from which we had kept ourselves aloof by the Senate's rejection of the Treaty of Versailles. Secretary Hughes's proposal was rejected by France; but a year later, when the disastrous consequences of the Ruhr occupation became apparent, France agreed with Great Britain to accept it.

The American government refused to be officially represented on the two expert committees appointed by the Reparations Commission, but declared that it would "view with favor the acceptance by American experts of invitations to participate in the work of the committees." Three Americans were finally chosen with the approval of Secretary Hughes. They were General Charles G. Dawes, Owen D. Young, and Henry M. Robinson. General Dawes was chosen chairman of the first committee whose task was to consider ways and means of balancing the German budget and the measures to be taken to stabilize German currency. Reginald McKenna, a British banker, presided over the second committee to determine the amount of German capital abroad with a view to bringing about its return to Germany. The committees began their work on January 14, 1924, and submitted their findings to the Reparations Commission on April 9 of that year.

The Dawes Commission

The Dawes Plan

Under the provisions of the Dawes Plan, as the work of the first committee became known, it was recommended that Germany should make reparations payments from the following sources: (1) from her ordinary budget, (2) from a transport tax, (3) from interest and amortization on German railway bonds, and (4) from interest and amortization on German industrial bonds. The annuities were to start at 1,000,000,000 gold marks in the first year and rise to 2,500,000,000 gold marks in the fifth or standard year.[19] The Dawes Plan provided for the creation of a Transfer Committee consisting of six members including an executive officer known as the Agent General for Reparations Payments.[20] One of the main functions of this Committee was the safeguarding of German foreign exchange and the stability of German currency. The Plan was officially accepted at a conference of the interested powers in London in August, 1924, and led to the French and Belgian evacuation of the Ruhr. The Dawes Plan did not attempt a solution of the whole reparation problem; it merely constituted "a settlement extending in its application for a sufficient time to restore confidence."[21] Nor was Germany's total reparations bill examined by the experts; Germany, save for certain minor adjustments, still was legally bound by the figures which the Reparations Commission fixed in 1921.

Accepted by the interested powers

After the Dawes Plan had functioned for four years the reparations creditors felt convinced that the time had come for a comprehensive and definitive settlement of the reparations problem. Accordingly the governments of Germany, Belgium, France, Great Britain, Italy, and Japan appointed a committee of financial experts which met in Paris on February 9, 1929. Four months of stren-

The Young Plan supersedes the Dawes Plan

[19]The size of the annuities was dependent to some extent on the level of commodity prices and the general economic development of Germany. For a detailed discussion, see Moulton and Pasvolsky, *War Debts and World Prosperity*, Chapter IX.

[20]Owen D. Young was the first Agent General for Reparations Payments. He was succeeded by S. Parker Gilbert, who held that office until the end of the reparations régime under the Dawes Plan.

[21]Reparations Commission, The Experts' Plan for Reparations Payments, p. 39.

uous negotiations followed, and on June 7, 1929, they signed a series of recommendations called officially the New Plan, but popularly known as the Young Plan after the American chairman, Owen D. Young. It superseded the Dawes Plan,[22] and provided for a schedule of annuities rising in the course of thirty-seven years from 1.7 billion to a maximum of a little over 2.4 billion reichsmarks; then for a further period of twenty-two years the annuities were to fall from about 1.6 billion to some 900 million reichsmarks. Germany, further, recovered financial autonomy and was given full responsibility for raising reparations. An agency, known as the Bank for International Settlements, was created to act as a trustee for the creditor powers in receiving reparations from Germany, thus replacing the Reparations Commission set up by the Treaty of Versailles.[23]

United States continues to deny any connection between debts and reparations

The United States steadfastly denied that there was any connection between reparations payments by Germany and war-debt payments by the Allies to the United States.[24] Notwithstanding our attitude, the reparations creditors of Germany regarded the economic relationship between these two sets of obligations to be so close as to influence their policy towards both. In accordance with the Balfour note, Great Britain consistently espoused

[22]The Young Plan went into effect officially May 17, 1930.

[23]For a discussion of the Young Plan see Moulton and Pasvolsky, *War Debts and World Prosperity*, Chapter X.

[24]Despite this denial, Secretary of the Treasury Mellon, chairman of the World War Foreign Debt Commission, in a letter to President Hibben of Princeton University, March 15, 1927, wrote: "It is obvious that your statement that the debt agreements which we have made impose a tremendous burden of taxation for the next two generations on friendly countries, is not accurate, since the sums paid us will not come from taxation but will be more than met by the payments to be exacted from Germany." This statement was later modified to exclude Great Britain.

The Committee on Ways and Means of the House of Representatives in recommending to Congress the ratification of the debt-funding agreement with France contended that the settlement was based on France's capacity to pay. In determining capacity one of the principal considerations taken into account, the Committee stated, was the Dawes payment from Germany to France. Cf. Combined Annual Reports, p. 267.

proposals for the cancellation of debts, and in this respect she occupied a strategic position, for she is not only a debtor to the United States but she is a larger creditor of many nations, having loaned her Allies during the war approximately $10,000,000,000. The British debt-funding agreements with two of her principal debtors, France and Italy, for example, were governed by two basic considerations: (1) the amount she would need for her debt payments to the United States, and (2) the financial capacity of the individual debtor.[25] As for France, unlike Great Britain she did not at any time declare a definite policy towards her debtors, but in her debt-funding agreements with them she was exceedingly lenient. Her responsible statesmen on numerous occasions declared that France favored a complete cancellation of all war debts as between the Allied and Associated Powers.

Great Britain steadily urges general cancellation

France supports British position

The payments on war debts to the United States were made according to the agreements up to and including the payments due on June 15, 1931. The amounts received by that date from foreign governments reached a total of $2,627,580,897,[26] which is a little over one-quarter of the original sum loaned. This figure represented $725,300,411 as repayment in principal and $1,902,280,486 in interest.[27] These sums were in part applied to the retirement of the public debt of the United States which had increased from approximately $2,975,618,585 in 1917 to a peak of $26,596,701,648 in 1919, an increase of $23,621,083,063 in two years. In 1930 the public debt figure was $16,185,000,000, showing a decrease of $10,411,701,648 in a ten-year period,[28] the reduction coming in part from war-debt repayments but chiefly from surplus revenues.

Payments made to United States through June 15, 1931

[25]See Moulton and Pasvolsky, *War Debts and World Prosperity,* Chapter VI.

[26]Release by the Treasury, July 1, 1931.

[27]*Ibid.*

[28]Daily statement of the United States Treasury, October 31, 1930.

American loans to Europe during this period

During the period the European nations were making their payments to the United States, American bankers were simultaneously making large and frequent loans to Europe. It has been estimated that American bankers and investors loaned $4,929,277,000 to Europe, $1,420,957,000 of which went into Germany.[29] These private loans stimulated American export trade and contributed to the era of prosperity, as well as to the restoration of the gold standard on the Continent, and the economic rehabilitation of Europe. Above all, these loans helped to make possible the payment of German reparations to the Allies, which in turn made possible payments of war debts to the United States.[30] Thus Germany received by way of American loans well over half of her reparations payments, and these same loans plus loans to the Allies practically equaled American war-debt receipts. In addition to loans to the German government, private loans were also made to German municipalities and industrial corporations, *et cetera*. All these loans fattened the German economy. Credits established here enabled the Germans to purchase raw and other materials destined to increase German national wealth. Part of this increase was siphoned to the ex-Allies in the form of reparations payments, which, in the ex-Allies' view, were the source of war-debt payments to the United States. American foreign loan policy, for the time being at least, helped to conceal the true nature of the intergovernmental debt problem. When the world depression began with the collapse of the New York stock market in October, 1929, and the American bankers ceased lending abroad, the

Loans made practically equaled debt payments received

True nature of debt obscured

[29]Annual Report of the Secretary of Commerce for the fiscal year ending June 30, 1931.

[30]From 1924 to 1931 inclusive, payments credited Germany on account of reparations totalled $2,480,000,000. (The War Debts, Supplement to the *Economist*, London, November 12, 1932.) Total receipts by the United States on intergovernmental debts during that period amounted to $2,627,580,897. These figures suggest that the Allies were paying their debts to America with what they were receiving from Germany.

debt problem came into its proper perspective.[31] The illusion that war debts had been settled by the debt-funding agreements, and reparations by the Young Plan, was destroyed when the nation realized that it was American private loans to Europe that had helped to support the whole intergovernmental debt structure.

World depression stopped lending

The deepening world-wide depression resulting in a catastrophic drop in prices was intensified by a series of major financial crises in Europe in 1931. In May, the Austrian government revealed that the Kredit Anstalt, one of the great financial houses in Austria with far-flung connections, was in a desperate plight. In June and July, Germany suffered a banking crisis which aggravated her special difficulties. With foreign loans at an end, her whole economy had slowed down. This, as is usual, was most noticeably revealed in budget difficulties. On June 5, the German Chancellor, Dr. Heinrich Bruening, promulgated an emergency decree—his third within eleven months—in an endeavor to bring order out of the budgetary chaos. At the same time he brought Germany's plight to the attention of the world by declaring that "the limits of the privations we have imposed upon our people have been reached," and that Germany must have "relief from the unbearable reparations obligations."[32] Though loans had ceased Germany had still to pay on reparations along with the new commercial debt burden which had become two-thirds as great as reparations.

European financial crises of 1931

Germany's need of relief from reparations payments

American creditors had the largest stake in the solvency of Germany. This stake was equal to that of all the rest

[31]The amazing decline in the volume of new long-term foreign issues offered in the New York market is shown by the following table which appeared in the New York *Times*, December 18, 1932:

1928	$1,251,000.000
1929	671,000,000
1930	905,000,000
1931	229,000,000
1932	none

[32]New York *Times*, June 6, 1931.

The Hoover Moratorium

of the world combined. It was to America's interest therefore to take measures to maintain the solvency of Germany. Accordingly on June 20, 1931, President Hoover, after consultation with Congressional leaders of both political parties, proposed the postponement for "one year of all payments on intergovernmental debts, reparations and relief debts, both principal and interest, of course not including obligations of governments held by private parties."[33] The President declared that the object of the plan was "to give the forthcoming year to the economic recovery of the world." Mr. Hoover repeated the declared policy of the American government on the connection between debts and reparations:

> Our government has not been a party to, or exercised any voice in determination of reparations obligations. . . . The repayment of debts due to us from the Allies for the advances of war and reconstruction was settled upon a basis not contingent upon German reparations or related thereto. Therefore reparations is necessarily wholly a European problem with which we have no relation.

France not consulted

The whole world applauded the proposal—the whole world but France. Mr. Hoover had not consulted the French government before proposing a moratorium. Neither had he appraised fully the French regard for the sanctity of the Young Plan for reparations payments which his proposal violated. There followed fast and furious negotiations between the two countries, which resulted in an agreement in principle on July 6, 1931, postponing intergovernmental debts from July 1, 1931, to June 30, 1932, but obliging the German government to continue the payment of the unconditional annuities, provided for by the Young Plan, in the form of deposits in the Bank for International Settlements.[34] The Bank in turn was

---

[33] *Ibid.*, June 21, 1931. See Moulton and Pasvolsky, *War Debts and World Prosperity*, pp. 322–324.

[34] By a Joint Resolution of December, 1931, Congress provided the authority to postpone payments to the United States and authorized the Secretary of the

to invest these funds in government guaranteed bonds of the German railways, and the railways in turn were to pass to the government the amounts received from the Bank. This circuitous transaction preserved in French eyes the literal sanctity of the unconditional portion of the Young annuities.

France preserved unconditional annuities under Young Plan

The economic cyclone which started in Austria and moved on to Germany struck England about the middle of July, 1931. The crisis in England was characterized by heavy withdrawals of balances due to foreign creditors in London. The tradition that the City of London is the world's financial fortress of security was shaken when it was learned in August that a 250 million dollar credit from Paris and New York was supporting the pound sterling. But the drain of gold was too heavy and the August credit was exhausted by August 23. Five days later another loan of 400 million dollars was granted by bankers of Paris and New York. Not even this was sufficient to stem the tide of heavy withdrawals and on September 20 the British government announced the suspension of the gold standard.

Great Britain goes off the gold standard

The British departure from gold left the United States and France as the two great creditor nations, the defenders of the gold standard. It became obvious that if the gold standard was to remain as the basis of currency, these two nations would have to coöperate to that end. Accordingly, M. Laval, the French Premier, was invited to come to the United States, in the words of President Hoover "to discuss . . . the question of such further arrangements as are imperative during the period of the depression in respect to intergovernmental debts."[35]

The arrival of the French Premier in America on October 22, 1931, signalized to the world the political and

Treasury to conclude agreements providing for repayment of the postponed amounts over a period of ten years beginning July 1, 1933, with interest at the rate of four per cent per annum.

[35]New York *Times*, October 7, 1931.

Premier Laval visits President Hoover

economic power to which France had risen, giving her a pre-eminent position in the economic destiny of Europe and making her an indispensable partner in the American effort to maintain the gold standard and pursue a common policy to that end. The results of the Hoover-Laval conversations were embodied in a joint statement issued in Washington on October 25, 1931. From the statement it appeared that the crux of the conversations turned on war debts and reparations, styled "intergovernmental obligations," and the maintenance of the gold standard. The pronouncement on the war-debt problem read:

Their statement on the debt problem

> In so far as intergovernmental obligations are concerned, we recognize that prior to the expiration of the Hoover year of postponement some agreement regarding them may be necessary covering the period of business depression, as to the terms and conditions of which the two governments make all reservations. The initiative in this matter should be taken at an early date by the European powers principally concerned within the framework of the agreements existing prior to July 1, 1931.[36]

Significance of this statement

While the words used were sufficiently broad and vague, they were generally interpreted to mean that in bracketing war debts and reparations the President had acknowledged the existence of some kind of link between the two and their relation to the business depression. This apparent recognition of the connection between debts and reparations was a distinct departure from the policy which the American government had pursued since the problem arose at the Peace Conference of 1919.[37] The joint statement indicated further that reparations were to be dealt with in the framework of the Young Plan, and the initiative was to be taken by the principal powers concerned —Germany and France. Thus it would seem that Premier Laval succeeded in establishing (1) a connection

[36]New York *Times*, October 26, 1931. See Walter Lippmann and William O. Scroggs, *The United States in World Affairs*, 1931, Appendix IV, for the text of the statement.

[37]See, however, Mr. Mellon's letter to President Hibben, *supra*, p. 796, note 24.

between debts and reparations, and (2) in obtaining a declaration from President Hoover that if any modifications were to take place they would be within the framework of the Young Plan which the American President ignored some four months earlier in his moratorium.

Congress ratifies moratorium with qualifying resolution

President Hoover had proposed his moratorium on intergovernmental debts when Congress was not in session. He had, however, obtained assurances from several of the Congressional leaders of both parties that they favored a moratorium and would support him on it. When Congress convened in December, it ratified the moratorium but attached to the resolution of ratification a declaration that it is "against the policy of Congress that any of the indebtedness of foreign countries to the United States should be in any manner cancelled or reduced, and nothing in this joint resolution shall be construed as indicating a contrary policy, or implying that favorable consideration will at any time be given to a change in policy hereby declared."[38]

European governments seemed to ignore the qualifying resolution

It is difficult to estimate how seriously the European governments took the declaration by Congress. On its face it appeared an outright repudiation of the President's conversations with the French Premier, as well as a clear warning to European creditors that the door to cancellation or reduction of war debts was locked and double locked. The attitude of Congress, it may be said, reflected popular opinion throughout the country. Notwithstanding the decision of Congress, the suggestion set out in the Hoover-Laval joint statement, that the initiative be taken by the European powers principally concerned, prompted the German government to invoke the machinery of the Young Plan. At Lausanne[39] on

---

[38]H. J. Resolution 147, 72nd Congress, 1st Session.

[39]Originally the Lausanne conference was called to deal with reparations and other measures necessary to solve the economic and financial difficulties responsible for the world crisis. The United States refused to send delegates because she feared that in participating in a conference dealing with German

Germany invoked Young Plan machinery

June 16, 1932, the reparations creditors and debtors[40] met to evolve a "lasting settlement" of the reparation question. The steps taken at Lausanne marked another and the final stage in the financial liquidation of the war. The reparations creditors agreed to wipe out over nine-tenths of Germany's reparation obligation. With a bill of about 25 billion dollars still owed by Germany under the Young Plan, the new agreement called for the delivery to the Bank of International Settlements of German government bonds to the amount of 3 billion gold marks bearing interest at five per cent with a sinking fund of one per cent. The Lausanne agreement was hailed as an important contribution towards world recovery. It caused world markets to take heart again. Yet its ratification was, by a "gentlemen's agreement" between the principal creditors, made to depend upon the conclusion of a satisfactory arrangement on war debts with the United States. With German reparations virtually cancelled, the thought in Europe's mind was what would be the future American policy with respect to war debts.

German reparations reduced nine-tenths

Reduction dependent upon satisfactory arrangements with the United States

From the time that the Lausanne agreement was signed on July 9, 1932, until the American Presidential election was over on November 8, the European governments refrained from taking steps looking towards a review of the régime of war debts for fear of complicating the election. However, within forty-eight hours after the American voters had elected Franklin D. Roosevelt, the Democratic candidate to the Presidency, the British government addressed a note[41] to Secretary Stimson stating that the

reparations and general economic problems she would be drawn into a consideration of war debts. To surmount this obstacle, a separate conference was proposed by the British to meet in London at some future date with an agenda agreeable to the United States. This was accepted by us.

[40]The designated American "observer" attended the Lausanne Conference and participated in drafting the agreements.

[41]The British note was dated November 10. Dept. of State, Papers Concerning Intergovernmental Debts, November–December 1932, p. 33.

war debts "as now existing must be reviewed," and asking for "an exchange of views at the earliest possible moment." Anticipating a favorable reply, the British government asked "for a suspension of the payments[42] due from them for the period of the discussions now suggested . . ." Some twenty-four hours after the British note was received, a similar request came from the French government. The note[43] recalled that France, basing her action upon the principles expressed in the joint statement on October 25, 1932, by President Hoover and Premier Laval, "agreed to very heavy sacrifices at Lausanne." In making these sacrifices, she had acted "in close accord with the ideas of the American government." The note concluded by proposing a further study of the debt question and asked for an extension of the suspension of payments pending the study.[44]

Britain asks for review of war debts

France sends similar note

Both request extension of moratorium

The situation created by the British and French notes was critical indeed and was anxiously watched by the whole country. Whatever policy would be worked out towards the debt problem by President Hoover, who was to be succeeded by Franklin D. Roosevelt in a few months, would necessarily run over into the next administration. President Hoover therefore asked Governor Roosevelt, as he then was, to consult with him. Governor Roosevelt accepted the invitation, suggesting that the meeting be wholly informal and personal, and cautiously pointed out that "in the last analysis the immediate question raised by the British, French, and other notes creates a responsibility which rests upon those now beset with the executive and legislative authority."[45] The historic meeting[46] between the President and the President-elect resulted in

President Hoover confers with President-elect Roosevelt

[42]An instalment on the British debt was due December 15.

[43]*Op. cit.*, p. 23.

[44]Belgium, Czechoslovakia, and Poland sent somewhat similar notes. *Ibid.*, pp. 1, 9, and 71.

[45]New York *Times*, November 15, 1932.

[46]The meeting took place on November 22, 1932.

no joint public announcement, but the next day President Hoover issued a statement reviewing the history of the debts and asserting again that there was no connection between debts and reparations. He believed that the changed world situation and the universal precipitous fall in commodity prices, which had increased the burden of debt, offered some justification for the creation of an agency to exchange views with each nation individually on the adjustment of its debt. President-elect Roosevelt, however, opposed the creation of a new agency and stated that the existing diplomatic service of the government offered an adequate channel for an exchange of views. It was his belief that no action by Congress could limit the constitutional power of the President to conduct negotiations with foreign governments, and saw an advantage in this method for debtor nations to bring to the attention of the American government new conditions and facts affecting any phase of their indebtedness.[47]

President Hoover again denies connection between war debts and reparations

Secretary Stimson's reply refuses support for moratorium extension

On November 23[48] Secretary Stimson replied to the British note of November 10 stating that the President contemplated the creation of an agency to consider the problem individually with each government. As to the suspension of the installment of the British debt due December 15, the Secretary of State declared that no authority lies in the President to grant such an extension, and moreover "no facts have been placed in our possession which could be presented to the Congress for favorable consideration." The note made clear that our government and people attached such importance to the maintenance in force of the original agreement by the payment on December 15 as far to outweigh any reasons for its suspension. "The prospects of a satisfactory approach to the whole question," the Secretary wrote, "would be

[47]New York *Times*, November 24, 1932. See also Walter Lippmann, *The United States in World Affairs*, 1932, pp. 179–180.

[48]Dept. of State, Papers Concerning Intergovernmental Debts, November-December, 1932, p. 35.

greatly increased" by meeting the payment when due.[49]

British note of December intended for Congress and the American people

On December 1, the British government in a lengthy note[50] supplied the facts which would be likely to induce Congress to act favorably on the debt problem. While in form it was a note to the American government, in fact it was an appeal to Congress and to the American people to coöperate with Great Britain "to make the first and essential step towards averting disaster, financial, economic, and political." The resumption of the war-debt payments as they existed before the Hoover moratorium, it was contended, would deepen the world-wide depression by further falls in commodity prices with disastrous consequences to all. The British government believed that a discussion with us would bear fruitful results for revival of world prosperity. It again asked for the postponement of the December 15 installment pending review of the whole question.[51] The note conceded that a scaling down of war debts would bear heavily on the American taxpayer, but such a loss could not be measured in the same scale as the untold loss of wealth and human misery caused by the economic crisis.

Postponement of December installment again requested

> It will not profit a creditor country to collect a few million pounds or dollars if it thereby perpetuates a world disorder which reacting on itself involves losses of revenue many times greater [through loss of foreign trade]; and a settlement, however generous it may seem, which relieves the economic machinery of the world by clearing up these intergovernmental payments, would be repaid again and again by the contribution which it would make to world revival.

If Great Britain were to resume payment to the United States, she would be obliged to reopen the question of payments from her own debtors; the debtor countries

[49]A similar note was sent to the French government on the same day. The replies to the Belgian, Polish, and Czechoslovak governments were in a similar vein.

[50]Dept. of State, Papers Concerning Intergovernmental Debts, November-December, 1932, p. 37.

[51]The French note of December 1 was to the same effect. *Ibid.*, p. 26.

in turn would have to demand payment by Germany of her obligations under the Young Plan and Great Britain would have to do likewise. This would undo the Lausanne agreements, unsettle the whole reparations problem, and lead to grave political consequences.

To resume payments would undo the Lausanne agreements

If we measure the reception given to the British note by the American public from press opinion, we are obliged to say that it was on the whole favorable to an examination of the British case. But in Congressional circles the note was not sympathetically received, and when Congress reconvened the sentiment in both houses against reopening the debt question was clear. President Hoover therefore abandoned the idea of a Congressional commission and fell back on the alternative plan of appointing his own commission.[52]

American press favorable to a review

Congress opposed

In England opinion on war debts was divided; some felt that the integrity of Britain's credit dictated honoring an obligation freely made no matter what the consequences might be, but this was by no means unanimous. Certain Cabinet members, notably Neville Chamberlain, then Chancellor of the Exchequer, favored repudiation. Viscount Snowden, former Chancellor of the Exchequer in two Labor governments, asserted that Britain was not in equity bound to pay[53] and also urged repudiation. In France, where there had always been strong opposition to the payment of war debts, and where the Franco-American debt-funding agreement was approved by the Chamber of Deputies on condition that payments under it be conditional upon the sums Germany was to pay on account of reparations, public opinion on the whole favored repudiation.

English opinion divided between paying and repudiating

French opinion generally for repudiation

[52]In the creation of such a commission which Hoover believed would not complete its work before the end of his term of office, the President sought the coöperation of President-elect Roosevelt in selecting the members. Mr. Roosevelt, however, felt that he could not accept such a responsibility. New York *Times*, December 23, 1932.

[53]See his article in the New York *Times*, November 17, 1932.

During the exchange of notes between our government and its debtors, the one insisting on payment and the others asking for relief by way of postponement and review, the nation watched with great anxiety the approaching 15th of December. On that day, Secretary of the Treasury Mills announced[54] that Great Britain, Italy, Czechoslovakia, Finland, Latvia, and Lithuania had met their payments; and that France, Belgium, Estonia, Hungary, and Poland had defaulted.[55]

Six nations make the installment payment

Five default

When President Roosevelt entered the White House, the war-debt policy of the United States was still uncertain. There were a few indications that American sentiment had softened. These lay chiefly in the aggressive plans of the new administration to relieve the pressing debt burdens of the American people. But the country as a whole did not seem to be drifting into a frame of mind that would promote a settlement consonant with the Lausanne agreement. Such a settlement would mean, according to Europe, the acceptance by the United States of a lump sum payment to the amount of something under two billion dollars, i. e., the amount in principal and interest Germany was still to pay by way of reparations. To this idea the new administration did not seem inclined. Rather it was veering to the negotiation of settlements with each debtor separately, these settlements to be based upon a *quid pro quo* of trade privileges as a means of making the solution of the war-debt problem palatable to the American nation.

President Roosevelt's policy turns toward trade agreements as a means of settlement

In 1933, Great Britain, Italy, Latvia, Lithuania, and Czechoslovakia made "token payments" toward interest on their war debts, hoping thereby to avoid the stigma of default. The new Roosevelt Administration took measures to scale down debt payments in proportion

Token payments

[54]Dept. of State, Papers Concerning Intergovernmental Debts, November–December, 1932, p. 80.

[55]The French government characterized their action as "deferring" payment.

as German reparation payments had been reduced by the Allies at the Lausanne Conference of June, 1932. Austria, Belgium, Estonia, France, Greece, Hungary, Poland, and Yugoslavia had made no payments at all since the Hoover moratorium. There was great pressure by the European nations for a solution of the whole debt problem. Mr. Ramsay MacDonald, the Prime Minister of Great Britain, visited President Roosevelt in April, 1933, to discuss, *inter alia,* the agenda for the World Economic Conference which was to be held in London in June, 1933. He and the President agreed that war debts would have no place on the agenda. Mr. MacDonald, however, introduced the subject at the World Economic Conference notwithstanding his agreement with the President. The question of the war debts, he declared to the assembled delegates, must be dealt with before every obstacle to general recovery could be removed, and must be taken up without delay by the nations concerned. There was much truth in Mr. MacDonald's contention, but for the moment neither Congress nor the American people were in the mood to scale down or write off the war debts. Such exploratory negotiations as the State Department did conduct led it to infer that it would be inexpedient to submit to Congress for acceptance the proposals it had discussed.

War debtors press for solution

Congress and people opposed to scaling down debts

A solution of a sort was soon provided for this vexing problem of war debts. On April 4, 1934, Congress passed, and on April 13 the President signed, what is commonly known as the Johnson Act, which forbids the making of loans within the jurisdiction of the United States to any foreign government, or its subdivision, which had defaulted on its debts to the United States. This was not the kind of legislation which bankers and economists thought constructive. It was vindictive legislation, but it expressed the feeling of a vindictive public. When the June 15, 1934, payment date neared, the Italian govern-

The Johnson Act

ment stated in a note[56] that it had been prepared to make another token payment until "a law recently passed"—meaning the Johnson Act—deprived the token payment of its symbolic and practical meaning. Those nations in default since the Hoover moratorium were not stimulated into paying by the Johnson Act, and when June 15, 1934, came around, defaulted again. Earlier, on June 4, 1934, Great Britain had announced that she would "suspend" further payments pending a settlement which had prospects of success.

Defaults and suspensions

Semi-annually the State Department, in order to keep the record straight, sends reminders to the debtors that payments are due. Semi-annually the Treasury Department adds the defaulted interest to the already defaulted interest. The likelihood that these debts with the accumulating interest thereon will ever be paid grows more remote daily.

---

[56]Department of State, Press Release, June 16, 1934.

PART VIII

THE UNITED STATES IN AN ERA OF POWER POLITICS AND WAR

CHAPTER XXXV

COMMERCIAL POLICY

THE economic disorganization wrought by the World War stimulated trade restrictions, but not until the full force of the world-wide economic depression began to be felt did protectionism and foreign trade controls take on the aspect of *sauve qui peut.*

Fordney-McCumber tariff

The first general tariff enacted after the war, the Fordney-McCumber Act of 1922, carried high rates. It came at a time when, as a result of the war, the traditional debtor-creditor relationship which the United States bore towards Europe had been completely reversed.[1] The large loans extended by private bankers and the American government for the purchase of war materials and supplies in this country had resulted in so great an expansion of our exports that these exceeded imports by many billions of dollars.[2] By the end of 1919, the total of all capital obligations due the United States was approximately 18 billion dollars.[3] This transformation from a debtor to a leading creditor position was not accompanied by a corresponding adjustment of American financial and commercial policy. In the new role of a leading world creditor, the United States for the most part followed the pre-war policy of economic nationalism which had been dictated by her position as a debtor nation. This policy found expression particularly in high tariff walls to protect the home market against foreign competition, and in

The United States a leading world creditor

[1]National Industrial Conference Board, *The International Financial Position of the United States*, pp. 17–34.

[2]*Ibid.*, pp. 36, 37.

[3]*Ibid.*, p. 48.

the promotion of export trade by official and private agencies. The Fordney-McCumber tariff was followed in 1930 by the Hawley-Smoot tariff, which carried some of the highest rates in the history of American protectionism and accentuated the position of the United States as one of the extreme protectionist nations in the world. The 1930 tariff was in part an effort to forestall the rush of foreign goods which might have resulted from the effects of the world-wide fall of commodity prices soon after the collapse of the stock market boom in Wall Street in 1929. The protests against the Hawley-Smoot bill by Latin-American and European countries were of no avail. The world depression had driven the Hoover administration to seek shelter under a higher tariff wall, so strong was its belief in America's economic self-sufficiency.

Hawley-Smoot tariff

The rising trade barriers

The Hawley-Smoot Act let loose a tariff orgy; other nations raised their tariffs upward and invoked import restrictions and prohibitions not only to hit back at the United States but to protect themselves from the violent decline in world prices. There were various motives for throwing up trade barriers. The need for safeguarding national gold reserves prompted nations to seek a balance between exports and imports, imports for which payment had to be made abroad in gold. It was believed that by keeping out foreign goods unemployment would be checked and domestic prices maintained. In September, 1931, England abandoned the gold standard, and before the close of that year, Canada, India, the Scandinavian countries, and Japan followed England's course. The departure from "gold" increased the number of trade restrictions, and led those still on "gold" to impose controls on dealings in foreign exchange. In November, 1931, came the crowning event in the annals of protectionism—Great Britain abandoned her traditional policy of free trade and imposed duties as high as 50 per cent *ad valorem* on a long list of articles.

Great Britain abandons free trade

The figures published by the Department of Commerce[4] showed that world trade in 1932—both exports and imports—declined to $26,160,000,000, a reduction of 34 per cent in value and 26 per cent in volume from the preceding year. The total trade in 1932 was the lowest for any year since 1910—it had amounted to $39,597,000,000 in 1931; to $54,921,000,000 in 1930; and to $68,290,000,000 in 1929. In percentage terms, the total world trade in 1932 was 52.5 per cent under 1930 and 61.7 per cent under 1929. This heavy decline in international trade was attributed in part to a shrinkage in demand resulting from the impairment of purchasing power by the economic depression, and partly to artificial restrictions on trade. That the tariff war was an important factor contributing to the paralysis of world trade and to the profound disturbance of the world's economic equilibrium is now generally recognized.

The decline in world trade

In the face of a deepening depression and the depreciation of many currencies which led to so-called exchange dumping, however, the high tariffs which hampered international trade soon appeared[5] inadequate to protect the shrinking home market from foreign competition. Hence the quota system, which limited imports of an article to a specific amount, came into being to buttress the tariff device. While this system had the merit of simplicity, as well as certainty, in practice the allocation of quotas between nations clamoring for a share in the market led to recriminations and economic warfare.

The quota system

In addition to tariffs and quotas certain nations resorted to exchange control,[6] more as a measure of monetary defense to prevent a drain on gold reserves than as a means of trade protection. By restricting the amount of

Exchange control

[4]*Commerce Reports*, April 8, 1933, p. 211.

[5]League of Nations, *World Economic Survey*, 1936, p. 138.

[6]Andreas Predöhl, "The Experience of the Countries Practicing Exchange Control," Joint Committee Carnegie Endowment, International Chamber of Commerce, *The Problem of Monetary Stabilization.*

foreign exchange available to importers to pay for their purchases abroad, exchange control did in effect check rigidly the volume of import trade. In Germany particularly it led to clearing agreements, which have spread to most of the nations of Europe and Latin America.[7] One of the results of the clearing agreements method of controlling foreign exchange has been for a nation resorting to this system to balance its trade with each nation with which it deals. It created a bilateral balancing of international trade and destroyed the triangular or multilateral type upon which international trade flourished. This type of trade and its effect upon a nation's commerce can be compared to a manufacturer who buys his raw materials and hires his workmen only from those who buy his products.

The connection between war debts and tariffs

Intimately connected with American tariff policy was the problem of war debts. So long as extensive foreign loans were made to Europe by our private bankers, so long as millions were spent by American tourists abroad, and large sums were sent home by immigrants living in the United States, just so long were the debtor nations able to make payments on account of war debts, notwithstanding the restrictive effect on trade of the Fordney-McCumber Act of 1922. But when these loans ceased, when tourist trade shrank, and remittances abroad fell, the tariff policy revealed its true effect. The connection between our tariff policy and the payment of debts was recognized by Franklin D. Roosevelt who, as Democratic candidate for the presidency in 1932,[8] declared:

> The debts will not be a problem—we shall not have to cancel them—if we are realistic about providing ways in which pay-

[7]For a survey of clearing agreements and their effects, cf. League of Nations, *Enquiry into Clearing Agreements.*

[8]President Hoover, Republican nominee, favored the existing tariff barriers, and, if anything, was prepared to raise them. He was opposed to cancellation of war debts, but favored remitting particular payments on them in return for larger purchases of American goods by Europe.

ment is possible through the profits arising from the rehabilitation of trade. . . . Our policy declares for payment, but at the same time for lowered tariffs and resumption of foreign trade which opens the way for payment.

President Roosevelt made known to Congress after it convened on March 9, 1933, that he would ask authority to negotiate tariff agreements in order "to break through trade barriers and establish foreign markets for farm and industrial products." But for the moment the economic conditions of the nation were so critical that both he and Congress turned their attention to the more immediate problem of bringing domestic order out of chaos.

The banking crisis

In March, 1933, the nation was already in its third year of an economic depression, world wide in extent and effect, and in the throes of a nation-wide banking crisis. In his first inaugural address President Roosevelt asked "a stricken nation in the midst of a stricken world" to cast aside fear and unite to conquer the depression "as a trained and loyal army willing to sacrifice for the good of a common discipline." It was an emergency more serious than war. Suffering was widespread, not at a time of scarcity, but of plenty. The number of unemployed had reached an unprecedented peak, estimated anywhere from 10,000,000 to 14,000,000, and what with the fall in commodity prices and the volume of business losses, the credit structure of the nation was shaken to its foundations. The anxieties which beset the nation led many to wonder whether the economic structure could endure the havoc which was being inflicted. To be sure, the nation had been through depressions before. In the years following 1837, 1873, 1893, and 1907, it had experienced depressions of varying degrees of intensity. Then, the shocks of unemployment and increased agricultural production were absorbed by free land and by an expanding foreign market. But in 1933 the economic dislocation was deeper and wider than

Wide economic dislocation

any this nation had experienced; there was no free land, and foreign trade had shrunk to an incredibly low level.

Emergency finance measures

To stave off the collapse of the nation's credit structure the President, on March 6, ordered all the banks of the United States closed. When Congress met in special session three days later, it enacted in one day the Emergency Banking Act by which the President continued the proclamation closing the banks.[9] On March 10 the President prohibited[10] the export of gold, and on April 5 he forbade the hoarding of gold and ordered the delivery of gold or gold certificates to the Federal Reserve Bank. Despite the financial crisis here, and the restrictive operation of the gold standard, the foreign exchange value of the dollar at first remained stable. But when on April 20 an embargo was imposed by executive order[11] upon the shipment of gold, the dollar—left free to find its own level—depreciated, notwithstanding the nation's favorable balance of international payments.[12]

Thus far the emergency monetary measures dealt essentially with the banking crisis within the nation. It was believed at first that the gold embargo was temporary and that devaluation of the dollar was not contemplated. The Thomas Amendment to the Agricultural Adjustment Act, which became law on May 12, 1933, made it evident, however, that a new monetary policy had come into being. President Roosevelt in his radio address of May 7 described it thus: "The Administration has the definite objective of raising commodity prices to such an extent that those who have borrowed money will, on the average, be able to repay that money in the same kind of dollar which they borrowed."[13] By the Thomas Amend-

[9] *Annual Report of the Secretary of the Treasury,* 1934, p. 202.

[10] *Ibid.*

[11] *Ibid.*

[12] *Federal Reserve Bulletin,* June, 1933, p. 342.

[13] New York *Times,* May 8, 1933.

ment, the President was authorized, *inter alia*, to reduce the gold content of the dollar by not more than 50 per cent. The growing sentiment in Congress for inflation as a means of raising prices was satisfied, and more drastic legislative measures were forestalled.

The first pragmatic test of Mr. Roosevelt's foreign policy in the economic sphere was provided by the World Monetary and Economic Conference which met in London in June and July of 1933. In a message cabled to fifty-four heads of state on May 16, 1933, before the Conference convened, President Roosevelt declared that it "must establish order in place of the present chaos by a stabilization of currencies; by freeing the flow of world trade, and by international action to raise price levels."[14] Whatever hope there was that the Conference would succeed arose from the fact that the forces of economic chaos in the financial and commercial world were so appalling that the Conference could not afford to fail. The Preparatory Commission of Experts had thought it necessary to call attention to the gravity of the situation in the following words:

President calls for stabilization of currencies

> Unemployment has recently been estimated as involving at least 30 million workers. Even this huge total, which does not include the workers' families or other dependents, is probably an underestimate. The burden of suffering and demoralization resulting from unemployment of such proportions is appalling. Wholesale commodity prices—expressed in gold—have declined since October, 1929, by roughly a third; raw material prices on the average by 50 to 60 per cent. In the middle of December, at Winnipeg, the price of wheat fell to the lowest level recorded in any primary market for wheat during the past four centuries. . . . Industrial production has been drastically curtailed, particularly in those trades producing capital equipment. The depths which have been reached in some instances are illustrated by the position of the United States steel industry which, at the close of 1932, was operating at only 10 per cent capacity. The international flow of goods, hindered by currency disorders and restricted by a multiplicity of new governmental interven-

[14]Department of State, Press Release, May 20, 1933.

tion, has been reduced to incredibly low levels. . . . Failure in this critical undertaking threatens a world-wide adoption of ideals of national self-sufficiency which cut unmistakably athwart the lines of economic development. Such a choice would shake the whole system of international finance to its foundations, standards of living would be lowered, and the social system as we know it could hardly survive.[15]

American delegation declines to consider currency stabilization

To what extent the President's domestic program of national rehabilitation would conflict with or be retarded by his program for the Conference was apparently not considered. But one month after the message to the heads of state saw the American delegation in London declining to consider immediate currency stabilization. It was explained that the American efforts "to raise prices are the most important contribution that it can make and that anything that would interfere with these efforts and possibly cause a violent price recession would harm the Conference more than the lack of an immediate agreement for temporary stabilization."[16] The "gold bloc" countries—France, Italy, Switzerland, Holland, Belgium—insisted that precedence be given to monetary stabilization, since in their view currency stabilization was the key to removing trade barriers. With a further decline in the exchange value of the dollar during the last week in June the "gold bloc" renewed its effort to secure an agreement on monetary stabilization, and failing an agreement sought an immediate adjournment of the Conference. This led to the drafting of a declaration which was designed to

Compromise proposed

effect a compromise on the conflicting aims between the United States and the "gold" countries. The nations on the gold standard were to maintain the free working of that standard at current gold parities; while those "off gold," without in any way prejudicing their future ratios to gold, declared it their intention to bring back an inter-

---

[15]League of Nations, Draft annotated agenda submitted by the Preparatory Commission of Experts, pp. 5–6.

[16]Department of State, Press Release, June 24, 1933.

national standard based on gold. In addition the nations "off gold" were to adopt measures to limit exchange speculations.

The President rejects the compromise

The compromise reached by the American delegation was sharply and unexpectedly reversed by the President, who declared that he "would regard it as a catastrophe amounting to a world tragedy" if the Conference should "allow itself to be diverted by the proposal of a purely artificial and temporary experiment affecting the monetary exchange of a few nations only." He went on to say that, "The sound internal economic system of a nation is a greater factor in its well-being than the price of its currency in changing terms of the currencies of other nations. . . . So, too, old fetishes of so-called international bankers are being replaced by efforts to plan national currencies with the objective of giving those currencies a continuing purchasing power which does not greatly vary in terms of commodities and needs of modern civilization. . . ."[17]

Those who remembered the President's statement to the heads of state on May 16 when he declared that the forthcoming World Economic Conference "must establish order in place of present chaos by the stabilization of currencies, by freeing the flow of world trade, and by international action to raise price levels," were dismayed and confused by this sharp statement. What had happened in the interval between the President's declaration of May 16 and July 3 was a shifting of emphasis from exchange stabilization which promised to enlarge the outlets for American surpluses, to a "sound internal economic system" as a more desirable factor in national well-being. As for "freeing the flow of world trade," that too was set aside in a large measure, and for the time being, by the National Industrial Recovery Act which authorized the President, *inter alia*, to raise customs duties to protect the

[17]Department of State, Press Release, July 8, 1933.

price and wage increases to be brought about by the new legislation. When the Conference adjourned on July 27, 1933, there was deep disappointment over its failure. The problems of monetary exchange, tariffs, and other trade barriers were left unsolved. Yet it is not surprising that the Conference was barren of accomplishments. It met at a time when the United States had embarked upon a policy of inflation and was averse to any provisional stabilization of her currency which would hamper the execution of the new policy, and when economic nationalism was rampant throughout the world.

The Conference a failure

The President secures authority to negotiate trade agreements

It was not until March 2, 1934, that the President asked Congress for authority to enter into trade agreements in order to modify, "within carefully guarded limits," existing tariff restrictions. The domestic recovery program launched a year earlier had resulted in rising commodity prices and a general improvement in business. Such improvement as did take place was largely confined to industries producing for home consumption. In asking Congress for authority to deal with tariffs as a means of restoring foreign trade the President sought to broaden the field of national economic recovery. There was some debate and opposition to giving the President such wide powers over tariffs, but on the whole the nation and Congress were ready to do his bidding. His resolute and forthright measures to combat the crisis of the previous year, by what became known as the "New Deal" program of recovery, inspired public confidence and brought him popular favor.

The traditional trade policy of the United States has been not to discriminate between foreign nations, but to extend equality of treatment to all who do not discriminate against this nation's trade. This was the policy embodied in the Trade Agreements Act which became law on June 12, 1934. Under it a concession on a given article in a trade agreement with a foreign nation (other than Cuba) was to apply also to the same product from any third nation, unless that third nation was found to discriminate against the products of the United States. The same treatment for American products was required of the other party to the trade agreement. This principle of equality of treatment, reciprocal in nature, rests upon the belief that multilateral trade and payments are best calculated to free the world of trade restrictions, expand the world's real income and thus raise the standard of living of peoples everywhere.

The Trade Agreements Act

The Act authorized the President to conclude trade agreements with foreign governments where the existing tariff rates were unduly burdening and restrictive to the foreign trade of the United States. It gave the President the power to negotiate trade agreements altering existing tariff duties, under certain limitations, by as much as 50 per cent.[18] The agreements were to go into effect by Presidential proclamation without further Congressional action. The Act extended to all nations, unless they should discriminate against the commerce of the United States, every advantage secured by any[19] particular nation entering into a reciprocal trade agreement with us. Thus by the method of trade agreements the Roosevelt administration proposed to effect a downward revision of tariff rates, through reciprocal concessions exchanged between two nations and the extension of these concessions to other nations through the most-favored nation policy. For the first time in our history, the American government was in a position to adapt its tariff policy to the needs of the nation in the light of world conditions.[20]

[18]The Act provided for open hearings and for interdepartmental consultations. Public notice must be given before any agreement is concluded in order that those interested may be given an opportunity to present their views.

[19]Cuba is specially treated.

[20]The McKinley Tariff Act of 1890 authorized the President, "with a view to secure reciprocal trade" to impose duties on five articles then on the free list coming from countries charging duties against American goods which he found to be "reciprocally unequal and unreasonable." Under this Act ten

Tariff rates in hands of experts

Tariff making by this Act was removed from the lobbies of the Capitol to the offices of government experts; national welfare was to replace the predatory and selfish interests of small groups in determining the rates to be imposed. To lay the groundwork for negotiating the new trade treaties, a difficult and complex task, an elaborate administrative machinery was set up in Washington. The painstaking and scientific manner with which the Government undertook to formulate tariff rates, and the broad concern for national welfare which inspired its work, was in striking contrast to the log-rolling and sinister lobbying methods which dominated the making of the Smoot-Hawley Act of 1930, the Fordney-McCumber Act of 1922, and the others in our history.

Trade agreements made with fifteen nations by the end of 1936

Within a year of its coming into force, the Roosevelt administration had concluded trade agreements with five countries[21] and was conducting negotiations with thirteen others. These nations accounted for 40 per cent of the foreign trade of the United States. By the end of 1936, the number had risen to fifteen, and these included Canada and France. "The Hull reciprocity program," pointed out the Republican New York *Herald Tribune* in referring to the agreement with France, "remains about the only practical contribution now being made in the world toward the amelioration of world entanglements,

---

reciprocity agreements were concluded; the results were meager, however, since the concessions were confined to a small number of articles.

The Dingley Tariff Act of 1897 (Section 3) empowered the President to conclude reciprocal trade agreements, without Senatorial approval, with restricted concessions to minor duty reductions on a limited number of articles. The results were not significant because the bargaining power placed in the hands of the Executive was so limited. Section 4 of the Tariff Act of 1897 did authorize the negotiation of trade treaties of much wider scope. But these agreements required the approval of the Senate. The agreements negotiated were never reported out of the Senate Committee on Foreign Relations.

It is interesting to note, however, that the reciprocal trade agreements idea was first developed under a Republican Party administration. Cf. Francis B. Sayre, *Five Years of the Trade Agreements*.

[21]Cuba, August 24, 1934; Brazil, February 2, 1935; Belgium, February 27, 1935; Haiti, March 28, 1935; and Sweden, May 25, 1935. Department of State, *Treaty Information Bulletin*, No. 68, May, 1935.

and as such its influence is of greater value than the specified concessions suggest."[22] With the new tariff policy, the Roosevelt administration secured concessions from other countries on hundreds of exportable items and at the same time reduced the tariff rates on several hundred imported items. But in spite of these reductions, the rates still remained at a high level of protection. The process of reconstructing the foreign market was a gradual one and at the end of two years of tariff bargaining the trade agreements had not brought about any profound change in our economic life, and none was expected.

The Roosevelt administration hopes for world economic appeasement

In addition to improving trade, the reciprocal trade policy sought to bring about world appeasement. The economic warfare, which reached such enormous proportions during the depression years, was in large measure responsible for the alarming disintegration of all international relationships which the world was witnessing. President Roosevelt hoped that the removal of trade restrictions would be "of some assistance in discouraging the economic source of war and therefore a contribution toward the peace of the world."[23] He did not claim that a more liberal international trade would stop war, but pointed out that war was a natural sequence without more liberal international trade.

The German trade policy

While the United States was engaged in an effort to free international trade through the reduction of trade barriers, the totalitarian states, more notably Germany, embarked upon a policy of "economic self-containment." On the 9th of September, 1936, Herr Hitler, at a Nazi Party rally at Nürnberg, announced the inauguration of a four-year plan to make Germany self-sufficient in raw materials. The proposal was that Germany's chemists produce substitutes from materials to be found in her

---

[22]New York *Herald Tribune,* May 14, 1936.

[23]Address at Chautauqua, New York, August 14, 1936. See New York *Times,* August 15, 1936.

mines and factories and thus render her independent of all imports at the end of four years. General Herman Goering was placed in charge. Under his command the entire nation's economic system was subordinated to the exigencies of the plan to limit as far as possible Germany's dependence on the outside world for her supply of foodstuffs and military raw materials in case of prolonged war or blockade.[24]

German trade policy linked to preparation for war

Whether such a policy was economically wise, not to ask whether it was possible of achievement, was secondary to the aim of freeing the nation of dependence upon the outside world for raw materials in case of war. Self-sufficiency envisaged economic isolation, with foreign trade cut to the bone. What foreign trade there was left followed a policy of bilateral balancing. In Germany, for example, the government, by means of clearing and compensation agreements, directed the importation of raw materials in accordance with her rearmament needs from countries whose trade balance with her was active. Other nations—forced to meet the German threat and to prepare themselves similarly for war—also resorted to controlling their foreign commerce by means of clearing and compensation agreements, but it was in Germany and Italy where the practice was developed with the greatest ingenuity destructive of international trade and in conflict with the American trade agreements program.

Trade agreements not made with totalitarian nations

Of the twenty-two reciprocal trade agreements negotiated up to the present time,[25] none has been concluded with authoritarian nations. Under the Trade Agreements Act, the President may deny the benefits of tariff reduction to any nation discriminating against the United States. On October 15, 1935, the President directed that

---

[24]Italy, too, was endeavoring to develop her economy on a self-sufficient basis similar to that of Germany. The Italian dictator ordered imports restricted and replaced by substitutes of Italian manufacture.

[25]January 10, 1940.

the trade agreement duties no longer be applied to imports from Germany because of her discrimination against imports from the United States.[26] Germany has been on the American "black list" ever since, and her products have been subject to the maximum rates under the Hawley-Smoot tariff of 1930. The table below shows the course German-American trade has taken following the German trade policies under the Hitler régime and the retaliatory measures taken by the United States:

United States Exports to and Imports from Germany[27]
(value in thousands of dollars)

	Exports	*General Imports*
1929	410,449	254,688
1933	140,024	78,185
1934	108,738	68,805
1935	91,981	77,792
1936	101,956	79,679
1937	125,884	92,644
1938	107,130	64,550
1939	47,374	52,447

Republicans opposed to reciprocal trade agreements

In the Presidential campaign of 1936 the trade agreements policy came in for a good deal of debate. The Republican National Convention in its platform declared: "We will repeal the present Reciprocal Trade Agreement Law. It is futile and dangerous. Its effect on agriculture and industry has been destructive. Its continuation would work to the detriment of the wage earner and the farmer." In place of reciprocity it proposed to restore "the principle of the flexible tariff in order to meet changing economic conditions here and abroad." The National Democratic Convention platform was a justification of the reciprocal trade agreement policy and a promise to con-

[26]U. S. Treasury Department, Treasury Decision, T. D. No. 47898.

[27]Department of Commerce, Bureau of Foreign and Domestic Commerce, Trade of the United States with Germany, 1938; and Monthly Statistical Statement No. 1703, December, 1939. The boycott of German goods by American Jewish groups and others was a factor in the reduced trade.

tinue it. "We shall continue to foster the increase in our foreign trade which has been achieved by this administration; to seek by mutual agreement the lowering of those tariff barriers, quotas and embargoes which have been raised against our exports of agricultural and industrial products, but continue as in the past to give adequate protection to our farmers and manufacturers against unfair competition or the dumping on our shores of commodities and goods produced abroad by cheap labor or subsidized by foreign governments."

The attack by the Republicans on the Administration's tariff policy was directed at the Middle West and Northwest, and it centered about the Reciprocal Trade Agreement between the United States and Canada signed November 15, 1935, because of the concessions made on competitive agricultural imports from Canada. The arguments of the critics apparently did not make much headway with the farmers, for on election day they voted to return Franklin D. Roosevelt to the White House for a second term.

Trade agreement with France

One of the real tests of the reciprocal trade policy was the Administration's ability to conclude agreements with industrialized nations of Europe. The pact with France signed on May 6, 1936, was such a test. For the Administration it represented a signal victory; it not only increased trade between the two nations but it put an end to commercial warfare which had flared up from time to time during the past decade between the two countries.

The agreement with Great Britain, negotiated simultaneously with the new Canadian agreement, signed on November 17, 1938, was by far the most important single accomplishment in the whole series of agreements. It crowned the efforts of Secretary of State Hull to achieve tariff reduction and promote a freer international trade. The agreements between the United States, Great Britain and Canada covered the world's greatest trading area, the

United States and the British Empire alone furnishing about 40 per cent of the world's international commerce. Great Britain removed her duty on American wheat, thus enabling our farmers to compete with Canadian and Australian wheat growers on an equal footing. Duties on American lard and certain fruit juices were removed; and duties on rice, oatmeal, rolled and flaked oats, apples, pears, and many canned and dried fruits were reduced. Great Britain agreed to the continued free entry of our raw cotton, sulphur, resin, and fur skins. Additional concessions were granted to our fishery products, electrical and office machinery, lumber and wood manufactures, automobiles, and scores of other items. In return the United States offered concessions on some 600 different items, consisting chiefly of textiles, and metals and their manufactures. We reduced our rates on earthenware, china, glass, leather goods, sport goods, and pipes, and stabilized the rates on whiskey and gin. The Anglo-American-Canadian agreements were significant in that they reversed the protectionist trend which appeared in the British Empire in 1930. Whereas in that year Great Britain admitted no less than 83 per cent of her imports duty free, as a result of the Imperial Economic Conference at Ottawa, Canada, in 1932, the free list amounted to only 25 per cent.

Trade agreement with Great Britain and Canada

The agreements with Great Britain and Canada came at a time when the prestige of the democracies struck a new low in the defeat they suffered by the Munich Accord[28] of September, 1938, and were not without some political significance in demonstrating to the totalitarian dictatorships the solidarity of the democratic countries. The system of autarchy and the sweeping economic controls Germany adopted, under which foreign trade is directed into bilateral channels, were strikingly in conflict with the

[28]See *infra*, pp. 974–985.

reciprocal trade agreements program which sought to free trade by lowering our own tariff barriers as well as those of others. The nations with which the United States now[29] has reciprocal trade agreements represent about 60 per cent of this nation's total foreign trade. During the period of operation of the trade agreements program increases have occurred in both our exports and our imports. "Taking the average figures for the years 1934 and 1935 and the years 1937 and 1938, we find that, while our exports rose by one billion dollars, our imports increased by 671 millions. In 1937 and 1938 the excess of exports over imports averaged 700 million dollars. In 1939 the picture has been approximately the same."[30] The basic ideas underlying this tariff policy are that exports and imports are interdependent; nations cannot sell without buying. The imports of one nation are the exports of other nations. To induce other nations to mitigate their excessive obstructions to exports, we must, of necessity, stand ready to adjust our own excessive trade restrictions. In the five and one-half years of operation the trade agreements program has borne fruit. The principle of the American trade policy, it should be pointed out, has not made any headway with nations where foreign trade is a state monopoly, such as Russia, or where imports are subordinated in a nation's economy to the military program, as is the case with Germany and Italy. In a state-controlled economy of the Russian or German type, where market forces and private initiative are suppressed, the principle of equality of treatment has no place. The successful operation of the principle presupposes an economic organization based upon private capitalism. In a world headed steadily in the direction of economic nationalism and closed economy the United States made a

The balance sheet of the trade agreements policy

[29]As of January 10, 1940.

[30]Secretary of State Cordell Hull, before the House Committee of Ways and Means, New York *Times*, January 12, 1940.

valiant effort and a contribution towards reversing the trend.

The unstable currency conditions

The high tariffs, import quotas, and exchange controls, which the American reciprocal trade agreement policy was endeavoring to modify, were directly related to the unstable condition of currencies throughout the world. Ever since 1931, when Great Britain went off gold the currencies of the European nations have been in a state of disequilibrium. Norway, Sweden, Denmark, Finland, Portugal, Argentina, and many of the British dominions, known as the "sterling bloc" because of their commercial ties with Great Britain, also abandoned the gold standard, and tied their currencies to the pound. France, Belgium, Holland, Italy, Switzerland, and Luxembourg—known as the "gold bloc"—adhered to the gold standard. When the United States suspended the gold standard in March, 1933, and then devalued the dollar on January 31, 1934, by giving a gold value equivalent to 59.06 per cent of its former level, it added to the existing monetary difficulties throughout the world. In a world financially interdependent it was not surprising that the independent effort of one nation to remedy its internal price structure by depreciating its currency should throw out of balance the currencies of other nations. Whether unstable currencies demoralized trade and brought on restrictions, or whether the decline in trade incident to the world depression had undermined the currencies, there was no agreement. Whichever view one took, as Sir Henry Strakosh pointed out, there could be no lasting stability of the exchanges without establishing the internal economic equilibrium in the nations concerned by balancing their budgets and solving their over-extended foreign and domestic credit problem.[31] But nations not unlike individuals find that the pressure of events quite often compels decision and action in conflict with counsels of perfection.

[31]The (London) *Economist*, October, 1936.

What the pressure of events was, when on September 25 and 26, 1936, there came announcements from Paris, London, and Washington that France, Great Britain, and the United States had entered into a monetary "agreement," is not known. The motive, as stated in the announcement, was "a common desire to foster those conditions which safeguard peace and will best contribute to the restoration of order in international economic relations and to pursue a policy which will tend to promote prosperity in the world and to improve the standard of living of peoples."[32] France, her Minister of Finance announced simultaneously, had decided to reduce the gold content of the franc and set up an exchange equalization fund to prevent fluctuations in the exchange rates, as had Great Britain and the United States. The tripartite "agreement" which preceded the decision of the French government was a promise on the part of each "to continue to use appropriate available resources so as to avoid as far as possible any disturbance of the basis of international exchange resulting from the proposed readjustment."[33] The announcement went on to state that: "The government of the United States is moreover convinced, as are also the governments of France and Great Britain, that the success of the policy set forth above is linked with the development of international trade. In particular it attaches the greatest importance to action being taken without delay to relax progressively the present system of quotas and exchange controls with a view to their abolition."[34] Belgium, Holland, and Switzerland adhered to the tripartite accord. Germany declined. The "gentlemen's agreement" marked the end of the "gold bloc." While it was not a stabilization agreement, it called for coöperation among its adherents to maintain

The tripartite agreement

[32]Department of Treasury, Press Release, September 25, 1936.

[33]*Ibid.*

[34]*Ibid.*

"the greatest possible equilibrium in the system of international exchange."[35] National monetary policies were not changed by the "agreement"; it merely prevented them from becoming dangerously competitive. Gold, as an internal standard of value, began to disappear when Great Britain went off gold in 1931, and by 1937 it had well-nigh vanished. Its function, as was so signally evidenced by the "agreement," had become not one of maintaining the fixity of exchanges, but of adjusting deficits in balances of payments.

The banking crisis in the United States in 1933 gave rise to a series of emergency monetary measures which culminated in the devaluation of the dollar on January 31, 1934, pursuant to the Gold Reserve Act approved by the President the preceding day. The Act gave the President power to alter the gold value of the dollar and vested in the United States title to all the gold held by the Federal Reserve system. Since February 1, 1934, the Secretary of the Treasury has been buying gold at $35 per ounce. Revaluation by legislative fiat of the gold holdings at $35 per ounce, as compared with the previous price of $20.67 per ounce, netted the Federal Government $2,808,000,000. Of this sum $2,000,000,000 was set aside as a stabilization fund.[36]

The influx of gold

There has been a great influx of gold from abroad into the United States since the beginning of 1934 resulting in an accumulation from a total of $4,000,000,000, or 30 per cent of the world supply, to a total of $17,600,000,000, or about 60 per cent, at the end of September, 1939.[37] Of this total increase of $13,600,000,000 about $2,808,000,000 represent the result of revaluation of the $4,000,000,000 in the nation in 1934; and $200,000,000 was acquired under the gold buying program prior to revaluation. The

[35] *Annual Report of the Secretary of the Treasury,* 1937, p. 259.
[36] *Federal Reserve Bulletin,* March, 1934, p. 141.
[37] *Ibid.,* January, 1940.

balance of $10,700,000,000 is what has been added since 1934.[38]

Reasons for the influx of gold

There were a number of circumstances which gave rise to the gold flow to the United States during this period. Of the $9,700,000,000 of gold and $1,000,000,000 of silver which have found their way to the United States from January, 1934, to October, 1939, $2,200,000,000 represent goods and services sold by us to foreign countries in excess of goods and services which we purchased from them. This sum, in other words, represents our favorable balance of trade for that period. Of the remainder, $5,500,000,000 has been attributed to the political and economic uncertainties abroad; and $3,000,000,000 to unidentified transactions.[39]

Gold a problem

The presence of this vast amount of gold in the United States, and its continuing inflow, present problems baffling to economists and statesmen. Fear even has been expressed by some that gold will lose its character as money if the world's stock continues to flow and accumulate in the United States. To stem the flow of gold would create as many problems as it would solve; to reduce the price of gold would generate deflationary tendencies injurious to our economic structure as a whole; to create an excess of imports over exports would reduce the stock of gold, but such a course would necessitate lowering of our tariff barriers to a point the nation would not but might be forced to accept. "It seems, therefore, that the problem of our huge gold stock is likely to stay with us for a long while, and that it may even increase—if gold continues to flow into this country. No simple solution to the problem can be devised. The ultimate solution will have to be a part of the answer to the much broader problems of restoration of world stability and international

[38] *Federal Reserve Bulletin,* January, 1940, pp. 11, 60.

[39] *Ibid.,* p. 12. Cf. *Federal Reserve Bulletin,* February, 1939, pp. 92–96, and Treasury Department, Press Service, March 23, 1939.

trade. It will also be bound up with rationalization of our own economy."[40]

Defaulted foreign dollar bonds

Between 1920 and 1931, it has been estimated, approximately $10,500,000,000 of foreign dollar bonds were floated in the United States. They were issued or guaranteed by governments, or their subdivisions, and by private corporations at a time when there was no government supervision over the issuance of these bonds. As the Foreign Bondholders Protective Council, Inc. stated, "it is natural that some of the loans made should have been wise and others unwise."[41] On December 31, 1938, there were outstanding $5,527,947,838 in principal amount. Of this sum $2,028,753,017, or 36.7 per cent, was in default.[42] Their grouping according to areas was as shown in the table on page 840.[43]

American policy with reference to defaulted investments

The traditional policy[44] of our government in the past has been that such loan and investment transactions were primarily private affairs and should be handled by the persons directly concerned. Within the proper limits of international law and international amity, our government has in the past endeavored to protect the interests of our nationals abroad from unfair treatment or from discrimination in favor of other creditors. The controversy in 1934 and 1935 over the unfair treatment accorded

[40] *Ibid.*

[41] Foreign Bondholders Protective Council, Inc.; *Annual Report*, 1934, p. 9.

[42] *Ibid.*, p. 1138.

[43] *Ibid.*

[44] The United States has adhered to her traditional policy of not interfering where there is no discrimination against American nationals, viewing the dollar loans floated in the United States as private matters to be handled by the parties directly concerned. Yet the amount of defaulted bonds was so great and the need for protecting the large number of American nationals who held these securities so urgent that the Roosevelt Administration invited a group on October 20, 1933, to form what became known as the Foreign Bondholders Protective Council, Inc., a private non-profit-making organization to protect American holders of foreign securities. The task of the Council was and remains arduous in view of the depression and the disorganization of world trade. In many instances it has secured the resumption of interest and sinking fund payments, and in others it has disclosed that nations in default were financially able to resume payments on interest and sinking funds.

	Outstanding		In Default		
	No. of Issues	*Principal Amount*	*No. of Issues*	*Principal Amount*	*Per Cent in Default*
Latin America	178	$1,600,530,070	155	$1,233,806,487	77.1
Europe	133	1,544,223,086	82	705,712,030	45.7
Far East and Africa	19	510,824,331	1	2,102,000	.4
Canada	307	1,872,370,351	37	87,132,500	4.7
	637	$5,527,947,838	275	$2,028,753,017	36.7

Their grouping according to issues was as follows:[45]

	No. of Issues	*Principal Amount*	*No. of Issues*	*Principal Amount*	*Per Cent in Default*
National	148	$2,990,138,757	87	$1,213,997,497	40.6
State, etc.	194	1,085,201,190	82	364,672,990	33.6
Municipal	174	531,514,685	54	201,694,800	37.9
Corporate (Government Guarantee)	121	921,093,206	52	248,387,730	27.0
	637	$5,527,947,838	275	$2,028,753,017	36.7

[45]Foreign Bondholders Protective Council, Inc.; *Annual Report*, 1934. A substantial number of these bonds are held by citizens of other countries and the figures given should not be interpreted as indicating the amount of bonds held by American investors nor the amount of American foreign investments. But it is believed that American citizens own a major portion of these defaulted securities.

by Germany to its American creditors illustrated the extent to which our government was prepared to go in protecting its nationals.

Germany discriminates against our nationals

On June 9, 1933, the German government declared a transfer moratorium on interest and sinking fund payments on most public and private foreign obligations. When The Netherlands and Switzerland threatened to retaliate by impounding German balances arising out of her trade with them Germany modified her moratorium towards them. The United States protested at this discriminatory treatment, but not having an unfavorable trade balance with Germany, she could not threaten to retaliate. After the German Finance Minister explained that Germany could pay only in proportion as her creditors bought from her, President Roosevelt summoned the German Ambassador to the White House and requested that the American creditors be accorded the same treatment as creditors of other nations.[46] But they were not. On June 14, 1934, the German government announced to all creditor governments the suspension of the service of the medium-term and long-term foreign loans, including the Dawes and Young loans,[47] which were described as "political" in character. Again those countries indebted to German creditors on trade balances were in a favorable position; they could resort to reprisals by impounding German credit balances and by applying them to the service of the German loans held by their nationals. The United States, however, had no such weapon.[48] She was in no better position with respect to the German suspension of service on the medium and long-term loans than she was with respect to the German transfer moratorium on interest and sinking-fund payments. On June 27,

[46]Department of State, Press Release, January 27, 1934.

[47]*Ibid.*, June 15, 1934.

[48]On June 27, 1934, Congress passed Public Resolution 53, suspending remaining payments to German nationals for property sequestered during the war. Cf. United States Statutes at Large, vol. 48, Part I, pp. 1267–1269.

1934, our government in a sharp note[49] objected to Germany branding American loans to her as "political." The note pointed out that the loans were made "in accordance with loan contracts and arrangements which stated that the proceeds were to be applied for productive purposes." They were financial engagements entered into voluntarily by "a mature industrial and trading state" well aware "of the dangers incident to disturbances in the capital market in the event of loss of confidence in its affairs." Germany could find the foreign exchange for the repatriation of German securities held abroad at depressed prices and for the importation of a vast amount of materials for her rearmament, but could not find the foreign exchange to meet her debts. "The asserted anxiety of the German government to make every effort to meet its obligations," the note went on to say, "cannot be proven by a mere display of its depleted balances, but must be evident from an examination of the whole trend and operation of German policy." The note was reinforced by a memorandum on November 23, 1934, citing specific instances of discrimination against American creditors. Notwithstanding the strong language of the note, the United States—the largest creditor—failed to secure for her nationals treatment similar to that of Great Britain, Switzerland, France, Sweden, Italy, The Netherlands, and Belgium—the other chief creditors.

The United States protests to Germany

The United States makes her position known on Austrian debts

Austria ceased to exist as an independent nation when Germany annexed her on March 13, 1938. Immediately there arose the question as to whether Germany would take over the debts due our government and nationals. The United States was quick to inform her,[50] on April 6, that we would look to her for payment of the debt of $24,055,708.92 incurred by Austria for flour sold to her under the authority of the Act of Congress approved

[49]Department of State, Press Release, June 27, 1934.

[50]Department of State, Press Release, April 6, 1938.

March 30, 1920. In addition dollar loans had been made to the Austrian government, provinces, municipalities, and corporations, totaling $36,879,900.[51] Many of these dollar bonds were held by American investors. The American government asked for prompt assurances on those debts as well. When our Ambassador to Germany delivered the note, he was informed that the German government was under no legal obligation to take over the external debts of the Austrian government. To this contention, our government—not receiving any response to its note of April 6—replied on June 9, 1938:[52] "It is believed that the weight of authority clearly supports the general doctrine of international law founded upon obvious principles of justice that in case of absorption of a state, the substituted sovereignty assumes the debts and obligations of the absorbed state, and takes the burdens with the benefits. A few exceptions to this general proposition have sometimes been asserted, but these exceptions appear to find no application to the circumstances of the instant case." But here, as in the case of the German debts owed to American citizens, the United States was at a disadvantage because of her trade position. Germany had no trade balance here which the United States could impound and apply to the servicing of the Austrian debt. A united front of the creditors, who had joined in the postwar financial reconstruction of Austria, might have succeeded in compelling Germany to honor Austria's obligations, had not Great Britain entered into a separate arrangement with her without regard for the position of the other governments and without consulting them. Agreements to pay the holders of Austrian bonds were made by Germany with her other important creditors—but none with the United States.

The German reply

The discrimination by Germany towards American

[51]Foreign Bondholders Protective Council, *Annual Report*, 1938, p. 649.

[52]Department of State, Press Release, June 17, 1938.

creditors created ill will between the two nations. Not much was needed to exacerbate that feeling, for the American public was already aroused over the suppression of civil liberties in Germany and the ruthless methods of her dictatorship. The open and continuous persecution of Jews, the repressive measures against the Catholic and Protestant churches evoked bitter resentment. The German government was not pleased at the way the American public responded to the methods of dictatorship. Its controlled press, resentful of our criticism, carried threatening and vile attacks against the United States, our public officials including the President, and our system of government. Under the circumstances relations between the two nations were strained to the breaking point.

German dictatorship methods create ill will

Future trade policy of the United States dependent upon other nations' policies

The international trade policy of the United States in the future is in no small part dependent upon the economic systems of the nations with which it trades. Germany, Italy, Spain, Japan, and other nations have adopted rigid governmental controls over private enterprise, and Russia has resorted to state socialism. Private enterprise in the totalitarian systems exists on paper, and business has become an instrument of the state. Foreign trade, in the sense that individuals may buy and sell in foreign countries in competition with each other, has been done away with. For these states foreign trade has become an instrument of national policy and not of free economic enterprise. Upon the outbreak of war in Europe in September, 1939, Great Britain and France also resorted to a rigid control over production and foreign trade. To what extent such measures of government control of state economy will be discarded or kept when the war emergency is over it is not possible to predict. When the various forms of foreign trade controls were first instituted to supplement and replace tariffs, they were regarded as temporary measures adopted under crisis conditions and destined to disappear as soon as the emergency which brought them into being should pass. Not only have these controls not disappeared, but they have been tightened and woven into the fabric of national economies. If the chief commercial nations of the world should permanently make foreign trade a state monopoly, American foreign trade based on free economic enterprise would become untenable. The United States will then, it seems, be faced with the necessity either of abandoning foreign trade as a vital part of her economy or of setting up similar internal controls to cope with totalitarian competition.

Possible threat to American foreign trade

CHAPTER XXXVI

THE GOOD NEIGHBOR

The Monroe Doctrine an affair of the United States

OLD policies die hard and new ones are not readily accepted. For years the policy of the United States towards the Latin-American countries was the object of distrust and suspicion. Latin-American statesmen saw the Monroe Doctrine slowly extended from a policy of protecting the continent from colonization by any European powers to one of "international police power." In the formulation, definition, interpretation, extension, and application of the Doctrine they had had no part. The policy embodied in the Doctrine was exclusively an affair of the United States, and the New World her domain.[1] They have resented the Doctrine as an affront to their sovereignty and as a device for American economic and political penetration and intervention.[2]

The policy of the good neighbor

In his inaugural address of March 4, 1933, President Roosevelt couched the foreign policy of the new Administration in the following terms: "In the field of world policy, I would dedicate this nation to the policy of the good neighbor—the neighbor who resolutely respects himself and, because he does so, respects the rights of others; the neighbor who respects his obligations and respects the sanctity of his agreements in and with a world of neighbors." This general statement, lofty in purpose,

[1]Cf. Charles Evans Hughes, Address, *American Journal of International Law*, vol. 17 (1923), pp. 611, 616.

[2]A Latin-American critic has expressed this resentment in the following words: "It is one of the ironies of modern history that the Doctrine which was advanced to prevent European intervention should be known, today, as the cloak of United States hegemony and intervention in that same part of the New World which it was originally, and supposedly, intended to protect from the ambitions of the Old." Gaston Nerval, *Autopsy of the Monroe Doctrine*, p. 182.

was followed by words more concrete. On December 28, 1933, the President declared that "the definite policy of the United States with respect to Latin America from now on is one opposed to armed intervention." Our South American neighbors had reason to suspect the genuineness of the change in policy which the President's utterance implied. On many previous occasions they had heard statesmen from the United States in lofty phrases give lip service to democracy and the equality of all nations before the law. Yet when the time came, the United States had not hesitated to set those principles aside by using troops or naval pressure to collect debts due her nationals. The Roosevelt declaration, though hailed by Latin America as an advance step toward the outlawry of intervention, remained to be translated into action. Good intentions must be coupled with good deeds.

The United States abrogates the Platt Amendment

A concrete demonstration of the new policy came on May 29, 1934, when the treaty embodying the Platt Amendment[3] was abrogated by the negotiation of a new treaty between Cuba and the United States. The provision with respect to maintaining or acquiring coaling or naval stations, of which Guantanamo is one, was, however, retained in the new treaty.[4] The abrogation followed a statement made by President Roosevelt on November 24, 1933, that he was desirous "of showing by deed our intention of playing the part of a good neighbor to the Cuban people."[5] With a speed rare in its history, the Senate, two days after the treaty was signed, gave its advice and consent, with only one Senator casting a negative vote, to the ratification of the treaty. When ratifications were exchanged on June 9, the Cubans celebrated the event for three days. President Mendietta of Cuba, along with other heads of Latin-American govern-

[3]See *infra*, pp. 512–513.

[4]See *infra*, p. 674.

[5]Cf. *Congressional Record*, 73rd Congress, Second Session, p. 10145.

ments, reciprocated President Roosevelt's "conviction that the relations of our respective countries have entered upon a new phase which will be marked by frank cordiality and a spirit of mutual coöperation and understanding."[6]

The United States and Cuba sign trade agreement

Following the abrogation of the Platt Amendment, Cuba and the United States concluded a new trade agreement on August 24, 1934, under the Trade Agreements Act of June 12, 1934.[7] It went into effect on September 3. This was the first agreement to be negotiated under the Trade Agreements Act. While a preferential tariff system had already existed between Cuba and the United States—a preference which by stipulation was confined to these two nations only and not to be extended to others through the most-favored nation clause—the new trade pact carried these arrangements further.

The good neighbor policy in Haiti

When President Roosevelt came to office Haiti was the only Caribbean country still under control of United States marines. Pan Americanism on the intervention model in that country was carried to an extreme not known in the others in that region. The United States had maintained marines there since 1915, had supervised public finances, controlled customs revenues, and organized a native police force under the command of United States marine officers. Here was the acid test of Mr. Roosevelt's new policy of the good neighbor. By an executive agreement of August 7, 1933,[8] American marines were to be withdrawn by the end of October, 1934, and Haitian officers were promptly to replace American officers in the *Garde d'Haiti*.[9] Financial control to insure the servicing of

---

[6]Department of State, Press Releases, June 9 and 16, 1934.

[7]See Chapter XXXV.

[8]Agreement between the United States of America and Haiti, signed August 7, 1933, Executive Agreement Series, No. 46.

[9]President Roosevelt paid a brief visit to Haiti in July, 1934. As a gesture of good will the President agreed to the evacuation of Haiti by our marines in August instead of October. Cf. Agreement between the United States of America and Haiti, Modifying the Agreement of August 7, 1933, signed July 24, 1934. Executive Agreement Series, No. 68.

Haiti's external funded debt, was not relinquished. This was to remain until 1952 as provided under the terms of an agreement by which Haiti had secured a loan in 1922.

Haiti regains control over her finances

If military occupation was to go under the good neighbor policy of the Roosevelt Administration, why should financial control of Haiti remain? This was the argument of President Sténio Vincent of Haiti. On April 17, 1934, President Roosevelt and President Vincent, who had come to Washington to free his country of dollar diplomacy, announced that they had discussed a new form of financial administration.[10] By an agreement concluded on the 28th, with the approval of the State Department, the National City Bank of New York—which had floated the 1922 loan—was to sell the Bank of Haiti to the Haitian government. The supervision of the government's finances, hitherto exercised by American officials, was likewise to be transferred to the Haitian government.[11] When the Haitian National Assembly ratified the agreement, direct control of Haitian finances by American interests came to an end, and with it was liquidated a source of ill feeling against the United States.[12]

The good neighbor policy modifies the non-recognition doctrine

The device of refusal of diplomatic recognition, as a weapon to discourage and suppress revolutions, was explicitly agreed to by the five Central American countries themselves in the Additional Convention to the General Treaty of Peace and Amity signed at the Central American Conference held in Washington in 1907.[13] Sixteen years later the same body continued and strengthened the nonrecognition policy to be applied against governments coming into power as a consequence of revolution or a *coup d'état*. While the United States was not a party

[10]Department of State, Press Release, April 17, 1934.

[11]On July 9, 1935, the Bank of Haiti was transferred to the Haitian government under stipulations designed to protect the interests of the bondholders.

[12]Papers Relating to the Foreign Relations of the United States, 1907, part 2, 696. See *infra*, pp. 560–562.

[13]*Ibid.*

to these agreements, she nevertheless applied and interpreted the principles contained therein whenever recognition of a Central American government was involved. When, in December, 1931, General Maximiliano Martinez, the Minister of War, became President of El Salvador, following a *coup d'état*, our government refused to recognize the *de facto* government of that country. The Martinez régime desired to regularize its existence and in December of 1932 served notice of its intention to denounce the 1923 agreement. Costa Rica took similar action and extended recognition to the Martinez régime. Guatemala, Nicaragua, and Honduras followed the same course on January 25, 1934. On the following day, the United States joined the four Central American countries by recognizing the Martinez régime.[14] The justification for our action was that since the 1923 treaty was no longer operative as to El Salvador there was no longer any purpose in adhering to a policy which arose out of a treaty now defunct. Thus consistency served a double purpose; it permitted recognition which in turn served to strengthen the policy of the good neighbor.

The treaty of March 2, 1936, modifies our relations with Panama

The desire for improving relations with Panama was manifested by a series of agreements signed on March 2, 1936, designed to eliminate the friction and discord which for many years had clouded our relations with the Isthmian Republic. By the Canal Treaty negotiated in 1903 the United States guaranteed the independence of Panama and reserved the right to intervene to preserve order.[15] To the Panamanians this agreement constituted an infringement of their sovereignty and an injury to their dignity. The general treaty of March 2, 1936, modified and reinterpreted certain provisions of the 1903 treaty, and the supplementary conventions dealt with radio rights, communications, and construction of a highway

[14]Department of State, Press Release, January 27, 1934.

[15]William M. Malloy, *Treaties*, vol. 2, p. 1349.

across the Isthmus. By the general treaty of March 2, 1936, the United States renounced the right to intervene to maintain the defense of the Canal as well as the right to acquire, by the exercise of the right of eminent domain, lands or properties in or near the cities of Panama and Colon, and substituted the obligation of joint coöperation and responsibility for the protection of their common interests. The United States also agreed to pay the Canal rental, amounting to $250,000 a year, in Panama currency at the old gold-dollar rate of exchange instead of basing the rental, as the Treasury Department had previously proposed, upon the devalued United States currency.

The Senate delays ratification

The Senate Committee on Foreign Relations held hearings on the treaty in executive session. Japan's withdrawal from the London Naval Conference preceding the negotiation of the agreements with Panama caused some anxiety on the part of military and naval officials as to whether or not modifications of the 1903 treaty should be approved; they feared that changes in the *status quo* in the Canal Zone at this time might prove injurious to the defense of the Canal. In April, 1936, consideration of the treaty was suspended,[16] and not until July 25, 1939, did the Senate give its advice and consent to ratification. Meanwhile, Panama had ratified it along with the three conventions on December 24, 1936. Thus the Roosevelt Administration gave further evidence of its desire to liquidate the policy of intervention in the affairs of Latin-American states.

These concrete demonstrations of neighborliness were based on a mixture of self-interest and idealism. The policy of the good neighbor found favor with the American public, and inspired confidence in the Latin-American governments. Yet the twenty Latin-American republics were not unmindful that the good neighbor, by whatever

[16]For text of treaty see *Congressional Record*, 76th Congress, First Session, July 24, 1939, p. 1.

idealism it was motivated, still remained the most powerful of all the republics. Nor were they unmindful of the economic motives by which the new policy was in part inspired. There was a considerable difference in the response which the individual Latin-American states indicated they would make to the proposal for closer inter-American coöperation. The smaller nations, particularly those of Central America and the Caribbean, which had experienced intervention by the United States, realized that they were not strong enough to stand alone in a world where the weak are the ready prey of ambitious dictators bent on conquest. To these, the shadow of the Colossus of the North afforded some comfort. There were other states, however, such as Argentina, Chile, Colombia, Mexico, Peru, and Uruguay, which, at this time, felt themselves strong enough to stand alone and which were neither ready nor willing to give up their political and economic ties with Europe in favor of closer relations with the United States.

Latin-American nations respond to good neighbor policy

President Roosevelt suggests conference of Latin-American states

On January 30, 1936, President Roosevelt addressed letters to the heads of the twenty Latin-American republics declaring that the signatures of Bolivia and Paraguay[17] to the Chaco peace protocol of June 12, 1935, afforded a favorable opportunity for all to consider further their joint responsibility and their common need to prevent conflicts and to promote the cause of permanent peace "on this Western Continent." He suggested that a conference meet at Buenos Aires to consider whether the peace of the Americas might be best safeguarded, (1) by "prompt ratification of all the inter-American peace instruments already negotiated"; (2) by "amend-

[17]While fighting had ceased in 1935, the century-old quarrel between the two nations over the Chaco region was not settled until October 10, 1938, when an arbitration commission, consisting of members from Argentina, Brazil, Chile, Peru, the United States, and Uruguay, announced the boundary settlement which, by the agreement of the two governments signed at Buenos Aires on the 21st of July, 1938, was to be final.

ment of existing peace instruments in such manner as experience has demonstrated to be most necessary"; or, (3) "perhaps through the creation by common accord of new instruments of peace additional to those already formulated."[18] This was not to be a rival of the League of Nations, for if the conference was fruitful, its work, the President declared, "would supplement and reinforce the efforts of the League of Nations and of all other existing or future agencies in seeking to prevent war."[19]

Expansion of German, Italian, and Japanese influence creates anxiety

There were a number of reasons motivating the President to call the conference at this time. The good neighbor policy had borne friendly fruit; suspicion on the part of the Latin-American states had been allayed, and resentment was vanishing in the face of concrete demonstrations of sincerity on the part of the good neighbor of the North. Against this background a conference such as the President had in mind might further and strengthen the interests of the United States which were threatened from various directions. The rapid expansion of German, Italian, and Japanese influence, while then primarily economic in character, was not without serious political implications to the democratic powers, particularly to our own country. There were disturbing signs of the inroads Germany was making into Latin-American trade at the expense of the United States by the use of the *Aski* mark system[20] and direct export subsidies. In 1936 Germany displaced us in Brazil and Chile as the chief source of imports, a position held by us since the World War. Japan, while a relatively minor factor in Latin-American trade, had also made large gains. In the year 1929 she supplied 0.5 per cent of the total Latin-American

---

[18]Department of State, Press Release, February 15, 1936.

[19]*Ibid.*

[20]*Aski* marks are used by German importers to pay exporters for specified goods shipped to Germany and can be used only to purchase certain German products. Cf. H. Gerald Smith, "German Trade Competition in Latin America," *Commercial Pan-American*, October, 1936.

imports; in 1936, she supplied 2.2 per cent.[21] There were also definite signs that Europe was drifting into war, a development creating the need for closer inter-American coöperation to insure the security of the Western hemisphere for the defense of its neutral rights. There was a fear even that the totalitarian fascist dictatorships might, if thwarted in Europe and Africa, turn to South America for territorial expansion.

Conference convenes at Buenos Aires

The President's suggestion was unanimously approved by the heads of the twenty Latin-American nations, and after ten months of preparatory work, the Inter-American Conference for the Maintenance of Peace convened in Buenos Aires on December 1, 1936. This was an extraordinary conference in that it took place between two regularly planned International Conferences of American States—the one that met in Montevideo in 1933, and the one scheduled to be held in Lima in 1938. President Roosevelt journeyed to Buenos Aires on the cruiser *Indianapolis* to participate in the opening ceremonies.

President Roosevelt attends

The ovation he received upon arrival was described as "the largest and most jubilant" ever given to anyone in Argentina.[22] He opened the Conference with an appeal to the republics of the New World to help the Old World avert the impending catastrophe:

> You who assemble today carry with you in your deliberations the hopes of millions of human beings in other less fortunate lands. Beyond the ocean we see continents rent asunder by old hatreds and new fanaticism. We hear the demand that injustice and inequality be corrected by resorting to the sword and not by resorting to reason and peaceful justice. We hear the cry that new markets can be achieved only through conquest. We read that the sanctity of treaties between nations is disregarded.
>
> We know, too, that the vast armaments are rising on every side and that the work of creating them employs men and

[21]Cf. Latin-American Trade Statistics: League of Nations, *Review of World Trade*, 1935 and 1936.

[22]New York *Times*, December 1, 1936.

women by the millions. It is natural, however, for us to conclude that such employment is fake employment, that it builds no permanent structures and creates no consumers goods for the maintenance of lasting prosperity. We know that nations guilty of these follies inevitably face the day either when their weapons of destruction must be used against their neighbors or when an unsound economy like a house of cards will fall apart.

In either case, even though the Americas become involved in no war, we must suffer too. The madness of a great war in other parts of the world would affect us and threaten our good in a hundred ways. And the economic collapse of any nation or nations must of necessity harm our own prosperity.[23]

President Roosevelt stresses common action against aggressors

The President was convinced that peace in the Western World could best be maintained through the processes of constitutional democratic government. "In our determination to live at peace among ourselves," he declared, "we in the Americas make it at the same time clear that we stand shoulder to shoulder in our final determinations that others who, driven by war madness or land hunger might seek to commit acts of aggression against us, will find a hemisphere wholly prepared to consult together for our mutual safety and our mutual good." He affirmed his faith in democracy as a way of life. "If we in our generation can continue its successful application in the Americas," he said, "it will spread and supersede other methods by which men are governed and which seem to most of us to run counter to our ideals of human liberty and human progress."

To the Latin Americans the reference by Mr. Roosevelt to common action against aggressors was of particular significance. They wondered whether Mr. Roosevelt had in mind making the unilateral Monroe Doctrine the common possession of all the American republics. When at the Santiago Conference in 1923, and again in 1928 at the Havana Conference, a number of the Latin-American nations had sought to secure a redefinition of

[23]Department of State, Press Release, November 30, 1936.

the Monroe Doctrine, the United States had frowned on the idea. Was the United States, through the person of her President, proposing to Pan-Americanize the Monroe Doctrine?

Latin-American nations agree to consult in the event peace is menaced

The extent to which the President's reference to common action against aggressors found expression in treaty form may be seen from the Convention for the Maintenance, Preservation, and Re-establishment of Peace, the most significant agreement adopted at the Buenos Aires Conference.[24] Article I deals in general terms with the situation arising "in the event that the peace of the American Republics is menaced . . . any of the Governments of the American Republics . . . shall consult with the other Governments of the American Republics . . . for the purpose of finding and adopting methods of peaceful coöperation." At the Conference, Brazil—with the support of the United States—sought to secure the inclusion in the treaty text of the language of the original message of President Monroe in 1823 and a reference to the possible interposition of a non-American power in any American country. But to include such language in the treaty, it was felt by Argentina, would be interpreted as a challenge to Europe. Hence it was omitted.

Article 2 of the Convention for the Maintenance, Preservation, and Re-establishment of Peace is broader than the Monroe Doctrine. "In the event of war, or a virtual state of war between American States, the Governments of the American Republics represented at this Conference shall undertake without delay the necessary mutual consultations, in order to exchange views and to seek . . . a method of peaceful collaboration; and,

[24]The texts of the agreements adopted at the Conference are to be found in Inter-American Conference for the Maintenance of Peace, *Report on the Proceedings of the Conference, submitted to the Governing Board of the Pan-American Union by the Director General* (Washington, Pan-American Union, February, 1937).

in the event of an international war outside America which might menace the peace of the American Republics, such consultation shall also take place to determine the proper time and manner in which the signatory states, if they so desire, may eventually coöperate in some action tending to preserve the peace of the American Continent." Two eventualities are contemplated under this article: (1) a war between American states, and (2) an international war outside America. In the first eventuality, there is an obligation to consult for the purpose of finding and adopting methods of peaceful coöperation within the terms of the Pact of Paris of 1928 and the Treaty of Non-Aggression and Conciliation of 1933. In the second eventuality, i.e., a war outside America, the language is non-committal, and guarded. Yet the agreement to consult on coöperative measures constitutes a step forward in "continentalizing" the Monroe Doctrine and constitutes an important contribution to the peace machinery of this hemisphere. What the signatories will do with this convention when the occasion arises to apply it, it is difficult to say.

Intervention becomes inadmissible

The smaller American States were wary about a collective agreement to consult. At conference tables big powers have a way of dominating and influencing little ones, not always to their benefit. In adopting the Additional Protocol Relative to Non-Intervention the Buenos Aires Conference went a long way to allay such fears. Article 1 of the Additional Protocol provides that "The High Contracting Parties declare inadmissible the intervention of any one of them, directly or indirectly, and for whatever reason, in the internal or external affairs of any other of the Parties." The second paragraph of this Article provides that "The violation of the provisions of this Article shall give rise to mutual consultation, with the object of exchanging views and seeking methods of peaceful adjustment." Thus intervention by one nation is made the collective concern of all the others and sets up the procedure of consultation to find a peaceful solution. The United States accepted this Additional Protocol without reservations.

The United States attitude on intervention undergoes a change

America's attitude on this subject had undergone a significant change since 1933. At the Seventh Pan-American conference at Montevideo in 1933, when the question was debated in connection with a convention[25] on the rights and duties of states, the American delegation sought to avoid discussion of the subject and suggested the appointment of a committee of jurists to consider and define the terms. But the Latin-American states, particularly those which had experienced intervention, were opposed to this course. As the debate proceeded in Montevideo, with one delegation after another condemning intervention, Secretary Hull rose and declared: "I feel safe in undertaking to say that under our support of the general principle of non-intervention as has been suggested, no government need fear any intervention on the part of the United States under the Roosevelt Administration." Three years later, the qualification "under the Roosevelt Administration" disappeared.

Of equal importance to the United States, was the subject of furthering trade relations through the trade agreements program.[26] The world depression affected the economic position of the Latin-American states and led them to resort to tariff increases, exchange controls, import quotas, clearing agreements, and multiple tariffs.[27] At Montevideo, Mr. Hull sought closer economic coöperation through lower tariff barriers and acceptance of the principle of equal treatment as the basis of commercial policy. But the divergent views and policies of the

[25]Article 8 of that convention is as follows: No state has the right to intervene in the internal or external affairs of another.

[26]See Chapter XXXV.

[27]Cf. Henry Chalmers, "Foreign Tariffs and Commercial Policies in Latin America during 1935," *Bulletin of the Pan-American Union, May, 1936.*

nations, based on different economic needs, led the Seventh Pan-American Conference to adopt Mr. Hull's resolution as merely a pious hope upon which to build. At Buenos Aires our delegation proposed two resolutions dealing with the abolition or reduction of trade barriers and with the principle of equality of treatment. But the aims sought by these resolutions were not in line with the practices of the leading Latin-American states. The resolutions were passed, however, with a qualification that the signatories should adopt the policies "to the extent that the several national economies permit."

Trade practices of Latin-American states stand in way of principle of equality of treatment

The Convention to Coördinate, Extend, and Assure the Fulfillment of Existing Treaties Between the American States, another product of the Conference, was based on a draft convention prepared by the United States delegation. The draft convention contemplated the creation of a "Permanent Inter-American Consultative Committee," to be made up of the Foreign Ministers of the American republics whose duty it would be to assist states in the observance of treaty obligations and to collaborate on ways and means of preventing conflicts. The body was to meet at regular intervals to exchange information and views concerning action to be taken in pursuance of the neutrality provisions of the treaty. To the Argentine delegation the proposal of the United States to set up a Consultative Committee was objectionable because it saw in it a "political organization" of the continent under the primacy of the United States, as well as an attempt to set up an American League of Nations as a rival to the one at Geneva. As a result of the objections raised by Argentina and others the proposal was dropped and in its stead was substituted the obligation to consult without reference to any consultative body.

Argentina thwarts proposal of the United States to set up consultative body

The provisions of the Convention to Coördinate, Extend, and Assure the Fulfillment of the Existing Treaties dealing with the machinery of peace recited five major treaties already in existence: The Gondra Treaty of 1923, a product of the fifth Pan-American Conference held in Santiago, which provided for the submission of controversies to commissions of inquiry; the Pact of Paris of 1928, sometimes referred to as the Kellogg-Briand Pact on the outlawry of war; the Inter-American Conciliation Convention of 1929, which empowered the *ad hoc* commissions of inquiry to undertake conciliation as well as investigation of controversies; the Inter-American Arbitration Treaty of 1929, which called for compulsory arbitration for the settlement of legal disputes; and the Argentine Anti-War Pact of 1933, which, *inter alia*, condemned wars of aggression and pledged the parties thereto not to recognize territorial changes brought about by other than pacific means.[28] The signatories pledged themselves to adhere to these five existing treaties dealing with the machinery of peace.

The Latin-American states pledge themselves to adhere to the existing peace machinery

The Latin-American states decline to follow proposal of the United States delegation on common policy of neutrality

In addition, the Convention to Coördinate, Extend, and Assure the Fulfillment of the Existing Treaties embodied provisions looking to the adoption of a common policy of neutrality in the event the peace machinery failed. Here again the Conference refused to follow the proposals submitted by the United States delegation. The United States sought an agreement which in essence would embody the principles of her own neutrality legislation,[29] i.e., an embargo on lethal weapons and loans, leaving the neutrals free to extend the embargo on trade in a manner and to an extent consonant with their domestic policies. As finally adopted, the Convention reduced the proposal of the United States to a recognition that in the event of war, the contracting parties will consult and adopt "in their character as neutrals a common and solidary attitude, in order to discourage or prevent the

[28]For texts, see U. S. Department of State, Treaty Series Nos. 752, 780, 886, 887 and 906.

[29]See Chapter XXXIX.

spread or prolongation of hostilities." It left the signatories free to impose embargoes on war materials and loans and other financial help and permitted states members of the League of Nations to fulfill their obligations under the Covenant.

Conference adopts measures to promote closer cultural relations

The Conference also took measures to promote closer intellectual and cultural relations between the American states. Five conventions and twenty-seven resolutions were reported to the Conference by the Committee on Intellectual Coöperation. The most significant of the agreements dealing with educational measures was the Convention for the Promotion of Inter-American Cultural Relations providing for the interchange annually of professors and students among the twenty-one nations. To further "moral disarmament" the Conference adopted the Convention Concerning Peaceful Orientation of Public Instruction wherein the signatories agree "to organize, in their public educational establishments, the teaching of the principles of pacific settlement of international disputes and the renunciation of war as an instrument of national policy, as well as the practical applications of these policies." Our delegation, however, did not sign this Convention on the ground that the matter of education lies largely outside the sphere of activities of the Federal Government.

United front lacking at Conference

The success of an international conference cannot be judged by output alone. International engagements mean much or little, depending upon the will of the parties, the circumstances which brought them into being, and the circumstances which exist when they are to be applied. At Buenos Aires there was no united front of the nations gathered there. The United States sought a stronger regional grouping of the American states, but met resistance, particularly on the part of Argentina, and a warm response on the part of Brazil. The explanation for the attitudes of these two nations towards the United

States is in the main economic. While the United States is Brazil's best customer for coffee, she is Argentina's competitor in meat and grains and has shut her products out of the United States market by the Hawley-Smoot tariff of 1930. Latin-American trade, like trade generally, is a two-way street and the architects of our tariff barriers forgot this principle in giving way to domestic pressure groups.

Democracy everywhere on defensive

When the Buenos Aires Conference met, democracy everywhere was on the defensive. In South America, where representative government has had a chequered career at best in its struggle to supplant military dictatorship, the growing Fascist and Nazi economic penetration was causing us concern lest it be followed by political penetration. Democracy in South America too was yielding ground in the face of a shattered economic structure creating social unrest and a crop of military revolts. Hardly a nation south of Panama had escaped serious political or military uprisings since 1930. The fall in the price of coffee, nitrates, tin, copper, and other staple products of these republics resulted in mass unemployment, numerous bankruptcies, and general discontent, out of which Fascism made its appearance. It was not without significance that the President, on his visit to South America, should have appealed to his listeners to "maintain and defend the democratic form of constitutional government" and that the Conference should have stressed democracy as the condition of amicable relations among nations. In his closing address to the Conference, Secretary Hull stated that the American republics "have undertaken to assume a common and solidary attitude toward an attack from abroad."[30]

This reference to "an attack from abroad" was not a fanciful idea on the part of the Secretary of State and

[30]Department of State, *Report of the Delegation of the United States of America to the Inter-American Conference for the Maintenance of Peace,* Buenos Aires, Argentina, December 1–23, 1936, p. 94.

was not made for the purpose of frightening the delegates who heard him. Obviously the delegates from the South American republics understood the full import of Mr. Hull's words. The Roosevelt administration saw in the growing fascist penetrations in South America not only a German and Italian threat to the form of government of the Latin-American states, but the undermining of our influence in that region as well. The course of events in Europe which impelled President Monroe to make his declaration to Congress on December 2, 1823, was not unlike that which prompted Mr. Hull to rally the Latin-American states to the defense of this hemisphere. Said President Monroe: "The political system of the Allied Powers is essentially different . . . from that of America. This difference proceeds from that which exists in their respective governments. . . . It is impossible that the Allied Powers should extend their political system to any portion of either continent without endangering our peace and happiness; nor could anyone believe that our southern brothers, if left to themselves, would adopt it of their own accord. It is equally impossible, therefore, that we should behold such interposition, in any form, with indifference. . . ." President Monroe's declaration was a warning to a reactionary alliance of absolutist powers, unilateral in character and designed to protect the newborn democratic régimes of Latin America, as well as our own. Mr. Hull's statement, predicated on the Convention for the Maintenance, Preservation, and Re-establishment of Peace, "continentalized" the Monroe Doctrine in warning the European dictators that "in the event that the peace of the American Republics is menaced" the American Republics will meet the menace by collective action, since "the national security of each individual American republic has become the common interest of all."[31]

Secretary Hull warns that American republics will act collectively against attack from abroad

[31] *Ibid.*, p. 95.

On May 26, 1937, President Roosevelt submitted to the Senate for its advice and consent the following instruments signed at the Inter-American Conference for the Maintenance of Peace at Buenos Aires in December, 1936:

1. Convention for the Maintenance, Preservation, and Reestablishment of Peace.
2. Inter-American Treaty on Good Offices and Mediation.
3. Additional Protocol Relative to Non-Intervention.
4. Convention to Coördinate, Extend, and Assure the Fulfillment of the Existing Treaties between the American States.
5. Treaty on the Prevention of Controversies.
6. Convention on the Pan-American Highway.
7. Convention Concerning Artistic Exhibitions.
8. Convention for the Promotion of Inter-American Cultural Relations.

The Senate, acting with great dispatch and without a record vote, advised ratification[32] on June 29, 1937, thus making the United States one of the first signatories to ratify the agreements and "thereby giving a further indication of the sincerity of the good neighbor policy,"[33] as the President urged when he sent the treaties to the Senate.

The United States proposes to lease war vessels to Brazil

There was at this time in Washington a disposition to press further the policy of the good neighbor toward the Latin-American states. As a step in the direction of "collective action" Senator Walsh of the Senate Committee on Naval Affairs introduced, at the request of Secretary Hull, a joint resolution giving the President power to lease over-age and decommissioned naval vessels to Latin-American states. The immediate object of this legislation was to lease six decommissioned destroyers to Brazil, and the underlying reasons were the critical events in Europe and the possible threat to South America from the totalitarian powers. In his letter to Senator Walsh, the Secretary of State wrote:

[32] *Congressional Record*, 75th Congress, First Session, pp. 8420–8435.
[33] Department of State, Press Release, May 26, 1937.

Recently the government of Brazil has informed this government of its increasing concern with certain tendencies of the world political situation. The desire on the part of some nations for access to raw materials and the forceful action taken by those nations to consummate these desires have made Brazil, a country of vast territory and relatively small population, particularly apprehensive. The government, therefore, has thought it the part of prudence to improve its relatively modest national defense, but, being deficient in trained military or naval personnel and equipment, it finds its task a considerable one.

With respect to naval defense, the Brazilian government is constructing certain vessels and purchasing others abroad. Upon the construction or delivery of these vessels, the government will be the possessor of what it considers to be necessary naval material, but, unless steps are taken meanwhile, there will be a dearth of trained personnel to operate its ships. In order to remedy this deficiency the government of Brazil has inquired whether the government of the United States would be disposed to lease six of its decommissioned destroyers until its own vessels are ready.[34]

Argentina objects to proposal

The proposal was not favorably received. Here in the United States the move was characterized as a step in encouraging armament competition among the South American countries. Germany believed the move was designed to check her trade and influence in Brazil.[35] Argentina, Brazil's rival for South American leadership, raised strong objections and requested that the proposed leases be held in abeyance pending consultation with the other South American nations. In apparent embarrassment the United States and Brazil, in a joint statement,[36] sought to explain that "The proposal [the leasing of destroyers] envisaged, of course, merely the offer of a neighborly service to such of the other American nations as might desire it, and in this way to promote understanding, friendliness, and mutually beneficial relationships between all of the American nations." The two governments were not disposed "to encourage inter-

[34] *Congressional Record*, 75th Congress, First Session, p. 11219.

[35] New York *Times*, August 11, 1937.

[36] Department of State, Press Release, August 20, 1937.

national controversy relative to some entirely minor and temporary phase of that [good neighbor] policy," nor "to modify their understanding" with regard to the pending proposal. Congress adjourned without acting on the joint resolution, and the likelihood that the succeeding Congress would act was dissipated when, on November 10, 1937, President Getulio Vargas of Brazil assumed dictatorial powers by abolishing the Constitution adopted in 1934 and the national, state, and municipal legislatures. A "corporative" state was proclaimed by the new Constitution, giving sanction to the "Leader" principle, and lodging in him the supreme authority in the state.

The Vargas coup creates uneasiness

The Vargas coup came shortly after Italy had adhered to the German-Japanese anti-Comintern Pact, which strengthened the camp of the fascist powers. It was a significant portent. Was the Vargas régime modeled on the German or Italian pattern? Or was it just one of those caricatures of the European types, possessing the labels but not the content of fascist totalitarianism? Was Brazil, a country with an area larger than the United States and a population of 47,000,000, to join the ranks of fascism, taking other Latin-American states with her? Perhaps this was only an old line of *caudillo* dictatorship of the type common among our southern neighbors, and not unlike the dictatorships of Diaz of Mexico, Cabrera of Guatemala, and Gomez of Venezuela, each of which enjoyed close and friendly relations with the United States. At any rate there was widespread fear in the United States that an alliance between a South American dictatorship and a European fascist state was not beyond the realm of possibility. The Under-Secretary of State, Mr. Sumner Welles, chided the American press for misinterpreting what had happened in Brazil and for passing judgment "upon what our American neighbors are doing within the realm of their strictly domestic affairs." In the same address he warned those with designs upon South America by saying:

> Any attempt on the part of non-American powers to exert through force their political or material influence on the American continent would be immediately a matter of the gravest concern not only to the United States but to every other American republic as well, and appropriate action would undoubtedly at once be determined upon as the result of common consultation between them.[37]

Relations between the United States and Mexico a test of good neighbor policy

To judge and test the policy of the United States towards her neighbors, Latin-American States keep a close watch upon Mexican relations with the United States. Nowhere has the policy of the good neighbor been so subjected to strain as with Mexico. The revolution of 1910, with the slogan "Mexico for the Mexicans," under the leadership of the National Revolutionary Party whose founders ousted Diaz, has had an uneven course. The National Revolutionary Party sought an end of foreign influence and interests in Mexico, expropriation of big landed estates, and their redistribution to small village commonwealths (*ejidos*). It sought to remove the social and political influence of the Catholic Church in the affairs of the nation, to broaden suffrage, and to establish a free public school system. Because of civil strife, political chaos, and betrayal on the part of some of its leaders, the program of reform remained but partially executed. Under Plutarco Elias Calles, leader of the National Revolutionary Party, who became President in 1924 on a platform to continue the work of the revolution, the program of radical reform was slowed down for a program of collaboration with foreign capital, more particularly with American interests after the appointment of Dwight Morrow as United States Ambassador in 1927. Calles relinquished his office as President in 1928, but continued to be the most powerful

[37] Department of State, Press Release, December 6, 1937.

person in Mexico until 1934, when, as president-maker, he designated Lázaro Cárdenas for the office.

Cárdenas carries forward the revolution

The disciple was more sincere about revolutionary reform than his master and the political bosses who helped him to obtain power. Soon after Cárdenas became President—December 1, 1934—he began in earnest the execution of the six-year plan of the National Revolutionary Party to set up a "coöperative system toward socialism"—a program of reform embodied in the platform on which he was elected.[38] The plan, among other things, called for the establishment of two thousand rural schools, twelve hundred new libraries, children's parks, and technological institutions. This nation was little aware of the far-reaching social and economic transformation that went on in Mexico during the first four years of the Cárdenas régime until the news of the expropriation of the properties of British and American oil companies on March 18, 1938, burst upon the world. For two decades the Mexican government, in execution of its agrarian reforms, had been expropriating farm lands belonging to American citizens, promising compensation to the owners. Not a single claim had been adjusted and none had been paid, according to our State Department, notwithstanding the repeated requests of our Government for settlement.[39] On June 24, 1937, the Mexican government nationalized the railroads,[40] which had a bonded indebtedness of some $240,000,000 already in default, two-thirds of which was held by British and American nationals. Here, as in the case of land, the Government promised to compensate the owners, but no compensation has thus far been forthcoming.

---

[38]Cárdenas got rid of all Calles adherents in his Cabinet, and after Calles had retired from public life caused him to leave Mexico.

[39]Department of State, Press Release, July 21, 1938.

[40]Gilberto Bosques, *The National Revolutionary Party of Mexico and the Six-Year Plan*, pp. 323–325, 340.

Washington anxious about expropriation

Under the Cárdenas Administration, the socialization of Mexico's economy proceeded at a much faster tempo than under previous administrations. Official Washington was not disposed to intervene in the affairs of Mexico, but it watched developments south of the Rio Grande with anxiety. In a note[41] addressed to the Mexican government relative to compensation for the expropriation of agrarian properties of our citizens, this Government stated it was "entirely sympathetic to the desires of the Mexican government for the social betterment of its people," but felt that it could not accept the idea of social reform carried forward at the expense of American citizens, any more than the American government would feel justified in carrying forward its plans for social betterment at the expense of Mexican citizens.

Mexico expropriates British and American oil companies

The economic program of "Mexico for Mexicans" was extended on March 18, 1938, to four British and thirteen American oil companies. On that day President Cárdenas announced that the Mexican government would take over the oil properties, and by a decree of the 19th of March the properties of the seventeen companies were declared expropriated for "public utility."[42] Payment was to be made to the companies within ten years from a percentage—to be determined later—of the petroleum and by-products taken from the expropriated wells, such payment to be figured on the basis of the taxable value of the properties taken. The immediate occasion for the expropriation was an award made to the oil workers by the Board of Arbitration and Conciliation increasing wages and granting benefits, which the oil companies contended would bankrupt them if they abided by the award; the real reason for the expropriation may be said to be Mexico's desire to carry forward the social revolution, *inter alia*, by wresting control and ownership

Payment promised

[41]Department of State, Press Release, July 21, 1938.

[42]*Diario Oficial*, March 19, 1938.

of the industry from the foreign companies and doing away with foreign exploitation.

Expropriation a severe test of good neighbor policy

How far the policy of the good neighbor had carried the United States in her relations with Latin-American states generally, and Mexico particularly, can be gathered from the attitude of our State Department toward Mexican oil expropriation. A generation ago so direct a challenge to American interests by a Latin-American country would have meant intervention; in 1938, intervention was unthinkable without destroying the fabric of Inter-American solidarity the Roosevelt administration had been striving to build.[43] Pressed by the American oil companies who charged that their rights under Mexican law had been violated to an extent making the expropriation a denial of justice in international law, Secretary Hull dispatched a note of protest on March 27. In a public statement on March 30, he said:

> This government has not undertaken and does not undertake to question the right of the Government of Mexico in the exercise of its sovereign power to expropriate properties within its jurisdiction. This government has, however, on numerous occasions and in the most friendly manner pointed out to the Government of Mexico that in accordance with every principle of international law, of comity between nations and of equity, the properties of its nationals so expropriated are required to be paid for by compensation representing fair, assured, and effective value to the nationals from whom these properties were taken.[44]

Secretary Hull hopes for equitable solution

The expropriation of the oil properties belonging to American citizens, the Secretary of State said, was but one incident in a long series of incidents of this character and accordingly raised no new question, and it was his hope that an equitable solution would soon be found by the Mexican government.

---

[43]The British government's reaction to the Mexican government's expropriation of oil properties was violent and brought on a rupture of diplomatic relations.

[44]Department of State, Press Release, April 2, 1938.

Mexico's reply, dated March 31, and signed by President Cárdenas himself, stated that the attitude of President Roosevelt and the people of the United States had won the esteem of the Mexican people. The note assured the American government that "Mexico will know how to honor its obligations of today and its obligations of yesterday." While the exchange of notes served to clear the air and to place Mexico on record with respect to compensation there was grave doubt whether she could make immediate payment. In fact, her capacity for deferred payment on any scale likely to satisfy the oil companies was regarded with considerable scepticism. The policy of the good neighbor did not permit of the use of diplomatic pressure nor of economic coercion. Friendship of Latin-American nations, in the light of the world situation, dictated a course of conduct which would avoid hostile reaction. Negotiations between the two governments on a settlement of the oil question are still going on at the present writing. The difficulties in the way of an equitable solution are enormous. There is a wide difference of opinion as to the value of the property taken and grave doubts as to whether the Mexican government, in the present state of the nation's economy, can find the means to pay. The boycott instituted by American and British oil companies has forced the Mexican government, pressed for revenue, to find a market for Mexican oil in Germany and Italy; this has not helped Mexico's financial position.

Mexico lacks capacity to make immediate payment

The American government's note of July 21, 1938, to the Mexican government, while dealing with agrarian expropriation, pointed to a possible future course of United States policy with respect to the expropriated oil properties. It demanded effective compensation to the owners and proposed arbitration, pursuant to the provisions of the General Treaty of Arbitration of January 5, 1929, of "the question whether there has been compliance by the Gov-

The United States proposes arbitration

ernment of Mexico with the rule of compensation as prescribed by international law in the case of the American citizens whose farm and agrarian properties in Mexico have been expropriated . . . and if not, the amount of, and the terms under which, compensation should be made by the Government of Mexico."[45]

Eighth Pan-American Conference meets

The Lima Conference, officially entitled the Eighth International Conference of American States, met from December 9 to 27, 1938, in Lima, Peru, at a time when two dangers were threatening inter-American relations. There was the threat to the good neighbor policy arising from Mexico's expropriation policy—a policy which it was feared other Latin-American countries might be tempted to emulate; and there was the threat to inter-American coöperation and friendship from the fascist Powers. In the face of a critical world situation, with only an armistice—as one observer characterized it[46]—established by the Munich Agreement, the United States delegation to the Lima Conference aimed at developing continental solidarity against political and ideological penetration and possible armed aggression by the fascist nations.

In Europe, Fascism had gained enormous strength and prestige. General Francisco Franco, with the military

---

[45]Department of State, Press Release, July 21, 1938. In a note dated November 9, 1938 (Department of State, Press Release, November 12, 1938), Secretary of State Hull proposed that a commission composed of one representative from each of the governments fix the values of the expropriated American-owned agrarian properties, and, in the event of a disagreement, the question be referred to a third person selected by the Permanent Commission as established by the so-called Gondra Treaty of 1923. The two commissioners were to hold their first meeting in the City of Mexico on December 1, 1938, and were to complete their work on evaluation not later than May 31, 1939. On that date, the Mexican government was to pay the sum of $1,000,000 as a first payment of the indemnities to be determined, and subsequent annual payments in no event less than $1,000,000, until the total indemnity was liquidated.

The Mexican government accepted the proposals in a note to the American government dated November 12, 1938. (Department of State, Press Release, November 12, 1938.)

[46]Hamilton Fish Armstrong, "Armistice at Munich," *Foreign Affairs,* January, 1939.

aid of Germany and Italy was destroying Republican Spain. Adolf Hitler had emerged as the master of the European continent when he wrested the Sudetenland from Czechoslovakia by the Munich Agreement of September, 1938. Secretary of State Hull, in his opening address at the Lima Conference, declared that an "ominous shadow falls athwart our own continent." Stressing the fixed purpose of the American nations to oppose military or ideological invasion of the Western Hemisphere, he declared that "there must not be a shadow of a doubt anywhere as to the determination of the American nations not to permit the invasion of this hemisphere by the armed forces of any power or any possible combination of powers."[47]

Fascism gains in strength and prestige

Secretary Hull warns against invasion of the Western Hemisphere

The United States program for a stronger American front against external aggression did not propose an inter-American policy of isolation from Europe; for since culturally and economically many of the Latin-American states are more closely tied to Europe than to the United States, a policy of isolation would have been unacceptable to them. Argentina, for example, is linked culturally to Europe by her large European population and economically by her dependence on the European markets. She was not disposed to run the risk of losing her markets abroad just to please the United States. As an outstanding wheat-producing, cattle-raising and meat-exporting nation, her products are in competition with those of the United States; the quarantine and trade restrictions which we imposed upon her products was a source of ill-will and resentment. Nor did the United States seek an alliance, or an all-American defense pact; what she did desire was solidarity by strengthening the Consultative Pact signed at the Buenos Aires Conference of 1936 to make certain of concerted action in the event of a "non-

American delegation seeks solidarity of Latin-American states

[47]The text of Mr. Hull's speech is reported in the New York *Times*, December 11, 1938.

American menace." But some of the Latin-American states, notably Argentina, Paraguay, Uruguay, Chile, and Bolivia, were not disposed to follow the United States. Unanimity was an essential requisite for solidarity. What emerged from the Conference was a compromise of the conflicting aims of the various nations represented, acceptable to all. It was officially styled "the Declaration of Lima," and was the most outstanding achievement of the Eighth Pan-American Conference.

The Declaration of Lima

The preamble of the Declaration states in part "that the peoples of America have achieved spiritual unity through the similarity of their republican institutions, their unshakeable will for peace, their profound sentiment of humanity and tolerance, and through their absolute adherence to the principles of international law, of the equal sovereignty of States and of individual liberty without religious or racial prejudices." It goes on to state that "The Governments of the American States declare:

First. That they reaffirm their continental solidarity and their purpose to collaborate in the maintenance of the principles upon which the said solidarity is based.

Second. That faithful to the above-mentioned principles and to their absolute sovereignty, they reaffirm their decision to maintain them and to defend them against all foreign intervention or activity that may threaten them.

Third. And in case the peace, security, or territorial integrity of any American Republic is thus threatened by acts of any nature that may impair them, they proclaim their common concern and their determination to make effective their solidarity, coördinating their respective sovereign wills by means of the procedure of consultation, established by conventions in force and by declarations of the Inter-American Conferences, using the measures which in each case the circumstances may make advisable. It is understood that the Governments of the American Republics will act independently in their individual capacity, recognizing fully their juridical equality as sovereign states.

Fourth. That in order to facilitate the consultations established in this and other American peace instruments, the Ministers for Foreign Affairs of the American Republics, when deemed desirable and at the initiative of any one of them, will meet in their several capitals by rotation and without protocolary character. Each Government may, under special circumstances or for special reasons, designate a representative as a substitute for its Minister for Foreign Affairs."[48]

The Declaration of American Principles

The second outstanding achievement of the Lima Conference was the Declaration of American Principles. This set forth eight rules of conduct which the twenty-one American Republics pledged to observe: (1) intervention of one state in the affairs of another is inadmissible; (2) all differences of an international character should be settled by peaceful means; (3) the use of force as an instrument of national or international policy is proscribed; (4) relations between states should be governed by the precepts of international law; (5) treaties should be faithfully observed and revised by agreement of the contracting parties; (6) peaceful collaboration and intellectual interchange should be sought among the peoples of the Americas; (7) economic reconstruction as a contribution to national and international well-being as well as to peace should be fostered; and (8) international coöperation as a necessary condition to the maintenance of the aforementioned principles should be encouraged.

Conference adopts measures opposed to ideological penetration and political activities of foreigners

Of more immediate concern to the Conference than a possible armed attack, was the problem of the increasing spread of German and Italian propaganda, and the disrupting influence of minorities preserving political allegiance to their countries of origin. Here the United States was joined by Brazil, Argentina, Uruguay, and others in proclaiming determined opposition to ideological penetration. The Conference adopted a resolution on foreign minorities[49] and another on the political activities of foreigners.[50] The resolution on foreign minorities

[48]Department of State, Press Release, December 24, 1938.

[49]Pan-American Union, *Report on the Results of the Conference*, 1939, p. 61.

[50]*Ibid.*, p. 61.

declared that "residents who, according to domestic law, are considered aliens, cannot claim collectively the condition of minorities"; and that dealing with political activities of foreigners called upon the Governments of the American Republics to "consider the desirability of adopting measures prohibiting the collective exercise within their territory, by resident aliens, of political rights invested in such aliens by the laws of their respective countries."

Eighth Pan-American Conference fruitful in resolutions

While the Eighth Pan-American Conference approved over a hundred resolutions, it did not conclude a single treaty, convention, or protocol. Problems dealing with the application of sanctions, the definition of an aggressor, and the disposition of pecuniary claims, and many others, were postponed or referred back for further study. In the sense that no treaties were entered into, this Conference was perhaps not so constructive as previous ones; but if we view the Declaration of Lima as a political program on which the American republics can develop joint action for the consideration and solution of their common problems, it will have been commensurate in the affairs of nations to a hundred treaties.

Fascist victory in Europe a threat to our position in Western Hemisphere

That a victory of the fascist powers in Europe means a definite threat to the South American republics and to our position in the Western Hemisphere is fully appreciated by our government. President Roosevelt's declaration calling for "the protection of the whole American Hemisphere against invasion or control or domination by non-American nations" reflects the sentiment of the majority of the American people. South American statesmen have admitted that if their continent should be threatened by invasion, they would have to look to the United States for protection.

It has been a difficult and trying task for the United States, the most powerful nation in the Western Hemisphere, to persuade her neighbors to the south that her goal in relation with them is expansion of inter-American trade on a mutually profitable basis in an atmosphere of political coöperation, and nothing more. The good neighbor policy toward Latin America has overcome many obstacles and has brought about a change in the conception of Pan Americanism. Yet, notwithstanding all the difficulties that have been surmounted, many remain, and some of these are basic in character. The differences in language, race, and culture between Haiti and Chile, let us say, are hardly less pronounced than those between the United States and Mexico. Culturally the Latin-American nations orientate toward Europe—France and Italy as well as Spain and Portugal. Politically there is the lack of a common underlying conception of the meaning of democracy. Economically the primary issue involved for the United States in her dealings with Latin America is a frank recognition that our tariff on competitive products must be lowered before the goal of trade on a mutually profitable basis can be achieved. The idealism inherent in the good neighbor policy is not enough to compensate the Latin-American republics for the economic advantages which they secure elsewhere.

The task of the good neighbor is trying and difficult

CHAPTER XXXVII

THE "NEW ORDER" IN ASIA

Tangku truce leaves Japan in controlling position in North China

THE terms of surrender dictated by Japan in what is known as the Tangku truce was signed by the Nanking government on May 13, 1933. It marked for the time being the end of the undeclared war which Japan had conducted against China since the Mukden "incident" of September 18, 1931. By its terms China agreed to demilitarize the greater part of North China from Peiping to the Great Wall, thus tacitly abandoning the Manchurian provinces to Japan. The truce was brought about by Japanese military pressure against China in the face of the Stimson declaration of non-recognition of the fruits of aggression and the verdict of the League of Nations—whose members were neither prepared nor willing to challenge Japan's *fait accompli;*[1] it left Japan in a controlling position in North China free to exert continuous pressure on China by the ever-present threat of further invasion of her territory.

Chinese boycott drives Japan to seek markets in competitive areas

The invasion of Manchuria intensified Chinese nationalism and the Chinese economic boycott against Japan. In pursuance of her general policy of increased national industrialization, combined with a shrinking market in China, Japan sought outlets for export trade in other Asiatic and African markets, a great number of which were within the orbit of the British Empire. The British attempted to meet this competition by drastic tariff protection in regions where she exerts political influence. In India, the area of most intense Japanese-British competition, the preference given to British cotton textiles

[1]In a note dated March 27, 1933, Japan formally notified the Secretary-General of her intention to withdraw from the League of Nations.

rose from 5 per cent in 1931 to 50 per cent in 1933. As justification for this step the British pointed out the advantage afforded Japan in her depreciated *yen*, and the cheaper production costs resulting from lower wages as compared with those paid in the Lancashire mills. This and similar measures in other British dependencies aroused bitter resentment on the part of the Japanese, who were already suffering from a sense of frustration because of foreign opposition to their endeavors to expand. The more Japan was thwarted in her effort to seek markets in the rest of the world the more she was forced back upon the policy of turning East Asia into an exclusive Japanese preserve as an essential element in the solution of her economic problem.

Russia and Japan face each other along extended frontier

With the conquest of Manchuria, Soviet Russia and Japan were brought face to face along an extended frontier, intensifying Russian concern as to how far Japan intended to carry her expansionist ambitions on the mainland of Asia. As in the case of her European neighbors with whom she entered into non-aggression pacts, Russia proposed a similar pact to Japan, but the latter has steadily declined the offer, suggesting a prior settlement of existing controversies. Of these there were several—the Russian-owned Chinese Eastern Railway in "Manchukuo" (Manchuria), definition of boundaries, and Japanese fishing rights in Russian territorial waters. The Russians found themselves unable to defend the railway against the constant depredations of "bandits," which took the form of burning rolling-stock, cutting lines, robbing and kidnapping passengers, and even murdering employees of the road. Moscow suspected Japanese complicity in the activities of the "bandits." There was nothing to do but to get rid of the road on the best obtainable terms or fight to defend it, and the Russians did not want to fight. They offered the road to "Manchukuo" for 250 million gold rubles. After some eighteen months of bargaining they sold it, on January 22, 1935, for 140 million *yen* plus 35 million *yen* to be paid in compensation to dismissed Russian railway employees. By the purchase of the Chinese Eastern Railway, Japan succeeded in removing Russian influence in Manchuria and thwarting Russian ambitions for a short connection to the warm-water ports of the Pacific.

Russia sells Chinese Eastern Railway to Japan

While the controversy over Japanese fishing rights in Russian territorial waters has of recent years become a hardy perennial, its existence has served to aggravate the more serious problem of boundaries. It is a cardinal principle of the Soviet government, as it is of other governments, to maintain the integrity of its frontiers. Perhaps the Soviets express their sensitiveness about the integrity of their boundaries more forcefully than do others, for they believe that territory once under Communism should not readily be given up to capitalist exploiters. There has been considerable foundation for the Soviet fear that Japanese imperialists desired not only to drive Russia back as far into the Siberian hinterland as possible, but to wrest from her the maritime provinces of Siberia as well. Each has been concentrating troops and building vast military works in the neighborhood of their respective frontiers. Notwithstanding numerous Japanese provocations, the Soviets have succeeded in avoiding war with Japan.

Japanese aims conflict with Russian interests

On April 17, 1934, the Japanese government, through its Foreign Office spokesman in Tokyo, Mr. Eiji Amau, made what might be termed one of the most important declarations[2] of Japanese policy in regard to China. It was designed as a warning to the United States and other

[2]The following is a translation of the more important parts of the Amau statement which the Japanese Foreign Office handed the British Ambassador in Tokyo:

"Owing to the special position of Japan in her relations with China, her views and attitude respecting matters that concern China may not agree in every point with those of foreign nations; but it must be realized that Japan is called upon to exert the utmost effort in carrying out her mission and in

nations with interests in the Far East to refrain from any activities in China which the Japanese might regard as prejudicial to their own interests. The "special responsibilities in East Asia" which Japan had incurred placed upon her the primary obligation for maintaining peace and order in that region. Her "position and mission" in that area, meaning China primarily, placed upon her the duty to "act alone on her own responsibility" if that was found to be necessary, and she alone was to be the judge of what was necessary. Exploitation of China "undertaken by foreign powers, even in the name of technical or financial assistance" must cease. The

The Amau statement of Japanese policy

fulfilling her special responsibilities in East Asia. Japan has been compelled to withdraw from the League of Nations because of their failure to agree in their opinions on fundamental principles of preserving peace in East Asia. Although Japan's attitude towards China may at times differ from that of foreign countries, such difference cannot be evaded owing to Japan's position and mission.

"It goes without saying that Japan at all times is endeavoring to maintain and promote her friendly relations with foreign nations, but at the same time we consider it only natural that to keep peace and order in East Asia we must even act alone on our own responsibility, and it is our duty to perform it. At the same time there is no country but China which is in a position to share with Japan the responsibility for maintenance of peace in East Asia.

"Accordingly, unification of China, preservation of her territorial integrity, as well as restoration of order in that country, are most ardently desired by Japan. History shows that these can be attained through no other means than awakening and voluntary efforts of China herself.

"We oppose, therefore, any attempt on the part of China to avail herself of the influence of any other country in order to resist Japan; we also oppose any action taken by China calculated to play off one Power against another. Any joint operations undertaken by foreign Powers even in the name of technical or financial assistance at this particular moment after Manchurian and Shanghai incidents are bound to acquire political significance. . . .

"Japan therefore must object to such undertakings as a matter of principle, although she will not find it necessary to interfere with any foreign country negotiating individually with China on questions of finance or trade as long as such negotiations benefit China, and are not detrimental to peace in East Asia.

"However, supplying China with war aeroplanes, building aerodromes in China, and detailing military instructors or military advisers to China or contracting a loan to provide funds for political uses would obviously tend to alienate friendly relations between Japan, China, and other countries, and to disturb peace and order in Eastern Asia. Japan will oppose such projects.

"The foregoing attitude of Japan should be clear from the policies she has pursued in the past, but on account of the fact that positive movements for joint action in China by foreign Powers under one pretext or another are reported to be on foot, it was deemed not inappropriate to reiterate her policy at this time." Cf. *Parliamentary Debates,* House of Commons, vol. 288, p. 1366, April 23, 1934.

Japanese Ambassador at Washington, in explaining the Amau statement, declared that "Japan must act and decide alone what is good for China," and advised that all "legitimate foreign interests should consult Tokyo before embarking on any adventures there."[3] The declaration, sweeping in character and puzzling in the form in which it was made, aroused acute interest and concern. By it Japan gave notice that she had assumed unilaterally the role of sole arbiter of the destinies of China in disregard of the Nine-Power Treaty and the principle of the open door. While the declaration of Japan's special mission for the preservation of peace in East Asia was not a new departure, and the difference of opinion existing between her and the other interested Powers as to the conditions on which peace depended not of recent origin, the novel element was the warning to the world that the assistance which the Powers were rendering to China constituted a threat to peace. What this danger to peace was, as conceived by Japan, she did not clearly reveal; but the interpretive comments which appeared in the Japanese press indicated that she feared a rehabilitated China would be capable of resisting her mission on the continent of Asia, and that the continued economic assistance to China, particularly in the form of loans, might culminate in foreign intervention. To prevent these dangers from arising the Japanese government arrogated to itself what amounted to the right of veto over China's foreign relations.

Japan regards assistance by the Powers as threat to peace in East Asia

The immediate background and the ostensible cause which prompted this declaration related to the various plans for assistance to China. In May, 1933, the Chinese Minister of Finance arranged in Washington for a three-year, fifty million dollar wheat and cotton credit from the Reconstruction Finance Corporation. There was also

[3]Similar statements were made by Japan's official representatives in Berlin and Geneva.

discussion of a reconstruction loan to China under the auspices of the League of Nations. The United States Department of Commerce, through its Aeronautics Trade Division, had helped American aircraft firms to select a number of American aviation officers to establish training schools for Chinese pilots. In addition, our airplane manufacturers had carried on a lively business with China during this period. The China National Aviation Corporation, 45 per cent of whose stock was held by Americans and the remainder by the Chinese government, had developed an extensive air service in China.[4] Sales in airplanes—military and civil, including accessories—rose from $157,515 in 1932 to $1,762,247 in 1933.[5] For the year 1934 the figure rose to $3,778,262.[6] These were some of the activities engaged in by American firms, as well as firms of other nationals, that caused Japanese officials, who had other plans for the exploitation of the Chinese markets, great concern. Particularly distasteful to Japan was the emergence of the internal unification of China which the Western powers were encouraging and nourishing by financial and economic assistance.

Japan fears internal unification of China

The British Ambassador to Japan was the first of the plenipotentiaries of the Western powers to make a "friendly inquiry" of the Japanese Foreign Minister, on April 23, 1934, reminding him that the principle of equal rights in China was explicitly guaranteed by the Nine-Power Treaty, and that Article VII of this treaty created a duty upon each of the contracting parties to consult with the others whenever a situation arose involving the rights of the parties. Four days later, April 29, 1934, the United States, through her ambassador, took account of the Japanese declaration in a note delivered to the

Great Britain seeks explanation of Amau declaration

[4]Cf. Memorandum on American Civil Aviation in the Pacific, American Council, Institute of Pacific Relations, New York, May 4, 1934.

[5]U. S. Senate, Hearings before the Special Committee Investigating the Munitions Industry, Part 6, pp. 1465–69.

[6]Department of Commerce, *Aeronautical World News*, February 15, 1936, p. 2.

Japanese Foreign Minister.[7] The note pointed out that recent indications of Japan's attitude with reference to China, coming from sources so authoritative as to preclude their being ignored, made it necessary for the American government to reaffirm its position with regard to its rights and interests involved. The United States, the note indicated, was associated with China or with Japan or with both, together with certain other countries, in multilateral treaties relating to rights and obligations in the Far East, and in one great multilateral treaty to which practically all the countries of the world are parties. These treaties can be terminated or modified only by processes prescribed or recognized or agreed upon by the parties to them. No nation can, without the assent of the other nations concerned, rightfully endeavor to make conclusive its will in situations where there are involved the rights, obligations, and legitimate interests of other sovereign states. The American government, in its relations with other states, seeks to be considerate of the legitimate interests of other countries, and expects similar consideration from them.

The United States reminds Japan of the treaty structure relating to the Far East

The American note did not call for a reply and none was made. But the British request for an explanation of the meaning of the Amau declaration did elicit a reply from the Japanese government. According to the statement[8] made in the House of Commons by the Secretary of State for Foreign Affairs on April 30, 1934, the Japanese Foreign Minister in his reply, which has not been published, assured the British Ambassador that Japan would loyally observe the Nine-Power Treaty and that she continued to attach the greatest importance to the maintenance of the open door.[9] While the assurances given

Japan assures Great Britain

[7]Department of State, Press Release, May 5, 1934.

[8]*Parliamentary Debates*, House of Commons, vol. 289, 14, April 30, 1934.

[9]France and Italy, two other signatories to the Nine-Power Treaty, addressed notes to Japan requesting explanations and received similar assurances.

disclaimed any intention of disregarding treaties or infringing the treaty rights of others in China, there was no denial or withdrawal of the sweeping claims made in the Amau declaration.

The United States is cautious about taking lead in opposing Japan

But neither the United States nor Great Britain desired to go beyond making clear their respective positions on the designs of Japan towards China, nor was the Roosevelt administration inclined to assume leadership in opposing Japan's aims in China, as Secretary of State Stimson under the Hoover administration had done in the Manchurian crisis of 1931–1932.[10] Reluctance to take the initiative may well have been due to the disappointment the American government experienced in the Manchurian crisis when the British failed to follow our strong lead for more effective measures to check the Japanese invasion.[11] If the British government, whose stake in China and the Far East exceeds that of any other signatory to the Nine-Power Treaty, including the United States, was diplomatically "content to leave this particular question where it is,"[12] i.e., the question of the Amau declaration, the United States would likewise have to be content, since she was not of a mind at that time to take a lone stand for effective diplomatic pressure as a prelude to naval and military action if that became necessary.

Japan denounces Washington Naval Treaty

The equilibrium of political and economic rights established by the Washington Treaties received its first jolt when Japan invaded Manchuria and set up the puppet state of Manchukuo.[13] The second jolt came when Japan denounced the Washington Naval Treaty on December 29, 1934,[14] giving the parties the required two years' notice of her intention to terminate her obligations

---

[10]See Chapter XXXIII.
[11]Henry L. Stimson, *The Far Eastern Crisis,* pp. 101–102.
[12]*Parliamentary Debates,* House of Commons, vol. 289, 14, April 30, 1934.
[13]See Chapter XXXIII.
[14]Department of State, Press Release, December 30, 1934.

under it. What Japan now wanted was the abolition of the ratio principle and the establishment of a common upper limit for the Powers concerned. Her demands obviously reflected her policy to establish and maintain hegemony in the Far East to the virtual exclusion of Western political and economic influence. The Japanese phrases—"special position and mission" in China, "a new order for East Asia"—were merely different ways of saying the same thing. Drawing to a close was the Pacific régime constructed at the Washington Conference which, in the language of Professor Toynbee, "substituted the rights and needs of China for the demands and ambitions of Japan as the principal concern of international diplomacy in the Far East."

Japan eyes other Chinese provinces

A glance at the map of China discloses that the province of Hopei in Northern China contains the important cities of Peiping and Tientsin. The province of Hopei lies within the Great Wall. To the north of Hopei and adjoining it is Chahar, a province of Inner Mongolia. Strategically this area is of vast importance. An army in control of Chahar is in a position to check a flanking movement by Russia directed against Manchuria, and interrupt communications between China and Russia, and China and Inner Mongolia. To control Hopei is to control China proper. Hence these regions of China became the next objective of the Japanese army leaders.

In the summer of 1935, while the world witnessed Italian preparations for an attack on Ethiopia, Japanese army leaders demanded that the Chinese government remove its troops from Hopei and Chahar, along with certain high local officials in Hopei whom they regarded as unfriendly to Japan; and that it suppress all local party organizations. When, in the fall of 1935, the

Japan seizes Chinese provinces

Western powers were making efforts to check Italian aggression against Ethiopia, the Japanese military seized the opportunity, under the guise of an "autonomy" movement, to place under its control the provinces of Hopei, Chahar, Suiyuan, Shansi, and Shantung. These ominous events in the Far East prompted Secretary of State Cordell Hull to issue a statement to the press on December 5, 1935, setting forth this government's reaction. "There is going on in and with regard to North China a political struggle which is unusual in character and which may have far-reaching effects. . . . Whatever the origin, whoever the agents, be what they may be the methods, the fact stands out that an effort is being made—and is being resisted—to bring about a substantial change in the political status and condition of several of China's northern Provinces. . . . In the area under reference . . . there are located, and our rights and obligations appertain to, a considerable number of American nationals, some American property, and substantial American commercial and cultural activities. The American government is closely observing what is happening there. . . . As I have stated on many occasions, it seems to this Government most important in this period of world-wide political unrest and economic instability that governments and peoples keep within principles and pledges. This Government adheres to the provisions of treaties solemnly entered into for the purpose of facilitating and regulating, to reciprocal and common advantage, the contracts between and among the countries signatory."[15] Here, as in the case of the Japanese invasion of Manchuria and Jehol, our Government sought to define its position for the sake of keeping the record clear in case, at some future time, it should decide to meet these violations of its treaty rights by action other than note-writing.

The American government states its concern over Japan's action

[15]Department of State, Press Release, December 6, 1935. On the same day, the British Foreign Minister stated in the House of Commons that "it is unfortunate that events should have taken place which, whatever the truth of the matter may be, lend color to the belief that Japanese influence is being exerted to shape Chinese internal political developments and administrative arrangements." *Parliamentary Debates*, House of Commons, vol. 307, p. 336, December 5, 1935.

Japanese encroachments weld Chinese people

These steady Japanese encroachments upon Chinese independence and territorial integrity were not without their effect upon the Chinese people and government. A new Chinese spirit was arising—a spirit of resistance and opposition to the Japanese militarists, which was welding the numerous factions into a concerted effort to resist Japanese domination of China. Students and others throughout the country demonstrated not only against Japanese aggression but against the policy of non-resistance of the Nanking government under the leadership of General Chiang Kai-shek. They denounced the Nanking dictatorship and the suppression of civil liberties and called for united Chinese military resistance to Japan. The nationalist sentiment aroused by those demonstrations found response in the southern provinces under the influence of the Canton government where opposition to the policy of non-resistance of General Chiang Kai-shek was already strong. The quarrels between Nanking and Canton were composed under the impact to resist the invader. Moreover, by abandoning the silver standard[16] and adopting a form of managed currency,[17] deflation was checked and economic conditions began to improve.

Japan fears China's growing unity as obstacle to her aims

The growing political unity of China, the approaching reconciliation between the Nanking government and the Chinese Communist forces, and the improvement in Chinese economy were interpreted in Tokyo as barriers to Japanese aims for the hegemony of East Asia. There still remained open to Japanese conquest a substantial part of China, which, according to the military leaders dominating Japanese foreign policy, it would be a more difficult task to absorb if China were allowed political and economic development. On the eve of a fresh Japanese

[16]Sir Frederic Leith-Ross, chief British economic adviser, was sent by his Government to China in 1935 to advise on the reform of Chinese currency.

[17]The Silver Purchase Act passed by Congress in 1934 attracted a large amount of that metal to the United States, depleting Chinese bank reserves, causing a decline of commodity prices and demoralization of foreign trade.

assault there was a considerable difference of opinion in Japan over the means to further the expansionist policy on the continent of Asia. The issue revolved about means and not ends. One section of Japanese opinion favored the use of military force to reduce China to a state of vassalage, and the other argued for "moral suasion" plus intimidation to bring about the same end. Since the rapid development of Chinese nationalism and the consolidation of its energies into the direction of a common national will to resist Japan led to the belief that means short of violence would not be effective, a decision was taken in favor of violence. The march of conquest was resumed July 7, 1937.

Japan launches a large-scale offensive against China proper

This time the incident which provided the occasion for a fresh Japanese military offensive on a grand scale occurred at Lukachiao, on the outskirts of Peiping, on the night of July 7, 1937, when Japanese troops[18] engaged in nocturnal manoeuvers encountered Chinese troops stationed nearby. Shots were exchanged resulting in a few casualties on both sides. The incident in and of itself, whether deliberately provoked by one side or the other, did not justify a major conflict; but the Japanese military chose this incident, when attempts to settle it failed, to launch a large-scale offensive and in so doing convicted themselves of being the primary authors of the conflict which grew out of the affray. A nation bent on war need not be too ingenious to find a pretext. Japan put herself on a war basis and began pouring troops into China. Her large-scale military operations appeared to be the result of a careful plan. On August 9 came a provocative incident at Shanghai which again provided the Japanese with the necessary pretext for making an attack by land, sea, and air on the Chinese troops stationed in the area around

[18]Japan was permitted to station troops in the Peiping and Tientsin area pursuant to the protocol of September 7, 1901, which dealt with the settlement of the Boxer rebellion. The Chinese claimed Lukachiao was outside the area in which the Japanese were entitled to station troops.

that city. The fighting in and around Shanghai raged for three months, with a heavy loss in lives and property. During the fighting, many Americans and nationals of other countries lost their lives. President Roosevelt urged our nationals to leave and warned that those who chose to remain would do so at their own risk.[19] The Americans in the Far East protested against the President's warning as an abandonment of American rights and interests in China, and several days later Secretary of State Hull gave public assurances that our nationals would be protected to the limit of the Government's ability.[20]

The United States and Great Britain take parallel action in the Far East

Profiting by the diplomatic experience of the Manchurian crisis five years earlier,[21] the policy which the Roosevelt administration pursued in the early stages of the Sino-Japanese conflict was a cautious and circumspect one. The Government insisted on the observance of its treaty rights, but refused to risk the use of force. It consulted with Great Britain and other interested powers from time to time but it was careful to point out—in view of the hostility on the part of the American public towards any suggestion for joint action in international affairs—that its action in the Far East was "parallel" and not "joint." It sought to persuade the belligerents to end hostilities and to settle their differences by peaceful means, reminding them before the struggle got under way in full swing that an armed conflict would be a great blow to the cause of peace and world progress.

When the peace efforts of the United States, like those of other interested powers, proved ineffectual, and it became clear that the struggle was assuming the propor-

[19]New York *Times*, September 6, 1937.

[20]New York *Times*, September 10, 1937. When hostilities broke out there were some 10,000 American nationals in China. At the end of October, 1937, there were still 5800 left. Cf. Department of State, Press Releases, October 2, November 6, 1937.

[21]See Chapter XXXIII.

tions of a major conflict, the United States was faced with the problem of whether or not to invoke the Neutrality Act of May, 1937.[22] Here certainly was a war on a scale as large as, if not larger than, the Italo-Ethiopian conflict, or the Spanish conflict. In the Italo-Ethiopian conflict, although there was no formal declaration, the President proclaimed that a state of war "within the intent and meaning of the joint resolution" existed, and applied the arms embargo; in the Spanish civil war he sought and obtained special legislation to apply an embargo to both sides. In the case of the Sino-Japanese war, the President refrained from invoking the Act. The Administration had several reasons for its course of action. It was felt that an embargo would injure China, which was the victim of aggression and towards whom this nation was sympathetic, and would help Japan which was the aggressor. Japan, commanding the seas, could take advantage of the "cash-and-carry" provisions of the Neutrality Act, and by the same token, in the exercise of belligerent rights, prevent supplies from reaching her enemy. Moreover, the Act if invoked, it was feared, might provide Japan with the excuse to launch the final torpedo into the Nine-Power Washington Treaty which embodied the principle of the open door. While this treaty structure had been battered by Japan almost beyond recognition, it was still afloat and the American government was not disposed to see the wreck disappear altogether.

President Roosevelt refrains from invoking Neutrality Act

On September 12, 1937, China appealed to the League of Nations under Articles 10, 11 and 17 of the Covenant. She had appealed to the League when Japan invaded Manchuria in 1931. Her appeal then and the action of the League in branding Japan an aggressor did not check Japanese aggression, nor prevent the conquest of Manchuria. In 1931 the League enjoyed great prestige; its strength for dealing with a major breach of the peace

China appeals to the League of Nations

[22]See *infra*, pp. 951–953.

was still untried. But in the interval between 1931 and 1937, the League of Nations had undergone a sad metamorphosis. It was discredited by its failure in the Sino-Japanese conflict over Manchuria, and later, when Italy invaded Ethiopia. It had failed to secure world limitation of armament. Both Japan and Germany were no longer members of the League, but were allied in an "ideological" arrangement known as the anti-Comintern pact, entered into on November 25, 1936, to save European civilization from the Communist menace.[23] Italy and Germany had intervened in the Spanish civil war to help insurgent fascist General Francisco Franco destroy the Spanish Republic and had thus created a tense political atmosphere in Europe. Great Britain and France, fearing the spread of war from the challenge of the fascist dictatorships, were fully preoccupied in Europe in an effort to localize the Spanish conflict. The outlook for effective League help to China was well-nigh hopeless.

The League Assembly condemns Japan for bombing open towns

China's appeal was referred to the League's Far Eastern Advisory Committee which had been constituted in 1933 to follow the events with respect to Manchuria, but which had been dormant since 1934. The United States designated our Minister to Switzerland to sit in as an observer.[24] The Assembly of the League condemned Japanese bombings of open towns in China. In this condemnation the United States concurred. The findings of the sub-committee of the Far Eastern Advisory Committee constituted a condemnation of Japan on a charge of breaking treaty obligations and of engaging in military operations against China by land, sea, and air, out of all proportion to the incident which occasioned the conflict. Neither on the basis of the existing treaty structure nor on the right of self-defense were the measures taken justified. In

[23]Italy adhered to this pact on November 6, 1937.

[24]The State Department was careful to point out that it was merely coöperating with the League to coördinate League efforts with that of non-member states. Cf. Department of State, Press Release, September 25, 1937.

taking the law into her hands Japan had contravened her obligations under the Nine-Power Treaty and the Pact of Paris. But the report was careful not to label Japan as the aggressor in the conflict,[25] and it recommended that members of the League who were parties to the Nine-Power Treaty initiate consultation as provided for in Article 7 of that treaty.

President Roosevelt declares United States cannot save itself by isolation or neutrality in a world of anarchy

On the very day when the Far Eastern Advisory Committee of the League received the reports of its subcommittee and laid them before the League Assembly, which adopted them,[26] President Roosevelt delivered an address in Chicago in the course of which he declared: "The peace-loving nations must make a concerted effort in opposition to these violations of treaties and those ignorings of humane instincts which today are creating a state of international anarchy and instability from which there is no escape through mere isolation or neutrality."[27]

While the President made no direct mention of Japan, he denounced, by implication, her invasion of China in the strongest terms yet used since the conflict began. ". . . The landmarks and traditions which have marked the progress of civilization toward a condition of law, order, and justice are being wiped away." Referring again by implication to the Japanese slaughter of women and children by bombs from the air, to German and Italian intervention in Spain, and to Italian piracy in the Mediterranean, he went on to say: "If those things come to pass in other parts of the world, let no one imagine that America will escape, that it may expect mercy, that this Western Hemisphere will not be attacked and that it will continue tranquilly and peacefully to carry on the ethics and the arts of civilization. . . .

---

[25] League of Nations Publications, A. 78, 1937, VII and A. 80, 1937, VII.

[26] Department of State, Press Release, October 5, 1937.

[27] The State Department on October 6, 1937, issued a statement that it was in general accord with the conclusions of the Assembly of the League of Nations.

"It seems to be unfortunately true that the epidemic of world lawlessness is spreading. When an epidemic of physical disease starts to spread, the community approves and joins in a quarantine of the patients in order to protect the health of the community against the spread of disease."

The quarantine analogy

It was the President's use of the word "quarantine" in the setting of a powerful and impassioned address which attracted wide attention. In Geneva it gave rise to the hope that the United States would support international action against an aggressor, and it stimulated the Advisory Committee in the use of strong language in condemning Japan. Fervent advocates of collective action against dictatorships saw in it the dawn of a new day; and the isolationists saw in it "involvement" and the sacrifice of peace. To the nation as a whole the President's "manifesto," as two historians[28] characterized it, came as a surprise, for the public had not expected the Government to take any strong action in the Far Eastern conflict, and the sentiment, as registered through the poll-takers, was hostile to adventures abroad. In one of his "fireside chats" over the radio on October 12th, the President sought to allay the nation's fears by carefully avoiding any mention of concerted action and by emphasizing that a solution of the Sino-Japanese conflict would be sought by agreement at the forthcoming Brussels Conference[29] to be held under the terms of the Nine-Power Treaty.

The Brussels Conference meets

At the Brussels Conference which opened November 3, 1937, with delegates from nineteen countries present—Japan refusing to attend—three currents were discernible. The delegates from Great Britain, France, and the United States declared that the aim of the Conference was the restoration of peace by mediation on a basis fair

---

[28]Charles A. and Mary Beard, *America in Midpassage*, p. 486.

[29]In addition to the League member signatories of the Nine-Power Treaty, invitations were sent to other nations interested in the Far East, including Germany, Japan, the United States, and Soviet Russia. Germany declined the invitation.

to each and acceptable to both contestants. No concrete suggestions were made towards this end. M. Litvinoff, representing Soviet Russia, joined by the delegate from China, believed the purpose of the Conference to be not merely the restoration of peace, but the restoration of a just peace; this meant collective action against the aggressor, somewhat in line with the President's suggestions in his Chicago "quarantine" speech. The Italian delegate, who was believed to be Japan's mouthpiece at the Conference, and whose nation had been the object of League sanctions in the Italo-Ethiopian dispute, derided the idea of applying collective action against Japan. He urged the Conference to come to grips with the realities of the situation and limit its work to the task of bringing "the two parties into direct contact with each other, after which we have nothing further to do."[30]

European tension frustrates work of Conference

If the nations interested in the Far East were unwilling to take collective measures against Japan when she invaded Manchuria in 1931, the likelihood that they would do so in 1937 was even more remote. In 1931 there was no Adolf Hitler to challenge the European order as it was constructed by the Peace of Versailles. Nor was there a German-Japanese-Italo anti-Comintern pact whose aim, *inter alia*, was to revise the territorial *status quo*. Great Britain could ill afford to have her navy operating in Far Eastern waters with Germany and Italy ready to plunge Europe into war, the one seeking hegemony on the continent of Europe, not to say world dominion, and the other restoration in the Mediterranean of the glory of ancient Rome. The tense European situation, the British and French governments indicated, made them unwilling to undertake commitments in the Far East which might involve the use of their navies in that region. The United States, it was made clear, would have to take the initiative

---

[30] *Bulletin of International News*, XIV, 442, November 13, 1937.

and bear a heavy, if not the sole, burden of checking Japan. And this the United States was unwilling to do.

Conference suggests mediation to Japan

Mediation and conciliation appeared the only course left for the Conference to pursue. It accordingly sent a second invitation to Japan to attend, proposing mediation through a small committee of delegates. The invitation was again declined. The Conference then formulated a declaration denying Japan's assertion that the conflict concerned Japan and China alone; affirming that the powers viewed the problem "not in terms simply of relations between two countries in the Far East but in terms of law, orderly processes, world security, and world peace"; and warning that the states must "consider what is to be their common attitude" in a situation in which Japan denied their competence to act under the Nine-Power Treaty. The Conference further reaffirmed the validity of the principles of the Nine-Power Treaty,[31] urged the suspension of hostilities and a resort to peaceful processes. It recessed on November 24, 1937. The results achieved in terms of words were even less effective than those which the Advisory Committee of the League had adopted on October 5, 1937. In view of the debacle at Brussels, it was useless to set the machinery at Geneva in motion again.

The Conference fails

The diplomatic *ennui* which followed the "recess" of the Brussels Conference was broken when the American gunboat *Panay* and three American tankers which it was escorting on the Yangtze River were attacked and sunk by Japanese airplanes on December 12, 1937, several persons killed, and a score of others wounded.[32] The nation was aroused at the outrage, and on December 13, the day following the attack, the President took the dramatic step—with a view perhaps to forestalling any shifting of responsibility between the Japanese Cabinet

Japanese planes sink American ships

[31]Department of State, Press Release, November 27, 1937.

[32]Navy Department, Press Releases, December 24 and 25, 1937.

and the military—of addressing himself to the Japanese Emperor as the supreme authority. He instructed the Secretary of State to tell the Japanese Ambassador:

> 1. That the President is deeply shocked and concerned by the news of indiscriminate bombing of American and other non-Chinese vessels[33] on the Yangtze, and that he requests that the Emperor be so advised.[34]
>
> 2. That all the facts are being assembled and will shortly be presented to the Japanese government.
>
> 3. That in the meantime it is hoped the Japanese government will be considering definitely for presentation to this government:
>
> *a.* Full expression of regret and proffer of full compensation;
>
> *b.* Methods guaranteeing against a repetition of any similar attack in the future.[35]

Japanese government's claim of error of mistaken identity disallowed

The Japanese government hastened to express its apologies even before our authorities could lodge a protest, explained that its navy fliers mistook the *Panay* and the oil vessels for Chinese boats, and accepted full responsibility for the bombing. But the reports of eyewitnesses which appeared in the American press and were later confirmed in the statement of the commanding officer of the gunboat *Panay* and by the findings of the Special Court of Inquiry[36] cast much doubt, to say the least, on the Japanese government's version of mistaken identity. Visibility was so clear that the aviators could hardly have failed to see the large American flags displayed on deck.[37] In addition the Japanese authorities had been apprised in advance of the *Panay's* movements up the Yangtze. Furthermore similar outrages committed upon British ships on the Yangtze

[33]Several British ships were likewise attacked by the Japanese on the same day.

[34]The underscoring is the President's. The word "requests" was substituted by him for "suggests."

[35]Department of State, Press Release, December 13, 1937.

[36]Department of State, Press Release, December 25, 1937.

[37]It was later disclosed that when the sinking ship was abandoned, a motor launch approached and fired on her. The Japanese soldiers from the launch went aboard the *Panay* but left again a few minutes later. Cf. *Ibid.*

that same day were hardly in keeping with the version of mistaken identity.

The United States demands complete indemnification

On December 14 Secretary Hull sent a strong note[38] of protest demanding a formal expression of regret, complete indemnification and assurances that specific measures would be taken to insure that American interests and property would not be subjected henceforth to attack or unlawful interference. The note pointed out that the American vessels were on the Yangtze "by uncontested and incontestable right" and were "engaged in their legitimate and appropriate business" when they were attacked. Despite repeated assurances by the Japanese government and of various Japanese authorities at various points, the note went on to observe, American rights had been violated, lives endangered and property destroyed. On previous occasions the Japanese government had expressed regrets and tendered assurances that precautions would be taken against a recurrence of such incidents. Yet Japanese armed forces, "in complete disregard of American rights" had killed American nationals and destroyed American property. The Japanese government tendered a formal apology, promised indemnity for all losses, appropriate punishment for those responsible for the attack, and assurances that strict orders had been issued to prevent the recurrence of such incidents.[39] The incident was closed on December 25, when Secretary Hull instructed Ambassador Grew to accept the Japanese assurances, but not the Japanese version of the attack.[40]

Japan tenders formal apology

In an earlier period of our history, an incident such as the *Panay* might well have led to war. But the public shrank from the thought of war over such a provocation.

---

[38]Department of State, Press Release, December 14, 1937.

[39]*Ibid.*

[40]On April 22, 1938, the Japanese government paid $2,214,007.36 as indemnification for deaths, injuries, and property loss suffered by our citizens and the Government arising from the *Panay* incident.

On the contrary, the *Panay* affair gave impetus to a growing sentiment for the withdrawal of American armed forces from China, and served to move the proposed constitutional amendment[41] of Representative Ludlow of Indiana from the House Committee on the Judiciary, where it had been resting for three years, to the floor of the House. The debate on the amendment was brief but bitter, and in the end the proposal was defeated in the House by a narrow margin of 209 to 188. The fact that the Ludlow proposal was debated on the floor of the House at this time showed how strong isolationist sentiment was in the country and to what lengths it was ready to go to curb the authority of the Executive in the conduct of foreign affairs. "Such an amendment to the Constitution as that proposed would cripple any President in his conduct of our foreign relations, and it would encourage other nations to believe that they could violate American rights with impunity," wrote the President to William Bankhead, Speaker of the House of Representatives.[42]

The *Panay* affair and the Ludlow amendment

The *Panay* affair strengthened the movement for boycotting Japanese goods, and Japanese bombings of Canton in the spring of 1938 prompted numerous peace organizations, in a nation-wide campaign, to demand an embargo on the export of war materials to Japan. It was pointed out that 54 per cent of Japan's imports of war materials had been obtained from the United States and one half of the gas and oil used by Japanese bombers in their attacks on Canton were probably sold by American exporters.[43] How, it was asked, could our Government

The *Panay* affair strengthens movement for boycott and embargo

[41]The Ludlow Resolution as finally revised provided that: Except in case of attack by armed forces, actual or immediately threatened, upon the United States or its territorial possessions, or by any non-American nation against any country in the Western Hemisphere, the people shall have the sole power by a national referendum to declare war or to engage in warfare overseas. Congress, when it deems a national crisis to exist in conformance with this article, shall by concurrent resolution refer the question to the people.

[42]Department of State, Press Release, January 15, 1938.

[43]Cf. Senator Pope in the *Congressional Record*, Seventy-Fifth Congress, Third Session, p. 11172.

condemn Japan's aggression in China on the one hand, and permit the export of essential war materials which contributed so markedly to aggression on the other hand?

President Roosevelt asks for larger navy

With the attack upon one of our gunboats in the Far East still fresh in the minds of our citizens, the President on January 28, 1938, asked Congress for a 20 per cent increase in the existing naval authorizations,[44] an increase which placed the United States navy limits for the first time beyond the limitations imposed by the Washington and London Naval Treaties of 1922 and 1930 which expired on December 31, 1936.[45]

Japanese aims unfold

As the course of the undeclared war spread, the intention of Japan to interpose herself between China and the Western Powers became painfully clear. Military measures taken by the Japanese only to liquidate the incident near Peiping in July, 1937, blossomed forth into a vast program for the "stabilization" of Eastern Asia and the creation of a new Chinese régime under Japanese domination. The open door in Manchuria was closed, and it was beginning to close in the Japanese occupied territories of China proper. American merchants were excluded from their places of business, while Japanese nationals were permitted to return to theirs.[46] In North China the Japanese virtually monopolized the natural resources and ousted foreign traders. The same policy of Japanese discrimination and exclusion was employed in Central and South China. In a note to Japan October 6, 1938, Secretary Hull pointed out that the numerous practices of the Japanese government in China, including trade controls and restrictions, tariffs and monopolies, and currency manipulation, contravened the rights of Americans in China. These practices the Secretary of State

Secretary Hull protests against Japanese practices

[44] *Ibid.*, p. 1585.

[45] See Chapter XXXVIII.

[46] The State Department protested vigorously against such practices, citing specific instances in its note of May 31, 1938, to Japan. Cf. Department of State, Press Release, June 4, 1938.

characterized as "unlawful interference" and "unwarranted restrictions," which clearly indicated a purpose "to establish in areas which have come under Japanese military occupation general preference for, and superiority of, Japanese interests, an inevitable effect of which will be to frustrate the practical application of the principle of the open door and deprive American nationals of equal opportunity." Since the Japanese government had given repeated assurances to respect the maintenance of the open door, the note asked that such assurances be implemented.[47]

Japan denies discrimination against American nationals and regrets inconveniences

The Japanese reply of November 18, 1938, was in the nature of a general denial of discrimination against American nationals and those of other countries and an assertion that the participation of the interested powers in the reconstruction of China would be welcomed by Japan. The inconveniences suffered by American citizens, the reply stated, regrettably arose out of necessary military operations and measures for preserving peace and order. Japan was resolved in her purpose to establish a new order "based on genuine international justice throughout East Asia" and "any attempt to apply to the conditions of today and tomorrow inapplicable ideas and principles of the past would neither contribute toward the establishment of a real peace in East Asia, nor solve the immediate issue."[48] Secretary Hull described this reply as "not responsive," and in another note to Japan, dated December 31, 1938, he reaffirmed the American position. "The Government of the United States," the note said,

---

[47]Department of State, Press Release, October 29, 1938.

[48]Department of State, Press Release, November 19, 1938. On the occasion of the birthday of the Emperor of Japan, on November 3, 1938, the Japanese government issued a statement, drafted jointly by the Ministries of War, Navy, and Foreign Affairs, with the sanction of the Emperor, proclaiming its purpose to coördinate China and "Manchukuo" culturally, politically, and economically in the Japanese system, wherein others would be expected to adapt their attitude to the new conditions prevailing in East Asia. Cf. text in New York *Times*, November 3, 1938.

The United States asserts that Japan's action runs counter to treaty provisions

"expresses its conviction that the restrictions and measures under reference not only are unjust and unwarranted but are counter to the provisions of several binding international agreements, voluntarily entered into, to which both Japan and the United States, and in some cases other countries, are parties."[49] The United States deprecated the fact that Japan had chosen to embark upon a course directed toward the arbitrary creation, by methods of its own selection and in contravention of treaty pledges and established rights of other powers concerned, "of a 'new order' in the Far East." Our government warned Japan that: "Whatever may be the changes which have taken place in the situation in the Far East and whatever may be the situation now, these matters are of no less interest and concern to the American government than have been the situations which have prevailed there in the past, and such changes as may henceforth take place there, changes which may enter into the producing of a 'new situation' and a 'new order' are and will be of like concern to this Government. This Government is well aware that the situation has changed. This Government is also well aware that many of the changes have been brought about by action of Japan. This Government does not admit, however, that there is need or warrant for any one power to take upon itself to prescribe what shall be the terms and conditions of a 'new order' in areas not under its sovereignty and to constitute itself the repository of authority and the agent of destiny in regard thereto."[50] The note went on to say that the United States has at all times regarded agreements as susceptible of alteration, but that alterations can rightfully be made only by orderly processes of negotiation and agreement among the parties thereto, and it was prepared to discuss with the representatives of those powers, including China and

The United States denies Japan's right to prescribe terms and conditions of a "new order" in China

[49]Department of State, Press Release, December 31, 1938.

[50]*Ibid.*

Japan, changes based on justice and reason with due regard for the rights and obligations of all the parties directly concerned.

Japan fails to crush China after two years of fighting

When the Sino-Japanese war, which broke out on July 7, 1937, was nearing its second anniversary Japan could show on the black side of the ledger Japanese-dominated régimes at Peiping, Shanghai, Hankow, Nanking, and Canton—local centers surrounded by hostile populations; and on the red side of the ledger, a staggering war debt, a declining standard of living of its population (already low before the war), unforeseen prolongation of hostilities, and a growing determination on the part of the Chinese to continue the struggle. On the eve of this anniversary Japan could show very little effective exploitation or development of China's resources because her military expenditures continued to eat up such large amounts of capital—this too was on the red side of the ledger. Thus, a war which the Japanese militarists believed would crush China in a few months had developed into one of attrition by which China hoped to wear down the invader and emerge as victor.[51]

Japan seeks revision of status of the International Settlement at Shanghai and at Amoy

The war on China had bogged down, and a turn in Japan's strategy became necessary to demonstrate to her people reasons for the unexpected prolongation of hostilities. On May 3, 1939, the Japanese government, in an *aide-memoire* to our Government and to Great Britain, requested a revision of the regulations governing the status of the International Settlement at Shanghai. As if to back up the desire, as well as to provide a test case for the larger issues at stake in Shanghai, Japanese soldiers were landed on May 13, 1939, on Kulangsu, island center of the International Settlement at Amoy, and a demand was made for revision of the Kulangsu administration. Not only was the Japanese request rejected by both British and

[51]Cf. Walter H. Mallory, "The Strategy of Chiang Kai-Shek," *Foreign Affairs*, July, 1939, pp. 699–711.

American[52] governments, but the challenge was instantly countered by a concentration of American, French, and British naval vessels off the island, with the landing of patrol forces and a combined display of military force in the Settlement to thwart a possible Japanese *coup*. There the matter was allowed to rest.

The combined Anglo-American-French front in defense of their interests in the International Settlement was not without meaning to the Japanese army leaders. Tientsin was therefore chosen as an easier objective, where neither the United States nor France has jurisdictional interests, but where Britain has. While Great Britain was being pressed hard in Europe by another impending German blow—this time against Poland—the Japanese instituted a blockade of the British Concession at Tientsin on June 14, 1939. The pretext was the assassination of a puppet Chinese customs inspector on April 9, 1939, by four Chinese suspects who sought safety in the Concession and whom the British refused to surrender. The Concession was barricaded, British subjects were stripped, humiliated, and beaten, an anti-British campaign was whipped up throughout North China, and British nationals were forced to evacuate a number of cities. By these means Japanese army leaders sought to coerce "British coöperation in establishing the new order in East Asia." In concrete terms "coöperation" meant: (1) Japanese participation with Great Britain in policing the Concession —the first entering wedge in destroying the system of foreign-controlled areas in China; (2) Great Britain's abandonment of support of China's national currency, thus weakening China economically; and, (3) British pressure on China to lay down arms on Japanese terms.

Japan blockades Tientsin

Our Government expressed concern over the "broader aspects" of the Japanese attack on Tientsin, and when the British in the course of their negotiations appeared

[52]Department of State, Press Release, May 20, 1939.

to be giving in to the Japanese demands, it served notice on Japan, on July 26, 1939, that it would terminate six months hence the 1911 Japanese-American treaty of commerce and navigation, "with a view to better safeguarding and promoting American interests."[53] It was a stiff warning to Japan and an encouragement to Britain to resist Tokyo's demands.[54] By giving such notice the United States placed herself in a position to impose drastic economic penalties against Japan.

The United States serves notice to terminate commercial treaty with Japan

Within a month after the United States served notice that she would terminate her trade treaty with Japan came the announcement of the Soviet-German non-aggression pact, on August 23, 1939. Germany's desertion of the anti-Comintern front, in which Japan was a leading member, confused the Japanese army extremists and other elements which desired to transform the anti-Comintern front into a military alliance with Germany. The pact, for the time being at least, freed Soviet Russia from the threat of a simultaneous attack by Germany in the West and by Japan in the East, thus strengthening Russia's position in the Far East. It was a diplomatic defeat of the first magnitude for Japan.

Soviet-German pact a diplomatic defeat for Japan

The war which broke out in Europe in September, 1939, has limited the freedom of action of the Western powers in the Far East and has increased the responsibility of the United States in that region. At this present writing the United States is the one great power free to oppose Japanese ambitions in the Pacific and play a decisive role in the outcome of the Far Eastern conflict. But she

The United States the only power free to oppose Japan

[53]Department of State, *Bulletin,* July 20, 1939, p. 81.

[54]The British agreed to a measure of coöperation with the Japanese in maintaining law and order in Tientsin and handed over the four Chinese for trial in a puppet Chinese court. The demands by Japan on Great Britain, that Chinese national currency be banned within the Tientsin Concession and that Chinese silver reserves in Tientsin and in the diplomatic quarter of Peiping be handed over, were communicated to our Government and the French. The negotiations on these demands broke down when the startling announcement came that Soviet Russia and Germany had concluded a non-aggression pact on August 23, 1939.

cannot play that role without considering the effect her action will have upon the balance of forces in the European conflict.

Note on the Philippines

Independence has long been a desire of the Filipinos. After years of agitation Philippine leaders and American agricultural and labor interests were successful in having Congress enact the Hawes-Cutting bill for Philippine independence on January 17, 1933. The Filipinos sought independence at the lowest economic price to which the United States could be induced to agree, and certain agricultural interests, particularly the producers of beet sugar, cottonseed oil and cordage, urged and supported independence because they wanted Philippine products put outside the American tariff wall. Organized labor made common cause with the American farmers because it wanted Filipino labor placed under immigration restrictions applicable to foreign countries as a protection from the competition of cheap labor. The act was passed over the objections of the Hoover Administration at a time when Japan was on the warpath in the Far East. On the eve of the Congressional vote overriding the veto, President Hoover and four of his Cabinet Secretaries attacked the bill as a betrayal of the trust the United States had assumed towards the Filipinos. Secretary of State Stimson contended that the withdrawal of American sovereignty would be attended by hazard and uncertainty involving the welfare of the Filipinos on the one hand and the prestige and future interests of the United States on the other. The aims contemplated in the bill, he pointed out, would profoundly disturb the political equilibrium throughout the Western Pacific and Eastern Asia. The Philippine legislature, whose consent was prerequisite to the granting of independence, expressed dissatisfaction with certain provisions of the Act and rejected it.

Congress enacts Hawes-Cutting bill for Philippine independence

Congress overrides President Hoover's veto

At the request of President Roosevelt, who urged certain amendments to the Hawes-Cutting Act which would make the act acceptable to the Filipinos, Congress returned to the subject, and on March 22, 1934, passed the Tydings-McDuffie bill. The President signed it on March 24, and the Philippine legislature adopted it on May 1, 1934. Under the terms of the Act a constitutional convention met at Manila and drew up a constitution which the President approved as being within the terms of the Act. The new constitution was ratified by the qualified electors in the Philippines on May 14, 1935, and on November 15, 1935, the new government was inaugurated under Manuel L. Quezon, the first President of the Commonwealth of the Philippines.

Congress passes the Tydings-McDuffie bill

Commonwealth of the Philippines comes into being

Under the Tydings-McDuffie Act the Philippines are to enjoy a commonwealth status for a period of 10 years, at the expiration of which full and complete independence is granted. During that interval, foreign affairs of the islands remain under the direct supervision and control of the United States. No loans are to be contracted elsewhere than in the Philippines or in the United States without our approval. All military forces of the islands may be called into the service of the United States which continues to have the right to maintain military and naval establishments. During the ten-year period of transition, the United States reserves the right to intervene to preserve government under the constitution. After the ten-year period, the Act declares that the United States shall "withdraw and surrender all right of possession, supervision, jurisdiction, control or sovereignty" in and over the Philippines. American naval stations and reservations are excepted. The Act recommends that the President enter into negotiations at the earliest practicable date with foreign nations with a view to the conclusion of a treaty "for the perpetual neutralization of the Philippine Islands if and when independence shall

Tydings-McDuffie Act contemplates independence for Philippines after ten years

have been achieved." The decision to give the Filipinos their independence in 1946 was epoch-making in the diplomacy of the Pacific since it contemplated reducing to the vanishing point American commitments in that region. It opened up the prospect of a far-reaching change in the balance of power in the Far East at a time when Japan was engaged in the process of subjugating China and closing the open door to the Western powers.

Future of the Philippines uncertain

The future of the Islands, in the light of Japan's aggression in China and her program of expansion in the Orient generally, has become increasingly uncertain. In the Philippines and in the United States certain sections of opinion, fearing that Japan will attempt to dominate the Islands economically or by conquest after American withdrawal, have indicated that the question of independence should be reappraised.[55] Filipino politicians have expressed a desire to continue the commonwealth status for an indefinite duration.[56] Another section of the American public has pointed to the Philippine link as providing the greatest danger of involvement in a war with Japan and has urged withdrawal from the Islands.[57] In the last analysis the future development of Philippine-American relations must conform to the general pattern of America's foreign policy in the Far East.

---

[55]Cf. U. S., 74th Congress, First Session, Investigation of Conditions in the Philippines: Reports of Senators McKellar and Gibson, Senate Document, No. 57.

[56]Cf. the statements of President Quezon, New York *Times*, March 17, 1938, and March 12, 1939.

[57]Nicholas Roosevelt, "Laying Down the White Man's Burden," *Foreign Affairs*, July, 1935.

CHAPTER XXXVIII

REARMAMENT

IN ADDITION to the difficulty of reconciling the "security" and "disarmament" conceptions of the organization of peace, the Disarmament Conference was faced with the problem of the German demand for equality in armaments. On October 14, 1933, two days before another session was to open in Geneva, the German government suddenly announced its withdrawal from the Conference and from membership in the League of Nations,[1] and declared its determination to stay away from Geneva until "equality is no longer withheld." The Nazi Party, under the leadership of Adolf Hitler, had come to power in Germany on January 30, 1933, and with it came the policy of national "renewal" whose avowed aim, *inter alia*, was to free Germany from the Treaty of Versailles. The withdrawal from the League of Nations and the Conference was the first overt act of the new Third Reich in fulfilling that objective.

Germany withdraws from Conference and League of Nations

Several hours before this startling announcement reached Geneva, Sir John Simon, the British Secretary of Foreign Affairs, had presented to the General Commission of the Conference a program which would permit the gradual realization of Germany's equality status and leave the way open for negotiation on certain other German demands—such as the right to construct immediately all the types of weapons the other signatories did not agree to abandon. The British proposal had the support of the French, Italian, American, and many other

British propose gradual rearmament for Germany

[1]Formal notification was received by the Secretary-General of the League of Nations on October 21, 1934.

important delegations, and was in effect the first detailed and concrete program, other than vague statements of general principles, to receive such strong support.

British plan to serve as general framework

The British draft convention,[2] originally submitted by Prime Minister Ramsay MacDonald on March 16, 1933, with the modifications suggested by Sir John Simon to meet in part the German desire for equality, was to serve as the general framework of the future disarmament treaty. It is interesting to examine its principal political provisions and to note in retrospect the extent to which the American delegation was prepared to go to secure an arms agreement, particularly in the light of the traditional American policy.

British plan differentiates European security from security generally

Part I of the draft attempted to provide a solution of the vexing problem of security. The security problem of Continental Europe was differentiated from the security problem generally. There was a provision for a security pact between the European states, under which they would have assumed definite obligations to enforce the sanction provisions of the Covenant of the League of Nations. As for the non-European states, there was a provision for consultation between members of the League and non-members in the event of a breach or threatened breach of the Pact of Paris. In other words, the sanctions provisions were confined to European nations, and the consultation provision was universal.

American government ready to consult in case of breach of Pact of Paris

The compromise was made possible by the American offer to consult with other powers in the event of a breach of the Pact of Paris.[3] Mr. Norman Davis, American Ambassador at Large, explained to the Conference that in the event of a breach or of a threatened breach of the Pact of Paris, the United States would be ready to confer with

[2]League of Nations, Conference for the Reduction and Limitation of Armaments, Draft Convention, Conference Documents, 163.

[3]League of Nations, General Commission, Provisional Minutes of the Sixty-first Meeting, pp. 473–475.

a view to maintaining peace; and should the powers in consultation decide on the aggressor, and should the United States concur in the decision "on the basis of its own independent judgment" then the United States "will undertake to refrain from any action and to withhold protection from its citizens if engaged in activities which would tend to defeat the collective effort which the states in consultation might have decided upon against an aggressor." In other words, we were prepared to withhold the exercise of our neutral rights to permit the League a free hand in applying sanctions against an aggressor. We were willing to make this contribution to the organization of peace if a disarmament treaty were signed. But, we were not to be asked to put the pledge to consult in treaty form. The pledge to consult would be made by a Presidential declaration of policy.

Non-involvement in Europe conditions American disarmament policy

American coöperation in the Disarmament Conference was in the main confined to the task of finding a formula for the mutual and gradual reduction of armaments. Being primarily a naval power, situated between two oceans which afford her an enviable security, the United States clung to the thesis that disarmament was an end in itself. She would have nothing to do, therefore, with European political issues.[4] The problem of disarmament in Geneva was viewed by her as one belonging in the realm of arithmetic, disassociated from political considerations. We need only look at the Washington Naval Treaty and its Nine-Power Treaty corollary, however, to realize that in the Far East, where her immediate vital interests come into play, the United States regarded the problem of disarmament as inextricably tied up with the balance of power in the Pacific. The disarmament policy of this

[4]The 1933 draft convention dealt mainly with the problem of stabilizing the navies not subject to the Washington and London Naval Treaties, and left the final settlement to a Conference to be held simultaneously with that scheduled in 1935 under the London Naval Treaty of 1930.

nation *vis-a-vis* Europe throughout its participation in the Disarmament Conference was conditioned by the tradition of non-involvement in European political problems.

Germany's withdrawal from League and Conference creates tension

With the withdrawal of Germany from the League and the Conference, at a time when the nations appeared to be nearer an agreement on armaments than ever before, political tension in Europe mounted. Security through disarmament and political arrangements, so far as Germany's neighbors were concerned, now appeared inadequate. The problem which confronted them was no longer a world-wide agreement on armaments but how to meet the menace of impending German rearmament. The United States was not willing to take part in any decision upon the problem for fear of involving herself in a course of action toward Germany, if the solution arrived at should fail.

Task of persuading Germany to return falls upon Great Britain and Italy

The main task of persuading Germany to return to the Conference fell upon Great Britain and Italy, and their efforts were principally directed towards bringing the French and the Germans into some measure of agreement on the latter's desire to rearm. The "parallel and supplementary efforts" of the European powers to span the gulf between France and Germany, carried on between January and May, 1934, during a recess of the Disarmament Conference, were without success. The French refused to consent to immediate German rearmament, and in a memorandum[5] to the British, dated April 17, cited

[5]British Command Paper, 4559, Further Memoranda on Disarmament. "In reality," the French memorandum stated, "the German government, without awaiting the results of the negotiations which were in progress, has wished to impose its determination to continue every form of rearmament, within limits of which it claims to be the sole judge, in contempt of the provisions of the Treaty, which, in the absence of any other convention, continue to govern the level of its armaments. The German government intends to increase immediately on a formidable scale not only the strength of its army, but also [that] of its navy and its aviation. So far as this last is concerned, it is all the less permissible for the neighbors of Germany to disregard the menace that hangs over them, in that numerous aerodromes have recently been organized in the demilitarized zone, also in violation of the Treaty.

"Whatever explanation may be advanced after the event, facts of such

German figures showing an increased expenditure for armaments amounting to 352 million marks—an increase which the French contended had occurred during the negotiations to bring Germany back to the Conference and in violation of the Treaty of Versailles. There the deadlock remained.

France accuses Germany of rearming

The Disarmament Conference reconvened May 29, 1934—after a recess of seven months. The statesmen who had gathered in Geneva could not disguise from themselves the fact that the prospect of an arms limitation agreement was darker than ever before. "The gradual fading away of the Disarmament Conference absolved the statesmen of the world from attendance at a painful deathbed scene, but by the autumn of 1935 they were hard put to it to maintain the official fiction that the case was merely one of suspended animation. The realities of the situation were symbolized in the action of the American government, who announced on the 14th of September their decision to close the offices of their delegation at Geneva and reduce the delegation to one man."[6] The Conference had failed in its purpose to secure an arms limitation agreement. The distrust and anxiety which beset the nations of Europe as a result of the rebirth of German military power, and the waning confidence in the League Covenant as an agency of security, particularly after the mortal blow which Japan had dealt the League by her invasion of Manchuria, led them to increase their armaments and to resort to alliances on the pre-World War models. An era of acute international and political tension set in.

The Disarmament Conference fails

The Disarmament Conference did not concern itself primarily with naval armaments, which were already subject to restriction by the Washington and London

---

exceptional gravity can lead to only one observation and conclusion. They prove that the German government, whether of set purpose or not, has made impossible the negotiations, the basis of which it has by its own act destroyed."

[6]Arnold J. Toynbee, assisted by V. M. Boulter, *Survey of International Affairs, 1935*, vol. 1, p. 57.

Naval Treaties so far as the five leading naval powers were concerned. What discussion did take place revolved chiefly around the vain attempt to distinguish between "offensive" and "defensive" arms. The Japanese delegates, however, did suggest a higher naval ratio for themselves,[7] combined with a heavy reduction in "offensive" vessels. By the time the League had demonstrated its impotence in the Manchurian incident, they went further and announced that Japan would not accept a renewal of the Washington and London naval limitation agreements on the 5 : 5 : 3 basis[8] upon their expiration.

Disarmament Conference not concerned with naval armaments

The London Naval Treaty of 1930,[9] which was to expire in 1936, obligated the signatories thereto to meet in 1935 "to frame a new treaty to replace and to carry out the purposes of the present Treaty." As a prelude to the 1935 conference, preparatory conversations took place in London in 1934 between American, British, and Japanese representatives. The three signatories outlined their positions in great detail, against a background of conflicting aims in the Far East. With Japan's conquest of Manchuria and her claim to a "special position and mission" in China "to keep peace and order in East Asia"—which the United States has refused to recognize or admit[10] — the preliminary naval conversations in London lacked a propitious setting.

The three largest naval powers hold preparatory conversations in London

The British proposal

The British proposed a reduction in the size of battleships, the abolition of the submarine, or a drastic limitation of its number, asked for twenty additional cruisers over and above the fifty limit[11] set by the London Treaty, and a continuation of the naval ratios. The Japanese

[7]League of Nations, *Conference for the Limitation of Armaments*, 1932–33, Conf. D. 94, December 9, 1932.

[8]*Op. cit.*, Minutes of the General Commission, vol. II, pp. 504–505.

[9]See Chapter XXX, pp. 709–712.

[10]See Chapter XXXVII.

[11]Hearing before the Committee on Foreign Relations, United States Senate, relative to a Treaty for the Limitation of Naval Armaments, etc., May 14, 1936, p. 17.

delegation proposed the abandonment of the ratio system hitherto in force and the establishment of a common upper limit of global tonnage for all naval powers, with each nation free to allot its tonnage to any category of ship in any amount desired within the total. In addition, the Japanese advocated an all-round reduction of naval tonnage, and the abolition of "offensive" vessels, by which it meant battleships, aircraft carriers, and heavy cruisers, but not submarines, which it defined as "defensive" in character. The object of these proposals, they said, was to create a "condition of non-menace and non-aggression."[12] The use of the term "naval parity" or "naval equality" with Great Britain and the United States, was studiously avoided, but the desire was there, nevertheless, and it was expressed by Admiral Yamamoto in the following language:

The Japanese proposal

> Our aim is not merely to bring the navies of Great Britain and the United States down to our level; we should like to reduce our navy too. In view of the great importance of the work of disarmament, all the powers concerned must be ready to make sacrifices. We believe, though, that the strongest parties should make the greatest sacrifices. We, too, will make sacrifices, and we expect the same of France and Italy as well.[13]

Japan's determination to secure naval parity reflected its purpose to become the sole arbiter in the affairs of Eastern Asia. She had already served notice[14] on the rest of the world to accept her "special position" in that area, and her demand for naval equality was a further warning that she would support that claim by force against any Power which sought to challenge it.

The American proposal

Our delegation was in accord with the principle of an all-round reduction of naval armament, but insisted on maintaining "the essential balance between the fleets,"[15] i.e., a reduction "in such a manner as not to change the

[12]*Ibid.*, p. 18.

[13]New York *Times*, November 4, 1934.

[14]See *infra*, pp. 880–885.

[15]U. S. Department of State, *The London Naval Conference*, Conference Series No. 24, pp. 52–53.

relative strength of the nations concerned."[16] Essentially what the United States demanded was a continuation of the 5 : 5 : 3 ratio principle embodied in the Washington Naval Treaty of 1922 and continued for the most part in the London Naval Treaty of 1930. The naval equilibrium established in 1922 was part of a series of political agreements dealing with the Far East and formed a "collective system of coöperation for the maintenance of peace"[17] in that region. To alter the naval symbols would disturb the political arrangements which it helped to support. That was the thesis of the American proposal.

Japan's demand for naval equality not reconcilable with United States demand for equality of security

In terms of strategy Japan sought a naval agreement which would make her mistress of the East and free her from the menace of other naval powers who might some day challenge her ambition in that area, either singly or in combination. But American naval policy as expounded by the General Board of the Navy includes, *inter alia*, the creation of a naval fleet "in sufficient strength to support the national policies and commerce" of the United States. If the maintenance of the principle of the open door is one of those national policies,[18] the implication is clear that American naval strength must be at a level capable of supporting that policy.[19] Japan's demand for naval equality could not be reconciled with the American demand for "equality of security."

British incline to concessions

The British, at the beginning of the negotiations, desired to placate the Japanese and were disposed to make concessions on the equality issue. Whether the British attitude was influenced by a desire to shift the burden of opposing Japan's aims in Asia upon the United States

[16]Norman H. Davis, "The Disarmament Problem," *Foreign Affairs*, Special Supplement, April, 1935.

[17]*Ibid.*

[18]See Chapter XXXVII.

[19]Certain naval writers are agreed that the ratio 5:3 would operate to give Japan a decided advantage in case of an American-Japanese conflict in the Western Pacific. Cf. H. C. Bywater, "Japanese and American Naval Power in the Pacific," *Pacific Affairs*, July, 1935, pp. 168–175.

alone, it would be difficult to state with certainty. Mr. J. L. Garvin, the well-informed editor of the London *Observer*, rebuked those members of the British Cabinet who encouraged Japan in the belief that she could drive a wedge between the United States and Great Britain, and asserted that an "Anglo-American understanding must be the firm principle, unswerving aim, and impregnable foundation of British policy."[20] In a vain attempt to find a face-saving compromise the British proposed that Japan be given naval equality in principle, subject to an understanding that she would not in fact build up to the British and American level for the duration of the agreement. This proposal was promptly rejected by the Japanese, and the conversations came to an end December 19, 1934.

Japan gives notice to terminate Washington Naval Treaty

Ten days after the preliminary conversations in London ended, the Japanese Ambassador in Washington informed the American government that Japan would terminate her obligations under the Washington Naval Treaty on December 31, 1936.[21] Whether by design or coincidence, on the day Japan denounced the Washington Naval Treaty the Navy Department announced that the American fleet would hold manoeuvres in Pacific waters in May of 1935. This, added to the policy embodied in the Vinson Bill of March 27, 1934, to build up the navy to full treaty strength, caused a painful impression upon Japanese military and naval leaders who were now fully convinced that the balance of the fleets as established by the naval treaties offered no security for Japan.

In the years following the Washington and London Naval Treaties, neither Great Britain nor the United States maintained a naval strength at the levels permitted by these agreements.[22] The Vinson-Trammell Act author-

[20]The *Observer* (London), November 4, 1934.

[21]Department of State, Treaty Information, December, 1934, pp. 4–9.

[22]In July, 1934, the United States was free to lay down 78 more ships with a total of 136,975 tons; Great Britain, 44 more ships with a total of 132,963 tons; Japan, one ship of 1500. Cf. Secretary of the Navy, *Annual Report*, 1934.

ized the Navy Department to build up to the maximum treaty levels. The program called for the construction of one aircraft carrier, 99,200 tons of destroyers, and 35,530 tons of submarines, in addition to 6 cruisers previously authorized—a total of 102 vessels. Provision was also made for replacement of certain over-age vessels and of existing capital ships after December 31, 1936, should no new agreement be concluded in the meantime. This was the largest construction program authorized since 1916, and its cost was estimated at sums ranging from $590,000,000 to $1,000,000,000. Judged from the vast program projected, the Vinson-Trammell Act was one of the most significant measures in American naval history. Upon signing the bill, President Roosevelt declared that it was the policy of his Administration to favor continued limitation of naval armaments and pointed out that the law was merely an authorization bill and that the completion of its program depended upon appropriations by future Congresses.

Vinson-Trammell Act authorizes vast naval construction program

The rate of naval building in the United States since 1922 had been much slower than in either Japan or Great Britain. The American fleet thus contained a larger proportion of over-age vessels than the fleets of the other two powers. There were various motives, however, which prompted the Roosevelt Administration to take steps to build up the navy to the Washington and London Treaty levels. One was to put the United States in a better bargaining position in a future conference; another was to provide employment and help industry; but the strongest motive was to serve warning—which would be implicit in the construction program—that Japan's demand for naval equality would start a new race in naval armaments, and in this race the United States was determined to win.

The United States slower than Japan or Great Britain in building up to treaty limits

Following the failure of the preliminary naval conversations in London in 1934, diplomatic negotiations were resumed in 1935 between Great Britain and Japan in the hope of still holding a naval conference in that year. The conference met in London in December, 1935; it was attended by delegates from Great Britain, France, Italy, the United States, and Japan. Here, as in the preliminary conversations held in 1934, the Japanese position on "global limitation" and the American position on maintaining the existing naval ratios were far apart. While there were earnest efforts to explore the possibilities of compromise, both delegations remained firm. Japan's internal political situation and desire to impress China with her independence of the Western Powers led her to maintain an uncompromising position. From the standpoint of the United States, recognition of naval parity would give tacit approval to Japan's policies in the Far East. When the powers refused to accord naval parity to her, Japan withdrew from the conference.

The London Naval Conference meets in 1935

Japan withdraws from Conference

But the Japanese withdrawal did not wreck the conference, as was feared. On March 25, 1936, the United States, Great Britain, and France signed the London Naval Treaty of 1936. In addition there was an Anglo-American exchange of letters which recorded an understanding that there would be no competitive naval building between them, and that the principle of parity as between the fleets of the British Commonwealth and the United States would remain unchanged.[23] On May 18, 1936, the Senate unanimously gave its advice and consent to ratification.

Great Britain, France, and the United States sign naval treaty

The treaty, which comprised stipulations with respect to definitions, qualitative limitations, advance notification, and exchange of information, was not of much value because of the escape clauses which the signatories put in to protect themselves against building by those not parties to it.[24] It contained no provision with respect to

Treaty contains many escape clauses

[23] *The London Naval Conference*, 1935, cited, pp. 443–444.

[24] U. S. Department of State, "Treaty between the United States of America and Other Powers Signed at London, March 25, 1936," Treaty Series, No. 919.

quantitative limitation, thus leaving the signatories free to build as many ships as they pleased in each class. Great Britain could by this agreement build cruisers in number and type most useful for her needs. The United States succeeded in keeping the 35,000-ton battleships as well as a free hand in outbuilding Japan to maintain the existing ratios.

Great Britain announces vast rearmament program

On March 3, 1936, during the naval negotiations in London, Great Britain announced her rearmament program and outlined the conditions which necessitated it.[25] The policy of "taking risks for peace" was officially repudiated because it had not, in her opinion, removed the dangers of war. Conditions in the international field had deteriorated to an alarming extent. Germany's rapid rate of rearming threatened the security of her neighbors and rapidly produced a situation where peace was being imperilled. The fatal race of unlimited armaments competition was once more on. Europe found herself heading towards the same goal to which the unrestricted competition in armaments had driven her in the years preceding August 1914.

Germany launches stupendous rearmament program

Germany occupied the central position in the European race to rearm. In March of 1935, with universal military service revived and a new air force created, Germany launched a rearmament program unprecedented in modern times. On the eve of bolting the Disarmament Conference, she sought to expand her army of 100,000 men —the number allowed under the Treaty of Versailles— to 300,000. By the end of December, 1935, her forces had swelled to a total of over 600,000 men. On March 7, 1936, German troops marched into the demilitarized Rhineland zone. The far-reaching expansion in land forces was matched by increases in aerial and naval forces.[26]

---

[25]Statement Relating to Defense, Cmd. 5107 (1936).

[26]Under the Anglo-German naval accord of June 18, 1935, since denounced by Germany, Germany agreed to a fleet 35 per cent of Britain's total tonnage.

In September, 1936, Herr Hitler proclaimed a four-year plan by which his nation would become self-sufficient. Germany was to endeavor to free herself from dependence upon the outside world by finding substitutes for cotton, wool, rubber, petroleum, lead, nickel, tin, and other essential materials. It was a plan designed to organize the entire nation for war. By the end of 1936, less than two years after the first formal repudiation of the disarmament clauses of the Versailles Treaty, Germany had risen again to a commanding military position in Europe.

France increases her armaments

Across the Rhine to the west, France responded by increasing her military budget to a peace level unknown in French history and took steps to nationalize her war industries. The "Maginot line" of fortifications, completed in 1935, was extended down to the Swiss frontier because of a possible German invasion through Switzerland and up along the Belgium frontier in anticipation of another German violation of Belgium neutrality. The conscript term of one year was raised, in 1935, to two years, and a vast program was launched to motorize the army and expand the naval and air forces.

Italy follows Germany's model

Totalitarian preparations for war in Italy displayed some striking similarities to those in Germany. To carry forward a vast program of armament and to develop a system of self-sufficiency, she, too, placed her national economy on a basis of autarchy. In case of war, Italy was determined not to be at the mercy of countries rich in raw materials. How a nation poorer even than Germany in industrial raw materials was to achieve self-sufficiency was answered by the boast that Il Duce performs miracles. The Italian dictator stated at Avellino on August 30, 1936, at the conclusion of annual army manoeuvres, that Italy was "always in a position, in the course of a few hours and at a simple word of command, to mobilize 8,000,000 men—a formidable *bloc* which fourteen years of Fascist régime has brought to the necessary high temperature of sacrifice and heroism." And at Bologna, on the 24th of October, Mussolini boasted that the olive branch of peace which he offered to the world sprouted "from the forest of eight million sharp bayonets wielded by youths of dauntless heart."

Russia expands her armaments

Faced with a threat of war in Europe and in the Far East, Soviet Russia too was rapidly expanding her man power and materials. From an army of 562,000 in 1933 the number rose to 1,300,000 in 1936.[27] The frenzied speed and the scale of her military preparations were reflected in the budgets for national defense. In 1933 the cost was 1.5 billion rubles; in 1936 it rose to 14.8 billion rubles; and in 1937 it reached 20 billion rubles.[28]

Japan increases her armaments

The "emergency" character of the armament program of Japan which resulted from the Manchurian campaign of 1931–1932 and which was thought to be temporary proved illusory. Her military naval budget rose from 454.6 million yen in 1932 to 1,021.5 million yen in 1936, or 50 per cent of the total budget.[29] The "China incident," which began in 1937, inspired a new twelve-year "armament improvement plan" for increasing the air force, strengthening the Manchurian garrison, mobilizing supply facilities, and securing strategic materials. To the regular budget for national defense, which was 1,412 million yen in 1937, was added the item of 2,529 million yen for the China war.[30] For the year 1938 the Japanese government allotted 1,246 million yen to national defense, and 4,850 million yen to the China war. These two items represented about 72 per cent of Japan's total authorized expenditure, and 46 per cent of her national income.

---

[27]See the statement of Marshall Tukachevsky, New York *Times*, January 16, 1936.

[28]Gregory T. Grinko, Finance Commissar, in statement to Central Executive Committee, New York *Times*, January 12, 1937.

[29]Cf. League of Nations, *Armaments Year Book*, 1936, p. 566.

[30]*Oriental Economist*, Supplement, "Trade and Industry in 1937–1938."

Smaller nations follow same course

The smaller countries in Europe pursued the same tragic course as the big ones. They turned to costly defense programs, and to new alignments because of the failure of the Disarmament Conference, of the League of Nations' action to check Japan in Manchuria, and of sanctions against Italy in her war on Ethiopia. Belgium and Holland embarked upon the construction of elaborate fortifications on their frontiers facing Germany. Switzerland, fearing that she might become a second Belgium in another world war, reorganized her national defense system. Poland (which was soon to be partitioned by Nazi Germany and Soviet Russia), Austria, and Czechoslovakia (which were also to be the objects of German conquest) were feverishly increasing their national defenses. Such arming in an atmosphere of ever-increasing political tension was bound to lead to war. Short of war, such arming was certain to bring national bankruptcy. "And it was a sweet paradox for the Devil to roll his tongue over—the hope of avoiding armed conflict by piling up munitions! Yet lunacy, bankruptcy, and paradox notwithstanding, there was not a responsible statesman the world over, trustee for the lives and welfare of his people, who dared to take chances on any other course."[31]

Rising cost of world armaments is stupendous

In 1934 the world armament expenditure was in excess of $5,000,000,000; in 1935 it rose to $8,776,000,000; in 1936 it was $12,976,000,000; in 1937 it was $15,468,000,000; and in 1938 it reached a total of $17,581,000,000. Eighty per cent of this outlay was due to the armament programs of the seven great powers—Great Britain, France, the United States, Germany, Italy, Japan, and the Soviet Union.[32] During the decade preceding the World War, the armament costs of these same seven nations had risen

[31]Whitney H. Shepardson and William O. Scroggs, *The United States in World Affairs,* An Account of American Foreign Relations, 1936.

[32]League of Nations, *Armaments Year Book,* 1936; William T. Stone, "Economic Consequences of Rearmament," *Foreign Policy Reports,* XIV, October 1, 1938.

from approximately $1,500,000,000 to $2,400,000,000.[33] The economic consequences of the flow of capital into war industry, with increasing state participation and intervention in the economic structure of the nation, raised the question whether capitalism can arm for totalitarian war and survive in anything like its present form.

The United States also in rearmament ferment

The United States was not a silent spectator in this world rearmament ferment. The naval appropriation bill for 1937–1938 provided for an expenditure of $516,258,808. The speed with which this appropriation was passed by the House—within four days after its introduction, and without a record vote—showed that Congressional sentiment was strongly in favor of strengthening the navy. The army appropriation bill for 1937–1938 called for an expenditure of $415,263,154, making a combined army and navy total of $931,521,962. Compared with the budget of the preceding year, this one was only 2.3 per cent higher; compared with the budgets of the great military powers of Europe, ours was small; compared with the army and navy figures of the first Franklin D. Roosevelt administration, this one was nearly twice as large. But before the year was over President Roosevelt, in a letter dated December 28, 1937, to Representative Taylor, Chairman of the Appropriations Committee, expressed his anxiety over the course of world events and indicated that he would ask Congress for a more extended armaments program.

President Roosevelt sounds warning

In his annual message to Congress on January 3, 1938, the President expressed the prevailing sentiment of the nation when he said: "We must keep ourselves adequately strong in self-defense. . . . There is a trend in the world away from the observance of both the letter and the spirit of treaties. We propose to observe, as we have in the past, our own treaty obligations; but we cannot be certain of reciprocity on the part of others." The cost

[33]Cf. *The Economist* (London), Armaments Supplement, October 19, 1929.

of national defense for the year ending June 30, 1939, he estimated to be $991,000,000, and he was careful to add that he might be obliged to ask Congress for additional sums later.

The naval building program, as set out in the Vinson-Trammell Act of 1934, was designed to bring the American navy up to the Washington and London Naval Treaty limits by 1940, that is, by a gradual expansion over a period of years. Whether this expansion would take place depended upon the willingness of Congress annually to appropriate the necessary funds for construction. When Congress, therefore, appropriated $547,000,000 for naval expenditures for the fiscal year 1938–1939, the largest amount since 1920–1921, it was carrying out the policy of the Act in building the navy up to the treaty limits even though those limits were no longer binding. Before the 1938–1939 naval appropriation had become law—the House had acted, but the Senate had not—President Roosevelt, in a second message to Congress, on January 28, 1938, asked for a 20 per cent increase in the existing authorizations. He told Congress that the nation could no longer be certain that its defense would be limited to one ocean or to one coast, or that the Panama Canal would be safe. An adequate national defense, in his opinion, meant "the protection not only of our coasts but also of our communities far removed from the coast. We must keep any potential enemy many hundred miles away from our continental limits." The Administration had decided, "in the light of the increasing armaments of other nations" to build a navy beyond the limits fixed by the Washington and London Naval Treaties of 1922 and 1930 which expired at the end of 1936. This decision, reached after careful deliberation, was historic. The great experiment in the control of naval armaments begun in 1922, and which formed the backbone of the security system in the Pacific through the stabilization of the three greatest

President Roosevelt asks for further authorizations

A navy second to none

fleets, was now to be supplanted by a policy of "a navy second to none."

The recommendations of the President were embodied in a bill[34] which provided for a general increase of 20 per cent in naval armament. It proposed an increase in the authorized number of battleships from fifteen to eighteen; cruisers from thirty-nine to forty-seven; airplane carriers from six to eight; and destroyers from one hundred thirty-two to one hundred forty-seven. In addition, the maximum number of naval planes was increased from some 2000 to 3000,[35] and a provision was made for increasing personnel.

It was Admiral William D. Leahy, Chief of Naval Operations, who explained to the committees of the House and Senate the need for a stronger and enlarged navy. Under our system of government, according to which the President and Congress formulate policy, Admiral Leahy had perforce to confine his testimony to matters bearing on the broad task of naval operations which confronted the navy in guarding the nation's defense lines and repelling a hostile fleet before it could reach our shores.[36] But behind the testimony there were international political factors which were vitally affecting the military position of the United States, and which called for an orientation in our military policy. The chief factors were the changing balance of power on the continent of Europe, with Germany as the dominant nation; the restriction on

Factors affecting our military position

[34]H. R. 9218, Seventy-fifth Congress, Third Session.

[35]The bill as finally passed made 3000 the minimum instead of the maximum.

[36]The Secretary of the Navy in his annual reports states the "fundamental naval policy" without any legislative or executive authorization. The core of this policy is to maintain a navy in sufficient strength to support the national policies and commerce and to guard the continental and overseas possessions of the United States. Cf. United States Navy Department, *Annual Report of the Secretary of the Navy, 1933*. This was amended so as to provide for a navy suitable for operations in either or both oceans, protection of American lives and assistance in evacuating Americans from danger zones, and maintenance of uninterrupted communications with and for American nationals, i.e., protecting American foreign commerce. Cf. United States Navy Department, *Annual Report of the Secretary of the Navy, 1938*.

British sea power and freedom of action by the military ascendency of Germany; the German and Italian ideological and commercial penetration in Latin America; and the Japanese attempt to establish hegemony in the Far East.[37]

Naval program arouses fear of isolationists

For the proponents of "a navy second to none," the Administration's rearmament program was in the nature of a field day; for the isolationists and peace advocates, it raised fears and suspicion that our government was getting ready for a foreign venture. These fears, at a time when Congress was considering the enlarged naval program, were heightened by the visit of the Chief of the Navy Department's War Plans Division to London to confer with high ranking British naval officers, and the participation of three American cruisers in the ceremonies opening the new British naval base at Singapore. The visit, the State Department explained, was for the purpose of consulting the French and the British on the advisability of asking Japan for information on her naval building program; the three cruisers in Singapore were merely making a courtesy call.

Senator Johnson sees involvement

Behind the euphemism "parallel action"—a phrase used by the State Department to explain what appeared to be joint action with Great Britain, particularly in the Far East—the isolationists thought they saw "involvement." This fear was real in the mind of Senator Hiram Johnson of California, who introduced a resolution[38] calling upon the Secretary of State to tell the Senate whether or not "any alliance, agreement, or understanding exists or is contemplated with Great Britain relating to war or the possibility of war"; whether or not "there is any understanding or agreement, express or implied, for the use of the navy of the United States in conjunction with any other nation"; whether or not "there is any understanding or agreement, express or implied, with any

[37]Cf. Major George Fielding Eliot, *Defending America.*

[38]*Congressional Record,* Seventy-fifth Congress, Third Session, pp. 1977, 2096.

nation, that the United States Navy, or any part of it, should police or patrol or be transferred to any particular waters or any particular ocean." The three inquiries were each answered by the Secretary of State with an unequivocal "no" before the Senate acted on the resolution.[39] But Mr. Hull's "no" did not convince the Senator from California, who later told the Senate that he was "for a good navy, a large navy, and for the navy bills which are now pending," but was against "this navy of ours being used in connection with any other country on earth," and against "any alliance with any other country on earth."[40]

Representative Tinkham seeks investigation of State Department

In the House, Representative Tinkham from Massachusetts, who asserted that he had voted for every military and naval appropriation for twenty-three years but would not vote for this one, flatly stated that he did not believe what had been said by Admiral Leahy or by Secretary Hull.[41] He preferred to believe Mr. Winston Churchill, who was quoted in a newspaper as having said that "an excellent arrangement" existed between the United States and Great Britain. In the Congressman's opinion "a sinister secret diplomacy" was now directing American foreign policy with "collusive political engagements between the United States and Great Britain." He went so far as to introduce a resolution calling for an investigation to determine to what extent the Department of State "is dominated and controlled by the British Foreign Office" and "the character of the intrigue or collective political engagement which apparently has been entered into with Great Britain." In the upper House, Senator Bone sought to establish "a defensive sea area" around the United States beyond which the

[39]Cf. Letter of Cordell Hull to Senator Key Pittman, Chairman of Senate Committee on Foreign Relations, Department of State, Press Release, February 12, 1938.

[40]*Congressional Record,* Seventy-fifth Congress, Third Session, pp. 2097, 2334.

[41]*Ibid.,* p. 4413.

navy would not be permitted to operate except in case of an attack on the United States or a violation of the Monroe Doctrine. But every attempt to hamper the Administration or to cut down the authorizations was defeated. In the House, the bill passed by a vote of 294 to 100; in the Senate, by a vote of 56 to 28.[42] The President signed the bill on May 17, 1938.

Congress increases strength of army

Because of the insular character of our defense policy, conditioned by our geographical position, the navy has attracted more attention than the army. The army, however, has not been neglected; far from it. The long-range program of reorganization and modernization initiated by General Douglas MacArthur soon after President Roosevelt took office in 1933 has continued. In 1939 the regular enlisted strength was brought up to 165,000,[43] and in that year Congress responded to the President's request by raising the authorized strength of the army to 202,500 enlisted men and to 16,719 commissioned officers.[44] By 1940 the National Guard is expected to reach a total of 210,000.[45] Added training facilities have also been provided for reserve officers.[46] The appropriation for the army for the fiscal year 1938–1939 was $459,000,000, the largest since 1921, and there were indications that bigger demands would soon be forthcoming.

Nor has the United States in recent years neglected the airplane, which today is in the forefront of the revolution in military technique. The airplane has gone through a swift technical development since the World War; its strength, mobility, and destructive power, used in conjunc-

---

[42] *Op. cit.*, pp. 4992, 8181.

[43] United States, War Department, *Report of the Chief of Staff*, U. S. Army, 1938.

[44] U. S. 76th Congress, First Session, Hearings before the Senate Committee on Military Affairs on H. R. 3791.

[45] *Ibid.*, House Report No. 119, on the Military Establishment Appropriation Bill, 1940, p. 10.

[46] *Ibid.*, Hearings before the Subcommittee of the House Committee on Appropriations on the Military Establishment Appropriation Bill for 1940, pp. 553ff.

Congress authorizes increase in planes

tion with a mechanized army, make it one of the decisive weapons in modern warfare. On January 12, 1939, President Roosevelt urged Congress to strengthen the air corps by at least 3000 planes, at a cost estimated at $300,000,000.[47] The War Department was authorized to spend $170,000,000 of this sum for the building of planes, with an upper limit of 6000.[48] In addition, in response to the new concept of hemispheric defense, the army intends to build widely dispersed operating bases, strategically located. Thus the army and the navy combined will in a few years possess a total of some 8500 planes. There was virtually no opposition to this vast program. The fear which gripped all of Europe during the days preceding the British and French capitulation to Germany at Munich[49] spread to this country and dampened opposition to increased armaments. The nation had sensed the overwhelming power of air armaments with which Hitler had wrested Sudetenland from Czechoslovakia in September, 1938, in what has become known as the Munich Accord.

War plan contemplates mobilization of nation's wealth and man power

The far-reaching modernization of the army was geared in 1937 to a new basic war plan or industrial mobilization plan in which the War Department has earmarked some 12,000 factories as potential wartime producers of munitions and equipment. This plan contemplates the mobilization of the nation's resources in men and materials in the support of the military and naval forces in case the nation becomes involved in a major conflict. Recognizing that modern war cannot be waged except by totalitarian control, the plan envisages the subordination of the normal pattern of political, economic, and social existence to the aim of winning the conflict. The system of controls set up in the plan would modify the constitutional liberties

[47] *Congressional Record*, January 12, 1939, p. 300.

[48] H. R. 3791, approved April 3, 1939.

[49] See *infra*, pp. 974–986.

we enjoy in peace time—to what extent it is not now possible to state. While the wartime super-agencies proposed by the plan would enjoy dictatorial powers for the duration of a war, it is not possible to predict to what degree our liberties would be modified when the conflict was over. War today is a catalytic force in social change and not infrequently is a prelude to revolution.

House Committee proposes another naval increase

When the interlude of "peace" ended in Europe in September, 1939, Representative Vinson, with the approval of the President, the Navy Department, and the majority of the House Committee on Naval Affairs, announced on November 4, 1939, plans for the third great authorization program of the Roosevelt Administration. The 1934 and 1938 expansion programs proved inadequate in the light of the Far Eastern and European conflicts; the 1939 project was bigger and the most costly thus far of any in the Franklin D. Roosevelt era. It called for an expenditure within the succeeding four years of $1,300,000,000 on 127 ships. Upon completion of this program in 1944 the total tonnage of the navy would be 2,154,000. The new program was urged upon the nation by the Chairman of the House Naval Committee on the ground that the existing fleet and the projects under way were adequate only "against any single aggressor," and this latest additional strength was necessary to provide protection against "possible combinations." What was this "possible combination" against which official Washington had set out to build "a navy second to none"? A German victory in Europe would mean the end of British and French naval power and a redistribution of French and British colonies in Africa, or perhaps even a change in the ownership of important Portuguese or Spanish islands in the Atlantic, readily accessible to the South American coast. A victory for Japan in the Far East would provide a threat to the United States from the Pacific. If the two victors combined, they would very likely challenge the Monroe Doctrine. From time to time the nation has been discreetly told that the President has in his possession information which has made him and those in his confidence apprehensive of the aims of the totalitarian powers which desire to destroy the existing political and territorial arrangements in both oceans. With Germany as the center of dynamic tendencies in Europe, and Japan in Asia, and profound issues affecting the distribution of power everywhere, the nation as a whole has approved the vast outlays for armaments. But where will this vast armada be used? In distant waters to protect economic and political policies, or in the waters adjacent to the Western Hemisphere? If the neutrality legislation correctly mirrors the sentiment of the nation, the American people desire to guard their position in the Western Hemisphere and to avoid being drawn into conflicts in distant areas. The nation recoils from the thought of "involvement," diplomatic or military, which would be necessary to affect power relationships in Europe or in Asia. Temporary intervention, such as was engaged in by this nation in the First World War, was not enough, and today there appears to be no universal desire on the part of the American people to go even as far as they did in 1917. Whether this sentiment will continue is in no small measure dependent upon who the victors in Europe may be.

Nation approves naval increase

The United States faces a vastly different military problem

The military problem facing the United States in 1939 was very different from the one she faced during the World War. Then she had only the European theater to consider. Asia was quiet and Japan was not looked upon as an enemy. In 1939 the United States faced the possibility of war in the Atlantic and the Pacific. In addition, the development of modern weapons, particularly aircraft with its increased range and speed, has lessened our sense of security and has in considerable part necessitated a new concept of defense, known as hemispheric defense, that is, the maintenance of a military machine adequate to prevent the establishment of hostile forward bases in the Western Hemisphere. It was in response to this fear (or threat) that the Roosevelt Administration in 1939 set out to provide the greatest peacetime armaments program in American history in which the element of cost assumed a distinctly secondary role.[50]

[50]*Congressional Record*, January 12, 1939, pp. 300–301.

CHAPTER XXXIX

NEUTRALITY LEGISLATION

Congress turns to neutrality legislation

THE failure of the Disarmament Conference, and Germany's resurgence in Europe—marked by the advent of Adolf Hitler to power in January, 1933, and by the reintroduction of compulsory military service in Germany in March, 1935 in violation of the Treaty of Versailles—aroused Congressional interest in legislation designed to insulate the United States from a possible European war. Moreover, the findings of the Nye investigation which disclosed the activities of the armament manufacturers, the bankers, and other profiteers during the years before the United States entered the World War, gave rise to a widespread belief that the United States had been drawn into the War solely to protect the interests of bankers and munition manufacturers.

Italy prepares to attack Ethiopia

The unmistakable signs that Premier Mussolini of Italy was preparing to attack Ethiopia created anxiety that this might furnish the spark for another European conflagration. Both Italy and Ethiopia were members of the League of Nations. Both were signatories to the Pact of Paris. Great Britain, France, and Italy, in a tripartite convention entered into in 1906, had agreed to make every effort to preserve the integrity of Ethiopia and to act together to safeguard their interests in that country. Moreover, Italy and Ethiopia had concluded a Treaty of Amity and Arbitration in 1928 to safeguard and respect each other's independence and "to submit to a procedure of conciliation or arbitration any questions which may arise between them and which it has not been possible to settle by the usual diplomatic means, without having recourse to the force of arms."[1]

On December 5, 1934, when a border dispute arose[2] between these two nations, Italy's obligation to refrain from separate action and from the use of force against Ethiopia was therefore fourfold in character. Unavailing efforts were made by the Great Powers and the League Council to arbitrate and conciliate. Contemptuous of efforts to settle his differences with Ethiopia amicably, Mussolini was bent on a "totalitarian solution" of the Ethiopian affair "with Geneva, without Geneva, or against Geneva," as it was expressed in an unsigned article—the author of which was believed to be Mussolini—appearing in the *Popolo d'Italia* of July 31, 1935. Italian military preparations for an invasion of Ethiopia proceeded at a feverish pace.

Anti-war sentiment in the United States spreads

As the Italian legions poured through the Suez Canal in the summer of 1935 on their way to Eritrea and Italian Somaliland to start their attack on a member of the League of Nations, anti-war sentiment spread throughout the United States. The American people demanded of their representatives legislation which would keep the nation from being drawn into the impending hostilities. On August 24, 1935, Congress passed, and on August 31, 1935, President Roosevelt signed the so-called Neutrality Act.[3]

Congress passes the Neutrality Act of 1935

The Act provided that upon the outbreak or during the progress of war between two or more foreign states "the President shall proclaim such fact." Following such a proclamation, the export from the United States of "arms, ammunition, or implements of war" to a belligerent was prohibited. The President was empowered to enumerate

[1]League of Nations, Treaty Series, XCIV, 413.

[2]The border affair at the oasis of Walwal resulted in the death of some thirty Italians and over one hundred Ethiopians. League of Nations Publications, Official Document C. 49, M. 22, 1935, VII.

[3]Public Resolution, No. 67, 74th Congress (S. J. Res. 173).

Act provides for arms embargo

the articles covered by the embargo. It should be noted that under these terms, a measure of discretion was given to the President in determining when a state of war exists and in enumerating the articles to be embargoed. These provisions were temporary in character, expiring, under the terms of the Act, on February 29, 1936.

Munitions Control Board created

The Act also set up a permanent National Munitions Control Board consisting of the Secretaries of State, War, Navy, and Commerce. Every person engaged in the business of manufacturing, exporting, or importing any of the arms, ammunition, and implements of war, referred to in the Act,[4] was required to register with the Secretary of State, and to furnish a list of the arms, ammunition, and implements of war which he manufactures, imports, or exports. Export or import of such articles without a license from the Board was made unlawful. The creation of the Board was the first significant step the Federal Government had taken in the direction of controlling the activities of munitions makers and merchants.[5]

The Act made it unlawful for American vessels to carry to, or for the use of, the belligerents any of the articles listed in the proclamation. Other provisions empowered the President, in the exercise of his discretion, to prohibit travel by American citizens on ships of the belligerents, except at their own risk; and to prescribe conditions for, or to prohibit, the use of American ports by belligerent submarines.

The so-called Neutrality Act of 1935 reflected in some measure the lessons which had been brought home to us by our experiences in the World War. The authors of the Act apparently felt that the United States had become

[4]The President's proclamation of the articles to be considered as "arms, ammunition, and implements of war" was to be made upon the recommendation of the Board. (On September 25, 1935, President Roosevelt proclaimed such a list.)

[5]The office of Arms and Munitions Control, lodged in the Department of State, was established September 21, 1935.

involved in that war because of her efforts to protect American trade with the belligerents. American exports to Europe for the year ending June 30, 1914, had reached the unprecedented figure of $1,486,000,000. In the calendar year 1916, that export figure rose to $3,813,000,000.[6] It was not only our trade with the belligerents which expanded enormously, but that with the neutrals as well. Not being able to secure merchandise from belligerents, the neutrals—especially those outside of Europe—turned to American manufacturers. Exports to countries other than those of Europe and Canada doubled in 1916.[7] By 1917 the nation's industry and agriculture had geared its production to the demands of the belligerents and was profiting immensely from trade with the Allies. To have ended that trade, some felt, would have brought on an economic depression of the first magnitude.[8]

Neutrality Act reflects belief that the United States went to war to protect trade interests

Whatever the causes which brought this nation into war on the side of the Allies in 1917—and historians differ as to what they were[9]—the Neutrality Act of 1935 attempted, in part, to stop the traffic in arms in the apparent belief that the law would keep this nation from being drawn into another European war.

Italy attacks Ethiopia

The long heralded attack on Ethiopia came on October 3, 1935. The Council of the League of Nations was summoned to meet on October 7 to determine whether Italy

[6]U. S. Department of Commerce, *Statistical Abstract of the United States, 1932*, p. 444.

[7]*Ibid.*, p. 444.

[8]See Ambassador Page's dispatch in *U. S. Foreign Relations, 1917*, Supplement 2, vol. 1, p. 516, in support of this view; as well as Ray Stannard Baker, *Woodrow Wilson, Life and Letters*, Neutrality, 1914–1915, vol. 5, p. 181.

[9]Charles Seymour, in his *American Neutrality, 1914–1917*, believes it was the German submarine campaign which brought the United States into the war. Newton D. Baker, Secretary of War in President Wilson's Cabinet, expressed a similar belief; see his article, "Why We Went to War," *Foreign Affairs*, October, 1936, pp. 83–84. See also, Samuel Flagg Bemis, *Diplomatic History of the United States*, p. 660. J. Duane Squires, in his *British Propaganda at Home and in the United States from 1914 to 1917*, believes it was superior British propaganda. Robert Lansing, in his *War Memoirs*, p. 19, ascribes it to the threat a German victory would hold to the Anglo-Saxon basis of the American way of life.

was the aggressor. President Roosevelt issued two proclamations dated October 5 invoking the provisions of the Neutrality Act. In one of the proclamations the President declared an export embargo against both belligerents on arms, ammunition, and implements of war;[10] and in the other, he admonished "all citizens of the United States to abstain from traveling on any vessel of either of the belligerent nations" and gave notice that any citizen traveling "contrary to the provisions of the said Joint Resolution will do so at his own risk." But the President did not think his duty ended merely with invoking the law. "In these specific circumstances," he declared in a statement issued through the State Department, "I desire it to be understood that any of our people who voluntarily engage in transactions of any character with either of the belligerents do so at their own risk."[11]

President Roosevelt invokes Neutrality Act

This statement certainly presented a departure from the traditional American policy of upholding the doctrine of the "Freedom of the Seas." American trade with nations at war, in the Italo-Ethiopian conflict at least, was not going to receive the protection of the American government. Far-reaching indeed was the executive renunciation of what Jefferson called "inalienable rights" and what Wilson termed "acknowledged rights," slogans which had involved this nation in the War of 1812 and in the World War.

League of Nations imposes sanctions

The way was now clear for the League of Nations to bring into operation the sanctions provisions of the Covenant without fear of America's insistence on her rights as a neutral. On October 7 the League Council took the momentous step of approving its special committee's report finding that the Italian government had resorted to war in violation of its obligations under the

[10] The proclamation carried six detailed categories.

[11] Department of State, Press Release, October 5, 1935.

Covenant[12] and thus had opened the way for the invocation of sanctions under Article XVI of the Covenant. The step was momentous because sanctions were to be invoked for the first time in the League's history, and collective action against an aggressor was to be given the first real test. On November 18—more than five weeks after the League Council had declared that "the Italian government has resorted to war in disregard of its covenants under Article XII of the Covenant of the League of Nations"—the sanctions came into operation in the form of an embargo on arms, credits, and exports, and a boycott of imports of Italian origin.[13] Coal, oil, and copper, it should be stated, were not included in the list.

The United States eases way for League sanctions

The United States pursued an isolationist policy in the Italo-Ethiopian dispute. But her initiative in invoking the embargo on arms and in discouraging exports of non-embargoed goods to the belligerents gave moral support to the League and perhaps stimulated it into imposing sanctions. Without knowing what American policy would be with respect to "neutral rights," members of the League would have been reluctant to risk the imposition of sanctions. Moreover, had our exporters remained free to carry on trade with the belligerents, the League members would themselves not have been willing to renounce trade with Italy. Thus the United States gave advance notice, so to speak, of its policy and left the League members free to take whatever steps they thought wise to discharge the obligations imposed upon them in upholding the Covenant against an aggressor.

Textually the embargo on arms favored neither Italy nor Ethiopia; in effect, however, Italy was disadvantaged by it. Well prepared before hostilities began, Italy in

---

[12]League of Nations Publications. Official No. C. 411 (1). M. 207 (1). L 935, VII.

[13]On November 18, 1935, the Italian government applied counter sanctions against countries imposing sanctions on Italy.

opposing a poorly armed people was, in reality, caused little embarrassment by our embargo. The exertion of "moral pressure" to discourage "abnormal" trade with Italy, however, aroused the Italian government and there were intimations even that an embargo by our government on oil would be regarded as a "hostile act."

The Administration seeks to discourage trade in essential war materials

The Roosevelt Administration endeavored to reinforce League action by discouraging American trade with the belligerents. From time to time warnings by the President and other government officials[14] made it clear that while there was no legal prohibition against general trade with the belligerents, the American government regarded trade in certain commodities such as oil, copper, trucks, tractors, scrap iron, and scrap steel—essential war materials, although not actually "arms, ammunition, or implements of war"—as directly contrary to its policy and the general spirit of the Neutrality Act.

The Rickett oil affair

A concrete illustration of the Government's policy was the manner in which it handled the Rickett Oil Concession. On September 4, 1935, a month before the outbreak of hostilities, came the announcement that Emperor Haile Selassie of Ethiopia had granted to Francis M. Rickett, a British promoter, on behalf of the African Exploration and Development Company—a Standard Oil subsidiary—the right to exploit oil and mineral resources in an area of some 150,000 square miles, covering about half of Ethiopia, for a period of 75 years. This grant was made by the Emperor presumably in the hope that it would draw in Great Britain and the United States to oppose Italian aggression. The Department of State informed the Standard Vacuum Oil Company that the concessions "had been the cause of great embarrassment not only to the Government but to other governments who are making strenuous and sincere efforts for

[14]See Department of State, Press Releases, October 12, November 2, 9, 16, 1935.

the preservation of peace" and that "it was highly desirable that the necessary steps should be taken at the earliest possible moment to terminate the present concession."[15] The company withdrew from the concession, and President Roosevelt was able to declare that the Rickett affair was "another proof that since March 4, 1933, dollar diplomacy is no longer recognized by the American government."[16]

Exports to Italy rise

But in spite of such "moral pressure" as was exerted by the Administration in the Rickett case,[17] exports to Italian Africa, particularly of oil—so vital for motorized transportation and airplane attack—rose markedly during the months of October and November, 1935, over the comparable months of the previous year.[18]

President dissatisfied with inflexible provisions of Neutrality Act of 1935

When President Roosevelt signed the Neutrality Act of 1935, he did so reluctantly and pointed out that "further careful consideration of neutrality needs is most desirable."[19] He was not satisfied with the Act because its inflexibility was fraught with danger. He felt that the Executive should be given discretion in adapting the system to the needs of preserving peace or equally, the interests of the United States. This, of course, might mean discretion to impose an embargo against an aggressor and give help to the victim of aggression. Hence, when Congress convened on January 3, 1936, the President addressed it and the country over a nation-wide radio network. He deplored the fact that "the temper and the purposes of the rulers of many of the great populations in Europe and Asia have not pointed the way either to

[15]Department of State, Press Release, September 7, 1935.

[16]New York *Times*, September 5, 1935.

[17]The Department of Commerce notified the owners of ships on which the Government had placed mortgages that the transportation of essential war materials to either of the belligerents was contrary to national policy. In the case of the tanker *Ulysses* the Government threatened to foreclose the mortgage on the tanker if it sailed to Italy with a cargo of 12,000 tons of oil.

[18]Department of Commerce, News Release, November 23, 1935.

[19]Department of State, Press Release, August 31, 1935.

peace or to good-will among men." Certain rulers, he said (he refrained from naming Chancellor Hitler of Germany and Premier Mussolini of Italy), had "impatiently reverted to the old belief in the law of the sword, or to the fantastic conception that they, and they alone, are chosen to fulfill a mission, and that all the others among the billion and a half of human beings must and shall learn from them and be subject to them." The Government of the United States opposed the spread of autocracy and the persecution of peoples. The President was referring to Germany's persecution of the Jews and her efforts to destroy organized religion and substitute the doctrine of "people, blood, and race" with a new tribal paganism in place of Christianity. International relations had deteriorated; insecurity had spread among nations, and rearmament was proceeding apace. The President called upon Congress for a "two-fold neutrality"—an embargo on arms and an embargo on export, in excess of normal commerce, of other materials used in the conduct of war.

President asks for new neutrality legislation

The bill which was introduced was an attempt to placate the various conflicting schools of thought, from isolationist to internationalist. It carried provisions which reflected, in some measure, the President's views as expressed in his message to Congress. But it failed to win support. The isolationist Congress felt that it did not go far enough in prescribing a mandatory embargo on all exports, loans, and credits. Some decried it because it was a surrender of the principle of the freedom of the seas; and others because it hampered the Executive in acting in concert with other nations to maintain peace. Since the embargo provisions of the Neutrality Act of 1935 were to expire on February 29, 1936, with Italy and Ethiopia still at war and the fear ever present that other nations might be drawn in, time was too short for protracted debate on an issue which revealed such fundamental differences of points of view. The expedient Congress resorted to was to extend the Act of 1935 to May 1, 1937, with three amendments. It forbade the granting of loans or credits to belligerents; it exempted American republics from the operation of the Act if they engage in a war against a non-American state; and it made mandatory what was hitherto the discretionary power of the Executive to extend the arms embargo to additional states when they became involved in war.

Congress extends 1935 Act with amendments

The Neutrality Act of February 29, 1936, made no mention of an arms embargo in the event of *civil war*, and when civil war broke out in Spain in July, 1936, the President found himself powerless to act. As the international aspects of the Spanish civil war became evident, the danger that the conflict might spread through the intermeddling of some other nation prompted the French government to propose a non-intervention agreement by which the European powers would desist from sending arms and munitions to either party in Spain. In Russia, there was sympathy with the established Spanish government; in Italy and in Germany the sympathy was with the rebels. How to prevent these nations from testing out new weapons as well as their fascist and communist ideologies in Spain became a critical problem for Europe. The International Committee for the Application of the Agreement regarding Non-intervention in Spain,[20] to which twenty-seven nations adhered, came into being for the purpose of localizing the conflict and preventing intervention by those interested in using Spain as a proving ground for their new armaments as well as their ideologies.

Civil war breaks out in Spain

The civil war in Spain aroused the interest and feeling of the public in this country. The traditions of democracy embedded in the American character of over a hundred

[20] The Non-intervention Committee was not effective. Italy and Germany, notwithstanding their assurances, sent "volunteers" and war materials to the rebels, and Russia sent mechanics and airmen to the Loyalists.

and fifty years of history are repugnant to fascist ideology. The Spanish conflict provided an opportunity for anti-fascist groups, some of them communist, to come to the aid of the Spanish Republic. Soon several thousand Americans were fighting in the front lines in Spain for the Spanish government. Organizations sprang up to collect funds, food, clothing, and medical supplies and to enlist the services of doctors and nurses. On the other hand pro-fascist sympathizers, believing that the rebel leader, General Francisco Franco, was carrying on a war against Communism, set up rival organizations. The interest which the Spanish conflict created gave rise to anxiety on the part of those who felt that a mere arms and credit embargo was not sufficient in a major crisis to impose neutrality upon the American people who enjoy freedom of speech, freedom of the press, and other constitutional rights.[21]

Spanish civil war arouses American interest

Nevertheless, the Roosevelt administration, not desiring to hamper the efforts of Great Britain and France to localize the war in Spain through the Non-intervention Committee, and in the absence of any legislation applicable to the Spanish civil war, used "moral suasion" to discourage American exporters from shipping munitions to either side in the conflict. As soon as Congress convened, the President, in his message of January 6, 1937, asked that the Neutrality Act be amended "to cover specific points raised by the unfortunate civil strife in Spain."[22] Congress acted quickly, and on January 8 the President signed the joint resolution prohibiting the export of arms, muni-

Joint resolution imposes arms embargo on Spain

[21]Anti-fascist picketing of the German and Italian embassies led the Secretary of State, on complaints by the German and Italian embassies, to recommend legislation to prevent picketing of foreign embassies, legations, and consulates. By joint resolution, approved February 15, 1938, the display of banners and the commission of certain specified offensive or intimidating acts within five hundred feet of any building or premises within the District of Columbia used or occupied by any foreign government or its representatives as an embassy, legation, or consulate, or for other official purposes, was prohibited.

[22]*Congressional Record*, January 6, 1937, p. 87.

tions, and implements of war to Spain, or to any other foreign country for trans-shipment to Spain, and cancelled export licenses previously granted for this purpose.

Wisdom of embargo against Spanish government questioned

This resolution applied only to the Spanish civil war. It was passed not without some misgivings on the part of many Congressmen.[23] A particular nation was singled out. Was this a wise step to take in view of our Latin-American policy to suppress revolts by giving aid to the established government? Was not our government injuring the democratic cause to the advantage of fascism in imposing an embargo against the Spanish government and the rebels but not against Germany and Italy which were actually engaged in helping the Spanish rebels to overthrow a duly constituted government? If Germany and Italy were openly engaged in sending men and munitions to the rebels why should not the United States prohibit the sale of arms and ammunition to them? There was ample evidence from which the President could conclude that both Italy and Germany had committed acts of war against the Republic of Spain, even though the formal declaration was lacking. The absence of a formal declaration of war between Italy and Ethiopia in October, 1935, did not deter the President from invoking the embargo against them. During the time when both Germany and Italy were deeply involved in giving aid to the Spanish rebels, both of these countries were buying arms freely in this country.[24] Why did not the President extend the arms embargo to them? For the President to have invoked the embargo against Italy and Germany would have been tantamount to pronouncing a moral judgment on their acts. Such a course would not only have embarrassed the Non-intervention Committee which shut its eyes to the acts of Germany and Italy, but would

[23]See *Congressional Record,* January 6, 1937, pp. 95ff.

[24]See First Annual Report of National Munitions Control Board, Washington, Government Printing Office, 1937.

have placed the United States in an exposed position. This the President was unwilling to do. He felt he could go no further than the Non-intervention Committee without incurring grave international dangers.

With the arms embargo resolution on Spain out of the way, Congress turned its attention to the enactment of a "permanent" neutrality law which would come into operation when the 1935 Act, as amended and extended on February 29, 1936, should expire on May 1, 1937.

The nation divided on the type of neutrality legislation

The discussion which followed in and out of Congress disclosed that the nation was overwhelmingly in favor of legislation which would keep us out of war, but as to what this should contain there were many differences of opinion. There were some who proposed an unlimited mandatory embargo as to all belligerents. There were others who urged a mandatory embargo on the outbreak of war, while still others felt that the President should be given discretion to impose the embargo. John Bassett Moore argued for a return to the traditional system of neutrality which America had espoused since the days of Washington.[25] Others urged a policy of "trade at your own risk" without any protection whatsoever from the Government, a policy declared by President Roosevelt on the outbreak of the Italo-Ethiopian War. Then there were some who came forward with the "cash-and-carry" type of neutrality—a system whereby exporters could sell anything except lethal weapons so long as payment was made in cash and transportation was made on non-American ships, with title passing to the buyer before the goods were shipped.

Mandatory embargo versus discretionary embargo

There was intense debate in and out of Congress on the issue of the mandatory versus the discretionary type of embargo. Should the Executive be given discretion to impose an embargo on the outbreak of war? Should the law be drawn so as to set forth in detail the course of

[25]Cf. his pamphlet, "Pending 'Neutrality' Proposals: Their False Conceptions and Misunderstandings."

conduct the President should follow in any and all situations? Or should it be drawn so as to permit him discretion and freedom in setting the embargo machinery in motion?

The Neutrality Act of 1937 represents compromise

The measure which was finally passed, after it had been reported out of the Senate and House conference and signed by the President May 1, 1937, represented a compromise between the mandatory and the discretionary schools of thought with a slight margin of victory for the discretionary school. Those Senators who voted against the bill[26] feared giving the President discretion over so many provisions. Senator Bone of Washington objected because it gave the President "a discretionary power that I would not give my own father,"[27] while Senator Borah of Idaho, who had been the Senate's watchdog in matters of foreign policy for nearly three decades and who voted for the bill, insisted that "there must be large discretion in any workable neutrality law" and that "the more discretion within reason the better, for where you are dealing with war conditions it is impossible to foresee what course a nation should pursue."[28]

Act of 1937 further restricts enjoyment of neutral rights

The Neutrality Act of May 1, 1937, which superseded the Neutrality Acts of August 31, 1935, and of February 29, 1936, was designed to be permanent, save for the "cash-and-carry" provisions which were to expire at the end of two years. Under the Act of May 1, 1937, "whenever the President shall find that there exists a state of war between, or among two or more foreign States, the President shall proclaim such and it shall thereafter be unlawful": (1) to export or to attempt to export "arms, ammunition, or implements of war from any place in the United States" to any belligerent named in such proclamation,

---

[26]The Senate vote was 41 for and 15 against the bill. See *Congressional Record*, 75th Congress, First Session, pp. 5168–5182.

[27]*Ibid.*, p. 5155.

[28]*Ibid.*, p. 5156.

or to any neutral State for trans-shipment to, or for the use of, any such belligerent; (2) "to purchase, sell, or exchange bonds, securities, or other obligations of the government of any belligerent," or of any political subdivision thereof, or of any person or faction acting for or on behalf of the government of such State, with the proviso that the President may exempt "ordinary commercial credits and short-term obligations in aid of legal transactions and of a character customarily used in normal peacetime commercial transaction" from the operation of this section;[29] (3) to carry any arms, ammunition, or implements of war on any American vessel to any belligerent; (4) for any citizen of the United States to travel on any vessel of a belligerent, except in accordance with such rules and regulations as the President shall prescribe; (5) for any American vessel engaged in commerce with belligerents "to be armed or to carry any armament, arms, ammunition, or implements of war, except small arms and ammunition therefor which the President may deem necessary"; and (6) to export arms, ammunition, or implements of war to a State where civil strife exists.

Act permits belligerents to buy on cash-and-carry basis

Under the Act, the President was empowered, in his discretion, to prohibit the use of American ports as a base of supply for belligerent states; to forbid submarines and armed merchant vessels of a foreign State from entering American ports or territorial waters except under such conditions and limitations as he may prescribe; to prohibit the export of any goods to a belligerent "until all right, title, and interest therein shall have been transferred to some foreign government," or national; and to prohibit the transport of any article on an American vessel to any belligerent State. The Act specifically

[29]The renewal or adjustment of such indebtedness as may exist on the day the President invokes the embargo, as well as the solicitation of funds to be used "for medical aid" or "for food and clothing to relieve human suffering" by any person or organization not acting for or on behalf of any belligerent, was likewise exempt from the operation of this section.

exempted from its operation "an American republic or republics engaged in war against a non-American State or States, provided the American republic is not coöperating with a non-American State or States in such war." It continued the National Munitions Control Board, consisting of the Secretaries of State, Treasury, War, Navy, and Commerce, with authority to license the manufacture and export of arms, ammunition, and implements of war.

Act seeks to reduce provocative incidents which might lead to involvement

Thus a comparison of the three neutrality statutes shows a successive growth of restrictions in an endeavor to reduce provocative incidents which might lead to our "involvement." Starting with an embargo on arms in the Act of 1935, the Act of 1937 added other articles which the President might designate. Whereas there were no restrictions on financial transactions with belligerents under the 1935 Act, loans or credits were forbidden under the 1936 and 1937 Acts. While the President was authorized under the 1935 Act to withdraw protection from American citizens traveling on belligerent ships, the Act of 1937 empowered him to forbid such travel except in accordance with such rules and regulations as he should prescribe.

Cash-and-carry provision in Act designed to protect American trade

The so-called "cash-and-carry" provision in the Act was one of its most interesting features. The Acts of 1935 and 1936 were silent on the export of steel, copper, oil, cotton, and other such commodities. From the standpoint of "involvement" the export of these commodities is as dangerous as the export of lethal weapons. But an embargo on all materials used for war purposes—and in a modern war, where the entire nation is in arms, the distinction between materials for war purposes and non-war purposes is worn thin—would result in deepening economic distress in the United States where some ten millions were unemployed. The "cash-and-carry" device offered a partial way out of the dilemma. It was a device designed to protect American war trade on the one hand with the least possible likelihood of "involvement" on the other. International bankers and munitions manufacturers were shut out, however. Senator Borah summed it up when he said: "We seek to avoid all risks, all danger, but we make certain to get all the profits."[30]

Cash-and-carry provision favors belligerent in control of seas

The Act of 1937 was neutrality in form only. The "carry" aspect of the principle obviously favored the belligerents in control of the seas, such as Great Britain with her large navy and large merchant marine. The "cash" aspect would provide no serious obstacle to her; with enormous investments here which could be made liquid, Great Britain would be in a position to buy what she needed from us.

Cash-and-carry provision a warning to the fascist dictatorships

The Act was framed and debated against a European background of recurring political crises and impending war, with Great Britain and France aligned against Germany and Italy, the would-be aggressors. Congress was not indifferent to the swift-moving events in Europe and its action reflected in large measure the sentiment of the nation towards would-be aggressors. The "cash-and-carry" principle was not only designed to reduce the danger of our "involvement" in Europe, but also to give notice to the fascist dictatorships of Germany and Italy that the American arsenal and granary would not be open to them in case of war since they lacked the financial resources with which to buy, and the vessels with which to carry away the goods.

Neutrality Act of 1937 incompatible with certain treaty obligations

It was obvious that the Neutrality Act of 1937 was incompatible with certain treaty obligations which we had assumed, particularly towards Latin-American nations. The Convention of Rights and Duties of States in the Event of Civil Strife, adopted at Havana on February 20, 1928, and ratified by us on May 21, 1930, obliges the United States as well as the Latin-American states, in the event of civil strife, "to forbid the traffic in arms and

[30] *Congressional Record*, March 1, 1939, p. 2099.

war material, except when intended for the government, while the belligerency of the rebels has not been recognized. . . ." Apart from treaty obligations our government in an effort to discourage revolutions has followed a policy of not permitting the export of arms to rebels in Latin-American states, but has allowed the shipment of arms to the constituted authorities. Under the Neutrality Act, the arms embargo, in the event of civil strife, must apply to the existing government and to rebels alike; under the Havana Convention, the United States assumed an obligation to apply an arms embargo against the rebels only. Were some foreign powers to instigate a revolt or give aid to a revolutionary faction in a Latin-American state, as the Italian and German dictators did in Spain, the President under the Neutrality Act of 1937 would be hamstrung; he would have to invoke the embargo against the recognized government as well as against the rebels.[31]

The Neutrality Act of 1937 and the collective peace machinery

Nor was Congress concerned with the effect that its neutrality policy might have on the collective peace machinery which had been built since the Treaty of Versailles. The fear that an arms embargo might hinder members of the League of Nations from resorting to sanctions against an aggressor was of no moment to Congress. The failure of sanctions in the Italo-Ethiopian conflict led to widespread belief that the League had been so weakened that sanctions would not very likely be attempted again.

In the summer of 1937 the neutrality principle was again put to the test when Japan launched an attack on China.

[31]In an effort to remove the conflict between our Latin-American policy with respect to arms embargoes and the Neutrality Act of 1937, an amendment was introduced in Congress exempting Latin-American countries from the application of the Act "unless the President shall find, after consultation with the governments of other American republics and after consideration of all the circumstances," that the application of the Neutrality Act would "tend toward the re-establishment of peace or the protection of the commercial interests of the United States." Cf. *Congressional Record*, 75th Congress, First Session, pp. 8916, 8987. Congress, however, adjourned before acting on the proposal.

Military operations by land, sea, and air were carried on on an extensive scale and over a wide area, without formal declaration of war by either side. There was no doubt that the military activity in China constituted war in fact, if not in legal theory. Yet, President Roosevelt did not "find" a state of war to exist as a condition preceding the invocation of the Act. He did declare that government-owned merchant vessels would not be permitted to transport arms, ammunition, or implements of war either to China or to Japan, and that "any other merchant vessels, flying the American flag, which attempt to transport any of the listed articles to China or Japan will, until further notice, do so at their own risk."[32]

President Roosevelt fails to invoke Neutrality Act in Sino-Japanese conflict

Senator Pittman gives reasons for not invoking Neutrality Act

The Administration's reason for not invoking the Act was given in a formal statement by Senator Key Pittman, Chairman of the Foreign Relations Committee, on July 29, 1939. Not every armed conflict was a state of war, the Senator contended. If the conflict continued beyond immediate hope "of a peaceful solution, then a state of war exists." "If today," said the Senator, "the President should declare a state of war to exist between China and Japan, it would be his duty to place in effect as to both such governments all of the provisions of the Neutrality Act. If then an armistice is declared tomorrow or any subsequent date shortly thereafter, his decision that a state of war exists would be erroneous under the interpretation intended in our Neutrality Act. Certainly, the second the Neutrality Act is put in force and effect, the influence of the President in bringing about a cessation of hostilities in China would be greatly depreciated and his great power for the protection of our citizens impaired. If either government declares war,[33] his discretion ends.

[32]Department of State, Press Release, September 14, 1937.

[33]Neither side in the Italo-Ethiopian conflict declared war, yet the President did not hesitate to find that a state of war did exist, and he invoked the Neutrality Act of 1935 within a few days of the outbreak of hostilities.

Such a declaration, however, must be made by a government."[34]

Embargo on China and Japan not feasible

But the Sino-Japanese armed conflict continued beyond immediate hope of a peaceful solution and yet the President did not invoke the Act. There was pressure on the Administration from all sides for and against the application of the law. In the summer of 1937 American industry bogged down, domestic buying power had contracted, and the nation was in a state of economic depression. To clamp an embargo on both belligerents would have meant the disruption of American trade with China and Japan, with possibly a blockade by Japan of the Chinese coast followed by the publication in both countries of contraband lists covering almost every important article of commerce. Invoking the Neutrality Act would simply have intensified the depression here, since Japan—a heavy buyer of scrap iron, oil, cotton, and other commodities—would undoubtedly have retaliated against an embargo on munitions and loans. And so, to lessen the danger of becoming involved and of aggravating the economic depression, the Administration failed to invoke the Neutrality Act but warned that merchant vessels carrying munitions and implements of war would do so at their own risk.[35]

Roosevelt Administration seeks to strengthen cash-and-carry provisions

When war seemed imminent in Europe early in 1939, the Roosevelt Administration sought to prepare the country for it by urging a repeal of the arms embargo, as well as a reinstatement and strengthening of the "cash-and-carry" provisions of the 1937 Act which were about to expire. Congress refused to accept the Administration's proposals for revision because it did not share the Administration's fear of a war in Europe. While the President did not approve of the embargo on arms in the 1935 Act, he later endorsed the principle as a desirable

[34] *Congressional Record*, 75th Congress, First Session, p. 10165.

[35] See *infra*, pp. 890–891 for other considerations for not invoking the Act.

part of our neutrality policy. He urged the arms embargo in the Spanish civil war, and in his annual message to Congress on January 3, 1936, he declared that as part of a consistent policy the United States declines "to encourage the prosecution of war by permitting belligerents to obtain arms, ammunition, or implements of war from the United States." The President then, of course, had in mind the wars in Spain and Ethiopia, and believed that an arms embargo in those situations would promote the interests of peace. In so far as it concerned the European war, the President, as we shall see, was to urge a different course upon Congress.

President Roosevelt invokes Neutrality Act on outbreak of war in Europe

Upon the outbreak of war in Europe in September, 1939, the President invoked the Neutrality Act of 1937 which imposed upon him the duty of prohibiting the export of arms, ammunition, and implements of war to any of the belligerents or to any neutral state for transshipment to a belligerent.[36] The Neutrality Act of 1937 did not authorize him to put our trade on a "cash-and-carry" basis when the European war broke out: that provision had expired in May, 1939. In addition to the measures taken under the Neutrality Act of 1937, the President on September 8, 1939, issued a "proclamation of national emergency in connection with and to the extent necessary for the proper observance, safeguarding, and enforcing of the neutrality of the United States and the strengthening of our national defense within the limits of peace-time authorizations."[37]

[36]On September 5, 1939, President Roosevelt issued two proclamations: the first was based on our rights as a neutral under international law, and the second was under the Neutrality Act of 1937. Cf. Department of State, *Bulletin*, September 9, 1939.

[37]The authority for this proclamation was based on the Espionage Act of June 15, 1917, U.S. Statutes at Large, vol. 40, Part I, p. 220, et seq. Under these emergency powers, the President, by executive orders of the same day (Department of State, *Bulletin*, September 9, 1939) authorized an increase in the United States Army to 227,000 and the National Guard to 235,000 men; an increase in the enlisted strength of the United States Navy to 145,000 and the Marine Corps to 25,000 men; and an increase in the personnel of the Federal Bureau of Investigation not exceeding 150 men.

Secretary Hull notifies belligerents that the United States has not abandoned rights as neutral under international law

Lest it be thought that the United States had abandoned her rights as a neutral, and in order to keep the record clear, Secretary of State Hull, on September 14, served notice on the European belligerents that the United States "has not abandoned any of its rights as a neutral under international law. . . . The restrictive measures taken in accordance with domestic legislation do not and cannot constitute a modification of principles of international law. On the contrary, this government, adhering as it does to these principles, reserves all rights of the United States and its nationals under international law and will adopt such measures as may seem practical and prudent when those rights are violated by any of the belligerents."[38] Thus to the extent prohibited by law, our neutral rights were, so to speak, put in cold storage.

President Roosevelt urges repeal of arms embargo

In his message to Congress which convened in special session on September 21, 1939, the President declared that the existing arms embargo was "most vitally dangerous to American neutrality, American security and American peace. . . . Repeal of the embargo and a return to international law are the crux of this issue."[39] The repeal of the arms embargo was debated in and out of Congress for six weeks. There was general agreement on the need for measures which would "protect the neutrality, the safety and the integrity of our country, and at the same time keep us out of war," but there was no agreement as to the best means of achieving these objectives. Behind the controversy lay the essentially different attitudes towards the European conflict. A German victory, the President and his advisers felt, would gravely jeopardize the vital interests of the United States. The disappearance of British naval power and with it the British Empire

[38]Department of State, *Bulletin*, September 16, 1939.

[39]Cf. President's message to Congress, *Congressional Record*, September 21, 1939.

would expose the United States to dangers in this hemisphere, and would force us to maintain a two-ocean navy and an enormous army and air fleet. Were Great Britain and France to be defeated, this nation would be one of the few surviving democracies in a world dominated by totalitarian dictatorships whose aims and methods are known to be inimical to our way of life and who seek to refashion the world in their own image. These were the threatened dangers which the President and his advisers saw and sought to avoid. To protect our vital interests he pressed for a policy which would enable the European democracies, fighting for their existence, to buy arms, munitions, war materials, and airplanes in the American market. A majority of Congress agreed with the President that the United States would be safer if the democracies defeated Germany; and were the democracies to lose, the proponents of repeal contended, the repeal of the arms embargo would have set up in the United States a war-making industry essential to greater national defensive measures necessitated by Germany's victory. Those who opposed the President's policy were equally convinced that the best interests of the United States would be served by keeping out of another world war at all costs. They weighed the possible defeat of Great Britain and France as it would affect our position in the Western Hemisphere against the peril to our democratic institutions in consequence of participation in a war, and concluded that staying out of the European struggle would serve our interests best and would, at any rate, be the lesser of two evils.

Arguments for and against changing the rules

In addition to the issues over policy, the legal problem of changing the "rules of the game" while a foreign war was in progress was also debated. Those who opposed changes in the neutrality law contended that it would be an unneutral act since the changes contemplated were motivated by a desire to help one belligerent as against another.[40] International law does not prohibit changes if made for the purpose of safeguarding neutral rights and interests or to fulfill neutral obligations.[41] Lifting an arms embargo, however, was not one of those changes which could be justified under international law. When in the World War, Germany and Austria-Hungary requested the United States to stop the shipment of arms, our Government replied to the Central Powers that "any change in its own laws of neutrality . . . which would affect unequally the relations of the United States with the nations at war would be an unjustifiable departure from the principle of strict neutrality."[42] This contention was met by the argument that as long as the changes applied in law to all belligerents alike, there could be no complaint that the changes were unneutral in character.[43] While, to be sure, the economic and military effects resulting from a nation's neutrality may in fact prove more beneficial to one or the other of the belligerents, the neutral's obligation of impartiality was met under international law when its own domestic laws treated the belligerents equally.

Public opinion advocates change

Whatever the merits of the respective legal arguments were, considerations of policy prevailed. Public opinion on the whole was not disposed to deprive the sea Powers of their advantage to resort to the American market for supplies; nor did it appear much concerned that the proposed changes in the legislation would not work out in an impartial manner, for the American people were far from impartial in their thoughts. To them the European war appeared to be a struggle of the forces of freedom and peace against the forces of tyranny, oppression, and per-

[40]Cf. Letters of Professors Charles Cheney Hyde and Philip C. Jessup, in the New York *Times*, September 21, 1939, and October 5, 1939.

[41]"Rights and Duties of Neutral States in Naval and Aerial War," *American Journal of International Law*, July, 1939, pp. 316–329.

[42]*U.S. Foreign Relations*, 1915, Supplement, p. 162.

[43]Cf. Letters of Professor Clyde Eagleton in the New York *Times*, September 25, 1939, and October 15, 1939, and his editorial comment in the *American Journal of International Law*, January, 1940, pp. 99–104.

secution. Congress reflected that opinion. In the preamble to the Neutrality Act of 1939,[44] which became law on November 4, 1939, Congress expressly reserved "the right to repeal, change, or modify this joint resolution, or any other domestic legislation in the interests of peace, security, or welfare of the United States and its people." Repeal of the arms embargo is practically the only feature which involves a return to our traditional policy of neutrality. Beyond this, the curbs on the exercise of American neutral rights go further than those which existed on the outbreak of hostilities in Europe in September. The main structure of the Act rests on the "cash-and-carry" provisions concerning trade between the United States and the nations at war.

Main structure of Neutrality Act of 1939 rests on cash-and-carry provisions

The Act empowers the President, whenever he, or Congress by concurrent resolution, finds that there exists a state of war, to define combat areas into or through which it becomes unlawful for an American citizen or vessel to proceed. Combat areas are to apply to vessels as well as to aircraft, and they may be modified, altered, or abolished at the President's discretion.

American citizens and vessels are prohibited from entering combat areas

When the Act is invoked, it becomes unlawful for any American vessel to carry any passengers or any articles or materials to any belligerent, subject to certain exceptions which are set out in Section 2. It becomes likewise unlawful to export or transport to any belligerent any articles or materials "until all right, title, and interest therein shall have been transferred to some foreign government, agency, institution, association, partnership, corporation, or national." Losses incurred by our citizens in connection with the sale or transfer of title of such articles shall not be made the basis of any claim put forward by the American government.

Under the Act it is unlawful for any person to purchase, sell or exchange bonds, securities, or other obligations of

[44]Public Resolution, No. 54, 76th Congress, Second Session.

a belligerent state named in the Presidential proclamation, if the obligations are issued after the date of such proclamation. Renewal or adjustment of existing indebtedness is specifically permitted, however. Private individuals or enterprises in belligerent states may secure credit if they do not act in behalf of their governments.

The Neutrality Act of 1939 imposes embargo on loans and credits

Such are some of the chief safeguards which the Act sets up against "involvement." The American government has gone far in its desire to avoid the possibility of being drawn into the European war; its neutrality legislation has, to a large extent, set aside the traditional American policy of the freedom of the seas. It must be observed that however great the sacrifices which the 1939 Act entails, no legislation can anticipate all contingencies or protect the nation against every future development, particularly in a world-wide complex of strife. To what extent our legislative neutrality policy will keep us from "involvement" must, as these lines are written, remain a large interrogation mark.

Neutrality legislation has its limits

CHAPTER XL

PRELUDE TO WAR IN THE WEST

Hitler's rise to power a turning point in Western civilization

WHEN President Hindenburg named Adolf Hitler Reichskanzler of Germany on January 30, 1933, a new era began for Europe, and for that matter, for the world at large. In retrospect Hitler's rise to power was a turning point in the history of Western civilization. Terrorism moved swiftly. Within a year Hitler destroyed the Weimar Constitution, suppressed all opposition parties, crushed the trade unions and forbade all strikes, began an open and continuous persecution of the Jews, and shot, beheaded or imprisoned liberal critics even of the German race. Hitler made good his campaign promise that "heads would roll." A government and nation of social democracy was transformed overnight, so to speak, into a government by despotism, imposing upon its peoples a cult of savagery, superstition, and paganism the like of which a European nation has not known for centuries. Hitler was soon to usher into the relations between Germany and other nations the same political technique which brought him into authority in Germany—the technique of power politics. The advent of Hitler to supremacy in Germany marked the beginning of the end of the European order created at Versailles in 1919.

Hitler's basic assumptions concerning the place of Germany in the family of nations and her diplomatic objectives were stated by him in his book entitled *Mein Kampf*,[1] published originally in two volumes, in 1925 and 1927,

---

[1]The references are to the edition published by Reynal & Hitchcock, New York, 1939. Reprinted by permission of Houghton Mifflin Co.

respectively. It is the best evidence of the program of Hitler and his government and contains the principles which have guided Germany's foreign policy since his rise to power. So closely has he pursued this program that a few of the significant passages from *Mein Kampf* are set out as samples for an understanding of the most startling phenomenon of our times—Hitlerism.

Hitler's program set forth in *Mein Kampf*

If, in its historical development, the German people had possessed this group unity as it was enjoyed by other peoples, then the German Reich would today probably be the mistress of this globe. World history would have taken a different course, and no one would be able to decide if in this way there would not have arrived what today so many blinded pacifists hope to beg for by moaning and crying: *A peace, supported not by the palm branches of tearful pacifist professional female mourners, but founded by the victorious sword of a people of overlords which puts the world into the service of a higher culture.*[2]

One must be perfectly clear about the fact that the regaining of the lost regions will not come about through solemn appeals to the dear Lord or through pious hopes in a League of Nations, but only by force of arms.[3]

Today I am guided by the sober knowledge that one does not regain lost territories by means of the glibness of tongue of sharp parliamentarian gobblers, but that one must regain them by means of a sharp sword, that is, through a bloody struggle.[4]

State frontiers are man-made and can be altered by man.

The reality of a nation having managed a disproportionate acquisition of territory is no superior obligation for its eternal recognition. It proves at most the might of the conqueror and the weakness of the victim. And, moreover, this might alone makes right. If the German people today, penned into an impossible area, face a wretched future, this is as little Fate's command as its rejection would constitute a snub to Fate. Just as little as some superior power has promised another nation more soil and territory than the German, or would be insulted by the fact of this unjust division of territory. Just as our forefathers did not get the land on which we are living today as a gift from Heaven, but had to conquer it by risking

[2] *Op. cit.*, p. 599.

[3] *Ibid.*

[4] *Ibid.*, p. 912.

their lives, so no folkish grace but only the might of a triumphant sword will in the future assign us territory, and with it life for our nation.

Much as we all today recognize the necessity for a reckoning with France, it will remain largely ineffective if our foreign policy aim is restricted thereto. It has and will retain significance if it provides the rear cover for an enlargement of our national domain of life in Europe.[5]

Germany will be either a world power or will not be at all. To be a world power, however, it requires that size which nowadays gives its necessary importance to such a power, and which gives life to its citizens..

The political testament of the German nation for its dealings with the outside world, however, should and must always read substantially:

Never tolerate the establishment of two continental powers in Europe. See an attack on Germany in any such attempt to organize a military power on the frontiers of Germany, be it only in the form of the creation of a State capable of becoming a military power, and, in that case, regard it not only a right, but a duty, to prevent the establishment of such a State by all means including the application of armed force, or, in the event that such a one be already founded, to repress it. See to it that the strength of our nation is founded, not on colonies, but on the European territory of the homeland. Never regard the Reich as secure while it is unable to give every national offshoot for centuries his own bit of soil and territory. Never forget that the most sacred right in this world is the right to that earth which a man desires to till himself, and the most sacred sacrifice that blood which a man spills for this earth.[7]

Hitler's aim is to make Germany militarily powerful

Essential to the success of Hitler's foreign policy was a mighty Germany, and a mighty Germany could not be created without first destroying the European system of public law created by the Treaty of Versailles. The aim was to make Germany, not rich, but powerful in the belief that when you have the power you can acquire riches by force. Complete control of the state with production for war as its chief concern was the means by which the new master of Germany set about fulfilling

[5]*Ibid.*, p. 949.

[6]*Ibid.*, p. 950.

[7]*Ibid.*, pp. 962–963.

his program of national resurgence. Militarization in all its forms, such as army expansion and rearmament, first secret and then overt, proceeded apace. Hitler's first chief step in foreign policy was the announcement on October 14, 1933, of Germany's withdrawal from the League of Nations and the Disarmament Conference. The announcement rocked the Disarmament Conference to its foundations. By this act Germany renounced the international system of collaboration which came into being after the World War as a means of organizing peace. The significance of the step in the light of Herr Hitler's aims for Germany was fully understood in all the capitals of the world, particularly in those of the European countries.

Germany withdraws from the League and the Disarmament Conference

While Secretary of State Cordell Hull opposed German rearmament and laid at Germany's door the blame for imperilling the entire disarmament movement, the Administration was not willing to have it appear that it was allying itself with France and Great Britain in a common political front against Germany. In the light of the crisis, it proceeded to make its policy clear at the Disarmament Conference. Said Mr. Norman Davis, the American delegate:

The United States restates its policy on disarmament

> We are in Geneva solely for disarmament purposes. While there is a possibility of successfully carrying on disarmament negotiations we will gladly continue to do our part. We are not, however, interested in the political element or any purely European aspect of the picture. We again make it clear that we are in no way politically aligned with any European powers. Such unity of purpose as has existed has been entirely on world disarmament matters.[8]

Senatorial fears were thus allayed. The hopes for political collaboration of those who saw in the League an instrument for saving the peace were dashed. With this declaration, the American government withdrew from active participation in the disarmament discussions. It would

[8]Department of State, Press Release, October 30, 1933.

have nothing to do with the deadlock resulting from Germany's withdrawal, which, to our government, appeared to be a European affair. The policy of the United States was one of political isolation from disturbances abroad, and economic insulation against the impact of external forces, at a time when the Roosevelt Administration was seeking social and economic reconstruction for this nation by national means.

Germany repudiates disarmament clauses of the Treaty of Versailles

Of as startling a character as the bolting of the Disarmament Conference and the League of Nations by Germany was her unilateral repudiation of the disarmament sections of the Treaty of Versailles by promulgating a law on March 16, 1935, which introduced the prohibited universal military service. This, together with the admission of the Soviet Union to membership in the League of Nations, with a permanent seat on the Council, on September 18, 1934, and the announcement of the signing of the Franco-Russian Treaty of Mutual Assistance on May 2, 1935,[9] were perhaps the three most significant events in the European cauldron. The heart of the European treaty system following the World War had now stopped beating. Hitler had posed a challenge through power to the West; Great Britain appeared willing to condone it; France was unable to meet it single-handed.[10] The fears and distrust which seized the nations of Europe following Germany's abrupt withdrawal, the waning confidence in the League

[9]On May 16, 1935, Russia and Czechoslovakia signed a similar pact of mutual assistance.

[10]Professor Arnold J. Toynbee, assisted by V. M. Boulter, in their *Survey of International Affairs,* 1935, vol. 1, p. 154, have this illuminating comment on French policy: "Throughout the fourteen years preceding Herr Hitler's advent to power in 1933 it had been the consistent foreign policy of France to sacrifice everything else for the sake of retaining the power—without the will—to make a preventive war upon Germany if and when the occasion should arise; and now [re-establishment by Germany of universal compulsory military service], when the occasion had arisen—and this very largely as the result of French intransigeance—France acted on her feelings, at the price of stultifying her policy, by refraining from playing the trump card which she had insisted, at such cost, upon keeping in her hand. It was astonishing to see her persist, even after this, in rejecting the last fleeting opportunities of accommodation with a Germany who was now rapidly rearming without asking French leave."

of Nations, and the disintegration of international solidarity, caused a return to the pre-war system of alliances to thwart the danger of German expansion.[11] The protagonist and the leader in the scramble for allies was France.

The Stresa Conference regrets Germany's unilateral repudiation

A meeting of the three great powers, Great Britain, France, and Italy, at Stresa on April 11–14, 1935, to consider a plan of action against Germany, was the device next best to a preventive war—a war which the French had unsuccessfully urged upon the British. The Stresa Conference regretted the unilateral repudiation adopted by the German government; recognized the necessity of maintaining the independence and integrity of Austria—which was being threatened by Germany in pursuit of her new program to unite all Germans into one great and powerful Reich; and agreed to oppose, by all practicable means, any unilateral repudiation of treaties which might endanger the peace of Europe.[12] From Stresa the delegates of the three powers adjourned to Geneva to attend an extraordinary session of the League Council on April 15 when a similar act was staged. The condemnation of Germany by the League Council was resolutely rejected by the German government.

The British inclination to appease the German government, at the expense of French security, was manifested by the Anglo-German Exchange of Notes on June 18, 1935, by which the German navy was reëstablished at 35 per cent of the strength of the British navy with the right of equality in respect to submarines.[13] Notwithstanding the declarations and the common diplomatic front at Stresa and at Geneva on the observance of treaty obliga-

[11]When the German military budget for 1934–1935 was published in March, 1934, it called for an increase in aerial armaments from 78,000,000 marks in 1933–1934 to 210,000,000 marks. The figure for the Reichswehr rose from 344,900,000 marks in 1933–1934 to 574,500,000 marks. At this time Germany had not renounced the disarmament clauses of the Treaty of Versailles.

[12]Cf. British White Paper, Cmd. 4080 (1935).

[13]*Documents on International Affairs*, edited by John W. Wheeler-Bennett and Stephen Held, 1935, vol. 1.

tions, Great Britain was willing to coöperate with Germany in her repudiation of the disarmament provisions of the Treaty of Versailles. The British justified their action on the ground that Germany would build a larger navy if no top limit was set. Since Great Britain was not disposed to compel observance of the arms limitations clauses of the Treaty of Versailles, be they land, sea, or air, she felt a 35 : 100 navy ratio was better than a 100 : 100 ratio. By the agreement, however, Great Britain sanctioned a German navy nearly as large as the French and three times the size permitted under the Versailles Treaty. Thus what had been sternly denied to democratic Germany, weak and defenceless, was gladly given to Nazi Germany, which was rapidly arming and openly preparing for war. It was suspected that Great Britain was giving general support to the restoration of German power in order to counterbalance French power in Europe, and was at the same time seeking to draw Germany into a Western orientation in opposition to the Soviet Union. In France, there was indignation over this British coöperation in treaty-breaking. The French Minister of Marine declared: "A serious event has just altered the equilibrium of the European naval forces. What has surprised us in the Anglo-German agreement is decidedly not the fact of fresh rearmament on Germany's part—a move which it was easy to foresee. What has surprised us is the precipitate adhesion of England to this German act—and this in conditions which might make us doubtful, not indeed of England's friendship, but of her traditional prudence. . ."[14]

Great Britain agrees to German naval rearmament

The implications of the course of political events in Europe were clear to the United States. The scramble for allies and the feverish rearmament race could only lead to war. If the number of bills introduced in Congress in 1935 to keep the United States from being drawn into "the next war" was a guide to American opinion in its

[14]*Ibid.*

reaction to the events in Europe, then this nation was more determined than ever before to pursue a course of political isolation by means of legislative neutrality. It was not interested in theoretical discussions about visit and search, freedom of the seas, or contraband, issues which involved us in a war in 1812 and in 1917; it was eager only for insulation against war which seemed imminent. The tension in Europe and the impending invasion of Ethiopia by Italy crystallized isolationist sentiment. The Neutrality Act of August 31, 1935,[15] expressed the desire of the people of the United States to keep this nation from becoming involved in war.

The United States seeks insulation against war

On the eve of the Italian invasion of Ethiopia, Emperor Haile Selassie called upon the United States, on July 3, 1935, to invoke the Pact of Paris, of which Italy and Ethiopia were signatories. The appeal of the Emperor, in the light of previous invocations by the United States,[16] seemed proper. But the Roosevelt Administration, remembering that the response to the initiative of the Hoover Administration in invoking the Pact of Paris in the Sino-Japanese dispute had been disappointing, was not disposed to risk a rebuff. In reply, therefore, our Government stated it "would be loath to believe that either of them [Italy or Ethiopia] would resort to other than pacific means as a method of dealing with this controversy or would permit any situation to arise which would be inconsistent with the commitments of the pact."[17] For Ethiopia there was nothing but cold comfort in these words. When the announcement came that Italian armies had commenced their invasion of Ethiopia on October 3, 1935, President Roosevelt—on October 5—invoked the Neutrality Act of August 31, 1935, against

Emperor of Ethiopia calls upon the United States to invoke Pact of Paris

[15]See Chapter XXXIX.

[16]The Hoover Administration had taken the lead in invoking it in the Russo-Japanese dispute in 1929 (see *infra*, pp. 757–760), and in the Sino-Japanese dispute over the Manchurian affair of 1931 (see *infra*, Chapter XXXIII).

[17]Department of State, Press Release, July 6, 1935.

Italy and Ethiopia. The way was thus paved for collective action by the League of Nations, without fear that the United States would insist on neutral rights.

League of Nations imposes sanctions

The course of diplomatic events in Europe during the Italo-Ethiopian war was keenly watched by official Washington. After the League had found that Italy "resorted to war in disregard of its covenants," it proceeded to the consideration and imposition of sanctions. If the League of Nations was not to crumble under the impact of the flagrant aggression of Italy—as it very nearly did from the blow given it by the Japanese invasion of Manchuria—a strong stand was necessary in defense of the Covenant. Despite the risks involved in applying sanctions against a major power, the alternative of standing by and doing nothing, it seemed, involved greater risks and more serious consequences. While the sanctions imposed upon Italy were by no means exhaustive, this first essay in international coöperation to penalize an aggressor was an extraordinary achievement. In its initial stages, at any rate, this effort was an expression of the aims sought by those inspired by the vision of Woodrow Wilson to enforce peace through collective action.

Oil not included in list of sanctions

The hopes generated in the hearts of those who saw in the application of sanctions a new world order were short lived. Oil was not included in the sanctions imposed by the members of the League. Yet an embargo on oil would have crippled, and perhaps put an end to the Italian invasion of Ethiopia. Moreover, a sincere effort to apply the provisions of the Covenant would have meant aid to the victim of aggression and progressive pressure through economic strangulation upon the aggressor. This was not done. On the contrary, the French government's plan, to which the British government adhered, was to make sanctions as innocuous as possible and avoid snatching from Mussolini a victory over Ethiopia. Pierre Laval,

Premier of France, calculated that in a possible struggle against Germany Italian friendship would be worth more to France than the League would be. That France and Great Britain were disposed to overlook their obligations under the Covenant was manifested by the abortive Hoare-Laval agreement,[18] euphemistically termed an "Outline of an Agreed Settlement of the Italo-Ethiopian Conflict." By this agreement Italy was to secure about half of the territory of Ethiopia along with a zone for "economic expansion and settlement," which of course meant ultimate political dominion of the rest of Ethiopia; in return she was to call off her war. The Hoare-Laval scheme was cynical to the extreme. It proposed to buy off the aggressor and in addition to secure the League's blessing for the scheme in order to clothe it with respectability. The popular outcry against it was so great in Great Britain and in France that both governments abandoned it. In the end, Italy conquered Ethiopia, but instead of joining France in support against Germany she eventually joined Germany, first in an arrangement known as the "Rome-Berlin Axis," which was later transformed into an offensive and defensive military alliance. Great Britain and France alienated Italy because they had been forced by popular clamor to make an effort to apply the principles of collective security. Yet by their insincere and half-hearted application of sanctions—in the desire to win over a doubtful ally—they scuttled the Covenant of the League.

The Hoare-Laval agreement

The disintegration of the principle of collective security through League action continued apace following the abortive Hoare-Laval plan, and before many months passed a new crisis developed in Europe—the crisis arising from Germany's abrogation of the Locarno Pact.[19]

Hitler repudiates the Locarno Pact

[18]British White Paper, Cmd. 5044 (1935).

[19]By Articles 42–44 of the Treaty of Versailles Germany was forbidden to maintain or construct any fortifications, to maintain or assemble armed forces, and to construct permanent works for mobilization within a specified area on either bank of the Rhine River. A violation by Germany of any of these prohi-

On the morning of March 7, 1936, by the method of shock diplomacy which Europe had already grown to dread, Hitler announced the end of the Locarno Pact and the military reoccupation of the demilitarized zone on the Rhine. This unilateral repudiation of a solemn engagement, freely entered into to preserve the peace in one of the danger spots of Europe, confronted the Powers with the crucial issue of the strength of law against the claims of force—an issue which was to become more critical for the peace of Europe as German military strength grew by leaps and bounds. The Council of the League, on March 19, 1936, declared Germany guilty of a breach of the Versailles and Locarno Treaties. Beyond this, however, nothing effective happened. Great Britain and France were at loggerheads on how to meet the German menace; and Italy, alienated by League sanctions, was on the threshold of a rapprochement with Germany. Germany had calculated admirably—her enemies were divided and confused.[20]

British role crucial

The success of the Nazi offensive was in considerable measure due to the crucial role of British foreign policy at this time. If Great Britain had taken a decisive stand with France, the Soviet Union, and the smaller states for

---

bitions was to be regarded as a hostile act against the signatories of the Treaty. By the Locarno Pact of October 16, 1925, Germany, France, and Belgium pledged themselves to non-aggression and pacific settlement. Great Britain, France, Germany, Italy, and Belgium guaranteed the inviolability of the German-Belgian and Franco-German frontiers as fixed by the Treaty of Versailles as well as the demilitarization of the Rhineland [British White Book, Final Protocol of the Locarno Conference, 1925, Cmd. 2525 of 1925]. Following the signing of the Locarno Pact, Germany joined the League of Nations. At the time the Locarno Pact was entered into it was hailed as a notable achievement in the stabilization of peace in Europe.

[20]The United States made no protest. While not a party to the Treaty of Versailles she did reserve to herself certain rights and privileges under that Treaty by the Treaty of Berlin signed August 25, 1921. (Malloy, *Treaties, Conventions, International Acts, Protocols, and Agreements between the United States and Other Powers*, 1776–1923, vol. 3, p. 2596.) The Roosevelt Administration, on the occasion of the Locarno crisis as on the occasion of Germany's open rearmament in 1935, was isolationist and avoided invoking American treaty rights for fear of involving the United States in European political questions.

the collective maintenance of peace, the consequent balance of forces for peace might have compelled Germany to enter a system of collective security. But British policy, under strong pro-Nazi influence, tipped the balance the other way at every critical point. With every success of the Nazi offensive, attended by British acquiescence in some instances and tacit support in others, the resistance of the smaller states became progressively weaker.

Hitler's "peace plan"

To soften the blow of the unilateral repudiation of the Locarno Treaty, Hitler, on March 31, 1936, put forward a European "peace plan" whereby Germany offered to conclude a new security pact with the Western powers, and bilateral non-aggression pacts with her Eastern neighbors, excluding Russia. The bilateral non-aggression pacts, it was observed, did not provide for mutual assistance to the victim of aggression, and significantly did not include a clause suspending validity in the event of aggression by either signatory against a third party. This kind of commitment, in contradistinction to the mutual guarantee, would thus in effect immobilize and paralyze collective defense against aggression and would enable Germany to devour her victims one at a time. It suited Hitler's conception of the "localization of war" which was revealed in his speech before the Reichstag on May 21, 1935.[21] His "peace plan" was not accepted.

The state of humiliation of losing a war in which the German people had lived since 1918 was, as a result of the violent successes of power politics of the Hitler régime, replaced by a state of tension. It was a tension which could not continue, and which would, it was generally feared, sooner or later seek an outlet through war.[22] With his western frontier remilitarized, Hitler turned his attention to France's eastern allies. At the National Socialist Party Rally at Nürnberg, in September, 1936, Herr

[21]Cf. New York *Times*, May 22, 1935.

[22]Hamilton Fish Armstrong, *We or They*, pp. 3–25.

Hitler de-
nounces
Bolshevism

Hitler intensified the campaign—that later turned out to be an elaborate pretense—of saving civilization from Bolshevism. The Nürnberg *Partei Tag* took for its theme the denunciation of Bolshevism. Said Herr Hitler, "If we had at our disposal the incalculable wealth and stores of raw materials of the Ural Mountains and the unending fertile plains of the Ukraine, to be exploited under National Socialist leadership, then we would produce, and our German people would swim in plenty."[23] An expression of this character by the head of a nation prior to 1914 would have been followed with incalculable consequences; in 1936 the Europeans could only gasp at the approaching peril with incredulity, dismay, and fear.

Germany
enters into
anti-Com-
munist Pact
with Japan

The counter-weight to the Soviet Union, at that moment the ally of France, was Japan, and on November 25, 1936, Germany and Japan announced their agreement against the Communist International.[24] The appearance of this Fascist front[25] to save civilization from Bolshevism fooled

[23]New York *Times*, September 13, 1936. This passage, which appeared in the German newspaper *Völkische Beobachter* of September 14, 1936, was recast as follows: If the Urals with their incalculable wealth of raw materials, the rich forests of Siberia, and the unending cornfields of the Ukraine *lay in Germany* under National Socialist leadership the country would swim in plenty.

[24]Its ostensible purpose was stated in the preamble as follows:

"The government of the German Reich and the Imperial Japanese government, recognizing that the aim of the Communist International, known as the Comintern, is to disintegrate and subdue existing States by all the means at its command; convinced that the toleration of interference by the Communist International in the internal affairs of the nations not only endangers their internal peace and social well-being, but is also a menace to the peace of the world; desirous of coöperating in the defence against Communist subversive activities; have agreed as follows:

Article 1

The High Contracting States agree to inform one another of the activities of the Communist International, to consult with one another on the necessary preventive measures, and to carry these through in close collaboration.

Article 2

The High Contracting Parties will jointly invite third States whose internal peace is threatened by the subversive activities of the Communist International to adopt defensive measures in the spirit of this agreement or to take part in the present agreement." Cf. *Documents on International Affairs*, edited by John W. Wheeler-Bennett and Stephen Held, 1936, pp. 297–299.

[25]Italy adhered to the anti-Comintern pact on November 6, 1937.

no one, least of all the Soviet government. Here was an ideological device which sought to conceal the designs and aims of its artificers—an association in pursuit of territorial aggrandizement, as well as intervention in the affairs of nations accused by these powers of Bolshevist deviltry. But the objective of territorial conquest could not be dramatized without alarm, whereas a crusade against Communism might find favor. Not only Communism came in for tirades at the hands of National Socialist Germany, but Democracy as well. One might have believed that Herr Hitler included the democracies in his desire to save civilization from Communism. But Herr Hitler attached an esoteric meaning to "civilization," a meaning which, in the light of his philosophy as revealed in *Mein Kampf* and the practice to which he put it in Germany, was as dangerous to Democracy as it appeared to be to Communism.

Germany launches reign of terror to overthrow Dollfuss and to coördinate Austria

The "union of all Germans in a greater Germany" was an important article of faith in the Nazi program, and soon after Hitler came to power the possibility of *Anschluss* with Austria, forbidden by the peace treaties, became a disturbing factor in European politics. Nazi Germany and her agents in Austria launched a reign of terror to overthrow the régime of Chancellor Englebert Dollfuss and "coördinate" Austria. On July 25, 1934, Dollfuss was murdered by supporters of the German Nazi régime as a prelude to what proved to be an abortive Nazi *Putsch*.[26] While Hitler washed his hands of Austria after the Dollfuss assassination, partly because of her apparently unexpected resistance to the *Putsch*, and perhaps more because of Premier Mussolini's support of his neighbor, he did not give up his design to incorporate Austria into the German Reich; he merely deferred it to a more opportune moment.

[26] Sidney B. Fay, "Dollfuss: Victim of Nazi Crime," *Current History*, September, 1934.

Hitler's designs in Austria and Czechoslovakia

In an address to his Reichstag on February 20, 1938, Hitler said:

> There are more than ten million Germans in states adjoining Germany which before 1866 were joined with the bulk of the German nation by a national link. Until 1918 they fought in the Great War shoulder to shoulder with the German soldiers of the Reich. Against their own free will they were prevented by peace treaties from uniting with the Reich.
>
> This was painful enough, but there must be no doubt about one thing: political separation from the Reich may not lead to deprivation of rights; that is, the general rights of racial self-determination which were solemnly promised to us as a condition for the armistice. We cannot disregard it just because this is a case concerning Germany.
>
> In the long run it is unbearable for a World Power, conscious of itself, to know there are racial comrades at its side who are constantly being afflicted with the severest suffering for their sympathy or unity with the whole nation, its destiny, and its philosophy! . . .
>
> But just as England stands up for her interests all over the globe, present-day Germany will know how to guard its more restricted interests. To these interests of the German Reich belong also the protection of those German peoples who are not in a position to secure along our frontiers their political and philosophical freedom by their own efforts.[27]

Ten million Germans, seven in Austria and three in Czechoslovakia, though neither country was mentioned by name, became the object of Herr Hitler's program. Here was continental conquest under the guise of racial pretension. What position were France and Great Britain to take on Germany's expansion in Central Europe? France was divided and in the throes of a domestic crisis, and without British support, would not venture to check Germany. Great Britain appeared disposed to give Germany a free hand in that region of Europe. Thus, even before Hitler's address to the Reichstag on February 20, the London *Times*, a source close to the British government, in an editorial on February 17, 1938, foreshadowed what British policy would be:

[27]New York *Times*, February 21, 1938.

It is the predominant British view that any aim which Germany may legitimately set herself beyond her Eastern borders can be accomplished by peaceful means and could only risk defeat in a general upheaval if attempted by other means. "Expansion"—meaning the extension of German influence—is guaranteed by the economic preponderance of Germany as a great and highly organized area of industrial production and a great market, exerting a natural attraction upon complementary communities. It can be no part of British policy to resist expansion in that sense or the relations that will develop along with it.

Germany annexes Austria

On March 12, 1938, German troops marched into Austria, and on March 13 Hitler proclaimed the end of the Federal State of Austria and henceforth "a land of the German Reich."

The United States reaction to annexation is one of caution

American official reaction to the German annexation of Austria was one of caution. The disappearance of a sovereign independent state was officially regarded as having been brought about by means not contrary to the covenants and obligations of the Pact of Paris, and therefore not calling for the application of the Stimson doctrine of non-recognition. Isolationist feeling, if anything, was strengthened as the peril of international anarchy spread. The impulse to stay aloof from danger found expression in the many proposals considered by Congress in the effort to draw a legislative asbestos curtain around the frontiers of the United States. The response of the American public to the sensational "quarantine" address[28] of President Roosevelt in Chicago on October 5, 1937, delivered at the time Japan was invading China, to test, *inter alia*, the relative strengths of the opposing schools of thought on international affairs—isolation or collective action—left little doubt that sentiment of the American people was strongly for isolation and against action which might lead to involvement.

The destruction of the Austrian State placed Czechoslovakia in a perilous position. That central European

[28]See *infra*, pp. 893 f.

republic was now surrounded by Germany on three sides of its vital military and industrial areas. The three million Sudeten Germans in Czechoslovakia had, by Hitler's speech of February 20, 1938, become his "wards," as had the Austrians whose liberty and state he destroyed on March 12. On what better basis could Herr Hitler stake his claim to the areas in which the Sudeten Germans lived than that of self-determination? The Sudetens were never a part of the German Reich, and before the World War were included in the Austro-Hungarian Empire. But self-determination had a righteous sound, and it was a principle which Hitler must have thought the Western democracies could not very well deny to him. In a speech which was awaited by the whole world, he told the Nürnberg Nazi Congress, on September 12, 1938:

Czechoslovakia in a perilous position

> Today we again see plotters, from democrats down to Bolsheviki, fighting against the Nazi State. . . . These [Sudeten] Germans, too, are creatures of God. The Almighty did not create them that they should be surrendered by a State construction made at Versailles to a foreign power that is hateful to them. . . . They are being oppressed in an inhuman and intolerable manner. . . . I can only say to representatives of the democracies that this is not a matter of indifference to us. And I say that if these tortured creatures cannot obtain rights and assistance by themselves, they can obtain both from us. An end must be made of depriving these people of their rights. . . . I demand that the oppression of 3,500,000 Germans in Czechoslovakia shall cease and be replaced by the free right of self-determination.[29]

Hitler commits Germany to free the Sudetens

Thus in a speech full of frenzy, venom, and distortion of truth, the head of the German state committed himself to free the Sudetens. Since France and Russia were bound to Czechoslovakia by alliances, would Hitler risk a war with them over the Sudeten question? As for Great Britain, what would her position be, and would she stand by France? Again an "indiscreet" editorial in

[29] New York *Times*, September 13, 1938.

the London *Times*, which enjoyed the confidence of the Government of the day, gave Hitler a clue. After indicating that a solution of the Sudeten problem within the framework of the Czechoslovak state might not prove satisfactory, the editorial went on to say: "In that case it might be worth while for the Czechoslovak government to consider whether they should altogether exclude the project, which has found favor in some quarters, of making Czechoslovakia a more homogeneous state by the secession of that fringe of alien populations who are contiguous to the nation with which they are united by race."[30] Thus, five days before his speech at Nürnberg in which he threatened a violent solution of the question, Hitler was apprised by a responsible British newspaper of the workings of the British Foreign Office mind. Great Britain would not fight over Czechoslovakia. Notwithstanding the British Foreign Office repudiation of the editorial, the events which followed proved that the writer of the editorial had accurately forecast British policy.

Violence spreads in the Sudetenland

The Sudeten crisis had already reached a violent stage before Hitler made his September 12th speech. The rioting in the Sudetenland, provoked and instigated by the Sudeten extremists, who were aided and abetted by the German Nazis and the German controlled press, had reached such a pitch of violence that the Czechoslovak government imposed a form of martial law in the disturbed districts.[31] After the Nürnberg speech the rioting and disorder increased to such an extent that the Czechoslovak government was obliged to extend martial law and disband the Sudeten German Party and the Free Corps—a storm troop organization modelled on the pattern of its Hitler counterpart. By September 14, 1938, German troops had drawn up along the Czechoslovak frontier ready to

[30]London *Times*, September 7, 1938.

[31]Cf. British White Paper; Correspondence respecting Czechoslovakia, Cmd. 5847 (1938).

invade that nation.[32] On the following day the British Prime Minister, Neville Chamberlain, flew to Germany to talk to Hitler "with a view to trying to find a peaceful solution" of the "increasingly critical situation." The world later learned from Mr. Chamberlain that "Herr Hitler made it plain that he had made up his mind that the Sudeten Germans must have the right of self-determination and of returning, if they wished, to the Reich. If they could not achieve this by their own efforts, he said, he would assist them to do so and he declared categorically that, rather than wait, he would be prepared to risk a world war."

The British Prime Minister flies to Germany to confer with Hitler

The British and French governments yield to Hitler's threat

The British and French governments accepted Hitler's principle of self-determination, and on September 19 presented to Czechoslovakia a proposal[33] bluntly informing her that the maintenance of peace and the safety of Czechoslovakia's vital interests could not effectively be assured without handing over to Germany the Sudeten area, "mainly inhabited by Sudeten Deutsch." The areas to be transferred, the joint British-French proposal asserted, "would probably have to include areas over 50 per cent of German inhabitants." Great Britain, "as a contribution to the pacification of Europe," would be prepared "to join in an international guarantee of the new boundaries of the Czechoslovak State against unprovoked aggression" on the condition that Czechoslovakia give up her alliances with France, Soviet Russia, Rumania, and Jugoslavia. Since the British Prime Minister was to resume conversations with Herr Hitler on Wednesday—the joint proposal was delivered to the Czechoslovak government on Monday the 19th of September, 1938—the proposal asked for an answer at the

[32]Cf. Prime Minister Chamberlain's speech of September 28, 1938, in New York *Times*, September 29, 1938.

[33]*Ibid.* The text is contained in the British White Paper, Correspondence respecting Czechoslovakia, Cmd. 5847.

earliest possible moment, i.e., within forty-eight hours. This was, to say the least, a veiled ultimatum, presented by two great powers to an ally of one of these powers at the behest of another great power, and unprecedented in the annals of diplomacy. Czechoslovakia asked for the application of the Treaty of Arbitration of October 16, 1925, between herself and Germany, but the British and the French governments brushed this request aside and demanded instant surrender as the only means of avoiding a German invasion.[34] On the 21st of September the Czechoslovak government "under extraordinary pressure" from the British and French governments surrendered to the proposal; and on the following day Prime Minister Chamberlain flew to Godesburg, Germany, to meet Herr Hitler and to present him with Sudetenland. But the gift was to be handed to Herr Hitler in his own way. In the famous Godesberg Memorandum he insisted on German military occupation of the areas to be ceded, by October 1—areas which included some Czech majorities. Herr Hitler agreed "to permit a plebiscite to take place" by November 25 in areas to be defined later in which persons resident on October 28, 1918, or born there prior to that date could vote. "The evacuated Sudeten German area," Hitler demanded, "is to be handed over without destroying or rendering unusable in any way military, commercial, or traffic establishments. . . ." No "foodstuffs, goods, cattle, raw materials, etc." were to be removed.

The Czechoslovak government yields

Hitler increases demands

These conditions shocked the British Prime Minister. He had accepted the first ultimatum, but could not bring himself to accept the second. What was the essential difference between the first and the second ultimatum? In the first, upon the amputation of the Sudetenland from Czechoslovakia, an international guarantee, with Great

[34]Cf. Hamilton Fish Armstrong, "Armistice at Munich," *Foreign Affairs*, January, 1939.

Britain participating, would secure the new state and replace the existing military alliances of Czechoslovakia. In the second, i.e., in the Godesberg Memorandum, Hitler demanded military occupation of the Sudetenland by October 1 and made no mention of guarantees to Czechoslovakia. Neither the British nor the French were disposed to press the Czechoslovak government to accept the Godesberg ultimatum and neither could any longer advise her not to mobilize. Czechoslovakia did reject the Godesberg demands, and, in view of Herr Hitler's apparent determination to attack, mobilized on September 23, 1938. Great Britain and France likewise redoubled their own war measures.[35] A European war, perhaps a world war, hung in the balance. Czechoslovakia was willing to settle the Sudeten issue on the basis of the Franco-British proposal, by negotiation; Herr Hitler preferred the use of military force notwithstanding the fact that virtually all of his demands had been conceded. An "authoritative statement" issued from the British Foreign Office on September 26 declared: "The German claim to the transfer of the Sudeten areas has already been conceded by the French, British, and Czechoslovak governments, but if in spite of all efforts made by the British Prime Minister a German attack is made upon Czechoslovakia, the immediate result must be that France will be bound to come to her assistance, and Great Britain and Russia will certainly stand by France."[36]

Czechoslovakia rejects Godesberg demands

This European drama which reached its climax in the capitulation of France and Great Britain at Munich on September 29, 1938—and culminated in the final destruction of Czechoslovakia as an independent state in March, 1939—was watched from this side of the ocean with

[35]At this point the British began digging trenches in their city parks and in the countryside and were preparing to evacuate women, children, and old men from London.

[36]New York *Times*, September 27, 1938.

intense feeling and anxiety. President Roosevelt on September 26, 1938, sent an appeal to Herr Hitler and to President Benes: "On behalf of 130 millions of people of the United States of America, and for the sake of humanity everywhere, I most earnestly appeal to you not to break off negotiations looking to a peaceful, fair, and constructive settlement of the questions at issue." He reminded them of their obligations under the Pact of Paris not to resort to war. He ended his appeal by stating, "I earnestly repeat that so long as negotiations continue, differences may be reconciled. Once they are broken off reason is banished and force asserts itself. . . . And force produces no solution for the future good of humanity."[37] President Benes replied promptly and sympathetically to the President's appeal by stating that he desired nothing other than to settle the controversy by arbitration, and that his government would never do anything to violate the Pact of Paris. Herr Hitler's reply uncompromisingly refused responsibility if war should come and placed it on Czechoslovakia's door. "The possibilities of arriving at a just settlement by agreement," Herr Hitler declared, "are therefore exhausted with the proposals of the German [Godesberg] memorandum. It does not rest with the German government, but with the Czechoslovak government alone to decide whether it wants peace or war."[38]

President Roosevelt appeals to Hitler and Benes

In another plea to Herr Hitler, on September 29, President Roosevelt declared:

President Roosevelt pleads with Hitler again

The question before the world today, Mr. Chancellor, is not the question of errors of judgment or of injustices committed in the past. It is the question of the fate of the world today and tomorrow. The world asks of us who at this moment are heads of the nations the supreme capacity to achieve the destinies of nations without forcing upon them as a price the

---

[37]Department of State, Press Release, October 1, 1938.

[38]*Ibid.*

mutilation and death of millions of citizens. Resort to force in the Great War failed to bring tranquillity. Victory and defeat were alike sterile. . . .

The President emphasized that continued negotiations remain the only way by which the Sudeten problem can be disposed of upon any lasting basis. He concluded:

Allow me to state my unqualified conviction that history, and the souls of every man, woman, and child whose lives will be lost in the threatened war will hold us and all of us accountable should we omit any appeal for its preservation.

The government of the United States has no political involvements in Europe, and will assume no obligations in the conduct of the present negotiations. Yet in our own right we recognize our responsibilities as a part of a world of neighbors.

The conscience and the impelling desire of the people of my country demand that the voice of their government be raised again and yet again to avert and to avoid war.[39]

The British Prime Minister appeals to Hitler and Mussolini

The British Parliament met on September 28, 1938, to hear the Prime Minister's account of the Sudeten crisis, which was swiftly moving to the breaking point. He disclosed that he had sent the German Chancellor a communication that very morning offering to come to Berlin "to discuss arrangements for transfer with you and representatives of France and Italy if you desire" since "I feel certain that you can get all essentials without war and without delay."[40] He disclosed also that he had sent a communication to the Italian Premier urging him to prevail upon the German Chancellor "to agree to my proposal which will keep all our peoples out of war. I have already guaranteed that Czech promises shall be carried out and feel confident full agreement could be reached in a week."[41] While the Prime Minister was revealing to the House his efforts to save the peace of Europe, a message was placed in his hands—a message

---

[39]*Ibid.*

[40]British White Paper, Further Documents respecting Czechoslovakia, Cmd. 5848 (1938).

[41]*Ibid.*

from Herr Hitler "inviting me to meet him at Munich tomorrow morning. He has also invited Signor Mussolini and M. Daladier. Signor Mussolini has accepted and I have no doubt M. Daladier will also accept. I need not say what my answer will be."[42] The scene in the House of Commons was dramatic. The world heaved a sigh of relief; those condemned to die had received a stay of execution.

The Munich settlement

The Munich agreement[43] dated September 29, 1938, signed by the heads of the German, British, French, and Italian governments—Czechoslovakia, whose national existence was vitally affected, was shut out of the Munich negotiations—gave Hitler essentially what he had demanded at Godesberg. His deadline—October 1—was virtually met, for on that day the German military occupation of the Sudeten territory was to begin. Instead of the occupation of the entire territory on October 1, as he had insisted at Godesberg, the Munich settlement provided for military occupation by successive stages to be completed by October 10. The demands of Poland and Hungary upon slices of the Czechoslovak state—demands which Hitler had championed—were to be settled by the nations concerned, if possible, within three months; otherwise, they were to be settled by the heads of the governments signatories to the Munich agreement. The offer of Great Britain and France to join in a guarantee of Czechoslovakia's new boundaries against unprovoked aggression was repeated. Germany and Italy agreed to give a guarantee to Czechoslovakia "when the question of the Polish[44] and Hungarian minorities in Czechoslovakia

[42]New York *Herald Tribune,* September 29, 1938.

[43]British White Paper, *loc. cit.*

[44]Poland however did not wait to settle her dispute with Czechoslovakia. She sent an ultimatum demanding the Teschen area by noon of October 1—the same day German troops began their occupation. Prague yielded and Polish troops marched in on October 2. Hungary received a portion of Slovakia by the German-Italian award of November 2, 1938.

has been settled."[45] Thus Hitler imposed his own solution of the Sudeten question by methods slightly milder than those he demanded at Godesberg; and Mr. Chamberlain achieved—if it can be called an achievement—a bloodless surrender by Czechoslovakia. With this partition Czechoslovakia became a quasi-totalitarian vassal of Hitler's Reich, and it marked her end as a bulwark against the German *Drang nach Osten.*

Czechoslovakia a vassal of Hitler's Reich

The Munich settlement a defeat for Great Britain and France

Germany emerged from the Munich conference as the dominant power on the continent of Europe. Hitler had succeeded in destroying the alliances between France and Czechoslovakia, between Czechoslovakia and Russia, and the system of alliances of the little Entente. He now had a free hand in Eastern Europe. The Munich Accord was an unmitigated defeat for Great Britain and France. In the language of Winston Churchill it was "a disaster of the first magnitude" and in the language of a British historian it marked "a turning point not only in British history but in world history too."[46] The public events of September, 1938, were momentous. They recalled the observations made by Sir Eyre Crowe of the British Foreign Office in 1907 in a "Memorandum on the Present State of British Relations with Germany":

> [But] the action of Germany toward this country . . . might be likened not inappropriately to that of a professional blackmailer whose extortions are wrung from his victim by the threat of some vague and dreadful consequence in case of refusal. To give way to the blackmailer's menaces enriches him; but it has long been proved by uniform experience that, although this may secure for the victim temporary peace, it is certain to lead to renewed molestation and higher demands after ever shortening periods of amicable forbearance. The blackmailer is usually ruined by the first resolute stand made against his exactions and the determination to face all risks of a possible disagreeable situation rather than to continue in the path of

[45] British White Paper, *loc. cit.*

[46] Arnold J. Toynbee, "A Turning Point in History," *Foreign Affairs*, January, 1939.

endless concessions. But, failing such determination, it is probable that the relations between the two parties will grow steadily worse.

There is one road which, if past experience is any guide to the future, will most certainly not lead to any permanent improvement of relations with any power, least of all Germany, and which must therefore be abandoned; that is the road paved with graceful British concessions—concessions made without any conviction either of their justice or of their being set off by equivalent counter-services. The vain hopes that in this manner Germany can be "conciliated" and made more friendly must be definitely given up. . . .

These melancholy forecasts unhappily proved to be true.[47]

Repercussions of Munich agreement in the United States

For the United States the Munich agreement was not without far-reaching significance. Great Britain had yielded to force and her primacy as a world power had been shaken, if not eclipsed. The world was now confronted with the prospect of a German bid for world domination. British naval power which stood behind British prestige for a century or more had helped the United States to support two basic principles of her foreign policy—the Monroe Doctrine and the open door. With Great Britain preoccupied in Europe, the United States had to reconsider her position in world affairs, particularly in the Far East and in the Western Hemisphere. The immediate answer was a further expansion of the vast American rearmament program.[48]

Germany invades the provinces of Bohemia and Moravia

The British Conservative government, and its policy of appeasement towards the European dictators, had a rude awakening when German troops on March 15, 1939,

[47]In 1938, Winston Churchill, another British statesman who, like Sir Eyre Crowe, understood the German mind, wrote: "Undoubtedly the Government could make an agreement with Germany. All they have to do is to give her back her former colonies or such others as she may desire; to muzzle the British Press and platforms by law of censorship; to give Herr Hitler a free hand to spread the Nazi system and dominance far and wide through Central Europe. After an interval, long or short, we should be drawn into a war, but by that time we should be confronted with an antagonist overwhelmingly powerful and find outselves deprived of every friend." Cf. Winston Churchill, *While England Slept*.

[48]See *infra*, pp. 926–928.

invaded the non-German provinces of Bohemia and Moravia—the remnants of the once magnificently armed and fortified Czechoslovak state. By decree, dated March 16, Hitler proclaimed that the provinces belonged hereafter to the German Reich and came under her protection under the title of "The Protectorate of Bohemia and Moravia." No nation in Europe, small or large, could henceforth feel itself secure from some new adaptation of Nazi *Weltanschauung*, accompanied by blackmail, aggression, and oppression. By the destruction of Czechoslovakia in deliberate violation of the Munich agreement which he had signed not quite six months before, Hitler cynically discarded his own theory of racial purity and appeared under his true colors as an unprincipled menace to European peace and liberty. His action brought to a close the British policy of appeasement and marked a turning point in the struggle for a new balance of power in Europe.

Destruction of Czechoslovakia ends British policy of appeasement

With the destruction of Czechoslovakia as an independent state, Great Britain resumed her traditional policy of preparing to checkmate any nation aspiring to hegemony of the European continent. The Anglo-French alliance, gradually taking shape since March, 1936, was the main instrument of the "stop Hitler" coalition. Its weakness lay in the fact that it was no bar to Germany's eastward expansion. The first move to remedy this weakness came on March 31, 1939, when the British government announced that it had pledged support to Poland in the event of a threat to her independence.[49]

Great Britain gives pledges to Poland, Greece, Rumania, and Turkey

[49]Referring to the events leading up to the partition of Czechoslovakia, Prime Minister Chamberlain stated in the House of Commons on April 3, 1939: "At that time it was possible to quote . . . the assurances that had been given me by Herr Hitler, and not to me but to the world, that the foreign policy of the German government was limited, that they had no wish to dominate other races, and that all they wanted was to assimilate Germans living in territory adjacent to their country. We were told that when that was done that was to be the end, and there were to be no more territorial ambitions to be satisfied. Those assurances have now been thrown to the winds. That is the new fact which has destroyed confidence and which has forced the British government

Similar announcements were made on April 13 of pledges to Greece and Rumania by both Great Britain and France[50] followed by a pledge to Turkey on May 12.[51] An effort to bring Russia into the "stop Hitler" coalition, however, failed.

Germany and Italy enter into a military alliance

To counteract the British coalition, described by Herr Hitler as "encirclement," Germany and Italy on May 22, 1939, transformed the Rome-Berlin Axis of 1936 into a formal military alliance.[52] Unlike the pre-war Triple Alliance between Germany, Austria-Hungary, and Italy, which was defensive in character, and at Italy's express desire excluded war against Britain, this agreement was offensive as well as defensive. These two partners, according to comments in the Italian controlled press on the occasion of the signing of the alliance, were to find "living space" in areas alleged to have been carved out by the respective parties—Germany in the Baltic, Central, and Eastern Europe, and Italy in the Balkans, the Mediterranean, and Africa.

President Roosevelt appeals to Hitler

Next on the time table of Nazi aggression was Danzig and the Polish Corridor, and soon after the conquest of Czechoslovakia the German government turned its active attention toward a solution of that question. As the battle lines in Europe were closing in over the Danzig issue, President Roosevelt once again made a direct appeal[53] to the German Chancellor on April 14, 1939:

to take this great departure of which I gave the first intimation on Friday." (*Debates*, House of Commons, vol. 345, April 3, 1939.) The great departure referred to by Mr. Chamberlain was the announcement by him in the House of Commons on March 31, 1939, that in the event of any action which clearly threatened Polish independence, and which the Polish government considered it vital to resist with its national forces, Great Britain would come to the aid of Poland with all the support in her power. France gave a similar assurance. (Documents concerning German-Polish Relations and the Outbreak of Hostilities between Great Britain and Germany on September 3, 1939, Cmd. 6106, pp. 36–39.)

[50] *Debates*, House of Commons, vol. 346, April 13, 1939.

[51] *Ibid.*, vol. 347, May 12, 1939.

[52] For text, cf. New York *Times*, May 23, 1939.

[53] Department of State, Press Release, April 15, 1939.

You realize I am sure that throughout the world hundreds of millions of human beings are living today in constant fear of a new war or even a series of wars.

The existence of this fear—and the possibility of such a conflict—is of definite concern to the people of the United States for whom I speak, as it must also be to the peoples of the other nations of the entire Western Hemisphere.

Three nations in Europe [Austria, Czechoslovakia, Albania] and one [Ethiopia] in Africa have seen their independent existence terminated. A vast territory in another independent nation [China] of the Far East has been occupied by a neighboring state. Reports, which we trust are not true, insist that further acts of aggression are contemplated against still other independent nations. Plainly the world is moving toward the moment when this situation must end in catastrophe unless a more rational way of guiding events is found.

You have repeatedly asserted that you and the Germany people have no desire for war. If this is true there need be no war.

I am convinced that the cause of world peace would be greatly advanced if the nations of the world were to obtain a frank statement relating to the present and future policy of governments.

Are you willing to give assurance that your armed forces will not attack or invade the territory or possessions of the following independent nations: Finland, Estonia, Latvia, Lithuania, Sweden, Norway, Denmark, The Netherlands, Belgium, Great Britain and Ireland, France, Portugal, Spain, Switzerland, Lichtenstein, Luxembourg, Poland, Hungary, Rumania, Yugoslavia, Russia, Bulgaria, Greece, Turkey, Iraq, the Arabias, Syria, Palestine, Egypt, and Iran.

President Roosevelt asks Hitler for assurance of non-aggression

Since the United States was not involved in the immediate controversies in Europe, the President asked Herr Hitler to make such a statement of policy to him in order that he might, as a friendly intermediary, communicate such a declaration to the other nations apprehensive as to the course German policy may take. The President further asked that Herr Hitler's assurance of non-aggression be for a period of ten years at least, and a quarter of a century if possible, to permit a more permanent peace to be worked out. Were Herr Hitler to give such an undertaking, the President stated he would transmit it to the governments of the nations named, asking them for similar assurances towards the German government. In addition, the President declared to Herr Hitler that if such a pledge were given, the United States would participate in a conference on disarmament to relieve the peoples of the world of the crushing burden of armaments and to discuss ways and means looking towards the most practical manner of opening up avenues of international trade to the end that every nation may be enabled to buy and sell on equal terms in the world market as well as to possess assurance of obtaining the materials and products of peaceful economic life.

"Heads of great governments," the President went on to state, "in this hour are literally responsible for the fate of humanity in the coming years. They cannot fail to hear the prayers of their peoples to be protected from the foreseeable chaos of war. History will hold them accountable for the lives and the happiness of all—even unto the least."

The prelude to war

No direct reply was made to the President's note. The pattern of events preceding the outbreak of war between Germany and Poland began to take shape in the summer of 1939 and bore a striking resemblance to that which culminated in the partition of Czechoslovakia the previous year, and in her disappearance as an independent state in March, 1939. The German-controlled press carried wild tales of German minority persecutions by Polish authorities and Poles. A suffocating fanaticism was stirred up over highly synthetic "incidents" manufactured for the occasion to bring national "honor" into question. This deliberate German provocation, whipped up by an efficient and sinister propaganda machine in accordance with fixed policy, exacerbated feeling between the two nationalities. It was done with the object of creating a war spirit in Germany, impressing public opinion abroad, and provoking defeatism or apparent aggression in Poland.

Sir Nevile Henderson, British Ambassador to Germany, has made the following observation on the effect of atrocity propaganda on Herr Hitler:

> People are apt, in my opinion, to exaggerate the malign influence of Herr von Ribbentrop [German Minister of Foreign Affairs], Dr. Goebbels]Minister of Propaganda and Enlightenment], Herr Himmler [Chief of Secret Police], and the rest. It was probably consistently sinister, not because of its suggestiveness (since Herr Hitler alone decided policy), nor because it merely applauded and encouraged, but because, if Herr Hitler appeared to hesitate, the extremists of the party at once proceeded to fabricate situations calculated to drive Herr Hitler into courses which even he at times shrank from risking. The simplest method of doing this was through the medium of a controlled press. Thus what happened in September last year [on the occasion of the partition of Czechoslovakia], was repeated in March this year [on the occasion of the annexation of what was left of Czechoslovakia], and again in August [on the occasion of the invasion of Poland]. Dr. Goebbels' propaganda machine was the ready tool of these extremists, who were afraid lest Herr Hitler should move too slowly in the prosecution of his ultimate designs.
>
> The 1938 stories of Czech atrocities against its German minority were rehashed up almost verbatim in regard to the Poles. Some foundation there must necessarily have been for a proportion of these allegations in view of the state of excitable tension which existed between the two peoples. Excess of zeal on the part of individuals and minor officials there undoubtedly was—but the tales of ill-treatment, expropriation, and murder were multiplied a hundredfold.[54]

Germany demands Danzig and the Corridor

Events in the summer of 1939 proceeded with the inexorable fatality of the Greek tragedy. Germany demanded the return of the Free City of Danzig as well as of the Corridor, unconditionally and without compromise. On August 21, the British Ambassador to Berlin reported that "carefully concealed German military concentrations were already in progress, and that instructions had been given to complete them by the 24th of August."[55] On the 22nd of August the world learned that negotiations

[54]British White Paper, Germany No. 1 (1939), pp. 257–258.

[55]*Ibid.*, p. 259.

had been concluded for the signature of a Russo-German non-aggression pact and that Herr von Ribbentrop would fly to Moscow on the 23rd to sign it. If the purpose of this agreement was to deter Great Britain from honoring her obligation to Poland, the Germans were very much mistaken, for in his letter[56] to the German Chancellor of August 22, 1939, the British Prime Minister stated:

The Russo-German pact

Whatever may prove to be the nature of the German-Soviet Agreement, it cannot alter Great Britain's obligation to Poland which His Majesty's government have stated in public repeatedly and plainly, and which they are determined to fulfill.

It has been alleged that, if His Majesty's government had made their position more clear in 1914, the great catastrophe would have been avoided. Whether or not there is any force in that allegation, His Majesty's government are resolved that on this occasion there shall be no such tragic misunderstanding.

If the case should arise, they are resolved, and prepared, to employ without delay all the forces at their command, and it is impossible to foresee the end of hostilities once engaged. It would be a dangerous illusion to think that, if war once starts, it will come to an early end even if a success on any one of the several fronts on which it will be engaged should have been secured.

. . . I cannot see that there is anything in the questions arising between Germany and Poland which could not and should not be resolved without the use of force, if only a situation of confidence could be restored to enable discussions to be carried on in an atmosphere different from that which prevails today.

The British Ambassador, in his report to the British Foreign Minister, wrote as follows of an interview with Herr Hitler on August 23rd:[57]

I spoke of the tragedy of war and of his immense responsibility, but his answer was that it would be all England's fault. I refuted this only to learn from him that England was determined to destroy and exterminate Germany. He was, he said, 50 years old; he preferred war now to when he would be 55 or 60. I told him that it was absurd to talk of extermination.

[56]Documents concerning German-Polish Relations and the Outbreak of Hostilities between Great Britain and Germany on September 3, 1939, Cmd. 6106, pp. 96–97.

[57]*Ibid.*, pp. 100–101.

Nations could not be exterminated and a peaceful and prosperous Germany was a British interest. His answer was that it was England who was fighting for lesser races whereas he was fighting only for Germany: the Germans would this time fight to the last man: it would have been different in 1914 if he had been Chancellor then. . . . In referring to the Russian non-aggression pact he observed that it was England which had forced him into agreement with Russia.

President Roosevelt appeals to the King of Italy, the German Chancellor, and the President of Poland

On the 23rd of August, President Roosevelt appealed to King Victor Emanuel of Italy, in the hope that through the Italian Monarch, the Italian Prime Minister would intervene with Herr Hitler, his ally, to avert the outbreak of war. The following day the President importuned Herr Hitler and the President of Poland to settle their controversy by direct negotiation, by impartial arbitration, or through the procedure of conciliation, selecting as a conciliator a national of one of the American Republics free from any connection with European political affairs. "The people of the United States," the President reminded the German Chancellor, "are as one in their opposition to policies of military conquest and domination. They are as one in rejecting the thesis that any ruler or any people possess the right to achieve their ends or objectives through the taking of action which will plunge countless of millions into war. . . ." Upon receiving the Polish President's reply that his government was willing to agree to solve the controversy by direct negotiation or by conciliation, President Roosevelt again appealed to Herr Hitler on August 25, urging him to agree to a peaceful solution.

Similar appeals were made by the King of the Belgians in the name of the Heads of States of Denmark, Finland, Luxembourg, Norway, Sweden, The Netherlands, and on his own behalf, on August 23. This was followed by a joint offer of mediation by the King of the Belgians and by the Queen of The Netherlands on August 28. His Holiness, the Pope, also broadcast an appeal for peace on August 24. All were to no avail.

Germany unleashes a lightning attack on Poland

In the early hours of September 1, the German forces, without any declaration of war, crossed the frontier and unleashed a lightning attack by land and air upon Polish towns, aerodromes, and lines of communication. Hitler issued a proclamation to the German army declaring that the Polish State had refused a peaceful settlement and had appealed to arms. This accusation was echoed and reechoed in every German newspaper. At 10 : 30 in the morning of that day Hitler met the assembled members of his Reichstag and similarly announced that he had been "forced to take up arms in defence of the Reich." As the British Ambassador to Germany wrote: "The die had in fact been cast and never can there have been or ever be a case of more deliberate and carefully planned aggression."[58]

Great Britain and France declare war on Germany

On learning of the German attack upon Poland, Great Britain and France, on September 1, informed the German government that both were prepared to come to Poland's assistance unless satisfactory assurances were forthcoming that it had suspended all aggressive action against Poland and was prepared promptly to withdraw its forces from Polish territory.[59] Germany rejected the French and British demands, and on September 3, 1939, Great Britain and France were at war with Germany for the second time in twenty-five years.

President Roosevelt addresses the nation by radio

On September 3, 1939, President Roosevelt addressed the nation by radio. He told his listeners that he had hoped against hope that some miracle would bring to an end the invasion of Poland by Germany and prevent a devastating war in Europe. "For four long years," he said, "a succession of actual wars and constant crises have shaken the entire world and have threatened in each case

---

[58]British White Paper, Germany No. 1 (1939), p. 275.

[59]Cf. Documents concerning German-Polish Relations and the Outbreak of Hostilities between Great Britain and Germany on September 3, 1939, Cmd. 6106, pp. 157–158.

to bring on the gigantic conflict which is today unhappily a fact.[60] He asked the nation to "master at the outset a simple but unalterable fact in modern foreign relations. When peace has been broken anywhere, peace of all countries everywhere is in danger." A significant passage in the address which revealed the President's attitude towards the conflict was the following:

> This nation will remain a neutral nation, but I cannot ask that every American remain neutral in thought as well. Even a neutral has a right to take account of facts. Even a neutral cannot be asked to close his mind or his conscience.[61]

Promises to keep the United States out of war

The President closed his address with the promise that every effort of the government would be directed towards keeping the nation out of war. "As long as it remains within my power," he declared, "there will be no blackout of peace in the United States." On September 5, he invoked the Neutrality Act of 1937.[62] The President, however, did not like the arms embargo provision of the 1937 Act, and called a special session of Congress to convene on September 21 to consider its repeal. After a historic debate which lasted six weeks, Congress passed, and on November 4 the President signed, the Neutrality Act of 1939.[63]

During our history as a nation of a century and a half we have witnessed the rise and fall of empires and through the pursuit of a continental policy by which we have kept ourselves free from involvement, we have utilized the turmoils abroad to strengthen our position in the Western Hemisphere. The continental policy was suited to the

[60]Text of address in the New York *Times*, September 4, 1939.

[61]Twenty-five years ago President Wilson called upon the American people to "be impartial in thought as well as in action," to "put a curb upon our sentiments as well as upon every transaction that might be construed as a preference of one party to the struggle before another." Cf. Papers Relating to the Foreign Relations of the United States, 1914, Supplement, The World War, p. 552.

[62]See *infra*, p. 954.

[63]*Ibid.*, pp. 955–959.

times and to the genius and welfare of our people, and enabled us to emerge as the most powerful nation in the world.

Time has brought great changes since the United States began to think in national terms. "Her entire geography, for one thing, has altered; where she once looked out on one ocean, she now looks out on two. While she held at first but a fringe along the shoreline, she now spreads across a continent, and since the acquisition of Hawaii, Porto Rico, and the Philippines, and the building of the Panama Canal, her shadow falls far beyond the confines of the Union. As she has reached out to make contact with the world, the world with its steamships, aircraft, cables, and radios has advanced to meet her, until distance no longer decides the relationship between herself and the rest of mankind."[64]

The United States facing an uncertain future

As a result of the wars now raging in the Far East and in Europe, the United States faces an uncertain and an uneasy future. The American people have perhaps never been more isolationist than they are today, as respects their reluctance to go to war. Yet never before have the American people been so unneutral in partisanship as they are today, for their sympathies are listed almost wholly against the totalitarian powers whose concept of civilization differs so radically from ours. It may be asked of what interest is it to us who wins. The answer is that the security of the United States and her way of life as well as her position of primacy in the Western Hemisphere are not likely to remain unaffected by a victory of the totalitarian powers. For the United States then the issue which seems to dominate all others is the choice between guarding our position in the Western Hemisphere whatever the outcome of the present struggles may be, or throwing in our lot with Great Britain and France in an effort to secure victory for the Western democracies.

---

[64]John W. Davis, *The Permanent Bases of Foreign Policy*, p. 101 (published by the Council on Foreign Relations, Inc., 1931).

INDEX